THE
SPIRITUAL MAN

Watchman Nee

IN THREE VOLUMES

Christian Fellowship Publishers, Inc.
New York

Reprinted As a Combined Edition, 1977

Available from the Publishers at:

11515 Allecingie Parkway

Richmond, Virginia 23235

THE SPIRITUAL MAN
Volume I

EXPLANATORY NOTES

The Spiritual Man is a translation of the only book of any substantial size which brother Watchman Nee himself ever wrote. At the time of writing it he felt this work might be his last contribution to the church, although since then God has graciously overruled. Long after the book's initial publication in Chinese our brother once was heard to express the thought that it should not be reprinted because, it being such a "perfect" treatment of its subject, he was fearful lest the book become to its readers merely a manual of principles and not a guide to experience as well. But in view of the urgent need among the children of God today for help on spiritual life and warfare, and knowing our brother as one who is always open to God's way and most desirous to serve His people with all that God has given him, we conclude that he would doubtless permit it to be circulated in English. Hence this translation.

Translations used. The Revised Standard Version (RSV) of the Bible has been used throughout the text unless otherwise indicated. Additional translations where employed are denoted by the following abbrevations:

Amplified—*Amplified Old Testament*
ASV—American Standard Version (1901)
AV—Authorized Version (King James)
Darby—J. N. Darby, *The Holy Scriptures, a New Translation*
Young's—Young's *Literal Translation*

Soulical and Soulish. The adjectives "soulical" and "soulish" have been used to convey distinctly different meanings. "Soulical" as herein employed pertains to those proper, appropriate, legitimate, or natural qualities, functions, or expressions of man's soul which the Creator intended from the very beginning for the soul uniquely to possess and manifest. "Soulish" appears in these pages to describe that man *in toto* who is so governed by the soulical part of his being that his whole life takes on the character and expression of the soul.

Contents

VOLUME I

EXPLANATORY NOTES   6
FIRST PREFACE   7
SECOND PREFACE   15

PART ONE: INTRODUCTION ON
    SPIRIT, SOUL AND BODY

1 Spirit, Soul and Body   21
2 Spirit and Soul   31
3 The Fall of Man   43
4 Salvation   55

PART TWO: THE FLESH

1 The Flesh and Salvation   69
2 The Fleshly or Carnal Believer   83
3 The Cross and the Holy Spirit   95
4 The Boastings of the Flesh   108
5 The Believer's Ultimate Attitude
    towards the Flesh   119

PART THREE: THE SOUL

1 Deliverance from Sin and the Soul Life   133
2 The Experience of Soulish Believers   153
3 The Dangers of Soulish Life   167
4 The Cross and the Soul   179
5 Spiritual Believers and the Soul   193

Preface

To THE LORD Whom I serve I offer my heartfelt thanks, for He has given me the privilege of writing this book. I had always hoped another more capable would undertake this work, yet it pleases the Lord to call me to it. If the choice were left to me I should be the last of all to write; for I have the least desire to do such a book. My hesitation lies not in withdrawal from duty but rather in the realization that such a book touching on the way of spiritual life and the stratagem of spiritual warfare is surely beyond the possibility of one whose experience of the Lord has been less than ten years long. The Bible does permit a believer to relate his experience; the Holy Spirit even leads one to do so; how much better though if such experiences as "caught up into the third heaven" be mentioned after "fourteen years." Now I do not have a "third heaven" experience, neither have I received great revelation, but I have learned through His grace to follow the Lord in the small things of the day. In this work, therefore, my attempt is but to impart to the children of God that which I have received from the Lord in these years.

It was about four years ago that I felt called to write such a book. At that time I was resting from physical weakness in a small hut by the river, praying and reading the Word. I felt the urgent need for a book—based on the Word and on experience—which would give God's children a clear understanding of spiritual life in order that the Holy Spirit might use it in leading the saints onward and in delivering them from groping in darkness. It was then that I knew I was commissioned by the Lord to undertake this task. I began to compose the chapters which discuss the differentiation of spirit, soul and body, a chapter on the body, and also the first part of the chapter dealing with soul life. But I soon discontinued writing. I had many other claims upon my time besides this one. That was not the main deterrent, however, for I could still find opportunity to write. I lay down my pen chiefly because up to that time many truths were yet to be written which had not been fully proven in my experience. This lack I knew would lessen the value as well as the power of the book. I would prefer to learn more before the Lord and prove His truths through experience. What I wrote would then be spiritual realities instead of merely spiritual theories. Thus the work was suspended for three years.

I can say that during these three years I had the book daily in my heart. Although some might consider the publishing of this work long overdue, I could clearly see the hand of the Lord. Within these few years the truths contained in this book, especially those in the last volume, have liberated many from the power of darkness, demonstrating that we had touched spiritual reality. By the special grace of the Lord I was enabled to understand more of the purpose of God's redemption in dividing the new and the old creations. I praise the Lord for that. The Lord also gave me opportunities to meet many of his choicest ones during my various travels. This increased my observation, knowledge and experience. In my contacts with people the Lord showed me not only what is genuinely lacking among His children but what is the revealed remedy in His Word as well. Let me therefore tell my readers that this is a manual on spiritual life, every point of which can be experimentally proven.

Due to my special experience in the physical body during these few years, it has been given me to know more of the reality of eternity and, likewise, the great debt I owe the church of God. Thus I hoped I would be able to finish this book within a short period. Thanks to God the Father and to some of my friends in the Lord, I was provided with a quiet place for resting and writing. Within a few months I had finished Parts I through IV. Although I have not yet begun the other parts, I am sure God the Father will supply the necessary grace at the needed time.

Now that this volume is shortly to be published and the other volumes will soon follow, let me speak frankly: learning the truths in this book was not easy; writing them down was even harder. I may say that for two months I lived daily in the jaws of Satan. What battling! What withstanding! All my powers of spirit, soul and body were summoned to contend with hell. Such battles are now temporarily suspended, but more parts must be written. You who are Moses on the hill, please do not forget Joshua in the plain. I know the enemy hates this work deeply. He will try every means to prevent it from reaching people's hands and to hinder them from reading it. Oh, that you would not allow the enemy to succeed here.

This book, which will contain three volumes, is not written in sermonic or expositive form. Differences occur in the length of treatment of various subjects and this the readers should notice. Although all volumes deal with spiritual life and warfare, some sections may lay more stress on spiritual *life* while others may lay more on spiritual *warfare*. The book as a whole is prepared to serve as a guide; hence its emphasis is principally a matter of how to walk in this way rather than that of persuading people initially to take this walk. It is written not so much to urge individuals to seek the spiritual way as to help those who *are* seeking to *know* the way. May all whose hearts are out to the Lord find help in its pages.

I am deeply aware that the spiritual life of the readers of this book may vary greatly. If you should therefore come to some points difficult to understand, please neither reject them nor try to fathom them mentally. Such truths should be reserved for more matured life. Upon re-reading that difficult part later (say after two weeks or a whole month), you may perhaps grasp it better. Nevertheless, this book deals wholly with spiritual life as an experience. In no other way can it be understood. What appears to be tasteless in the beginning may come to be most precious later. You will understand when you reach that stage. But is it necessary to wait until reaching that stage before understanding? If such were the case, what will be the use of this book! A great mystery surrounds the spiritual experience of a believer. The Lord always gives a foretaste of the outline of a deeper life before He leads him into the full experience of it. Many believers mistake their foretaste for the fullness, not realizing that the Lord is just beginning to lead them in. The teaching in this book will meet the need of those who have tasted but not yet fully drunk.

One thing we must guard against: we should never use the knowledge we acquire from this book as an aid in analyzing ourselves. If in God's light we see light, we shall know ourselves without losing our freedom in the Lord. But if all day long we analyze ourselves, dissecting our thoughts and feelings, it will hinder us from losing ourselves in Christ. Unless a believer is deeply taught by the Lord he will not be able to know himself. Introspection and self-consciousness are harmful to spiritual life.

It would be well to reflect upon God's redemptive design. God's purpose is that through the new life given us at the time of regeneration He might be able to deliver us from (1) sin, (2) the natural, and (3) the supernatural, that is, the satanic force of evil in the unseen realm. These three steps of deliverance are necessary; none can be omitted. If a Christian limits God's redemptive work by being content with merely overcoming sin, he falls far short of the purpose of God. The natural life (the good self) must be overcome, and so too must the supernatural enemy. It certainly is well to overcome sin, but the work is not complete if the petty self and the supernatural evil are left unconquered. The cross can afford us such victory. I hope through God's grace I can emphasize these points as we go along.

Aside from the last Part of the concluding volume which will discuss the body, this book may be considered Biblical psychology. We base everything on the Bible and prove all by spiritual experience. The result of our findings, both through studying the Word and through experience, tells us that for every spiritual experience (for example, the new birth) there is a special change in our inward man. We conclude that the Bible divides man into three parts—spirit, soul and body. We shall see further how different are the functions and the realms of these three parts, particularly those of spirit and soul. In this connection, a few words need to be said concerning Part One of this first volume. The differentiation of spirit and soul as well as the difference in their functions are necessary knowledge to those who seek to grow in spiritual life. Only after knowing what is the spirit and what is spiritual can we walk according to the spirit. Because of the great lack of such teachings, I have attempted to explain in detail. To believers with some background this first Part will not present any difficulty to their understanding; but those who are unfamiliar with such a study need only remember the conclusions and may then proceed to the second Part. Part One, consequently, does not deal specifically with spiritual life; it merely supplies us with some necessary knowledge basic to spiritual life. This Part may be better understood if it is reread after the entire book is first finished.

I am not the first to advocate the teaching of the dividing of spirit and soul. Andrew Murray once said that what the church and individuals have to dread is the inordinate activity of the soul with its power of mind and will. F. B. Meyer declared that had he not known about the dividing of spirit and soul, he could not have imagined what his spiritual life would have been. Many others, such as Otto Stockmayer, Jessie Penn-Lewis, Evan Roberts, Madame Guyon, have given the same testimony. I have used their writings freely since we all have received the same commission from the

Lord; therefore I have decided to forego notating their many references.*

This book is written not only for the believers as such, but also to help those who are younger in the Lord's service than I. We who are responsible for the spiritual life of others ought to know from what and into what we lead them—from whence to where. If we help people, negatively, not to sin and, positively, to be zealous; will that be all the Lord wants us to do? Or is there perhaps something deeper? I personally feel the Bible has given a most definite judgment. God's purpose is that His children are to be delivered wholly from the old creation and are to enter fully into the new creation. No matter how the old creation may appear to man, it is utterly condemned by God. If we workers know what ought to be destroyed and what ought to be built, then we are not the blind leading the blind.

New birth—receiving God's own life—is the starting point of all spiritual life. How useless it is if the end result of all our exhortation, persuasion, argument, explanation and study is but to induce some understanding in the mind, some determination in the will, some feeling in the emotion. It has not assisted people to receive God's life into their spirit. But if we who are responsible for preaching the gospel truly perceive that unless people receive God's life into the depths of their beings we have not done anything profitable, then what a drastic reformation will there be in our work! Indeed, such knowledge will bring us to the realization that many who do profess to believe in the Lord Jesus have never actually done so. Tears, penitence, reform, zeal and labor: these are not the hallmarks of a Christian. Happy are we if we know that our responsibility is to bring man to receive God's uncreated life.

As I recall how the enemy has tried to hinder me from learning the truths written in the last volume, I cannot but be apprehensive that some, though possessing the book, will be

---

*Citations will be added where the direct quotations can be found.— Translator.

hindered by Satan from reading it; or if they do read it, will be made to soon forget it. Therefore let me warn my readers: you should ask God to keep Satan from preventing your reading it. Pray as you read; turn what you read into prayer. Pray that God will cover you with the helmet of salvation lest you forget what you read or simply fill your mind with innumerable theories.

A few words to those who already possess the truths set forth in the following pages. If God has graciously liberated you from the flesh and the power of darkness, you, in turn, ought to bring these truths to others. So after you have digested the book thoroughly and the truths have become your own, will you gather a few saints together and teach them the truths. If it is too much to use the entire book, then one or two parts would be profitable. The hope is that the truths herein will not be left unnoticed. Even lending the book to others to read would be a profitable thing.

Now that this small treatise is in the Lord's hand, if He is pleased with it, may He bless it toward spiritual growth and spiritual victory in me as well as in many of my brothers and sisters. May the will of God be done. May His enemy be defeated. May our Lord Jesus soon return to reign. Amen.

Shanghai   Watchman Nee
June 4, 1927

Second
Preface

MOST HAPPY AM I TODAY for I have completed the last Part
of the book. I recall when I wrote the earlier preface I had
completed but the first four parts. With these last six now
done I find I have much yet to share with my readers. Hence
this second preface.

Many months have passed since I commenced writing this
final portion of the book. I can truthfully say that during
these months the burden of this work has been upon me
daily. It is natural for the enemy to hate the spreading of
God's truth. As a consequence I have been attacked and
assaulted incessantly. Thanks be unto God, His grace has
hitherto sustained me. Often I thought it would be impossible to continue writing because the pressure upon my spirit
was too heavy and the stamina of my body too weak; yea, I
even despaired of life itself. As often as I despaired, however,
just as often was I strengthened by the God whom I serve,
according to His promise and through the prayers of many.
Today the task is finished and the burden is discharged.
What comfort I now experience!

Today I reverently offer this book to our God. Since He has
performed that which He began, my prayer before Him is
that He may bless these pages to fulfill its God-given mission
in His church. I am asking God to bless every reader that he
may find the straight path and learn to follow the Lord perfectly. My spirit together with my prayer henceforth follows the outgoing of this work. May God use it according to
His most excellent will.

Brethren, it is considered politic for a writer not to show too much enthusiasm for his own work, but I shall now proceed to disregard this human convention. I do this not because I wrote the book but because of the deposit of truth in the book. Had it been written by another I think I would be freer to draw people's attention to it. I must therefore beg your pardon for being beside myself. I know the importance of the truths herein contained and, according to the best of my knowledge of God's will, I feel they will meet the urgent need of this age. No matter how mistaken I may be, of one thing I am certain: I did not have the slightest intention of undertaking this task: I wrote only because I was commissioned by the Lord so to do. The truths in these pages are not mine; they were given me by God. Even when I was writing He blessed me with many new blessings.

I desire my readers to understand thoroughly that this work is in no way to be considered a treatise on the *theory* of spiritual life and warfare. I myself can testify that I have learned these truths through much suffering, trial and failure. It can almost be said that every one of these teachings has been branded with fire. And these words are not used lightly; they come from the depth of the heart. God knows from whence these truths do come.

When composing the volumes I did not attempt to group similar and related principles together. I have simply mentioned them as the need arose. Out of consideration for their extreme importance, I may have touched upon one truth or another many times, hoping the children of God would thereby better remember. Only through repetition will the truth be retained and only by reviewing will it be learned. "Therefore the word of the Lord will be to them precept upon precept, precept upon precept, line upon line, line upon line, here a little, there a little" (Is. 28.13).

I realize there are many apparent inconsistencies in the work, but the reader should remember that they are indeed apparent, not actual. Because this book treats of matters in the spiritual realm, there are bound to be many apparent theoretical contradictions. Spiritual things do often seem to be contradictory (2 Cor. 4.8,9). However, these all find their perfect harmony in experience. Hence, though there are places which seem to defy understanding, my request is that you try your best to understand. If anyone desires to misunderstand, he can surely read into these pages that which I have not intended.

I deeply sense that only one class of people will actually understand this book. My original purpose was to supply the need of many believers; obviously only those who have need will be able to appreciate the book. Such ones will find here a guidebook. Others will either look upon these truths as ideals or criticize them as inappropriate. According to the measure of his need shall be the believer's understanding of what is written here. Unless the reader has personal need he will not find any problem solved through the reading of these pages. This is what the reader must guard against.

The deeper the truth the easier is it to become theoretical. Apart from the working of the Holy Spirit, none can arrive at deeper truth. Thus some will treat these principles as a sort of ideal. Let us therefore be careful lest we accept the teachings in the book with our mind and deceive ourselves into thinking we have possessed them already. This is most dangerous, for deception which comes from the flesh and the evil spirit shall increase day by day.

The reader also should be watchful lest he misuse the knowledge he obtains from these pages to criticize others. It is very easy for us to say this is of the spirit and that is of the flesh; but do we not know we ourselves are no exception? Truth is given to set people free, not to find fault. In criticizing we prove ourselves to be not one bit less soulish or carnal than the criticized. The danger is most serious; consequently we need to exercise great caution.

In my first preface I mentioned one matter which deserves to be repeated and elaborated upon here. It is of the utmost importance that we never try to analyze ourselves. Upon reading such a treatise as this, we may quite unconsciously

become over-active in self-analysis. In observing the condition of our inward life we tend to over-analyze our thoughts
and feelings and the movements of the inner man. This may
result in much apparent progress, yet actually it renders
treatment of the self life that much more difficult. If we persistently turn within ourselves we shall lose our peace completely, for we shall soon discover the discrepancy which
exists between our expectation and our actual condition.
We expect to be filled with holiness but we are found wanting in holiness. This makes us uncomfortable. God never
asks us to be so introspective. To do so constitutes one of
the main reasons for spiritual stagnation. Our rest lies in
looking to the Lord, not to ourselves. In the degree that
we look off unto Him to that degree are we delivered from
self. We rest on the finished work of the Lord Jesus Christ,
not on our own shifting experience. True spiritual life depends not on probing our feelings and thoughts from dawn
to dusk but on "looking off" to the Savior!

Let not any reader be misled into thinking he must resist
all supernatural occurrences. My aim is simply to impress upon you the necessity of testing whether or not something is
of God. I most sincerely believe many supernatural experiences come from God; I have witnessed a great number of
them. However, I must acknowledge that today many supernatural phenomena are false and deceptive. I do not have the
slightest intention of persuading any to refuse everything
supernatural. I merely point out in this book the basic
differences in principle between these two types of manifestation. When a believer is faced with any supernatural phenomenon, he ought to examine it carefully according to the
principles revealed in the Bible before he decides to accept
or to reject it.

As to the matter of soul, I honestly feel most Christians
swing from one extreme to the other. We on the one hand
usually consider emotion as soulish; consequently those who
are easily moved or excited we normally categorize as soulish.
On the other hand we forget that being *rational* does not at

all constitute one as being spiritual. This misjudgment of spiritualizing a rational life must be guarded against equally as much as against that of mistaking a predominantly emotional life for spirituality. Proceeding one step further, we should never reduce the function of our soul to deadly inactivity. Formerly we may never have viewed our soulish feeling and excitement with any degree of concern and thus we walked accordingly. Later, however, and recognizing our former error, we now suppress these emotions altogether. Such an attitude to us may appear to be quite good, but it will not make us a whit more spiritual. If my reader should misunderstand on this point, and no matter how minor may be this misunderstanding, then I know his life is going to become very "dead." Why? Because his spirit, without any opportunity to express itself, will be imprisoned by a deadened emotion. And beyond this lies a further danger; namely, that in overly-suppressing his emotion, the believer will develop eventually into a rational, not a spiritual, man; and thus, though in another form, he still remains soulish. Yet the excitement of the soul, if it expresses the *spirit's* feeling, is extremely valuable; and the thought of the soul, if it reveals the *spirit's* mind, can be most instructive.

I would like to say something about the concluding Part of the book. Considering the frailty of my body, I would seem to be the least qualified to write on such a matter; perhaps, though, this very frailty affords me a deeper insight since I suffer more weakness, sickness and pain than most people. Countless times my courage has seemed to fail but, thank God, I have been able to finish writing this portion. I hope those who have had similar experiences in their earthly tents will accept what I have written as offering some light out of the darkness through which I have gone. Naturally innumerable are the controversies which have revolved around divine healing. Since this is a book which deals primarily with principles, I refrain from entering into argument with other believers on details. I have said in the book what I feel led to say. What I now request of my reader is that in the phenomena of sicknesses he discern and distinguish as to which come from God and which from self.

I confess there is much which is incomplete in this work; nevertheless, having done my best, I offer that best to you. Knowing the seriousness of the message herein, I asked God with fear and trembling to lead me through it all. What I have set down I present to the conscience of God's children— for them to weigh what is said.

I recognize that a work which seeks to uncover the wiles of the enemy shall certainly incur the hostility of the power of darkness and the opposition of many. I have not written with the thought of courting the approval of men. This opposition I consider therefore as of no account. I also realize that if God's children derive help from reading this book they may think more of me than is proper. Let me speak honestly that I am but a man, the weakest of all men. The teachings of these pages reveal the experiences of my weaknesses.

The book is today in the readers' hands. This is wholly God's grace. Should you have the courage and perserverance to read through the first Part and continue on with the others, perhaps God will bless you with His truth. If you already have finished reading the whole work, may I entreat you to reread it after some time has elapsed. Beloved, let us turn our hearts once again to our Father, cast ourselves upon His bosom by faith and draw from Him His life. Let us confess anew that we are poor but He is rich, that we have nothing but He has everything. Except we are given grace we are but defenseless sinners. May we thank Him with gratitude in our hearts, for the Lord Jesus has given us grace.

Holy Father, what You have entrusted to me is now here in this book. If it seems good to You, may You bless it. May You in these last days keep Your children from corrupted flesh and wicked spirits! Father, may You build Your Son's Body, destroy Your Son's enemy, and hasten the coming of Your Son's Kingdom! Father God, I look to You, I cast myself upon You, and I desire after You!

Shanghai, June 25, 1928   Watchman Nee

PART ONE

INTRODUCTION ON SPIRIT, SOUL AND BODY

1 Spirit, Soul and Body

2 Spirit and Soul

3 The Fall of Man

4 Salvation

CHAPTER 1

SPIRIT, SOUL AND BODY

THE ORDINARY CONCEPT of the constitution of human beings is dualistic—soul and body. According to this concept soul is the invisible inner spiritual part, while body is the visible outer corporal part. Though there is some truth to this, it is nevertheless inaccurate. Such an opinion comes from fallen man, not from God; apart from God's revelation, no concept is dependable. That the body is man's outward sheath is undoubtedly correct, but the Bible never confuses spirit and soul as though they are the same. Not only are they different in terms; their very natures differ from each other. The Word of God does not divide man into the two parts of soul and body. It treats man, rather, as tripartite—spirit, soul and body. 1 Thessalonians 5.23 reads: "May the God of peace himself sanctify you wholly; and may your spirit and soul and body be kept sound and blameless at the coming of our Lord Jesus Christ." This verse precisely shows that the whole

man is divided into three parts. The Apostle Paul refers
here to the complete sanctification of believers, "sanctify
you *wholly*." According to the Apostle, how is a person
wholly sanctified? By his spirit and soul and body being
kept. From this we can easily understand that the *whole*
person comprises these three parts. This verse also makes
a distinction between spirit and soul; otherwise, Paul would
have said simply "your soul." Since God has distinguished
the human spirit from the human soul, we conclude that man
is composed of not two, but three, parts: spirit, soul and
body.

Is it a matter of any consequence to divide spirit and soul?
It is an issue of *supreme* importance for it affects tremendously the spiritual life of a believer. How can a believer
understand spiritual life if he does not know what is the
extent of the realm of the spirit? Without such understanding
how can he grow spiritually? To fail to distinguish between
spirit and soul is fatal to spiritual maturity. Christians often
account what is soulical as spiritual, and thus they remain in
a soulish state and seek not what is really spiritual. How can
we escape loss if we confuse what God has divided?

Spiritual knowledge is very important to spiritual life. Let
us add, however, that it is equally as, if not more, important
for a believer to be humble and willing to accept the teaching of the Holy Spirit. If so, the Holy Spirit will grant him
the experience of the dividing of spirit and soul, although
he may not have too much knowledge concerning this truth.
On the one hand, the most ignorant believer, without the
slightest idea of the division of spirit and soul, may yet
experience such a dividing in real life. On the other hand,
the most informed believer, completely conversant with the
truth concerning spirit and soul, may nonetheless have no
experience of it. Far better is that person who may have both
the knowledge and the experience. The majority, however,
lack such experience. Consequently, it is well initially to lead
these to know the different functions of spirit and soul and
then to encourage them to seek what is spiritual.

Other portions of the Scriptures make this same differentiation between spirit and soul. "For the word of God is living and active, sharper than any two-edged sword, piercing
to the division of *soul and spirit*, of joints and marrow, and
discerning the thoughts and intentions of the heart" (Heb.
4.12). The writer in this verse divides man's non-corporal
elements into two parts, "soul and spirit." The corporal part
is mentioned here as including the joints and marrow—organs
of motion and sensation. When the priest uses the sword to
cut and completely dissect the sacrifice, nothing inside can
be hidden. Even joint and marrow are separated. In like
manner the Lord Jesus uses the Word of God on His people
to separate thoroughly, to pierce even to the division of the
spiritual, the soulical, and the physical. And from this it
follows that since soul and spirit can be *divided*, they must
be different in nature. It is thus evident here that man is
a composite of three parts.

THE CREATION OF MAN

"And Jehovah God formed man of dust from the ground,
and breathed into his nostrils the breath of life; and man
became a living soul" (Gen. 2.7 ASV). When God first
created man He formed him of dust from the ground, and
then breathed "the breath of life" into his nostrils. As soon
as the breath of life, which became man's spirit, came into
contact with man's body, the soul was produced. Hence the
soul is the combination of man's body and spirit. The Scriptures therefore call man "a living soul." The breath of life
became man's spirit; that is, the principle of life within him.
The Lord Jesus tells us "it is the spirit that gives life" (John
6.63). This breath of life comes from the Lord of Creation.
However, we must not confuse *man's* spirit with God's Holy
Spirit. The latter differs from our human spirit. Romans 8.16
demonstrates their difference by declaring that "it is the Spirit
himself bearing witness *with* our spirit that we are children
of God." The original of the word "life" in "breath of life"

is *chay* and is in the *plural*. This may refer to the fact that the
inbreathing of God produced a twofold life, soulical and
spiritual. When the inbreathing of God entered man's body
it became the spirit of man; but when the spirit reacted with
the body the soul was produced. This explains the source of
our spiritual and soulical lives. We must recognize, though,
that this spirit is not God's *Own* life, for "the breath of the
Almighty gives me life" (Job 33.4). It is not the entrance of
the uncreated life of God into man, neither is it that life of
God which we receive at regeneration. What we receive at
new birth is God's Own life as typified by the tree of life.
But our human spirit, though permanently existing, is void
of "eternal life."

"Formed man of dust from the ground" refers to man's
body; "breathed into his nostrils the breath of life" refers to
man's spirit as it came from God; and "man became a living
soul" refers to man's soul when the body was quickened by
the spirit and brought into being a living and self-conscious
man. A complete man is a trinity—the composite of spirit,
soul and body. According to Genesis 2.7, man was made up
of only two independent elements, the corporeal and the
spiritual; but when God placed the spirit within the casing
of the earth, the soul was produced. The spirit of man touching the dead body produced the soul. The body apart from
the spirit was dead, but with the spirit man was made alive.
The organ thus animated was called the soul.

"Man became a living soul" expresses not merely the fact
that the combination of spirit and body produced the soul;
it also suggests that spirit and body were completely *merged*
in this soul. In other words, soul and body were combined
with the spirit, and spirit and body were merged in the soul.
Adam "in his unfallen state knew nothing of these ceaseless
strivings of spirit and flesh which are matters of daily experience to us. There was a perfect *blending* of his three natures
into one and the soul as the uniting medium became the
cause of his individuality, of his existence as a distinct being."
(Pember's *Earth's Earliest Age*) Man was designated a

living soul, for it was there that the spirit and body met
and through which his individuality was known. Perhaps we
may use an imperfect illustration: drop some dye into a cup
of water. The dye and water will blend into a third substance
called ink. In like manner the two independent elements of
spirit and body combine to become living soul. (The analogy
fails in that the soul produced by the combining of spirit and
body becomes an independent, indissoluble element as much
as the spirit and body.)

God treated man's soul as something unique. As the angels
were created as spirits, so man was created predominantly
as a living soul. Man not only had a body, a body with the
breath of life; he became a living soul as well. Thus we
find later in the Scriptures that God often referred to men
as "souls." Why? Because what the man is depends on how
his soul is. His soul represents him and expresses his individuality. It is the organ of man's free will, the organ in which
spirit and body are completely merged. If man's soul wills to
obey God, it will allow the spirit to rule over the man as
ordered by God. The soul, if it chooses, also can suppress the
spirit and take some other delight as lord of the man. This
trinity of spirit, soul and body may be partially illustrated
by a light bulb. Within the bulb, which can represent the
total man, there are electricity, light and wire. The spirit
is like the electricity, the soul the light, and body the wire.
Electricity is the cause of the light while light is the effect of
electricity. Wire is the material substance for carrying the
electricity as well as for manifesting the light. The combination of spirit and body produces soul, that which is unique to
man. As electricity, carried by the wire, is expressed in light,
so spirit acts upon the soul and the soul, in turn, expresses
itself through the body.

However, we must remember well that whereas the soul
is the meeting-point of the elements of our being in this
present life, the spirit will be the ruling power in our resurrection state. For the Bible tells us that "it is sown a physical
body, it is raised a spiritual body" (1 Cor. 15.44). Yet here

is a vital point: we who have been joined to the resurrected Lord can even now have our spirit rule over the whole being. We are not united to the first Adam who was made a living soul but to the last Adam Who is a life-giving spirit (v.45).

RESPECTIVE FUNCTIONS OF SPIRIT, SOUL AND BODY

It is through the corporal body that man comes into contact with the material world. Hence we may label the body as that part which gives us *world-consciousness*. The soul comprises the intellect which aids us in the present state of existence and the emotions which proceed from the senses. Since the soul belongs to man's own self and reveals his personality, it is termed the part of *self-consciousness*. The spirit is that part by which we commune with God and by which alone we are able to apprehend and worship Him. Because it tells us of our relationship with God, the spirit is called the element of *God-consciousness*. God dwells in the spirit, self dwells in the soul, while senses dwell in the body.

As we have mentioned already, the soul is the meeting-point of spirit and body, for there they are merged. By his spirit man holds intercourse with the spiritual world and with the Spirit of God, both receiving and expressing the power and life of the spiritual realm. Through his body man is in contact with the outside sensuous world, affecting it and being affected by it. The soul stands between these two worlds, yet belongs to both. It is linked with the spiritual world through the spirit and with the material world through the body. It also possesses the power of free will, hence is able to choose from among its environments. The spirit cannot act directly upon the body. It needs a medium, and that medium is the soul produced by the touching of the spirit with the body. The soul therefore stands between the spirit and the body, binding these two together. The spirit can subdue the body through the medium of the soul, so that it will obey God; likewise the body through the soul can draw the spirit into loving the world.

Of these three elements the spirit is the noblest for it joins with God. The body is the lowest for it contacts with matter. The soul lying between them joins the two together and also takes their character to be its own. The soul makes it possible for the spirit and the body to communicate and to cooperate. The work of the soul is to keep these two in their proper order so that they may not lose their right relationship —namely, that the lowest, the body, may be subjected to the spirit, and that the highest, the spirit, may govern the body through the soul. Man's prime factor is definitely the soul. It looks to the spirit to give what the latter has received from the Holy Spirit in order that the soul, after it has been perfected, may transmit what it has obtained to the body; then the body too may share in the perfection of the Holy Spirit and so become a spiritual body.

The spirit is the noblest part of man and occupies the innermost area of his being. The body is the lowest and takes the outermost place. Between these two dwells the soul, serving as their medium. The body is the outer shelter of the soul, while the soul is the outer sheath of the spirit. The spirit transmits its thought to the soul and the soul exercises the body to obey the spirit's order. This is the meaning of the soul as the medium. Before the fall of man the spirit controlled the whole being through the soul.

The power of the soul is most substantial, since the spirit and the body are merged there and make it the site of man's personality and influence. Before man committed sin the power of the soul was completely under the dominion of the spirit. Its strength was therefore the spirit's strength. The spirit cannot itself act upon the body; it can only do so through the medium of the soul. This we can see in Luke 1.46-47: "My soul magnifies the Lord, and my spirit has rejoiced in God my Saviour" (Darby). "Here the change in tense shows that the spirit first conceived joy in God, and then, communicating with the soul, caused it to give expression to the feeling by means of the bodily organ." (Pember's *Earth's Earliest Age*)

To repeat, the soul is the site of personality. The will, intellect and emotions of man are there. As the spirit is used to communicate with the spiritual world and the body with the natural world, so the soul stands between and exercises its power to discern and decide whether the spiritual or the natural world should reign. Sometimes too the soul itself takes control over man through its intellect, thus creating an ideational world which reigns. In order for the spirit to govern, the soul must give its consent; otherwise the spirit is helpless to regulate the soul and the body. But this decision is up to the soul, for therein resides the personality of the man.

Actually the soul is the pivot of the entire being, because man's volition belongs to it. It is only when the soul is willing to assume a humble position that the spirit can ever manage the whole man. If the soul rebels against taking such a position the spirit will be powerless to rule. This explains the meaning of the free will of man. Man is not an automaton that turns according to God's will. Rather, man has full sovereign power to decide for himself. He possesses the organ of his own volition and can choose either to follow God's will or to resist Him and follow Satan's will instead. God desires that the spirit, being the noblest part of man, should control the whole being. Yet, the will—the crucial part of individuality—belongs to the soul. It is the will which determines whether the spirit, the body, or even itself is to rule. In view of the fact that the soul possesses such power and is the organ of man's individuality, the Bible calls man "a living soul."

THE HOLY TEMPLE AND MAN

"Do you not know," writes the Apostle Paul, "that you are God's temple and that God's Spirit dwells in you?" (1 Cor. 3.16) He has received revelation in likening man to the temple. As God formerly dwelt in the temple, so the Holy Spirit indwells man today. By comparing him to the temple

we can see how the tripartite elements of man are distinctly
manifested.

We know the temple is divided into three parts. The first
is the outer court which is seen by all and visited by all. All
external worship is offered here. Going further in is the Holy
Place, into which only the priests can enter and where they
present oil, incense and bread to God. They are quite near
to God—yet not the nearest, for they are still outside the
veil and therefore unable to stand before His very presence.
God dwells deepest within, in the Holy of Holies, where
darkness is overshadowed by brilliant light and into which no
man can enter. Though the high priest does enter in once
annually, it nonetheless indicates that before the veil is rent
there can be no man in the Holy of Holies.

Man is God's temple also, and he too has three parts. The
body is like the outer court, occupying an external position
with its life visible to all. Here man ought to obey every
commandment of God. Here God's Son serves as a substitute
and dies for mankind. Inside is man's soul which constitutes
the inner life of man and which embraces man's emotion,
volition and mind. Such is the Holy Place of a regenerated
person, for his love, will and thought are fully enlightened
that he may serve God even as the priest of old did. Innermost, behind the veil, lies the Holy of Holies into which no
human light has ever penetrated and no naked eye has ever
pierced. It is "the secret place of the Most High," the dwelling place of God. It cannot be reached by man unless God
is willing to rend the veil. It is man's spirit. This spirit lies
beyond man's self-consciousness and above his sensibility.
Here man unites and communes with God.

No light is provided for the Holy of Holies because God
dwells there. There is light in the Holy Place supplied by the
lampstand of seven branches. The outer court stands under
the broad daylight. All these serve as images and shadows
to a regenerated person. His spirit is like the Holy of Holies
indwelt by God, where everything is carried on by faith,
beyond the sight, sense or understanding of the believing

one. The soul resembles the Holy Place for it is amply enlightened with many rational thoughts and precepts, much knowledge and understanding concerning the things in the ideational and material world. The body is comparable to the outer court, clearly visible to all. The body's actions may be seen by everyone.

The order which God presents to us is unmistakable: "your spirit and soul and body" (1 Thess. 5.23). It is not "soul and spirit and body," nor is it "body and soul and spirit." The spirit is the pre-eminent part, hence it is mentioned first; the body is the lowest and therefore is last mentioned; the soul stands between, so is mentioned between. Having now seen God's order, we can appreciate the wisdom of the Bible in likening man to a temple. We can recognize the perfect harmony which exists between the temple and man in respect to both order and value.

Temple service moves according to the revelation in the Holy of Holies. All activities in the Holy Place and in the outer court are regulated by the presence of God in the Holiest Place. This is the most sacred spot, the place upon which the four corners of the temple converge and rest. It may seem to us that nothing is done in the Holiest because it is pitch dark. All activities are in the Holy Place; even those activities of the outer court are controlled by the priests of the Holy Place. Yet all the activities of the Holy Place actually are directed by the revelation in the utter quietness and peace of the Holy of Holies.

It is not difficult to perceive the spiritual application. The soul, the organ of our personality, is composed of mind, volition and emotion. It appears as though the soul is master of all actions, for the body follows its direction. Before the fall of man, however, the soul, in spite of its many activities, was governed by the spirit. And this is the order God still wants: first the spirit, then the soul, and lastly the body.

CHAPTER 2
SPIRIT AND SOUL

SPIRIT

IT IS IMPERATIVE that a believer know he has a spirit, since, as we shall soon learn, every communication of God with man occurs there. If the believer does not discern his own spirit he invariably is ignorant of how to commune with God in the spirit. He easily substitutes the thoughts or emotions of the soul for the works of the spirit. Thus he confines himself to the outer realm, unable ever to reach the spiritual realm.

> 1 Corinthians 2.11 speaks of "the spirit of the man
>   which is in him."
> 1 Corinthians 5.4 mentions "my spirit."
> Romans 8.16 says "our spirit."
> 1 Corinthians 14.14 uses "my spirit."
> 1 Corinthians 14.32 tells of the "spirits of prophets."
> Proverbs 25.28 refers to "his own spirit." Darby
> Hebrews 12.23 record "the spirits of just men."
> Zechariah 12.1 states that "the Lord . . . formed the
>   spirit of man within him."

The above Scripture verses sufficiently prove that we human beings do possess a human spirit. This spirit is not synonymous with our soul nor is it the same as the Holy Spirit. We worship God in this spirit.

According to the teaching of the Bible and the experience of believers, the human spirit can be said to comprise three parts; or, to put it another way, one can say it has three main functions. These are conscience, intuition and communion.

→ The *conscience* is the discerning organ which distinguishes right and wrong; not, however, through the influence of knowledge stored in the mind but rather by a spontaneous direct judgment. Often reasoning will justify things which our conscience judges. The work of the conscience is independent and direct; it does not bend to outside opinions. If man should do wrong it will raise its voice of accusation.
→ *Intuition* is the sensing organ of the human spirit. It is so diametrically different from physical sense and soulical sense that it is called intuition. Intuition involves a direct sensing independent of any outside influence. That knowledge which comes to us without any help from the mind, emotion or volition comes intuitively. We really "know" through our intuition; our mind merely helps us to "understand." The revelations of God and all the movements of the Holy Spirit are known to the believer through his intuition. A believer must therefore heed these two elements: the voice of con-
→ science and the teaching of intuition. *Communion* is worshiping God. The organs of the soul are incompetent to worship God. God is not apprehended by our thoughts, feelings or intentions, for He can only be known *directly* in our spirits. Our worship of God and God's communications with us are directly in the spirit. They take place in "the inner man," not in the soul or outward man.

We can conclude then that these three elements of conscience, intuition and communion are deeply interrelated and function coordinately. The relationship between conscience
✓ and intuition is that conscience judges according to intuition; it condemns all conduct which does not follow the directions
⚹ given by intuition. Intuition is related to communion or worship in that God is known by man intuitively and reveals
⟍ His will to man in the intuition. No measure of expectation or deduction gives us the knowledge of God.

From the following three groups of Scripture verses it can readily be observed that our spirits possess the function of conscience (we do not say that the spirit *is* conscience), the function of intuition (or spiritual sense), and the function of communion (or worship).

A) *The Function of Conscience in Man's Spirit*

"The Lord your God *hardened* his spirit" Deut. 2.30
"Saves the *crushed* in spirit" Ps. 34.18
"Put a new and *right* spirit within me" Ps. 51.10
"When Jesus had thus spoken, he was *troubled* in spirit" John 13.21
"His spirit was *provoked* within him as he saw that the city was full of idols" Acts 17.16
"It is the Spirit himself bearing *witness* with our spirit that we are *children* of God" Rom. 8.16
"I am present in spirit, and as if present, I háve already *pronounced judgment*" 1 Cor. 5.3
"I had no *rest* in my spirit" 2 Cor. 2.13 AV
"For God did not give us the spirit of *timidity*" 2 Tim. 1.7

B) *The Function of Intuition in Man's Spirit*

"The spirit indeed is *willing*" Matt. 26.41
"Jesus *perceiving* in his spirit" Mark 2.8
"He *sighed* deeply in his spirit" Mark 8.12
"He was deeply *moved* in spirit" John 11.33
"Paul was *pressed* in the spirit" Acts 18.5 AV
"Being *fervent* in spirit" Acts 18.25
"I am going to Jerusalem, *bound* in the spirit" Acts 20.22
"What person *knows* a man's thoughts except the spirit of the man which is in him" 1 Cor. 2.11
"They *refreshed* my spirit as well as yours" 1 Cor. 16.18
"His spirit was *refreshed* by you all" 2 Cor. 7.13 AV

C) *The Function of Communion in Man's Spirit*

"My spirit *rejoices* in God my Savior" Luke 1.47
"The true worshipers will *worship* the Father in spirit and truth" John 4.23
"Whom I *serve* with my spirit" Rom. 1.9
"We *serve* . . . in the new life of the spirit" Rom. 7.6
"You have received the spirit of sonship when we *cry* Abba Father" Rom. 8.15
"The Spirit himself bearing witness *with* our spirit" Rom. 8.16
"He who is *united* to the Lord becomes one spirit with him" 1 Cor. 6.17
"I will *sing* with the spirit" 1 Cor. 14.15
"If you *bless* with the spirit" 1 Cor. 14.16
"In the spirit he *carried me away*" Rev. 21.10

We can know by these Scriptures that our spirit possesses at least these three functions. Although unregenerated men do not yet have life, they nevertheless possess these functions (but their worship is of evil spirits). Some people manifest more of these functions while others less. This does not however imply that they are not dead in sins and transgressions. The New Testament does not consider those with a sensitive conscience, keen intuition or a spiritual tendency and interest to be saved individuals. Such people only prove to us that aside from the mind, emotion and will of our soul, we also have a spirit. Prior to regeneration the spirit is separated from God's life; only afterwards does the life of God and of the Holy Spirit dwell in our spirits. They then have been quickened to be instruments of the Holy Spirit.

Our aim in studying the significance of the spirit is to enable us to realize that we as human beings possess an independent spirit. This spirit is not man's mind, his will or his emotion; on the contrary, it includes the functions of conscience, intuition and communion. It is here in the spirit that God regenerates us, teaches us, and leads us into His rest. But sad to say, due to long years of bondage to the soul many Christians know very little of their spirit. We ought to tremble before God, asking Him to teach us through experience what is spiritual and what is soulish.

Before the believer is born again his spirit becomes so sunken and surrounded by his soul that it is impossible for him to distinguish whether something is emanating from the soul or from the spirit. The functions of the latter have become mixed up with those of the former. Furthermore, the spirit has lost its primary function—towards God; for it is dead to God. It thus would appear that it has become an accessory to the soul. And as the mind, emotion and volition grow stronger, the functions of the spirit become so eclipsed as to render them almost unknown. That is why there must be the work of dividing between soul and spirit after a believer is regenerated.

In searching the Scriptures it does seem that an unregenerated spirit functions no differently from the way the soul does. The following verses illustrate this.

"His spirit was troubled" Gen. 41.8
"Then their spirit was appeased toward him" Judges 8.3 Darby
"He that is hasty of spirit exalteth folly" Prov. 14.29 Darby
"A downcast spirit dries up the bones" Prov. 17.22
"Those who err in spirit" Is. 29.24
"And shall wail for anguish of spirit" Is. 65.14
"His spirit was hardened" Dan. 5.20

These show us the works of the *unregenerated* spirit and indicate how similar are its works to those of the soul. The reason for not mentioning soul but spirit is to reveal what has occurred in the very depth of man. It discloses how man's spirit has become controlled and influenced completely by his soul with the result that it manifests the works of the soul. The spirit nonetheless still exists because these works come from the spirit. Though ruled by the soul the spirit does not cease to be an organ.

SOUL

Aside from having a spirit which enables him to commune with God, man also possesses a soul, his self-consciousness. Hs is made conscious of his existence by the work of his soul. It is the seat of our personality. The elements which make us human belong to the soul. Intellect, thought, ideals, love, emotion, discernment, choice, decision, etc., are but various experiences of the soul.

It has been explained already that the spirit and the body are merged in the soul which, in turn, forms the organ of our personality. That is why the Bible sometimes calls man "soul," as though man has only this element. For example, Genesis 12.5 refers to people as "souls" (ASV). Again, when Jacob brought his entire family down to Egypt, it is recorded that "all the souls of the house of Jacob, that came into Egypt, were threescore and ten" (Gen. 46.27 ASV). Numerous instances occur in the original language of the Bible where "soul" is used instead of "man." For the seat and essence of the personality is the soul. To comprehend a man's personality is to comprehend his person. Man's existence, characteristics and life are all in the soul. The Bible consequently calls man "a soul."

That which constitutes man's personality are the three main faculties of volition, mind and emotion. Volition is the instrument for our decisions, revealing our power to choose. It expresses our willingness or unwillingness: "we will" or "we won't." Without it, man is reduced to an automaton. Mind, the instrument for our thoughts, manifests our intellectual power. Out of this arise wisdom, knowledge and reasoning. Lack of it makes a man foolish and dull. The instrument for our likes and dislikes is the faculty of emotion. Through it we are able to express love or hate and to feel joyful, angry, sad or happy. Any shortage of it will render man as insensitive as wood or stone.

A careful study of the Bible will yield the conclusion that these three primary faculties of personality belong to the soul. Too many Scripture passages exist to quote them all. Hence only a few selections can be enumerated here.

A) *The Soul's Faculty of Volition*

"Give me not up to the will (original, "soul") of my adversaries" Ps. 27.12
"Thou dost not give him up to the will (original, "soul") of his enemies" Ps. 41.2
"Delivered you to the greed (original, "soul") of your enemies" Ezek. 16.27
"You shall let her go where she will (original, "soul")" Deut. 21.14
"Aha, we have our heart's desire (original, "soul")" Ps. 35.25
"Or swear an oath to bind himself (original, "soul") by a pledge" Num. 30.2
"Now set your mind and heart (original, "soul") to seek the Lord your God" 1 Chron. 22.19
"They desire and *lift up* their soul to return to dwell there" Jer. 44.14 Amplified
"These afflictions my soul *refuses* to touch" Job 6.7 Amplified
"My soul *chooseth* strangling, death, rather than my bones" Job 7 15 Darby

The "will" or "heart" here points to the human will. "Set the heart," "lift up their soul," "refuse" and "choose" are all exercises of the will, having their springs in the soul.

B) *The Soul's Faculty of Intellect or Mind*

> "Whereunto they *lift up* their soul, their sons and their daughters" Ezek. 24.25 Darby
> "That a soul be without *knowledge* is not good" Prov. 19.2 Darby
> "How long must I bear pain (Syriac:Hebrew: *hold counsels*) in my soul?" Ps. 13.2
> "Marvelous are thy works; and that my soul *knoweth* right well" Ps. 139.14 Darby
> "My soul continually *thinks* of it" Lam. 3.20
> "*Knowledge* will be pleasant to your soul" Prov. 2.10
> "Keep sound *wisdom* and discretion . . . and they will be life for your soul" Prov. 3.21,22
> "Know that *wisdom* is such to your soul" Prov. 24.14

Here "knowledge," "counsel," "lift up," "think," etc., exist as the activities of man's intellect or mind, which the Bible indicates as emanating from the soul.

C) *The Soul's Faculty of Emotion*

1) EMOTIONS OF AFFECTION

> "The soul of Jonathan was *knit* to the soul of David, and Jonathan *loved* him as his own soul" 1 Sam. 18.1
> "You whom my soul *loves*" Song 1.7
> "My soul *magnifies* the Lord" Luke 1.46
> "His life *abhorreth* bread, and his soul dainty food" Job 33.20 Darby
> "Who are *hated* by David's soul" 2 Sam. 5.8
> "My soul was *vexed* with them" Zech. 11.8 Darby
> "You shall *love* the Lord your God . . . with all your soul" Deut. 6.5
> "My soul is *weary* of my life" Job 10:1 Darby
> "Their soul *abhorreth* all manner of food" Ps. 107:18 Darby

2) EMOTIONS OF DESIRE

> "For whatever thy soul *desireth* . . . or for whatever thy soul *asketh* of thee" Deut. 14.26 Darby
> "What thy soul may *say*" 1 Sam. 20.4 Darby
> "My soul *longs*, yea, *faints* for the courts of the Lord" Ps. 84.2

"Your soul's *longing*" Ezek. 24.21 Darby
"So *longs* my soul for thee, O God" Ps. 42.1
"My soul *yearns* for thee in the night" Is. 26.9
"My soul is *well pleased*" Matt. 12.18

3) EMOTIONS OF FEELING AND SENSING

"A sword will *pierce through* your own soul also" Luke 2.35
"All the people were *bitter* in soul" 1 Sam. 30.6
"Her soul is *bitter* and *vexed* within her" 2 Kings 4.27 Amplified
"His soul was *grieved* for the misery of Israel" Judges 10.16 Darby
"How long will ye *vex* my soul" Job 19.2 Darby
"My soul shall *exult* in my God" Is. 61.10
"*Gladden* the soul of thy servant" Ps. 86.4
"Their soul *fainted* within them" Ps. 107.5
"Why are you *cast down*, O my soul" Ps. 42.5
"Return, O my soul, to your *rest*" Ps. 116.7
"My soul is *consumed* with longing" Ps. 119.20
"*Sweetness* to the soul" Prov. 16.24
"Let your soul *delight* itself in fatness" Is. 55.2 Amplified
"My soul *fainted* within me" Jonah 2.7
"My soul is very *sorrowful*" Matt. 26.38
"Now is my soul *troubled*" John 12.27
"He was *vexed* in his righteous soul day after day" 2 Peter 2.8

We can discover in the above observations touching upon man's various emotions that our soul is capable of loving and hating, desiring and aspiring, feeling and sensing.

From this brief Biblical study it becomes quite obvious that the soul of man contains in it that part known as will, that part known as mind or intellect, and that part known as emotion.

THE SOUL LIFE

Some Bible scholars point out to us that three different words are employed in the Greek to designate "life": (1) *bios* (2) *psuche* (3) *zoe*. They all describe life but convey very different meanings. *Bios* has reference to the means of life or living. Our Lord Jesus used this word when He commended the woman who cast into the temple treasury her whole living. *Zoe* is the highest life, the life of the spirit. Whenever the Bible speaks of eternal life it uses this word. *Psuche* refers to the animated life of man, his natural life or the life of the soul. The Bible employs this term when it describes the human life.

Let us note here that the words "soul" and "soul life" in the Bible are one and the same in the original. In the Old Testament the Hebrew word for "soul"—*nephesh*—is used equally for "soul life." The New Testament consequently employs the Greek word *psuche* for both "soul" and "soul life." Hence we know "soul" not only is one of the three elements of man but also is man's life, his natural life. In many places in the Bible, "soul" is translated as "life."

> "Only you shall not eat flesh with its life, that is, its blood" Gen. 9.4,5
> "The life of the flesh is in the blood" Lev. 17.11
> "Those who sought the child's life are dead" Matt. 2.20
> "Is it lawful on the sabbath—to save life or to destroy it?" Luke 6.9
> "Who have risked their lives for the sake of our Lord Jesus Christ" Acts 15.26
> "I do not account my life of any value" Acts 20.24
> "To give his life as a ransom for many" Matt. 20.28
> "The good shepherd lays down his life for the sheep" John 10.11, 15,17

The word "life" in these verses is "soul" in the original. It is so translated because it would be difficult to understand otherwise. The soul actually is the very life of man.

As we have mentioned, "soul" is one of the three elements of man. "Soul life" is man's natural life, that which makes him exist and animates him. It is the life whereby man today lives; it is the power whereby man becomes what he is. Since the Bible applies *nephesh* and *psuche* both to soul and to man's life, it is evident to us that these two, though distinguishable, are not separable. They are distinguishable inasmuch as in certain places *psuche* (for example) must be translated either as "soul" or as "life." The translations cannot be interchanged. For instance, "soul" and "life" in Luke 12.19-23 and Mark 3.4 are actually the same word in the original, yet to translate them with the same word in English would be meaningless. They are inseparable, however, because these two are completely united in man. A man without a soul does not live. The Bible never tells us that a natural man possesses a life other than the soul. The life of man is but the soul permeating the body. As the soul is joined to the body it becomes the life of man. Life is the phenomenon of the soul. The Bible considers man's present body a "soulical body" (1 Cor. 15.44 original), for the life of our present body is that of the soul. Man's life is therefore simply an expression of the composite of his mental, emotional and volitional energies. "Personality" in the natural realm embraces these different parts of the soul but only that much. Soul life is man's natural life.

That the soul is man's life is a most important fact to recognize for it bears greatly upon the kind of Christian we become, whether spiritual or soulish. This we shall explain further on.

SOUL AND MAN'S SELF

Inasmuch as we have seen how soul is the site of our personality, the organ of volition and the natural life, we can easily conclude that this soul is also the "real I"—I myself. Our self is the soul. This too can be demonstrated by the Bible. In Numbers 30, the phrase "bind himself" occurs ten times. In the original it is "bind his soul." From this we are led to understand that the soul is our own self. In many other passages of the Bible we find the word "soul" is translated as "self." For instance:

"You shall not defile yourselves with them" Lev. 11.43
"You shall not defile yourselves" Lev. 11.44
"For themselves and for their descendants" Esther 9.31
"You who tear yourself in your anger" Job 18.4
"He justified himself" Job 32.2
"But themselves go into captivity" Is. 46.2
"What every one (original, "every soul") must eat, that only may be prepared by you" Ex. 12.16
"Who kills any person (original, "kill any soul") without intent" Num. 35.11,15

"Let me (original, "let my soul") die the death of the righteous" Num. 23.10

"When any one (original, "any soul") brings a cereal offering" Lev. 2.1

"I have . . . quieted myself" Ps. 131.2 AV

"Think not that in the king's palace you (original, "soul") will escape" Esther 4.13

"The Lord God has sworn by himself (original, "sworn by his soul")" Amos 6.8

These Scriptures from the Old Testament inform us in various ways how the soul is man's own self.

The New Testament conveys the same impression. "Souls" is the original rendering for "eight *persons*" in 1 Peter 3.20 and for "two hundred and seventy-six *persons*" in Acts 27.37. The phrase in Romans 2.9 translated today as "every human being who does evil" is given in the original as "every soul of man that works evil." Hence, to warn the soul of a man who works evil is to warn the evil man. In James 5.20, saving a soul is considered to be saving a sinner. And Luke 12.19 treats the rich fool's speaking words of comfort to his soul as speaking to himself. It is therefore clear that the Bible as a whole views man's soul or soul life as the man himself.

A confirmation of this can be found in the words of our Lord Jesus, given in two different Gospels. Matthew 16.26 reads: "For what will it profit a man, if he gains the whole world and forfeits *his life* (*psvche*)? Or what shall a man give in return for *his life* (*psvche*)?" Whereas Luke 9.25 renders it: "For what does it profit a man if he gains the whole world and loses or forfeits *himself* (*eautov*)?" Both Gospel writers record the same thing; yet one uses "life" (or "soul") while the other uses "himself." This signifies that the Holy Spirit is using Matthew to explain the meaning of "himself" in Luke and Luke the meaning of "life" in Matthew. Man's soul or life is the man himself, and vice versa.

Such a study enables us to conclude that, to be a man, we must share what is included in man's soul. Every natural man possesses this element and whatever it includes, for the soul is the common life shared by all natural men. Before regeneration, whatever is included in life—be it self, life, strength, power, choice, thought, opinion, love, feeling—pertains to the soul. In other words, soul life is the life a man inherits at birth. All that this life possesses and all that it may become are in the realm of the soul. If we distinctly recognize what is soulical it will then be easier for us later on to recognize what is spiritual. It will be possible to divide the spiritual from the soulish.

THE FALL OF MAN

THE MAN GOD FASHIONED was notably different from all other created beings. Man possessed a spirit similar to that of the angels and at the same time had a soul resembling that of the lower animals. When God created man He gave him a perfect freedom. He did not make man an automaton, controlled automatically by His will. This is evident in Genesis 2 at the time God instructed the original man what fruit he could eat and what not. The man God created was not a machine run by God; instead he had perfect freedom of choice. If he chose to obey God, he could; if he decided to rebel against God, he could do that too. Man had in his possession a sovereignty by which he could exercise his volition in choosing to obey or to disobey. This is a most important point, for we must realize that in our spiritual life God never deprives us our freedom. Unless we actively cooperate, God will not undertake anything for us. Neither God nor the devil can do any work without first obtaining our consent, for man's will is free.

Man's spirit was originally the highest part of his entire being to which soul and body were to be subject. Under normal conditions the spirit is like a mistress, the soul like a steward, and the body like a servant. The mistress commits matters to the steward who in turn commands the servant to carry them out. The mistress gives orders privately to the steward; the steward in turn transmits them openly to the servant. The steward appears to be the lord of all, but in actuality the lord over all is the mistress. Unfortunately man

has fallen; he has been defeated and has sinned; consequently, the proper order of spirit, soul and body has been
confused.

God bestowed upon man a sovereign power and accorded
numerous gifts to a human soul. Thought and will or intellect
and intention are among the prominent portions. The original
purpose of God is that the human soul should receive and
assimilate the truth and substance of God's spiritual life. He
gave gifts to men in order that man might take God's knowledge and will as his own. If man's spirit and soul would
maintain their created perfection, healthiness and liveliness,
his body would then be able to continue forever without
change. If he would exercise his will by taking and eating the
fruit of life, God's Own life undoubtedly would enter his
spirit, permeate his soul, transform his entire inner man,
and translate his body into incorruptibility. He then would
literally be in possession of "eternal life." In that event his
soulical life would be filled completely with spiritual life,
and his whole being would be transformed into that which
is spiritual. Conversely, if the order of spirit and soul would
be reversed, then man would plunge into darkness and the
human body could not last long but would soon be corrupted.

We know how man's soul chose the tree of the knowledge
of good and evil rather than the tree of life. Yet is it not clear
that God's will for Adam was to eat the fruit of the tree of
life? Because before He forbade Adam to eat the fruit of the
tree of good and evil and warned him that in the day he ate
he should die (Gen. 2.17), He first commanded man to eat
freely of every tree of the garden and purposely mentioned
the tree of life in the midst of the garden. Who can say that
this is not so?

"The fruit of the knowledge of good and evil" uplifts the
human soul and suppresses the spirit. God does not forbid
man to eat of this fruit merely to test man. He forbids it because He knows that by eating this fruit man's soul life will
be so stimulated that his spirit life will be stifled. This means
man will lose the true knowledge of God and thus be dead

to Him. God's forbiddance shows God's love. The knowledge of good and evil in this world is itself evil. Such knowledge springs from the intellect of man's soul. It puffs up the soul life and consequently deflates the spirit life to the point of losing any knowledge of God, to the point of becoming as much as dead.

A great number of God's servants view this tree of life as God offering life to the world in His Son the Lord Jesus. This is eternal life, God's nature, His uncreated life. Hence, we have here two trees—one germinates spiritual life while the other develops soulish life. Man in his original state is neither sinful nor holy and righteous. He stands between the two. Either he can accept God's life, thus becoming a spiritual man and a partaker of divine nature; or he can inflate his created life into becoming soulish, consequently inflicting death on his spirit. God imparted a perfect balance to the three parts of man. Whenever one part is over-developed the others are afflicted.

Our spiritual walk will be greatly helped if we understand the origin of soul and its life principle. Our spirit comes directly from God for it is God-given (Num. 16.22). Our soul is not so directly derived; it was produced after the spirit entered the body. It is therefore characteristically related to the created being. It is the created life, the natural life. The soul's usefulness is indeed extensive if it maintains its proper place as a steward, permitting the spirit to be mistress. Man can then receive God's life and be related to God in life. If, however, this soulical realm becomes inflated the spirit is accordingly suppressed. All man's doings will be confined to the natural realm of the created, unable to be united to God's supernatural and uncreated life. The original man succumbed to death in that he ate of the fruit of the knowledge of good and evil, thereby abnormally developing his soulical life.

Satan tempted Eve with a question. He knew his query would arouse the woman's thought. If she were completely under the spirit's control she would reject such questioning.

By trying to answer she exercised her mind in disobedience to the spirit. Doubtless Satan's question was full of errors, for his prime motive was merely to incite Eve's mental exertion. He would have expected Eve to correct him, but alas, Eve dared to change God's Word in her conversation with Satan. The enemy accordingly was emboldened to tempt her to eat by suggesting to her that, in eating, her eyes would be opened and she would be like God—knowing good and evil. "So when the woman saw that the tree was good for food, and that it was a delight to the eyes, and that the tree was to be desired to make one wise, she took of its fruit and ate" (Gen. 3.6). That was how Eve viewed the matter. Satan provoked her soulical thought first and then advanced to seize her will. The result: she fell into sin.

Satan always uses physical need as the first target for attack. He simply mentioned eating fruit to Eve, an entirely physical matter. Next he proceeded to entice her soul, intimating that by indulging, her eyes would be opened to know good and evil. Although such searching for knowledge was perfectly legitimate, the consequence nonetheless led her spirit into open rebellion against God because she misconstrued God's forbiddance as arising from an evil intention. Satan's temptation reaches initially to the body, then to the soul and lastly to the spirit.

After being tempted Eve gave her verdict. To begin with, "the tree was good for food." This is the "lust of the flesh." Eve's flesh was the first to be stirred up. Second, "it was a delight to the eyes." This is "the lust of the eyes." Both the body and her soul were now enticed. Third, "the tree was to be desired to make one wise." This is "the pride of life." Such desire revealed the wavering of her emotion and will. Her soul was now agitated beyond control. It no longer stood by as a spectator but had been goaded into desiring the fruit. How dangerous a master human emotion is!

Why should Eve desire the fruit? It was not merely the lust of the flesh and the lust of the eyes, but also curiosity's urge for wisdom. In the pursuit of wisdom and knowledge, even of so-called "spiritual knowledge," activities of the soul often can be detected. When one tries to increase his knowledge by doing mental gymnastics over books without waiting upon God and looking to the guidance of the Holy Spirit, his soul is plainly in full swing. This will deplete his spiritual life. Because the fall of man was occasioned by seeking knowledge, God uses the foolishness of the cross to "destroy the wisdom of the wise." Intellect was the chief cause of the fall; hence, in order to be saved one must believe in the folly of the Word of the cross rather than depend upon his intellect. The tree of knowledge causes man to fall, so God employs the tree of folly (I Peter 2.24) to save souls. "If any one among you thinks that he is wise in this age, let him become a fool that he may become wise. For the wisdom of this world is folly with God" (1 Cor. 3.18-20; also see 1.18-25).

Having carefully reviewed the account of the fall of man, we are able to see that in rebelling against God, Adam and Eve developed their souls to the extent of displacing their spirits and plunging themselves into darkness. The prominent parts of the soul are man's mind, will and emotion. Will is the organ of decision, therefore the master of the man. Mind is the organ of thought, while emotion is that of affection. The Apostle Paul tells us "Adam was not deceived," indicating that Adam's mind was not muddled on that fatal day. The one who was feeble-minded was Eve: "the woman was deceived and became a transgressor" (1 Tim. 2.14). According to the record of Genesis it is written that "the woman said, 'The serpent beguiled me and I ate' " (Gen. 3.13); but that "the man said, 'The woman gave (not beguiled) me fruit of the tree and I ate' " (Gen. 3.12). Adam obviously was not deceived; his mind was clear and he knew the fruit was from the forbidden tree. He ate because of his affection for the woman. Adam understood that what the serpent said was nothing more than the enemy's deception. From the words of the Apostle we are led to see that Adam sinned deliberately. He loved Eve more than himself. He made her his idol, and for her sake he was willing to rebel against the commandment of his Creator. How pitiful that his mind was overruled by his emotion; his reasoning, overcome by his affection. Why is it that men "did not believe the truth?" Because they "had pleasure in unrighteousness" (2 Thess. 2.12). It is not that the truth is unreasonable but that it is not loved. Hence when one truly turns to the Lord he "believes with his heart (not mind) and so is justified" (Rom 10.10).

Satan moved Adam to sin by seizing the latter's will through his emotion, while he tempted Eve to sin by grasping her will through the channel of a darkened mind. When man's will and mind and emotion were poisoned by the serpent and man followed after Satan instead of God, his spirit, which was capable of communing with God, suffered a fatal blow. Here we can see the law which governs the work of Satan. He uses the things of the flesh (eating fruit) to entice man's soul into sin; as soon as the soul sins, the spirit descends into utter darkness. The order of his working is always such: from the outside to the inside. If he does not start with the body, then he begins by working on the mind or the emotion in order to get to the will of man. The moment man's will yields to Satan he possesses man's whole being and puts the spirit to death. But not so the work of God; His is always from the inside to the outside. God begins working in man's spirit and continues by illuminating his mind, stirring his emotion, and causing him to exercise his will over his body for carrying into execution the will of God. All satanic works are performed from the outside inward; all divine works, from the inside outward. We may in this way distinguish what comes from God and what from Satan. All this additionally teaches us that once Satan seizes man's will, then is he in control over that man.

We should carefully note that the soul is where man expresses his free will and exerts his own mastery. The Bible therefore often records that it is the soul which sins. For example, Micah 6.7 says, "the sin of my soul." Ezekiel 18.4,20 reads, "the soul that sins." And in the books of Leviticus and Numbers mention frequently is made that the soul sins.

Why? Because it is the soul which chooses to sin. Our description of sin is: "The will acquiesces in the temptation." Sinning is a matter of the soul's will; atonement accordingly must be for the soul. "Ye give the heave-offering of Jehovah to make atonement for your souls" (Ex. 30.15 Darby). "For the soul of the flesh is in the blood; and I have given it to you upon the altar to make atonement for your souls, for it is the blood that maketh atonement for the soul" (Lev. 17.11 Darby). "To make atonement for our souls before Jehovah" (Num. 31.50 Darby). Since it is the *soul* which sins, it follows that the *soul* needs to be atoned. And it can only be atoned, moreover, by a soul:

> it pleased Jehovah to bruise him; he hath subjected him to suffering . . . thou shalt make his soul an offering for sin . . . He shall see of the fruit of the travail of his soul, and shall be satisfied . . . he hath poured out his soul unto death . . .; and he bore the sin of many, and made intercession for the transgressors. (Is. 53.10-12 Darby)

In examining the nature of Adam's sin we discover that aside from rebellion there is also a certain kind of independence. We must not lose sight here of free will. On the one hand, the tree of life implies a sense of *dependence*. Man at that time did not possess God's nature, but had he partaken of the fruit of the tree of life he could have secured God's life; man could have reached his summit—possessing the very life of God. This is dependence. On the other hand, the tree of the knowledge of good and evil suggests *independence* because man strived by the exercise of his will for the knowledge not promised, for something not accorded him by God. His rebellion declared his independence. By rebelling he did not need to depend upon God. Futhermore, his seeking the knowledge of good and evil also showed his independence, for he was not satisfied with what God had bestowed already. The difference between the spiritual and the soulish is crystal clear. The spiritual depends utterly upon God, fully satisfied with what God has given; the soulish steers clear of God and covets what God has not conferred, especially "knowledge." Independence is a special mark of the soulish. That thing—no matter how good, even worshiping God— is unquestionably of the soul if it does not require complete trust in God and instead calls for reliance upon one's own strength. The tree of life cannot grow within us together with the tree of knowledge. Rebellion and independence explain every sin committed by both sinners and saints.

SPIRIT, SOUL AND BODY AFTER THE FALL

Adam lived by the breath of life becoming spirit in him. By the spirit he sensed God, knew God's voice, and communed with God. He had a very keen awareness of God. But after his fall his spirit died.

When God spoke to Adam at the first He said, "in the day that you eat of it (the fruit of the tree of good and evil) you shall die" (Gen. 2.17). Adam and Eve nevertheless continued on for hundreds of years after eating the forbidden fruit. This obviously indicates that the death God foretold was not physical. Adam's death began in his spirit.

What really is death? According to its scientific definition, death is "the cessation of communication with environment." Death of the spirit is the cessation of its communication with God. Death of the body is the cutting off of communication between spirit and body. So when we say the spirit is dead it does not imply there is no more spirit; we simply mean the spirit has lost its sensitivity towards God and thus is dead to Him. The exact situation is that the spirit is incapacitated, unable to commune with God. To illustrate. A dumb person has a mouth and lungs but something is wrong with his vocal cords and he is powerless to speak. So far as human language is concerned his mouth may be considered dead. Similarly Adam's spirit died because of his disobedience to God. He still had his spirit, yet it was dead to God for it had lost its spiritual instinct. It is still so; sin has destroyed the spirit's keen intuitive knowledge of God and rendered man spiritually dead. He may be religious, moral, learned, capable, strong and wise, but he is dead to God. He may even talk about God, reason about God and preach God, but he is still dead to Him. Man is not able to hear or to sense the voice of God's Spirit. Consequently in the New Testament God often refers to those who are living in the flesh as dead.

The death which began in our forefather's spirit gradually spread until it reached his body. Though he lived on for many years after his spirit was dead, death nevertheless worked incessantly in him until his spirit, soul *and* body were all dead. His body, which could have been transformed and glorified, was instead returned to dust. Because his inward man had fallen into chaos, his outward body must die and be destroyed.

Henceforth Adam's spirit (as well as the spirit of all his descendants) fell under the oppression of the soul until it gradually merged with the soul and the two parts became closely united. The writer of Hebrews declares in 4.12 that the Word of God shall pierce and divide soul and spirit. The dividing is necessary because spirit and soul have become one. While they are intimately knit they plunge man into a psychic world. Everything is done according to the dictates of intellect or feeling. The spirit has lost its power and sensation, as though dead asleep. What instinct it has in knowing and serving God is entirely paralyzed. It remains in a coma as if non-existent. This is what is meant in Jude 19 by "natural, not having spirit" (literal).* This certainly does not mean the human spirit ceases to exist, for Numbers 16.22 distinctly states that God is "the God of the spirits of all flesh." Every human being still has in his possession a spirit, although it is darkened by sin and impotent to hold communion with God.

However dead this spirit may be towards God it may remain as active as the mind or the body. It is accounted dead to God but is still very active in other respects. Sometimes the spirit of a fallen man can even be stronger than his soul or body and gain dominion over the whole being. Such persons

---

* The spirit here does not point to the Holy Spirit but to the human spirit, for it is preceded by the word "natural," which literally is, "soulish." As "soulish" pertains to man, so "spirit" also pertains to man.

are "spiritual" just as most people are largely soulical or physical, because their spirits are much bigger than that of
ordinary individuals. These are the sorceresses and the witch-
es. They indeed maintain contacts with the spiritual realm;
but these do so through the evil spirit, not by the Holy Spirit.
The spirit of the fallen man thus is allied with Satan and his
evil spirits. It is dead to God yet very much alive to Satan
and follows the evil spirit which is now at work in him.

In yielding to the demand of its passions and lusts the soul
has become a slave to the body so that the Holy Spirit finds
it useless to strive for God's place in such a one. Hence the
Scripture declares, "My Spirit shall not always plead with
Man; for he indeed is flesh" (Gen. 6.3 Darby). The Bible
refers to the flesh as the composite of the unregenerated soul
and the physical life, though more often than not it points to
sin which is in the body. Once man is completely under the
dominion of the flesh he has no possibility of liberating himself. Soul has replaced the spirit's authority. Everything is
done independently and according to the dictates of his
mind. Even in religious matters, in the hottest pursuit of God,
all is carried on by the strength and will of man's soul, void
of the Holy Spirit's revelation. The soul is not merely independent of the spirit; it is additionally under the body's control. It is now asked to obey, to execute and to fulfill the lusts,
passions and demands of the body. Every son of Adam is
therefore not only dead in his spirit but he is also "from the
earth, a man of dust" (1 Cor. 15.47). Fallen men are governed completely by the flesh, walking in response to the desires of their soulish life and physical passions. Such ones are
unable to commune with God. Sometimes they display their
intellect, at others times their passion, but more often both
their intellect and passion. Unimpeded, the flesh is in firm
control over the total man.

This is what is unfolded in Jude 18 and 19 — "mockers,
walking after their own lusts of ungodlinesses. These are they
who set themselves apart, natural men, not having spirit"
(Darby). Being soulish is antagonistic to being spiritual. The

spirit, that noblest part of us, the part which may be united
to God and ought to regulate the soul and body, is now under
the dominion of the soul, that part of us which is earthly in
both its motive and aim. The spirit has been stripped of its
original position. Man's present condition is abnormal.
Wherefore he is pictured as not having spirit. The result of
being soulish is that he becomes a mocker, pursuing ungodly
passions and creating divisions.

1 Corinthians 2.14 speaks of such unregenerated persons
in this fashion: "The natural (soulish) man does not receive
the gifts of the spirit of God, for they are folly to him, and he
is not able to understand them because they are spiritually
discerned." Such men as are under the control of their souls
with their spirits suppressed are in direct contrast to spiritual
people. They may be exceedingly intelligent, able to present masterful ideas or theories, yet they do not consent to
the things of the Spirit of God. They are unfit to receive revelation from the Holy Spirit. Such revelation is vastly different from human ideas. Man may think human intellect
and reasoning are almighty, that the brain is able to comprehend all truths of the world; but the verdict of God's Word is,
"vanity of vanities."

While man is in his soulish state he frequently senses the
insecurity of this age and so he too seeks the eternal life of
the coming age. But even if he does, he is still powerless to
uncover the Word of life by his much thinking and theoriz-
ing. How untrustworthy are human reasonings! We often observe how very clever persons clash in their different opinions. Theories easily lead man into error. They are castles in
the air, tumbling him into eternal darkness.

How true it is that without the guidance of the Holy Spirit
intellect not only is undependable but also extremely dangerous, because it often confuses the issue of right and wrong.
A slight carelessness may cause not merely temporary loss
but even everlasting harm. The darkened mind of man frequently leads him to eternal death. If only unregenerated
souls could see this, how good it would be!

While man is fleshly he may be controlled by more than just the soul; he may be under the direction of the body as well; for soul and body are closely entwined. Because the body of sin is abounding in desires and passions, man may commit the most hideous of sins. As the body is formed of the dust, so its natural tendency is towards the earth. The introduction of the serpent's poison into man's body turns all its legitimate desires into lusts. Having once yielded to the body in disobeying God, the soul finds itself bound to yield every time. The base desires of the body may therefore often be expressed through the soul. The power of the body becomes so overwhelming that the soul cannot but become the obedient slave.

God's thought is for the spirit to have the pre-eminence, ruling our soul. But once man turns fleshly his spirit sinks into servitude to the soul. Further degradation follows when man becomes "bodily" (of the body), for the basest body rises to be sovereign. Man has then descended from "spirit-control" to "soul-control," and from "soul-control" to "body-control." Deeper and deeper he sinks. How pitiful it must be when the flesh gains dominion.

Sin has slain the spirit: spiritual death hence becomes the portion of all, for all are dead in sins and trespasses. Sin has rendered the soul independent: the soulish life is therefore but a selfish and self-willed one. Sin has finally empowered the body: sinful nature accordingly reigns through the body.

CHAPTER 4
SALVATION

CALVARY'S JUDGMENT

DEATH ENTERED THE WORLD through the fall of man. Reference here is to spiritual death which separates man from God. Through sin it came in the beginning and so has it ever come since then. Death always comes through sin. Note what Romans 5.12 tells us about this matter. First, that "sin came into the world through one man." Adam sinned and introduced sin into the world. Second, that "death (came into the world) through sin." Death is sin's unchanging result. And lastly, that therefore "death spread to all men because all men sinned." Not merely has death "spread *to*" or "passed *upon*" (Darby) all men, but literally "to all men the death did pass *through*" (Young's). Death has permeated the spirit, soul and body of all men; there is no part of a human being into which it has not found its way. It is therefore imperative that man receive God's life. The way of salvation cannot be in human reform, for "death" is irreparable. Sin must be judged before there can be rescue out of death. Exactly this is what has been provided by the salvation of the Lord Jesus.

The man who sins must die. This is announced in the Bible. No animal nor angel can suffer the penalty of sin in man's stead. It is man's triune nature which sins, therefore it is man who must die. Only humanity can atone for humanity. But because sin is in his humanity, man's own death cannot atone for his sin. The Lord Jesus came and took human nature upon himself in order that *He* might be judged instead of humanity. Untainted by sin, His holy human nature could therefore through death atone for sinful humanity. He died a substitute, suffered all penalty of sin, and offered his life a ransom for many. Consequently, whoever believes on Him shall be judged no more (John 5.24).

When the Word became flesh He included all flesh in Himself. As the action of one man, Adam, represents the action of all mankind, so the work of one man, Christ, represents the work of all. We must see how inclusive Christ is before we can understand what redemption is. Why is it that the sin of one man, Adam, is judged to be the sin of all men both present and past? Because Adam is humanity's head from whom all other men have come into the world. Similarly the obedience of one man, Christ, becomes the righteousness of many, both of the present and the past, inasmuch as Christ constitutes the head of a new mankind entered into by a new birth.

One incident in Hebrews 7 may illustrate this point. To prove that the priesthood of Melchizedek is greater than the priesthood of Levi, the writer reminds his readers that Abraham once offered a tithe to Melchizedek and received from him a blessing and so concluded that Abraham's tithe offering and blessing were Levi's. How? Because "he (Levi) was still in the loins of his ancestor (Abraham) when Melchizedek met him" (v.10). We know that Abraham begot Isaac, Isaac Jacob, and Jacob Levi. Levi was Abraham's great grandson. When Abraham offered the tithe and received a blessing, Levi was not yet born, nor even were his father and grandfather. Yet the Bible considers Abraham's tithe and blessing as Levi's. Inasmuch as Abraham is lesser than Melchizedek, Levi too is of less account than Melchizedek. This incident can help us to understand why Adam's sin is construed to be the sin of all men and why the judgment upon Christ is counted as judgment for all. It is simply because at the time Adam sinned, all men were presently in his loins. Likewise, when Christ was judged, all who will be regenerated were present in Christ. His judgment is hence

taken as their judgment, and all who have believed in Christ
shall no longer be judged.

Since humanity must be judged, the Son of God—even the
man Jesus Christ—suffered in his spirit, soul and body on the
cross for the sins of the world.

Let us first consider his physical sufferings. Man sins
through his body and there enjoys the temporary pleasure of
sin. The body must accordingly be the recipient of punishment. Who can fathom the physical sufferings of the Lord
Jesus on the cross? Are not Christ's sufferings in the body
clearly foretold in the Messianic writings? "They have
pierced my hands and feet" (Ps. 22.16). The prophet Zecha-
riah called attention to "him whom they have pierced" (12.
10). His hands, His feet, His brow, His side, His heart were
all pierced by men, pierced *by* sinful humanity and pierced
for sinful humanity. Many were His wounds and high ran His
fever for, with the weight of His whole body hanging unsup-
ported on the cross, His blood could not circulate freely. He
was extremely thirsty and therefore cried out, "My tongue
cleaves to my jaws"—"for my thirst they gave me vinegar to
drink" (Ps. 22.15, 69.21). The hands must be nailed, for they
love to sin. The mouth must suffer, for it loves to sin. The feet
must be pierced, for they love to sin. The brow must be
crowned with a thorny crown, for it too loves to sin. All that
the human body needed to suffer was executed upon His
body. Thus He suffered physically even to death. It was within His power to escape these sufferings, yet He willingly offered His body to endure immeasurable trials and pains,
never for a moment shrinking back until He knew that "all
was now finished" (John 19.28). Only then did He dismiss
his spirit.

Not His body only, His soul as well, suffered. The soul
is the organ of self-consciousness. Before being crucified,
Christ was administered wine mingled with myrrh as a seda-
tive to alleviate pain, but He refused it as He was not willing
to lose His consciousness. Human souls have fully enjoyed the
pleasure of sins; accordingly in His soul Jesus would endure

the pain of sins. He would rather drink the cup given Him by God than the cup which numbed consciousness.

How shameful is the punishment of the cross! It was used to execute runaway slaves. A slave had neither property nor rights. His body belonged to his master; he could therefore be punished with the most shameful cross. The Lord Jesus took the place of a slave and was crucified. Isaiah called Him "the servant"; Paul said He took the form of a slave. Yes, as a slave He came to rescue us who are subject to the lifelong bondage of sin and Satan. We are slaves to passion, temper, habits and the world. We are sold to sin. Yet He died because of our slavery and bore our entire shame.

The Bible records that the soldiers took the garments of the Lord Jesus (John 19.23). He was nearly naked when crucified. This is one of the shames of the cross. Sin takes our radiant garment away and renders us naked. Our Lord was stripped bare before Pilate and again on Calvary. How would His holy soul react to such abuse? Would it not insult the holiness of His personality and cover Him with shamefulness? Who can enter into His feeling of that tragic moment? Because every man had enjoyed the apparent glory of sin, so the Savior must endure the real shame of sin. Truly "thou (God) hast covered him with shame . . . with which thy enemies taunt, O Lord, with which they mock the footsteps of thy anointed"; He nonetheless "endured the cross, despising the shame" (Ps. 89.45,51; Heb. 12.2).

No one can ever ascertain how fully the soul of the Savior suffered on the cross. We often contemplate His physical suffering but overlook the feeling of His soul. A week before the Passover He was heard to mention: "Now is my soul troubled" (John 12.27). This points to the cross. While in the Garden of Gethsemane Jesus was again heard to say: "My soul is very sorrowful, even to death" (Matt. 26.38). Were it not for these words we would hardly think his soul had suffered. Isaiah 53 mentions thrice how His soul was made an offering for sin, how His soul travailed, and how He poured out His soul to death (vv.10-12). Because Jesus bore the

curse and shame of the cross, whoever believes in Him shall
no more be cursed and put to shame.

His spirit too suffered immensely. The spirit is that part of
man which equips him to commune with God. The Son of
God was holy, blameless, unstained, separated from sinners.
His spirit was united with the Holy Spirit in perfect oneness.
Never did there exist a moment of disturbance and doubt,
for He always had God's presence with Him. "It is not I
alone," declared Jesus, "but I and he who sent me . . . And
he who sent me is with me" (John 8.16,29). For this reason
He could pray, "Father, I thank thee that thou hast heard me.
I knew that thou hearest me always" (John 11.41-42). Nevertheless, while He hung on the cross—and if there ever were
a day when the Son of God desperately needed the presence
of God it must be that day—He cried out, "My God, my God,
why hast thou forsaken me?" (Matt. 27.46) His spirit was
split asunder from God. How intensely He felt the loneliness,
the desertion, the separation. The Son was still yielding, the
Son was still obeying the will of the Father-God, yet the Son
was forsaken: not for His Own sake, but for the sake of
others.

Sin affects most deeply the spirit; consequently, holy as the
Son of God was, still He had to be wrenched away from the
Father because He bore the sin of others. It is true that in the
countless days of eternity past "I and the Father are one"
(John 10.30). Even during His days of earthly sojourn this
remained true, for *His* humanity could not be a cause of separation from God. Sin alone could separate: even though that
sin be the sin of others. Jesus suffered this spiritual separation
for us in order that our spirit could return to God.

When he surveyed the death of Lazarus, Jesus might have
been thinking of His Own approaching death, and so "he was
deeply moved in spirit and troubled" (John 11.33). Upon
announcing that He would be betrayed and die on the cross,
He was again "troubled in spirit" (John 13.21). This tells us
why, when He received God's judgment on Calvary, He cried
out: "My God, my God, why hast thou forsaken me?" For "I

think of God and I moan; I meditate, and my spirit faints"
(Matt. 27.46 echoing Ps. 22.1; Ps. 77.3). He was deprived
of the mighty strengthening through the Holy Spirit in His
spirit (Eph. 3.16) because His spirit was torn away from the
Spirit of God. Therefore He sighed, "I am poured out like
water, and all my bones are out of joint; my heart is like wax,
it is melted within my breast; my strength is dried up like a
potsherd, and my tongue cleaves to my jaws; thou dost lay
me in the dust of death" (Ps. 22.14-15).

On the one side, the Holy Spirit of God deserted Him; on
the other, the evil spirit of Satan mocked him. It seems apparent that Psalm 22.11-13 refers to this phase: "Be not far
from me . . . there is none to help. Many bulls encompass me,
strong bulls of Bashan surround me; they opened wide their
mouths at me, like a ravening and roaring lion."

His spirit endured God's desertion on the one side and resisted the evil spirit's derision on the other. Man's human
spirit has so separated itself from God, exalted itself, and
followed the evil spirit that man's spirit must be totally brok-
en in order that it may no longer resist God and remain allied
with the enemy. The Lord Jesus became sin for us on the
cross. His inner holy humanity was completely smashed as
God passed judgment upon unholy humanity. Forsaken by
God, Christ thus suffered sin's bitterest pain, enduring in
darkness the punitive wrath of God on sin without the support of the love of God or the light of His countenance. To be
forsaken by God is the consequence of sin.

Now our sinful humanity has been judged completely because it was judged in the sinless humanity of the Lord
Jesus. In Him, holy humanity has won its victory. Whatever
judgment should come upon the body, soul and spirit of sinners has been poured upon Him. He is our representative. By
faith we are joined to Him. His death is reckoned as our
death, and His judgment as our judgment. Our spirit, soul
and body have altogether been judged and penalized in Him.
It would not be any different had we been punished in per-

son. "There is therefore now no condemnation for those who are in Christ Jesus" (Rom. 8.1).

This is what He has accomplished for us and such is now our standing before God. "For he who has died is freed from sin" (Rom. 6.7). Positionally we already have died in the Lord Jesus; it only awaits the Holy Spirit to translate this fact into our experience. The cross is where the sinner—spirit, soul and body—is altogether judged. It is through the death and resurrection of the Lord that the Holy Spirit of God is able to impart God's nature to us. The cross bears the sinner's judgment, proclaims the sinner's worthlessness, crucifies the sinner, and releases the life of the Lord Jesus. Henceforth anyone who accepts the cross shall be born anew by the Holy Spirit and receive the life of the Lord Jesus.

REGENERATION

The concept of regeneration as found in the Bible speaks of the process of passing out of death into life. A man's spirit before regeneration is far away from God and is considered dead, for death is dissociation from life and from God Who is the fountain of life. Death is hence separation from God. Man's spirit is dead and therefore unable to commune with Him. Either his soul controls him and plunges him into a life of ideas and imaginations, or the lusts and habits of his body stimulate him and reduce his soul to servitude.

Man's spirit needs to be quickened because it is born dead. The new birth which the Lord Jesus spoke about to Nicodemus is the new birth of the spirit. It certainly is not a physical birth as Nicodemus suspected, nor is it a soulical one. We must note carefully that new birth imparts God's life to the *spirit* of man. Inasmuch as Christ has atoned for our soul and destroyed the principle of the flesh, so we who are joined to Him participate in His resurrection life. We have been united with Him in His death; consequently it is in our spirit that we first reap the realization of His resurrection life. New birth is something which happens entirely within the spirit; it has no relation to soul or body.

What makes man unique in God's creation is not that he possesses a soul but that he has a spirit which, joined to the soul, constitutes the man. Such union marks out man as extraordinary in the universe. Man's soul is not related directly to God; according to the Bible, it is his spirit that relates itself to God. God is Spirit; all who worship Him, therefore, must worship in spirit. It alone can commune with God. Only spirit can worship Spirit. We thus find in the Bible such statements as: "serving with my spirit" (Rom. 1.9, 7.6, 12.11); "knowing through the spirit" (1 Cor. 2.9-12); "worshiping in spirit" (John 4.23-24; Phil. 3.3); "receiving in spirit the revelation of God" (Rev. 1.10; 1 Cor. 2.10).

In view of this fact, let us remember that God has ordained He will deal with man through his spirit alone and that by man's spirit His counsels are to be realized. If such be the case, how necessary for the spirit of man to continue in constant and living union with God, without for a moment being affected into disobeying divine laws by following the feelings, desires, and ideals of the outward soul. Otherwise, death shall set in immediately; the spirit will be denied its union with God's life. This does not signify that man would no longer have a spirit. It simply means, as we have discussed previously, that the spirit would abdicate its lofty position to the soul. Whenever a person's inner man heeds the dictates of the outer man, he loses contact with God and is rendered dead spiritually. "You were dead through the trespasses and sins in which you once walked" by "following the desires of body and mind" (Eph. 2.1-3).

The life of an unregenerated person almost entirely is governed by the soul. He may be living in fear, curiosity, joy, pride, pity, pleasure, delight, wonder, shame, love, remorse, elation. Or he may be full of ideals, imaginations, superstitions, doubts, suppositions, inquiries, inductions, deductions, analyses, introspections. Or he may be moved—by the desire for power, wealth, social recognition, freedom, position, fame, praise, knowledge—into making many daring decisions, into personally arbitrating, into voicing stubborn opinions, or even into undergoing patient endurance. All these and other like things are merely manifestations of the soul's three main functions of emotion, mind and will. Is not life composed pre-eminently of these matters? But regeneration can never arise out of these. To be penitent, to feel sorry for sin, to shed tears, to even make decisions does not bring in salvation. Confession, decision, and many other religious acts can never be and are not to be construed as new birth. Rational judgment, intelligent understanding, mental acceptance, or the pursuit of the good, the beautiful, and the true are merely soulical activities if the spirit is not reached and stirred. Although they may serve well as servants, man's ideas, feelings and choices cannot serve as masters and are consequently secondary in this matter of salvation. The Bible hence never regards new birth as being severity to the body, impulsive feeling, the demand of the will, or reform through mental understanding. The Biblical new birth occurs in an area far deeper than human body and soul, yea, even in man's spirit, where he receives God's life through the Holy Spirit.

The writer of Proverbs tells us that "the spirit of man is the lamp of the Lord" (20.27). During the time of regeneration the Holy Spirit comes into man's spirit and quickens it as though kindling a lamp. This is the "new spirit" mentioned in Ezekiel 36.26; the dead old spirit is quickened into life when the Holy Spirit infuses it with God's uncreated life.

Before regeneration the soul of man is in control of his spirit while his own "self" rules his soul and his passion governs his body. Soul has become the life of the body. At regeneration man receives God's Own life into his spirit and is born of God. As a consequence, the Holy Spirit now rules man's spirit which in turn is equipped to regain control over the soul and, through the soul, to govern his body. Because the Holy Spirit becomes the life of man's spirit, the latter becomes the life of man's whole being. The spirit, soul and body are restored to God's original intention in every born-again person.

What then must one do to be born anew in one's spirit? We know that the Lord Jesus died in the sinner's place. He suffered in His body on the cross for all the sins of the world. God views the death of the Lord Jesus as the death of all the world's people. His holy humanity suffered death for all unholy humanity. But something does remain for man himself to do. He must exercise faith in committing himself—spirit, soul and body—into union with the Lord Jesus. That is to say, he must reckon the death of the Lord Jesus as his own death and the resurrection of the Lord Jesus as his own resurrection. This is the meaning of John 3.16: "Whoever believes into (literal) him should not perish but have eternal life." The sinner must exercise faith and a believing into the Lord Jesus. By so doing, he is united with Him in His death and resurrection and receives eternal life (John 17.3)—which is spiritual life—unto regeneration.

Let us be careful not to separate into distinct matters the death of the Lord Jesus as our substitute and our death with Him. Those who stress mental understanding will surely so do, but in spiritual life these two are inseparable. Substitutionary death and co-death should be distinguished but never separated. If one believes in the death of the Lord Jesus as his substitute he already has been united with the Lord Jesus in His death (Rom. 6.2). For me to believe in the substitutionary work of the Lord Jesus is to believe that I already have been punished in the Lord Jesus. The penalty of my sin is death; yet the Lord Jesus suffered death for me; therefore I have died in Him. There can be no salvation otherwise. To say that He died for me is to say that I already have been penalized and have died in Him. Everyone who believes in this fact shall experience its reality.

We may say then that the faith by which a sinner believes in the death of the Lord Jesus as substitute is "believing into" Christ and thus union with Him. Though a person may be concerned only with the penalty for sin and not with the power of sin, his being united with the Lord is nonetheless the common possession he shares with all who believe in Christ.

He who is not united with the Lord has not yet believed and therefore has no part in Him.

In believing, one is united with the Lord. To be united with Him means to experience everything He has experienced. In John 3 our Lord informs us how we are united with Him. It is by our being united with Him in His crucifixion and death (vv.14-15). Every believer at least positionally has been united with the Lord in His death, but obviously "if we have been united with him in a death like his, we shall certainly be united with him in a resurrection like his" (Rom. 6.5). Hence he who believes in the death of the Lord Jesus as his substitute is likewise positionally raised up with Christ. Though he may not yet fully experience the meaning of the death of the Lord Jesus, God nevertheless has made him alive together with Christ and he has obtained a new life in the resurrection power of the Lord Jesus. This is new birth.

We should beware lest we insist that a man is not born anew unless he has experienced death and resurrection with the Lord. The Scriptures deem anyone who believes in the Lord Jesus as already regenerated. "All who received him, who believed in his name . . . were . . . born of God" (John 1.12-13). Let it be understood that to be raised together with the Lord is not an experience antecedent to the new birth. Our regeneration is our union with the Lord in His resurrection as well as in His death. His death has concluded our sinful walk, and His resurrection has given us a new life and initiated us into the life of a Christian. The Apostle assures us that "we have been born anew to a living hope through the resurrection of Jesus Christ from the dead" (1 Peter 1.3). He indicates that every born-again Christian has been resurrected already with the Lord. However, the Apostle Paul in Philippians still urges us to experience "the power of His resurrection" (3.10). Many Christians have been born anew and been thus raised with the Lord, even though they are lacking in the manifestation of resurrection power.

Do not confuse, then, position with experience. At the time one believes in the Lord Jesus he may be most weak and ig-

norant; he is nonetheless placed by God in the perfect position of being considered dead, raised and ascended with the
Lord. He who is accepted *in* Christ is as acceptable *as* Christ.
This is position. And his position is: all that Christ has experienced is his. And position causes him to experience new
birth, because it hinges not on how deep he has known experimentally the death, resurrection and ascension of the
Lord Jesus, but on whether he has believed in Him. Even if
experimentally a believer is totally ignorant of the resurrection power of Christ (Phil. 3.10), he has been made alive
together with Christ, raised up with Him and seated with
Him in the heavenly places (Eph. 2.5-6).

Still another matter should be carefully noticed with respect to regeneration; namely, that far more became ours
than simply what we had in Adam before the fall. On that day
Adam possessed spirit; yet it was created by God. It was not
God's uncreated life typified by the tree of life. No life relationship existed at all between Adam and God. His being
called "the son of God" is similar to the angels being so
called, for he was created directly by God. We who believe in
the Lord Jesus, however, are "born of God" (John 1.12-13).
Accordingly, there is a life relationship. A child born inherits
his father's life; we are born of God; therefore, we have His
life (2 Peter 1.4). Had Adam received the life which God
offered in the tree of life, he immediately would have obtained the eternal uncreated life of God. His spirit came from
God, and so it is everlasting. How this everlasting spirit
shall live depends upon how one regards God's order and
upon what choice he makes. The life we Christians obtain in
regeneration is the same which Adam could have had but
never had: God's life. Regeneration not only retrieves out of
chaotic darkness the order of man's spirit and soul; it additionally affords man the supernatural life of God.

Man's darkened and fallen spirit is made alive through
being strengthened by the Holy Spirit into accepting God's
life. This is new birth. The basis upon which the Holy Spirit
can regenerate man is the cross (John 3.14-15). The eternal

life declared in John 3.16 is the life of God which the Holy Spirit plants in man's spirit. Since this life is God's and cannot die, it follows that everyone born anew into possessing this life is said to have eternal life. As God's life is totally unfamiliar with death, so the eternal life in man never dies.

A life relationship is established with God in new birth. It resembles the old birth of the flesh in that it is once and for all. Once a man is born of God he can never be treated by God as not having been so born of Him. However endless eternity may be, this relationship and this position cannot be annulled. This is because what a believer receives at new birth is not contingent upon a progressive, spiritual and holy pursuit after he believes but is the pure gift of God. What God bestows is eternal life. No possibility exists for this life and position to be abrogated.

Receiving God's life in new birth is the starting point of a Christian walk, the minimum for a believer. Those who have not yet believed on the death of the Lord Jesus and received supernatural life (which they cannot possess naturally), are deemed in the sight of God to be dead, no matter how religious, moral, learned or zealous they may be. Those who do not have God's life are dead.

For those who are born anew, there is great potentiality for spiritual growth. Regeneration is the obvious first step in spiritual development. Though the life received is perfect, it waits to be matured. At the moment of new birth life cannot be full-grown. It is like a fruit newly formed: the life is perfect but it is still unripe. There is therefore boundless possibility for growth. The Holy Spirit is able to bring the person into complete victory over body and soul.

TWO KINDS OF CHRISTIANS

The Apostle in 1 Corinthians 3.1 divides all Christians into two classifications. They are the spiritual and the carnal. A spiritual Christian is one in whom the Holy Spirit dwells in his spirit and controls his entire being. What is meant, then, by being carnal? The Bible employs the word "flesh" to describe the life and value of an unregenerated man. It comprises everything which issues from his sinful soul and body (Rom. 7.19). Hence a carnal Christian is one who has been born anew and has God's life, but instead of overcoming his flesh he is overcome by the flesh. We know the spirit of a fallen man is dead and he is dominated by his soul and body. A carnal Christian, therefore, is one whose spirit has been quickened, but who still follows his soul and body unto sin.

If a Christian remains in a carnal condition long after experiencing new birth, he hinders God's salvation from realizing its full potential and manifestation. Only when he is growing in grace, constantly governed by the spirit, can salvation be wholly wrought in him. God has provided full salvation in Calvary for the regeneration of sinners and complete victory over the believer's old creation.

PART TWO

THE FLESH

1 The Flesh and Salvation
2 The Fleshly or Carnal Believer
3 The Cross and the Holy Spirit
4 The Boastings of the Flesh
5 The Believer's Ultimate Attitude towards the Flesh

CHAPTER 1

THE FLESH AND SALVATION

THE WORD "FLESH" is *basar* in Hebrew and *sarx* in Greek. Seen often in the Bible, it is used in various ways. Its most significant usage, observed and made most clear in Paul's writings, has reference to the unregenerated person. Speaking of his old "I," he says in Romans 7: "I am fleshly" (v.14 Darby). Not merely his nature or a particular part of his being is fleshly; the "I"—Paul's whole being—is fleshly. He reiterates this thought in verse 18 by asserting "within me, that is, in my flesh." It follows clearly that "flesh" in the Bible points to all an unregenerated person is. In connection with this usage of "flesh" it must be remembered that in the very beginning man was constituted spirit, soul and body. As it is the site of man's personality and consciousness, the soul is connected to the spiritual world through man's spirit. The soul must decide whether it is to obey the spirit and hence be united with God and His will or is to yield to the body and all the temptations of the material world. On the occasion of man's fall the soul resisted the spirit's authority and became enslaved to the body and its passions. Thus man became a fleshly, not a spiritual, man. Man's spirit was denied its noble position and was reduced to that of a prisoner. Since the soul is now under the power of the flesh, the Bible deems man to be fleshly or carnal. Whatever is soulical has become fleshly.

Now aside from the use of "flesh" to designate all that an unregenerated person is, sometimes it is written to denote the soft part of the human body as distinct from blood and bones. It may be employed to mean additionally the human body. Or at still other times it may be used to signify the totality of mankind. These four meanings are all very closely related. We should therefore note briefly these other three ways of using "flesh" in the Bible.

First, "flesh" as applied to the soft part of the human body. We know that a human body is composed of flesh, bones and blood. Flesh is that part of the body through which we sense the world around us. Therefore a fleshly person is one who follows the world. Beyond simply having flesh, he walks after the sense of his flesh.

Second, "flesh" as applied to the human body. Broadly speaking, flesh means the human body whether living or dead. According to the latter part of Romans 7 sin of the flesh is related to the human body: "I see in my members another law at war with the law of my mind and making me captive to the law of sin which dwells in my members" (v. 23). The Apostle then continues in Chapter 8 by explaining that if we would overcome the flesh we must "put to death the deeds of the body" by the Spirit (v.13). Hence, the Bible uses the word *sarx* to indicate not only psychical flesh but physical flesh as well.

Third, "flesh" as applied to the totality of mankind. All men in this world are born of the flesh; they are all therefore fleshly. Without exception the Bible views all men to be flesh. Every man is controlled by that composite of soul and body called the flesh, following both the sins of his body and the self of his soul. Thus whenever the Bible speaks of all men its characteristic phrase is "all flesh." *Basar* or *sarx* consequently refers to human beings *in toto*.

HOW DOES MAN BECOME FLESH?

"That which is born of the flesh is flesh." So asserted the Lord Jesus to Nicodemus long ago (John 3.6). Three questions are answered by this succinct statement: (1) what flesh is; (2) how man becomes flesh; and (3) what its quality or nature is.

(1) *What is flesh?* "That which is born of the flesh is flesh." What is born of the flesh? Man; therefore man is flesh; and everything a man naturally inherits from his parents belongs to the flesh. No distinction is made as to whether the man is good, moral, clever, able and kind or whether he is bad, unholy, foolish, useless and cruel. Man is flesh. Whatever a man is born with pertains to the flesh and is within that realm. All with which we are born or which later develops is included in the flesh.

(2) *How does man become flesh?* "That which is *born* of the flesh is flesh." Man does not become fleshly by learning to be bad through gradual sinning, nor by giving himself up to licentiousness, greedy to follow the desire of his body and mind until finally the whole man is overcome and controlled by the evil passions of his body. The Lord Jesus emphatically declared that as soon as a man is born he is fleshly. He is determined neither by his conduct nor by his character. But one thing decides the issue: through whom was he born? Every man of this world has been begotten of human parents and is consequently judged by God to be of the flesh (Gen. 6.3). How can anyone who is born of the flesh not be flesh? According to our Lord's word, a man is flesh because he is born of blood, of the will of the flesh, and of the will of man (John 1.13) and not because of how he lives or how his parents live.

(3) *What is the nature of flesh?* "That which is born of the flesh *is* flesh." Here is no exception, no distinction. No

amount of education, improvement, cultivation, morality or religion can turn man from being fleshly. No human labor or power can alter him. Unless he is not generated of the flesh, he will remain as flesh. No human device can make him other than that of which he was born. The Lord Jesus said "is"; with that the matter was forever decided. The fleshliness of a man is determined not by himself but by his birth. If he is born of flesh, all plans for his transformation will be unavailing. No matter how he changes outwardly, whether from one form to another or through a daily change, man remains flesh as firmly as ever.

THE UNREGENERATED MAN

The Lord Jesus has stated that any unregenerated person born but once (i.e., born only of man), is flesh and is therefore living in the realm of the flesh. During the period we were unregenerated we indeed "lived in the passions of our flesh, following the desires of body and mind, and so we were by nature children of wrath, like the rest of mankind" because "it is not the children of the flesh who are the children of God" (Eph. 2.3; Rom. 9.8). A man whose soul may yield to the lusts of the body and commit many unmentionable sins may be so dead to God (Eph. 2.1)—"dead in trespasses and the uncircumcision of . . . flesh" (Col. 2.13)—that he may have no consciousness of being sinful. On the contrary he may even be proud, considering himself better than others. Frankly speaking, "while we were living in the flesh, our sinful passions, aroused by the law, were at work in our members to bear fruit for death" for the simple reason that we were "carnal, sold under sin." We therefore with our flesh "serve the law of sin" (Rom. 7.5, 14, 25).

Although the flesh is exceedingly strong in sinning and following selfish desire it is extremely weak towards the will of God. Unregenerated man is powerless to fulfill any of God's will, being "weakened by the flesh." And the flesh is even "hostile to God; it does not submit to God's law, indeed it cannot" (Rom. 8.3, 7). This however does not imply that the flesh totally disregards the things of God. The fleshly sometimes do exert their utmost strength to observe the law. The Bible moreover never treats the fleshly as synonymous with the law-breakers. It merely concludes that "by works of the law shall no flesh be justified" (Gal. 2.16 ASV). For the fleshly not to keep the law is certainly nothing unusual. It simply proves they are of the flesh. But now that God has ordained that man shall not be justified by works of law but by faith in the Lord Jesus (Rom. 3.28), those who attempt to follow the law only disclose their disobedience to God, seeking to establish their own righteousness in lieu of God's righteousness (Rom. 10.3). It reveals further that they belong to the flesh. To sum up, "those who are in the flesh cannot please God" (Rom. 8.8), and *this* "cannot" seals the fate of the fleshly.

God looks upon the flesh as utterly corrupt. So closely is it linked with lust that the Bible often refers to "the lusts of the flesh" (2 Peter 2.18 Darby). Great though His power, God nonetheless cannot transform the nature of the flesh into something pleasing to Himself. God Himself declares: "My spirit shall not always strive in man forever, for he is flesh" (Gen. 6.3 Young's). The corruption of the flesh is such that even the Holy Spirit of God cannot by striving against the flesh render it unfleshly. That which is born of the flesh is flesh. Man unfortunately does not understand God's Word and so he tries continually to refine and reform his flesh. Yet the Word of God stands forever. Due to its exceeding corruption, God warns His saints to hate "even the garment spotted by the flesh" (Jude 23).

Because God appreciates the actual condition of the flesh He declares it is unchangeable. Any person who attempts to repair it by acts of self-abasement or severity to the body shall fail utterly. God recognizes the impossibility of the flesh to be changed, improved or bettered. In saving the world, therefore, He does not try to alter man's flesh; He instead gives man a new life in order to help put it to death. The flesh must die. This is salvation.

GOD'S SALVATION

"God," asserts the Apostle, "has done what the law, weakened by the flesh, could not do: sending his own Son in the likeness of sinful flesh and for sin, he condemned sin in the flesh" (Rom. 8.3). This uncovers the actual situation of that moral class of the fleshly who may perhaps be very much intent on keeping the law. They may indeed be observing quite a few of its points. Weakened by the flesh, however, they cannot keep the whole law.* For the law makes it quite clear that "he who does them shall live by them" (Gal. 3.12 quoting Lev. 18.5) or else he shall be condemned to perdition. How much of the law, someone may ask, shall he keep? The entire law; for "whoever keeps the whole law but fails in one point has become guilty of all of it" (James 2.10). "For no human being will be justified in his sight by works of the law since through the law comes knowledge of sin" (Rom. 3.20). The more one desires to observe the law the more he discovers how full of sin he is and how impossible for him to keep it.

God's reaction to the sinfulness of all men is to take upon Himself the task of salvation. His way is in "sending his own Son in the likeness of sinful flesh." His Son is without sin, hence He alone is qualified to save us. "In the likeness of sinful flesh" describes His incarnation: how He takes a human body and links Himself with mankind. God's only Son is referred to elsewhere as "the Word" that "became flesh" (John 1.14). His coming in the likeness of sinful flesh is the "became flesh" of that verse. Therefore our verse in Romans 8.3 tells us as well in what manner the Word became flesh. The emphasis here is that He is the Son of God, consequently sinless. Even when He comes in the flesh, Gods' Son does not become "sinful flesh." He only comes in "the *likeness* of sinful flesh." While in the flesh, He remains as the Son of God and is still without sin. Yet because He possesses the likeness

---

*We should of course note that there is another class, recognized in Romans 8.7, who do not in the least care to keep God's law: "the mind that is set on the flesh is hostile to God; it does not submit to God's law, indeed it cannot."

of sinful flesh, He is most closely joined with the world's sinners who live in the flesh.

What then is the purpose of His incarnation? As a "sacrifice for sins" is the Biblical explanation (Heb. 10.12), and this is the work of the cross. God's Son is to atone for our sins. All the fleshly sin against the law; they cannot establish the righteousness of God; and they are doomed to perdition and punishment. But the Lord Jesus in coming to the world takes this likeness of sinful flesh and joins Himself so perfectly with the fleshly that they have been punished for their sin in His death on the cross. He need not suffer for He is without sin, yet He does suffer because He has the likeness of sinful flesh. In the position of a new federal head, the Lord Jesus now includes all sinners in His suffering. This explains the punishment for sin.

Christ as the sacrifice for sin suffers for everyone who is in the flesh. But what about the power of sin which fills the fleshly? "He condemned sin in the flesh." He who is sinless is made sin for us, so that He dies for sin. He is "put to death in the flesh" (1 Peter 3.18). When He dies in the flesh, He takes to the cross the sin in the flesh. This is what is meant by the phrase "condemned sin in the flesh." To condemn is to judge or to mete out punishment. The judgment and punishment of sin is death. Thus the Lord Jesus actually put sin to death in His flesh. We therefore can see in His death that not only our *sins* are judged but *sin itself* is even judged. Henceforth sin has no power upon those who are joined to the Lord's death and who accordingly have sin condemned in their flesh.

REGENERATION

God's release from the penalty and power of sin is accomplished in the cross of His Son. He now lays before all men this salvation so that whoever wills to accept may be saved.

God knows no good resides in man; no flesh can please Him. It is corrupted beyond repair. Since it is so absolutely hopeless, how then can man please God after he has believed in His Son unless He gives him something new? Thank God,

He has bestowed a new life, His uncreated life, upon those who believe in the salvation of the Lord Jesus and receive Him as their personal Savior. This is called "regeneration" or "new birth." Though He cannot alter our flesh God gives us His life. Man's flesh remains as corrupt in those who are born anew as in those who are not. The flesh in a saint is the same as that in a sinner. In regeneration the flesh is not transformed. New birth exerts no good influence on the flesh. It remains as is. God does not impart His life to us to educate and train the flesh. Rather, it is given to overcome the flesh.

Man in regeneration actually becomes related to God by birth. Regeneration means to be born of God. As our fleshy life is born of our parents so our spiritual life is born of God. The meaning of birth is "to impart life." When we say we are born of God it signifies we receive a new life from Him. What we have received is a real life.

We have seen previously how we human beings are fleshly. Our spirit is dead and our soul is in full management of the entire being. We are walking according to the lusts of the body. No good is in us. In coming to deliver us, God first must restore the spirit's position within in order that we may have fellowship with Him again. This occurs when we believe in the Lord Jesus. God puts His life into our spirit, thus raising it up from death. The Lord Jesus now declares that "that which is born of the Spirit is spirit" (John 3.6). At this juncture God's life, which is the Spirit, enters our human spirit and restores it to its original position. The Holy Spirit takes up His abode in the human spirit; and man is thereby transferred into the spiritual realm. Our spirit is quickened and reigns once again. The "new spirit" mentioned in Ezekiel 36.26 is the new life we receive at the time of regeneration.

Man is not regenerated by doing something special but by believing the Lord Jesus as his Savior: "to all who received him, who believed in his name, he gave power to become children of God; who were born, not of blood nor of the will of the flesh nor of the will of man, but of God" (John

1.12-13). Those who believe the Lord Jesus as Savior are born of God and are therefore His children.

Regeneration is the minimum of spiritual life. It is the basis upon which later building up takes place. One can neither speak of spiritual life nor expect to grow spiritually if he is not regenerated, since he has no life in his spirit. Just as no one can construct a castle in the air so we cannot edify those who are unregenerated. If we attempt to teach an unregenerate to do good and to worship God, we are simply teaching a dead man. We are attempting to do what God cannot do when we try to repair and reform the flesh. It is vital that each believer know beyond doubt he has been regenerated already and has received a new life. He must see that new birth is not an attempt to tinker with the old flesh or to transform it into spiritual life. On the contrary, it is receiving a life which he never had and could not have had before. If one is not born anew he cannot see the kingdom of God. He can never perceive the spiritual mysteries and taste the heavenly sweetness of God's kingdom. His destination is but to wait for death and judgment; for him there is nothing more.

How can one know he is regenerated? John tells us man is born anew by his believing on the name of the Son of God and receiving Him (1.12). The name of God's Son is "Jesus" which means "he will save his people from their sins" (Matt. 1.21). Believing on the name of the Son of God is hence equivalent to believing in Him as the Savior, believing that He died on the cross for our sins in order to free us from the penalty and power of sin. To so believe is to receive Him as Savior. If one desires to know whether he is regenerated or not, he simply need ask himself one question: Have I come to the cross as a helpless sinner and received the Lord Jesus as Savior? If he answers affirmatively he is regenerated. All who believe in the Lord Jesus are born anew.

THE CONFLICT BETWEEN THE OLD AND THE NEW

It is essential for a regenerated person to understand what he has obtained through new birth and what still lingers of his natural endowment. Such knowledge will help him as he continues his spiritual journey. It may prove helpful at this point to explain how much is included in man's flesh and likewise how the Lord Jesus in His redemption deals with the constituents of that flesh. In other words, what does a believer inherit in regeneration?

A reading of several verses in Romans 7 can make clear that the components of the flesh are mainly "sin" and "me": "sin that dwells in me . . . , that is, in my flesh" (vv. 14,17-18 Darby). The "sin" here is the power of sin, and the "me" here is what we commonly acknowledge as "self." If a believer would understand spiritual life he must not be confused about these two elements of the flesh.

We know the Lord Jesus has dealt with the sin of our flesh on His cross. And the Word informs us that "our old self was crucified with him" (Rom. 6.6). Nowhere in the Bible are we told to be crucified since this has been done and done perfectly by Christ already. With regard to the question of sin, man is not required to do anything. He need only consider this an accomplished fact (Rom. 6.11) and he will reap the effectiveness of the death of Jesus in being wholly delivered from the power of sin (Rom. 6.14).

We are never asked in the Bible to be crucified for sin, that is true. It *does* exhort us, however, to take up the cross for denying self. The Lord Jesus instructs us many times to deny ourselves and take up the cross and follow Him. The explanation for this is that the Lord Jesus deals with our sins and with ourselves very differently. To wholly conquer sin the believer needs but a moment; to deny the self he needs an entire lifetime. Only on the cross did Jesus *bear* our sins; yet throughout His life the Lord *denied* Himself. The same must be true of us.

The Galatian letter of Paul delineates the relationship between the flesh and the believer. He tells us on the one hand that "those who belong to Christ Jesus have crucified the flesh with its passions and desires" (5.24). On the very day one becomes identified with the Lord Jesus then his flesh also is crucified. Now one might think, without the Holy Spirit's instruction, that his flesh is no longer present, for has it not been crucified? But no, on the other hand the letter says to us to "walk by the Spirit, and do not gratify the desires of the flesh. For the desires of the flesh are against the Spirit, and the desires of the Spirit are against the flesh" (5.16-17). Here we are told openly that one who belongs to Christ Jesus and has already the indwelling Holy Spirit still has the flesh in him. Not only does the flesh exist; it is described as being singularly powerful as well.

What can we say? Are these two Biblical references contradictory? No, verse 24 stresses the sin of the flesh, while verse 17 the self of the flesh. The cross of Christ deals with sin and the Holy Spirit through the cross treats of self. Christ delivers the believer completely from the power of sin through the cross that sin may not reign again; but by the Holy Spirit Who dwells in the believer, Christ enables him to overcome self daily and obey Him perfectly. Liberation from sin is an accomplished fact; denial of self is to be a daily experience.

If a believer could understand the full implication of the cross at the time he is born anew he would be freed wholly from sin on the one side and on the other be in possession of a new life. It is indeed regrettable that many workers fail to present this full salvation to sinners, so that the latter believe just half God's salvation. This leaves them as it were only half-saved: their sins are forgiven, but they lack the strength to cease from sin. Moreover, even on those occasions when salvation is presented completely sinners desire just to have their sins forgiven for they do not sincerely expect deliverance from the power of sin. This equally renders them half-saved.

Should a person believe and receive full salvation at the very outset, he will experience less failure battling with sin and more success battling with self. Rarely are such believers found. Most enter upon only half their salvation. Their conflicts are therefore mainly with sin. And some do not even know what self is. In this connection, the personal condition of the believer plays a part before regeneration. Many tend to do good even before they believe. They of course do not possess the power to do good nor could they be good. But their conscience seems to be comparatively enlightened, though their strength to do good is nevertheless weak. They experience what is commonly called the conflict between reason and lust. Now when these hear of God's total salvation they eagerly accept grace for release from sin even as they receive grace for forgiveness of sin. Others, however, before believing, harbor pitch-black consciences, sin terribly, and never intend to do good. Upon hearing of God's whole salvation they naturally grasp the grace of forgiveness and neglect (not reject) the grace for deliverance from sin. They will encounter much struggle over sin of the flesh afterwards.

Why is this latter case so? Because such a re-born man possesses a new life which demands him to overcome the rule of his flesh and to obey it instead. God's life is absolute; it must gain complete mastery over the man. As soon as that life enters the human spirit it requires the man to leave his former master of sin and to be subject entirely to the Holy Spirit. Even so, sin in this particular man is deeply rooted. Although his will is being renewed in part through the regenerated life, it is still tied to sin and self; on many occasions it bends towards sin. Inevitably great conflict will erupt between the new life and the flesh. Since people in this condition are numerous, we shall pay special attention to them. Let me remind my reader, however, that this experience of prolonged struggle and failure with sin (different from that with self) is unnecessary.

The flesh demands full sovereignty; so does the spiritual life. The flesh desires to have man forever attached to itself; while the spiritual life wants to have man completely subject to the Holy Spirit. At all points the flesh and spiritual life differ. The nature of the former is that of the first Adam, the nature of the latter belongs to the last Adam. The motive of the first is earthly; that of the second, heavenly. The flesh focuses all things upon self; spiritual life centers all upon Christ. The flesh wishes to lead man to sin, but spiritual life longs to lead him to righteousness. Since these two are so essentially contrary, how can a person avoid clashing continually with the flesh? Not realizing the full salvation of Christ, a believer constantly experiences such a struggle.

When young believers fall into such conflict they are dumbfounded. Some despair of spiritual growth thinking they are just too bad. Others begin to doubt they are genuinely regenerated, not aware that regeneration itself brings in this contention. Formerly, when the flesh was in authority without interference (for the spirit was dead), they could sin terribly without feeling any sense of sinfulness. Now new life has sprung up, and with it heavenly nature, desire, light and thought. As this new light penetrates the man it immediately exposes the defilement and corruption within. The new desire is naturally dissatisfied to remain in such a state and longs to follow the will of God. The flesh begins to contend with the spiritual life. Such battle gives the believer an impression that housed within him are two persons. Each has its own idea and strength. Each seeks victory. When the spiritual life is in ascendancy the believer is most glad; when the flesh gains the upper hand he cannot but grieve. Experience of this kind confirms that such ones have been regenerated.

The purpose of God is never to reform the flesh but to destroy it. It is by God's life given the believer at regeneration that the self in the flesh is to be destroyed. The life God imparts to man is indeed most powerful, but the regenerated person is still a babe—newly born and very weak. The flesh long has held the reins and its power is tremendous. Furthermore, the regenerated one has not yet learned to apprehend by faith God's complete salvation. Though he be saved, he is still of the flesh during this period. Being fleshly denotes being governed by the flesh. What is most pitiful is for a believer, hitherto enlightened by heavenly light to know the wickedness of the flesh and to desire with full heart victory over it, to find himself too weak to overcome. This is the moment when he sheds many tears of sorrow. How can he not be angry with himself, for though he harbors a new desire to destroy sin and to please God his will is not steadfast enough to subdue the body of sin. Few are the victories; many, the defeats.

Paul in Romans 7 voices the inner anguish of this conflict:

> I do not understand my own actions. For I do not do what I want, but I do the very thing I hate . . . For I know that nothing good dwells within me, that is, in my flesh. I can will what is right, but I cannot do it. For I do not do the good I want, but the evil I do not want is what I do. Now if I do what I do not want, it is no longer I that do it, but sin which dwells within me. So I find it to be a law that when I want to do right, evil lies close at hand. For I delight in the law of God in my inmost self, but I see in my members another law at war with the law of my mind and making me captive to the law of sin which dwells in my members. (vv.15-23)

Many will respond to his cry of nearly final despair: "Wretched man that I am! Who will deliver me from this body of death?" (v.24)

What is the meaning of this contention? It is one of the ways the Holy Spirit disciplines us. God has provided a whole salvation for man. He who does not know he has it will not be able to enjoy it, neither will he be able to experience it if he does not desire after it. God can only give to those who believe and receive and claim. When man hence asks for forgiveness and regeneration, God surely bestows it upon him. And it is through conflict that God induces the believer to seek and to grasp total triumph in Christ. He who was ignorant before will now seek to know; the Holy Spirit will then be afforded a chance to reveal to him how Christ has dealt with his old man on the cross so that he may now believe into possessing such triumph. And he who possessed not because he sought not will discover through such battle that all the truth he had was merely mental and consequently ineffectual. This will stir him to desire to experience the truth he only mentally had known.

This strife increases as the days go by. If believers will proceed faithfully without giving in to despair, they will incur fiercer conflict until such time as they are delivered.

CHAPTER 2
THE FLESHLY OR CARNAL BELIEVER

ALL BELIEVERS COULD, like Paul, be filled with the Holy Spirit at the moment of belief and baptism (cf. Acts 9.17-18). Unfortunately many still are controlled by the flesh as though not dead and raised up again. These have not truly believed in the accomplished fact of Christ's death and resurrection for them, nor have they sincerely acted upon the call of the Holy Spirit to follow the principle of death and resurrection. According to the finished work of Christ they have died and have been resurrected already; according to their responsibility as believers they should die to self and live to God; but in actual practice they do not do so. These believers may be considered abnormal. This abnormality is not to be understood as being limited only to our day, however. Long, long ago just such a condition among believers had confronted the Apostle Paul. The Christians at Corinth were one example. Listen to what he said of them:

> But I, brethren, could not address you as spiritual men, but as men of the flesh, as babes in Christ. I fed you with milk, not solid food; for you were not ready for it; and even yet you are not ready, for you are still of the flesh. For while there is jealousy and strife among you, are you not of the flesh, and behaving like ordinary men? (1 Cor. 3.1-3)

Here the Apostle divides all Christians into two classes: the spiritual and the fleshly or carnal. The spiritual Christians are not at all extraordinary; they are simply normal. It is the fleshly who are out of the ordinary, because they are abnormal. Those at Corinth were indeed Christians, but they were fleshly, not spiritual. Three times in this chapter Paul declares they were men of the flesh. Through the wisdom given him by the Holy Spirit the Apostle was made to realize that he first must identify them before he could offer them the message they needed.

Biblical regeneration is a birth by which the innermost part of man's being, the deeply hidden spirit, is renewed and indwelt by the Spirit of God. It requires time for the power of this new life to reach the outside: that is, to be extended from the center to the circumference. Hence we cannot expect to find the strength of "the young men" nor the experience of "the fathers" manifested in the life of a child in Christ. Although a newly born believer may proceed faithfully, loving the Lord best and distinguishing himself in zeal, he still needs time for opportunities to know more of the wickedness of sin and self and occasions to know more of the will of God and the way of the spirit. However much he may love the Lord or love the truth, this new believer still walks in the realm of feelings and thoughts, not yet having been tested and refined by fire. A newly born Christian cannot help being fleshly. Though filled with the Holy Spirit, he nevertheless does not know the flesh. How can one be liberated from the works of the flesh if he does not recognize that such works spring from the flesh? In assessing their actual condition, therefore, newly born babes are generally of the flesh.

The Bible does not expect new Christians to be spiritual instantaneously; if they should remain as babes after many years, however, then their situation is indeed most pitiful. Paul himself points out to the Corinthians that he had treated them as men of the flesh earlier because they were new born babes in Christ, and that by now—at the moment of his writing them—they certainly should be growing into manhood. They had instead frittered away their lives, remained as babes, and were thus still fleshly.

It does not necessitate as much time as we think today for one to be transformed from the fleshly into the spiritual. The believers at Corinth came out from a strictly sinful heathen background. After the lapse of only a few years the Apostle already viewed them as having been babes too long. They had been too long in the flesh, for by that time they ought to be spiritual. The purpose of Christ's redemption is to remove all hindrances to the Holy Spirit's control over the whole person so that he can be made spiritual. This redemption can never fail because the power of the Holy Spirit is superabundant. As a fleshly sinner can become a regenerated believer so a regenerated yet fleshly believer can be changed into a spiritual man. How lamentable to find modern-day Christians achieving no progress in their spiritual walk after several years, nay, even after decades. These moreover are filled with amazement if they find some who do enter upon a life of the spirit after a number of years. They consider it most unusual, not aware it is but normal—the regular growth of life. How long have you believed in the Lord? Are you spiritual yet? We should not become aged babes, grieving the Holy Spirit and suffering loss ourselves. All regenerated ones should covet spiritual development, permitting the Holy Spirit to rule in every respect so that in a relatively short period He may be able to lead us into what God has provided for us. We should not waste time, making no progress.

What then are the reasons for not growing? Perhaps there are two. On the one hand, it may be due to the negligence of those who, watching over the souls of the younger believers, may only speak to them of the grace of God and of their position in Christ but neglect to encourage them to seek spiritual experience. (Nay, those who watch over others may themselves be ignorant of life in the Spirit. How then could such ones ever lead others into more abundant life?) On the other hand, it may be because the believers themselves are not keen on spiritual affairs. Either they assume that it is sufficient enough merely to be saved or they have no spiritual appetite or they simply are unwilling to pay the price for advancement. As a deplorable consequence the church is over-stuffed with big babes.

What are the characteristics of the fleshly? Foremost among them is remaining long as babes. The duration of babyhood should not exceed a few years. When one is born anew by believing that the Son of God atoned for his sins on the cross, he simultaneously ought to believe that he has been crucified with Christ in order that the Holy Spirit may release him from the power of the flesh. Ignorance of this naturally will keep him in the flesh for many years.

The second characteristic of the fleshly is that they are unfit to absorb spiritual teaching. "I fed you with milk, not solid food; for you were not ready." The Corinthians grossly prided themselves on their knowledge and wisdom. Of all the churches in that period, that at Corinth was probably the most informed one. Paul early in his letter thanked God for their rich knowledge (1.5). Should Paul deliver spiritual sermons to them they could understand every word; however, all their understandings were in the mind. Although they knew everything, these Corinthians did not have the power to express in life that which they knew. Most likely there are many fleshly believers today who grasp so much so well that they can even preach to others but who are themselves yet unspiritual. Genuine spiritual knowledge lies not in wonderful and mysterious thoughts but in actual spiritual experience through union of the believer's life with truth. Cleverness is useless here, while eagerness for truth is insufficient too; the *sine qua non* is a path of perfect obedience to the Holy Spirit Who alone truly teaches us. All else is merely the transmission of knowledge from one mind to another. Such data will not render a fleshly person spiritual; on the contrary, his carnal walk actually will turn all his "spiritual" knowledge into that which is fleshly. What he needs is not increased spiritual teaching but an obedient heart which is willing to yield his life to the Holy Spirit and go the way of the cross according to the Spirit's command. Increased spiritual teaching will only strengthen his carnality and serve to deceive him into conceiving himself as spiritual.

For does he not say to himself, "How else could I possibly know so many spiritual things unless I were spiritual?" Whereas the real touchstone should be, "How much do you truly know from life or is it merely a product of the mind?" May God be gracious to us.

Paul wrote of yet another evidence of being fleshly when he affirmed that "while there is jealousy and strife among you, are you not of the flesh, and behaving like ordinary men?" The sin of jealousy and strife is eminent proof of carnality. Dissensions were rife in the church at Corinth, as is confirmed by such declarations as "I belong to Paul," "I belong to Apollos," "I belong to Cephas," "I belong to Christ" (1 Cor. 1.12). Even those who were contending for Christ by saying "I am of Christ" were included among the fleshly, for the spirit of flesh is always and everywhere jealous and contentious. For these to hold themselves up as being of Christ, but in that attitude of spirit, is inescapably carnal. However sweet the word may sound, any sectarian boasting is but the babbling of a babe. The divisions in the church are due to no other cause than to lack of love and walking after the flesh. Such an individual, supposedly contending for the truth, is simply camouflaging the real person. The sinners of the world are men of the flesh; as such, they are not regenerated; they are therefore under the rule of their soul and body. For a believer to be fleshly signifies that he too is behaving like an ordinary man. Now it is perfectly natural for worldly people to be fleshly; it is understandable if even newly born believers are fleshly; but if, according to the years during which you have believed in the Lord you ought to be spiritual, then how can you continue to behave as an ordinary man?

It is evident that a person belongs to the flesh if he comports himself like an ordinary man and sins often. No matter how much spiritual teaching he knows or how many spiritual experiences he purports to have had or how much effective service he has rendered: none of these makes him less carnal if he remains undelivered from his peculiar temperament, his temper, his selfishness, his contention, his vainglory, his unforgiving or unloving spirit.

To be fleshly or carnal means to behave "like ordinary men." We should ask ourselves whether or not our conduct differs very radically from ordinary men. If many worldly manners cling to your life then you are doubtless still of the flesh. Let us not argue over our being labeled as either spiritual or carnal. If we are not governed by the Holy Spirit what profit will the mere designation of spiritual be to us? This is after all a matter of life, not of title.

THE SINS OF THE FLESH

What the Apostle was experiencing in Romans 7 was a war against the sin which abides in the body. "Sin, finding opportunity in the commandment, deceived me . . . It was sin working death in me . . . sold under sin . . . but sin which dwells within me" (vv.11,13,14,17,20). While still in the flesh a believer often is overcome by the sin within him. Many are the battles and many, the sins committed.

The necessities of the human body may be classified into three categories: nourishment, reproduction, defense. Before man's fall these were legitimate requirements, unmixed with sin. Only after man fell into sin did these three become media for sin. In the case of nourishment, the world uses food to entice us. The first temptation of man is in this matter of food. As the fruit of the knowledge of good and evil enticed Eve, so drinking and feasting have become a sin of the flesh today. Let us not lightly regard this issue of food, for many fleshly Christians have stumbled on this point. The carnal believers at Corinth stumbled their brethren on just this matter of food. All who were therefore to be elders and deacons in those days were required to have overcome on this point (1 Tim. 3.3,8). Only the spiritual person appreciates the unprofitableness of devoting himself to eating and drinking. "So, whether you eat or drink, or whatever you do, do all to the glory of God" (1 Cor. 10.31).

Second, reproduction. Following the fall of man reproduction was changed into human lust. The Bible especially connects lust with the flesh. Even in the Edenic garden the sin of covetous eating immediately aroused lusts and shame. Paul puts these two together in his first letter to the Corinthians (6.13,15), and definitely relates drunkenness to unrighteousness (vv. 9-10).

Now as to defense. When sin has secured control, the body exhibits its strength in self-defense. It opposes anything which may interfere with its comfort and pleasure. What is commonly called temper and such of its fruits as anger and strife issue from the flesh and are therefore sins of the flesh. Because sin is the motivation behind self-defense, there has flowed forth directly and indirectly from it numerous transgressions. How many of the darkest sins in this world spring from self-interest, self-existence, self-glory, self-opinion, and whatsoever else there is of self.

An analysis of all the world's sins will demonstrate how they each relate to these three categories. A carnal Christian is one who is dominated by one, two, or all three of these items. While it amazes no one for a worldling to be ruled by the sin of his body, it ought to be viewed as very abnormal should a born-again Christian remain long in the flesh, fail to subdue the power of sin and live a life of ups and downs. A believer ought to allow the Holy Spirit to examine his heart and enlighten him as to what is prohibited by the law of the Holy Spirit and the law of nature, as to what hinders him from gaining temperance and self-control, and as to what rules him and deprives him of liberty in his spirit to serve God freely. Unless these sins are taken away, he cannot enter richly into spiritual life.

THE THINGS OF THE FLESH

The flesh has many outlets. We have learned how it is hostile to God and cannot possibly please Him. Neither believer nor sinner, however, can genuinely appreciate the complete worthlessness, wickedness, and defilement of the flesh as viewed by God unless he is shown by the Holy Spirit. Only when God by His Spirit has revealed to man the true condition of the flesh as God sees it will man then deal with his flesh.

The manifestations of the flesh manward are well-known. If a person is strict with himself and refuses to follow, as he once did, "the desires of body and mind" (Eph. 2.3), he will detect easily how defiled are these manifestations. The Galatian letter of Paul gives a list of these sins of the flesh so that none can be mistaken—"Now the works of the flesh are plain: immorality, impurity, licentiousness, idolatry, sorcery, enmity, strife, jealousy, anger, selfishness, dissension, party spirit (literally, "sect"), envy, drunkenness, carousing, and the like" (5.19-21). In this enumeration the Apostle declares that "the works of the flesh are plain." Whoever is willing to understand certainly shall recognize them. To ascertain whether one is of the flesh, he need but inquire of himself if he is doing any of these works of the flesh. It is of course unnecessary for him to commit all in the list in order to be carnal. Were he to do merely one of them he would establish himself beyond doubt as being fleshly, for how could he do any one of them if the flesh had relinquished its rule already? The presence of a work of the flesh proves the existence of the flesh.

These works of the flesh may be divided into five groups: (1) sins which defile the body, such as immorality, impurity, licentiousness; (2) sinful supernatural communications with satanic forces, such as idolatry, sorcery; (3) sinful temper and its peculiarities, such as enmity, strife, jealousy, anger; (4) religious sects and parties, such as selfishness, dissensions, party spirit, envy; and (5) lasciviousness, such as drunkenness and carousing. Every one of these is easily observed. Those who do them are of the flesh.

In these five groups we distinguish some sins as less sinful and others as more defiling; but however we may view them, whether more ugly or more refined, God discloses that all of them derive from one source—the flesh. Those who often commit the most defiling sins naturally know themselves as of the flesh, yet how difficult for those who triumph over these comparatively more defiling sins to acknowledge that they are carnal. They usually consider themselves superior to others and as not walking according to the flesh. They do not realize that however civilized the appearance may be, the flesh is still the flesh. "Strife, dissensions, party spirit, envy" convey a much cleaner appearance than that of "immorality, impurity, licentiousness, carousing." All nonetheless are fruits from the same tree. May we pray over these three verses until our eyes are opened to see ourselves. May we be humbled through prayer. Let us pray until we cry with many tears and mourn for our sins, until we know that we are only in name Christians—even "spiritual" Christians, but that our actual walk continues to be replete with the works of the flesh. May we pray until our hearts are aflame, willing to remove every carnal element.

The first step in the work of the Holy Spirit is to convince and convict us of our sins. As without the illumination of the Holy Spirit a sinner initially will never see the sinfulness of his sin and flee from the coming wrath into the obedience of Christ, so a believer subsequently needs to see his sin a second time. A Christian ought to blame himself for his sin. How can he ever become spiritual if he does not discern the utter wickedness and despicability of his flesh, so that he even abhors himself! Oh, in whatever way it may be that we sin, our belonging to the flesh remains the same. Now is the hour we should humbly prostrate ourselves before God, willing to be convicted afresh of our sins by the Holy Spirit.

THE NECESSITY FOR DEATH

To the degree that a believer is enlightened by the Holy Spirit into apprehending something of the pitiful condition of being fleshly, to that extent will his struggle with the flesh be intensified; and more often will be manifested his failures. In defeat he will be shown more of the sin and frailty of his

flesh in order that he may be aroused to an increased indigna-
tion at himself and an ardent determination to contend with
the sin of his flesh. Such a chain reaction may extend protractedly until at last, through experiencing the deeper work
of the cross, he is delivered. That the Holy Spirit should lead
us in just this way is truly fraught with meaning. Before the
cross can do its deeper work there must be an adequate
preparation. Struggle and failure supply just that.

Apropos the believer's experience, although he may agree
mentally with God's estimate of the flesh that it is corrupted
to the core and irredeemable, he nevertheless may lack that
clear spiritual insight which accurately appreciates the defilement and corruptness of the flesh. He may suppose what
God says to be true. But though the believer still would never
say so, he still tries to tinker with his flesh.

Many believers, ignorant of the salvation of God, attempt
to conquer the flesh by battling it. They hold that victory
depends upon the measure of power they have. These therefore earnestly anticipate God will grant them increased spiritual power to enable them to subdue their flesh. This battle
normally extends over a long period, marked by more defeats
than victories, until finally it seems complete victory over
the flesh is unrealizable.

During this time the believer continues on the one hand
to wage war and on the other to try improving or disciplin-
ing his flesh. He prays, he searches the Bible, he sets up many
rules ("do not handle, do not taste, do not touch") in the
vain hope of subduing and taming the flesh. He unwittingly
tumbles into the trap of treating the evil of the flesh as due
to the lack of rules, education and civilization. If only he
could give his flesh some spiritual training, thinks he, he will
be freed from its trouble. He does not comprehend that such
treatment is useless (Col. 2.21-23).

Because of the Christian's confusion in apparently desiring
the destruction of the flesh while concurrently trying to refine it, the Holy Spirit must allow him to strive, to be defeated, and then to suffer under self-accusation. Only after

he has had this experience over and over again will the believer realize that the flesh is irredeemable and his method
futile. He then will search out another kind of salvation. Thus
he now has come to appreciate in his experience what before
he merely came to know in his mind.

If a child of God faithfully and honestly believes in God
and sincerely entreats the Holy Spirit to reveal God's holiness
to him so that he may know his flesh in that light, the Spirit
certainly will do so. Henceforth he may perhaps be spared
many sufferings. But such believers are few. Most trust in
their own method, assuming that they are not that bad after
all. In order to correct this incorrect assumption, the Holy
Spirit patiently leads believers into experiencing little by
little the futility of their own devices.

We have observed that we cannot yield to the flesh; nor
can we repair, regulate, or educate it, because none of our
methods can ever alter in the slightest the nature of the flesh.
What then can be done? The flesh must die. This is God's
way. Not through any other avenue but death is it to be. We
would prefer to tame the flesh by striving, by changing it,
by exercising the will, or by innumerable other means; but
God's prescription is death. If the flesh is dead, are not all
problems automatically solved? The flesh is not to be conquered; it is to die. This is most reasonable when considered in relation to how we became flesh in the first place:
"that which is born of the flesh is flesh." We became flesh by
being born of it. Now the exit simply follows the entrance.
The way of possessing is the way of losing. Since we became
flesh by being born of the flesh, it naturally follows that we
shall be freed from it if the flesh dies. Crucifixion is the one
and only way. "For he who has died is freed from sin" (Rom.
6.7). Anything less than death is insufficient. Death is the
only salvation.

The flesh is most defiled (2 Peter 2.10-22); God accordingly does not attempt to change it. There is no method of
deliverance other than to put it to death. Even the precious
blood of the Lord Jesus cannot cleanse the flesh. We find in

the Bible how His blood washes our sin but never washes our flesh. It must be crucified (Gal. 5.24). The Holy Spirit can not reform the flesh; therefore He will not dwell in the midst of sinful flesh. His abiding in the believer is not for the purpose of improving, but for warring against, the flesh (Gal. 5.17). "It (the holy anointing oil which is a type of the Holy Spirit) shall not be poured upon the bodies of ordinary men" (Ex. 30.32). If such be the case, how absurd for us frequently to pray that the Lord will make us good and loving so that we may serve Him! How vain is that hope which aims at a holy position some day wherein we may be daily with the Lord and are able to glorify Him in all things! Indeed, we should never attempt to repair the flesh in order to make it cooperate with the Spirit of God. The flesh is ordained to death. Only by consigning the flesh to the cross may we be liberated from being enslaved permanently by it.

THE CROSS AND THE HOLY SPIRIT

MANY, IF NOT MOST, believers were not filled with the Holy Spirit at the moment they believed the Lord. What is even worse, after many years of believing they continue to be entangled by sin and remain carnal Christians. In these pages which follow, what we intend to explain regarding how a Christian may be set free from his flesh is based upon the experience of the believers at Corinth as well as that of many like believers everywhere. We moreover do not wish to imply that a Christian must first believe in the substitutionary work of the cross before he can believe in its identifying work. Is it not true, however, that many do not have a distinct revelation concerning the cross at the beginning? What they have received is but half the whole truth; and so they are compelled to receive the other half at a subsequent period. Now if the reader already has accepted the complete work of the cross, what is given here will concern him little. But if like the majority of believers he too has believed only half the whole then the remainder is indispensable for him. Yet we do want our readers to know that the two sides of the work of the cross need not be accepted separately; a second believing only becomes necessary because of incompleteness at the first.

THE DELIVERANCE OF THE CROSS

Upon reciting many deeds of the flesh in his Galatian letter, the Apostle Paul then points out that "those who belong to Christ Jesus have crucified the flesh with its passions and

desires" (Gal. 5.24). Here is deliverance. Is it not strange that
what concerns the believer vastly differs from what concerns
God? The former is concerned with "the works of the flesh"
(Gal. 5.19), that is, with the varying sins of the flesh. He is
occupied with today's anger, tomorrow's jealousy, or the day
after tomorrow's strife. The believer mourns over a particular
sin and longs for victory over it. Yet all these sins are but
fruits from the same tree. While plucking one fruit (actually
one cannot pick off any), out crops another. One after another they grow, giving him no chance for victory. On the
other hand God is concerned not with the *works* of the flesh
but with "the flesh" itself (Gal. 5.24). Had the tree been put
to death, would there be any need to fear lest it bear fruit?
The believer busily makes plans to handle sins—which are the
fruits, while forgetting to deal with the flesh itself—which is
the root. No wonder that before he can clear up one sin, another has burst forth. We must therefore deal today with the
source of sin.

Babes in Christ need to appropriate the deeper meaning
of the cross, for they are still carnal. The aim of God is to crucify the believer's old man with Christ with the result that
they who belong to Christ "have crucified the flesh with its
passions and desires." Bear in mind that it is the flesh together with its powerful passions and desires that has been
crucified. As the sinner was regenerated and redeemed from
his sins through the cross, so now the carnal babe in Christ
must be delivered from the rule of the flesh by the same cross
so that he can walk according to the Spirit and no longer according to the flesh. Thereafter it will not be long before he
becomes a spiritual Christian.

Here we find the contrast between the fall of man and the
operation of the cross. The salvation provided by the latter is
just the remedy for the former. How fitting indeed they are to
each other. Firstly, Christ died on the cross for the sinner to
remit his sin. A holy God could now righteously forgive him.
But secondly, the sinner as well died on the cross with Christ
so that he might not be controlled any longer by his flesh.

Only this can enable man's spirit to regain its proper rule, make the body its outward servant and the soul its intermediary. In this way the spirit, the soul, and the body are restored to their original position before the fall. If we are ignorant of the meaning of the death herein described we shall not be delivered. May the Holy Spirit be our Revealer.

"Those who belong to Christ Jesus" refers to every believer in the Lord. All who have believed Him and are born anew belong to Him. The deciding factor is whether one has been related to Christ in life, not how spiritual one is or what work he does for the Lord nor whether he has been freed from sin, has overcome the passions and desires of his flesh, and is now wholly sanctified. In other words, the question can only be: has one been regenerated or not? Has one believed in the Lord Jesus as his Savior or not? If he has, no matter what his current spiritual state may be—in victory or in defeat—he "has crucified the flesh."

The issue before us is not a moral one, nor is it a matter of spiritual life, knowledge, or work. It simply is whether he is the Lord's. If so, then he already has crucified the flesh on the cross. The meaning clearly is not that of going to crucify, or of in the process of crucifying, but *has crucified.*

It may be helpful to be more explicit here. We have indicated that the crucifixion of the flesh is not dependent upon experiences, however different they may be; rather is it contingent upon the fact of God's finished work. "Those who belong to Christ Jesus"—the weak as well as the strong—"have crucified the flesh with its passions and desires." You say you still sin, but God says you have been crucified on the cross. You say your temper persists, but God's answer is that you have been crucified. You say your lusts remain very potent, but again God replies that your flesh has been crucified on the cross. For the moment will you please not look at your experience, but just hearken to what God says to you. If you do not listen to His Word and instead look daily upon your situation, you will never enter into the reality of your flesh having been crucified on the cross. Disregard your feelings

and experience. God pronounces your flesh crucified; it therefore *has* been crucified. Simply respond to God's Word and
you shall have experience. When God tells you that "your
flesh has been crucified" you should answer with "Amen, indeed my flesh has been crucified." In thus acting upon His
Word you shall see your flesh is dead indeed.

The believers at Corinth had indulged in sins of fornication, jealousies, contentions, party spirit, lawsuits and many
others. They were plainly carnal. True, they were "babes in
Christ"; nevertheless they were of Christ. Can it actually be
said that these carnal believers had had their flesh crucified
on the cross? The answer undeniably is yes; even *these* had
had their flesh crucified. How is this so? We should realize
that the Bible never tells us to have ourselves crucified; it
informs us only that we "were crucified." We should understand that we are not to be crucified individually but that we
have been crucified together with Christ (Gal. 2.20; Rom.
6.6). If it is a crucifixion together then the occasion when the
Lord Jesus was Himself crucified is that moment when our
flesh too was crucified. Furthermore, the co-crucifixion is not
inflicted on us personally since it was the Lord Jesus who
took us to the cross at His crucifixion. Wherefore God considers our flesh as crucified already. To Him it is an accomplished fact. Whatever may be our personal experiences God
declares that "those who belong to Christ Jesus have crucified the flesh." In order to possess such death we must not
give too large a place to discovering how or to noticing our
experience; we should instead believe God's Word. "God says
my flesh has been crucified so I believe it is crucified. I acknowledge that what God says is true." By responding in this
fashion we shall soon encounter the reality of it. If we look at
God's fact first our experience will follow next.

From God's perspective these Corinthians did have their
flesh crucified on the cross with the Lord Jesus; but from
their point of view they certainly did not have such an experience personally. Perhaps this was due to their not knowing God's fact. Hence the first step towards deliverance is

to treat the flesh according to God's viewpoint. And what is that? It is not in trying to crucify the flesh but in acknowledging that it has been crucified, not in walking according to our sight but according to our faith in the Word of God. If we are well established on this point of acknowledging the flesh as already crucified, then we shall be able to proceed in dealing with the flesh experimentally. If we waver over this fact, the possibility of our definitely possessing it will escape us. In order to experience co-crucifixion we first must set aside our current situation and simply trust the Word of God.

THE HOLY SPIRIT AND EXPERIENCE

"While we were living in the flesh, our sinful passions . . . were at work in our members to bear fruit for death. But now we are . . . dead. . . ." (Rom. 7.5-6). Because of this the flesh has no rule over us any further.

We have believed and acknowledged that our flesh has been crucified on the cross. *Now*—not before—we can turn our attention to the matter of experience. Though we presently stress experience, we nevertheless firmly hold to the fact of our crucifixion with Christ. What God has done for us and what we experience of God's completed work, though distinguishable, are inseparable.

God has done what He could do. The question next is, what attitude do we assume towards His finished work? Not just in name but in actuality has He crucified our flesh on the cross. If we believe and if we exercise our will to choose what God has accomplished for us, it will become our life experience. We are not asked to do anything because God has done it all. We are not required to crucify our flesh for God has crucified it on the cross. Do you believe this is true? Do you desire to possess it in your life? If we believe and if we desire then we shall cooperate with the Holy Spirit in obtaining rich experience. Colossians 3.5 implores us to "put to death therefore what is earthly in you." This is the path towards experience. The "therefore" indicates the consequence of what precedes it in verse 3; namely, "you have died." The "you have died" is what God has achieved for us. Because "you have died," therefore "put to death what is earthly in you." The first mention of death here is our factual position in Christ; the second, our actual experience. The failure of believers today can be traced to a failure to see the relationship between these two deaths. Some have attempted to put their flesh to nought for they lay stress only upon the death experience. Their flesh consequently grows livelier with each dealing! Others have acknowledged the truth that their flesh in fact was crucified with Christ on the cross; yet they do not seek the practical reality of it. Neither of these can ever appropriate experimentally the crucifixion of the flesh.

If we desire to put our members to death we first must have a ground for such action; otherwise we merely rely upon our strength. No degree of zeal can ever bring the desired experience to us. Moreover, if we only know our flesh has been crucified with Christ but are not exercised to have His accomplished work carried out in us, our knowledge too will be unavailing. A putting to nought requires a knowing first of an identification in His death; knowing our identification, we must exercise the putting to death. These two must go together. We are deceiving ourselves should we be satisfied with just perceiving the fact of identification, thinking we are now spiritual because the flesh has been destroyed; on the other hand, it is an equal deception if in putting to nought the wicked deeds of the flesh we over-emphasize *them* and fail to take a death attitude towards the flesh. Should we forget that the flesh is dead we shall never be able to lay anything to rest. The "put to death" is contingent upon the "you have died." This putting to death means bringing the death of the Lord Jesus to bear upon all the deeds of the flesh. The crucifixion of the Lord is a most authoritative one for it puts away everything it encounters. Since we are united with Him in His crucifixion we can apply His death to any member which is tempted to lust and immediately put it to nought.

Our union with Christ in His death signifies that it is an accomplished fact in our spirits. What a believer must do now is to bring this sure death out of his spirit and apply it to his members each time his wicked lusts may be aroused. Such spiritual death is not a once for all proposition. Whenever the believer is not watchful or loses his faith, the flesh will certainly go on a rampage. If he desires to be conformed completely to the Lord's death, he must unceasingly put to nought the deeds of his members so that what is real in the spirit may be executed in the body.

But whence comes the power to so apply the crucifixion of the Lord to our members? It is "by the Spirit," insists Paul, that "you put to death the deeds of the body" (Rom. 8.13), To put away these deeds the believer must rely upon the Holy Spirit to translate his co-crucifixion with Christ into personal experience. He must believe that the Holy Spirit will administer the death of the cross on whatever needs to die. In view of the fact that the believer's flesh was crucified with Christ on the cross, he does not need today to be crucified once again. All which is required is to apply, by the Holy Spirit, the accomplished death of the Lord Jesus for him on the cross to any particular wicked deed of the body which now tries to rise up. It will then be put aside by the power of the Lord's death. The wicked works of the flesh may spring up at any time and at any place; accordingly, unless the child of God by the Holy Spirit continually turns to account that power of the holy death of our Lord Jesus, he will not be able to triumph. But if in this way he lays the deeds of the body to rest, the Holy Spirit Who indwells him will ultimately realize God's purpose of putting the body of sin out of a job (Rom. 6.6). By thus appropriating the cross the babe in Christ will be liberated from the power of the flesh and will be united with the Lord Jesus in resurrection life.

Henceforth the Christian should "walk by the Spirit" and should "not gratify the desires of the flesh" (Gal. 5.16). We always should remember that however deeply our Lord's cross may penetrate into our lives we cannot expect to avoid further agitations of the wicked deeds of our members without constant vigilance. Whenever one of God's own fails to follow the Holy Spirit he immediately reverts to following the flesh. God unveils to us the reality of our flesh through His Apostle Paul's delineation of the Christian's self in Romans 7 from verse 5 onward. The moment the Christian ceases to heed the Holy Spirit he instantly fits into the carnal life pattern described here. Some assume that because Romans 7 stands between Chapters 6 and 8 the activity of the flesh will become past history as soon as the believer has passed through it and entered into the life of the Spirit in Romans 8. ᵀn actuality Chapters 7 and 8 run concurrently. Whenever a believer does not walk by the Spirit as in Romans 8 he is immediately engulfed in the experience of Romans 7. "So then I of myself serve the law of God with my mind, but with my flesh I serve the law of sin" (7.25). You will notice that Paul concludes his description of his experience given before this verse 25 by using the phrase "so then." He encounters incessant defeat up through verse 24; only in verse 25 does he enter into victory: "Thanks be unto God through Jesus Christ our Lord" (v.25a). Upon gaining victory over constant defeat we read Paul saying: "I of myself serve the law of God with my mind." Here he is telling us that his new life desires what God desires. That, however, is not the whole story; for Paul immediately continues by declaring: "*but* with my flesh I serve the law of sin." And this we find him saying *just after* his victory of verse 25a. The obvious inference is that no matter how much his inner mind may serve God's law, his flesh always serves sin's law. However much he may be delivered from the flesh it remains unchanged and continues to serve sin's law (v.25), because the flesh is forever the flesh. Our life in the Holy Spirit may be deepened, but this will not alter the nature of the flesh or prevent it from serving the law of sin. If we therefore desire to be led of the Holy Spirit (Rom. 8.14) and freed from the oppression of the flesh, we must put to death the wicked deeds of the body and walk according to the Holy Spirit.

THE EXISTENCE OF THE FLESH

Let us note carefully that though the flesh may be so put to death that it becomes "ineffective" (the real meaning of "destroy" in Rom. 6.6), it endures nonetheless. It is a great error to consider the flesh eradicated from us and to conclude that the nature of sin is completely annihilated. Such false teaching leads people astray. Regenerated life does not alter the flesh; co-crucifixion does not extinguish the flesh; the indwelling Holy Spirit does not render it impossible to walk by the flesh. The flesh with its fleshly nature abides perpetually in the believer. Whenever opportunity is provided for its operation, it at once will spring into action.

We have previously seen how closely associated are the human body and the flesh. Until such time as we are freed physically from this body we shall not be able to be so delivered from the flesh that no more possibility of its activity exists. Whatever is born of the flesh *is* flesh. There is absolutely no eradication of it until this body corrupted from Adam is transformed. Our body is not yet redeemed (Rom. 8.23); it waits for redemption at the return of the Lord Jesus (1 Cor. 15.22, 23, 42-44, 51-56; 1 Thess. 4.14-18; Phil. 3.20-21). As long as we are in the body, therefore, we must be alert daily lest the flesh break forth with its wicked deeds.

Our life on earth can at best be likened to that of Paul, who remarked that "though we walk in the flesh, we do not war according to the flesh" (2 Cor. 10.3 ASV). Since he still possesses a body he walks in the flesh. Yet because the nature of the flesh is so corrupt he does not war according to the flesh. He walks in the flesh, yes; but he does not walk by the flesh (Rom. 8.4). Until a believer is set free from the physical body he is not entirely free from the flesh. Physically speaking he must live in the flesh (Gal. 2.20); spiritually speaking he need not and must not war according to the flesh. Now if by obvious inference from 2 Cor. 10.3, Paul, being in the body, remains susceptible to warring according to the flesh (though from v.4 we see he does not war that way), who then dares to say that he no longer has any potentially active flesh. The finished work of the cross and its continual application by the Holy Spirit are consequently inseparable.

We must pay unusual attention to this point for it brings in grave consequences. Should a believer come to assume that he is sanctified completely and has no more flesh, he will slip either into a life of pretension or into a life of indolence void of watchfulness. One fact needs to be underscored here. Children born of regenerated and sanctified parents are still of the flesh and in need of being born anew just as any other children are. None can say they are not of the flesh and have no need to be born anew. The Lord Jesus asserted that "that which is born of the flesh is flesh" (John 3.6). If what is born is flesh, it proves that what gives birth to it must likewise be flesh for only flesh can beget flesh. That children are fleshly bears concrete testimony that the parents are not delivered completely from the flesh. The saints transmit to their children their fallen nature only because it is theirs originally. They cannot impart the divine nature received at regeneration because that nature is not originally theirs but is received individually as a free gift from God. The fact that believers do communicate their sinful nature to their children indicates it is ever present in them.

Viewed from this approach, a new creature in Christ we realize never fully recovers in *this* life the position Adam had before the fall, for the body at least is still awaiting redemption (Rom. 8.23). A person who is a new creation continues to harbor the sinful nature within him; he is yet in the flesh. His feelings and desires are at times imperfect and they are less noble than those of Adam before the fall. Unless the human flesh is eradicated from within, he cannot have perfect feelings, desires or love. Man can never arrive at the position of being beyond the possibility of sin since the flesh persists. If a believer does not follow the Holy Spirit but instead yields to the flesh, he certainly will be under the reins of the flesh. Despite these realities, however, we should not emasculate the salvation fulfilled by Christ. The Bible informs us in many places that whatsoever has been begotten of God and is filled with God has no tendency towards sin. This though does not mean there is categorically no possibility of sinful desire. To illustrate. We say wood floats—that it does not have the tendency to sink; but surely it is not unsinkable. If the wood is soaked sufficiently enough in water it will sink of its own accord. Nevertheless the nature of a piece of wood clearly is not to sink. Similarly, God has saved us to the extent of not having the tendency to sin, but He has not saved us to the extent of our being unable to sin. Should a believer remain wholly bent toward sin, it proves he is of the flesh and has not yet appropriated full salvation. The Lord Jesus is able to bend us away from sin; but in addition we must be watchful. Under the influence of the world and the temptation of Satan the possibility of sinning stays with us.

Naturally a believer should understand that in Christ he is a new creation. As such, the Holy Spirit indwells his spirit; and this, together with the death of Jesus actively working in his body, can equip the believer to live a holy life. Such a walk is only possible because the Holy Spirit administers the cross upon the believer's flesh in putting to death the deeds of its members. It is then no longer active. This is not to imply, however, that he has no more flesh. For a believer continues to possess a sinful flesh and is conscious of its presence and defilement. The very fact that sinful nature is transmitted to the children has established beyond doubt that what we now possess is not the natural perfection of sinless Adam.

A believer must confess that even in his holiest hours there may be moments of weakness: evil thoughts may creep into his mind unconsciously; unbecoming words may escape his mouth unknowingly; his will may find it sometimes difficult to yield to the Lord; and he secretly may even endorse the thought of self-sufficiency. These are none but the works of the flesh. Therefore let it be known to believers that the flesh is able to exercise its power again at any time. It has not been eradicated from the body. But neither does the presence of the flesh mean sanctification is impossible to a believer. It is only when we have yielded our body to the Lord (Rom. 6. 13) that it is possible for us no longer to be under the dominion of the flesh but under the dominion of the Lord. If we

follow the Holy Spirit and maintain an attitude of not letting
sin reign over the body (Rom. 6.12), then our feet are freed
from stumbling and we experience sustained victory. Our
body thus delivered becomes the temple of the Holy Spirit
and is at liberty to do God's work. Now the way to *preserve*
one's freedom from the flesh must be exactly the way this
freedom is first obtained at that juncture of life and death
when the believer says "yes" to God and "no" to the flesh. Far
from it being an aoristic once for all event in time, the believer
must maintain throughout his life an affirmative attitude towards God and a negative response towards the flesh. No
believer today can arrive at the point of being beyond
temptation. How necessary to watch and pray and even to
fast that one may know how to walk according to the Holy
Spirit.

Nevertheless, the believer ought to dilute neither God's
purpose nor his own hope. He has the possibility of sinning,
but he must not sin. The Lord Jesus has died for us and crucified our flesh with Himself on the cross; the Holy Spirit indwells us to make real to us what the Lord Jesus has accomplished. We have the absolute possibility of not being
governed by the flesh. The presence of the flesh is not a call
for surrender but a summons to watchfulness. The cross has
crucified the flesh wholly; if we are minded to put to nought
the evil works of the body in the power of the Holy Spirit we
shall experience indeed the finished work of the cross. "So
then, brethren, we are debtors, not to the flesh, to live according to the flesh—for if you live according to the flesh you will
die, but if by the Spirit you put to death the deeds of the body
you will live" (Rom. 8.12-13). Since God has bestowed such
grace and salvation, the fault is altogether ours if we continue to follow the flesh. We are no longer debtors to it as
we once were before we knew such salvation. If we now persist in living by the flesh it is because we want so to live, not
because we must so live.

Many matured saints have experienced sustained victory
over the flesh. Though the flesh abides, its power is reduced
practically to zero. Its life with its nature and activities has

been laid to rest so consistently by the cross of the Lord in the power of the Holy Spirit that it is relegated to a state of existence as if not present. Due to the profound and persistent operation of the cross and the faithfulness of saints in following the Holy Spirit, the flesh, though existing, loses all its resistance. Even its power to stimulate believers seems to be nullified. Such a complete triumph over the flesh is attainable by all believers.

"If by the Spirit you put to death the deeds of the body you will live." The entire relationship expressed in this verse hangs upon that word "if." God has done all that is necessary; He cannot do anything more. It is now up to us to take a stand. If we neglect this perfect salvation, how then shall we escape? "If you live according to the flesh you will die"—this is a warning. Atlhough you are regenerated you nonetheless will lose out in your spiritual walk as though you are not alive. "If by the Spirit" you live, you also die, but you die in the death of Christ. Such a death is most authentic because that death will put to nought all the deeds of the flesh. One way or the other you will die. Which death do you choose: that which stems from lively flesh or that which issues in active spirit? If the flesh is alive the Holy Spirit cannot live actively. Which life do you prefer: that of the flesh or that of the Spirit? God's provision for you is that your flesh and its entire power and activities may be put under the power of Christ's death on the cross. What is lacking in us is none other than death. Let us emphasize it before we speak of life, for there can be no resurrection without prior death. Are we willing to obey God's will? Are we amenable to letting the cross of Christ come out practically in our lives? If so, we must by the Holy Spirit put to death all the wicked deeds of the body.

CHAPTER 4

THE BOASTINGS OF THE FLESH

THE OTHER SIDE OF THE FLESH

Do THE WORKS of the flesh include only what we hitherto mentioned? Or are there other fleshly works? Is the flesh now inactivated under the power of the cross?

Up to this point what we have stressed has been the sins of the flesh which are the lusts of the human body. But our attention now needs to be drawn to another side of the flesh. You will recall we stated earlier that the flesh comprises the works of the soul as well as the lusts of the body. Thus far we have touched upon the body side only, leaving the soul side nearly unscathed. The believer, it is quite true, must rid himself of the defiling sins of the body, but he also needs to resist the works of his soul; for these are no less corrupt in the eyes of God than the sins of the body.

According to the Bible the works of the "flesh" are of two kinds (though both are of the flesh): the unrighteous and the self-righteous. The flesh can produce not only defiling sins but also commendable morals: not only the base and the ignoble but the high and noble as well: not only sinful lust but good intention too. It is this latter side to which we must address ourselves now.

The Scriptures employ the word "flesh" to describe man's corrupt nature or life which embraces soul and body. In the creative act of God soul is placed between spirit and body, that is, between what is heavenly or spiritual and what is earthly or physical. Its duty is to mingle these two, according each its proper place yet making them intercommunicative, that through such perfect harmony man ultimately may attain full spirituality. Unfortunately the soul yielded to temptation which arose from the physical organs, thus releasing itself from the authority of the spirit and embracing instead the control of the body. Soul and body accordingly were joined together to be flesh. Not only is the flesh "devoid of the spirit"; it also is directly opposed to the spirit. The Bible consequently asserts that the "flesh lusts against the spirit" (Gal. 5.17 literal).

The opposition manifested by the flesh against the spirit and against the Holy Spirit is two-fold: (1) by way of committing sin—rebelling against God and breaking the law of God; and (2) by way of performing good—obeying God and following the will of God. The body element of the flesh, full of sin and lust, naturally cannot but express itself in many sins, much to the grief of the Holy Spirit. The soul part of the flesh, however, is not as defiled as the body. Soul is the life principle of man; it is his very self, comprising the faculties of will, mind and emotion. From the human viewpoint the works of the soul may not be all defiled. They merely center upon one's thought, idea, feeling, and like or dislike. Though these all are focused upon self, they are not necessarily defiling sins. The basic characteristic of the works of the soul is independence or self-dependence. Even though the soul side is therefore not as defiled as the body side, it nonetheless is hostile to the Holy Spirit. The flesh makes self the center and elevates self-will above God's will. It may serve God, but always according to its idea, not according to God's. It will do what is good in its own eyes. Self is the principle behind every action. It may not commit what man considers sin: it may even try to keep God's commandments with all its power: yet "self" never fails to be at the heart of every activity. Who can fathom the deceitfulness and vitality of this self? The flesh opposes the spirit not just in sinning against God, but now even in the matter of serving Him and pleasing Him. It opposes and quenches the Holy Spirit by leaning upon its own strength without wholly relying upon God's grace and simply being led by the Spirit.

We can find many believers around us who are by nature good and patient and loving. Now what the believer hates is sin; therefore if he can be delivered from it and from the works of the flesh as described in Galatians 5, verses 19 through 21, then is he content. But what the believer *admires* is righteousness; therefore he will try hard to act righteously, longing to possess the fruits of Galatians 5, verses 22 and 23. Yet, just here lies the danger. For the Christian has not come to learn how to hate the *totality* of his flesh. He merely desires to be liberated from the sins which spring from it. He knows how to resist somewhat the deeds of the flesh, but he does not realize that the entire flesh itself needs to be destroyed. What deceives him is that the flesh not only can produce sin but can also perform good. If it is still doing good it is evident it is yet alive. Had the flesh definitely died the believer's ability both to do good and to do evil would have perished with it. An ability to undertake good manifests that the flesh has not yet died.

We know that men originally belong to the flesh. The Bible distinctly teaches that there is no one in the world who is not of the flesh, for every sinner is born of the flesh. But we additionally recognize that many, before they are born anew, and even many who in their lifetime never believe in the Lord, have performed and continue to perform many commendable acts. Some seem to be naturally born with kindness, patience or goodness. Notice what the Lord Jesus says to Nicodemus (John 3.6); though the latter man is so good naturally, he is nonetheless regarded as of the flesh. This confirms that the flesh can indeed do good.

From the letter of Paul to the Galatians, we once more can see that the flesh is capable of doing good. "Having begun with the Spirit, are you now ending with the flesh?" (3.3). God's children in Galatia had descended into the error of doing good by the flesh. They had begun in the Holy Spirit; they did not continue therein to be made perfect. They wanted instead to be perfected through their righteousness, even the righteousness according to law. Hence it was that the Apostle put such a question to them. If the flesh in the Galatian believers could only do evil, Paul would not have needed to pose such a question, because they themselves would have known only too well that the sins of the flesh could not possibly perfect what was begun in the Holy Spirit. That they desired to perfect with their flesh what the Holy Spirit had initiated proves that to arrive at a perfect position they were depending upon the ability of their flesh to do good. They had truly made an arduous attempt to do good, but the Apostle shows us here that the righteous acts of the flesh and the works of the Holy Spirit are worlds apart. What one does by the flesh is done by himself. It can never perfect what the Holy Spirit has begun.

In the preceding chapter the Apostle can be found uttering another weighty word on this: "But if I build up again those things which I tore down, then I prove myself a transgressor" (2.18). He was pointing at those who, having been saved and having received the Holy Spirit, still insisted on gaining righteousness according to law (vv.16,17,21) through their own flesh. We have been saved through faith in the Lord and not through our works: these are what Paul meant by the things torn down. We know that he always had thrown down the works of sinners, treating such deeds as absolutely valueless in anyone's salvation. Now if by doing righteously we try to "build up again those things" which we have destroyed, then, Paul concludes, "we prove ourselves a transgressor." The Apostle is hence telling us that inasmuch as sinners cannot be saved through their efforts, so we who have been regenerated likewise cannot be perfected through any righteous acts of our flesh. How vain do such righteous deeds continue to be!

Romans 8 maintains that "those who are in the flesh cannot please God" (v.8). It implies that the fleshly have tried, but unsuccessfully, to please God. This of course refers specifically to the righteous acts of the flesh which utterly fail to please God. Let us become profoundly informed here of precisely what the flesh is able to do: it is able to perform righteous deeds, and to do them expertly. We often conceive of the flesh in terms of lust; we consequently consider it strictly defiled, not realizing that it includes more than the lust side. The activities of the various faculties of the soul may not be as defiled as lust. Furthermore, "lust" as sometimes used in the Bible has no connotation of defilement, as for example, "the flesh lusts against the Spirit, and the Spirit against the flesh" in Galatians 5.17 (Darby). We see that the Spirit also lusts—against the flesh. Lust in this instance simply conveys the idea of an intense desire.

All which one does or is able to do before regeneration is but the efforts of the flesh. Thus it can do good as well as evil. The error the believer makes lies right here in that he only knows that the evil of the flesh must be destroyed without appreciating that the good of the flesh needs to be done away with as well. He is unaware of the fact that the righteousness of the flesh belongs as much to the flesh as its evil. The flesh remains flesh, no matter how good or how bad. What imperils a Christian is his ignorance of, or his reluctance to face up to, the necessity of ridding himself of everything of the flesh, including what is good. He must positively recognize that the good of the flesh is not one bit more presentable than its evil, for both pertain to the flesh. Unless the good flesh is dealt with no Christian can ever hope to be freed from the dominion of the flesh. For by letting his flesh do good he will soon find it working evil. If its self-righteousness is not destroyed, unrighteousness shall surely follow.

THE NATURE OF THE GOOD WORKS OF THE FLESH

God opposes the flesh so drastically because He knows its actual condition thoroughly. He desires His children to be released completely from the old creation and enter fully upon the new in experience. Whether good or bad, flesh is still flesh. The difference between the good which proceeds from the flesh and the good which flows from the new life is that the flesh always has self at its center. It is my self who can perform and does perform good without the need of trusting in the Holy Spirit, without the necessity of being humble, of waiting on God, or of praying to God. Since it is I who wills and thinks and does without the need of God and who consequently considers how improved I am or how truly a somebody I have now become through my own efforts, is it not inevitable that I shall ascribe glory to myself? Obviously such deeds do not bring people to God; instead they puff up the self. God wants everyone to come to Him in a spirit of utter dependency, completely submissive to His Holy Spirit, and humbly waiting upon Him. Any good of the flesh which revolves around self is an abomination in the sight of God, for it does not proceed from the Spirit of the life of the Lord Jesus but is of self and glorifies self.

The Apostle protests in his Philippian letter that he "put no confidence in the flesh" (3.3). It tends to be self-confident. Because they themselves are so able, the fleshly do not need to trust in the Holy Spirit. Christ crucified is the wisdom of God, but how much confidence a believer reposes in his own wisdom! He can read and preach the Bible, he can hear and believe the Word, but all are executed in the power of his mind, without experiencing the slightest inner registration of a need to depend absolutely upon the instruction of the Holy Spirit. Many therefore believe they possess all the truth, though what they have comes merely from hearing others or from themselves searching the Scriptures. What is of man far exceeds what is of God. They do not have a heart to receive instruction from Him or to wait upon the Lord to reveal to them His truth in His light.

Christ crucified is also the power of God. But how much self-reliance obtains in Christian service. More effort is exerted in planning and arranging than in waiting upon the Lord. Double is the time expended on preparing the division and conclusion of a sermon than on receiving the power from on high. Yet not because the truth is unproclaimed or the person and work of Christ is unconfessed or the glory of God is unsought do all these works become dead before God, but because there is so much trust in the flesh. How we stress human wisdom and strive for satisfactory arguments in our messages: how we use appropriate illustrations and diverse other means to stir men's emotions: how we employ wise exhortations to induce men to make decisions! But where are the practical results? To what degree do we rely upon the Holy Spirit and to what degree upon the flesh? How can the flesh ever impart life to others? Is there actually any power in the old creation which can qualify people to inherit a part in the new creation?

Self-confidence and self-reliance, as we have said, are the notable traits of the good works of the flesh. It is impossible for the flesh to lean upon God. It is too impatient to tolerate any delay. So long as it deems itself strong it will never depend upon God. Even in a time of desperation the flesh continues to scheme and to search for a loophole. It never has the sense of utter dependency. This alone can be a test whereby a believer may know whether or not a work is of the flesh. Whatever does not issue from waiting upon God, from depending upon the Holy Spirit, is unquestionably of the flesh. Whatever one decides according to his pleasure in lieu of seeking the will of God emanates from the flesh. Whenever a heart of utter trust is lacking, there is the labor of the flesh. Now the things done may not be evil or improper; they in fact may be good and godly (such as reading the Bible, praying, worshiping, preaching); but if they are not undertaken in a spirit of complete reliance upon the Holy Spirit, then the flesh is the source of all. The old creation is willing to do anything—even to submit to God—if only it is permitted to live and to be active! However good the deed of the flesh may appear to be, "I", whether veiled or seen, always looms large on the horizon. The flesh never acknowledges its weakness nor admits to its uselessness; even should it become a laughingstock, the flesh remains unshaken in the belief in its ability.

"Having begun with the Spirit, are you now ending with the flesh?" This uncovers a great truth. One may begin well, in the Spirit, but not continue well therein. Our experience bears out the fact of the relative ease with which a thing may begin in the Spirit but end up in the flesh. Often a newly apprehended truth is imparted by the Holy Spirit; after awhile, however, this truth has turned into a boasting of the flesh. The Jews in the early days committed just such an error. How frequently in the matters of obeying the Lord, of denying one's self afresh, of receiving power to save souls, one genuinely may rely upon the Holy Spirit at the outset; yet not long afterwards that same person changes God's grace into his own glory, treating what is of God as his possession. The same principle holds true in our conduct. Through the working of the Holy Spirit at the beginning there occurs a mighty transformation in one's life whereby he loves what he previously hated and hates what he loved before. Gradually, though, "self" begins to creep in unawares. The person increasingly interprets these changes to be of his making and unto his own admiration; or he grows careless and gradually pushes on by self-trust rather than by dependence upon the Holy Spirit. Thousands of matters there are in the experiences of believers which begin well in the Spirit but terminate unfortunately in the flesh.

Why is it that many of God's dear children eagerly seek a wholly consecrated walk and most earnestly desire the more abundant life but nevertheless fail? Often when listening to messages, conversing with people, reading spiritual books, or praying privately, the Lord makes known to them how perfectly possible it is to have a life of fullness in the Lord. They are made to sense the simplicity and sweetness of such a life and they see no obstacle in the way to their securing it. Indeed they experience a blessing with power and glory which they have never before known. Oh, how good it is! But alas, how soon it all vanishes. Why? How? Is it because their faith is imperfect? Or their consecration not absolute? Surely their faith and consecration have been utterly towards the Lord. Then why such a failure? What is the reason for losing the experience and how can it be restored? The answer is simple and definite. They are trusting in the flesh and trying to make perfect by the flesh what was begun in the Spirit. They are substituting self for the Spirit. Self desires to lead the way while hoping that the Holy Spirit will come alongside and assist. The position and work of the Spirit have been replaced by that of the flesh. Absent is that complete reliance upon the Spirit's leading for accomplishment. Absent also is a necessary waiting upon the Lord. Attempting to follow Him without denying the self is the root of all failures.

THE SINS WHICH FOLLOW

Should a believer be so self-confident that he dares to complete the task of the Holy Spirit in the energy of the flesh, he will not come into full spiritual maturity. He will instead drift until the sins he previously had overcome return to him again in power. Do not be surprised by what is said here. It is a spiritual truism that wherever or whenever the flesh is serving God, there and then the power of sin is strengthened. Why did the proud Pharisees become slaves to sin? Was it not because they were too self-righteous and served God too zealously? Why did the Apostle chide the Galatians? Why did they manifest the deeds of the flesh? Was it not because they sought to establish their own righteousness by works and to perfect by the flesh the work which the Holy Spirit had begun? The hazard for young believers is to stop short of the putting to death of the power of the flesh in doing good by only knowing what the cross does for the sinful side of the flesh. In so doing they retreat again into the sins of the flesh. The greatest blunder Christians commit upon experiencing victory over sin lies in not using the way of victory to sustain it; instead they try to perpetuate the victory by their works and determination. It may perhaps succeed for a while. Before long though they shall find themselves sliding back into their former sins, which may differ in form but not in essence. They then either slump into despair by concluding that constant and persistent triumph is impossible to achieve or they try to camouflage their sins without honestly confessing that they have sinned. Now what is it that causes such failure? Just as the flesh gives you strength to do righteously so it also gives you the power to sin. Whether good acts or evil, all are but the expressions of the same flesh. If the flesh is not furnished opportunity to sin, it is willing to do good; and if once the opportunity to perform good is provided, the flesh will soon revert to sin.

Here Satan deceives God's children. If believers would habitually maintain the attitude of the flesh being crucified Satan could have no chance; for "the flesh is Satan's workshop." If the flesh in whole, not just in part, is truly under the power of the death of the Lord, Satan will be totally disemployed. He is consequently willing to allow the sinful part of our flesh to be offered unto death if he may only deceive us into retaining the good part. Satan is quite aware that should the good side remain intact the life of the flesh will continue to be kept alive. He still has a base from which to operate to recover that side which he has lost. He knows very well that the flesh could win and regain its victory in the realm of sin if the flesh succeeded in squeezing the Holy Spirit out in the matter of serving God. This explains why many Christians fall back into the service of sin after they have been set free. Should the spirit not actually be in complete and continuous control in the matter of worship, it will be unable to maintain dominion in daily life. If I have not yet entirely denied myself before God I cannot deny myself before men, and therefore I cannot overcome my hatred, temper and selfishness. These two are inseparable.

Through ignorance of this truth, the believers at Galatia fell into "biting and devouring one another" (Gal. 5.15). They attempted to perfect by the flesh what had been begun by the Holy Spirit, for they desired "to make a good showing in the flesh" in order that "they might glory in (their) flesh"

(6. 12, 13). Naturally their successes were very scanty in performing good by the flesh, while their failures in overcoming evil became quite numerous. Little did they realize that as long as they would serve God with their strength and ideas they doubtlessly would serve sin in the flesh. If they did not forbid the flesh to do good they could not prevent it from doing evil. The best way to keep from sinning is not to do any good by one's self. Being unconscious of the utter corruption of the flesh, the Galatian believers in their foolishness wished to make use of it, not recognizing that the same corruption marked the flesh in boasting of doing good as in following lust. They could not do what God wanted them to do because on the one hand they tried to accomplish what the Holy Spirit had begun and on the other they vainly attempted to rid themselves of the passion and lust of the flesh.

CHAPTER 5

THE BELIEVER'S ULTIMATE ATTITUDE TOWARDS THE FLESH

GOD'S VIEW OF THE FLESH

WE CHRISTIANS NEED to be reminded once again of God's judgment upon the flesh. "The flesh," says the Lord Jesus, "is of no avail" (John 6.63). Whether it be the sin of the flesh or the righteousness of the flesh, it is futile. That which is born of the flesh, whatever it may be, is flesh, and can never be "unfleshed." Whether it be the flesh in the pulpit, the flesh in the audience, the flesh in prayers, the flesh in consecration, the flesh in reading the Bible, the flesh in singing hymns, or the flesh in doing good—none of these, asserts God, can avail. However much believers may lust in the flesh, God declares it all to be unprofitable; for neither does the flesh profit the spiritual life nor can it fulfill the righteousness of God. Let us now note a few observations concerning the flesh which the Lord through the Apostle Paul makes in the letter to the Romans.

(1) "To set the mind on the flesh is death" (8.6). According to God's view there is spiritual death in the flesh. The only escape is to commit the flesh to the cross. Regardless how competent it is to do good or to plan and plot so as to draw down the approval of men, God has pronounced upon the flesh simply one judgment: death.

(2) "The mind that is set on the flesh is hostile to God" (8.7). The flesh is opposed to God. Not the slightest chance is there of peaceful co-existence. This holds true in regard not only to the sins which issue from the flesh but also to its noblest thoughts and actions. Obviously defiling sins are

hostile to God, but let us observe that righteous acts can be done independently of God as well.

(3) "It does not submit to God's law, indeed it cannot" (8.7). The better the flesh works the farther away it is from God. How many of the "good" people are willing to believe in the Lord Jesus? Their self-righteousness is not righteousness at all; it is actually unrighteousness. None can ever obey all the teaching of the Holy Bible. Whether a person is good or bad, one thing is certain: he does not submit to God's law. In being bad he transgresses the law; in being good he establishes another righteousness outside of Christ and thus misses the purpose of the law ("through the law comes knowledge of sin" 3.20).

(4) "Those who are in the flesh cannot please God" (8.8). This is the final verdict. Regardless how good a man may be, if the doing is out from himself it cannot please God. God is pleased with His Son alone; aside from Him and His work no man nor work can delight God. What is performed by the flesh may seem to be quite good; nevertheless, because it derives from self and is done in natural strength it cannot satisfy God. Man may devise many ways to do good, to improve, and to advance, but these are carnal and cannot please Him. This is not only true of the unregenerate; it is likewise true of the regenerated person. However commendable and effective should anything be that is done in his own strength the believer fails to draw down upon himself the approval of God. God's pleasure or displeasure is not founded upon the principle of good and evil. Rather, God traces the source of all things. An action may be quite correct, yet God inquires, what is its origin?

From these Scripture references we can begin to appreciate how vain and futile are the efforts of the flesh. A believer who is shown precisely God's estimation of it will not blunder easily. As human beings we distinguish between good works and evil works; God on the other hand goes behind and makes a distinction as to the source of every work. The most excellent deed of the flesh brings down upon it the same displeasure of God as would the most defiled and wicked work, for they all are of the flesh. Just as God hates unrighteousness, so He abhors self-righteousness. The good acts done naturally without the necessity of regeneration or union with Christ or dependence upon the Holy Spirit are no less carnal before God than are immorality, impurity, licentiousness, etc. However beautiful man's activities may be, if they do not spring from a complete trust in the Holy Spirit they are carnal and are therefore rejected by God. God opposes, rejects and hates everything belonging to the flesh— regardless of outward appearances and regardless whether done by a sinner or a saint. His verdict is: the flesh must die.

THE BELIEVER'S EXPERIENCE

But how can a believer see what God has seen? God is so adamant against the flesh and its every activity; yet the believer appears to reject only its bad features while clinging affectionately to the flesh itself. He does not reject categorically the whole thing: he instead continues to do many things in the flesh: he even assumes a self-confident and proud attitude about it as though he were now rich with God's grace and qualified to perform righteously. The believer literally is making use of his flesh. Because of such self-deceit the Spirit of God must lead him over the most shameful path in order to make him know his flesh and attain God's view. God allows that soul to fall, to weaken, and even to sin, that he may understand whether or not any good resides in the flesh. This usually happens to the one who thinks he is progressing spiritually. The Lord tries him in order that he may know himself. Often the Lord so reveals His holiness to such a one that the believer cannot but judge his flesh as defiled. Sometimes He permits Satan to attack him so that, out of his suffering, he may perceive himself. It is altogether a most difficult lesson, and is not learned within a day or night. Only after many years does one gradually come to realize how untrustworthy is his flesh. There is uncleanness even in his best effort. God consequently lets him experience

Romans 7 deeply until he is ready to acknowledge with Paul: "I know that nothing good dwells within me, that is, in my flesh" (v.18). How hard to learn to say this genuinely! If it were not for countless experiences of painful defeat the believer would continue to trust himself and consider himself able. Those hundreds and thousands of defeats bring him to concede that all self-righteousness is totally undependable, that no good abides in his flesh. Such dealing, however, does not terminate here. Self-judgment must continue. For whenever a Christian ceases to judge himself by failing to treat the flesh as useless and utterly detestable but assuming instead even a slightly self-flattering and vainglorious attitude, then God is compelled to run him again through fire in order to consume the dregs. How few are they who humble themselves and acknowledge their uncleanness! Unless such a state is realized God will not withdraw His dealings. Since a believer cannot be freed from the influence of the flesh for a moment, he should never cease exercising the heart to judge himself; otherwise he will step once more into the boasting of the flesh.

Many suppose the Holy Spirit's conviction of sin pertains just to the people of the world, for does He not convict them of their sins into believing the Lord Jesus? But Christians ought to know that such operation of the Holy Spirit is as important in the saints as it is in the sinners. Out of necessity He must convict the saints of their sins, not merely once or twice but daily and incessantly. May we more and more experience the conviction of the Holy Spirit so that our flesh can be put under judgment unceasingly and never be able to reign. May we not lose, even for a moment, the true picture of our flesh and God's estimation of it. Let us never believe in ourselves and never trust our flesh again, as though it could ever please God. Let us always trust the Holy Spirit and at no time yield the slightest place to self.

If ever there was one in the world who could boast of his flesh that person must be Paul, for as to righteousness under the law he was blameless. And if any could boast of his flesh

following regeneration, it certainly must be Paul again because he has become an apostle who has seen the risen Lord
with his own eyes and who is used greatly by the Lord. But
Paul dare not boast, for he knows his flesh. His Romans 7
experience enables him to realize fully who he is. God already has opened his eyes to see via his experience that there
dwells in his flesh no good, only sin. The self-righteousness
of which he boasted in the past he now knows to be refuse
and sin. He has learned and learned well this lesson; hence
he dare not trust the flesh again. But with this lesson he does
not in any wise cease. No, Paul continues to learn. And so the
Apostle declares that he can "put no confidence in the flesh.
Though I myself have reason for confidence in the flesh also.
If any other man thinks he has reason for confidence in the
flesh, I have more" (Phil. 3.3-4). Despite the many reasons
he can marshal for trusting his flesh (vv. 5-6), Paul
realizes how God regards it and well understands how
absolutely undependable and untrustworthy it is. If we continue reading Philippians 3 we shall discover how humble
Paul is with respect to trusting in himself: "not having a
righteousness of my own" (v.9): "that if possible I may attain the resurrection from the dead" (v.11): "not that I have
already obtained this or am already perfect; but I press on to
make it my own, because Christ Jesus has made me his own"
(v.12). Should a believer aspire to attain spiritual maturity
he must preserve forever that attitude which the Apostle
Paul maintained throughout his spiritual walk; namely, "not
that I have already attained." The Christian dare not entertain the slightest self-confidence, self-satisfaction or self-joy,
as though he could trust his flesh.

If the children of God honestly strive for the life more
abundant and are ready to accept God's assessment of the
flesh, they will not esteem themselves stronger and better
than others, notwithstanding their extensive spiritual progress. They will not utter such words as "I of course am different from the others." If these believers are disposed to let the
Holy Spirit reveal to them God's holiness and their corrup-

tion and do not fear to be shown too clearly, then hopefully they will come to perceive by the Spirit their corruption at an earlier time, with perhaps a consequent lessening of the painful experience of defeat. How lamentable it is, though, that even when one's intention may not be to trust the flesh, there may yet lurk beneath the surface some little impurity, for such a one still thinks he has some strength. In view of this, God must permit him to encounter diverse defeats in order to eliminate even that little confidence in himself.

THE CROSS AND THE DEEPER WORK
OF THE HOLY SPIRIT

Because the flesh is grossly deceitful, the believer requires the cross and the Holy Spirit. Once having discerned how his flesh stands before God, he must experience each moment the deeper work of the cross through the Holy Spirit. Just as a Christian must be delivered from the sin of the flesh through the cross, so he must now be delivered from the righteousness of the flesh by the same cross. And just as by walking in the Holy Spirit the Christian will not follow the flesh unto sin, so too by walking in the Holy Spirit he will not follow the flesh unto self-righteousness.

As a fact outside the believer the cross has been accomplished perfectly and entirely: to deepen it is not possible. As a process within the believer the cross is experienced in an ever deepening way: the Holy Spirit will teach and apply the principle of the cross in point after point. If one is faithful and obedient he will be led into continually deeper experiences of what the cross has indeed accomplished for him. The cross objectively is a finished absolute fact to which nothing can be added; but subjectively it is an unending progressive experience that can be realized in an ever more penetrating way.

The reader by this time should know something more of the all-inclusive character of his having been crucified with the Lord Jesus on the cross; for only on this basis can the Holy Spirit work. The Spirit has no instrument other than that cross. The believer by now should have a fresh understanding of Galatians 5.24. It is not "its passions and desires" alone which have been crucified; the flesh itself, including all its righteousnesses as well as its power to do righteously, has been crucified on the cross. The cross is where both passions and desires and the spring of those passions and desires are crucified, however admirable they may be. Except as one sees this and is ready to deny *all* his flesh, bad *or* good, can he in fact walk after the Holy Spirit, be pleasing to God, and live a genuinely spiritual life. Such readiness must not be lacking on his part, for though the cross as an accomplished fact is complete in itself its realization in a person's life is measured by his knowledge and readiness and faith.

Suppose the child of God refuses to deny the good of his flesh. What will be his experience? His flesh may appear to be extremely clever and powerful in undertaking many activities. But however good or strong, the flesh can never answer to God's demands. Hence when God actually summons him to prepare to go to Calvary and suffer, the Christian soon discovers his only response is to shrink back and to become as weak as water. Why did the disciples fail so miserably in the Garden of Gethsemane? Because "the spirit indeed is willing, but the flesh is weak" (Matt. 26.41). Weakness here causes failure there. The flesh can only display its apparently excellent power in matters which suit its taste. That is the reason the flesh draws back at God's call. Its death is therefore essential, else God's will can never be done.

Whatever has the intent and desire to develop ourselves that we may be seen and admired by others belongs to the flesh. There is natural good as well as natural bad in this flesh. John 1.13 informs us of "the will of the flesh." The flesh *can* will and decide and plan to execute good in order to receive God's favor. But it still belongs to human flesh and hence must go to the cross. Colossians 2.18 speaks of "the mind of his flesh" (Darby). The self-confidence of a Christian is nothing but trusting in his wisdom, thinking he knows every teaching of the Scriptures and how to serve God. And

✗ 2 Corinthians 1.12 mentions the "wisdom" of the flesh. It is highly dangerous to receive the truths of the Bible with human wisdom, for this is a hidden and subtle method which invariably causes a believer to perfect with his flesh the work of the Holy Spirit. A very precious truth may be stored securely in the memory; however, it is merely in the mind of the flesh! The Spirit alone can quicken, the flesh profits nothing. Unless all truths are enlivened continually by the Lord, they profit neither ourselves nor others. We are not discussing sin here but the inevitable consequence of the natural life in man. Whatever is natural is not spiritual. We must not only deny our righteousness but also our wisdom. This too must be nailed to the cross.

Colossians 2.23 speaks of a "worship" or "devotion" of the flesh. This is "worship" according to our opinion. Each method we devise to stir, seek, and acquire a sense of devotion is worship in the flesh. It is neither worship according to the teaching of Scripture nor worship under the guidance of the Holy Spirit. Hence the possibility of walking by the flesh always exists; whether in the matter of worship, or in Christian work, or in Biblical knowledge, or in saving souls.

The Bible frequently mentions the "life" of the flesh. Unless this is yielded to the cross it lives within the saint just as much as in the sinner. The only difference is that in the saint there is spiritual opposition to it. But the possibility remains for him to take that life and draw upon it. The life of the flesh may help him to serve God, to meditate upon truth, to consecrate himself to the Lord. It may motivate him to perform many good acts. Yes, the Christian can take his natural life as true life in such a way as to make him feel he is serving the will of God.

We must understand that within man two different life principles exist. Many of us live a mixed life, obeying one and then the other of these two different principles. Sometimes we entirely depend on the Spirit's energy; at other times we mix in our own strength. Nothing seems to be stable and steadfast. "Do I make my plans like a worldly man,

ready to say Yes and No at once?" (2 Cor. 1.17) A characteristic of the flesh is its fickleness: it alternates between Yes and
No and vice versa. But the will of God is: "Walk not according to the flesh (not even for a moment) but according
to the Spirit" (Rom. 8.4). We ought to accept God's will.

"In him also you were circumcised with a circumcision
made without hands, by putting off the body of flesh in the
circumcision of Christ" (Col. 2.11). We should be willing to
allow the cross, like a knife in circumcision, to cut off completely everything which pertains to the flesh. Such incision
must be deep and clean so that nothing of the flesh is left
concealed or can remain. The cross and the curse are inextri-
cable (Gal. 3.13). When we consign our flesh to the cross
we hand it over to the curse, acknowledging that in the flesh
abides no good thing and that it deserves nothing but the
curse of God. Without this heart attitude it is exceedingly
difficult for us to accept the circumcision of the flesh. Every
affection, desire, thought, knowledge, intent, worship and
work of the flesh must go to the cross.

To be crucified with Christ means to accept the curse our
Lord accepted. It was not a glorious moment for Christ to be
crucified on Calvary (Heb. 12.2). His being hanged on
the tree meant His being accursed of God (Deut. 21.23).
Consequently, for the flesh to be crucified with the Lord simply implies being accursed with the Lord. As we must receive the finished work of Christ on the cross, so must we
enter into the fellowship of the cross. The believer needs to
acknowledge that his flesh deserves nothing else than the
curse of death. His pratical fellowship with the cross begins after he sees the flesh as God sees it. Before the Holy
Spirit can take full charge over a person there first must be
the complete conmmittal of his flesh to the cross. Let us pray
that we may know what the flesh exactly is and how it must
be crucified.

Brethren, we are not humble enough to accept willingly
the cross of Christ! We refuse to concede we are so helpless,
useless, and utterly corrupt that we deserve nothing but
death. What is lacking today is not a better living but a bet-

ter dying! We need to die a good death, a thorough death. We have talked enough about life, power, holiness, righteousness; let us now take a look at death! Oh that the Holy Spirit would penetrate our flesh deeply by the cross of Christ that it might become a valid experience in our life! If we die correctly we shall live correctly. If we are united with Him in a death like His we shall certainly be united with Him in a resurrection like His. May we ask the Lord to open our eyes to behold the absolute imperative of death. Are you prepared for this? Are you willing to let the Lord point out your weaknesses? Are you ready to be crucified openly outside the gate? Will you let the Spirit of the cross work within you? Oh, may we know more of His death! May we completely die!

We should be clear that the death of the cross is continuous in its operation. We can never enter upon a resurrection stage which leaves death entirely out, for the experience of resurrection is measured by the experience of death. A peril among those who pursue the ascension life is that they forget the categorical necessity of continuously putting to nought the flesh. They forsake the position of death and proceed to resurrection. This results in either treating lightly as of no serious hazard to their spiritual growth the works of the flesh, or in spiritualizing them, that is, assuming the things of the flesh to be of the spirit. How essential to see that death is the foundation for everything. You may proceed to build but you should never destroy the foundation. The so-called risen and ascended realm will be unreal if the death of the flesh is not maintained continuously. Let us not be deceived into thinking we are so spiritually advanced that the flesh has no more power to entice us. This is merely the enemy's attempt to remove us from the basis of the cross in order to render us outwardly spiritual but inwardly carnal. Many such prayers as: "I thank you Lord, for I am no longer such and such but am now so and so" are simply echoes of the unacceptable prayer recorded in Luke 18.11-12. We are most susceptible to deception by the flesh when we are on the verge of being delivered from it. We must abide constantly in the Lord's death.

Our security is in the Holy Spirit. The safe way lies in our readiness to be taught, fearful lest we yield any ground to the flesh. We must submit ourselves cheerfully to Christ and trust the Holy Spirit to apply the dying of Jesus to us that the life of Jesus may be exhibited. Just as formerly we were filled with the flesh, so now we shall be filled with the Holy Spirit. When He is in complete control He will overthrow the power of the flesh and manifest Christ as our life. We shall be able then to say that the "life I now live in the flesh is no longer I who live, but Christ who lives in me." Yet the foundation of that life is and always will be that "I have been crucified with Christ" (Gal. 2.20)!

If we live by faith and obedience we can expect the Spirit to do a most holy and wonderful work in us. "If we live by the Spirit"—this is our faith, for we believe that the Holy Spirit abides in us; then "let us also walk by the Spirit"—this is our obedience (Gal. 5.25). We ought to believe simply and restfully that our Lord has given us His Spirit, now abiding in us. Believe in His gift and trust that the Holy Spirit indwells you. Take this as the secret of Christ's life in you: His Spirit dwells in your innermost spirit. Meditate on it, believe in it, and remember it until this glorious truth produces within you a holy fear and wonderment that the Holy Spirit indeed abides in you! Now learn to follow His leading. Such guidance emerges not from the mind or thoughts; it is something of life. We must yield to God and let His Spirit govern everything. He will manifest the Lord Jesus in our life because this is His task.

WORDS OF EXHORTATION

If we allow the Spirit of God to do a deeper work by the cross our circumcision will become increasingly real. "We are the true circumcision, who worship God in spirit, and glory in Christ Jesus, and put no confidence in the flesh" (Phil. 3. 3). That confidence in the flesh is relinquished through the circumcision performed without hands. The Apostle makes glorying in Christ Jesus the center of everything. He explains to us that there is danger on the one side yet security on the

other. Putting confidence in the flesh tends to destroy glorying in Christ Jesus, but worship in spirit gives us the blessed
joy of life and truth. The Holy Spirit uplifts the Lord Jesus
but humbles the flesh. If we genuinely desire to glory in
Christ and to let Him secure glory in us, we must receive the
circumcision of the cross and learn to worship in the Holy
Spirit. Do not be impatient for impatience is of the flesh. Do
not try different methods because they are useful solely in
helping the flesh. We must distrust the flesh entirely, however good or able it may be. We should trust instead the Holy
Spirit and submit to Him alone. With such trust and obedience the flesh will be humbly kept in its proper place of curse
and accordingly lose all its power. May God be gracious to
us that we may put no confidence in the flesh—yea, that we
may look down upon ourselves and acknowledge how unreliable and utterly fruitless is our flesh. This is a very real
death. Without it there can be no life.

"Do not use your freedom as an opportunity for the flesh"
(Gal. 5.13). We have obtained freedom in the Lord; let us
not therefore give any opportunity to the flesh, for its rightful place is death. Do not unconsciously construe the activity
of the Holy Spirit to be your own, but forever be on guard
lest the flesh should be revived. Do not usurp the glory of His
triumph and thereby afford the flesh a chance to resume operation. Do not grow overconfident following a few victories;
if so, your fall cannot be far away. When you have learned
how to overcome and the flesh has long lost its power, never
imagine that thereafter you are altogether triumphant over
it. Should you not rely upon the Holy Spirit you will soon be
thrown once more into a distressing experience. With holy
diligence you must cultivate an attitude of dependency, else
you will be the target of the flesh's attack. The least pride
will supply the flesh an opportunity. Do not be fearful over
the possibility you may lose face before others. The Apostle,
immediately after his teaching on the crucifixion of the flesh
and walking in the Spirit, said: "Let us not become vainglorious" (Gal. 5.26 Darby). If you humbly recognize how

worthless you are before God, then you will not attempt to vaunt yourself before men. Suppose you hide the weakness of your flesh before men in order to receive glory. Are you not unwittingly giving occasion to the flesh for its activity? The Holy Spirit can help and strengthen us, but He Himself will not supplant us in performing what is our responsibility. Therefore to fulfill that responsibility we on the one hand must maintain the attitude of rendering no occasion to the flesh; but on the other hand we must put that attitude into actual practice when called upon to deny the flesh in all the daily realities of our walk.

"Make no provision," exhorts Paul, "for the flesh" (Rom. 13.14). For the flesh to operate it needs a harbinger. That is why no provision ought to be made for it. If the flesh is to be kept confined to the place of curse, we must be watchful always. We must examine our thoughts continually to see whether or not we harbor the least self-conceit, for certainly such an attitude will give great opportunity to the flesh. Our thoughts are most important here because what is provided for in the secrecy of our thought life will come forth openly in words and deeds. The flesh must never be offered any ground. Even when conversing with others we need to be on the alert lest in many words the flesh is equipped to perform its work. We may love to say many things, but if these are not uttered in the Holy Spirit it is better to say nothing. The same applies to our deeds. The flesh can conjure up many plans and methods and be full of expectations. It has its opinions, power and ability. To others and even to ourselves, these may appear to be quite commendable and acceptable. But let us be reckless enough to destroy even the best of them for fear of violating the Lord's commandment. The best the flesh has to offer must be delivered mercilessly to death for the simple reason that it belongs to the flesh. The righteousness of the flesh is as abhorrent as is its sin. Its good acts should be repented of just as much and as humbly as its sinful deeds. We must always maintain God's view of the flesh.

In case we fail, we must examine ourselves, confess our sin, and resort to the cleansing of the precious blood. "Let us purify ourselves from every pollution of flesh and spirit" (2 Cor. 7.1 Darby). Not only must there be the work of the Holy Spirit and that of the precious blood; we ourselves must work towards cleansing too. We must search out all the uncleannesses of the flesh and consign them to the cross of our Lord. Even the best that is done—though it may not be sinful according to man—is nevertheless condemned by God as unclean. "That which is born of the flesh is flesh." This covers both the person and his deeds. God is not so much interested in the form or shape as in the source. Hence we must be purified not only from our sins but also from every deed of the flesh. "Beloved, I beseech you as aliens and exiles to abstain from the passions of the flesh" (1 Peter 2.11).

PART THREE

THE SOUL

1 Deliverance from Sin and the Soul Life
2 The Experience of Soulish Believers
3 The Dangers of Soulish Life
4 The Cross and the Soul
5 Spiritual Believers and the Soul

CHAPTER 1

DELIVERANCE FROM SIN AND THE SOUL LIFE

THE WAY OF DELIVERANCE

ROMANS 6 LAYS THE FOUNDATION for the Christian's deliverance from sin. Such deliverance God provides for every believer; all may enter in. Moreover, let us be unmistakably clear that this liberation from the power of sin may be experienced the very hour a sinner accepts the Lord Jesus as Savior and is born anew. He need not be a long-time believer and undergo numerous defeats before he can receive this gospel. Delay in accepting the gospel according to Romans 6 is due either to the incomplete gospel he has heard or to his unwillingness in wholly accepting and fully yielding to it. Whereas actually this blessing should be the common possession of all the newly born.

Chapter 6 begins with a call to reminisce, not to anticipate. It directs our attention to the past, to what is already
ours: "Knowing this, that our old man has been crucified with
him, that the body of sin might be annulled, that we should
no longer serve sin" (v.6 Darby). In this single verse we find
three major elements—

      (1) "sin" (singular in number);
      (2) "old man"; and
      (3) "body" (the body of sin).

These three are vastly different in nature and play unique
roles in the act of sinning. Sin here is that which commonly is
called the *root* of sin. The Bible informs us that we were
formerly slaves of sin. Sin had been the master. First of all
therefore, we need to recognize that sin possesses power, for
it enslaves us. It emits this power incessantly to draw us into
obedience to its old man so that we might sin. The old man
represents the sum total of everything we inherit from Adam.
We can recognize the old man by knowing what the new man
is, because whatever is not of the new man must belong to
the old. Our new man embraces everything which flows
newly from the Lord at our regeneration. Hence the old man
betokens everything in our personality which is outside the
new—our old personality and all which belongs to the old
nature. We sin because this old man loves sin and is under its
power. Now the body of sin refers to this body of ours. This
corporeal part of man has become the inevitable puppet in
all our sinning. It is labeled the body of sin because it likewise is subject to the power of sin, fully laden with the lusts
and desires of sin. And it is through this body that sin manages to express itself, else it will be merely an invisible power.
    To recapitulate then, sin is the power which pulls us to do
sin. Old man is the non-corporeal part of what we inherit
from Adam. The body of sin is the corporeal element we inherit from him.
    The process of sinning follows this order: first, sin; next, the
old man; lastly, the body. Sin exudes its power to attract man

and force him to sin. Since the old man delights in sin, he condones sin and bends to it, instigating the body to sin. Wherefore the body serves as the puppet and actually practices sin. It is through the joint enterprise of these three elements that sin is committed. Present always are the compulsion of sin's power, the inclination of the old man, and the practice of the body.

Now how can a man be delivered from sin? Some theorize that since sin is the first cause we must annihilate it in order to attain victory; accordingly they advocate "the eradication of sin." Once the root of sin is pulled out, think these, we never shall sin again and are obviously sanctified. Others argue that we must subdue our body if we desire to overcome sin, for is it not our body, they ask, which practices sin? So there arises in Christendom a group of people who promote asceticism. They use many techniques to suppress themselves for they anticipate that once they overcome the demands of their bodies they shall be holy. None of these is God's way. Romans 6.6 is transparent as to His way. He neither eradicates the root of sin within nor suppresses the body without. Rather, God deals with the old man in between.

GOD'S FACT

The Lord Jesus in going to the cross took with Him not only our sins but also our beings. Paul enunciates this fact by proclaiming "that our old man has been crucified with him." The verb "crucified" in the original is in the aorist tense, connoting that our old man was once and forever crucified with Him. As the cross of Christ is a fact accomplished, so our being crucified with Him is additionally an accomplished fact. Who ever questions the reality of the crucifixion of Christ? Why, then, should we doubt the reality of the crucifixion of our old man?

Many saints, upon hearing the truth of co-death, immediately assume that they ought to die, and so they try their best to crucify themselves. Either lack of God's revelation or lack of faith accounts for this attitude. They not only do this themselves; they teach others so to do as well. The results are too obvious: no power is theirs to be freed from sin and their old man they feel will not die.

This is a grievous misjudgment. The Bible never instructs us to crucify ourselves. Precisely the opposite are we told! We are taught that when Christ went to Calvary He took us there and had us crucified. We are not instructed to begin crucifying ourselves now; instead the Scriptures assure us that our old man was dealt with at the time Christ went to the cross. Romans 6.6 alone is sufficient to substantiate this. There is not the remotest idea conveyed of desiring to crucify ourselves, nor does the Word in the slightest sense imply that our crucifixion awaits realization. The verse in Romans 6 permits no room for doubt when it categorically pronounces that we were crucified with Christ, a fact already accomplished. This is truly the effect of the most precious phrase in the Bible—"in Christ." It is because we are in Him and are united with Him that we can say that when Christ went to the cross we went there in Him, that when Christ was crucified we too were crucified in Him. What a wonderful reality that we are in Christ!

Mere mental assimilation of these truths cannot withstand temptation, however. The revelation of God is positively essential. The Spirit of God must reveal how we are in Christ and how we are united with Him in one. He must also show us distinctly how our old man was crucified with Christ for the simple reason that we are in Christ. This cannot be simply a mental comprehension; it must be a disclosure of the Holy Spirit. When a truth is unfolded by God it most naturally becomes a power in man, who then finds himself able to believe. Faith comes through revelation. Without the latter the former is impossible. This explains why many do not have faith, for though they mentally understand they do not have God's revelation. Therefore, brethren, pray until God gives us revelation so that "knowing this" in our spirit we may truly confess "that our old man has been crucified with him."

What is the consequence of the crucifixion of our old man? Again the answer comes to us unequivocally—"that the body of sin might be annulled." "Annulled" should be rendered "withered" or "unemployed." Beforehand when sin stirred, our old man responded and consequently the body practiced sin. With the crucifixion of the old man and its replacement by the new man, sin may still stir within and attempt to exert its pressure, but it fails to find the consent of the old man in driving the body to sin. Sin can no longer tempt the believer for he is a new man; the old has died. The body's occupation was formerly that of sinning, but this body of sin is now disemployed because the old man was set aside. It is not able to sin and hence has been denied its job. Praise the Lord, this is what He has furnished us.

Why does God crucify our old man with Christ and render our body jobless? His purpose is that "we should no longer serve sin." What God has done in this regard makes it possible for us not to yield thereafter to the pressure of sin nor to be bound by its power. Sin will exercise no dominion over us. Hallelujah! We must praise God for this deliverance.

THE TWO ESSENTIALS

How shall we enter into such blessing? Two elements are indispensable. First, "reckon yourselves dead to sin and alive to God in Christ Jesus" (Rom. 6.11 Darby). This is the essential of faith. When God avows that our old man was crucified with Christ we believe His Word and "reckon ourselves as dead." How then do we die? "We reckon ourselves as dead to sin." When God affirms that we are resurrected with Christ we again trust His Word and "reckon ourselves alive." How then do we live? "We reckon ourselves as alive to God." This reckoning is none other than believing God according to His Word. When God says our old man was crucified, we account ourselves dead; when He insists we are made alive, we reckon ourselves as alive. The failure of many lies in the desire to feel, to see and to experience this crucifixion and resurrection before trusting in the Word of God.

These do not realize God has done it already in Christ and that if only they would believe His Word by reckoning that what He has done is true, His Holy Spirit would give them the experience. His Spirit would communicate to them what is in Christ.

Second, "neither yield your members instruments of unrighteousness to sin, but yield yourselves to God as alive from among the dead and your members instruments of righteousness to God" (Rom. 6.13 Darby). This is the essential of consecration. If we persist in holding on to something which God wants us to relinquish, sin shall have dominion over us, and our reckoning shall be futile. If we fail to yield our members as godly instruments of righteousness to speak and do what He desires and go where He directs, should we be surprised we are not yet delivered from sin? Whenever we refuse to relinquish or we offer resistance to God, sin shall return to its dominion. Under such circumstances we naturally lose the power to reckon, that is, to believe God's Word. In our ceasing to exercise faith and to reckon, can we still be said to be positionally in Christ? Yes, but we are living no longer in Him according to the sense of the "abide in me" of John 15. Accordingly we are unqualified to experience what is factual in Christ, even our crucifixion.

Now we may infer from any defeat of ours that it is due either to lack of faith or failure to obey. No other reason can suffice. Conceivably a defeat could flow from both these reasons; if not from both, then from one or the other. We ought to learn how to live in Christ by faith, never seeing or thinking of ourselves outside of Him. Learn to believe daily that we are in Christ and that whatever is true of Him is true of us. Likewise, through the power of God we must learn daily to keep our consecration unspotted. Count all things as refuse, for there is nothing in the world we cannot relinquish for the Lord and nothing that we should want to keep for ourselves. Let us be disposed to respond positively to God's demands, however difficult or contrary to the flesh they may be. For God no cost is too high. Anything can be sacrificed if only we may please Him. Let us daily learn to be obedient children.

Had we so reckoned and so yielded, we would now be enjoying what the Word of God has manifestly declared: "sin will have no dominon over you."

THE RELATION BETWEEN SIN AND THE BODY

A Christian enters a decidedly hazardous period of his life upon coming to know the truth of co-death and experiencing something of freedom from sin. If at this juncture he receives good instruction and permits the Holy Spirit to apply the cross to himself in a deeper way, he eventually will reach spiritual maturity. But if the believer is content to view his experience of victorious life over sin as the apogee of attainment and forbids the cross to contravene his soul life then he will abide in the soulical realm and mistake his soulical experience for a spiritual one. In spite of the fact his old man was dealt with, the believer's soul life remains untouched by the cross. The will, mind and emotion will therefore continue to function without any check; and the result: his experience is confined to the realm of the soul.

What we need to know is how far such deliverance from sin actually has affected our being—what it has touched but also what it has not yet touched which should be. More especially must we understand that sin has a very particular relationship to our body. Unlike many philosophers we do not consider the body intrinsically evil, but we do confess that the body is the province of sin's domination. In Romans 6.6 we find the Holy Spirit describing our body as "the body of sin," for it is nothing but that before we experience the treatment of the cross and yield our members to God as instruments of righteousness. Sin had seized our body and forced it into servitude. It became sin's fortress, instrument and garrison. Wherefore no designation is more fitting than that of "the body of sin."

A careful reading of Romans 6 through 8, which tell of deliverance from sin, will uncover not only what is the relation of the body to sin but also what is God's perfect salvation in releasing our body completely from serving sin into serving Him.

In Romans 6 the Apostle sets forth these statements:

"the sinful body might be destroyed" (v.6)
"let not sin therefore reign in your mortal bodies, to make you obey their passions" (v.12)
"do not yield your members to sin as instruments of wickedness" (v.13)
"yield . . . your members to God as instruments of righteousness" (v.13)

In Romans 7 God uses Paul to speak of the body in the following terms:

"at work in our members" (v.5)
"I see in my members another law" (v.23)
"making me captive to the law of sin which dwells in my members" (v.23)
"who will deliver me from this body of death?" (v.24)

In Romans 8 the pronouncements of the Holy Spirit through Paul are very plain:

"your bodies are dead because of sin" (v.10)
"will give life to your mortal bodies also through his Spirit which dwells in you" (v.11)
"if by the Spirit you put to death the deeds of the body you will live" (v.13)
"the redemption of our bodies" (v.23)

From these passages we can begin to discern God's particular concern towards our body. God is aware that the body is sin's special sphere of operation. Man has become a slave to sin because his body is sin's puppet. But the moment his body is disemployed from sin the person ceases to be its slave. A man thus freed from sin actually experiences the liberation of his body from its power and influence.

The purpose in crucifying the old man is to release the body from the dominion of sin. With the old man, sin's partner, crucified and the new man taking its place, sin's power over the body is broken, because without the cooperation of the old man sin cannot directly use the body.

It must be emphasized that to be delivered from the power
of sin merely means to have our body liberated. (Of course
our perfect redemption which also includes the deliverance
from the presence of sin lies in the future). Not yet dealt with
is the life of the soul upon which we lean. If we consider
victory over sin as life on the highest plateau then we are
most foolish. We are accepting the "annulling" or "wither-
ing" of the body as life supreme but ignoring the fact that
over and above the body of sin stands the natural soul which
requires as much dealing as does the body. A believer's spiritual odyssey is bound to be shallow if he only knows the body
unemployed (wonderful as that may be) but fails to experience the soul life denied.

Mention was made earlier of the active self or soul engaged
in the work of God. The body may be "withered" but the
soul remains quite active. It may express itself in many different ways yet it invariably centers upon self. Believers who
live in the soul incline towards either will or mind or emotion. They may even shift in their inclinations. But though
outward appearances may differ, the inward clinging to the
soul characterizes them all. Those who are disposed towards
volition will walk according to their own delight and refuse
the will of God. Those whose propensity is towards mind will
order their way according to their own wisdom and neglect
to receive with quietness the guidance of the Holy Spirit in
their intuition. While those whose natural disposition is emotional will seek for pleasures in their feelings. Whatever one's
bent, each will view his tendency as life supreme. No matter
the direction of the inclination, one thing is common to all
such people: all live in themselves: all live in what they naturally possessed before believing the Lord—whether talent,
ability, eloquence, cleverness, attractiveness, zealousness, or
whatever. In principle, soul life is natural strength; in manifestation, its expression is either by stubborn unyielding or
by self-conceit or by pleasure-seeking. If therefore a believer
lives by his soul he will draw naturally upon his reservoir of
strengths and will exhibit a particular strength in one or

more of these ways. Unless the believer offers his soul life to death, he shall cultivate that life, incur the displeasure of God, and miss the fruit of the Holy Spirit.

THE SOUL AS LIFE

When we say the soul is the natural life of man we mean it is the power which preserves us alive in the flesh. Our soul *is* our life. The original word employed in Genesis 1.21,24 for "living creature(s)" is "soul" because this soul is the life human beings and other living creatures share in common. This is the power we naturally possess and by which we live before our regeneration; it is the life which every man has. The Greek lexicon gives the original meaning of *psuche* as "animal life"; so that soul life is what makes man a living creature. It belongs to the natural. Though the soul life may not necessarily be evil—since many sins have been overcome by believers through their old man being crucified with Christ—yet it remains natural. It is the life of man; hence it is most human. It makes man a perfectly human being. Perhaps it is good, loving and humble. Nonetheless it is but human.

This life is entirely distinct from the new life the Holy Spirit gives us at new birth. What the Holy Spirit imparts is God's uncreated life; this other is but man's created life. The Holy Spirit grants us a supernatural power; this other is merely the natural. The Holy Spirit gives the *zoe;* this other is the *psuche.*

Life is that power within a man which animates every member of his body. Hence this inward soulical power finds expression through the outward physical activity. The outer activity is but the effect of the inner power. What therefore lies unseen behind the activity is the substance of life. All we naturally "are" is included in that life. This is our soul life.

SOUL AND SIN

Soul life supplies the energy for executing whatever is commanded. If the spirit rules, the soul will be directed by the spirit to exercise its volition to decide or to do on behalf of the spirit's desire; if however sin reigns in the body, the soul will be enticed by sin into using its volition to decide or to do what sin desires. The soul works according to its master, for its function is the execution of orders. Prior to man's fall it committed its power to the spirit's direction; but after the fall it responded completely to sin's coercion. Because man turned into a fleshly being this sin which afterwards reigned in the body became man's nature, enslaving the soul and the life of man and compelling him to walk after sin. In this way sin became man's nature while soul became man's life.

We often treat life and nature as synonymous and co-significant. Strictly speaking they are different. Life it would appear is much broader than nature. Each life possesses its special nature which, being the natural principle of existence, includes life's disposition and desire. While we are yet sinners our life is our soul and our nature is sin. By the soul we live and the disposition and desire of our life are according to sin. To put it another way, what decides our walk is sin but what supplies the strength to walk in that fashion (sinfully) is the soul. The nature of sin initiates while the life of the soul energizes. Sin originates, soul executes. Such is the condition of an unbeliever.

When a believer accepts the grace of our Lord Jesus in being his substitute on the cross, although he may remain woefully ignorant of his being crucified with Christ he is given God's life nonetheless and has his spirit quickened. This imparted new life brings with it a new nature as well. Hence there now exists both two lives and two natures in the believer: the soul life and the spirit life on the one side, the sin nature and God's nature on the other.

These two natures—old and new, sinful and godly—are fundamentally unalike, irreconcilable and unmixable. The new and the old daily strive for authority over the whole man. During this initial stage the Christian is a babe in Christ because he is yet fleshly. Most variable and most painful are his experiences, punctuated by both successes and failures. Later on he comes to know the deliverance of the cross and learns how to exercise faith in reckoning the old man as crucified with Christ. He is thereby freed from that sin which has paralyzed the body. With his old man crucified the believer is empowered to overcome and enjoys in actual experience the promise that "'sin will have no dominon over you."

With sin under his feet and all lusts and passions of the flesh behind his back, the believer now enters a new realm. He may picture himself wholly spiritual. When he turns to eye those others who remain entangled in sin he cannot but feel elated and wonder how he has reached the summit of spiritual life. Little does this one realize that far from being completely spiritual he still remains partially carnal; he is yet———

A SOULISH OR CARNAL CHRISTIAN

Why is this so? For we see that the soul life continues though the cross has dealt with the believer's sinful nature. It is true that every sin erupts from that sinful nature, with the soul simply a willing servant; nevertheless the soul as inherited from Adam cannot avoid being infected with Adam's fall. It may not be entirely defiled; however, it is natural and quite unlike God's life. The corrupted old man in the believer has died but his soul remains the power behind his walk. On the one hand the sinful nature has been drastically touched but on the other hand the self life still persists and therefore cannot escape being soulish. Although the old man may cease to direct the soul, the latter continues to energize the daily walk of man. Since God's nature has replaced his sinful nature all man's inclinations, desires and wishes are naturally good, so unlike his former unclean state. It must not be overlooked, however, that what executes these new desires and wishes continues to be the old soul power.

To depend upon the soul life to carry out the wish of the spirit is to use natural (or human) force to accomplish supernatural (or divine) goodness. This is simply trying to fulfill God's demand with self-strength. In such a condition the believer is still weak in positively doing right, even though negatively he has overcome sin. Few are those disposed hon-

estly to acknowledge their weakness and incapability and to
lean utterly upon God. Who will confess his uselessness if he
has not been humbled by the grace of God? Man takes pride
in his prowess. For this reason he can hardly entertain the
thought of trusting the Holy Spirit for doing right but is sure
to correct and improve his former behavior by his soul power.
The danger for him is in attempting to please God with his
own power instead of learning to be strengthened with might
in his spirit life through the Holy Spirit so that he may follow the dictates of his new nature. In point of fact his spiritual life is still in its infancy, not having grown yet to that maturity wherein he is able to manifest every virtue of God's
nature. If the believer fails to wait humbly and to rely entirely upon God he inevitably employs his natural, soulical vitality to meet God's requirements placed upon His children. He
does not understand that however good to the human outlook
his efforts may appear to be, they can never please God. Because by so doing, he is mingling what is of God with what
is of man, expressing heavenly desire by means of earthly
power. And the consequence? He fails miserably to be spiritual and continues to abide in the soul.

Man does not know what soul life is. Simply put, it is what
we customarily term self life. It is a serious mistake not to
distinguish between sin and self. Many of the Lord's people
view these two as one and the same entity. What they do not
recognize is that both in Biblical teaching and in spiritual experience they are distinctive. Sin is what defiles, is against
God and is totally wicked; self may not necessarily be so. On
the contrary, it can at times be very respectable, helpful and
lovely. Take, for example, the soul in relation to Bible reading, certainly a most commendable activity. Attempting to
understand the Holy Bible with one's native talent or ability
is not considered sinful; yet approaching the Bible in this
way is undeniably the work of self. Soul-winning, too, if accompanied by methods that accord merely with one's own
thought, will be full of self. And how often pursuit after
spiritual growth originates in the natural self perhaps only

because we cannot bear the thought of falling behind or because we seek some personal gain. Bluntly stated, the doing of good is not sin but the manner, methods, or motive in such good-doing may be surfeited with our self. Its source is man's *natural* goodness, not that supernatural kind given by the Holy Spirit through regeneration. Many are innately merciful, patient, and tender. Now for these to show mercy or patience or tenderness is not committing sin; but because these "good" traits belong to their natural life and are the work of the self they cannot be accepted by God as something spiritual. These acts are performed not by complete reliance upon God's Spirit but by trusting in self-strength.

These few examples illustrate how sin and self do differ from each other. As we proceed in our spiritual walk we shall discover many more instances of how sin may be absent but self fully present. It almost seems inevitable that self will creep into the most holy work and the noblest spiritual walk.

Having long been bound by sin the child of God easily construes freedom from its power to be life par excellence. Just here lurks the greatest danger in the days ahead for this one who now concludes that all pernicious elements within him have been rooted out. He is unaware that even if the old man has died to sin and the body of sin is withered, "sin" nevertheless has not died. It merely has become an unseated sovereign which if given the opportunity will put forth its best effort to regain its throne. The believer's experience of being delivered from sin may even continue but he is not thereby rendered perfect. He has yet to deal unremittingly with his "self."

How deplorable it is should Christians look upon themselves as wholly sanctified when, having sought sanctification, they experienced deliverance. They are ignorant of the truth that liberation from sin is only the first step in overcoming life. It is but the initial victory given by God as an assurance to them of the many more victories that are to follow. Triumph over sin is like a door: one step taken and you are in; triumph over self is like a pathway: you walk and walk for the rest of your days. Upon overthrowing sin we are called next to overcome ourselves—even the best of self, the zealous and religious self—daily.

If one knows only emancipation from sin but has had no experience of self-denial or loss of soul life, he places himself inescapably in the position of resorting to his natural soulical strength to accomplish God's will in his walk. He does not realize that, sin apart, two other powers reside within him, spirit power and soul power. Spirit power is God's power received spiritually at regeneration, while soul power is his own granted him naturally at birth.

Whether one is to be a spiritual man or not largely hinges upon how he handles these two forces within him. The believer enters the ranks of the spiritual by drawing upon the spiritual power to the exclusion of that of his soul. Should he use his soul power or even a combination of the two, the result inevitably shall be a soulish or carnal Christian. God's way is plain. We must deny everything originating in ourselves—what we are, what we have, what we can do—and move entirely by Him, daily apprehending the life of Christ through the Holy Spirit. Failure to understand or to obey leaves us no other alternative but to live hereafter by the power of the soul. A spiritual Christian therefore is one whose spirit is led by God's Spirit. He draws the power for his daily walk from the life given by the Holy Spirit Who indwells his spirit. He does not abide on earth seeking his own will but the will of God. He does not trust in his cleverness to plan and to perform service towards God. The rule of his walk is to dwell quietly in the spirit, no further influenced or controlled by the outer man.

The soulish Christian is eminently different. Though he is in possession of a spirit power he does not draw upon it for his life. In his daily experience he persists in making the soul his life and continues to lean upon his self power. He follows the dictates of his pleasure and delight because he has failed to learn to obey God. To God's work he brings his natural wisdom, devising many ingenious arrangements. His everyday existence is governed and affected by the outer man.

To recapitulate what has been said, the problem of the two natures has been answered but the problem of the two lives remains unsolved. The spirit life and the soul life co-exist within us. While the first is in itself exceedingly strong, the second manages to control the entire being because it is so deeply rooted in man. Unless one is disposed to deny his soul life and permit his spirit life to grasp the reins, the latter has little chance to develop. This is abhorrent to the Father for the child of God deprives himself of spiritual growth. He must be instructed that overcoming sin, blessed though it surely is, is but the bare minimum of a believer's experience. There is nothing astonishing in it. *Not* to overcome sin is what *ought* to astonish us. Does not the Scripture legitimately ask: "How can we who died to sin still live in it?" (Rom. 6.2) For to believe that the Lord Jesus died for us as our substitute is inseparable from believing that we have died with Him (Rom. 6.6). What should amaze us then is not the cessation of sinning in those who have died to sin but the continuance of that phenomenon in them as though yet alive. The first condition is quite normal; the second, altogether abnormal.

To be freed from sin is not a difficult task when viewed in the light of the finished, perfect and complete salvation of God. A believer must proceed to learn the more advanced and perhaps more formidable and deeper lesson of abhorring his life. Not only must we hate the sinful nature which comes from Adam but also the natural vitality upon which we now rely for our living. We must be willing to deny the good which is produced by the flesh as well as the evil of the flesh. Do not merely forsake all sins; in addition, deliver up this life of sin to death. A walk in the Holy Spirit is not only not committing sin but also not allowing self to abide. The Holy Spirit can manifest His power solely in those who live by Him. Whoever walks by his natural strength cannot expect to witness the mighty realities of the Holy Spirit. We need to be released from everything natural as well as from everything sinful. If we insist upon walking according to man—not just the sinful, but the all-inclusive natural, man—we reject the rule of the Holy Spirit in our lives. How can He exhibit His power if we are set free from sin and yet continue to think as "men" think, desire as "men" desire, live and work as "men" do? We are not leaning entirely upon the Holy Spirit of God to work in us. If we genuinely desire His fullness we first must break the all-pervasive influence of the soul.

THE EXPERIENCE OF A MIXED SOUL AND SPIRIT

We do not mean to imply that soulish believers experience nothing except what belongs to the soul; though saints of this type are plentiful. Soulish ones do enjoy some spiritual experiences. Those however are rather mixed, with the soulical mingling with the spiritual. These believers are acquainted with the outline of a spiritual walk because the Holy Spirit has led them so to do. But due to many hindrances they frequently fall back upon natural energy to supply strength for their living, expecting to fulfill the holy requirements of God by their flesh. These follow their desires and ideas and seek sensual pleasure and mental wisdom. While they may be spiritual in knowledge, in point of fact they are soulish. The Holy Spirit genuinely dwells in their spirit and has accorded them the experience of conquering sin through the operation of the cross. But He is not allowed to lead their lives. While some may be ignorant of the law of the Spirit many others may love their soul life just too much to give it up.

Now spirit and soul are easy to distinguish in experience. Spiritual life is maintained simply by heeding the direction of the spirit's intuition. If a believer walks according to God's Spirit he will not originate or regulate anything; he will instead wait quietly for the voice of the Holy Spirit to be heard in his spirit intuitively and assume for himself the position of a subordinate. Upon hearing the inner voice he rises up to work, obeying the direction of intuition. By so walking the believer remains a steadfast follower. The Holy Spirit alone is the Originator. Moreover he is not self-dependent. He does not employ his prowess in executing God's will. Whenever action is required the believer approaches God intently—fully conscious of his weakness—and petitions God to give him a promise. Having received God's promise he then acts, counting the power of the Holy Spirit as his. In an attitude such as this God will surely grant power according to His Word.

Precisely the opposite is the soulish life. Self is the center here. When a Christian is said to be soulish he is walking according to self. Everything originates from himself. He is governed not by the voice of the Holy Spirit in the inner man but rather by the thoughts, decisions and desires of his outer man. Even his feeling of joy arises from having his own wishes satisfied. It will be recalled that the body was said to be the shell of the soul, which in turn forms the sheath of the spirit. As the Holy Place is outside the Holy of Holies so the soul is outside the spirit. In such intimate proximity how easy it is for the spirit to be influenced by the soul. The soul has indeed been delivered from the tyranny of the body; it is controlled no longer by the lusts of the flesh; but a similar separation of the spirit from the control of the soul has not yet occurred in the soulish Christian. Before the believer had overcome his fleshly lusts his soul had been joint-partner with his body. They together constituted one enormous life, the other nature. As it was with soul and body so is it now with his spirit and his soul. The spirit is merged with the soul. The former provides the power while the latter gives the idea, with the result that his spirit is too often affected by his soul.

Because it is surrounded by the soul (even buried therein), the spirit is stimulated easily by the mind. A born-again person ought to possess unspeakable peace in the spirit. Unfortunately this tranquillity is disturbed by the stimulating lust from the soul with its numerous independent desires and thoughts. Sometimes the joy which floods the soul overflows into the spirit, inducing the believer to think he is the happiest person in the world; at other times sorrow pervades and he becomes the most unhappy person. A soulish Christian frequently encounters such experiences. This is because the spirit and the soul remain undivided. They need to be split asunder.

When such believers hear some teaching on the division of spirit and soul, they would like very much to know where their spirit is. They may search diligently, but they are unable to sense the presence of their spirit. Without any real experience there, they naturally are at a loss how to distinguish their spirits from their souls. Since these two are so closely linked it is common for them to treat soulish experiences (such as joy, vision, love, etc.) as superlative spiritual ones.

Before a saint arrives at the stage of spirituality he is sure to be dwelling in a mixed condition. Not content with a quietude in his spirit, he will seek a joyous feeling. In his daily living the believer sometimes will follow the leading of intuitive knowledge and sometimes his thought, sensation or wish. Such a mixture of spirit and soul reveals that two antithetical sources reside in the believer: one belongs to God, one belongs to man: one is of the Spirit, the other is of himself: one is intuitive, the other rational: one is supernatural, the other natural: one belongs to the spirit, the other belongs to the soul. If the child of God carefully examines himself beneath the beam of God's light, he will perceive the two kinds of power within him. He likewise will recognize that sometimes he lives by the one life and at other times by the other. On the one hand he knows he must walk in faith by trusting in the Holy Spirit; on the other hand, he reverts to walking according to himself on the basis of what he terms spiritual feelings. He lives far more in the soul than in the spirit. The degree of his soulishness varies according to (1) his understanding of the spirit life with its principle of cooperating with God and (2) his actual yielding to the soul life. He can live entirely in an emotional, ideational or activist world, or he can even live alternately by his soul and by his spirit. Unless he is instructed by God through the revelation of the Holy Spirit in his spirit, he shall be unable to abhor the soulish life and to love the spirit life. Whichever life he chooses determines the path he shall follow.

CHAPTER 2

THE EXPERIENCE OF SOULISH BELIEVERS

THE LIFE OF SOULISH BELIEVERS

THE SOUL VARIES inevitably from person to person. It cannot be stereotyped. Each of us has his particular individuality— a uniqueness which will extend on into eternity. It is not destroyed at our regeneration. Otherwise, in the eternity to come life will be most colorless indeed! Now since there is this variation in the *souls* of all men, it naturally follows that the life of *soulish* believers will likewise vary from person to person. Consequently, we can speak here only in general terms and shall merely present the more prominent features, against which God's children may then compare their experiences.

Soulish believers are inordinately curious. For example, simply for the sake of knowing what the future holds do they try to satisfy their curiosity by studying thoroughly the prophecies of the Bible.

Carnal Christians tend to show off their differences and superiorities in clothing, speech or deeds. They desire to shock people into a recognition of all their undertakings. Of course, such a tendency may have been theirs before conversion; but they find it hard ever afterwards to overcome this natural propensity.

Unlike spiritual Christians, who seek not so much the explanation as the experience of being one with God, these believers look diligently for an understanding in their mind. They like to argue and to reason. Failure of their life experience to catch up with their ideal is not what worries them;

it is their inability to *understand* this lack of spiritual experience which troubles them! They conjecture that knowing mentally is possessing experientially. This is a tremendous deception.

Most soulish believers assume an attitude of self-righteousness, though often it is scarcely detectable. They hold tenaciously to their minute opinions. It is doubtless correct to hold fast the basic and essential doctrines of the Bible, but certainly we can afford to grant others latitude on minor points. We may have the conviction that what we believe is absolutely right, yet for us to swallow a camel but also to strain out a gnat is not at all pleasing to the Lord. We ought to lay aside the small differences and pursue the common objective.

At times the mind of soulish Christians is assaulted by the evil spirit; hence their thinking becomes confused, mixed, and sometimes defiled. In their conversations they frequently answer what is not asked: their mind runs wild: they shift their topics of discussion ever so often, proving how scattered are their thoughts. Even when they pray and read the Bible their mind wanders far away. Although these Christians usually act without so much as exercising a single thought about it beforehand, they can tell others how they always act on principle and how carefully they consider every action, even citing some analogous incidents from their lives to corroborate their claims. Oddly enough, they occasionally do take an action after thinking thrice or even ten times. Their actions are truly unpredictable.

Carnal believers are moved easily. On one occasion they may be extremely excited and happy, on another occasion, very despondent and sad. In the happy moment they judge the world too small to contain them, and so they soar on wings to the heavens; but in the moment of sadness they conclude that the world has had enough of them and will be glad to be rid of them. There are times of excitement when their hearts are stirred as though a fire were burning within or a treasure had suddenly been found. Equally are there times of depression when the heart is not so stirred but rather gives way to a feeling of loss, making them most dejected. Their joy and their sorrow alike turn largely upon feeling. Their lives are susceptible to constant changes for they are governed by their emotions.

Over-sensitivity is another trait which generally marks the soulish. Very difficult are they to live with because they interpret every move around them as aimed at them. When neglected they become angry. When they suspect changing attitudes towards them, they are hurt. They easily become intimate with people, for they literally thrive on such affection. They exhibit the sentiment of inseparability. A slight change in such a relationship will give their soul unutterable pains. And thus these people are deceived into thinking they are suffering for the Lord.

God is cognizant of the weakness of the soulish when they make self their center and consider themselves special upon achieving a little progress in the spiritual realm. He accords them special gifts and supernatural experiences which enable them to enjoy times of such overwhelming bliss as well as times of such closeness to the Lord as though actually to have seen and touched Him. But He uses these special graces to humble them and bring them to the God of all grace. Unfortunately believers do not follow God's intent. Rather than glorifying God and drawing closer to Him, they grasp God's grace for their own boasting. They now regard themselves stronger than others; for, they privately imagine, who can be more spiritual than those who have had such encounters? Moreover, soulish believers have numerous sentimental experiences which induce them to deem themselves more spiritual, not realizing these are but evidences of their being carnal. Not by feeling but by faith do the spiritual live.

Oftentimes a carnal Christian is troubled by outside matters. Persons or affairs or things in the world around readily invade his inward man and disturb the peace in his spirit. Place a soulish one in a joyful surrounding and joyful he will be. Put him in a sorrowful environment and sorrowful will he be. He lacks creative power. Instead, he takes on the complexion peculiar to that with which or whom he may be associated.

Those who are soulish usually thrive on sensation. The Lord affords them the sense of His presence before they attain spirituality. They treat such a sensation as their supreme joy. When granted such a feeling, they picture themselves as making huge strides towards the peak of spiritual maturity. Yet the Lord alternately bestows and withdraws this touch that He might gradually train them to be weaned from sensation and walk by faith. These do not understand the way of the Lord, however, and conclude that their spiritual condition is highest when they can feel the Lord's presence and lowest when they fail to do so.

Carnal believers bear a common stamp—talkativeness. Few should be their words, they know, but they are goaded into endless discussion by their excited emotion. They lack self-control in speech; once their mouth is open their mind seems to lose all control. Words pour forth like an avalanche. Now the soulish Christian realizes he should not be long-winded, but somehow he is unable to withdraw once the conversation gains momentum. Then thoughts of all kinds swiftly invade the conversation, precipitating a continual shift in topic and an unfailing replenishment in words. And "when words are many, transgression is not lacking" says Proverbs 10.19. For the result will be either the loss of control through much speaking, the loss of peace through argument, or even the loss of love through criticism because secretly and hypocritically they will judge others who are loquacious and deem it most unbecoming in them. Fully aware that flippancy does not become the saint, the carnal person still loves to talk frivolously and hankers to speak and to hear coarse jests. Or he may go in for vivacious and gay conversations which he simply cannot afford to miss, no matter what. Although at times he does abhor such impious or unprofitable talk, it is not for long; for when the emotion is stirred once again, he automatically returns to his favorite old pastime.

Soulish believers also indulge in "the lust of the eyes." What often governs their attitudes is the particular artistic or aesthetic view momentarily current in the world. They have not yet assumed a death-attitude to human artistic concepts. Instead they pride themselves on possessing the insight of an artist. Now should they not be ardent admirers of art they may swing to the other extreme of being indifferent to beauty altogether. These will clothe themselves in rags as a token of their suffering with the Lord.

The intellectuals among those who live by the soul tend to view themselves as "Bohemians." On a windy morning or a moonlit night, for example, they are apt to be found pouring out their souls in sentimental songs. They frequently bemoan their lives, shedding many tears of self-pity. These individuals love literature and are simply ravished by its beauty. They also enjoy humming a few lyric poems, for this gives them a transcendent feeling. They visit mountains, lakes and streams since these bring them closer to nature. Upon seeing the declining course of this world they begin to entertain thoughts of leading a detached existence. How ascendant, how pure they are! Not like other believers who seem to be so materialistic, so pedestrian, so enmeshed. These Christians deem themselves most spiritual, not recognizing how incredibly soulish they actually are. Such carnality presents the greatest obstacle to their entering a wholly spiritual realm because they are governed so completely by their emotion. Of greatest hazard to them are an unawareness of their dangerous position and an utter self-content.

Carnal believers may be long on so-called spiritual knowledge but usually are short on experience. Hence they condemn others but do not correct themselves. When they hear the teaching of the dividing of soul and spirit their natural minds smoothly assimilate it. But what happens then? They set about discerning and dissecting the soulish thoughts and acts not in their own lives but in those of others. Their acquisition of knowledge has merely propelled them to judge someone else and not to help themselves. This propensity to criticize is a common practice among the soulish. They have the soulical capacity to receive knowledge but lack the spiritual capacity to be humble. In their association with people they leave one with the impression of being cold and hard. Their dealing with others possesses a certain stiffness about it. Unlike spiritual believers their outward man has not been broken and they are therefore not easy to approach or to accompany.

Christians who thrive on the soul life are very proud. This is because they make self the center. However much they may try to give the glory to God and acknowledge any merit as of God's grace, carnal believers have their mind set upon self. Whether accounting their lives good or bad their thoughts revolve around themselves. They have not yet lost themselves in God. These feel greatly hurt if they are laid aside either in work or in the judgment of others. They cannot bear to be misunderstood or criticized because they—unlike their more spiritual brethren—still have not learned to accept gladly God's orderings, whether resulting in uplift or in rejection. Unwilling are they to appear inferior, as being despised. Even after they have received grace to know the actual state of their natural life as most corrupt and even after they may have humbled themselves before God—counting their lives to be the worst in the world, these nevertheless ironically end up regarding themselves more humble than the rest. They boast in their humility! Pride is deeply bred in the bone.

THE WORKS OF SOULISH BELIEVERS

The soulish are second to none in the matter of works. They are most active, zealous and willing. But they do not labor because they have received God's order; they labor instead because they have zeal and capacity so to do. They believe *doing* God's work is good enough, unaware that only

doing the labor of God's *appointment* is truly commendable.
These individuals have neither the heart to trust nor the time
to wait. They never sincerely seek the will of God. On the
contrary, they labor according to their ideas, with a mind
teeming with schemes and plans. Because they diligently
work, these Christians fall into the error of looking upon
themselves as far more advanced than their leisurely brethren. Who can deny, however, that with God's grace the
latter can easily be more spiritual than the former?

The labor of soulish believers chiefly depends upon feeling.
They take to work only when they feel up to it; and if these
congenial feelings cease while working they will quit automatically. They can witness to people for hours on end without weariness if they experience within their hearts a burning and unspeakably joyful feeling. But if they sustain a
coldness or dryness within they will scarcely speak, or not
even speak at all, in the face of the greatest need—as, say,
before a death-bed situation. With tingling warmth they can
run a thousand miles; without it, they will not move a tiny
step. They cannot ignore their feelings to the extent of speaking when stomach is empty to a Samaritan woman or talking while eyes are drowsy to a Nicodemus.

Carnal Christians crave works; yet amid many labors they
are unable to maintain calm in their spirit. They cannot fulfill God's orders quietly as can the spiritual believers. Much
work disturbs them. Outer confusion causes inner unrest.
Their hearts are governed by outward matters. Being "dis-
tracted with much serving" (Luke 10.40) is the characteristic
of the work of any soulish believer.

Carnal Christians are readily discouraged in their exertions. They lack that quiet confidence which trusts God for
His work. Regulated as they are by their internal sensations
and external environments, they cannot appreciate the "law
of faith." Upon feeling that they have failed, though not
necessarily true, they give up. They faint when the surroundings appear dark and uninviting to them. They have not yet
entered into the rest of God.

Lacking in farsightedness, believers who trust in the soul easily become discouraged. Only what is immediately ahead can they see. Momentary victory begets them joy, temporary defeat renders them sad. They have not discovered how to see on to the end of a matter through the eyes of faith. They yearn for an immediate success as comfort for their heart; failure to achieve it renders them unable to press on unwearily and to trust God in continued darkness.

The soulish are experts at finding fault, although they are not necessarily stronger themselves. Quick are the soulish to criticize and slow are they to forgive. When they investigate and correct the shortcomings in others they exude a kind of self-sufficient and superior attitude. Their way in sometimes helping people is correct and legal, but their motivation is not always right.

The tendency to be hasty often stamps those who follow their souls. They cannot wait on God. Whatever is done is done hurriedly, precipitously, impetuously. They act from impulse rather than from principle. Even in God's work, these Christians are so propelled by their zeal and passion that they simply cannot stay for God to make clear His will and way.

The mind of the carnal is occupied wholly with their endeavors. They ponder and plan, plot and predict. At times they presage a bright future, hence are beside themselves with joy; at other moments they foreglimpse darkness and immediately become haunted by untold misery. Do they thereby think of their Lord? No, they think more of their labors. To them, working for the Lord is of supreme importance, but often they forget the Lord Who gives work. The Lord's *work* becomes the center, the *Lord* of work recedes to the background.

Soulish persons, lacking in spiritual insights, are guided by sudden thoughts which flash through the mind; their words and works are therefore often inappropriate. They speak, in the first place, not because need summons them to do so but solely because they surmise there ought to be such a need. And then, they may reproach when sympathy is called for or comfort when warning is in order. All these are due to their deficiency in spiritual discernment. They place too much reliance upon their limited and limiting thoughts. And even after their words have proved to be unprofitable, they still refuse to accept the verdict.

Because he possesses oceans of plans and mountains of opinions it is extremely trying to work with a carnal Christian. Whatever he deems to be good must be accepted as good by others. The essential condition for working with him is perfect agreement to *his* ideas or interpretations. The slightest interpretation is equated as a deep involvement in what he considers to be the faith once delivered to the saints. Any different opinion which is manifested he positively cannot tolerate. Although the soulish believer knows he should not *hold on to* opinions, he makes sure that whenever an opinion needs to die it is certainly not going to be his! Sectarianism, he will admit, is unscriptural; but it is never *his* particular sect which must die. Whatever such a believer does not accept he labels as heresy. (Is it any wonder that other Christians—soulish like himself—respond in kind by denying the authenticity of his faith?) He is deeply attached to *his* work. He loves his own small, so-called inner circle and is thus incapable of laboring together with other children of God. And he insists on denominating God's children according to his own affiliation.

When it comes to preaching, the soulish cannot rely entirely on God. They either repose their confidence in some good illustrative stories and witty words or in their personalities. Perhaps a few notable preachers can even completely rely upon themselves: because *I* have said it, people are bound to listen! They may depend on God, but they likewise depend on self. Hence all their careful preparations. They expend more time in analyzing, in collecting materials, and in hard thinking than on prayer, on seeking God's mind, and on waiting for the power from above. They memorize their messages and then deliver them verbatim. *Their* thoughts oc-

cupy a primary place in such work. With such an approach
as this these believers will naturally put more confidence in
the message than in the Lord. Instead of trusting the Holy
Spirit to reveal man's need and God's supply to their listeners,
they depend exclusively upon the words they deliver to move
human hearts. What these carnal believers stress and trust
are but their own words. Perhaps their speech does convey
truth, but without the quickening of the Holy Spirit even
truth is of small advantage. There shall be very little spiritual
fruit should anyone lean on words rather than on the Holy
Spirit. However much these articulations are acclaimed, they
only reach people's minds, not their hearts.

Soulish believers relish using high-sounding spectacular
words and phrases. At least in this respect they are trying
to imitate the genuinely spiritual ones who, having been
given so much experience, are able to teach with a distinc-
tiveness of which none of their predecessors may ever have
conceived. The carnal consider this highly attractive, hence
their delight in employing wonderful imaginations in preaching. Whenever a masterful idea comes upon them—while
walking, conversing, eating, or sleeping—they will jot it
down for future use. They never question whether such idea
is revealed in their spirit by the Holy Spirit or is merely a
sudden thought which burst upon their mind.

Some Christians who are indeed soulish find special delight in helping others. Since they have not yet reached
maturity, they do not know how to give food at the proper
time. This does not mean these do not have knowledge;
actually they have too much. Upon discovering any improper
element or when told of some difficulty, they immediately
assume the role of senior believer, eager to help with what
limited insight they have. They pour forth scriptural teachings and experiences of saints in lavish abundance. They are
inclined to tell all they know, nay, perhaps more than they
know, now reaching out into the realm of supposition. These
"senior" believers exhibit one after another everything which
has been stored in their minds, without at all inquiring

whether those to whom they speak really have such a need
or can absorb so much teaching in one session. They are
like Hezekiah who opened all his storehouses and showed
off all his treasures. Sometimes without any outside stimulus
but just because they are stirred by an inner emotion, they
will shower others with spiritual teachings, many of which
are mere theories. They wish to display their knowledge.

The above characteristic is not true, however, of all soulish
children of God. It varies with different personalities. Some
will keep quiet, uttering not so much as a syllable. Even in
the face of desperate need, when they ought to speak, they
will clamp their mouths shut. They have not yet attained
freedom from natural shyness and fear. They may sit next
to those talkative believers and criticize them in heart, but
their silence does not make them any less soulish.

Because they are not rooted in God and have not therefore learned how to be hidden in Him, carnal people long to
be seen. They seek prominent position in spiritual work. If
they attend meetings they expect to be heard, not to hear.
They experience unspeakable joy whenever recognized and
respected.

The soulish love to use spiritual phraseology. They learn
by heart a large spiritual vocabulary which they invariably
employ whenever convenient. They use it in preaching as
well as in praying, but without any heart.

A vaunting ambition marks out those who live in the realm
of the soul. The first place is often their desire. They are
vainglorious in the Lord's work. They aspire to be powerful
workers, greatly used by the Lord. Why? That they may gain
a place, obtain some glory. They like to compare themselves
with others: probably not so much with those whom they
do not know as with those with whom they work. Such contending and striving in the dark can be very intense. Those
who are spiritually behind they despise, regarding them as
too laggard; those who are spiritually great they downgrade,
visualizing themselves as almost equal. Their unceasing pursuit is to be great, to be the head. They hope their work

will prosper so that they may be well spoken of. These desires of course are deeply concealed in their hearts, barely detectable by others. Although these longings may indeed be well-nigh hidden and mingled with other and purer motives, the presence of such base desires is nonetheless an irrefutable fact.

The soulish are terribly self-satisfied. Should the Lord use them to save one soul they will explode with joy and consider themselves spiritually successful. They take pride in themselves if they succeed but once. A little knowledge, a little experience, a little success easily provokes them to feel as though they have achieved a great deal. This common trait among soulish believers can be likened to a small vessel easily filled. They do not observe how vast and deep is the ocean of water which remains. So long as their bucket is brimming they are satisfied. They have not been lost in God, else they would be able to take in their stride all things as nothing. Their eyes focus upon their petty selves and hence they are greatly affected by a simple little gain or loss. Such limited capacity is the reason why God cannot use them more. If such boasting erupts upon winning only ten souls to the Lord, what will happen should a thousand souls be saved?

After they have experienced some success in preaching, one thought lingers with soulish believers: they were truly wonderful! They derive great joy in dwelling upon their superiority. How distinct they are from others, even "greater than the greatest apostle." Now sometimes they are hurt in heart if others have not thus esteemed them. They bemoan the blindness of those who do not recognize that a prophet from Nazareth is here. At times when these soulish believers think their messages contain thoughts which no one has discovered before, they become troubled should the audience fail to appreciate the marvel of it. Following each success they will spend a few hours, if not a day or two, in self-congratulation. Under such deceit, it is no wonder that they often come to assume that the church of God shall soon see a great evangelist, revivalist or writer in them. What anguish for them it must be if people fail to take notice!

Carnal believers are those without principles. Their words and deeds do not follow fixed maxims. They live instead according to their emotion and mind. They act as they feel or think, sometimes quite contrary to their usual pattern. This change can be seen most vividly after preaching. They change to what they recently have preached. If for instance they speak on patience, then for a day or two afterwards they are unusually patient. If they exhort people to praise God, then they will begin to praise and praise. This will not last long, however. Since they act according to feeling, their own words will activate their emotion into behaving in such and such a way. But once the emotion has passed, all is over and done with.

Another special point concerning soulish Christians is that they are uncommonly gifted. Believers bound by sin are not so talented; neither are the spiritual ones. It seems that God bestows abundant gifts upon the soulish in order that they may deliver their gifts to death voluntarily and then reclaim them renewed and glorified in resurrection. Yet such saints of God are loathe to consign these gifts to death and instead try to use them to the maximum. God-given abilities ought to be used by God for His glory, but carnal believers often regard these as theirs. So long as they serve God in this frame of mind they will continue to use them in accordance with their ideas without letting the Holy Spirit lead them. And when successful they render all glory to themselves. Naturally such self-glorification and self-admiration are quite veiled; nevertheless, however much they may try to humble themselves and to offer glory to God, they cannot avoid being self-centered. Glory be to God, yes: but be it unto God— and to me!

Because the carnal are greatly talented—active in thought, rich in emotion—they readily arouse people's interest and stir the latter's hearts. Consequently, soulish Christians usually possess magnetic personalities. They can quickly win the acclamation of the common people. Yet the fact remains that they actually are lacking in spiritual power. They do not contain the living flow of the power of the Holy Spirit. What they have is of their own. People are aware that they possess something, but this something does not impart spiritual vitality to others. They appear to be quite rich; they are really quite poor.

In conclusion. A believer may have any one or all of the aforementioned experiences before he is delivered entirely from the yoke of sin. The Bible and actual experience together substantiate the fact that many believers simultaneously are controlled on the one hand by their body unto sin and influenced on the other by their soul to live according to themselves. In the Bible both are labeled as being "of the flesh." Sometimes in their lives Christians follow the sin of the body and sometimes the self-will of the soul. Now if one can encounter many of the delights of the soul while attendantly indulging no lesser amount of the lusts of the body, is it not equally possible for him as well to have great soulish sensations in association with many experiences of the spirit? (Of course it should not be overlooked that there are some who conclude one phase before entering upon other phases.) A believer's experience is consequently a rather complex matter. It is imperative that we determine for ourselves whether we have been delivered from the base and the ignoble. Having spiritual experiences does not render us spiritual. Only after we have been delivered from both sin *and* self can we ever be accounted spiritual.

CHAPTER 3
THE DANGERS OF SOULISH LIFE

THE MANIFESTATIONS OF SOUL LIFE

THE MANIFESTATIONS OF SOUL LIFE can be separated generally into four divisions: natural strength; self-conceit, hard and unyielding towards God; self-styled wisdom with many opinions and plans; and emotional sensation sought in spiritual experiences. These are due to the fact that the life of the soul is self, which in turn is natural strength, and that the faculties of the soul are will, mind and emotion. Because there are these various faculties in the soul, the experiences of many soulish Christians are bound to be extremely unalike. Some incline more to the mind while others to emotion or will. Although their lives are therefore greatly dissimilar, all nonetheless are soulish lives. Those who turn to the mind may be able to discern the carnality in those who fall under emotion, and vice versa. Both, however, belong to the soul. What is absolutely vital for believers to see is that they must have their true condition exposed by God's light so that they themselves may be liberated by the truth instead of their measuring others with new knowledge. Had God's children been willing to use His light for self-enlightenment their spiritual state would not be so low today.

The most prominent indication of being soulish is a mental search, acceptance and propagation of the truth. For Christians of this type the highest spiritual experience and the profoundest truth serve but to cultivate their minds. This does not necessarily mean that one's spiritual walk is not in any manner affected in a positive way; but it certainly de-

notes that the prime motive is to gratify the mind. While believers who are mastered by the mental faculty do indeed
have a great appetite for spiritual matters, yet for the satisfaction of this hunger they depend more upon their thoughts
than upon God's revelation. They consume more time and
energy in calculating than in praying.

Emotion is what believers mistake most for spirituality.
Carnal Christians whose tendency is emotional in character
habitually crave sensation in their lives. They desire to sense
the presense of God in their hearts or their sensory organs;
they yearn to feel a love-fire burning. They want to feel
elated, to be uplifted in spiritual life, to be prosperous in
work. True, spiritual believers sometimes do have such sensations, yet their progress and joy are not contingent upon
these. The soulish are quite different in this respect: with
such sensations, they can serve the Lord; without them, they
can scarcely move a step.

A very common expression of a soulish walk manifests itself in the will—that power of self-assertion. Through it believers who live in the soul make self the center of every
thought, word and action. They want to know for *their*
satisfaction, feel for *their* enjoyment, labor according to *their*
plan. The hub of their life is self and the ultimate aim is to
glorify themselves.

Previously we learned that the term "soul" in the Bible is
translated also as "living creature" or "animal." It simply connotes "the animal life." This should help to indicate to us
how soul power expresses itself. The most appropriate phrase
which can be selected to describe the life and work of
soulish believers is "animal activities" or "animal aliveness":
much planning, numerous activities, confused thinking, and
mixed emotions: the whole being, both within and without,
in agitation and turmoil. When emotion is activated the rest
of the being naturally follows suit. But if emotion is depressed or sensation has cooled somewhat, the mind will remain excited in its own right. The walk of a carnal Christian
is characterized by perpetual movement—if not physical

activity, then mental or emotional liveliness. Such a walk is bristling with "animal aliveness"; it is far from communicating the life of the spirit.

We may summarize by saying that the tendency of the fallen soul is to set believers to walking by their natural power, to serve God with their strength and according to their ideas, to covet physical sensation in knowing the Lord or experiencing the Lord's presence, and to understand the Word of God by the power of their minds.

Unless a Christian has received from God a view of his natural self, he unquestionably shall serve God in the energy of his created life. This inflicts great damage upon his spiritual life and results in his bearing little if any true spiritual fruit. Believers must be shown by the Holy Spirit the shamefulness of performing spiritual work with creaturely power. Just as we consider it disgraceful for an ambitious child to flatter himself, so similarly God regards our "animal activity" in spiritual service to be a disgrace. May we be rich in the experience of repenting in dust and ashes instead of striving for the first place before men.

THE FOLLY OF BELIEVERS

Countless saints are blind to the harmfulness inherent in soulish experience. They consider it right to resist and reject those obviously sinful deeds of the flesh because these defile the spirit, but at the same time are they not justified in walking by the energy of the soul which they share in common with all men and animals? What wrong is there for we men to live by our natural power provided we do not sin? As long as the teaching of the Bible concerning soul life does not touch their hearts they will be unable to see any reason for denying that life. If for instance they should transgress God's law and offend Him, they definitely know this is wrong; but if these same believers try their best to do good and to inspire their inborn virtue, how, they ask, can there be any objection? In performing God's work they may neither do it zealously nor depend upon His strength, but at least, they will argue, what we do is God's work! Perhaps many of these endeavors are not appointed by God; nevertheless, those activities are not sinful, claim these believers, but rather most excellent! What offense can that kind of work be? Since God has bestowed gifts and talents in abundance, why can we not work with them? Are we not to engage our talents? If we are not talented we can do nothing; if talented, we should employ them at every opportunity!

Their reasoning continues in another vein: we of course would be wrong to neglect God's Word, but can it now be wrong for us to search out diligently with our mind the meaning of the Scriptures? Can there be sin in reading the Bible? There are many truths of which we presently are ignorant; how unreasonably long we would have to wait to understand them if we did not use our brains! Is not our mind created by God for us to use? Since we are doing it for God and not for sinful ends why can we not use our mind to plan and plot God's work?

They go one step further. Our seeking for the consciousness of God's presence, they will insist, arises from an honest and sincere heart. When we feel dry and low in our life and labor is it not true that God frequently uplifts us by making us so aware of the love of the Lord Jesus as though He had set aglow a fire in our hearts and by giving us such joy and such a sense of His presence that we can almost touch Him? Can anyone deny this as the summit of spirituality? Why, then, judge it wrong if we earnestly seek and pray for the restoration of such feeling after it has been lost and our life has become cold and common?

These musings are just what numerous saints do turn over in their hearts. They do not distinguish the spiritual from the soulical. They have not yet received that personal revelation of the Holy Spirit which shows them the evil of their natural walk. They must be willing to wait upon God for instruction, petitioning the Holy Spirit for revelation as to the sundry evils of their natural good life. This needs to be done in honesty and humility, accompanied by a readiness to forsake everything which the Holy Spirit may uncover. At the appropriate time He will point out to them the utter corruption of their natural life.

The Holy Spirit will equip them to realize that all their work and walk are centered upon self and not upon the Lord. Their good deeds are done not only by their own efforts but primarily for their own glory as well. They have not sought God's will in their exertions. They are not disposed to obey God nor to undertake every matter according to His guidance and through His strength. They simply do what and as they feel like doing. All their prayers and striving after God's will are purely outward shows; they are utterly false. Though these believers use God-endowed talents, they nevertheless think only of how gifted they are, forgetting entirely the Giver of these gifts. They eagerly admire the Word of the Lord but seek knowledge only to satisfy the aspiration of their mind; they are reluctant to wait upon God for His revelation in due course. Their quest for the presence of God, for the consciousness of His mercy and nearness, is not for God's sake but for their happiness. By so doing they are not loving the Lord; rather, they are loving the feeling which refreshes them and affords them the glory of the third heaven. Their total life and labor elevate self as the center. They wish to enjoy themselves.

God's children are awakened to the folly of holding fast their soul life only after they have been enlightened by the Holy Spirit as to the abhorrent character of that life. Such enlightenment does not arrive all at once; it proceeds gradually; not once for all but on many occasions. When believers are illumined by the Spirit for the first time they repent beneath the Light and voluntarily deliver their self life to death. But human hearts are exceedingly deceitful. After a while, perhaps but a few days later, self-confidence, self-love and self-pleasure are reinstated. Hence, periodic illumination must continue so that believers may be willing to deny their natural life. What is truly distressing is to find few believers so possessed of the Lord's mind that they are amenable to yielding voluntarily to Him in these matters. Multiplied defeats and no less shame are always required to render believers willing and ready to forsake their natural propensities. How imperfect is our willingness and how fickle is our condition!

Christians ought to eliminate their folly. They ought to adopt God's view of the absolute impossibility for their natural walk to please Him. They must dare to allow the Holy Spirit to point out to them every corruption of the soul life. They must exercise faith in believing God's estimation of their natural life and must wait patiently for the Holy Spirit to reveal in them what the Bible says of them. Only in this manner will they be led in the way of deliverance.

THE DANGERS OF BEING SOULISH

Believers who are reluctant to, or who fail to, attain what God has ordained are subject to certain hazards. God's intent is for His children to walk by the spirit, not by the soul or body. Failure to live in the spirit incurs loss. Its dangers are at least threefold.

1. *The danger of the spirit being suppressed.* The perfect and complete order of God's operation is first to move in the human spirit, next to enlighten the mind of the soul, and finally to execute through the body. Such an arrangement is of vital significance.

Having been born again of the Holy Spirit, believers ought now to live by their spirit. Only so shall they be qualified to ascertain the will of God and to cooperate with His Spirit in overcoming every wile of the enemy. The believer's spirit ought to be very much alive to the movement of the Holy Spirit so as not to quench His movement but follow it in order that He may execute His purpose through the human spirit. God's Spirit needs the cooperation of the human spirit to lead believers into triumph in their daily walk and to prepare them for the good works appointed them by God. (We shall touch on this aspect of the spirit subsequently.)

Many of God's children, however, do not perceive the movement of the Holy Spirit. They cannot distinguish between the spiritual and the soulical. They often construe the soulical to be the spiritual and vice versa, consequently drawing much upon the energy of the soul for their walk and work to the detrimental suppression of the spirit. They assume they are walking according to the spirit while in truth they are walking according to the soul. Such foolishness throttles their spirit from cooperating with God's Spirit and thereby interrupts what He is wishing to do in their lives.

As long as Christians dwell in the soul they move according to the thoughts, imaginations, plans and visions of their mind. They covet joyful sensations and are mastered by their feelings. When they have sensuous experiences they are elated, but when bereft of such experiences they can hardly lift a finger. They are therefore powerless to live in the realm of the spirit. Their feelings become their life, and as their feelings change so do they too. This amounts to nothing more than walking after the sensations of their outward soul and body instead of living out from the center of their being which is the spirit. Their spiritual sensitivity, overpowered by the body and the soul, grows dull. These believers can only sense matters in the soul or in the body; they have lost the spiritual sense. Their spirit is disabled from cooperating with God and their spiritual growth is arrested. They are no longer capable of acquiring power and guidance in their spirit for warfare and worship. If a person denies to his spirit complete ascendancy over his being or fails to draw upon its power to live, he shall never mature. Spiritual sense is most delicate. It is not easy to recognize even for those who have learned to know and follow it. How much more difficult will it be to discern spiritual awareness if it is subject to constant disturbance from rough soulical sensation emanating from the outside! Not only can soulical sensation confuse, it can also suppress, spiritual sense.

2. *The danger of retreating into the body realm.* Many fleshly works enumerated in Galatians 5 naturally have their

origin in the lusts of the human body, but quite a few others indicate as well the activities of the soul. "Selfishness, dissension, party spirit" distinctly flow from man's self or personality. They are the consequence of the numerous diverse thoughts and opinions held on to among saints. What is important to note here is the fact that these exertions of the soul are listed together with such sins of the body as "immorality, impurity, licentiousness, drunkenness, carousing." This ought to remind us of how closely entwined are the soul and the body. These two in reality are inseparable, because the body we are now in is a "soulical body" (1 Cor. 15.44 literal). Should a believer therefore merely seek to subdue his sinful nature and not his natural life too, he shall find himself, after a short period of experiencing victory over sin, once again tumbling into the realm of the body of sin. Though he may not return to those uglier forms of sin, nevertheless he remains bound by sin.

We should understand that the cross is where God handles the "old creation." There is no partial dealing with the old creation at the cross, for the latter deals with it in its totality. Hence we cannot approach the cross and claim only salvation by substitution without also accepting deliverance through identification. Once receiving by faith the Lord as personal Savior, we shall be led by the indwelling Holy Spirit to desire the experience of co-death with Christ, regardless how much or how little we comprehend identification. Although we shall not lose our new life, we shall fail to enjoy the blessing of it, even the joy of salvation, if we persistently resist the inner desire for the new life. The cross never stops short of its outworking. Deeper and deeper will it operate in us until the old creation is completely crucified experientially. Its goal is the total setting aside of everything belonging to Adam.

Now should God's children, upon experiencing victory over sin, neglect to proceed to overcome the natural life by continuing to dwell in the realm of the soul, they shall discover the soul and body gradually being reunited and leading them back into the sins which once they had forsaken. It can be likened to sailing against the current: lack of advance means sure drift backward. Whatever has been done shall soon be undone if the cross fails to work thoroughly in us. This may explain why many fall back into their old state after having experienced triumph over sin for a while. Should the old creation's life (that of the soul) be allowed to continue, that life will rapidly reunite with the old creation's nature (sin).

3. *The danger of the power of darkness taking advantage.* The Letter of James, written to believers, distinctly delineates the relation between soul life and satanic work:

> Who is wise and understanding among you? By his good life let him show his works in the meekness of wisdom. But if you have bitter jealousy and selfish ambition in your hearts, do not boast and be false to the truth. This wisdom is not such as comes down from above, but is earthly, unspiritual (literally soulish), devilish. (3.13-15)

There is a wisdom which comes from Satan and it is the same as that which can arise at times out of the human soul. The "flesh" is the devil's factory; his operation in the soulical part of the flesh is as active as in the bodily part. These verses explain how bitter jealousy springs from the seeking of soulish wisdom. It is through the activity of the devil in the human soul. Christians are aware that the adversary can entice people to sin, but do they equally realize he can inject thoughts into man's mind? The fall of man was due to the love of knowledge and of wisdom. Satan is employing the same tactic today in order to retain the believer's soul as his operative center.

The scheme of Satan is to preserve for himself as much of our old creation as possible. If he fails to entangle believers in sin, he will next try to induce them to keep their natural life by taking advantage of their ignorance of his wiles or their unwillingness to yield to the Spirit. For if he does not succeed, all the armies of hell shall soon be totally disemployed. The more believers unite with the Lord in spirit

the more the life of the Holy Spirit shall flow into their spirit
and the more the cross shall work in them daily. Hence they
shall be delivered increasingly from the old creation and shall
yield less ground to Satan from which to operate. Let it be
known that all the endeavors of Satan, whether by enticement or by attack, are perpetrated in our old creation. He
dare not waste his energy on our "new creation," God's Own
life. That is the reason he unceasingly attempts to persuade
the children of God to retain something of the old creation—
be it sin or the beautiful natural life—so that he may continue
to operate. How he conspires against believers and confuses
them into loving their self life, despite the fact they have
hated sin.

While we Christians were yet sinners we "once lived in the
passions of our flesh (referring to sins which are related particularly to the body), following the desires of body and
mind (referring to soul life)" (Eph. 2.3). The preceding
verse informs us that both are being wrought upon by the
evil spirit. Now our aim in discussing this is to assist God's
children to understand that the body is not the only sphere
of Satan's pernicious operation, but that the soul too is the
preserve of the adversary. We wish to reiterate that believers
must be released not only from sin but also from their natural
realm. May the Holy Spirit open our eyes to see the gravity
of such a step. Were saints able to be liberated step by step
from the life of the soul as well as the power of sin, Satan
would meet with great defeat on all sides.

Because believers, carnal as they are, do not know how
to guard their minds, evil spirits can easily utilize man's
natural wisdom towards the realization of their plot. They
can smoothly and subtly introduce misunderstanding and
prejudice in man's mind so as to raise questions touching
God's truth and doubts as to the truthfulness of others. How
extensive the obsessed mind has obstructed the working of
the Holy Spirit in man is beyond telling. Although one may
have a good intention, his will is betrayed by his obsessed
mind. Beautiful ideals, too, hinder the Holy Spirit's action

just as does human foolishness. The evil spirits can even impart visions or lofty thoughts to believers, lulling them into thinking that since these are supernatural they must be of God. And so the saint slips into deeper and deeper deception. Before the self life is delivered to death the believer's mind is bound to be curious, desiring to search out, to grasp, to possess: all of which furnishes opportunity to the evil spirits.

The emotional part of the soul also can be aroused easily by the adversary. Since many believers crave joyful feelings and the sensations of having the Holy Spirit, of the loveliness of the Lord Jesus, and of the presence of God, evil spirits will supply their senses with many strange experiences. This is that their natural abilities might be stimulated and that the still small voice of the Holy Spirit, traceable only by man's delicate intuitive faculty in his spirit, might be suppressed. God willing, later we shall discuss these problems in detail.

Christians shall incur great loss in spiritual warfare if they have not dealt with their self. Revelation 12.11 enunciates one of the vital conditions in overcoming the devil—namely, God's people must not love their soul life even to the point of death. Unless self-love or self-pity is committed to the cross they shall surely be defeated by the adversary. Soldiers of Christ who love their lives shall forfeit the victory. The adversary shall conquer everyone whose heart is filled with self-consideration.

Any attachment to things reveals weakness to the enemy. The sole possibility of overcoming him is to yield the natural life to death. Satan can operate through undisciplined souls; he also can directly attack those who know nothing of the cross. Our soul life constitutes the adversary's fifth column within us. It gives ground to the enemy. Regardless how much we know the truth and earnestly contend for it, the soul is forever our vulnerable spot. What is painfully disturbing is the fact that to the degree believers become spiritual to that degree does their soulish life become difficult to detect! The lesser the soulish element, the tougher to treat it. There may be the merest speck of carnality mixed in with the spiritual life, but just this makes it extremely troublesome to distinguish between what is soulish and what is spiritual. Unless Christians are keenly alert in resisting the devil, they shall encounter great defeat through their self life.

That the Christian's soul life could be deceived and could be used by the devil is indeed beyond common expectation. The alarm must therefore be sounded. It is God's desire that we deny everything we inherit from Adam, even our life and nature. Disobedience to God invariably implies danger.

CHAPTER 4

THE CROSS AND THE SOUL

THE CALL OF THE CROSS

ON AT LEAST FOUR SEPARATE OCCASIONS and recorded in the four Gospels the Lord Jesus called His disciples to deny their soul life, deliver it to death, and then to follow Him. The Lord fully recognizes that this is the *sine qua non* for any believer who desires to follow Him and to be perfect like Him in serving men and in obeying God. The Lord Jesus mentions soul life in all these calls, yet He places a different emphasis upon each. Since soul life can express itself in various ways, the Lord stresses a different aspect each time. Anyone who would be a disciple of the Lord must give close attention to what He has said. He is summoning men to commit their natural life to the cross.

THE CROSS AND SOULICAL AFFECTION

"He who does not take his cross and follow me is not worthy of me. He who finds his (soul) life will lose it, and he who loses his (soul) life for my sake will find it" (Matt. 10. 38-39).

These verses beckon us to relinquish our soul life and hand it over to the cross for the Lord's sake. The Lord Jesus explains how a man's foes shall be those of his household; how the son, for the sake of the Lord, shall be torn away from his father, the daughter from her mother, the daughter-in-law from her mother-in-law. This constitutes a cross and the cross denotes being crucified. It is our natural inclination to cherish our beloved ones. We are happy to listen to them and willing to respond to their bidding. But the Lord Jesus calls us to not rebel against God because of our beloved ones. When the desire of God and the desire of man are in conflict, we must for the Lord's sake take up our cross by committing our soulical affection to death, even though the person we love is dear to us, and even though under ordinary circumstances we would be most reluctant to hurt him. The Lord Jesus beckons us in this way so that we may be purified from our natural love. It is for this reason that He therefore declares that the one "who loves father or mother more than me is not worthy of me; and he who loves son or daughter more than me is not worthy of me" (v.37).

"If anyone comes to me and does not hate his own father and mother and wife and children and brothers and sisters, yes, and even his own life, he cannot be my disciple. Whoever does not bear his own cross and come after me, cannot be my disciple" (Luke 14.26-27). Now Matthew shows us in the matter of affection how believers ought to choose loving the Lord first rather than one's family; while Luke signifies what attitude must be maintained towards the love which arises from our soul life—we ought to hate it. Strictly speaking, we are not to love just because the objects of our affection are those whom we would naturally love. Dear and near as parents, brothers, sisters, wives and children are to us, they are listed among the forbidden. Such human love flows from soul life which will cling to its heart desires and will call for love in return. The Lord maintains that such soul life needs to be delivered to death. Though we do not now see Him, He wants us to love Him. He desires us to deny our natural love. He wishes to rid us of our natural love towards others so that we will not love with our own love. Of course He wills that we should love others, but not with our natural soulical affection. If we love, let it be for the sake of the Lord and not for their sake. A new relationship comes to us in the Lord. We should receive from Him His love so that we may love others. In a word, our love must be governed by the Lord. Should He desire us to, we must love even our enemies: if He does not ask us to, we cannot love even the dearest of our household. He does not want our heart to be attached anywhere because He wants us to serve Him freely.

This new love relationship being the case, the soul life must be denied. That is a cross. In so obeying Christ as to disregard his natural affection, a believer's natural love suffers intensely. Such sorrow and pain becomes a practical cross to him. Deep are the heart wounds and many are the tears when one has to forfeit the one he loves. These inflict intense sufferings upon our lives. How very loathe the soul is to yield up its beloved for the Lord's sake! But through this very action is the soul delivered to death; yea, it even becomes willing to die; and thus the believer is liberated from the power of the soul. Upon losing its natural affection on the cross the soul cedes ground to the Holy Spirit that He may shed abroad in the believer's heart the love of God, and enable him to love in God and with the love of God.

Let it be observed that, humanly speaking, this expression of the soul is quite legitimate, for it is most natural and is not defiled as is sin. Is not the love we have mentioned shared by all men? What illegitimacy can there be in loving those of one's family? Hence we know that our Lord is summoning us to overcome the natural, even to denying man's legal right . . . for the sake of God. God wants us to love Him more than our Isaac. It is true that this soul life is given by the Creator; nevertheless, He desires us not to be governed by that life principle. People of the world cannot understand why; only the believer who is losing himself gradually into the life of God can comprehend its meaning. Who can appreciate God's asking Abraham to sacrifice Isaac whom God Himself had first given? Those who apprehend God's heart make no attempt to cling to God-imparted gifts; rather do they desire to rest in God, the Giver of all gifts. God wills for us to be attached to nothing aside from Him, whether it be man or a thing or even something conferred on us by Himself.

Many Christians are quite disposed to leave Ur of the Chaldees, but few there be who can see the need to sacrifice on Mount Moriah what God has given. This is one of the penetrating lessons of faith and relates to our being united with God. He requires His children to forsake everything that they may be wholly His. They must not only rid themselves of whatever they know to be harmful but also yield to the cross whatever is humanly legitimate—such as affection—in order that they may be entirely under the authority of the Holy Spirit.

Our Lord's demand is most meaningful, for is it not true that human affection is tremendously uncontrollable? Without consigning it to the cross and losing it, affection can become a formidable obstacle to spiritual life. Human feelings change as the world changes. Their easy excitement can occasion a saint to lose his spiritual balance. Their constant disturbance can affect a believer's peace in his spirit. Do not sorrows, moanings, sighs and tears usually result from hurt feelings? If the Lord is not pre-eminent in our affections He can hardly be Lord in other respects. This is a test of spirituality and a measure of its degree. We must accordingly hate our soul life and refuse its affections to have free rein. The Lord's demand differs completely from our natural desire. What was previously loved shall now be hated; and even the organ which generates love, our soul life, must be abhorred as well. Such is the spiritual way. If we verily bear the cross we shall be neither controlled nor influenced by soulical affection but shall be fit to love in the power of the Holy Spirit. Even so did the Lord Jesus love His family while on earth.

THE CROSS AND SELF

"Then Jesus told his disciples, 'If any man would come after me, let him deny himself and take up his cross and follow me. For whoever would save his life will lose it, and whoever loses his life for my sake will find it' " (Matt. 16.24-25). Again our Lord is calling His disciples to take up the cross by presenting their soul life to death. Whereas the emphasis in Matthew 10 is the affection of the the soul, here in

Matthew 16 the self of the soul is brought into view. From the preceding verses we learn that the Lord Jesus was at that time unfolding to His disciples His approaching rendezvous with the cross. Out of his intense love for the Lord Peter blurted out: "Lord, pity Yourself." Peter was mindful of man, urging his Master to spare Himself from the pains of the cross in the flesh. Peter failed to understand how man ought to be mindful of the things of God, even in such a matter as death on a cross. He failed to see that concern for God's will must far exceed the concern for self. His attitude went something like this: "Though by dying on the cross one shall obey God's will and fulfill God's purpose, yet ought not one to think of himself? Should he not be mindful of the pain he will have to bear? Lord, pity Yourself!"

What was the Lord's answer to Peter? He sternly rebuked him and declared that such an idea as self-pity could only have originated from Satan. Then he continued by saying to His disciples: "It is not I alone who will go to the cross, but all you who follow and desire to be disciples must also go there. As my way is, so shall your way be. Do not incorrectly imagine that I alone must do God's will; all of you as well shall do His will. In the same manner as I am not mindful of myself and unconditionally obey God's will even to the death of the cross, so shall you deny your self life and be willing to lose it in obedience to God." Peter told the Lord: "You must *pity Yourself!*" The Lord came back with: "You must *deny yourself.*"

There is a price to pay in following God's will. The flesh trembles at such a prospect. While soul life reigns supreme within us we are unfit to accept God's orders because it wishes to follow its will and not God's. When He calls us to deny ourselves through the cross and renounce all for His sake, our natural life instinctively responds with self-pity. This renders us unwilling to pay any cost for God. Hence whenever we choose the narrow way of the cross and endure for Christ's sake, our soul life shall suffer loss. This is how we lose that life. Only in this way can the spiritual life of Christ be enthroned pure and supreme, undertaking within us whatever is well-pleasing to God and beneficial to men.

Now if we take note of this incident between Peter and the Lord we can readily perceive how wicked can be the functioning of this soul life. Peter uttered those carnal words of his *immediately* upon receiving revelation from God to know the mystery hitherto unknown to men—that the lonely Jesus Whom they were following was indeed the Christ of the living God. Directly following such an awesome revelation Peter was led captive by his self life into attempting to persuade his Master to pity Himself. How this ought to impress us with the fact that no amount of spiritual revelation and lofty knowledge can ever guarantee freedom from the dominion of the soul. On the contrary, the higher our knowledge and the more profound our experience, the more hidden shall be our soul life, and the harder, consequently, to detect and eject. Unless the natural realm has been treated drastically by the cross it shall continue to be preserved within man.

Another lesson which we can learn from this instance with Peter is the utter uselessness of the natural life. On this particular occasion Peter's soul life is activated not for himself but for the Lord Jesus. He loves the Lord; he pities Him; he desires the Lord to be happy; he is deeply averse to the Lord suffering like that. His heart is alright and his intention is good, but it is founded upon human consideration derived from the soul life. All such considerations the Lord must reject. Even to desire after the Lord is not permitted if done by the flesh. Does this not demonstrate beyond doubt that we can indeed be soulish in serving and desiring the Lord? If the Lord Jesus Himself denies His soul life in service to God, He certainly does not want us to serve Him with that soul life. He beckons believers to commit their natural self to death, not simply because it loves the world, but also because it may even desire after the Lord. Our Lord never asks how much is done; He only inquires from whence it is done.

At the same time that Peter expresses his affection towards the Lord he is also unconsciously revealing his attitude towards himself. He esteems the physical body of the Lord more than the will of God. He tries to persuade the Lord Jesus to be careful for Himself. Peter's personality is therefore fully unveiled. How true it is that the self always operates independently of the will of God, for it loves to serve Him according to what it in itself deems to be good. Following God's wishes means the stripping away of the soul. Whenever His mind is obeyed, the soul's idea is crushed.

Because Peter on this occasion in Matthew 16 spoke out from His soul, the Lord Jesus called His disciples to forsake the natural life. But the Lord indicates additionally that what Peter has uttered is from Satan. We may therein realize how Satan can employ man's self life. As long as this is not delivered to death Satan possesses an operative instrument. Peter speaks because he cherishes the Lord, yet he is being manipulated by Satan. Peter prays the Lord to be kind to Himself, not knowing this prayer is inspired by the enemy. Satan can urge people to love the Lord or even teach people to pray. He is not apprehensive if people pray or love the Lord; what strikes fear in him is that they might not love the Lord or pray to Him with their natural energy. While soul life continues, his business prospers. May God show us how dangerous this life is, because believers may too quickly conclude that they are spiritual merely because they love the Lord or admire heavenly things. God's purpose cannot be accomplished as long as Satan continues to find opportunity to work through that soul life which remains uncommitted to the death of the cross.

Self-pity, self-love, fear of suffering, withdrawal from the cross: these are some of the manifestations of soul life, for its prime motivation is self-preservation. It is exceedingly reluctant to endure any loss. This is precisely why the Lord summons us to deny self and take up our cross so as to crush our natural life. Every cross which passes before us beckons us to forsake our selves. We should not harbor any self-love but lay down our lives by the power of God. The Lord says to us that this cross is ours, for we each receive from God our own particular cross. That is what we ought to bear. Although it is our cross, it nevertheless is closely connected with the cross of the Lord. If in the disposition which Christ displayed in relation to His cross we are willing to take up ours, then we shall find that the power of His cross abides in us and enables us to lose our natural life. Each time the cross is taken up, each time does the soul life suffer loss. Each time the cross is circumvented, each time is the soul life fed and preserved.

The Lord Jesus does not imply that dealing with our natural inclinations is a once for all matter. We find in Luke the word "daily" is added to our Lord's call to take up the cross. Cross-bearing is continuous. The cross which condemned sin to death is an accomplished fact: all which remains for us to do is to acknowledge and receive it. But the cross through which we forfeit our soul life is different. Self-denial is not a matter already and completely accomplished; this we must experience daily. Now this does not mean that the soul life will never be lost or only be lost slowly. It simply bespeaks the fact that the cross which deals with the soul life operates differently from that which deals with sin. And the reason? Because death towards sin is accomplished for us by Christ: when He died, we died with Him. But the denial of the soul life is not an accomplished matter. We are required to take up our own cross daily by the power of the cross of Christ and determine daily to deny self—until it is lost.

Renunciation of our natural life is not something which is done once and forever. As for sin, we only need take the ground of the cross (Rom. 6.6) and immediately we are freed from its power and our servitude to it. In a moment this can be experienced with a full and perfect victory. But the self life must be overcome step by step. The deeper the Word of God penetrates (Heb. 4.12), the deeper works the cross and the further the Holy Spirit completes the union of the life of our spirit with the Lord Jesus. How can believers deny the

self when it is yet unknown to them? They can deny only
that part of the soul life which they already recognize. God's
Word must lay bare more and more of our natural life so that
the work of the cross can probe deeper and deeper. That is
why the cross must be borne daily. To know more of God's
will and to know more of the self furnishes the cross increased ground to operate.

THE CROSS AND THE SOUL'S LOVE OF THE WORLD

Once again our Lord speaks: "Remember Lot's wife. Whoever seeks to gain his life will lose it, but whoever loses his
life will preserve it" (Luke 17.32-33). Although these are by
now familiar words to the reader, we must note the Lord here
lays stress upon self-denial in relation to the things of this
world. How irksome it seems for believers to have their hearts
detached from earthly possessions. We need to follow our
Lord's admonition to remember Lot's wife, for she was one
who did not forget her possessions even in a time of the
greatest peril. She was not guilty of having retraced a single
step towards Sodom. All she did was look back. But how revealing was that backward glance! Does it not speak volumes
concerning the condition of her heart?

It is possible for a believer outwardly to forsake the world
and leave everything behind and yet inwardly cling to those
very elements he had forsaken for the Lord's sake. It does not
require a consecrated person to return to the world or to re-
possess what he had forsaken in the world to indicate that the
soul life is still active. If he but casts one longing glance it is
sufficient to disclose to us that he does not truly recognize
where the world stands in relation to the cross.

When the soul life is genuinely crushed nothing of this
world can again move a believer's heart. Soul life is worldly;
hence it is attached to the things of the world. Only after one
is actually willing to offer his soul life to death will he be fit
to follow the "Sermon on the Mount" without flinching.
Though in that "sermon" we do not find the Lord Jesus mentioning the work of the cross, we nonetheless know for certain

that unless one experiences identification with Christ in death—not merely having died to sin but having died to the self life as well—he attempts in vain to keep our Lord's teachings enunciated on the Mount. He may appear to be following these instructions, but his heart is not one with his appearance. Only a Christian who has yielded his soul life can spontaneously and unpretentiously give away his cloak when he has been sued for his coat. He whose self life has been sacrificed to death is cut loose from the things of the world.

Gaining spiritual life is conditional on suffering loss. We cannot measure our lives in terms of "gain"; they must be measured in terms of "loss." Our real capacity lies not in how much we retain but in how much has been poured out. Those who can afford to lose the most are those who have the most to give. The power of love is attested by love's sacrifice. If our hearts are not separated from love of the world, our soul life has yet to go through the cross.

"And you joyfully accepted the plundering of your property" (Heb. 10.34). The believers referred to in this passage did not simply endure but even joyfully accepted the plundering of their goods. This is the work of the cross. The attitude of saints towards their possessions most assuredly signifies whether they continue to preserve their self life or whether they have consigned it to death.

If we desire to tread a pure spiritual path we must allow God to so operate in us that our hearts can be severed from everything pertaining to the world and be totally released from the intent of Lot's wife. This is the prerequisite for experiencing perfect life in Christ. We can despise all the things in the world only after the Holy Spirit has shown the reality of heaven and its perfect life. Matters below and matters above defy comparison. The experience of the Apostle in Philippians 3 begins with esteeming everything as loss and proceeds to suffering the loss of all things. Therein does the Apostle come to know Christ and the power of His resurrection. Such is the perfect way. Often we are unconscious how powerful our self is until tested in regard to material matters. At times it seems we require more grace to lose our wealth than to lose our life! Earthly things truly represent an acid test for soul life.

God's children who indulge in eating and drinking and in ease and comfort need a deeper cutting away of the cross to free their spirit from the bondage and influence of the soul and to be free to live in God. Any who still hanker after the things of the world have yet to learn how to lose their soul life through the deep penetration of the cross.

THE CROSS AND SOUL POWER

In the Gospel of John the Lord Jesus touches upon soul life once more. "Truly, truly, I say to you, unless a grain of wheat falls into the earth and dies, it remains alone; but if it dies, it bears much fruit. He who loves his life loses it, and he who hates his life in this world will keep it for eternal life" (12.24-25). He subsequently gives the explanation with these words: "And I, when I am lifted up from the earth, will draw all men to myself" (v.32). John 12 records the most prosperous moment in our Lord's life. Lazarus had been raised from the dead and many Jews believed in Him. Triumphantly He entered into Jerusalem and was acclaimed by the populace. Even Gentiles sought to see Him. From the human viewpoint Calvary would now seem to be quite unnecessary, for could He not easily attract all men to Himself without going to the cross? But He knew better. Although his work appeared to be prosperous, He realized He could not grant life to men without His going to death. Calvary was the only way of salvation. If He died, He would draw all men to Himself and could indeed give life to all.

In John 12 the Lord explicitly describes the operation of the cross. He compares Himself to a grain of wheat. If it does not fall into the earth and die it remains *alone*. But if He be crucified and die, He shall impart life to many. The one condition is death. No death, no fruit. No other way is there to bear fruit than through death.

Our purpose, however, is not simply to learn about the
Lord Jesus. We wish beyond this to draw particular attention to its relationship to *our* soul life. The Lord applies the
grain of wheat to Himself in verse 24, but in verse 25 He implies that every one of His disciples must follow in His footsteps. He pictures the grain as representing their self life.
Just as a grain is unable to bear fruit unless it dies, so there
can be no spiritual fruit until the natural life has been broken
through death. Here he emphasizes the matter of fruitfulness. While the soul life does possess tremendous power it
nevertheless cannot fulfill the work of fruit-bearing. All the
energies generated in the soul including talent, gift, knowledge and wisdom, cannot enable believers to bear spiritual
fruit. If the Lord Jesus must die to bear fruit so also must His
disciples die in order to produce fruit. The Lord regards
soulish power as of no help to God in His work of fruit-
bearing.

The greatest peril for us in Christian service is to lean upon
our selves and to draw upon our soul power—upon our talent,
gift, knowledge, magnetism, eloquence or cleverness. The experience of countless spiritual believers confirms that unless
our soulishness is definitely delivered to death and its life at
all times inhibited from operating, it will be most active in
service. If this is true of them, then how can those who are unwilling to yield up, or unwatchful in denying, their soul life
prevent the intrusion of that life? Everything pertaining to
our natural life must be handed over to death so that in no
sense may we depend upon any of it but be willing instead to
be led through death's darkness of no support, no sensation,
no sight, no understanding, and silently trust God Himself
to work until we emerge on the other side of resurrection to
possess a more glorious life. "He who hates his life in this
world will keep it for eternal life." Our soul is not annihilated; rather, by passing through death it affords God an opportunity to communicate His life to us. Not to lose the soul
life in death shall mean great loss for the believer; but in losing it he will save it for eternity.

Do not misunderstand this verse as signifying the inactivity of our mind and talent. The Lord clearly asserts that in losing our soul life we will keep it unto eternal life. Just as "the sinful body might be destroyed" (Rom. 6.6) does not mean the destruction of the hands, feet, ears and eyes of the human body, so too the committal of the soul life to death must not be construed as connoting the negation or destruction of any of its functions. Even though the body of sin has been destroyed, we still yield our "members to God as instruments of righteousness" (Rom. 6.13); just so, when natural life is sacrificed to death, we shall find renewal, revival and restraint of the Holy Spirit in all the faculties of our soul. It cannot therefore imply that henceforth we become wood and stone without feeling, thought or will because we must not or cannot use any of the parts of the soul. Every part of the body as well as every organ of the soul still exists and is meant to be fully engaged; only now they are being renewed, revived and restrained by the Holy Spirit. The point at issue is whether the soul's faculties are to be regulated by our natural life or by the supernatural life which indwells our spirit. These faculties remain as usual. What is unusual now is that the power which formerly activated them has been put to death; the Holy Spirit has made God's supernatural power their life.

Let us amplify this subject a bit more. The various organs of our soul continue after the natural life has been relinquished in death. To nail the soul life to the cross does not at all imply that thereafter we shall be completely lacking in our thought, emotion and will. We distinctly read in the Bible of *God's* thought, intent, desire, satisfaction, love and joy. Moreover, the Scriptures often record that our Lord Jesus "loved," "rejoiced," "was sorrowful"; it is even recorded that "Jesus wept," that He "offered up prayers and supplications with loud cries and tears" in Gethsemane's Garden. Were His soul faculties annihilated? And do we become cold and dead persons? Man's soul is man's own self. It is where one's personality resides and whence it is expressed. If the soul does not accept power from the spirit life, then it will draw its power for living from its natural soulical life. The soul as a composite of organs continues, but the soul as a life principle must be denied. That power must be consigned to death so that the power of the Holy Spirit alone may operate all the parts of the soul, without interference from the natural life.

Herein do we see resurrection life. Without the supernatural life of God there can be no resurrection after death. The Lord Jesus could go through death and yet be raised because resident in Him is God's uncreated life. This life cannot be destroyed: it instead will always emerge into the fullness and glory of resurrection. Jesus poured out His soul to death and committed His spirit (in which was God's life) back into the hands of God. His death set Him free from soul life and released God's spiritual life unto greater splendor.

It is difficult indeed to understand why God, upon transmitting His life to us, then requires us to experience co-death with Christ so that His life may be resurrected in us. This is nonetheless God's law of life. And once possessing God's life, we then are empowered to periodically go through death and continue to come out alive. By continuously losing our soul life in death, we may continuously gain more abundantly and gloriously of God's life in resurrection.

God's aim is to take our soul life through death in company with His Own life in us; whenever His life in us is resurrected in our daily experience our soul also is raised with Him and produces fruit to eternity. This is one of the most profound lessons in spiritual life. The Holy Spirit alone can unfold to us the necessity of death as well as that of resurrection. May the Spirit of revelation make us understand how much our spiritual experience shall suffer if we do not hate our natural life and deliver it to death. Only when our soul accompanied by God's indwelling life passes through death and resurrection can we bear spiritual fruit and keep it for life eternal.

CHAPTER 5

SPIRITUAL BELIEVERS AND THE SOUL

THE DIVIDING OF SPIRIT AND SOUL

OUR LENGTHY DISCUSSION as to the difference between spirit and soul and their respective operations has been to lead us to this present point. For a believer who strives after God the element to be apprehensive about is the inordinate activity of the soul beyond the measure set by God. The soul has been in ascendancy for such long duration that in the matter of consecration it even presumes to take upon itself the task of realizing that act to God's satisfaction. Many Christians are unaware how drastically the cross must work so that ultimately their natural power for living may be denied. They do not know the reality of the indwelling Holy Spirit nor that His authority must extend to gathering under His control the thoughts, desires and feelings of the entire being. Without their having an inner appreciation of this, the Holy Spirit is unable to accomplish everything He wishes to do. The greatest temptation for an earnest and zealous saint is to engage his own strength in God's service rather than to wait humbly for the Holy Spirit to will and to perform.

The call of the cross of the Lord Jesus is to beckon us to hate our natural life, to seek opportunity to lose, not to keep, it. Our Lord wants us to sacrifice self and be yielded wholly to the working of His Spirit. If we are to experience afresh His true life in the power and guidance of the Holy Spirit, we must be willing to present to death every opinion, labor and thought of the soul life. The Lord additionally touches upon the issue of our hating or loving our self life. The soul is in-

variably "self-loving." Unless from the very depth of our heart
we abhor our natural life, we shall not be able to walk genuinely by the Holy Spirit. Do we not realize that the basic
condition for a spiritual walk is to fear our self and its wisdom and to rely absolutely upon the Spirit?

This war between the soul and the spirit is waged secretly
but interminably within God's children. The soul seeks to
retain its authority and move independently, while the spirit
strives to possess and master everything for the maintenance
of God's authority. Before the spirit achieves its ascendancy
the soul has tended to take the lead in all regards. Should a
believer allow self to be the master while expecting the Holy
Spirit to help and to bless him in his work, he undoubtedly
will fail to produce spiritual fruit. Christians cannot anticipate a walk and work pleasing to God if they have not
crushed their soul life by persistently denying its authority
and unconditionally laying it in the dust. Except all power,
impatience, and activity of the natural life are deliberately
and one by one delivered to the cross and a ceaseless vigil is
maintained, it will seize every chance to revive itself. The
reason for so many defeats in the spiritual realm is because
this sector of the soul has not been dealt with drastically.
If soul life is not stripped away through death but is allowed
to mingle with the spirit, believers shall continue in defeat.
If our walk does not exclusively express God's power it shall
soon be vanquished by man's wisdom and opinion.

Our natural life is a formidable obstacle to spiritual life.
Never satisfied with God alone, it invariably adds something
extra to God. Hence it is never at peace. Before the self is
touched God's children live by very changeable stimulations
and sensations. That is why they exhibit a wavy up-and-
down existence. Because they allow their soulical energies
to mix in with spiritual experiences their ways are often unstable. They accordingly are not qualified to lead others.
Their unrelinquished soul power continually deflects them
from letting the spirit be central. In the excitement of soulical
emotion the spirit suffers great loss in freedom and sensation.

Joy and sorrow may imperil the believer's self-control and set self-consciousness on a rampage. The mind, if overly active, may affect and disturb the quietness of the spirit. To admire spiritual knowledge is good, but should it exceed spiritual bounds the result shall be merely letter, not spirit. This explains why many workers, though they preach the most excellent truth, are so cold and dead. Many saints who seek a spiritual walk share a common experience—one of groanings because their soul and spirit are not at one. The thought, will and emotion of their soul often rebel against the spirit, refuse to be directed by the spirit and resort to independent actions which contradict the spirit. The life in their spirit is bound to suffer in such a situation.

Now given a condition like this in the believer, the teaching in Hebrews 4.12 takes on paramount significance. For the Holy Spirit instructs us therein how to divide spirit and soul experientially. The dividing of these two is not a mere doctrine; it is pre-eminently a life, a must in the believer's walk. Just what is its essential meaning? It means, first of all, that by His Word and through His indwelling Spirit God enables the Christian to differentiate in experience the operations and expressions of the spirit as distinct from those of the soul. Thus he may perceive what is of the spirit and what is of the soul.

The dividing of these two elements denotes additionally that through willing cooperation the child of God can follow a pure spiritual path unimpeded by the soul. The Holy Spirit in Hebrews 4 sets forth the high-priestly ministry of the Lord Jesus and also explains its relationship to us. Verse 12 declares that "the word of God is living and active, sharper than any two-edged sword, piercing to the division of soul and spirit, of joints and marrow, and discerning the thoughts and intentions of the heart." And verse 13 follows by informing us that "before him no creature is hidden, but all are open and laid bare to the eyes of him with whom we have to do." These therefore tells us how much the Lord Jesus fulfills His work as High Priest with respect to our spirit and soul. The

Holy Spirit compares the believer to a sacrifice on the altar. During the Old Testament period when people presented an offering, they bound their sacrifice to the altar. The priest then came and killed it with a sharp knife, parting it into two and piercing to the division of the joints and marrow, thus exposing to view all that formerly had been hidden from human sight. Afterwards it was burned with fire as an offering to God. The Holy Spirit uses this event to illustrate the work of the Lord Jesus towards believers and the experience of the believers in the Lord. Just as the sacrifice of old was cut asunder by the priests's knife so that the joints and marrow were exposed and divided, even so the believer today has his soul and spirit split apart by the Word of God as used by our High Priest, the Lord Jesus. This is that the soul may no longer affect the spirit nor the spirit any more be under the soul's authority; rather, each will find its rightful place, with neither confusion nor mixture.

As at the first the Word of God had operated on creation by separating light from darkness, so now it works within us as the Sword of the Spirit, piercing to the separation of the spirit and soul. Hence the noblest habitation of God—our spirits—is wholly separated from the base desires of our souls. Wherefore we come to appreciate how our spirit is the dwelling place of God the Holy Spirit and how our soul with all its energy shall indeed do the will of God as revealed to the human spirit by the Holy Spirit. No room can there be then for any independent action.

As the priest of old split the sacrifice, so our High Priest today divides our soul and spirit. As the priestly knife was of such sharpness that the sacrifice was cut into two, piercing to the separation of the closely knit joints and marrow, so the Word of God which the Lord Jesus currently uses is keener than any two-edged sword and is able to split cleanly apart the most intimately related spirit and soul there may be.

The Word of God is "living" for it has living power: "active" because it knows how to work: "sharper than any two-edged sword" since it can pierce into the spirit. What God's Word has penetrated is much deeper than the soul; it reaches into the innermost spirit. God's Word leads His people into a realm more profound than one of mere sensation; it brings them into the realm of the eternal spirit. Those who wish to be established in God must know the meaning of this penetration into the spirit. The Holy Spirit alone can teach us what is soul life and what is spirit life. Only after we learn how to differentiate experientially these two kinds of life and come to apprehend their respective values, are we delivered from a shallow, loose, sensational walk into that which is deep, firm and spiritual. Only then do we come into rest. The soul life can never furnish us rest. But please note that this must be known *in experience;* simply understanding in the mind will merely make us more soulish.

We need to pay special attention to this piercing and dividing. The Word of God plunges into the soul as well as into the spirit in order to effect the division of these two. The Lord Jesus in His crucifixion had His hands and feet and side pierced. Are we willing to let the cross work in our soul and spirit? A sword pierced through Mary's soul (Luke 2. 35). Although her "Son" was given by God, she was required to let go of Him and to relinquish all her authority and demands upon Him. Even though her soul craved to cling tenaciously to Him Mary must deny her natural affection.

The cleaving of soul and spirit means not only their separation but also a cracking open of the soul itself. Since the spirit is enveloped in the soul, it cannot be reached by the Word of life save through a cracked shell. The Word of the cross plunges in and splits open a way into and through the soul so that God's life can reach the spirit within and liberate it from the bondage of its soulish shell. Having received the mark of the cross, the soul now can assume its proper position of subjection to the spirit. But if the soul fails to become a "thoroughfare" to the spirit, then the former surely will become the latter's chain. These two never agree on any matter. Before the spirit achieves its rightful place of pre-eminence it is challenged persistently by the soul. While the spirit is striving to gain freedom and mastery the strong soul power exerts its utmost strength to suppress the spirit. Only after the cross has done its work on the soulish life is the spirit liberated. If we remain ignorant of the damage this discord between the spirit and soul can bring or remain unwilling to forsake the pleasure of a sensuous walk, we shall make hardly any spiritual progress. As long as the seige thrown up by the soul is not lifted the spirit cannot be freed.

Upon carefully studying the teaching of this fragment of Scripture, we may conclude that the dividing of spirit and soul hinges upon two factors: the cross and God's Word. Before the priest could use his knife the sacrifice had to be placed on the altar. The altar in the Old Testament speaks of the cross in the New Testament. Believers cannot expect their High Priest to wield God's sharp Sword, His Word which pierces to the separation of soul and spirit, unless first they are willing to come to the cross and accept its death. Lying on the altar always precedes the plunging of the sword. Hence all who desire to experience the parting of soul and spirit must answer the Lord's call to Calvary and lay themselves unreservedly on the altar, trusting their High Priest to operate with His keen Sword to the dividing asunder of their spirit and soul. For us to lie on the altar is our free-will offering well-pleasing to God; to use the sword to divide is the work of the priest. We should fulfill our part with all faithfulness, and commit the rest to our merciful and faithful High Priest. And at the appropriate time He shall lead us into a complete spiritual experience.

We need to follow the footsteps of our Lord. As He was dying, Jesus poured out His soul to death (Is. 53.12) but committed His spirit to God (Luke 23.46). We must do now what He did before. If we truly pour out the soul life and commit our spirit to God we too shall know the power of resurrection and shall enjoy a perfect spiritual way in the glory of resurrection.

THE PRACTICE

We have just seen how the High Priest operates if we accept the cross. We shall consider next the practical side; that is, how we may arrive at the experience of having the Lord Jesus divide our soul and spirit.

(1) Know the necessity of having the spirit and soul divided. Without this knowledge no such request will be made. Christians ought to petition the Lord to show them the abhorrence of a mixed spirit-and-soul life and also the reality of that deeper walk in God which is wholly spirit and uninterrupted by the soul. They should understand that a mixed life is a frustrated life.

(2) Ask for the separation of soul and spirit. After knowing, there must be a genuinely earnest desire in the heart, a requesting that this mingled soul and spirit be cut apart. Just here the question rests with the human will. Should believers prefer to enjoy what they themselves consider the best life and not desire to have their soul and spirit divided, God will respect their personal rights and not force them into such experience.

(3) Yield specifically. If believers definitely desire the experience of having their soul and spirit separated, they must consign themselves to the altar of the cross in a specific manner. They must be willing to accept totally every consequence of the operation of the cross and be conformed to the death of the Lord. Before they encounter the cleaving of soul and spirit believers need to bend their will continuously and incessantly towards God and actively choose to have this cleavage. And as the High Priest accomplishes this division in them their heart attitude should be that He should not stay His hand.

(4) Stand on Romans 6.11. God's children need to watch lest in seeking to experience the separation of soul and spirit they fall back into sin. Remember that this separating is built upon their having died to sin. Hence they should maintain daily the attitude of Romans 6.11, considering them-

selves verily dead to sin. Additionally, they should stand on Romans 6.12 and not permit sin to reign in their mortal bodies. This attitude will deprive their natural life any opportunity to sin through the body.

(5) Pray and study the Bible. Christians ought to search the Bible with prayer and meditation. They should let God's Word penetrate thoroughly into their souls so as to enable their natural life to be purified. If they actually do what God says, their soul life shall not be able to continue its free activity. This is the meaning of 1 Peter 1.22: "having purified your souls by your obedience to the truth."

(6) Daily bear the cross. Because the Lord desires to sever our spirit and soul He arranges crosses in our everyday affairs for us to bear. To take up the cross daily, to deny self at all times, to make no provision for the flesh—not even for a moment, and to be shown constantly by the Holy Spirit what are the activities of the soul in our lives: this is spiritual life. Through faithful obedience we shall be led to encounter the dividing of soul and spirit so that we may experience a pure spiritual walk.

(7) Live according to the spirit. This is a condition not only for our preservation but also for a distinct cleavage between spirit and soul. We must seek to walk by our spirit in all respects, distinguishing what is of the spirit and what is of the soul and resolving as well to follow the former while rejecting the latter. Learn to recognize the working of the spirit and follow it.

These are the conditions which we on our side must fulfill. The Holy Spirit requires our cooperation. The Lord will not be able to do His part should we fail to do ours. But were we to discharge our responsibility, our High Priest would tear apart our spirit and soul with the sharp Sword of His Spirit in the power of His cross. Everything which belongs to emotion, sensation, mind and natural energy would be separated one after another from the spirit so as to leave no trace of fusion. To lie on the altar is what we must do, but to divide the soul from the spirit with the well-honed knife is

what our High Priest undertakes. If we truly commit ourselves to the cross our High Priest shall not fail to execute His
ministry in separating our spirit and soul. We need not worry
about His part. Upon seeing we have fulfilled the requirements for His working He shall part our spirit and soul at
the appropriate time thereafter.

Those who have apprehended the danger of a mixture of
these two organs cannot but seek deliverance. Open though
the road is to deliverance, it nevertheless is not without its
difficulties. Believers must persevere in prayer that they may
see clearly their own pitiful state and understand the indwelling, working, and demands of the Holy Spirit. They
need to know the mystery and reality of the Holy Spirit
dwelling within them. May they honor such holy presence;
may they be careful not to grieve Him; may they know that,
aside from sin, what grieves Him the most as well as what
harms themselves the deepest is to walk and labor according
to their own life. The first and original sin of man was to
seek what is good, wise and intellectual according to his
own idea. God's children today often make the same mistake.
They should realize that since they have believed in the Lord
and have the Holy Spirit indwelling them, they ought to
give the Spirit complete authority over their souls. Do we
think because we have prayed and asked the Holy Spirit to
reveal His mind and to work in us, that all shall accordingly
be done? That assumption is not the truth; for unless we deliver to death specifically and daily our natural life, together
with its power, wisdom, self, and sensation and unless we
equally desire honestly in our mind and will to obey and rely
upon the Holy Spirit, we shall not see Him actually performing the work.

The Lord's people should understand that it is the Word
of God which parts their soul and spirit. The Lord Jesus is
Himself the living Word of God, so He Himself effects the
division. Are we disposed to let His life and accomplished
work stand between our soul and spirit? Are we ready to
have His life so fill our spirit that the soul life is immobilized?

The Bible is God's written Word. The Lord Jesus uses the teaching of the Bible to separate our soul and spirit. Are we willing to follow the truth? Are we ready to do what the Scriptures teach? Can we obey the Lord in accordance with the teaching of Scripture without putting in our opinion as well? Do we consider the authority of the Bible as sufficient without seeking human help in our obedience? We must obey the Lord and everything He teaches us in His Word if we would desire to enter upon a true spiritual path. This is the Sword which is operative to the cleaving of our soul and spirit.

THE SOUL UNDER THE SPIRIT'S CONTROL

Very early in this volume we likened our whole being—spirit, soul, and body—to the ancient Jewish temple of God's habitation. God dwells in the Holy of Holies. A curtain separates it from the Holy Place. This curtain seems to enclose God's glory and presence within the Holy of Holies, barring His glory from the Holy Place. Men of that time therefore can only know the things outside the curtain in the Holy Place. Apart from faith they in their outward life cannot sense the presence of God.

This curtain, however, only exists temporarily. At the appointed hour, when the flesh of our Lord Jesus (which is the reality of the curtain, Heb. 10.20) was crucified on the cross, the curtain was rent from top to bottom. What separated the Holiest and the Holy Place was removed. God's aim was not to dwell permanently just in the Holy of Holies. Quite the contrary. He desired to extend His presence to the Holy Place too. He was merely waiting for the cross to complete its work, for it is the cross alone which can rend the curtain and permit God's glory to shine out from the Holiest Place.

God today would have His own enjoy such a temple experience in their spirit and soul: if only the cross is allowed to perfect its work in them. As they ungrudgingly obey the Holy Spirit the communion between the Holy and the Holiest grows deeper day by day until they experience a great change. It is the cross which effects the rending of the curtain; that is, the cross so functions in the life of the believer that he has a rent-curtain experience between his spirit and soul. His natural life renounces its independence and waits upon the spirit life for direction and supply.

The curtain was torn in two, "from *top* to bottom" (Mark 15.38). This has to be God's doing, not man's. When the work of the cross is finished God tears the curtain. This cannot be achieved either by our labors or by our strength, not even by our entreaty. The moment the cross accomplishes its task at that moment is the curtain rent. Let us therefore renew our consecration and offer ourselves to God without reservation. Let us be willing to have our soul life committed to death in order that the Lord Who dwells in the Holiest may finish His work. If he observes that the cross has wrought thoroughly enough in us the Lord shall indeed integrate the Holiest and the Holy within us just as He centuries ago rent the curtain by His might so that His Holy Spirit might flow out from His glorious body.

Thus shall the glory in the shelter of the Most High overwhelm our daily sensuous life. All our walk and work in the Holy Place shall be sanctified in the glory of the Holiest. Like our spirit is, so shall our soul too be indwelt and regulated by the Holy Spirit of God. Our mind, emotion and will shall be filled by Him. What we have maintained by faith in the spirit we now also know and experience in the soul, nothing lacking and nothing lost. What a blessed life is this! "And the glory of the Lord filled the temple. And the priests could not enter the house of the Lord, because the glory of the Lord filled the Lord's house" (2 Chron. 7.1-2). However lovely our activities of priestly service may have seemed in the Holy Place, they all shall cease in the glorious light of God. Henceforth His glory governs everything. No more is animal activity adored.

This brings us to the other, and equally significant, aspect of the dividing of spirit and soul. Insofar as the soul's influence and control of the spirit is concerned, the work of the cross is to effect the division of the two; but insofar as the spirit's filling and reigning is concerned, the cross

works towards the surrender of the soul's independence so
that it may be reconciled completely to the spirit. Believers
should seek to experience oneness of spirit and soul. Were
we to allow the cross and the Holy Spirit to operate thoroughly in us we would discover that what the soul has relinquished is scarcely a fraction of what it ultimately gains:
the dead has now come into fruition, the lost is now kept for
eternal life. When our soul is brought under the reins of the
spirit it undergoes an immense change. Beforehand it seems
to be useless and lost to God because it is employed for self
and often moves independently; afterwards God gains our
soul, though to man it may appear to be crushed. We become as "those who have faith and keep their souls" (Heb.
10.39). This is much more profound than what we commonly
term "saved," because it points especially to life. Since we
have learned not to walk by sensation and sight, we are now
able to save our life by faith into serving and glorifying God.
"Receive with meekness the implanted word, which is able
to save your souls" (James 1.21). As God's Word is implanted
we receive its new nature into us and are thus enabled to
bear fruit. We obtain the life of the Word from the Word of
life. Although the organs of the soul still remain, these organs
no longer function through its power; rather, they operate
by the power of God's Word. This is "the salvation of your
souls" (1 Peter 1.9).

Human nerves are rather sensitive and are easily stirred
by outside stimuli. Words, manners, environments and feelings greatly affect us. Our mind engages in so many thoughts,
plans and imaginations that it is a world of confusion. Our
will is agitated to perform many acts according to our sundry
delights. None of the organs of our soul can bring us into
peace. Singly or collectively, they disturb, they confuse, they
shift us around. But when our soul is in the spirit's hand we
can be released from such disturbances. The Lord Jesus implores us: "Take my yoke upon you, and learn from me; for
I am gentle and lowly in heart, and you will find rest for your
souls" (Matt. 11.29). If we are favorably inclined to yield to

the Lord, to take up His yoke, and to follow Him, our soul shall not be aroused inordinately. If we learn of Him by seeing how He, when despised by men, continued to follow God's will and not His Own, our soul shall return to tranquillity. The reason for our hurt feelings lies in the fact that we are not amenable to being treated as our Lord was and are loathe to submit ourselves to the will and ordering of God. Were we to deliver our natural energies to death and capitulate entirely to the Lord, our soul, though so nervously sensitive, would rest in the Lord and not misunderstand Him.

The soul which comes under the Holy Spirit's authority is a restful one. Once we busily planned, today we calmly trust the Lord. Once we were flushed with anxieties, today we are like a child quieted at its mother's breast. Once we entertained many thoughts and ambitions, today we consider God's will best and rest ourselves in Him. In obeying the Lord wholly, we rejoice in heart fully. With complete consecration comes perfect peace. "As bondmen of Christ doing the will of God from the soul" (Eph. 6.6 Darby). We do not rely upon the soul to execute God's will, rather we perform His will from the soul, that is, with our whole heart. The soul which once rebelled against God's desire is now perfectly committed to Him through the operation of the cross. That which carried out its own will, or tried to do God's will by its own idea, is now of one heart with God in all things.

A soul under the rule of the Holy Spirit never worries for itself. "Do not be anxious about your life (original, soul)" (Matt. 6.25). We now seek first the kingdom of God and His righteousness because we believe God will supply our daily need. Once touched by the cross through the Holy Spirit, the soul no longer is able to be anxious about itself. While self-consciousness is the soul's prime expression, yet believers actually lose their self in God; hence they can trust God utterly. Every work of the soul, including self-love, self-seeking and self-pride, have been so eliminated that believers are no longer self-centered.

Because the cross has done its task we do not busily plan any more for ourselves. Instead of suffering anxiety we can restfully seek God's kingdom and righteousness. We know if we care for God's cares that God will take care of our cares. Once we wondered at miracles, now we live by the God of miracles and know in experience how God provides every need. This all flows naturally since God's power is backing us. The cares of this life emerge as very small items indeed along our daily path.

"Therefore let those who suffer according to God's will do right and entrust their souls to a faithful Creator" (1 Peter 4.19). Many people know God as the Creator but not as Father; believers, though, should experience Him not only as Father but also as Creator. As the latter God reveals to us His power. By this we will understand and acknowledge that the whole universe is in fact in His hand. Formerly it was hard for us to believe the idea that things in the world could not move against His will; but now we know that every element in the universe—be it human, natural, or supernatural—is under His careful scrutiny and clever ordering. We now acknowledge that all things come to us either through His order or by His permission. A soul governed by the Holy Spirit is a trusting one.

Our soul ought to desire the Lord as well as to trust Him. "My soul clings to thee" (Ps. 63.8). No more do we dare be independent of God nor do we dare serve the Lord according to the idea of the soul. Rather, we today follow Him with fear and trembling and trail after Him closely. Our soul genuinely clings to the Lord. No more is there independent action, but instead a full surrender to Him. And this is not by compulsion; we do it gladly. What we henceforth hate is our life; what we wholly love is the Lord.

Such persons cannot but utter the cry of Mary: "My soul magnifies the Lord" (Luke 1.46). No longer is there self-importance, either in public or in private. These believers recognize and admit their incompetency and only wish to exalt the Lord with humbleness of heart. They will not steal the Lord's glory any further but magnify Him in their souls.

For if the Lord is not magnified in the soul, nowhere else is He magnified either.

Only such as these count not their life (original, soul) of any value (Acts 20.24) and can lay down their lives (original, souls) for the brethren (1 John 3.16). Unless self-love is abandoned the believer shall forever shrink back when called actually to take up the cross for Christ. He who lives a martyr's life and is willing to nail his self to the cross is able as well to die a martyr's death if ever the need should arise. He can lay down his life for his brother if occasion demands it because in ordinary days he has denied himself continuously and has not sought his own right or comfort but has poured out his soul for the brethren. True love towards the Lord and the brethren arises out of no love for self. He "loved me" and "gave Himself for me" (Gal. 2.20). Love flows from the denial of the self life. Blood-shedding is the source of blessing.

Such a life is in truth one of prosperity, as is written: "thy soul prospers" (3 John 2 Darby). This prosperity originates not with what self has gained but with what self has denied. A soul lost is not a life lost, for the soul is lost in God. Soul life is selfish and therefore binds us. But the soul renounced shall abide in the boundlessness of God's life. This is liberty, this is prosperity. The more we lose the more we gain. Our possessions are not measured by how much we receive but by how much we give. How fruitful is this life!

To forsake the soul life, however, is not as easy as deliverance from sin. Since it is *our life*, the choice is *ours* to make daily not to live by *it* but by the life of God. The cross needs to be borne faithfully and to be borne increasingly faithfully. Let us gaze upon our Lord Jesus Who "endured the cross, despising the shame": "Consider him . . . , that ye wax not weary, fainting in your souls" (Heb. 12.2-3 ASV). The race set before us is none other than that of His despising the shame and enduring His cross.

"Bless the Lord, O my soul; and all that is within me, bless his holy name!" (Ps. 103.1)

THE
SPIRITUAL MAN

Watchman Nee

IN THREE VOLUMES

Christian Fellowship Publishers, Inc.
New York

Reprinted As a Combined Edition, 1977

Available from the Publishers at:

11515 Allecingie Parkway

Richmond, Virginia 23235

PRINTED IN U.S.A.

THE SPIRITUAL MAN
Volume II

Contents

VOLUME II

EXPLANATORY NOTES   6

PART FOUR: THE SPIRIT

  1   The Holy Spirit and the Believer's Spirit   7
  2   A Spiritual Man   18
  3   Spiritual Work   35
  4   Prayer and Warfare   52

PART FIVE: AN ANALYSIS OF THE SPIRIT

  1   Intuition   67
  2   Communion   86
  3   Conscience   106

PART SIX: WALKING AFTER THE SPIRIT

  1   The Dangers of Spiritual Life   129
  2   The Laws of the Spirit   144
  3   The Principle of Mind Aiding the Spirit   163
  4   The Normalcy of the Spirit   172

PART SEVEN: THE ANALYSIS OF THE SOUL— EMOTION

  1   The Believer and Emotion   189
  2   Affection   202
  3   Desire   212
  4   A Life of Feeling   224
  5   The Life of Faith   240

EXPLANATORY NOTES

Volume II of *The Spiritual Man* is a continuation in this series of studies. While many other books have been compiled from his spoken messages, this book translated from the Chinese is the only one of any substantial size which brother Watchman Nee himself ever wrote. At the time of writing it he felt this work might be his last contribution to the church, although since then God has graciously overruled. Long after the book's initial publication in Chinese our brother once was heard to express the thought that it should not be reprinted because, it being such a "perfect" treatment of its subject, he was fearful lest the book become to its readers merely a manual of principles and not a guide to experience as well. But in view of the urgent need among the children of God today for help on spiritual life and warfare, and knowing our brother as one who is always open to God's way and most desirous to serve His people with all that God has given him, we conclude that he would doubtless permit it to be circulated in English. Hence this translation.

Translations used. The Revised Standard Version (RSV) of the Bible has been used throughout the text unless otherwise indicated. Additional translations where employed are denoted by the following abbreviations:

> Amplified—*Amplified Old Testament*
> ASV—American Standard Version (1901)
> AV—Authorized Version (King James)
> Darby—J. N. Darby, *The Holy Scriptures, a New Translation*
> Young's—Young's *Literal Translation*

Soulical and Soulish. The adjectives "soulical" and "soulish" have been used to convey distinctly different meanings. "Soulical" as herein employed pertains to those proper, appropriate, legitimate, or natural qualities, functions, or expressions of man's soul which the Creator intended from the very beginning for the soul uniquely to possess and manifest. "Soulish" appears in these pages to describe that man *in toto* who is so governed by the soulical part of his being that his whole life takes on the character and expression of the soul.

PART FOUR

THE SPIRIT

1 The Holy Spirit and
the Believer's Spirit

2 A Spiritual Man

3 Spiritual Work

4 Prayer and Warfare

CHAPTER 1

THE HOLY SPIRIT AND
THE BELIEVER'S SPIRIT

BELIEVERS TODAY very much lack knowledge as to the existence and operation of the human spirit. Many are unaware that in addition to their mind, emotion and will they also have a spirit. Even when they have heard of the spirit, many Christians either consider their mind, emotion or will as the spirit or else plainly confess they know not where their spirit is. Such ignorance enormously affects cooperation with God, control over self, and war against Satan, the performance of which in all cases requires the operation of the spirit.

It is imperative that believers recognize a spirit exists within them, something extra to thought, knowledge and imagination of the mind, something beyond affection, sensation and pleasure of the emotion, something additional to desire, decision and action of the will. This component is far more profound than these faculties. God's people not only must know they possess a spirit; they also must understand how this organ operates—its sensitivity, its work, its power, its laws. Only in this way can they walk according to their spirit and not the soul or body of their flesh.

The spirit and soul of the unregenerate have become fused into one; therefore they do not know at all the presence of the deadened spirit; on the other hand, they are very well aware of strong soulical sensation. This foolishness continues even after being saved. That is why believers sometimes walk after the spirit and sometimes after the flesh even though they have received spiritual life and have experienced to some degree victory over the things of the flesh. To be unaware of the demand, movement, supply, sense, and direction of the spirit naturally curtails the life of the spirit and allows the natural life of the soul to go unchallenged as the living principle of one's walk. The magnitude of this ignorance far exceeds common admission of it among believers. Because of their ignorance concerning the spirit's operation, those who honestly desire deeper experience upon having overcome sin may all too easily be led astray into seeking so-called "spiritual" Bible knowledge with their minds, or a burning sensation of the Lord's presence in their physical members, or a life and labor emanating from their will power. They are deceived into overly esteeming their soul experiences and thus fall into conceiving themselves as ever so spiritual. Their soul life is inordinately nourished. They become so subjective as to assess their experience as unquestionably spiritual. Accordingly, they are hindered from making any genuine spiritual progress. For this reason God's children must be very humble before Him and seek to know the teaching of the Bible and the functioning of the spirit through the Holy Spirit in order that they may walk by the spirit.

THE REGENERATION OF MAN*

Why must a sinner be born anew? Why must he be born from above? Why must there be a regeneration of the spirit?

---

*Compare Part One, Chapter 4.

Because man is a fallen spirit. A fallen spirit needs to be re-born that it may become a new one. Just as Satan is a fallen spirit, so is man; only he has a body. Satan's fall came before man's; we therefore can learn about our fallen state from Satan's plunge. Satan was created as a spirit that he might have direct communion with God. But he fell away and be-came the head of the powers of darkness. He now is sepa-rated from God and from every godly virtue. This, however, does not signify that Satan is non-existent. His fall only took away his right relationship with God. Similarly, man in his fall also sank into darkness and separation from God. Man's spirit still exists but is separated from God, powerless to commune with Him and incapable of ruling. Spiritually speaking, man's spirit is dead. Nonetheless, as the spirit of the sinful archangel exists forever so the spirit of sinful man continues too. Because he has a body his fall rendered him a man of the flesh (Gen. 6.3). No religion of this world, no ethics, culture or law can improve this fallen human spirit. Man has degenerated into a fleshly position; nothing from himself can return him to a spiritual state. Wherefore regen-eration or regeneration of the spirit is absolutely necessary. The Son of God alone can restore us to God, for He shed His blood to cleanse our sins and give us a new life.

Immediately the sinner believes in the Lord Jesus he is born anew. God grants him His uncreated life that the sin-ner's spirit may be made alive. The regeneration of a sinner occurs *in his spirit*. God's work begins without exception within the man, from the center to the circumference. How unlike Satan's pattern of work! He operates from the outer to the inner. God aims first to renew man's darkened spirit by imparting life to it, because it is this spirit which God orig-inally designed to receive His life and to commune with Him. God's intent after that is to work out from the spirit to per-meate man's soul and body.

This regeneration gives man a new spirit as well as quick-ens his old one. "A *new spirit* I will put within you"—"That which is born of the Spirit is spirit" (Ezek. 36.26; John 3.6).

The "spirit" in these passages has God's life in view, for it is not what we originally possessed; it is accorded us by God at our regeneration. This new life or spirit belongs to God (2 Peter 1.4) and "cannot sin" (1 John 3.9); but our spirit, though quickened, may yet be defiled (2 Cor. 7.1) and in need of being sanctified (1 Thess. 5.23).

When God's life (which can equally be called His Spirit) enters our human spirit, the latter is quickened out of its coma. What was "alienated from the life of God" (Eph. 4.18) is now made alive again. Hence "although your bodies are dead because of sin, your spirits are alive because of righteousness" (Rom. 8.10). What we are given in Adam is a spirit made dead; what we receive in Christ at regeneration is both the dead spirit quickened and the new spirit of God's life: the latter, something Adam never had.

In the Bible God's life is often labeled "eternal life." "Life" here is zoe in Greek, denoting the higher life or spirit life. This is what every Christian receives at his regeneration. What is the function of that life? "This is eternal life," prayed Jesus to His Father, "that they know thee the only true God, and Jesus Christ whom thou hast sent" (John 17.3). Eternal life means more than mere future blessing to be enjoyed by believers; it is equally a kind of spiritual ability. Without it no one can know God nor the Lord Jesus. Such intuitive knowledge of the Lord comes solely upon receiving God's life. With the germ of God's nature within him, an individual can ultimately grow into a spiritual man.

God's aim in a regenerated man is for that man by his spirit to rid himself of everything belonging to the old creation, because within his regenerated spirit lie all the works of God towards him.

THE HOLY SPIRIT AND REGENERATION

When regenerated, man's spirit is made alive through the incoming of God's life. The Holy Spirit is the prime mover in this task. He convinces the world of sin and of righteousness and of judgment (John 16.8). He prepares human hearts to

believe in the Lord Jesus as Savior. The work of the cross
has been fulfilled by the Lord Jesus, but it is left to the Holy
Spirit to apply this finished work to the sinner's heart. We
ought to know the relationship between the cross of Christ
and its application by the Spirit. The cross accomplishes all,
but the Holy Spirit administers to man what it has accom-   ✗
plished. The cross grants us position; the Holy Spirit gives us
experience. The cross brings in the fact of God; the Holy
Spirit brings about the demonstration of that fact. The work
of the cross creates a position and achieves a salvation by
which sinners can be saved; the task of the Holy Spirit is to
reveal to sinners what the cross has created and achieved so
that they may in fact receive it and be saved. The Holy Spirit
never functions independently of the cross: without the cross
the Holy Spirit has no proper ground from which to operate: ✴
without the Holy Spirit the work of the cross is dead, that is,
it produces no effect upon men even though it is already
effective before God.

While it is the cross which achieves the whole work of
salvation it is the Holy Spirit Who operates directly upon
men for their salvation. Hence the Bible characterizes our
regeneration as a work of the Holy Spirit: "that which is born
of the Spirit is spirit" (John 3.6). The Lord Jesus explains
further on that regenerated man is "every one who is born
of the Spirit" (v.8). Believers are born anew because the
Holy Spirit brings to bear the work of the cross upon them
and communicates God's life to their spirit. He is none other
than the Executor of God's life. "We live by the Spirit" (Gal.
5.25). If whatever men know comes through their brain without the Holy Spirit regenerating their spirit, then their knowledge will help them not one whit. If their belief rests in man's
wisdom and not in God's power, they are merely excited in
their soul. They will not last long, for they are not yet newly
born. Regeneration comes just to those who believe in their
heart (Rom. 10.10).

Besides bestowing life to believers at new birth, the Holy
Spirit executes a further work of *abiding* in them. How re-

grettable for us if we forget this! "A new heart I will give you and a new spirit I will put within you . . . and I will put my Spirit within you" (Ezek. 36.26-27). Note that immediately after the clause "a *new spirit* I will put within you" there follows this one of "I will put *my Spirit* within you." The first statement signifies that believers shall receive a new spirit through the renewal of their deadened spirit by the incoming of life. The second has reference to the indwelling or the abiding of the Holy Spirit in that renewed spirit of theirs. Believers at new birth obtain not only a new spirit but also the Holy Spirit dwelling within. Is it not sad that many fail to understand the newness of their spirit *and* the abiding of the Holy Spirit in their new spirit? Christians need not delay many years following regeneration and then suddenly wake up and seek the Holy Spirit; they have His entire personality *abiding* in them—not just visiting them—at the moment they are saved. The Apostle exhorts us on this wise: "Do not grieve the Holy Spirit of God, in whom you were sealed for the day of redemption" (Eph. 4.30). The use of the word "grieve" here and not "anger" reveals the Holy Spirit's love. "Grieve" it says and not "cause to depart," for "he dwells with you and will be in you" (John 14.17). While every born-again believer does have the Holy Spirit permanently residing in him, nevertheless the plight of the indwelling Spirit may not be the same in all saints—He may be either grieved or gladdened.

We should understand the relationship between regeneration and the indwelling Holy Spirit. Unless a new spirit is available to Him the Holy Spirit cannot find a place to abide. The holy dove found no place whereon to set her foot in the judged world; she could take up her abode only in the new creation (see Gen. 8). How positively essential regeneration is! Without it the Holy Spirit cannot at all dwell in man. God's children receive within them the permanent abiding of God's Spirit. Just as this new spirit emerges through a life-producing relationship with God and is therefore inseparable from Him, so the abiding of the Holy Spirit is eternally unchangeable. Few are those who know they have been born anew and thus possess new life; but fewer still are those who know that from the moment they believed in the Lord Jesus they have the Holy Spirit indwelling them to be their energy, their guide, their Lord. It is for this very reason that many young Christians are slow in spiritual progress and never seem to grow. This sad state reflects either the foolishness of their leaders or their personal faithlessness. Until God's servants dissolve their prejudice which holds that "the indwelling Holy Spirit is but for the spiritual," they can hardly lead people on to any degree of spirituality.

The regenerative work of the Spirit of God embraces far more than convincing us of sin and leading us to repentance and faith in the Savior. It verily confers upon us a new nature. The promise of the Holy Spirit indwelling us follows closely the promise of having a new spirit. Actually they form two parts of one promise. In convincing men of sin and leading them to believe in the Lord, the Spirit is just preparing the groundwork for His Own indwelling. The singular glory of this dispensation of grace is that God's Spirit indwells believers in order to manifest the Father and the Son. God already has imparted to His children His Spirit; they now should faithfully acknowledge the Holy Spirit and loyally submit themselves to Him. Both the Day of Resurrection and that of Pentecost have passed; the Spirit has long since come. But many simply experience new birth without knowing in addition His abiding in them. They are living on the wrong side of Resurrection and Pentecost!

Regardless the dullness of Christians in recognizing the dwelling of the Person of God's Spirit in them, God nonetheless has given Him to them. This is an immutable fact which no condition of the Christian can gainsay. Because they have been regenerated they automatically have become a holy temple fit for habitation of the Holy Spirit. If only these would claim by faith this part of God's promise as they did the other part, they would gloriously experience both. But if they should stress new birth and be content merely with possessing a new spirit, they shall forfeit the possibility of experiencing a vigorous and joyful life and miss many blessings which God has provided them in the Lord Jesus. If on the other hand they accept God's promise in its totality, trusting in the divine fact that at regeneration God has given a new life *plus* the indwelling of the very Person of the Holy Spirit, then their spiritual life shall advance tremendously.

By faith and obedience believers may experience the abiding presence of the Spirit on the same day they receive their new spirit. The Person Who dwells within shall reveal Christ in them, sanctify them, and lead them on to true spiritual heights. Even so, Christians often do not appreciate the exalted position which this Person occupies, and thus descend to despising His indwelling and to following instead the dictates of their mind. These individuals ought to humble themselves before such light, learn to respect such a Holy Presence, and be willing to allow Him to work. They should tremble before Him for love's sake, not daring to impose their will in the slightest but always remembering how God has highly exalted them by virtue of His abiding presence. Any who desire to abide in Christ and live a holy life like His must accept by faith and obedience God's provision for them. The Holy Spirit already is in our spirit. Therefore the question before us now is, are we willing to let Him work from within?

THE HOLY SPIRIT AND MAN'S SPIRIT

Having realized how the Holy Spirit comes and dwells in believers at new birth, we must next observe exactly where He does dwell. By so doing, it is our hope that we shall know better His operation within us.

"Do you not know that you are God's temple and that God's Spirit dwells in you?" (1 Cor. 3.16) The Apostle Paul implies here that the Holy Spirit dwells in us as God so did in the temple of old. Though the entire temple symbolizes the place of God's presence and serves as a general picture of God's habitation, it is nevertheless in the Holy of Holies where God actually dwells, with the Holy Place and the outer court standing for those spheres of divine activity which are in accordance with God's presence in the Holiest. Answering truly to this typology, God's Spirit dwells now in our spirit, the antitype in our time of the Holy of Holies.

The dweller and his dwelling must share the same character. Only man's regenerated spirit—and not the mind, emotion or volition of his soul and not his body either—is fit to be God's dwelling place. The Spirit is both a builder and a dweller. He cannot dwell where He has not built: He builds to dwell and dwells only in what He has built.

The holy anointing oil may not be poured on the flesh; accordingly, it is obvious that the Holy Spirit cannot make His home in man's flesh for it includes everything man had or was before regeneration. He cannot dwell even in the spirit of an unregenerated person, not to mention in the mind, emotion or will of his soul or in his body. Inasmuch as the holy anointing oil is not poured on the flesh, just so the Holy Spirit does not abide in any part of the flesh. He has no connection with the flesh other than striving against it (Gal. 5.17). Unless there is an element within man unlike the flesh, the Holy Spirit finds Himself unable to dwell in man. It is therefore indispensable for the spirit of man to be regenerated so that He may abide in the new spirit.

Why is it so important to understand that the Holy Spirit dwells in man's innermost depth, deeper within than his organs of thought, feeling and decision? Because unless the child of God perceives this, invariably he shall seek His guidance in his soul. With understanding he shall be delivered from the deception and error of looking to what is outward. The Holy Spirit lives in the remotest recess of our being; there and only there may we expect His working and obtain His guidance. Our prayers are directed to "our Father who art in *heaven*," but the heavenly Father guides from *within* us. If our Counsellor, our Paraclete, resides in our spirit then His guidance must come from within. How tragically deceived we will be if we seek dreams, visions,

voices, and sensations in our outer man rather than seeking
Him in our inner man!

Frequently many children of God turn within themselves,
that is, they look into their soul to determine whether they
have peace, grace or spiritual progress. This is most harmful
and is not of faith. It diverts them from gazing upon Christ to
a looking at themselves. There is a peering within, however,
which is completely different from the above. It is faith's
greatest act. It is a search for guidance by looking to the
Holy Spirit Who indwells their spirit. Although a believer's
mind, emotion and will cannot discern the things within, yet
he ought to believe, even when in darkness, that God has
given him a new spirit in which His Spirit dwells. Just as God
dwelling in the darkness behind the curtain of the Holy of
Holies was feared though not seen by those in the Holy
Place and outer court, even so is the Holy Spirit Who dwells
in man's spirit incomprehensible by the soul and the body.

Thus are we able to recognize what is authentic spiritual
life. It is not to be discovered or experienced in the many
thoughts and visions of the mind, nor in the many burning
and exhilarating feelings of the emotion, nor in the sudden
shaking, penetrating and touching of the body by outside
force. It is to be found in that life which emanates from the
spirit, from the *innermost* part of man. To walk truly after
the Spirit is to understand the movement of this most hidden
area and to follow it accordingly. However wonderful may be
those experiences which occur through the components of
the soul, they are not to be accepted as spiritually valid as
long as they remain in the outward and run no deeper than
sensations. Only what results from the operation of the Holy
Spirit within man's spirit can be accounted spiritual experience. Hence to live a spiritual life requires faith.

"It is the Spirit himself bearing witness with our spirit that
we are children of God" (Rom. 8.16). Man's spirit is the
place where man works together with God. How do we know
we have been born anew and are therefore children of God?
We know because our inner man has been quickened and

the Holy Spirit dwells therein. Our spirit is a regenerated, renewed one, and He Who dwells in, yet is distinct from, this new spirit is the Holy Spirit. And the two of them bear witness together.

CHAPTER 2
A SPIRITUAL MAN

A PERSON WHOSE SPIRIT is regenerated and within whom the Holy Spirit abides can still be fleshly for his spirit may yet be under the oppression of his soul or body. Some very definite actions are required if he is to become spiritual.

Generally speaking we will encounter at least two great perils in our life but are enabled to overcome not only the first but the second of them as well. These two perils with their corresponding triumphs are: that of remaining a perishing sinner or becoming a saved believer and that of continuing as a fleshly believer or developing into a spiritual one. As sinner-turned-believer is demonstrably realizable, so carnal-turned-spiritual is likewise attainable. The God Who can change a sinner into a Christian by giving him His life can equally transform the fleshly Christian into a spiritual one by giving him His life more abundantly. Faith in Christ makes one a regenerated believer; obedience to the Holy Spirit makes him a spiritual believer. Just as the right relationship with Christ generates a Christian, so the proper relationship with the Holy Spirit breeds a spiritual man.

The Spirit alone can render believers spiritual. It is His work to bring men into spirituality. In the arrangement of God's redemptive design the cross performs the negative work of destroying all which comes from Adam while the Holy Spirit executes the positive work of building all which comes from Christ. The cross makes spirituality possible to believers; but it is the Holy Spirit Who renders them spiritual. The meaning of being spiritual is to belong to the Holy

Spirit. He strengthens with might the human spirit so as to govern the entire man. In our pursuit of spirituality, therefore, we must never forget the Holy Spirit. Yet we must not set aside the cross either, because the cross and the Spirit work hand in hand. The cross always guides men to the Holy Spirit, while the Latter without fail conducts men to the cross. These two never operate independently of each other. A spiritual Christian must experimentally know the Holy Spirit in his spirit. He must pass through several spiritual experiences. For the sake of clarity we shall discuss them in a somewhat sequential fashion, although in actual practice they frequently occur simultaneously.

Quite a few remarks will be made concerning how to be spiritual, but let us not forget what we have learned heretofore.* We should realize by now that what hinders one from being spiritual is the flesh. So if a person maintains a proper attitude towards it he shall encounter no difficulty in making progress. It is surprisingly true that the more spiritual one becomes the more he knows the flesh, because he increasingly discovers it. Had he not known it, how could he be spiritual? Hence we cannot neglect what has been discussed earlier concerning the flesh, since it serves as the basis for seeking spirituality. Unless there is this fundamental dealing with the flesh, whatever progress one may make shall inevitably be superficial, shallow, and unreal. But if one knows how to resist his flesh in all things—denying its activity, power, and opinion—he may be regarded as already spiritual. Nevertheless we would still like to cite some positive measures which are related directly to the spirit.

THE DIVIDING OF SPIRIT AND SOUL**

The salient implication of Hebrews 4.12 is whether we are living by intuitive guidance in the spirit or by the naturally good or bad influence of the soul. The Word of God must

*See Part Two, Chapters 4 and 5, the latter Chapter particularly.
**Compare Part Three, Chapter 5.

judge in this particular respect, for only God's sharp Sword can differentiate the source of our living. As a man's knife cuts and divides joints and marrow, so God's Sword too pierces and separates the most intimately linked spirit and soul. Initially such dividing may be simply a matter of knowledge, but ·it is essential that it enter the realm of experience; otherwise it shall in fact never be understood. Believers should allow the Lord to introduce this cleaving of spirit and soul into their practical walk. Not only must they seek it positively with consecration, prayer, and yieldedness to the operation of the Holy Spirit and the cross, but also they must actually possess such experience. Their spirit needs to be liberated from the soul's binding enclosure. These two must be parted cleanly even as the spirit and soul of the Lord Jesus were not one bit mixed. The intuitive spirit needs to be freed wholly from any influence which may come from soulical mind and emotion. The spirit must be the sole residence and office of the Holy Spirit. It must be released from every disturbance of the soul.

The various experiences of having his outer and inner man divided will make a believer spiritual. A spiritual believer differs from others for the simple reason that his entire being is governed by his spirit. Such spirit-control connotes more than the Holy Spirit's authority over the soul and body of man; it also signifies that man's *own* spirit, upon being elevated as head over the whole man through the working of the Holy Spirit and the cross, is no longer ruled by the soul and body but is powerful enough to subject them to its rule.

The division of these two organs is necessary for entering spiritual life. It is that preparation without which believers shall continue to be affected by the soul and hence shall always pursue a mixed course: sometimes walking according to the spirit life but at other times walking according to the natural life. Their pathway fails to be marked by purity, for both spirit *and* soul are their life principles. This mixture holds believers fast within a soulish framework which damages their walk as well as hinders the important work of the Spirit.

Were a believer's outer and inner life definitely separated so that he walks not according to the former but according to the latter, he would sense instantaneously any movement in his soul and immediately shake off its power and influence as though being defiled. Indeed, everything belonging to the soulish is defiled and can defile the spirit. But upon experiencing the partition of soul and spirit, the latter's intuitive power becomes most keen. As soon as the soul stirs, the spirit suffers and will resist right away. The spirit may even be grieved at the inordinate stirring of the soul in others. It will in fact repulse a person's soulish love or natural affection as something unbearable. Only after experiencing such separation do Christians come into possession of a genuine sense of cleanliness. They then know that not sin alone, but all which belongs to the soulish, is defiled and defiling and ought to be resisted. Nay, it is far more than simply knowing, for any contact with what is soulish—whether in themselves or in others—causes their intuitive spirit to feel defiled and to demand instant cleansing.

UNITED TO THE LORD IN ONE SPIRIT

In his first Corinthian letter, Paul informed his readers that whoever "is united to the Lord becomes one spirit with him" (6.17). And note that he did not say, "one soul with him." The risen Lord is the life-giving Spirit (15.45). His union with the believer is therefore a union with the believer's spirit. The soul, the seat of man's personality, belongs to the natural. All it can and is to be is a vessel for expressing the fruit of the union between the Lord and the believer's inner man. Nothing in his soul partakes of the Lord's life; it is solely in the spirit that such a union is effected. The union is one of spirits with no place for the natural. Should it be mixed in with the spirit it will cause impurity to the union of spirits. Any action taken according to our thought, opinion or feeling can weaken the experimental side of this union.

Things of the same nature unite perfectly. Inasmuch as the spirit of the Lord is pure, ours likewise needs to be as pure in order to be united truly with Him. If a believer clings to his own wonderful ideas and is unwilling to lay aside his preference and opinion, his union with the Lord will not be expressed in experience. The union of spirits permits no adulteration from anything soulish.

Wherein lies this union? It is in identification with Christ in His death and resurrection. "If we have been united with him in a death like his, we shall certainly be united with him in a resurrection like his" (Rom. 6.5). This verse explains our union with the Lord as one of being united with His death and resurrection. This simply indicates we are completely one with Him. By accepting His death as our death we enter into this union with the Lord. By additionally accepting His resurrection we who have died with Him shall be resurrected as well. Through faith's acceptance of His resurrection we shall stand experientially in the place of resurrection. Because the Lord Jesus was raised from the dead according to the Spirit of holiness (Rom. 1.4) and was made alive in the spirit (1 Peter 3.18), we too, when united with Him in resurrection, actually are united with Him in His resurrected Spirit. Henceforth we are dead to everything pertaining to ourselves and alive to His Spirit alone. This requires our exercising faith.* Once identified with His death, we lose the sinful and the natural in us; once identified with His resurrection, we are united with His resurrection life. Thus our inner being which is now united with the Lord becomes one spirit with Him. "You have died . . . through the body of Christ, so that you may belong to another, to him who has been raised from the dead . . ., so that we serve . . . in the new life of the Spirit" (Rom. 7.4,6). Through Christ's death we are joined to Christ, even in His resurrected life. Such union enables us to serve in the new life of the Spirit, free from any adulteration.

---

*See Part Three, Chapter 1, on the two essentials for deliverance from sin.

How marvelous is the cross! It is the foundation for everything spiritual. The purpose and end of its working is to
unite the believer's spirit with the resurrected Lord into one
spirit. The cross must go deeply to rid him of the sinful and
the natural within him that he may be joined to the positive
resurrection life of the Lord and thus become one spirit
with Him. A believer's spirit, together with all which is
natural and transient in him, needs to pass through death so
that it may be purified and then united to become one
spirit with the Lord in the freshness and purity of resurrection. Spirit is joined with Spirit to become one spirit.
And the outcome will be: to serve the Lord in "newness of
spirit" (Rom. 7.6 Darby). What is of the natural, of self, and
of animal activities has no more place in the believer's walk
and labor. Both the soul and the body may then but exhibit
the purpose, work, and life of the Lord. The Spirit life leaves
its imprint on everything, and everything speaks of the out-
flowing of the Spirit of the Lord.

This is ascension life. The believer is joined to the Lord
Who sits at the right hand of God. The Spirit of the enthroned Lord flows into the spirit of the believer, who is on
the earth yet not of the world; the enthroned life is accord-   ✗
ingly lived out upon the earth. The Head and the body
share the same life. With such a union He is able to pour
forth the power of His life through the believer's spirit. As
a tube which is connected to a fountain is able to convey
living water, so too the believer's spirit which is united with
the Spirit of the Lord is capable of transmitting life. The
Lord is not just the Spirit; He is the *life-giving* Spirit as well.
When our spirit is joined intimately with the life-giving
Spirit, it is filled with life; and nothing can limit that life.   ✗
How we need to have this in our spirit that we may triumph
continually in our daily walk. Such a union clothes us with
the victory of the Lord Jesus. It gives us the knowledge of
His will and mind. It builds and expands the new creation
within us by the rich inflow of the Lord's vitality and nature.
Through death and resurrection our spirit ascends—even as

the Lord has ascended on high—and experiences "the heavenly places," having trodden all that is earthly underfoot. Our inner being is in ascendancy, far above any obstacle or disturbance. Yes, it is continually free and fresh and discerns everything with the transparent sight of heaven. How radically different this life of heaven on earth is from one that is swayed by emotion. The former kind displays heavenly nature and is persistently spiritual.

KNOWING THE INDWELLING OF THE HOLY SPIRIT

God's children already have the Holy Spirit abiding in them, but they may not recognize Him or obey Him. They need to do so completely. They must realize that this indwelling presence is a Person, One Who teaches, guides, and communicates the reality of Christ to them. Until they are willing to acknowledge the foolishness and dullness of their soul and are ready to be taught, they block the way of this Person. It is necessary for them to let Him regulate everything so as to reveal the truth. Except they know in the depth of their being that God's Holy Spirit is indwelling them and unless with their spirit they wait for His teaching, they will not welcome His operation upon their soul life. Only as they cease to seek anything by themselves and only as they take the position of the teachable shall they be taught by the Spirit truth which they are able to digest. We know He verily abides in us when we understand that our spirit, which is deeper than thought and emotion, is God's Holy of Holies by which we commune with the Holy Spirit and in which we wait for His communication. As we acknowledge Him and respect Him, He manifests His power out from the hidden part of our being by extending His life to our soulical and conscious life.

The Christians at Corinth were of the flesh. In exhorting them to depart from their carnal state, Paul repeatedly reminded them of the fact that they were God's temple and that the Holy Spirit lived in them. Knowing He indwells them helps Christians to overcome their carnal condition.

They must know and understand perfectly by faith that He abides in them. Christians should not be content merely with knowing mentally the doctrine of the Holy Spirit as given in the Bible; they also need to know Him experimentally. They will then commit themselves without reservation to Him for renewal and submit every part of their soul and body to His correction.

The Apostle put to those at Corinth this question: "Do you not know that God's Spirit dwells in you?" (1 Cor. 3.16) Paul seemed to be surprised at their ignorance of such a sure fact. He viewed the indwelling of the Holy Spirit as the foremost consequence of salvation, so how could they miss it? However low a Christian's spiritual measure may be, even as low as that of those Christians at Corinth (alas, many probably do not rise higher than that), he nevertheless ought to be clear on this fact without which he shall long remain carnal and never become spiritual. Even if you have not yet *experienced* His indwelling, could you not at least believe he *does* abide in you?

Can we refrain from worship, respect, and praise when we consider how the Holy Spirit—Who is God Himself, One of the three Persons in the Triune God, the very life of the Father and the Son—comes to live in us who belong to the flesh? What grace for the Holy Spirit to dwell in the likeness of sinful flesh just as the Lord Jesus once took upon Himself the same likeness!

THE STRENGTHENING OF THE HOLY SPIRIT

In order for man's innermost organ to gain dominion over the soul and the body and thus serve as channel for the life of the Spirit to be transmitted to others, there must be His strengthening. Paul prays for believers "that according to the riches of his glory he may grant you to be strengthened with might through his Spirit in the inner man" (Eph. 3.16). He so prays because he considers it infinitely important. He asks God to strengthen by His Spirit their "inner man," which is the new man in them after they have trusted in the Lord.

Therefore the prayer is that the believer's spirit may be strengthened by God's Spirit.

From this we may deduce that the spirits of some saints are weak while those of others are strong. Whether they are potent or impotent depends upon whether or not they have received His strengthening. Since those at Ephesus had been sealed already with the Holy Spirit (1.13-14), the Apostle's prayer for them must be concerned with a gift other than His indwelling. His prayer indicates they must have not only the Holy Spirit indwelling them but also have His special power inundating their spirit so as to render their inner man strong. It is possible for us to possess a weak spirit although having God indwelling us.

To be filled with might in the inner man is the urgent need of Christians. However, unless they appreciate how feeble theirs is they will not ask for the invigoration of the Holy Spirit. Often the children of God cannot rise up to answer the Lord's call to service simply because, though their physical condition is good, their feelings are low, cold, and reluctant. Or even when their emotions are quite high, passionate, and willing, they find themselves unable to serve the Lord because now the body reacts lazily. Such phenomena betray the weakness of the spirit in its dominion over feeling and the physical body. The disciples found themselves in precisely that situation in the Garden of Gethsemane: "the spirit indeed is willing, but the flesh is weak" (Matt. 26.41). Willingness by itself is not sufficient; the spirit also must be strong. If it is sturdy it can overcome the infirmity of the flesh. Why do believers sometimes find themselves dragging and failing while laboring for souls? Lack of power in their spirit is the explanation. The same holds true in the case of environment. How easily we are affected by the confusion of the outside world. Were our spirits hardy we would be able to meet the most disturbing situation with peace and rest. Prayer is the acid test of the inner man's strength. A strong spirit is capable of praying much and praying with all perseverance until the answer comes. A weak one grows weary and fainthearted in the maintenance of praying. A vigorous spirit can move forward in the midst of adverse environment or feeling, but a frail one is impotent to stand against opposition. Great is the need of power in the spirit for spiritual warfare with Satan. Only those who have might in the inner man understand how to exercise their spiritual strength in resisting and attacking the enemy. Otherwise the battle will be make-believe, fought in the imagination of the mind or the excitement of the emotion, and perhaps fought with the weapons of flesh and blood.

In order for the inner man to be strengthened with power through the Holy Spirit, the children of God must discharge their responsibility. They need to yield specifically to the Lord, forsake every doubtful aspect in their life, be willing to obey fully God's will, and believe through prayer that He will flood their spirit with His power. Without delay God will answer the expectation of their heart, once all obstacles on their part are removed. Believers do not need to wait for the Holy Spirit's filling, because He has descended already. What they need only wait for is for themselves to fulfill the condition for His filling, which is, they must let the cross perform a deeper incision upon them. Should they be faithful in believing and obeying, then within a very short time the power of the Holy Spirit will saturate their spirit and strengthen their inner man for living and for laboring. Some may receive His filling immediately upon once surrendering themselves to the Lord, for they already have met the conditions for such filling.

This invasion of God's power in us, this infilling of His Spirit, happens in the human spirit. It is the inner and not the outer man which is activated by His power and thence becomes strong. This is most important to recognize, for it helps us to exercise simple faith in our desire for the filling of the Holy Spirit (Gal. 3.14), rather than to anticipate some bodily sensations such as a shaking, a jerking, or a hurling to the ground. Yet Christians need to be watchful lest they use faith as an excuse for not experiencing the empowering of the Holy Spirit. The conditions for filling must be accomplished and the attitude of believers must be firm. God will fulfill His promise.

By reading what the Apostle affirms in the succeeding verses in Ephesians 3 about apprehending, knowing, and filling, we are certain this strengthening with might in the inner man renders it highly sensitive. Like the body, the spirit has its functions and consciousness. Prior to the mighty inflow of the Holy Spirit's power into their spirit, believers scarcely can detect its intuitive power; but afterwards its intuitive force becomes most distinctive and hence readily discovered. As the inner man is energized, its intuitive power is increased. Believers are able to sense its slightest movement.

The effect of having the spirit filled with God's power is to afford it full sway over the soul and the body. Every thought, desire, sensation and intent is now governed by the spirit. The soul can no longer act independently: it becomes instead the spirit's steward. Furthermore, through the believer's spirit the Holy Spirit is able to impart God's life to thirsty and dying men. However, this filling of the Holy Spirit differs from the baptism with the Holy Spirit, because the latter is for the purpose of service while the former solves the problem of life (naturally it will affect service too).

WALKING ACCORDING TO THE SPIRIT

Transformation from soulish to spiritual does not guarantee that believers never again will walk according to the flesh. On the contrary, an ever present danger exists of falling back into it. Satan is constantly alert to seize every opportunity to cause them to plunge from their lofty position to a life below par. It is therefore highly necessary for God's children to be watchful at all times and to follow the Spirit so that they may remain spiritual.

"In order that the just requirement of the law might be fulfilled in us, who walk not according to the flesh but according to the Spirit . . . (Now) those who live according to

the Spirit set their minds on the things of the Spirit. To set
. . . the mind on the Spirit is life and peace" (Rom. 8.4-6).
To follow the spirit is to walk contrary to the flesh. Not following the spirit is walking by the flesh. Many Christians
oscillate between these two: now following the one, now
following the other. They ought to walk according to the
inner man *alone*, which is, to walk according to the spirit's
intuition and not for a moment according to the soul or body.
In thus following the spirit they invariably shall "set their
minds on the things of the spirit." And the result shall be
"life and peace."

To live by the spirit means to walk according to intuition.
It is to have all one's life, service, and action in the spirit,
ever being governed and empowered by it. This preserves the
saint in life and peace. Since he cannot remain in a spiritual
state unless he walks according to the spirit, then at the very
least the saint must understand its various functions and laws
if he is to walk well.

To live after the spirit is the Christian's daily task. He
ought to perceive that we can live neither by the noblest of
feelings nor by the loftiest of thoughts. We must walk according to the guidance accorded us through our intuition.
The Holy Spirit expresses His feeling through our spirit's
delicate sense. He does not operate directly on our minds,
suddenly inducing us to think of something. All His works
are done in our innermost depths. If we desire to know His
mind we should conduct ourselves in accordance with the intuition of our spirit. At times, however, we may sense something there without comprehending what it means, what it
demands, or what it is communicating. Whenever this happens, we must commit ourselves to prayer, asking that our
mind may be given understanding. Once we apprehend the
meaning of what we have sensed intuitively, we thereafter
should behave accordingly. The mind can instantly be enlightened and made to understand the meaning of intuition;

---
*See Part Five, Chapter 1.

but abrupt thoughts which originate with the mind void of intuition ought not to be followed. Solely intuitive teaching represents the Spirit's thought. Only this should we follow.

Such a walk by the spirit requires *reliance* and *faith*. We have seen before how all good actions of the flesh exhibit an attitude of independence towards God. The very nature of the soul is independency. Should believers act in accordance with their thought, feeling and desire, they have no need to spend time before God, to wait for His guidance. Those who follow "the desires of body and mind" (Eph. 2.3) need not rely upon God. Except Christians realize how useless, how undependable, and how utterly weak they are in seeking to know the will of God, they shall never cultivate a heart of reliance upon Him. To receive God's guidance in their spirit they must wait upon Him therewith; they must refrain from taking their feeling or thought as a guide. Let us remember that whatever we do or can do without trusting, seeking, and waiting upon God is or will be done in the flesh. With fear and trembling we must rely upon God for guidance in the inner depths. This is the sole way to walk according to the spirit.

To walk in this fashion requires faith of the believer. The opposite of sight and feeling is faith. Now it is the soulish person who gains assurance by grasping the things which can be seen and felt; but the person who follows the spirit lives by faith, not by sight. He will not be troubled by the lack of human assistance, nor will he be moved by human opposition. He can trust God even in utter darkness for he has faith in God. Because he does not depend upon himself, he can trust the unseen power more than his own visible power.

Walking after the spirit involves both the initiation of a work by revelation and execution of it through the Lord's strength. Frequently believers beseech God for spiritual power to do a work which has not been revealed at all in their intuition. This is simply impossible, for what is of the flesh is flesh. On the other hand believers frequently know the will of God through revelation in their intuition but bring their own strength to the work to perform it.* This likewise is impossible, for how can they begin with the Holy Spirit and end up with the flesh? Those who follow the Lord must be brought to the place of no confidence in the flesh. They must confess they can originate no good idea and must admit they possess no power to fulfill the Holy Spirit's work. All thought, cleverness, knowledge, talent and gift—which the world superstitiously worships—must be set aside in order to enable one to trust the Lord wholly. The Lord's people should persistently acknowledge their own unworthiness and incompetency. They dare not initiate anything before receiving God's order nor attempt to execute God's command in self-reliance.

To live by the spirit we must move in accordance with the delicate sense of its intuition and depend on its enabling to accomplish the revealed task. Well do we begin if we follow intuition instead of thought, opinion, feeling or tendency; well do we end if we rely on the Spirit's power and not on our talent, strength or ability. Simply keep in mind that the moment we cease to follow our intuitive sense at that very moment we begin to walk after the flesh and end up minding the things of the flesh. This in turn injects death into the spirit. Only if we "walk not according to the flesh" can we walk "according to the spirit."

Our aim is to be a spiritual man but not a spirit. If we recognize this distinction our lives shall never be cut and dried. We today are human beings and shall be so eternally, yet the highest achievement of a human being is to develop into a spiritual man. The angels are spirits; they have neither body nor soul. But we humans possess both. We are to be spiritual *men* and not spirits. The spiritual man shall continue to retain his soul and body; otherwise, he would be reduced to being a spirit instead of a man. No, what is meant by being a spiritual man is that he is under the control of his spirit

*See Part Two, Chapter 4.

which has become the highest organ of his whole person. Let us not be mistaken on this point. A spiritual man retains his soul and body; being spiritual does not annihilate these organs nor their respective functions, because these make man what he is. So although the spiritual man does not live by them, he certainly has not annihilated them either. They instead have been renewed through death and resurrection so that they are perfectly united to the spirit and have become instruments for its expression. Hence the emotion, mind and will remain in a spiritual man but are subject entirely to the guidance of the intuition.

The emotion of a spiritual man is completely under his spirit's regulation, no longer asserting an independent course as it once did. It does not block the spirit nor resist its move because it does not insist upon its own affection and feeling. The emotion now rejoices solely in what the spirit likes, loves only what the spirit directs, feels merely what the spirit permits. It has become its life: when the spirit stirs, emotion responds.

The mind of the spiritual man likewise cooperates with the spirit, wandering no more as in the past. It does not object to the spirit's revelation by raising its reason and argument, neither does it disturb the peace of the spirit with many confused thoughts, nor does it rebel against the spirit by boasting in its own wisdom. Quite the reverse, the mind cooperates fully with the intuition in advancing on the spiritual journey. If the spirit unfolds any revelation the mind discerns its meaning. It will assist the spirit to fight should the latter plunge into warfare. If the Holy Spirit desires to teach any truth, the mind will help the spirit to understand. The latter, though, has the authority to stop the mind's thinking as well as to initiate it.

The spiritual man also retains his will, yet it too is no longer independent of God but now decides according to the dictate of the spirit, having abandoned self as its center. The will does not insist upon its desire as before. It consequently is fit to obey God. No more is it hard and stiff but is completely broken; hence it cannot resist God or strive against Him. It has been tamed of its wild nature. Today when the spirit receives revelation and apprehends God's wish, the will decides to follow. It stands at the spirit's door like a courier, awaiting its every command.

The body of a spiritual man is subjected to the spirit as well. Because it has been cleansed by the precious blood and has had its passions and lusts dealt with by the cross, it can serve today as an obedient servant to the spirit's order as that order is communicated to the body from the spirit through the soul. By no means does it entice the soul into many sins by its passions and lusts as it formerly did. Instead the body now answers swiftly all the spirit's directions. The latter through the renewed will has complete authority over the body. Gone are the days when the body pressed a weak inner man. The spirit of a spiritual man has grown strong and the body is under its power.

The Apostle Paul has described the authentic condition of a spiritual man in I Thessalonians: "May the God of peace himself sanctify you wholly; and may your spirit and soul and body be kept sound and blameless at the coming of our Lord Jesus Christ" (5.23). Hence the portrait of the spiritual man which can be drawn from everything which has been said is as follows:

(1) He has God dwelling in his spirit, sanctifying him totally. Its life inundates his entire person so that his every component lives by the spirit life and functions in the spirit's strength.

(2) He does not live by soul life. His every thought, imagination, feeling, idea, affection, desire and opinion is renewed and purified by the Spirit and has been brought into subjection to his spirit. These no longer operate independently.

(3) He still possesses a body, for he is not a disembodied spirit; yet physical weariness, pain, and demand do not impel the spirit to topple from its ascended position. Every

member of the body has become an instrument of righteousness.

To conclude, then, a spiritual man is one who belongs to
the spirit: the whole man is governed by the inner man: all
the organs of his being are subject completely to it. His
spirit is what stamps his life as unique—everything proceeds
from his spirit, while he himself renders absolute allegiance
to it. No word does he speak nor act does he perform according to himself; rather does he deny his natural power
each time in order to draw power from the spirit. In a word,
a spiritual man lives by the spirit.

CHAPTER 3
SPIRITUAL WORK

As A BELIEVER GOES on his spiritual way he gradually begins to realize that to live for himself is a sin, yea, the greatest sin of his life. To live for himself is as it were a grain of wheat which having fallen into the earth refuses to die and hence remains alone. To seek the filling of the Holy Spirit in order to be a powerful spiritual person is solely to please himself, to make himself happy. For were he to live purely for God and His work this believer would not consider his personal happiness or feeling. He certainly would understand the meaning of spirituality. But in the depth of his heart lodges instead a soul's self-love.

All God's children are God's servants. Each of them receives some gift from the Lord: none is excepted (Matt. 25.15). God places them in His church and apportions to each a ministry to fulfill. God's objective is not to make the believer's spirit a reservoir of spiritual life which withers after a little while: if God's life becomes stagnant in him he begins to feel parched. No, spiritual life is for spiritual work; spiritual work expresses spiritual life. The secret of that kind of living lies in the incessant flowing of that life to others.

Spiritual food of a believer is nothing more nor less than accomplishing God's work (John 4.34). The kingdom of God suffers greatly at the hands of "spiritual believers" who busy themselves with prayer and Bible study and attend only to *their* spiritual need. The Lord's people should simply trust God for the sustenance of both their physical and

spiritual needs. If they are willing to endure hunger in order
to accomplish what God wants them to do, they shall be
satisfied. Spiritual food is simply to do His will. Preoccupation with one's own supply causes lack, whereas concern
with God's kingdom brings satisfaction. He who is occupied
with the Father's business and not with his own shall find
himself perpetually full.

The child of God should not be overanxious to make new
gains; what he essentially requires is to keep what he already
has, for not losing is itself a gain. The way to retain what
he possesses is to engage it. Burying it beneath the earth
is a sure way to lose it. When a believer allows the life in
his spirit to flow freely, he not only shall gain others but
shall gain himself as well. One gains by losing self for others
and not by hoarding for oneself. The life within a spiritual
man must be released by performing spiritual labor. If one's
inner being is always open and free (it must of course be
closed to the enemy), the life of God shall flow out from
him to the salvation and edification of many. The moment
spiritual exertion ceases, at that precise moment spiritual
life is blocked. These two are inseparable.

No matter what earthly occupation the believer may
have, he is apportioned a measure of work by God as well.
One who is spiritual knows his place in the body of Christ;
as a consequence he also knows the limits of his work. Each
member has his usefulness; his work lies in discharging that
usefulness. Some gifts are dispensed to benefit particular
members; while others, the whole body. A Christian ought
to recognize the limits of his gift and to labor within those
bounds. But many fail. They either withdraw from their
work and thus stifle the development of their spiritual life,
or they overextend themselves to their harm. Misusing
hands and feet damages a person just as much as not using
his hands and feet at all. One sure means of losing life, as
we have seen, is to try to keep spiritual life to oneself; yet
to work indiscriminately can equally impede life.

SPIRITUAL POWER

We must desire to be filled with the Holy Spirit experientially if we desire to have power in witnessing for Christ and in combating Satan. More and more people are in hot pursuit of such experiences today. But the question should be raised as to what lies behind such a quest. How many covet *danger* that they may boast? How many desire more glory for their flesh? How many hope people will fall effortlessly under their power? We must discern clearly why we solicit the power of the Holy Spirit. If our motive is neither of God nor one with God, we certainly will not be able to obtain the power. God's Holy Spirit does not fall on man's "flesh"; He descends only on God's newly created spirit within the man. We cannot allow the outward man, that is, the flesh, to persist while petitioning God to immerse our inner man, the spirit, in His Spirit. So long as the flesh continues unscathed the Holy Spirit of God shall never descend upon man's spirit, for man would only grow more fleshly and boastful if power were granted him.

It is often observed that Calvary precedes Pentecost. The Holy Spirit is not willing to dispense power to men and women who have not been dealt with by the cross. The path which leads to the upper room in Jerusalem winds by way of Calvary. Only those who are conformed to the death of the Lord can receive the power of the Lord. The Word of God affirms that "upon man's flesh shall it (holy anointing oil) not be poured" (Ex. 30.32 Darby). God's Holy Oil will not be poured upon the flesh, whether it be exceedingly defiled or highly refined. Where the mark of the cross is lacking, there the oil of the Spirit is absent. Through the death of the Lord Jesus God pronounces His verdict upon all who are in Adam: "all must die." Just as the Heavenly Power did not descend until the Lord Jesus died, even so should the believer not expect that Power if he has yet to know the death of the Lord Jesus in experience. Historically, Pentecost followed Calvary; experientially, being filled with the power of the Holy Spirit follows the bearing of the cross.

The flesh is condemned forever before God and by God is sentenced to death. Are we not attempting the impossible if we desire not its death but rather seek to adorn the flesh with the Holy Spirit that it may be more powerful in service? What is our intention after all? Personal attraction? Fame? Popularity? The admiration of spiritual believers? Success? Being pleasing to man? Self-edification? People with mixed motives, those of double mind, shall not be able to receive the baptism in the Holy Spirit. We perhaps may judge our motive pure, but our High Priest, through different circumstances, will enable us to know our true heart. Not until the work in hand has failed and we are despised and rejected shall we begin to discern the intent of our heart. Any who are genuinely used by the Lord always have gone this way. The time when we receive the power is after the cross has performed its task.

But are there not many of God's children who, never having had the deeper experience of the cross, are yet powerful in witnessing and appear to be greatly used by the Lord? The Bible indicates that there is an oil very much like the holy anointing oil (Ex. 30.33). It is compounded *like* the holy anointing oil, but it is not the *holy* anointing oil. Do not be taken in or flattered by your own success or fame. Take note only as to whether or not the old creation, including everything which comes by birth, has gone through the cross. Any power we possess before the flesh is put to death is certainly *not* the power of the Holy Spirit. Those with spiritual insight who live on the other side of the curtain well appreciate that such success has not a shred of spiritual value.

Only after a person has actually condemned his flesh and begins to walk according to the spirit will he receive the real power from God. Otherwise it would be his flesh that would be endued with spiritual power. How can one's spirit receive special power if the flesh has not experienced death, since the flesh rules by its own energy and invariably suppresses the spirit? The power of God only descends upon that spirit which is full of His Holy Spirit. This is the sole possibility. No other way can there be for the dynamism of the Spirit to flow out. Is it not true that when a vessel is already full, any added power will naturally overflow? To receive power, therefore, it is necessary for us to die to the old creation and learn how to walk in the Spirit.

Every Christian ought to seek the power of the Holy Spirit. To understand it mentally is not enough. His spirit must be engulfed by the Heavenly Power. The effectiveness of one's work depends upon whether he has the experience of being so immersed in the Holy Spirit. God's Spirit requires an outlet, but alas, in how many can He actually find that outlet? There are hindrances of sin, of pride, of coldness, of self-will, or of reliance on the soul life. God's Power has no exit! We have too many other sources of energy besides His!

In seeking the might of the Holy Spirit we must keep our mind clear and our will alive, thereby guarding ourselves from the enemy's counterfeit. We also must let God purge from our life anything sinful, unrighteous or doubtful, that our total being may be presented to the Lord. We then should "receive the promise of the Spirit through faith" (Gal. 3.14). Rest in God trusting that He will fulfill His Word in due course. Do not, however, forget His promise. Should there be delay, use the opportunity for closer scrutiny of your life beneath His light. Gladly accept any feeling which does come with the power; but if God deems it suitable not to accompany power with feeling, simply believe He has indeed fulfilled His Word.

How does one judge whether he has received the promise or not? By looking into his experience. He who has received power has his spiritual senses sharpened and also possesses an utterance—not of this world—to witness for the Lord. His work is effective and bears lasting fruit. Power is the basic ingredient for spiritual service.

Upon receiving the enablement of the Holy Spirit a believer grows very sensitive to his spirit's senses. He should keep his inner man continually free, allowing the Holy Spirit to flow out His life in and through his being. To keep the inner man free is to maintain it in an operative condition for the Holy Spirit. Suppose God, for instance, sends a believer to lead a meeting. This one's spirit must be open. He should not come to the meeting with a spirit loaded down with many cares or weights, else this shall afflict the whole meeting with heaviness, creating a difficult and unbearable situation. The one who leads should not carry his burden to the meeting and expect the congregation to set him free. Anyone who relies on the response of the congregation to relieve him of his burden is doomed to failure. When he enters the meeting place the leader's spirit must be light and unbound. Many who attend are teeming with burdens. Hence the leader first must release them through prayer, hymn, or truth before he can deliver God's message. He cannot expect to unshackle others while he is himself bound with unbroken fetters.

/ It should be clearly borne in mind that a spiritual gathering is the communion of spirit with spirit. The messenger delivers his message out of his spirit, and the hearer receives God's Word with his. Were the spirit of the messenger or the hearer to be weighed down and under bondage, it would be powerless to open to God and respond to His Word. Accordingly, the leader's spirit should be free in order that initially he may unloose the spirit of the congregation and then may deliver God's message to them.

We must have the Heavenly Power to achieve powerful work; but we must keep our spirit constantly open to let that Power freely flow from our spirit. The manifestation of power varies in its measure. The experience a Christian has of Calvary measures that of Pentecost. If man's spirit is unbound, God's Spirit can work.

Occasionally in working one may experience his inner man being shut in, especially in performing personal work. This may be due to the condition of the other party. The latter may not have an open spirit or mind to receive the truth, or he may harbor improper thoughts which block the spirit's outflow. Such a state will hem in the spirit of the worker. We know quite often whether we are able to perform any spiritual service by merely observing the attitude of the other party. If we find our inner being is closed in by him, we are not able to deliver the truth to that one.

Now were we to force ourselves to labor upon encountering the shutting in of our spirit, we would probably work not with it but with our mind. Yet only work done with the spirit accomplishes lasting results. Whatever is produced by the mind lacks spiritual power. Our efforts shall lose their effectiveness if initially we do not prepare ourselves through prayer and by setting our spirit free for the delivery of God's Word. We must learn how to walk after the spirit so that eventually we may know how to work by it.

THE INAUGURATION OF SPIRITUAL WORK

To inaugurate a work is no small matter. Christians should never initiate anything presumptuously on the basis of need, profit, or merit. These may not indicate God's will in the slightest. Perhaps He will raise up others to undertake this task or He may suspend it till some other time. Men may feel regretful, but God knows what is best. Hence need, profit and merit cannot serve as indicators for our work.

The book of Acts is the best aid in approaching our work. We do not find there anyone consecrating himself as a preacher nor anyone deciding to do the Lord's work by making himself a missionary or a pastor. What we do see is the Holy Spirit Himself appointing and sending men out to do the work. God never enlists men to His service: He simply sends whom *He* wants. We do not see anyone choosing himself: it is God who chooses His worker. There is positively no ground for man's flesh. When God selects, not even a Saul of Tarsus can withstand; when God does not select, even a Simon cannot buy it. God is the sole master of His work, for He will not permit any human mixture in it. Never does man come to work, but it is always God Who *sends* out to do his work. Spiritual service consequently must be inaugurated by the Lord Himself calling us. It should not be initiated through the persuasion of preachers, the encouragement of friends, or the bent of our natural temperament. None who are shod with fleshly shoes can stand on the holy ground of God's service. Many failures and much waste and confusion which have resulted are due to men's *coming* to work, instead of being *sent out* to work.

The chosen worker is not free to move, even after he is chosen. From the fleshly viewpoint no labor is as restrained as spiritual labor. We read in the book of Acts such phrases as: "the Spirit said to him" (10.19); "being sent out by the Holy Spirit" (13.4); "having been forbidden by the Holy Spirit" (16.6). Other than obeying orders, one has no authority to decide anything. In those days the works of the Apostles were performed by heeding the mind of the Holy Spirit apprehended in their intuition. How simple it is! If spiritual work must be contrived and controlled by believers themselves, who then is competent save those who are naturally capable, clever, and learned? *But,* God has discarded all which belongs to the flesh. Believers *can* be used by the Lord to do the most effective work, but only if their spirits are holy, alive, and full of power before the Lord. God has never delegated to believers authority over the control of His work, because He desires them to listen to what He tells them in their spirit.

Despite a great revival in Samaria, Philip was not responsible for the follow-up labor of strengthening. He must leave immediately for the desert in order that a "heathen" eunuch might be saved. Ananias had not heard of Saul's conversion, but he could not refuse to go to pray for Saul when sent, though by standards of human judgment he was casting his life away by walking directly into the persecutor's hand. Peter could not resist what the Holy Spirit had set forth, even though Jewish tradition forbade Jews from visiting anyone of another nation and associating with him. Paul and Barnabas were sent by the Holy Spirit; yet He retained the authority to forbid them from entering Asia; subsequently, though, He did lead Paul to Asia and established the church at Ephesus. All acts are in the hands of the Spirit; believers simply obey. Had it been left to human thoughts and wishes, many places which ought to be visited would not have been, and many others would have been visited which ought not to be. These experiences from Acts inescapably tell us that we too must follow the guidance of God's Spirit in our intuition and not follow our thoughts, reasons or wishes. They also indicate that He does not guide us by our counsels, desires or judgments because these often contradict the guidance of the Holy Spirit in our spirits. How then dare we follow our mind, emotion or will if even the Apostles did not move on that basis?

All works which God calls us to accomplish are revealed in the intuition of the spirit.* We shall deviate from God's will if we follow the thought of our mind, the feeling of our emotion or the desire of our will. Only what is born of the Spirit is spirit; nothing else is. In all their labors Christians must wait on God until they receive revelation in their intuition; otherwise the flesh will assert itself. God will undeniably grant us the spiritual strength for the task He calls us to execute. Here, then, is an excellent principle to remember: never extend beyond the strength of our spirit. If we undertake more than what we there have, we will draw invariably upon our natural strength for help. This shall be the beginning of vexation. Overstretching in work hinders us from walking according to the spirit and disables us from achieving true spiritual accomplishment.

How people today have seized upon reason, thought, idea, feeling, wish and desire as the governing factors in work! These emanate from the soul and contain not an ounce of spiritual value. These can be good stewards but they most assuredly are not good masters. We shall be defeated if we follow them. Spiritual service must emerge from the spirit: nowhere else but here shall God reveal His will.

Workers must never permit soulical sensations to transcend spiritual relations while helping others. They should minister spiritual help in all purity; any soulical feeling can be harmful. This often is a danger and a snare to workers. Even our love, affection, concern, burden, interest and zeal must be

*See Part Five, Chapter 1.

entirely under the spirit's guidance. Negligence in keeping this law causes untold moral and spiritual defeats. If we allow natural attraction and human admiration or the lack of these to govern our efforts we will surely fail in our work and our lives shall be ruined. To obtain genuine fruitfulness we frequently need to disregard fleshly relationships or, in the case of those dearest to us, at least relegate them to a subordinate place. Our thoughts and desires must be offered completely to the Lord.

We will undertake whatever we know intuitively through the guidance of the Holy Spirit; the flesh has no possibility of participating in God's service. The measure of our spiritual usefulness depends upon how penetratingly the cross has cut into our flesh. Do not look at apparent success; rather, look at how much is done by God's crucified ones. Nothing can cover the flesh, not even good intention, zeal, or labor and though they be in the name of the Lord Jesus and for the sake of the kingdom of heaven. God Himself will work; He brooks no interference from the flesh. We should realize that in the matter of serving God there is even the possibility of offering "unholy fire," that which is unspiritual. This arouses God's wrath. Any fire which is not kindled by the Holy Spirit in our spirit is but unholy fire and is deemed sinful in God's sight. Not all deeds done for God are His deeds. Doing for Him is not enough; the question is, who is doing the doing? God will not recognize any labor as His if it simply reflects the believer's activity and is carried out in his strength. God's recognized work must be done by God Himself through the spirit of the believer. Whatever comes from the flesh shall perish with the flesh; only what comes from God remains forever. Doing what is ordered by Him can never fail.

THE AIM OF SPIRITUAL WORK

Spiritual work aims to give life to man's spirit or to build up the life in the spirit. Our labor will be nil in worth or effectiveness if it is not directed towards the spirit lying in the very depths of man. What a sinner needs is life, not some sublime thought. A believer needs whatever can nourish his

spiritual life, not mere Bible knowledge. If all we communicate are excellent sermonic divisions, wonderful parables,
transcendent abstractions, clever words, or logical arguments,
we are but supplying additional thoughts to people's minds,
arousing their emotions once again, or activating their will
to make one more decision. With a moribund spirit do they
come and with just as moribund a spirit do they depart despite our heavy labors on their behalf. A sinner needs to have
his spirit resurrected, not to be able to argue better, shed
profuse tears, or make a firmer resolve. Likewise a believer
does not require outward edification, since his real lack is inward life more abundant — how he can grow spiritually.
Should we focus our attention on the outward man and neglect the inward man, our work will be utterly vain and
superficial. Such work equals no work at all, and perhaps
it is even worse than no work, for a lot of precious time is undeniably wasted!

Man can be moved to tears, can confess his sins, can consider redemption reasonable, can profess his interest in religion, can sign a decision card, can read the Bible and pray,
can even testify with joy; but still his spirit has not received
God's life and therefore remains as dead as before. Why? Because man's soul is capable of performing all these things. To
be sure, we do not despise these motions; nevertheless we
recognize that except the spirit is quickened these pious acts
are but rootless blades which will be totally withered beneath
the scorching sun. When a spirit is born anew it may display
these same manifestations in the outward soul: in the depth
of its being, however, it receives a new life which enables
the person to *know* God and to know Jesus Christ Whom God
has sent. No work possesses any spiritual effectiveness save
that which quickens the spirit into an intuitive knowledge of
God.

We ought to perceive that it is quite possible to exercise
"false faith" and experience "false regeneration." Many confuse understanding with believing. The former simply means
the mind understands the reason of the truth and reckons it
believable. The latter, according to the spiritual sense, in-

volves being united; that is, by believing that the Lord Jesus died for us we unite ourselves with His death. People can understand doctrine without necessarily believing in the Lord Jesus. What we stress is that men are not saved by their good deed, rather do they obtain eternal life through believing the Son of God. Men must *believe* in God's Son. Many believe the doctrine of atonement but fail to believe in the Savior Who atones. Their regeneration is false should they only fill the basin with the blood of the lamb without applying it on the doors of their heart. Countless are the professing Christians who lack the intuitive knowledge of God, although they live like true regenerated Christians—clean, pious, helpful, frequently praying and reading the Bible, even attending services. They can hear and converse about God, yet they do not *know God*, they have no personal knowledge of Him. "My own know me . . . and they will heed my voice" (John 10.14, 16). Those who neither know the Lord nor heed His voice are not His sheep.

Since man's relationship with God begins at regeneration and is carried on completely in the spirit, it is evident that all our work must have its center here. To court apparent success by merely whipping up people's enthusiasm results in a work without God. Once having learned the central place of the spirit, our efforts should undergo a drastic change. We do not labor without objective, simply following what we think is good; we have a distinctive aim, that of building up man's inner depths. In the past we laid stress on the natural; now must we emphasize the spiritual. Spiritual service means nothing other than our working by our spirit for the quickening of the spirits of others. Nothing else can be so termed.

When in fact we recognize that nothing *we* have can impart life to man, then we shall discover how utterly useless we in ourselves are. When we cease depending upon ourselves and using what we have we will see indeed how very weak we are. Not until then will we learn how much power our inner man has. Since we usually rely so heavily on the soul by which to live, we naturally do not appreciate how weak our spirit actually is. Now that we trust solely in the spirit's power we come to perceive the real dynamic of our spiritual life. If we are determined to give life to man's spirit and not just assist the mind to understand, the emotion to be stirred, or the will to decide, we will realize instantly that unless the Holy Spirit verily uses us we are absolutely undone. "Who were born not of blood nor of the will of the flesh nor of the will of man, but of God" (John 1.13). How can we beget them if God does not beget them? We now know all works must be done by God; we are but *empty* vessels. Nothing in us is able to beget them: nothing in them is capable of self-begetting. It is God Who pours out His life through our spirit. Spiritual work is therefore God doing His work. Whatever is not done by Him is not accounted as such.

We should beseech God to reveal the nature and greatness of His work to us. If we understand how much His work requires His great power, we shall be ashamed of our ideas and abashed by our self-reliance. We shall see that all our efforts are but "dead works." Though at times God in special mercy blesses our labors far beyond their due, we should nonetheless refrain from interpreting this as a green light to proceed on that course. Whatever is achieved by ourselves is worthless as well as dangerous. We ought to recognize that God's work is accomplished neither by charged atmosphere, attractive environment, romantic thought, poetic imagination, idealistic view, rational suggestion, burning passion, nor excited will. These might well be suitable were spiritual work merely a dream and not a reality. But such an endeavor is to regenerate the spirit of man and to give resurrection life to him. It can accordingly be accomplished only by God Himself in that Power which raised the Lord Jesus from death.

Thus we see that unless we communicate *God's life* to men our labor merits no praise in heaven. Whatever does not originate in the inward man where God's Spirit dwells is powerless to impart life, no matter how compatible or how incompatible that work may be with reason and feeling. False spiritual enablement may produce results seemingly alike but it can never grant authentic life to man's dead spirit. It may achieve anything and everything except the one real objective of spiritual work.

If we truly aim to bring life to others the power we use must obviously be God's. But in case we employ soul power, failure is inevitable because the soul, though itself alive (Gen. 2.7 Darby), cannot quicken others; for "it is the spirit that gives life" (John 6.63). Note also that "the last Adam (the Lord Jesus) became a life-giving spirit" (1 Cor. 15.45). As the Lord Jesus "poured out his soul to death" (Is. 53.12), so everyone who would serve as a channel for His life must likewise deliver his natural life to death in order that he may work with spirit life for the regeneration of others. However attractive the soul life may be, it possesses no reproductive force. It is impossible to draw on natural power as the energizing force for performing spiritual labor. Old creation can never be the source for new creation, nor can the old serve as the helper to the new. If we labor by the revelation of the Holy Spirit and in His strength, our audience shall be convinced and have their spirits enlivened by God. Else what we give them simply becomes a masterful idea which may stimulate temporarily but leaves no lasting result. The same work may be employed in both cases, but what originates with spirit power becomes spiritual life while that which draws upon self-power turns into natural reasoning. Furthermore, whatever is done in the energy of our natural life will whet people's appetite for more of such feeling and reasoning, automatically and unavoidably drawing them to the one who supplies such needs. The ignorant regard this as spiritual success since many are being gathered; but the discerning can perceive that no life exists in their spirit. The effect of such endeavor in the realm of religion is similar to that of opium or alcohol on the body. Man needs life, not ideas or excitement.

The responsibility of Christians is consequently just this: to present their spirits to God as vessels and to consign to death everything pertaining to themselves. Should they neither block their spirit nor attempt to give to others what they have in and of themselves, God can use His children greatly as channels of life for the salvation of sinners and the upbuilding of the saints. Without that, then whatever the listener receives is but the thought, reason and feeling of the worker; he never accepts the Lord as Savior nor is his dead spirit quickened. Realizing that our aim is to furnish life to man's spirit, we ourselves obviously must be duly prepared. By genuinely relinquishing our soul life and relying entirely on the inner man, we shall see that the words the Lord speaks through *our* mouths continue to be "spirit and life" (John 6.63).

THE CESSATION OF SPIRITUAL WORK

Spiritual work invariably flows with the current of the Holy Spirit—never reluctantly, never under compulsion, hence without need of fleshly strength. This does not imply of course that there is no opposition from the world or attack from the enemy. It simply means the work is done in the Lord with the consciousness of having His anointing. If God still requires the work, the believer will continue to sense himself flowing in the current, no matter how difficult his situation may be. The Holy Spirit aims at expressing spiritual life. Labor accomplished in Him correspondingly develops life in the spirit. Unfortunately many of God's servants frequently are pressed by environment or other factors into working mechanically. As soon as the individual is aware of it, he ought to inquire whether such "mechanical work" is desired by the Spirit or whether God would call him away to other service. God's servants should know that a task begun spiritually— that is, in the Spirit—may not necessarily continue that way. Many works are initiated by Him, but after He has no more need of them men often desire to keep them going. To regard as forever spiritual whatever is begun by the Holy Spirit is inevitably to change the spiritual into the fleshly.

A spiritual Christian can no longer enjoy the anointing of the Spirit in a work that has become mechanical. When a task is already given up by God as unnecessary and yet is maintained by the Christian because of the outside organization (with or without form) which surrounds it, then it must be carried on by drawing upon his own resources rather than upon the power of God. Should a saint persist in laboring after the spiritual work is terminated, he must employ his soul power as well as physical power to continue on with it. In true spiritual service one must completely deny his natural talent and gift; only in this way can he produce fruit for God. If not, each effort not led by the Holy Spirit does collapse if not supported by one's brain, talent, or gift.

A worker must observe carefully which part of his labor the Holy Spirit anoints. Then he will be able to cooperate with Him and operate within the current of His power. The worker's duty is to discern the current of the Spirit and to follow it. A task should be discontinued if it no longer enjoys God's anointing, is out of His current, and creates a sluggish, languid feeling. Another undertaking should be found which flows with the current. The spiritual man discerns more quickly than others. The matter for him to determine is, where is the Holy Spirit's current? Where is it flowing? Any labor that oppresses spiritual life, that fails to express the life of the spirit, or that hinders God's Spirit from overflowing has become a definite obstacle, however well it began. That work should be either cancelled or corrected so that the believer can obey life in the spirit. The worker may have to alter his relationship to the work.

Many cases can be cited to illustrate how the Lord's people are entangled in "organization," to the detriment of their life. At first these servants of God received tremendous spiritual power and were mightily used by God to save and build up man. Later arose the need for some kind of "organization" or "method" to preserve the grace that was given. Due to needs, requests, and sometimes orders, these servants were required to undertake so-called "edifying" work. Thus they were bound by environment and no longer had the freedom to follow the Holy Spirit. Gradually their spiritual life ebbed, though the outside organized work still continued in prosperity. Such has been the story of numberless defeats.

What tragedy lurks within spiritual work today! Many consider their labor a burden. Are there not many who say: "I am so busy with work that I have little time to commune with the Lord. I hope I can find the opportunity to suspend the work temporarily so that I may repair my spirit for the next task." How fraught with danger this is! Our work ought to be the fruit of our spirit's fellowship with the Lord. Every task should be undertaken joyfully as the overflow of the life of the spirit. If it becomes a weight and separates the life of the spirit from the Lord Jesus, then it ought to be terminated. Since the current of the Spirit has changed its course, one must seek to discover its re-location and follow accordingly.

Wide is the disparity between the Holy Spirit terminating our work and Satan hindering it. Yet people frequently are confused by these two. If God should say "Stop" and the believer continue, he will descend from working with his spirit into maintaining the work with his brain, talent, and strength. He may attempt to resist the enemy; without the anointing of the Holy Spirit, however, he cannot succeed. The whole warfare becomes fake. Whenever a child of God encounters resistance in the spirit he should distinguish immediately whether this opposition emanates from God or from the enemy. Should it be the latter his resistance by the *spirit* through prayer will release his inner man and thus he can advance with God. But if it is not from the enemy, the believer shall find as he advances that his own spirit becomes more oppressed, heavily burdened, and void of liberty.

In sum, then, the servants of God today must set aside every work which is not appointed by Him, that should long have been forsaken, which monopolizes everything, that does not come from the spirit, which oppresses the spirit and deflects spiritual work, and that is even good but nonetheless deprives them of other and nobler tasks.

CHAPTER 4
PRAYER AND WARFARE

ALL PRAYER OUGHT TO BE SPIRITUAL. Unspiritual prayers
are not genuine and can produce no positive result. What
abundant spiritual success there would be were every prayer
offered by believers on earth in fact spiritual! But sad to say,
fleshly prayers are far too numerous. Self-will found therein
deprives them of spiritual fruitfulness. Nowadays Christians
appear to treat prayer as a means to accomplish *their* aims
and ideas. If they possessed just a little deeper understanding, they would recognize that prayer is but man uttering to
God what is *God's* will. The flesh, no matter where displayed,
must be crucified; it is not permitted even in prayer. No mixing of man's will in God's work is possible, for He rejects the
best of human intentions and man's most profitable prospects.
God does not will He should follow what man has initiated.
Other than following God's direction, we have no right to direct Him. We have no ability to offer save to obey God's
guidance. God will do no work which originates with man, no
matter how much man may pray. He condemns such praying
as fleshly.

As believers enter the true realm of the spirit, immediately
they shall see how empty they themselves are, for absolutely
nothing in them can impart life to others or work havoc upon
the enemy. Instinctively they will therefore reckon on God.
Prayer then becomes imperative. True prayer uncovers the
emptiness in the petitioner but the fullness in the Petitioned.
Unless the flesh has been reduced to a "vacuum" by the cross,
what use is prayer and what can it possibly signify?

Spiritual prayer does not proceed from the flesh nor the

thought, desire, or decision of the believer; rather does it follow purely from that which is offered according to the will of God. It is prayed in the spirit, that is to say, spiritual prayer is made after one has discerned the will of God in his intuition. The command insisted upon in the Bible is to "pray at all times in the spirit" (Eph. 6.18). If that is not the way we are praying we must be praying in the flesh. We should not open our mouths too hastily upon approaching God. On the contrary, we first must ask God to show us what and how to pray before we make our request known to Him. Have we not consumed a great deal of time in the past asking for what *we* wanted? Why not now ask for what *God* wants? Not what we want but what He wants. If such be the case, then the flesh is provided no footing here. It takes a spiritual man to offer true prayer.

All spiritual prayers have their source in God. God makes known to us what we ought to pray by unfolding to us the need and by giving that need as a burden in our intuitive spirit. Only an intuitive burden can constitute our call to pray. Yet how we have overlooked many delicate registrations in the intuition through carelessness. Our prayer should never exceed the burden in our intuition. Prayers which are not initiated or responded to in the spirit originate instead with the believer himself. They are therefore of the flesh. So that his prayer may not be fleshly but may be effectual in the spiritual domain, the child of God ought to confess his weakness that he does not know how to pray (Rom. 8.26), and petition the Holy Spirit to teach him. He next should pray according to His instruction. God gives us utterance to pray just as he gives us utterance to preach. The need for the former equals that of the latter. In acknowledging our total weakness, we then are able to depend on the movement of the Holy Spirit within our spirit for uttering His prayer. How empty that work is which is done by the flesh; how likewise fruitless is that prayer which is offered in the flesh.

Not only should we pray with the spirit; we should "pray with the mind also" (1 Cor. 14.15). In praying, these two must work together. A believer receives in his spirit what he needs to pray and understands in his mind what he has received. The spirit accepts the burden of prayer while the mind formulates that burden in prayerful words. Only in this way is the prayer of a believer perfected. How often the Christian prays according to the thought in his mind without possessing any revelation in his spirit. He becomes the origin of the prayer himself. But true prayer must originate from the throne of God. It initially is sensed in the person's spirit, next is understood by his mind, and finally is uttered through the power of the Spirit. Man's spirit and prayer are inseparable.

To be able to pray with the spirit a Christian must learn first to walk according to the spirit. No one can pray with his spirit if during the whole day he walks after the flesh. The state of one's prayer life cannot be too greatly disconnected from the condition of his daily walk. The spiritual condition of many too often disqualifies them from praying in the spirit. The quality of a man's prayer is determined by the state of his living. How could a fleshly person offer spiritual prayer? A spiritual person, on the other hand, does not necessarily pray spiritually either, for unless he is watchful he also shall fall into the flesh. Nonetheless, should the spiritual man pray often with his spirit, his very praying shall keep his spirit and mind continually in tune with God. Praying exercises the spirit which in turn is strengthened through such exercising. Negligence in prayer withers the inner man. Nothing can be a substitute for it, not even Christian work. Many are so preoccupied with work that they allow little time for prayer. Hence they cannot cast out demons. Prayer enables us first inwardly to overcome the enemy and then outwardly to deal with him. All who have fought against the enemy on their knees shall see him routed upon their rising up.

Now the spiritual man grows stronger through such exercises. For if a believer prays often with his spirit, his spiritual efficiency shall be increased greatly. He will develop sharp sensitivity in spiritual affairs and will be delivered from all spiritual dullness.

The current need of the spiritual Christian is to learn by God's revelation in his spirit how to detect the enemy's attack and subsequently through prayer to disclose it. He should quickly understand any movement in his spirit so that he may achieve immediately through prayer what God desires him to accomplish. Prayer is work. The experiences of many children of God demonstrate that it accomplishes far more than does any other form of work. It is also warfare, for it is one of the weapons in fighting the enemy (Eph. 6. 18). However, only prayer in the spirit is genuinely effectual.

Praying in the spirit is most productive in attacking the enemy or resisting his wiles. It can destroy as well as build up. Whatever issues from sin and Satan it destroys, but whatevery belongs to God it edifies. Prayer is thus one of the most significant instruments in spiritual work and warfare. Yes, spiritual work and warfare turn on the matter of prayer. If a believer fails in prayer, he in fact fails in everything.

SPIRITUAL WARFARE

Broadly speaking, a Christian who has not yet experienced the baptism in the Holy Spirit is rather vague about the reality of the spiritual realm. He is like the servant of Elisha whose eyes were closed to that sphere. He may receive instructions from the Bible, yet his understanding is confined to the mind because he still lacks revelation in his spirit. But upon experiencing the baptism his intuition becomes acutely sensitive and he discovers in his spirit a spiritual world opening before him. By the experience of the baptism in the Holy Spirit he not only touches the supernatural power of God but contacts God's Person as well.

Now it is just there that spiritual warfare begins. This is the period when the power of darkness disguises himself as an angel of light and even attempts to counterfeit the Person and the work of the Holy Spirit. It is also the moment when the intuition is made aware of the existence of a spiritual domain and of the reality of Satan and his evil spirits. The Apostles were taught in the Scriptures by the Lord after Calvary; but they were made conscious of the real existence of a spiritual realm following Pentecost. Spirit-baptism marks the starting point of spiritual warfare.

Once a believer has contacted the Person of God via the baptism in the Holy Spirit, he then has his own spirit released. He now senses the reality of the things and beings in the spiritual domain. With such knowledge (and let us call to mind that the knowledge of a spiritual man does not accrue to him all at once; some of it may, and usually does, come through many trials), he encounters Satan. Only those who are spiritual perceive the reality of the spiritual foe and hence engage in battle (Eph. 6.12). Such warfare is not fought with arms of the flesh (2 Cor. 10.4). Because the conflict is spiritual so must the weapons. It is a struggle between the spirit of man and that of the enemy—an engagement of spirit with spirit.

Before he arrives at such a juncture in his spiritual walk, the child of God neither understands, nor can he engage in, the battle of the spirits. Only after his inner man has been strengthened by the Holy Spirit does he know how to wrestle with the adversary in his spirit. As he spiritually advances he begins to discover the reality of Satan and his kingdom and then it is that he is given to understand how to resist and attack the foe with his spirit.

The reasons for such conflict are many, with the enemy's tactic of attack and blocking constituting the greatest. Satan frequently either unsettles the emotions of the physical bodies of spiritual believers, or he blocks the works of the spiritual ones, or he may disturb their environments. The need to fight for God forms still another reason for this warfare. As Satan plots in the air and works on earth against God, so His people fight back with spiritual power, destroying the enemy's plots and plans through their prayers. Though at times saints do not know for sure what Satan's scheme is nor what he is doing at the moment, they nevertheless continue to press the fight with no let up, for they understand who their antagonist is.

Beyond the above two explanations, spiritual combat has for its existence yet another cause: the need to be delivered from Satan's deception and to deliver deceived souls.* In

---

*Consult Part Eight, Chapter 3 and Part Nine, Chapter 4.

spite of the fact that their spirit's intuition becomes sharp and
sensitive after they are baptized in the Holy Spirit, believers
may nonetheless fall into deception. To preclude their plunging into the wiles of the adversary, they need not only spiritual sensitivity but also spiritual knowledge. Should they be
ignorant of the manner in which the Holy Spirit leads, they
may assume a passive position and thereby become captives *deception*
of the enemy. The easiest error Christians can commit at this
moment is to follow some irrational feeling or experience
rather than the leading in their inner man. Once baptised in
the Holy Spirit, they have entered the supernatural realm.
Unless believers appreciate their own weakness, that is,
know how incompetent they are in themselves to encounter
the supernatural, they shall be deceived.

The Christian's spirit can be influenced by either of two
forces: the Holy Spirit or the evil spirit. He commits a fatal
blunder who thinks his spirit can be controlled solely by the
Holy Spirit and not be so by the evil spirit too. Let it be forever known that aside from the Spirit that is from God, there
is additionally "the spirit of the world" (1 Cor. 2.12), which
is in fact the spiritual foe of Ephesians 6.12. Except the Christian shuts up his spirit to resist, he may find the evil one
usurping his spirit through deceit and counterfeit.

When a child of God becomes spiritual he is subject to the
influence of the supernatural world. At this point it is vital
for him to know the difference between "spiritual" and "supernatural," the confusion of which forms the cause of many
deceptions. Spiritual experiences are those which originate
with the believer's spirit, while those of the supernatural may
not necessarily come from there. They may arise from physical senses or from the soulical sphere. A Christian ought
never interpret a supernatural experience as always being a
spiritual one. He should examine his experiences and determine whether they enter through the outer sensual organs or
come via the inner spirit. Whatever emanates from outside,
however supernatural it may be, is never spiritual.

The Lord's saints should not receive everything supernatural unquestioningly, for Satan too can perform supernatural
deeds. No matter how the feeling is during the moment

of experience nor how the phenomenon appears or declares itself to be, believers should investigate its source. The charge of 1 John 4.1 must be strictly observed: "Beloved, do not believe every spirit, but test the spirits to see whether they are of God; for many false prophets have gone out into the world." The counterfeits of the adversary often exceed the believer's expectation. If the Lord's people will humble themselves by admitting that deception is quite possible to them, they will be the less deceived. Because of the counterfeits of the enemy, spiritual warfare looms inevitable. Unless *with their spirits* soldiers of Christ take to the field to meet the foe, they shall find him coming in to suppress their spiritual strength. In spiritual conflict the spirit of the Christian wars against the enemy evil spirit. Now should the Christian be deceived already, then he fights to regain his freedom. If not, then he strives to rescue others and to prevent the foe from attacking. He takes the positive stance of subjugating the enemy by opposing every one of Satan's plans and works.

Such battles are fought in the strength of the spirit. It requires power there to wage war. A Christian must understand how to wrestle against the assailant with his spirit. Otherwise he cannot detect how the enemy will attack or discern how God will direct him to fight. But if he walks by the spirit he learns how to pray incessantly therein against the wicked powers. And with each battle his inner man waxes that much stronger. He comes to realize that by applying the law of the spirit he not only can overcome sin but also Satan.

From that part of the Scriptures in which the Apostle touches on spiritual warfare we can readily estimate how important strength is in such conflict. Before he mentions the problem of spiritual warfare (Eph. 6.11-18), Paul first exhorts his readers to "be strong in the Lord and in the strength of his might" (v.10). Where should there be this strength of which he speaks? Paul tells us in Chapter 3: "strengthened with might through his Spirit in the inner man" (v.16). The inner man is man's center, the spirit of man. And right there is where the powers of darkness attack the man. Now if the inner man is weak everything else becomes weak. A frail spirit produces fear in the heart which automatically weakens the believer's stand in the day of evil. What he needs pre-eminently is a firm spirit. Except he understands the nature of the conflict a believer is not capable of resisting *in his spirit* against the principalities and the powers.

Many Christians find their spirit feathery and free when all is sweetness and light; but just let there be eruptive war, and their spirit becomes disturbed, fearful, and worried, until finally it is submerged. They do not know why they are defeated. Satan's aim is victory, and to this end he attempts to remove believers from their ascension position by causing their spirit to sink so that *he* can ascend. Position is a primary factor in battle. When the saint's spirit tumbles, he loses his heavenly position. Christians must consequently maintain a strong spirit and yield no ground to the enemy.

Upon realizing how his inner man is strengthened with might through God's Holy Spirit, a spiritual child of God learns the absolute necessity of overcoming the enemy. His inner man grows sturdier as he attacks the foe with prayer and wrestling. In the same manner that the muscles of the wrestler develop in physical combat, just so the strength of the believer's spirit increases as he battles the adversary. The latter mounts an assault in order to depress the believer's inner man and thus to afflict his soul. If the child of God has come to appreciate the wiles of his assailant, he will not surrender at any point but will instead resist; and his emotional soul is thereby protected. Resistance in the inner man forces the enemy to go on the defensive.

Resistance is one of the indispensable elements in spiritual combat. The best defense is a continuous offense. Oppose with the will as well as with the strength in the spirit. Giving opposition means struggling free from the power of suppression. The opponent will be routed if one fights his way out by the spirit. But should one allow the enemy to attack and not resist in return, then that one's spirit will surely be depressed, sink very low, and may require many days before it regains its ascendancy. The spirit that does not withstand the enemy is often a suppressed one.

How shall we resist? With the Word of God which is the Sword of the Holy Spirit. As a believer receives God's Word it becomes "spirit and life" to him. Hence he can employ this

as his weapon of resistance. A heavenly believer knows how
to use the Word of God advantageously to break down the
enemy's lie. Even now a battle is raging in the world of the
spirit. Though unobserved by the eyes of the flesh, it is sensed
and proven by those who are seeking heavenly progress.
Many who are deceived and bound by the enemy need to be
released. Not only is there need for release from sin and self-
righteousness; many who are bound as well by supernatural
experience need release also. Due to curiosity and the prospect of pleasant sensations, Christians gladly welcome these
supernatural phenomena, not recognizing that these merely
puff up their pride without producing any real or lasting result in terms of a holy and righteous life or spiritual work.
When the evil spirits succeed in their deceptions they gain
a footing in the believer. From this ground the enemy gradually enlarges his frontiers until finally he renders the believer
as one who walks in the flesh.

Now obviously he who himself is bound cannot possibly
set others free. Only when wholly freed experientially from
the powers of darkness can the believer himself overcome the
foe and rescue others. The incidence of the danger of deception increases in proportion to the number of those who experience the baptism in the Holy Spirit. The need today is
for a company of overcoming saints who know how to wage
war for the release of those under the enemy's deception.
The church of God shall be defeated if she lacks members
who know how to walk by the spirit and how to fight therewith against the enemy. May God raise up such!

SOMETHING TO GUARD AGAINST IN SPIRITUAL WARFARE

Each stage of the believer's walk possesses its particular
hazard. The new life within us wages a constant war against
all which opposes its growth. During the physical stage, it
is a war against sins; in the soulish phase, it is a battle against
the natural life; and lastly, on the spiritual level, it is an onslaught against the supernatural enemy. It is solely when a
Christian turns spiritual that the evil spirit in that realm
launches its assault against his spirit. Accordingly, this is
called spiritual warfare. It is fought between spirits and with

spirit. Such a phenomenon rarely if ever occurs with un-spiritual believers. Do not imagine for a moment, therefore, that when one actually reaches the spiritual plateau he is beyond conflict. A Christian life is an unending engagement on the battlefield. The Christian has no possibility of laying down his arms until he stands before the Lord. While soul-ish, he faces conflict with the flesh and its danger; when spiritual, he encounters spiritual warfare and its peculiar hazards. Initially there is the war against Amalek in the wilderness. Upon entering Canaan there is next the struggle against the seven tribes of Canaan, wherein the attack of Satan and his evil hosts against the believer's spirit is mount-ed only after the believer has become spiritual.

Since the enemy focuses particular attention on the spirit, how necessary for spiritual believers to keep their own spirit in its normal state and frequently to exercise it as well. They must control with utmost caution all bodily sensations and carefully distinguish all natural and supernatural phenomena. Their mind must be kept perfectly calm without any disturb-ance; their physical senses too must be maintained in quiet balance without agitation. Spiritual Christians should exer-cise their will to deny and oppose any falsehood and seek to follow the inner man with their whole heart. Should they at any time follow the soul instead of the inner man they have lost precious ground already in spiritual warfare. Further-more, they must be very careful to guard their spirit from being passive in this warfare.

Now we have mentioned before that all our guidance must proceed from the inner man: we must wait with our spirit for the guidance of the Holy Spirit. All this is fundamentally true; however, we need to exercise extreme prudence here lest we fall into grievous error. For while we are waiting in our spirit for the Holy Spirit to move and guide us, a danger readily arises wherein our spirit and our entire being may slide into a state of passivity. Nothing can provide more ground for Satan to work from than this state of inaction. On the one side we ought not to do anything in our own strength save to obey the Holy Spirit; yet on the other side we need to be watchful lest our spirit or any part of our being turns mechanical and plunges into inertia. Our inner man must vitally govern our total being and must cooperate actively with God's Spirit.

When our spirit tumbles into passivity the Holy Spirit is left with no way to use it. This is because His operation in a human life is absolutely diametrical to that of Satan. The Holy Spirit *requires man to cooperate livingly with Him.* He desires man to work actively with Him because He never violates the believer's personality. By contrast, Satan demands a full stop in man so that he may *take over* and do everything in man's stead. He wishes man to accept his work passively. Satan wants to turn man into an automaton. Oh, how we should guard against whatever is extreme and guard against misunderstanding in spiritual doctrine. We need not fear being radical in obeying the Lord, that is for sure; nor do we need to guard against being extreme in denying the works of the flesh. But most vigilant must we be that we not be led to any extremes through misconception.

We said most emphatically earlier that we ought to seek God's work, for vain are those things which belong to man and spring from him. We have said that no spiritual value is possible except from what is done by the Holy Spirit through our inner man and that we should therefore wait with our spirit for revelation from God. Yes, this that we have affirmed is quite true. And blessed is he who is willing to follow this truth. Nonetheless, herein lies one of the gravest perils of all—that of going to the extreme through misunderstanding. Countless believers mistake this truth that we have enunciated as the call to inertia. They conceive the idea that their mind should be emptied for the Holy Spirit to think for them, that their emotion should be suppressed in order for Him to put His affection in them, and that their will should make no decision so that He can decide for them. They mistakenly assume they should accept without question whatever comes to them. Their spirit should not cooperate actively with the Holy Spirit but should wait passively for His moving. And then if there be any movement, it automatically is assumed to be from Him.

This constitutes a very serious misjudgment. It *is* a fact that

God wants to destroy every work of our flesh, but He never desires to destroy our *personality*. He takes no pleasure in transforming us into automata; rather does He delight in having us cooperate with Him. God does not wish us to be a people void of thoughts, feelings, and decisions: He yearns for us to think what He thinks, feel what He feels, desire what He desires. The Holy Spirit never supplants us in thinking, feeling, and desiring; we ourselves must think, feel and desire, but all according to God's will. If our mind, emotion and will plunge into a state of quiescence—in which we are no longer active but idly waiting for an outside force to activate us, then our spirit too cannot escape being passive at the same time. And thus Satan benefits immeasurably when we are unable to exercise our spirit but expect instead to be prodded by some external force.

A fundamental difference obtains between the work of the Holy Spirit and that of the evil spirit. *The Holy Spirit moves people themselves to work, never setting aside man's personality; the evil spirit demands men to be entirely inactive so that he may work in their place, reducing man's spirit to a robot.* Hence a passive spirit not only provides the evil one an opportunity to function but binds the hand of the Holy Spirit as well, because He will not operate without the cooperation of the believer. Under these circumstances the evil power inevitably will attempt to exploit the situation. Before a Christian becomes spiritual he is not confronted by this danger of contacting the satanic power; but once he becomes spiritual the wicked one naturally will assault his inner man. The fleshly Christian never experiences this passivity of spirit; the spiritual alone encounters the hazard of developing an errant spirit.

Due to his misconception of the destruction of the flesh, a child of God may allow his inner man to sink into an inert state. This affords the evil one a chance to simulate the Holy Spirit. If the believer forgets that the enemy may influence his spirit as much as the Holy Spirit can, he unwittingly may accept every moving in his spirit to be from the Holy Spirit and thereby cede ground to Satan for pursuing his aim of destroying the moral, mental, and physical well-being of the saint and making him suffer unspeakable pains.

This is exactly what has happened to many who have experienced "the baptism in the Holy Spirit." They do not understand that such an experience necessarily initiates them into a closer relationship with the spirit world and exposes them to the influence of both the Holy Spirit *and* the evil spirit. While they are experiencing a baptism in the spirit they consider all supernatural experiences to be baptism in the Holy Spirit. Truly they have been baptised in the spirit, but the searching question is, in what spirit have they been baptised—in the Holy one or in the evil one? Both of these may be viewed as "baptised in the spirit." Not recognizing that the Holy Spirit requires *their* spirit's cooperation and that He never does violence to their personality, many saints allow their inner man to descend into passivity and to permit some outside force to burn, twist, or overthrow them. They, in a word, have been baptised in the evil spirit.

Some Christians genuinely have been baptised in the Holy Spirit, yet being unable to distinguish between spirit and soul they are deceived afterwards. Because of their special experience, they maintain that now that the Holy Spirit is in full control they should not take any active step but remain completely passive. And so their inner man is submerged in total inertia. Satan begins to feed them many excessive pleasant sensations and numerous visions, dreams, and supernatural experiences too. They receive them all as from the Holy Spirit, not realizing that their inert spirit like a magnet draws in these counterfeit experiences. Had they known how to distinguish the sensational and the supernatural from the spiritual, these believers would have examined those experiences. Now, however, because of a lack of discernment combined with a passive spirit, they settle deeper and deeper into the enemy's deception.

As the believer's spirit grows increasingly quiescent, his conscience of course follows suit. Once his conscience is rendered passive, he next expects to be led *directly* by the Holy Spirit, either by voice or by Scripture verse. He concludes that He no longer will lead him by his conscience or by decisions emanating from his intuition; instead he will be led in the highest way. The Holy Spirit, he now assumes, will speak either directly to him or indirectly through some Bible verses. By ceasing to employ his conscience and by letting it drop into inaction, the saint is deceived into minding Satan in his daily walk. The Holy Spirit, however, true to His Own working principle, will always refrain from taking over man's conscience and using it for him. Satan alone will seize the occasion to replace the guidance of the believer's conscience and intuition with supernatural voices and other devices.

As conscience grows more passive and the evil spirit supplies his guidance, some Christians begin to lower their moral standard—thinking they henceforth live according to a higher life principle, and therefore treat immoral matters as not quite so immoral any more. They also cease to make any progress in life or work. Instead of *exercising* their intuitive power to detect the thought of the Holy Spirit or of engaging their conscience to discern right and wrong, they simply follow the supernatural voice which comes from outside and reduce themselves to robots. These Christians mistake the supernatural voice for the voice of God. They disregard their reasoning, their conscience, and other people's advice. They turn out to be the most stubborn individuals in the world: they refuse to listen to anyone. They picture themselves as obeying a higher law of life than the rest of their spiritual confreres. How they fit perfectly the description of the Apostle: "whose consciences are seared"! (1 Tim. 4.2) Their consciences are void of conviction!

Hence to sum up: in our spiritual warfare we must ever and anon preserve our inner man in an active state—wholly yielded to the Holy Spirit, yet not in passive submission; otherwise we shall be deceived by the enemy. Even should the adversary not assault us, we still shall retreat into a shut-in position if our spirit is not operative and outstretched. For the enemy would have the chance anyway to seal off all outlets for our spirit to work, to serve, and to war. It would suffer as though suppressed. Our inner man must accordingly be active and outgoing. It must resist Satan constantly or else it will be attacked from all sides.

Another very important principle to learn in spiritual warfare is that we must attack Satan incessantly. This is to prevent ourselves from being attacked. When a believer has crossed into the domain of the spiritual he daily ought to maintain a combat attitude in his spirit, praying therewith for the overthrow of all the works of Satan done through the evil powers. If not, he shall discover his spirit shall fall from heaven, grow very weak and feeble, gradually lose its senses, and finally become scarcely detectable. This is all because the believer's inner man has collapsed into such a passive condition that it has ceased to launch out in attack. Hence ground is surrendered to the enemy from which to assail, surround and shut in his spirit. But if the Christian daily "lets out" his spirit and continually resists the foe, he will keep his spirit mobilized. And with each passing day it shall wax stronger and stronger.

A Christian must be delivered from every misconception with respect to spiritual life. He often surmises, before he enters the spiritual sphere, that if only he could be as spiritual as his brother how happy he would be! He visualizes the spiritual odyssey as a most happy affair; and so he contemplates spending his days in perfect joy. Little does he know that the opposite is the truth. The spiritual path does not yield any enjoyment to the person himself; it is instead a life of daily fighting. To remove warfare from a spiritual life is to render it unspiritual. Life in the spirit is a suffering way, filled with watching and laboring, burdened by weariness and trial, punctuated by heartbreak and conflict. It is a life utterly outpoured entirely for the kingdom of God and lived in complete disregard for one's personal happiness. When a Christian is carnal he lives towards himself and for his own "spiritual" enjoyment. Of little real value is he in God's hand. Only as he dies to sin and to his personal life shall he be able to be used by God.

A spiritual life is one of spiritual usefulness because it is lived to mount assault upon assault against God's spiritual enemy. We ought to be zealous for God, relentlessly attacking that enemy and never allowing this most useful spirit of ours to sink into passivity.

PART FIVE

AN ANALYSIS OF THE SPIRIT

1 Intuition
2 Communion
3 Conscience

CHAPTER 1

INTUITION

To UNDERSTAND more clearly what spiritual life is we must analyze the spirit explicitly and assimilate all its laws. Only after we are really acquainted with its different functions are we able to know the laws which govern them; only after we become familiar with those laws can we walk according to the spirit; that is, according to the laws of the spirit. This is indispensable for experiencing the spiritual life. We should never fear appropriating too much knowledge concerning the spirit; but we should be extremely apprehensive if we use our mind excessively in such pursuit.

God's glad tidings to men is that the fallen can be regenerated and the fleshly can receive a new spirit. This new spirit serves as the basis for new life. What we commonly term spiritual living is but to walk by this spirit which we obtain at regeneration. It is something to be deplored that

believers are so ignorant of the functions of the spirit as well
as of other matters pertaining to it. Although they may know
the relationship of the spirit to man in name, they are unable
to identify their spirit in experience. Either they do not
realize where their spirit is or else they interpret their own
feelings or thoughts to be functions of the spirit. An analysis
of its functions hence becomes absolutely essential, for without them no believer can move according to the spirit.

THE FUNCTIONS OF THE SPIRIT

Mention was made previously that the functions of the
spirit could be classified as intuition, communion, and
conscience. While these three *can* be distinguished, still,
they are closely entwined. It is therefore difficult to treat
of one without touching upon the others. When we talk for
example about intuition, we naturally must include communion and conscience in our discussion. Thus in dissecting
the spirit we necessarily must look into its triple functions.
Since we have seen already how the spirit comprises these
three abilities, we shall proceed next to uncover what these
exactly are in order that we may be helped to walk according to the spirit. We may say that such a walk is a walk by
intuition, communion and conscience.

These three are merely the *functions* of the spirit. (Furthermore, they are not the *only* ones; according to the Bible,
they are but the *main* functions of the spirit). None of them
is the spirit, for the spirit itself is substantial, personal, invisible. It is beyond our present comprehension to apprehend
the substance of the spirit. What we today know of its substance comes via its various manifestations in us. We will
not attempt here to solve future mysteries but only attempt
to discover spiritual life; sufficient for us is the knowledge
of these abilities or functions and of the way to follow the
spirit. Our spirit is not material and yet it exists independently in our body. It must therefore possess its own spiritual
substance, out of which arise various abilities for the performance of God's demands on man. Hence what we desire
to learn is not the substance but the functions of the spirit.

Previously we have compared man to the temple and
man's spirit to the Holy of Holies. We shall proceed further
with this metaphor by comparing the intuition, communion
and conscience of the spirit to the ark in the Holy of Holies.
First, within the ark lies the law of God which instructs the
Israelites what they should do; God thereby reveals Himself and his will through the law. In like manner God makes
Himself and His will known to the believer's intuition that
he may walk accordingly. Second, upon the ark and
sprinkled with the blood is the mercy seat whereon God
manifests His glory and receives man's worship. Similarly,
every person redeemed by the blood has the spirit quickened; through this quickened spirit he worships and communes with God. As God formerly communed with Israel
on the mercy seat, so He today communes with the believer
in his blood-cleansed spirit. Third, the ark is called "the Ark
of Testimony" because therein are kept the Ten Commandments as God's testimony to Israel. Just as the two tablets of
law silently accused or excused the doings of Israel, so the
believer's conscience, on which God's Spirit has written the
law of God, bears witness for or against the conduct of the
believer. "My conscience bears me witness in the Holy
Spirit" (Rom. 9.1).

Observe with what respect the Israelites paid the ark! In
crossing the Jordan River they had no other guidance save
the ark, but they followed it without hesitation. In fighting
against Jericho, they did nothing except march behind it.
Later, they could not stand before the Philistines when they
tried to use the ark according to their way. Was not Uzzah
smitten to death as he put out his fleshly hand to hold the
ark? How joyful Israel was when they had prepared a habitation for it (Ps. 132). These incidents ought to teach us to
be exceptionally careful with our ark, which is our spirit with
its threefold functions. If we walk in this fashion, we shall
have life and peace; if we allow the flesh to interfere, we can
encounter nothing but total defeat. Victory depended not on
what or how Israel thought but on where the ark led. Spirit-

ual usefulness lies in the teaching of our intuition, communion and conscience and not in the thought of man.

INTUITION

As the soul has its senses, so too has the spirit. The spirit is intimately related to the soul and yet is wholly unlike it. The soul possesses various senses; but a spiritual man is able to detect another set of senses—lodged in the innermost part of his being—which is radically dissimilar from his set of soulical senses. There in that innermost recess he can rejoice, grieve, anticipate, love, fear, approve, condemn, decide, discern. These motions are sensed in the spirit and are quite distinct from those expressed by the soul through the body.

We can learn about the sensing of the spirit and its many-sided character from the following verses:

"The spirit indeed is *willing*" Matt. 26.41
"*Perceiving* in his spirit" Mark 2.8
"He *sighed* deeply in his spirit" Mark 8.12
"My spirit *rejoices* in God my Savior" Luke 1.47
"The true worshipers will *worship* the Father in spirit and truth" John 4.23
"He was deeply *moved* in spirit and *troubled*" John 11.33
"When Jesus had thus spoken, he was *troubled* in spirit" John 13.21
"His spirit was *provoked* within him as he saw that the city was full of idols" Acts 17.16
"He had been instructed in the way of the Lord; and being *fervent* in spirit" Acts 18.25
"Paul *purposed* in the spirit" Acts 19.21 ASV
"I go *bound* in the spirit unto Jerusalem" Acts 20.22 ASV
"(Be) *fervent* in spirit" Rom. 12.11 ASV
"For what person *knows* a man's thoughts except the spirit of the man which is in him" 1 Cor. 2.11
"I will *sing* with the spirit" 1 Cor. 14.15
"If you *bless* with the spirit" 1 Cor. 14.16
"I had no *rest* in my spirit" 2 Cor. 2.13 Darby
"We have the same spirit of *faith*" 2 Cor. 4.13
"A spirit of *wisdom* and of *revelation*" Eph. 1.17
"Your *love* in spirit" Col. 1.8 literal

From these many passages we can see readily that the spirit clearly senses and that such sensing is manifold. The Bible is not telling us here how our heart senses but rather how our *spirit* does. And it would appear that the sensing of the spirit is as inclusive as that of the soul. The spirit like the soul has its thoughts, feelings, and desires. But how we must learn to distinguish the spiritual from the soulical! We shall come to appreciate this difference if we are matured through the deeper work of the cross and the Spirit.

It is while a Christian lives spiritually that his spiritual sense develops fully. Before he experiences the dividing of soul and spirit and union with the Lord in one spirit, his spiritual sense is rather dull. But once he has had the power of the Holy Spirit poured into his spirit, his inner man is strengthened and it possesses the sense of the matured. Only then can he fathom the various senses of his spirit.

This spiritual sensing is called "intuition," for it impinges *directly* without reason or cause. Without passing through any procedure, it comes forth in a *straight* manner. Man's ordinary sensing is caused or brought out by people or things or events. We rejoice when there is reason to rejoice, grieve if there is justification to grieve and so forth. Each of these senses has its respective antecedent; hence we cannot conclude them to be expressions of intuition or direct sense. Spiritual sense, on the other hand, does not require any outside cause but emerges directly from within man.

Great similarities do exist between the soul and the spirit. But believers should not walk according to the soul, that is, they should not follow its thoughts, feelings and desires. The way God ordains for His children is a walk after the spirit; all other paths belong to the old creation and hence possess no spiritual value. But how to walk after the spirit? It is living by its intuition because the latter expresses the thought of the spirit which in turn expresses the mind of God.

Oftentimes we think of a certain thing we have good reason to do and our heart delights in it and finally our will decides to execute it; yet somehow, in the inner sanctuary of our being there seems to arise *an unuttered and soundless voice* strongly opposing what our mind, emotion or volition has entertained, felt, or decided. This strange complex seems to infer that this thing ought not to be done. Now such an experience as this may change according to altered conditions. For at other times we may sense in the inner depths that same wordless and noiseless monitor greatly urging, moving and constraining us to perform a certain thing which we view as highly unreasonable, as contrary to what we usually do or desire, and as something which we do not like to do.

What is this complex which is so unlike our mind, emotion and will? It is the intuition of the spirit: the spirit is expressing itself through our intuition. How distinctive the intuition is from our emotional feeling. Frequently we feel inclined to execute a certain act, but this inward, unarticulated intuition sharply warns against it. It is totally counter to our mind. The latter is located in the brain and is of a reasoning nature, while intuition is lodged elsewhere and is often opposed to reasoning. The Holy Spirit expresses His thought through this intuition. What we commonly refer to as being moved by the Spirit is but the Holy Spirit making us know His will intuitively by working upon our spirit. Just here can we differentiate between what comes from God's Spirit and what from ourselves and Satan. Because the Holy Spirit dwells in our spirit which is at the center of our being, His thought, expressed through our intuition, must arise from that innermost region. How contrary this is to thought which originates at the periphery of our being. If a notion should come from our outward man—that is, from the mind or emotion— then we realize it is but our own and not that of the Holy Spirit; for whatever is His must flow from the depths. The same distinction applies to what comes forth from Satan (those of demon possession excepted). He dwells not in our spirit but in the world: "he who is in you (the Holy Spirit) is greater than he who is in the world (Satan)" (1 John 4.4). Satan can only attack us from the outside in. He may work through the lust and sensations of the body or through the mind and emotion of the soul, for those two belong to the outward man. It therefore behooves us to learn to distinguish

our feelings as to whether they originate with the inner, or
come from the outer, man.

THE ANOINTING OF GOD

The intuition of which we have been speaking is exactly
the locus where occurs the anointing that teaches: "you have
been anointed by the Holy One, and you all *know*. . . . But
the anointing which you received from him *abides in you*,
and you have *no need that any one should teach you;* as his
anointing teaches you about everything, and is true, and is
no lie, just as it has taught you, abide in him" (1 John 2.20,
27). This portion of Scripture informs us quite lucidly where
and how the anointing of the Holy Spirit teaches us.

But before we delve into this passage may we first explain
the meaning of "knowing" and "understanding." We usually
do not make a distinction between these two words; in spiritual matters, however, the difference between them is incalculable: the spirit "knows" while the mind "understands." A
believer "knows" the things of God by the intuition of his
spirit. Strictly speaking, the mind can merely "understand";
it can never "know." Knowing is the work of intuition; understanding, the task of the mind. The Holy Spirit enables
our spirit to know; our spirit instructs the mind to understand. It may appear difficult to distinguish these two in the
abstract, but they are as disparate as wheat from weed in
experience. So ignorant are modern believers in their quest
to know the thought of the Holy Spirit that they do not even
realize how to distinguish "knowing" from "understanding."

Is it not true that we frequently experience this indescribable sense within us which makes us *know* whether or not to
do a certain thing? We may say we know the mind of the
Holy Spirit in our spirit. Nevertheless our mind may still fail
to *understand* what the meaning of it all is. In spiritual matters it is possible for us to know without understanding it.
Are there not times when, reaching our wit's end, we receive
the teaching of the Holy Spirit in our spirit and jubilantly
shout "I know it!"? And are there not times when our mind

receives light and understands what the Holy Spirit has
meant *long after* we have obeyed and acted on what He has
expressed in our intuition? Do we not at that moment ex-
claim "*Now* I understand it"? These experiences show us that
we "know" God's thought in our spirit's intuition but "understand" His guidance in the mind of our soul.

The Apostle John speaks of the operation of intuition
when he asserts that the anointing of the Lord, Who dwells
in the believer, shall instruct him in all things and enable
him to know all so that he has no need for anyone to teach
him. The Lord gives the Holy Spirit to every saint in order
that He may dwell in him and lead him into all truth. How
does He lead? Through the intuition. He unfolds His mind in
the believer's spirit. Intuition possesses the inherent ability
to discern His movement and its meaning. Just as the mind
instructs us in mundane affairs, so intuition teaches us in
spiritual affairs. Anointing in the original signifies "applying
ointment." This suggests how the Holy Spirit teaches and
speaks in man's spirit. He does not speak thunderously from
heaven nor does He cast the believer to the ground by an
irresistible force. Rather does He work very quietly in one's
spirit to impress something upon our intuition. In the same
way that a man's body feels soothed when ointment is applied, so our spirit gently senses the anointing of the Holy
Spirit. When intuition is aware of something, the spirit is
apprehending what He is saying.

To perform God's will a Christian need simply heed the
direction of his intuition. There is no necessity to ask others,
nor even to ask himself. The Anointing teaches him concerning everything. Not once will the Anointing leave him
nor permit him to choose independently. Any who wish to
walk after the spirit ought to recognize this. Our responsibility *is* none other than to accept instruction from the
Anointing. We need not decide our own way; indeed, He
will not allow us so to do. Whatever is not of the leading of
the Anointing is but our doing. The Anointing functions independently; He does not require our help. He expresses His
mind independently of our mind's searching or our emotion's

agitating. The Anointing operates in man's spirit to enable intuition to know His thought.

DISCERNMENT

Reading the context of this same portion of Scripture reveals how the Apostle is concerned with many false teachings and antichrists. He assures his readers that the same Holy One Who anoints them also teaches them to differentiate truth from lies and what is of Christ from what is of the antichrists. Christians do not require other men to instruct them since the indwelling Anointing teaches them everything. This is spiritual discernment, something greatly needed today. If we must pore over many theological references and reason, compare, research, observe and think with our mind until we ultimately reach an understanding of what is lie or what is truth, then only Christians with good minds and education would escape deception. But God has no respect for the old creation; He concludes that all except the newly created spirit must die and be destroyed. Can the wisdom which God demands to be destroyed assist people to know good and evil? No, most emphatically no! God puts His Spirit in every believer's spirit, regardless how sinful or dull he is. The indwelling Spirit shall teach him what is of God and what is not. This is why sometimes we can conjure up no logical reason for opposing a certain teaching, yet in the very depth of our being arises a resistance. We cannot explain it, but our inner sense tells us this is an error. Or contrarily we may hear some teaching which is entirely different from what we generally hold and which we will not like to follow, but is there not occasionally a still small voice that speaks persistently within us and contends that this is the way, walk you in it? Though we may muster many arguments against it, even overwhelming it with reason, nevertheless this inner small voice still insists that we are wrong.

Such experiences inform us that our intuition, the organ for the working of the Holy Spirit, is capable itself of distinguishing good from evil without any assistance from the mind's observation and investigation. No matter what his natural intellect may be, any individual who honestly and faithfully follows the Lord will be taught by the Anointing. The most learned doctor shares in the same foolishness with the dullest country folk when it comes to spiritual affairs; nay, the learned may make more mistakes than the dullard. False teachings are currently rampant. Many there are who with deceiving words disguise lies as truths. How necessary is this power of discernment in the spirit! The most appealing teaching, the cleverest brain, and the most enlightened advisors are undependable; only those who adhere intuitively to the teaching of the Anointing are preserved from being deceived in this time of theological confusion and supernatural manifestations. We should ask the Lord to make our spirit more active and pure. We should follow the still small voice that comes from our intuition instead of being overawed by people's knowledge and drawn away from the warning sounded within us. Otherwise we shall fall into heresy or become fanatical. If we quietly follow the teaching of the Anointing we shall be delivered from the compulsion of a noisy emotion and a confused mind.

DEALING WITH PEOPLE

Never should we judge other people; yet we surely need to know them so that we may comprehend both how to live with them and how to assist them. The ordinary way for man to know others is to inquire, observe and investigate—all of which, unfortunately, often lead us to blunder. Now we are not suggesting that these are categorically useless, but we do affirm that they occupy merely a secondary place in the knowledge of people. A pure spirit frequently discloses unmistakable discernment. Well do we remember when as children how we made certain remarks concerning various individuals we saw. As time went on how accurate these remarks proved to be. Many years have now passed; our knowledge, experience and observation have altogether been increased; yet somehow our ability to know people seems to be diminishing. When we made those remarks as children we had no suitable reason to advance for doing so other than

that we felt that way in our hearts. Many years later our
"sense" of that time was shown to have been correct. As a
child we never spoke out after once having carefully inves-
tigated or inquired, nor could we have ever given any good
reason for so speaking. What was it then? It was the operation of a pure intuition. Obviously the example we have just
set forth pertains to the natural. Nonetheless, in the things of
God our spiritual condition must be converted and become
as a little child if we desire to discern spiritually.

Let us observe our Lord Jesus. "And immediately Jesus,
perceiving in his spirit that they thus questioned within
themselves, said to them" (Mark 2.8). Do we not see there
the working of intuition? The Scripture does not state that
the Lord Jesus thought or felt in his heart nor does it say the
Holy Spirit told Him. It was His spirit that displayed this
perfect ability. The spiritual sense in the man Jesus Christ
was exceedingly pure, sensitive and noble; hence His spirit
detected immediately how the surrounding people questioned in their heart. He spoke to them according to what He
intuitively knew. This ought to be the normal condition of
every spiritual person. Our spirit indwelt by the Holy Spirit
is free to work and, filled with the power of knowledge, it
can exercise control over our whole being. Just as the human spirit of the Lord Jesus operated during His earthly
pilgrimage, even so shall our spirit be activated by the indwelling Spirit.

REVELATION

To know things in our intuition is what the Bible calls
revelation. Revelation has no other meaning than that the
Holy Spirit enables a believer to apprehend a particular matter by indicating the reality of it to his spirit. There is but
one kind of knowledge concerning either the Bible or God
which is valuable, and that is the truth revealed to our spirit
by God's Spirit. God does not explain Himself via man's
reasoning; never does man come to know God through rationalization. No matter how clever man's mind is nor how
much it understands about God, his knowledge of God re-

mains veiled. All he can do is rationalize what is behind the veil, because he has not penetrated the reality hidden from view. Since he has not yet "seen," man can "understand" but never can he "know." If there is no revelation, personal revelation, Christianity is worth nothing. Everyone who believes in God must have His revelation in his spirit, or else what he believes is not God but mere human wisdom, ideals or words. Such a faith cannot endure the test.

This kind of revelation is not a vision, a heavenly voice, a dream, or an external force which shakes the man. One may encounter these phenomena and still not have revelation. Revelation happens in the intuition—quietly, neither hastily nor slowly, soundless and yet with a message. How many denominate themselves Christians, though the Christianity they embrace is simply a kind of philosophy of life or of ethics, a few articles of truth, or some supernatural manifestations. Such an attitude will issue neither in a new birth nor in a new spirit. Numerous are these "Christians" whose spiritual usefulness measures up to zero. Not so are those who have received Christ, for by the grace of God they have perceived in their spirit the reality of the spiritual realm, which opens to them like the lifting of a veil. What they today *know* is far more profound than what their mind has comprehended; yea, it seems as though a new meaning has been imparted to all which they had only understood or comprehended in the past. Now everything is thoroughly and genuinely known, because the spirit has seen it. "We speak of what we *know*, and bear witness to what we *have seen*" (John 3.11). This is Christianity. Searching with intellect never delivers men; revelation in the spirit alone gives true knowledge of God.

ETERNAL LIFE

Many say, "If we believe, we have eternal life." What is this life we secure? It does point, to be sure, to future blessing. But what does eternal life mean for *today?* "And *this* is eternal life, that they *know* thee the only true God, and Jesus Christ whom thou has sent" (John 17.3). This life constitutes

for the here and now a new ability to know God and the
Lord Jesus. This is indeed true. Whoever believes in the
Lord and enjoys eternal life has obtained an intuitive knowledge of God which he never possessed before. Having
eternal life is not a slogan; it is a reality which can be demonstrated and exhibited in this present hour. Those without this
life can rationalize about God but they enjoy no personal
knowledge of Him. Only after one has received new life in
regeneration does he intuitively and *actually know* God.
People may understand the Bible, yet their spirit abides in
death. They may be familiar with theology, still their spirit
remains unquickened. They may even zealously serve in the
name of the Lord, but no new life is engendered within their
spirit. The Bible perceptively asks, "Canst thou by searching find out God? Canst thou find out the Almighty unto perfection?" (Job 11.7 ASV) No amount of mental laboring
can equip us to know God. Apart from the quickened spirit
within man no one is able to apprehend Him, not even with
his brain. The Bible recognizes just one kind of knowledge,
and that is the knowledge in the spirit's intuition.

GOD'S WAY OF GUIDING

As at the beginning a believer acquires his first knowledge
of God in his spirit, even so must he continue to know God
in his spirit. In a Christian life nothing is of any spiritual
benefit unless it flows from revelation in the intuition. Whatever does not issue from the spirit is not of God's will. Whatever we think or feel or decide, if not preceded by revelation
in the spirit, is reckoned as dead in the eyes of God. Should
a believer follow his sudden thought, the "burning fire" in
his heart, his natural inclination, his perfect reason, or his
rationalization, he is but activating his old man again. God's
will is not to be so known; He reveals Himself solely to man's
spirit. What is not revealed there is purely human activity.

The head is where God's will is understood, but it is never
the source of His will. The will of God originates in Himself,
Who by His Holy Spirit reveals it to the spirit of man. In
turn the latter causes the outward man to understand

through the mind what the inner man has known. Thus the
Christian is able to practice God's will. Now if instead of
seeking His purpose in the spirit a Christian should daily
search his mind, he will be confused, since thoughts often
change. He who follows his mind is not capable of saying at
any moment, "I *truly* know this is the will of God." Such
deep faith and assurance emerges only when one has received revelation in his spirit.

The revelation of God in our spirit is of two kinds: the
direct and the sought. By direct revelation we mean that
God, having a particular wish for the believer to do, draws
nigh and reveals it to the latter's spirit. Upon receiving such
a revelation in his intuition the believer acts accordingly. By
sought revelation we mean that a believer, having a special
need, approaches God with that need and seeks and waits
for an answer through God's movement in his spirit. The
revelation young believers receive is mostly the sought type;
that of the more matured ones is chiefly the direct kind. We
should quickly add, however, that these are not exclusively
so, only predominantly so. There lies the difficulty with the
young believer. While he ought to wait before the Lord, denying his thought, feeling and desire, he often becomes impatient waiting for His revelation and substitutes his own
disguised will for that of God. As a consequence he falls
under the accusation of his conscience. Granted that he genuinely has a heart to follow God's intent, he nonetheless unwittingly follows the thought of his mind because he lacks
spiritual knowledge. Who can avoid mistakes if he walks
without revelation?

Now we find true spiritual knowledge in this: only what
is appropriated in the spirit is spiritual knowledge; the rest
is wholly the mental kind. Let us inquire a moment, how
does God know things? How does He make His judgment?
By what knowledge does He control the universe? Does He
ascertain with His mind like man? Does He need to think
carefully before He understands? Does God depend upon
philosophy, logic and comparison to know a matter? Must
He search and investigate before He hits upon the solution?

Is the Almighty compelled to rely upon His brain? Decidedly not. God has no necessity to indulge in such sweating exercises. His knowledge and judgment is intuitive. As a matter of fact intuition is the common faculty of all spiritual
beings. The angels obey what they know as God's will intuitively; they do not arrive at a conclusion by way of argument, reason or contemplation. The difference between
knowing intuitively and knowing mentally is immeasurable.
Upon this very distinction hangs the outcome of spiritual
success or defeat. If it had been intended that a believer's
action or service was to be governed by rationalization and
common sense, no one would ever have attempted to carry
out those many glorious spiritual works of the past and the
present, because all of them supersede human reasoning.
Who would have dared do them if he had not first known
God's will intuitively?

Everyone who walks intimately with God, enjoying secret
communion and spiritual union, will receive God's revelation in his intuition and know unmistakably what he should
do. His actions obviously will attract no sympathy from men,
for they know not what he has seen. According to worldly
wisdom, his actions are utterly meaningless. Do not spiritual
believers suffer many oppositions of this kind? Have not the
worldly-wise labeled them as mad? Even their fleshly
brethren pass similar judgment on them. And the reason?
Because the old created life in worldly people or in believers
cannot understand the way of the Holy Spirit. How the
more rational believers do in fact criticize their less rational
brethren as "blindly zealous," not realizing that these "blindly zealous" are the truly spiritual ones, walking by the
revelation they intuitively have received.

We should be careful not to confuse intuition with emotion. In their zeal emotional Christians may display many
phenomena similar to those of spiritual Christians, but the
origin of these phenomena cannot be traced to intuition. Likewise in discernment rational Christians may act in many
ways like those who are spiritual, yet once again no revelation in intuition is involved. As emotional believers are souli-

cal, so are the rational. The spirit possesses a zeal which surpasses the emotional kind. The spiritual are "justified in the
spirit" (1 Tim. 3.16 ASV), not approved by the affections or
reasons of the flesh. Should we drop from the exalted position of the spirit into following the feeling and reasoning of
the flesh, we shall lose ground instantly and shall retreat, like
Abraham of old, into the visible and tangible Egypt for
help. The spirit and the soul move independently. As long
as the spirit has not yet ascended to hold sway over the total
man, the soul shall never cease to strive against it.

When a person's spirit has been quickened and subsequently strengthened by the power and discipline of the
Holy Spirit, his soul cedes its usurped place and returns to
submission. Increasingly the soul becomes the spirit's servant; similarly, the body, once subdued, becomes the soul's
servant. The spirit receives revelation of God in its faculty
of intuition, while the soul and the body unitedly execute
the will of the spirit. There is no end to such progress. Some
of the Lord's people may have more to deny than others,
for their spirit is not as pure because they have been far too
long saturated with mental knowledge and affections. Many
are so full of prejudice that they do not enjoy an open spirit
to accept God's truth. What they need are those requisite
dealings which can free their intuition to receive everything
from God.

We need to appreciate how fundamental is the difference
between spiritual and soulical experiences: spiritual experience is so designated because it begins with *God* and is
known in our *spirit*: soulical experience arises from the *man
himself* and does *not* emerge through the spirit. It is therefore quite possible for an unregenerated man to know fully
the Bible, to grasp accurately and expertly the essential
doctrines of Christianity, to apply zealously all his talents to
service, and to sway his audience with wonderful eloquence,
and yet remain within the realm of the soul without so much
as having crossed over one step, his spirit as dead as ever.
People shall never enter the kingdom of God through our
encouragement, persuasion, argument, inducement, excite-

ment, or attraction; entrance can be gained only by new birth, by nothing less than the resurrection of the spirit. The new life which invades us at regeneration brings with it many inherent abilities, not the least of which is the intuitive power of knowing God.

Does it hence mean that man's mind or brain is totally useless? Of course not. It obviously has its part to play. But we need to remember that intellect is of secondary, not of primary, importance. We do not sense God and the realities of God by our intellect; else eternal life would be meaningless. This eternal life or new life is the spirit mentioned in John 3. We apprehend God through this newly obtained eternal life or spirit. The mind's role is to explain to our outward man what we know in our spirit and additionally to form it into words for others to understand. Paul stresses most emphatically in his letters that the gospel he preaches does not originate with man: it is not acquired wholesale from one man's mind and retailed to the mind of others but is discovered through revelation. Although a believing man may have the best of minds, his teaching is nevertheless not to be derived from his thinking, whether sudden or progressive. His mind merely cooperates with his spirit in communicating to others the revelation his intuition has received. The brain is but the transmitting, not the receiving, mechanism of spiritual knowledge.

God communes with us entirely in the spirit. Save by its intuition there is no way of knowing God. In his spirit man soars into the eternal unseen realm of God. Intuition may be characterized as the brain of the inner sanctuary. When we say man's spirit is dead, we are indicating his intuition is insensitive to God and His realities. When we say the spirit controls the whole man, we mean the various parts of the soul and all the members of the body adhere closely to God's intuitively known will. We wish to underscore our point that regeneration is totally indispensable. Man's soulical faculties cannot perceive God: nothing else can be a substitute for intuition. Except a man receives a new life from God and has his intuition resurrected, he is eternally separated from God.

How fundamental new birth is. It is not just a term, nor is it purely a moral alteration, but the life of God actually enters our spirit and quickens its intuition. How utterly impossible for man to please God with his good deeds: they are simply the operations of the soul: his intuition is dead to God. Equally impossible is it for man to beget himself anew, because there is nothing in him which can produce new life. Unless God generates him he is not able to beget himself. Also worthless in the work of God is man's understanding of teachings, for the work must be done by *God*. What then can man do other than deliver himself into the hands of God for Him to work? His spirit shall remain forever dead unless he confesses that everything pertaining to man is useless and unless he stands in the place of death with the Lord Jesus and accepts His life.

Man's way cannot envisage acceptance of the Lord Jesus as Savior and a quickening of his spirit's intuition, but insists on substituting his mind for intuition. He thinks and cogitates until he creates many philosophies, ethics, or religions. But what is God's pronouncement? "As the heavens are higher than the earth, so are my ways higher than your ways and my thoughts than your thoughts" (Is. 55.9). However intensively man may contemplate, his thoughts are earthly and not heavenly. After regeneration, God enables our intuition to know His thought and to apprehend His way so that we may follow Him. Yet how forgetful believers are! We forget what we learned at regeneration. Countless are those saints who daily walk by their head and heart. In service we still attempt to move people's mind, emotion and will by our intellect, zeal and effort. God desires to teach us the fact that in service the soul, ours and everyone else's, is void of any spiritual value or worth. He actually allows us to be defeated in spiritual work and to become despondent, cold and fruitless in order that He may destroy our natural life with its wisdom, fervor, and ability. Such a lesson as this cannot be learned in one or two days. God must instruct us throughout our lifetime in order to make us realize that apart from following the spirit's intuition everything else is vain.

Now comes the crisis. Which will we follow when intuition and soul clash in their opinions? This will determine who is to rule over our life and which way we shall go. Our outer man and our inner man—the man of the flesh and the man of the spirit—are struggling for supremacy. In the early days of our Christian walk our spirit fought with the lusts of our flesh; today it is a battle between our spirit and our soul. Formerly the engagement was over the issue of sin; presently it is not a matter of good and evil but of natural good versus God's goodness. We contended for the quality of things before, but now we are concerned with the source of things. It is a conflict of the inward against the outward man, a war between God's will and man's good intention. To learn how to walk after the spirit is a lifetime's occupation for the new man. If one wholly follows the spirit, he shall overcome the man of the flesh completely. Through the strengthening by the Holy Spirit of the spirit in the new man, the believer shall be able to destroy totally his minding of the flesh so as to mind the things of the spirit. This is life and peace.

CHAPTER 2
COMMUNION

WE COMMUNICATE with the material world through the body. We communicate with the spiritual world through the spirit. This communication with the spiritual is not carried on by means of the mind or emotion but through the spirit or its intuitive faculty. It is easy for us to understand the nature of the communion between God and man if we have seen the operation of our intuition. In order to worship and fellowship with God man must possess a nature similar to His. "God is *spirit,* and those who worship him must worship in *spirit* and truth" (John 4.24). There can be no communication between different natures; hence both the unregenerate whose spirit obviously has not been quickened and the regenerate who does not use his spirit to worship are equally unqualified to have genuine fellowship with God. Lofty sentiments and noble feelings do not bring people into spiritual reality nor do they forge personal communion with God. Our fellowship with Him is experienced in the deepest place of our entire being, deeper than our thought, feeling and will, even in the intuition of our spirit.

A close scrutiny of 1 Corinthians 2.9-3.2 can provide a very clear view of how man communes with God and how man knows the realities of God through the spirit's intuition.

THE HEART OF MAN

"What no eye has seen, nor ear heard, nor the heart of man conceived, what God has prepared for those who love him" (v.9). The larger context of this one verse speaks of

God and the things of God. What He has prepared can neither be seen or heard by man's outward body nor conceived by his inward heart. The "heart of man" includes among other facets man's understanding, mind and intellect. Man's thought cannot envisage God's work, for the latter transcends the former. It is therefore evident that he who desires to know and commune with God cannot depend solely upon his thought.

THE HOLY SPIRIT

"God has revealed to us through the Spirit. For the Spirit searches everything; even the depths of God" (v.10). This verse sets forth the fact that the *Holy Spirit searches* everything and not that our mind conceives all. Only the Holy Spirit knows the depths of God. He knows what man does not know. By His intuition the Spirit searches everything. God is thus able to reveal through Him what our heart has never conceived. This "revealing" is not acquired after much thinking, for our heart cannot even conceive it. It is a revelation; it does not require the help of our thought.

The next two verses tell us how God reveals Himself.

THE SPIRIT OF MAN

"For what person knows a man's thoughts except the spirit of the man which is in him? So also no one comprehends the thoughts of God except the Spirit of God. Now we have received not the spirit of the world, but the Spirit which is from God, that we might understand the gifts bestowed on us by God" (vv.11 and 12). No one knows man's thoughts except the spirit of man; likewise, no one knows the things of God but the Holy Spirit. Man's spirit as well as God's Spirit apprehend things directly, not by deducing or searching. They perceive through the faculty of intuition. Since the Holy Spirit alone knows the things of God, we must receive the Holy Spirit if we also would know those things. The spirit of the world is cut off from communication with God. It is a dead spirit: it cannot effect communion with Him. The Holy Spirit, on the other hand, comprehends the things of God; therefore, by receiving in our intuition what the Holy Spirit knows, we too shall understand the realities of God. "We have received . . . the Spirit which is from God, that we might understand the gifts bestowed on us by God."

How then do *we know?* Verse 11 tells us man knows by his spirit. The Holy Spirit unfolds to our spirit what He knows intuitively so that we too may know intuitively. When the Holy Spirit discloses the matters pertaining to God He does so not to our mind nor to any other organ but to our spirit. God knows this is the sole place in man which can apprehend man's things as well as His things. The mind is not the place for knowing these things. While it is true that the mind can think and conceive many matters, it nonetheless cannot *know* them.

From this we can appreciate how highly God esteems the regenerated spirit of man. Before new birth man's spirit was dead. God had no way of unfolding His mind to such a man. The cleverest brain fails to know the mind of God. Both God's fellowship with man and man's worship of God are contingent upon the regenerated spirit of man. Without this revitalized component God and man are hopelessly separated—neither can come or go to the other. The first step towards communion between God and man must be this quickening of man's spirit.

Because man enjoys a free will he has authority to decide his own matters. That explains why he continues to encounter many temptations following new birth. Due to his foolishness or perhaps his prejudice he may not yield the rightful position to his spirit and its intuition. God accepts this spirit as the one place where He will commune with man and man with Him. But the believer still walks by his mind or emotion. How many times he completely ignores the voice of intuition. His principle of living is to adhere to what he himself considers reasonable, beautiful, delightful, or interesting. Even should he have a heart to do God's will, he usually will take either his impulsive idea or his more logical thought as the mind of God, not realizing that what he ought to follow is the thought expressed by the Holy

Spirit in his intuition. He sometimes may be willing to hear the voice of intuition, but failing to keep his feelings quiet he finds that voice blurred and confused. Walking after the spirit consequently becomes an occasional affair instead of forming a daily continuous experience in the Christian's life.

If the *initial* knowing of God's will is so difficult, who can wonder at the lack of further and more profound revelation? How then can we ever truly know in our spirit God's plan for the end of this age, the reality of spiritual warfare, and the deeper truths of the Bible? For our worship merely corresponds to what we think is best or what we feel on the spur of the moment. And to commune with the Lord in our intuition naturally becomes an unheard of phenomenon.

A believer must recognize that the Holy Spirit alone comprehends the things of God—and that intuitively. He is the one Person Who can convey this knowledge to man. But for anyone to obtain such knowledge he must appropriate it through the proper means; namely, he must receive with his intuition what the Holy Spirit intuitively knows. The conjunction of these two intuitions enables man to apprehend the mind of God.

"And we impart this in words not taught by human wisdom but taught by the Spirit, interpreting spiritual truths to those who possess the Spirit" (v.13). How are we going to impart to others the things of God which we have discerned in our spirit's intuition? Having come to know the realities of God, our responsibility now is to proclaim them. The Apostle Paul declares he does not transmit them in terms taught by human wisdom. That wisdom belongs to a man's mind and is the product of man's brain. Paul categorically asserts that he does not employ the words which come from the mind to communicate what his spirit knows concerning the things of God. Paul in himself possesses great wisdom. He is perfectly able to formulate many new and wonderful phrases and to deliver his message eloquently with good organization and illustrative parables. He knows how to make his audience understand what he means to say. He nevertheless refuses to use the terminology taught by human wisdom. This declaration and attitude of the Apostle Paul indicate that man's mind is not only useless in *knowing* the things of God but is also secondary in *imparting* spiritual knowledge.

The Apostle articulates God's realities in phraseology taught by the Spirit. In his intuition he receives His instruction. Nothing in the life of a Christian is of any value save that which is in his spirit. Even in relating spiritual knowledge he needs to employ spiritual words. Intuition appropriates not only the thing which the Holy Spirit unfolds but also the words taught by the same Spirit, in order to explain to others what has been revealed. How often a believer tries to impart to others what has been revealed so clearly to him by God; yet try as he may, he finds no words to convey the fundamental meaning of what has been disclosed. Why? Because he has not received words in his spirit. At other times, as he waits before the Lord, the believer senses something rising in the center of his being—perhaps but a few words. With those few words, however, he is able to communicate adequately at a meeting what has been revealed to him. He comes to realize how God actually uses him to testify for the Lord.

Such experiences attest the importance of the "utterance" given by the Holy Spirit. There are two kinds of utterance, the natural and the Spirit-given. The type of utterance recorded in Acts 2.4 is indispensable in spiritual service. However eloquent our natural utterance, it remains powerless to truly communicate the things of God. We may view ourselves as having spoken quite well; yet we have not succeeded in expressing the thought of the Spirit. Spiritual words, that is, terminology received in the spirit, can alone articulate spiritual knowledge. If we are burdened with the message of the Lord in our spirit, as though a fire were burning within, and yet have not the means to discharge that burden, we should wait for the "utterance" to be given by the Spirit so that we may proclaim the message of our spirit and discharge that burden. Should we inadvertently employ language taught by human wisdom instead of waiting for the words bestowed intuitively by the Holy Spirit, we shall find our spiritual effectiveness comes to nought. Speech merely grounded in earthly wisdom can only move people to say that the theory advanced is indeed good. Sometimes we enjoy many spiritual experiences, but we are at a loss how to articulate them until other believers unlock them with a word. This is because until the moment we heard others uttering our experience in simple terms, we still had not received in our spirit explicit words from the Lord.

Spiritual truths must be explained with spiritual phrases. We must employ spiritual means to reach spiritual ends. This is what the Lord especially wishes to teach us today. Spiritual goals need to be perfected through corresponding spiritual processes. The fleshly as fleshly will never become spiritual. If we hope to arrive at our spiritual objectives with our minds and emotions, we as it were are expecting sweet water to pour forth from fountains of bitter water. All matters pertaining to God—such as seeking His will, obeying His commandments, proclaiming His message—are effective only if they arise out of fellowship with God in the spirit. Whatever is performed through our thoughts, talents or methods is accounted by God as dead.

THE SOULICAL AND THE SPIRITUAL

"The unspiritual (original, *soulical*) man does not *receive* the gifts of the Spirit of God, for they are folly to him, and he is not able to *understand* them because they are spiritually discerned" (v.14). The soulical are those who have not yet been born anew and who hence do not possess a new spirit. Since their intuitive faculty is dead to God, all which they have are the faculties of the soul. They are well able to decide what they like through reason and affection but, not having a regenerated spirit, they are powerless to receive the things of the Spirit of God. Although these individuals can think and observe, they still lack basic intuitive power; they cannot take in what God reveals exclusively to man's spirit. How utterly inadequate are the natural endowments of man. He truly has much, but nothing can substitute for the operation of intuition. Because man is dead to God, no organ exists in him by which he can take in the things of God. Nothing in a soulical man is capable of communing with Him. Man's most respectable mind, intellect and reasoning are as corrupt as his lusts and passions; both equally are incompetent to apprehend God. Even a regenerated man, if he attempts to communicate with God by using his mind and observation (just as the unregenerate does) instead of exercising his renewed spirit, is absolutely impotent to perceive the realities of God. Those elements which belong to us naturally do not change their operations following regeneration. A mind is still a mind and a will, a will: these can never be turned into organs capable of communion with God.

Not only can the soulical person not receive the things of God, he even regards them as folly. According to the valuation of his mind, matters known by intuition are downright foolishness because they are all unreasonable, against human nature, contrary to worldly wisdom, or in conflict with common sense. The mind delights in whatever is logical, open to analysis, and psychologically appealing. God, however, is not governed by man's law and hence His actions are folly to the soulical. The folly mentioned in this particular chapter unquestionably refers to the crucifixion of the Lord Jesus. The word of the cross speaks not only of the Savior Who died in our stead but also of the believers who have died with the Savior. Everything naturally belonging to believers must go through the death of the cross. The mind may accept this as a theory, but it surely will oppose it as a practice.

Since the soulical person does not welcome this word of the cross, he obviously cannot comprehend what it is all about. Reception precedes knowledge. The ability or inability to receive tests the presence or absence of a quickened spirit. The capacity or incapacity to know manifests the vital or the moribund character of the intuitive faculty. The spirit first must be quickened before one is able to take in the things of God. With an enlivened spirit one is also given the intuitive ability to appropriate the things of God. Who knows a man's thoughts except the spirit of the man? A soulical person cannot discern God's realities because he does not enjoy that new spirit which carries within it the intuitive power of discernment.

The Apostle Paul proceeds to explain why the soulical man is incompetent to receive and to know matters pertaining to God: "Because they are spiritually discerned." Do we not notice how the Holy Spirit repeatedly stresses the fact that man's spirit is the place of communion with God? The focal point of this particular portion of Scripture is to prove and demonstrate that man's spirit is basic to, and exclusive in, any fellowship with God and the knowledge of divine matters.

Each element has its own particular use. The spirit is employed to know the heavenly realities. Now we are not trying to disparage the use of the soul's faculties. They *are* useful, but here they must play a *secondary* role. They should be under control and not be the controller. The mind should submit to the spirit's rule and should follow what intuition fathoms of the will of God. It ought not conceive its own ideas and then demand that the whole man comply. Emotion too should obey the dictates of the spirit. Its love or hate must follow the affection of the spirit and not its own. The will also should bend to what God has revealed intuitively in the spirit. It must not prefer those choices which are other than the will of God. Were these soulical faculties kept in secondary position the believer would make tremendous strides in his spiritual walk. Unfortunately most Christians give them first place, thus eliminating the spirit's position. Is it any wonder that they do not live a spiritual life nor are of any spiritual worth? The spirit needs to be restored to its ordained position. A believer must learn to wait *in the spirit* for the revelation of God. Unless it ascends to its rightful place a man is barred from knowing what the spirit alone can know. That is why verse 13 adds, "interpreting spiritual truths to those who possess the Spirit," for only the spiritually sensitive can know things in the spirit.

"The spiritual man judges all things, but is himself to be judged by no one" (v.15). The spiritual man is one whose spirit dominates and who has a highly sensitive intuition. It is qualified to perform its functions because its quietness is undisturbed by the mind, emotion and will of the soul.

Why can the spiritual man judge all matters? Because his intuition leans on the Holy Spirit for its knowledge. Why is he not judged by anyone? Simply because no one knows how and what the Holy Spirit imparts to his intuition. If a believer's knowledge depends on his intellect, then besides those who are naturally talented no one can judge in all respects. Learning and worldly education would be indispensable. And such a learned one would also be judged by those who are as wise or even wiser than he, for they certainly could understand the train of his thought. Spiritual knowledge, however, is based on the spirit's intuition. There is no limit to a Christian's knowledge if he is spiritual and possesses a sensitive intuition. His mind may be dull but the Holy Spirit is able to lead him into spiritual reality and his spirit is able to enlighten his mind. The way the Spirit reveals Himself does indeed surpass the expectation of man.

"For who has known the mind of the Lord so as to instruct him? But we have the mind of Christ" (v.16). Here is posed a problem. No one in the world has known the mind of the Lord so as to instruct Him because all men are soulical. The only way to apprehend God is by intuition. How can a person whose spirit is dead ever know the mind of God? This explains why no such persons as this can judge the spiritual man, for none of these have known the mind of the Lord. These are naturally the soulical people. On the other hand, the spiritual ones know the mind of the Lord for they have a responsive intuition. But the soulical cannot know because their intuition is not operative; hence they enjoy no fellowship with God. The meaning here is that the soulical can neither know the mind of the Lord nor that of those spiritual ones who are fully committed to Him.

"But we . . ." indicates that the "we" is different from those soulical people. "We" includes all the saved believers, many of whom perhaps continue to be fleshly. "But we have the mind of Christ." We who have been regenerated, whether babes or grownups, possess the mind of Christ and discern His thoughts. Because we have a resurrected intuition we are able to know and have known already what Christ has prepared for us in the future (v.9). The soulical do not know, but we, the regenerate, do know. The difference is in having or not having the spirit.

THE SPIRITUAL AND THE FLESHLY

"But I, brethren, could not address you as spiritual men, but as men of the flesh, as babes in Christ. I fed you with milk, not solid food; for you were not ready for it; and even yet you are not ready" (3.1-2). These words are closely related to the preceding verses and their teaching follows the line laid down above which speaks of the spirit of man. Now we all recognize that the dividing of the Scriptures into chapters and verses was contrived for the convenience of the readers and was not something at all revealed by the Holy Spirit. These words of verses 1 and 2 of 1 Corinthians 3 should be read in connection with those of the preceding chapter.

How incisive is Paul's spiritual sense. He is acquainted with all his readers, whether they are spiritual or fleshly, whether wholly controlled by the spirit or frequently governed by the flesh. He does not therefore disregard the condition of his readers' receptivity and pour out his thoughts at random simply because he is speaking of spiritual affairs. He will only communicate "spiritual things with spiritual" (v.13 RSV marginal). Paul's communication depends not on how much *he* knows, but on how much his *readers* can assimilate. There is no boasting here of his own knowledge. The Apostle has spiritual phraseology as well as spiritual knowledge; he accordingly knows how to deal with believers of all kinds. Not all terms which articulate the deep mystery of God are spiritual terms; only those which are taught in the spirit by the Holy Spirit are. And they are not necessarily profound words: they may in fact be very common and ordinary: yet *these* words are taught by the Holy Spirit and apprehended in the

spirit. When these are uttered they then produce considerable spiritual results.

What the Apostle writes in these two verses and in verse
15 of the previous chapter resolves one interesting paradox;
namely, if the spirit of man knows the things which belong to
man and the spiritual man judges all things, why then are
there so many spirit-renewed Christians who nonetheless
do not sense that they have a spirit or who are not able to
know the deep things of God through their spirit? The answer
is: "the *spiritual* man judges all things" (v.15). Though all
Christians *possess* a regenerated spirit, not all Christians are
spiritual. Many are still fleshly. Man's intuition has in truth
been quickened, but man must give intuition its rightful
place, providing it opportunity to operate. Or else it will be
suppressed, unable to commune with God, or to know what
it could know. Spiritual Christians do not walk by their soul
life; they have delivered all its faculties to the cross and
relegated them to a position of submission so that their intuition can receive God's revelation freely. Afterwards their
mind, emotion and will voluntarily comply with this revelation. Such is not the case with fleshly Christians. Regenerated
and alive to God intuitively, they have every opportunity to
be spiritual; but they remain bound to the flesh instead. The
lusts of the flesh remain so exceedingly powerful as to drive
these Christians to sin. Their carnal mind is still full of wandering thoughts, reasons and plans; their emotion runs wild
with many carnal interests, desires and tendencies; and their
will formulates many worldly judgments, arguments and
opinions. They are so occupied in following the flesh that they
have neither time nor inclination to listen to the voice of
intuition. Since the voice of the spirit is usually very soft,
it cannot be heard unless it is listened to attentively with
everything else quieted. How then can it be heard if the various parts of the flesh are inordinately active? When believers
are governed by the flesh they become influenced by it to
such an extent that their spirit grows dull and they are
unable to take solid food.

The Bible compares a newly regenerated believer to a baby. The life in his spirit which he newly possesses is as tiny and weak as a baby naturally born. There is nothing wrong with his being a baby as long as he does not remain too great a time in that stage. Every adult must begin as a child. But should he persist as such very long, his spirit never progressing beyond what it was when he was first regenerated some years before, then something is drastically wrong. Man's spirit can grow; the spirit's intuition is able to wax stronger. A newly regenerated person is like a new-born baby who has no self-consciousness and whose nerves are wobbly in function. His spirtual life may be compared to a spark of fire. His intuitive power is extremely weak and not effective. But a baby must grow daily. His knowledge must increase continuously through exercise, training, and growth until he has become fully self-conscious and knows how to skillfully exercise all his senses. Even so must a believer. Upon regeneration he needs to gradually exercise his intuition. Each exercise means an increase in experience, knowledge and spiritual stature. Just as a man's senses are not born with matured awareness, so a believer's intuition is not born highly sensitive.

All this does not signify, however, that the soulish Christians who long remain babes have no outward dealings with their sins, experience no increase in their knowledge of the Bible, exert no effort to serve the Lord, or receive no gift of the Holy Spirit. The saints at Corinth encountered all of these. They "were enriched in (Christ) with all speech and all knowledge . . . not lacking in any spiritual gift" (1 Cor. 1.5,7). From the human point of view, are these not signs of growth? We probably would regard the Corinthian believers as most spiritual; yet the Apostle viewed them as babes, as men of the flesh. Why is it that the increase in speech, knowledge and gifts was not considered growth? This uncovers an intensely significant fact, which is, that though the saints at Corinth grew in these outward endowments they failed to grow in their *spirit*. Their intuition did not wax stronger. Increase in preaching eloquence, Bible

knowledge and spiritual gift is not reckoned as increase of
spiritual life! If the believer's spirit—that which is capable
of communing with God—does not grow stronger and keener, God judges that he has not grown at all!

How many of the Lord's people today are developing in
the wrong direction! Many assume that upon being saved
they must seek higher Bible knowledge, better utterance in
preaching, and more spiritual gifts. They forget it is their
spirit that must advance. Speech, knowledge and gift are
purely outward matters; by contrast intuition is inward.
Quite sad is the sight of that Christian who allows his spirit
to persist as a babe, but who concomitantly fills his soul life
with speech, knowledge and gift. These articles are valuable,
but how can they be compared with the value of the spirit?
What God has newly created in us is this spirit (or spiritual
life), and what should develop into matured manhood is
likewise this spirit. Should we commit the serious mistake of
seeking the enrichment of the soul life instead of the increase
of this spiritual life with its intuition, we shall have made
no progress at all in God's eye. God considers our spirit all-
important; and so He cares for its growth. No matter how
much our mind, emotion and will may gain by speech,
knowledge and gift, it is all deemed by God as vain if our
spirit is not developing.

We daily expect to have more power, more knowledge,
more gifts, more eloquence; yet the Bible contends that even
if we have more of these elements we do not necessarily
progress in spiritual life. On the contrary, our spiritual walk
may remain the same without advancing a mile. Paul candidly reminds the believers at Corinth: "You were not ready
for it; and *even yet* you are not ready." In what were they
unprepared? They were not prepared to serve God with their
intuition, to know more of God intuitively, to receive His
revelation in their intuition. They were obviously not ready
when they first believed in the Lord; but now years later,
though enriched in speech, knowledge and gifts, they still
were not so. By those two words—"even yet"—the Apostle
signified that though they were replete with outward en-

richments their spiritual life had made no progress since they first believed. Real advancement is measured by the growth of the spirit and its intuition; the rest belongs to the flesh. This should be impressed indelibly on our hearts.

How sad that believers today seem to achieve progress in almost every sphere except in that of their spirit. After trusting the Lord for many years, they continue to lament: "I do not feel I have a spirit." The difference between our mind and God's mind is wide. We, like those at Corinth, try successfully to garner much so-called spiritual knowledge by exercising the intellect of our mind. Unfortunately the increase of our mind does not and cannot substitute the maturing in our intuition. To God we appear unchanged. We must henceforth remember that the increase God pre-eminently desires is not in our outward man but in the inward man and its intuition. He expects the new life which we receive at regeneration to enlarge. And all which belongs to the old creation He expects to be denied.

A believer fails to be spiritual because he is influenced too much by the flesh. Only one whose intuition is alive and who enjoys uninterrupted communion with God knows the deep truths of God. If the intuitive power is weak, what else can be absorbed except milk? Milk is pre-digested food. What this denotes is that the soulish believer cannot maintain clear fellowship with God in the spirit's intuition and hence must depend upon other more advanced Christians for the things of God. Matured Christians fellowship with God in their intuition and then transform what they have been shown into milk for the babes in Christ. The Lord permits such a thing in the life of a beginner, but He takes no pleasure in having His people remain dull and powerless in communing directly with Him. Feeding on milk indicates the person is far less capable of communing with God directly and instead relies on others to transmit God's message to himself. The matured has his intuition fully exercised to distinguish good from evil. We are of no spiritual utility if we have many ideas but do not possess the ability to commune with God and know His realities with our intuition.

The Christians at Corinth ranked high in speech, knowledge, gifts, but how was their spiritual life? Almost totally inactive. The church at Corinth was a carnal church, for all she had she had in the mind.

Many of the Lord's people currently commit the same error as did the saints at Corinth. The words of the Lord are spirit and life, but these people do not accept the words accordingly. They investigate theological problems with a very cold mind and search the hidden meaning of the Bible with the design of presenting the best interpretation. They satisfy their lust for knowledge. They communicate what they have found by writing and preaching. Excellent though their thoughts, arguments and outlines may be, seemingly most spiritual too, God nevertheless looks on these achievements as dead weights because they have not been achieved in the spirit. They have simply passed from one man's mind to another man's mind. Some readers or hearers may protest that they are helped, but the question is, *what* is helped? Beyond assisting the mind to acquire additional ideas, nothing else has happened. Such knowledge adds nothing to spiritual effectiveness. Only what comes from the spirit can enter the spirits of others; that which comes from the mind can only reach the minds of others. Finally, what comes from the Holy Spirit enters our spirit, and whatever the Holy Spirit transmits through our spirit can reach the spirits of others.

THE SPIRIT OF WISDOM AND REVELATION

In our communion with God the spirit of wisdom and revelation is imperative. "The God of our Lord Jesus Christ, the Father of glory, may give you a spirit of wisdom and of revelation in the knowledge of him" (Eph. 1.17). When a new spirit is received at regeneration its functions await development, for they presently lie dormant there. The Apostle Paul prayed for the regenerated believers at Ephesus, desiring that they receive the spirit of wisdom and revelation so that they might know God intuitively. Whether

COMMUNION 101

this ability is a hidden function of the believer's spirit which is activated through prayer or whether it is something added by the Holy Spirit to the believer's spirit as a result of prayer, we do not know. Yet one thing is certain: this spirit of wisdom and revelation is essential to one's communion with God. We also recognize that it can be obtained through prayer.

Although our intuition is capable of communing with God it requires wisdom and revelation. We need it to know what is of God and what is of ourselves. We must have wisdom to discern the enemy's counterfeit as well as his attack. We also require it to know how to conduct ourselves among men. In a thousand different ways we need God's wisdom, for we are foolish and prone to make mistakes. How difficult for us to execute God's will in all matters, but He will grant us the necessary equipment. He does not impart it to our brain; rather, He dispenses the spirit of wisdom to us so that we may have wisdom in our spirit. God gives it to our intuition for He will lead us through intuition into the way of wisdom. While our mind may indeed remain dull, our intuition is full of wisdom. Often when our own wisdom seems to have reached its end, there gradually rises from within us another kind to guide us. Wisdom and revelation are closely linked because all God's disclosures are those of wisdom. If we live naturally we have no way to figure out God. Nothing but darkness resides in the natural man. God and matters divine stretch far beyond the reaches of our mind. And although our spirit may even be quickened, it still dwells in darkness if there is no unfolding from the Holy Spirit. A *quickened* spirit only indicates that it is *at last capable of receiving God's revelation. It does not mean that it can now move independently.*

In our communion with God He frequently gives revelation. We ought to pray for such. The spirit of revelation implies that God reveals in the spirit. The spirit of wisdom and revelation signifies where God reveals Himself and how He imparts to us His wisdom. An impulsive thought is not to be interpreted as belonging to the spirit of revelation. Only what we intuitively know of the mind of God through the operation of the Holy Spirit in our spirit ever constitutes the spirit of revelation. God communes with us there and nowhere else.

The spirit of wisdom and revelation affords us true knowledge of God; all else is skin deep, imaginary, superficial, and therefore false. We frequently speak of God's holiness, righteousness, mercy, love, and other virtues. Man's mind *is* capable of conceiving these attributes of God, yet such mental knowledge is like looking through a stone wall. When however a believer has received revelation from God concerning His holiness, he sees himself corrupted to the core and void of any cleanliness before the light of God's dwelling in unapproachable light where no sinful, natural man can draw nigh. Oh, that many among us might be given such an experience as *that*. And thereafter let us compare the one who has received such a disclosure of God's holiness with the other who has no such experience yet easily speaks of His holiness. They may perhaps employ the same terminology, but the word articulated by the first seems to be many times weightier than that of the second person. The first one appears to speak with his whole being and not just with his lips. The spirit of revelation alone explains it. And this applies equally to all other truths in the Bible. Sometimes we understand a certain truth and recognize its importance, but only after that particular truth is gradually unfolded by God to our spirit are we able to speak with a special emphasis.

Whatever we gather outwardly which is not inwardly disclosed can neither move ourselves nor others. Revelation in the spirit alone contains spiritual potency. To commune with God is to receive His revelation in the spirit. Rare are God's disclosures for many of us because rarely do we wait on Him for them. How can we compare a preoccupied natural life with a life walked according to revelation? But if we are willing to provide God the opportunity, we shall receive revelation quite often indeed. The life of the Apostles abundantly substantiates this assertion.

SPIRITUAL UNDERSTANDING

There is a soulish as well as a spiritual wisdom. The first springs from man's mind while the second is supplied to the spirit by God. Education may remedy any lack of understanding and wisdom in a natural man, but it cannot alter his natural endowment. Spiritual wisdom, though, may be realized through believing prayer (James 1.5). One thing which we ought to keep in mind is, that in redemption "God shows no partiality" (Acts 10.34). He places all sinners, wise or foolish, on the *same* footing, and confers upon them the *same* salvation. As the entire being of the wise is totally corrupted so is that of the foolish. In God's sight the mind of the wise is as nonefficacious as that of the foolish. Both need the regeneration of the spirit; and after that it is no easier for the wise man than for the foolish to know the words of God. Now of course it is quite difficult for a very foolish person to know God; but is it less difficult for the wisest among men? Not at all, because God must be known in the spirit by everyone. Their minds may be unalike, yet both their spirits are dead and hence equally foolish and deficient in divine matters. Man's natural cleverness does not help him to know God and God's truth. No doubt the wise one is easier to reason with and is quicker in understanding, but it is altogether limited to the mental realm, utterly contrary to intuitive knowledge.

Do not assume that after regeneration the wise have advantage over the foolish in making spiritual progress. Unless they are more faithful and submissive, their better mental comprehension adds nothing to their intuitive knowledge. Man's old creation never serves as the source of the new creation. Spiritual advancement is measured by faithful obedience. Natural endowment does not affect spiritual life one way or the other, although it yields priority to the flesh. In spiritual experience everybody begins at the same starting point, passes through the same processes, and obtains the same results. All regenerated believers, including the naturally wise, must consequently seek spiritual understanding, without which no one can maintain normal fellowship with God. Nothing can take the place of spiritual understanding.

"That you may be filled with the knowledge of his will in all spiritual wisdom and understanding, to lead a life worthy of the Lord, fully pleasing to him, bearing fruit in every good work and increasing in the knowledge of God" (Col. 1.9-10). This is what Paul prayed for on behalf of the saints at Colossae. In this prayer we find that true knowledge of God's will is preceded by spiritual understanding and followed by: (1) leading a life worthy of the Lord, fully pleasing to Him; (2) bearing fruit in every good work; and (3) increasing in the knowledge of God.

No matter how good man's natural endowment is, he cannot know God's will by that means. It requires spiritual comprehension to know His will and to commune with Him. Only spiritual understanding can penetrate the spiritual realm. The natural kind may grasp some teachings but these stay in the mind and are unable to flow as life. Because spiritual understanding comes from the spirit it can transform what is understood into life. Have we now perceived that all true knowledge emerges from the spirit? The spirit of revelation moves hand in hand with spiritual understanding. God grants us the spirit of wisdom and revelation as well as spiritual comprehension. The wisdom and revelation we obtain in the spirit needs to be understood spiritually. Revelation is what we receive from God; understanding assists us to comprehend what is revealed. Spiritual understanding furnishes us the meaning of all the movements within our spirit so that we may comprehend God's will. Communion with God includes receiving His revelation in the spirit—that is, in the spirit's intuition—and then apprehending the meaning of this revelation by spiritual understanding. Our comprehension does not arise naturally but is enlightened by the spirit.

It is clear from these two verses in Colossians that if we desire to please God and to bear fruit we must know God's will in our spirit. Our spirit's relationship with God is the foundation for pleasing Him and bearing fruit. How vain for us to expect God's pleasure while walking according to the soul. God is pleased with nothing but His Own will. Nothing else can satisfy His heart. Our anguish is that we do not know God's will. We search and think, yet we seem unable to touch His mind. We should therefore remember that the way to know God's mind lies not in much searching and judging but in spiritual understanding. Nothing but man's spirit can judge God's will, for it has an intuitive power to discern His movement.

If we apprehend God in this way continuously we shall increase in the knowledge of Him. Intuition can grow and grow. It knows no bounds. Its development means the development of the believer's entire spiritual life. Each true communion we have with God trains us to commune better next time. We should seek to be perfect; accordingly, we must seize every opportunity to train our spirit to know God better. Today our need is to *truly* know Him, to appropriate Him in the depth of our being. How often we think we have discerned His will and yet later we discover we have been mistaken. Since our need is to know God and His will, we must seek to be filled with the knowledge of that will in all spiritual understanding.

CONSCIENCE

BESIDES THE FUNCTIONS OF INTUITION and communion, our spirit performs still another important task—that of correcting and reprimanding so as to render us uneasy when we fall short of the glory of God. This ability we call conscience. As the holiness of God condemns evil and justifies good, so a believer's conscience reproves sin and approves righteousness. Conscience is where God expresses His holiness. If we desire to follow the spirit (and since we never reach a stage of infallibility), we must heed what our inward monitor tells us regarding both inclination and overt action. For its works would be decidedly incomplete if it were only *after* we have committed error that conscience should rise up to reprove us. But we realize that even before we take any step—while we are still considering our way—our conscience together with our intuition will protest immediately and make us uneasy at any thought or inclination which is displeasing to the Holy Spirit. If we were more disposed today to mind the voice of conscience we would not be as defeated as we are.

CONSCIENCE AND SALVATION

While we were sinners our spirit was thoroughly dead; our conscience was therefore dead as well and unable to function normally. This does not mean the conscience of a sinner stops working altogether. It does continue to operate, though in a state of coma. Whenever it comes out of this coma it does nothing but condemn the sinner. It has no strength to lead men to God. Dead as it is to Him, God nonetheless desires the conscience to perform some feeble work in the heart of man. Hence in man's dead spirit conscience appears to do a little more work than the other functions of the spirit. The death of intuition and of communion seems to be a greater one than that of conscience. There is of course a reason for the variation. As soon as Adam ate the fruit of the tree of the knowledge of good and evil his intuition and communion died completely towards God, but his power of distinguishing good and evil (which is the function of conscience) was increased. Even today, while the intuition and communion of a sinner are altogether dead to God, his conscience retains something of its movement. This does not imply that man's conscience is alive; for according to the Biblical meaning of aliveness only that which has the life of God is reckoned as living. Anything void of God's life is considered dead. Since the conscience of a sinner does not embrace the life of God it is accounted dead, though it may appear to be active according to man's feeling. Such activity of the conscience augments the anguish of a sinner.

In initiating His work of salvation the first step of the Holy Spirit is to awaken this comatous conscience. He uses the thunders and lightnings of Mount Sinai to shake and enlighten this darkened conscience so as to convince the sinner of his violation of God's law and of his inability to answer God's righteous demand and additionally to convict him as one who is condemned and who deserves nothing but perdition. If one's conscience is willing to confess whatever sins have been committed, including the sin of unbelief, it will be sorrowful in a godly way, earnestly desiring the mercy of God. The tax-collector in our Lord's parable who went up to the temple to pray illustrates such a work of the Holy Spirit. It is what the Lord Jesus meant in his statement: "When (the Holy Spirit) comes, he will convince the world of sin and of righteousness and of judgment" (John 16.8). Should a man's conscience be closed to the conviction, however, then he can never be saved.

The Holy Spirit illuminates a sinner's conscience with the light of God's law so as to convict him of sin; the same Spirit also enlightens man's conscience with the light of the gospel so as to save him. If a sinner, upon being convicted of his sin and hearing the gospel of God's grace, is willing to accept the gospel and by faith take it, he will see how the precious blood of the Lord Jesus answers all the accusations of his conscience. Doubtless there is sin, but the blood of the Lord Jesus has been shed. What ground is left for accusation since sin's penalty has been fully paid? The blood of the Lord has atoned for all the sins of a believer; hence there is no more condemnation in the conscience. "If the worshipers had once been cleansed, they would no longer have any consciousness of sin" (Heb. 10.2). We may stand before God without fear and trembling because the blood of Christ has been sprinkled on our conscience (Heb. 9.14). Our salvation is confirmed by the fact that the precious blood has quieted this voice of condemnation.

Since the terrifying light of the law and the merciful light of the gospel both shine upon it, dare we overlook man's conscience in the preaching of the Word? Is our aim in preaching merely to make people understand in their mind, be moved in their emotion, and decide with their will without in the slightest touching their conscience? The Holy Spirit cannot do the work of regeneration through the precious blood if one's conscience has not been convicted of sin. We must stress the precious blood and the conscience proportionally. Some strongly insist on the latter but overlook the former; consequently sinners try hard to repent and to do good, hoping in this way to propitiate God's wrath with their own merits. Others emphasize the precious blood but neglect conscience. This results in a mental acceptance of the blood and a rootless "faith" because their conscience has not been reached by the Holy Spirit. Thus these two must be presented equally. Whoever is aware of an evil conscience will accept the full meaning of the precious blood.

CONSCIENCE AND COMMUNION

"How much more shall the blood of Christ, who through the eternal Spirit offered himself without blemish to God, purify your conscience from dead works to serve the living God" (Heb. 9.14). In order to commune with God and to

serve Him one first must have his conscience cleansed by
the precious blood. As a believer's conscience is cleansed he
is regenerated. According to the Scriptures the cleansing
by the blood and the regeneration of the spirit occur simultaneously. Here we are informed that before one can serve
God he must receive a new life and have his intuition
quickened through the cleansing of the conscience by the
blood. A conscience so cleansed makes it possible for the
intuition of the spirit to serve God. Conscience and intuition
are inseparable.

"Let us *draw near* with a true heart in full assurance of
faith, with our hearts sprinkled clean from an evil conscience
and our bodies washed with pure water" (Heb. 10.22). We
do not draw near to God physically as did the people in the
Old Testament period, for our sanctuary is in heaven; nor
do we draw near soulically with our thoughts and feelings
since these organs can never commune with God. The regenerated spirit alone can approach Him. Believers worship
God in their quickened intuition. The verse above affirms
that a sprinkled conscience is the basis for communion with
God intuitively. A conscience tinged with offense is under
constant accusation. That naturally will affect the intuition,
so closely knit to the conscience, and discourage its approach to God, even paralyzing its normal function. How infinitely necessary to have "a true heart in full assurance of
faith" in a believer's communion with God. When conscience
is unclear one's approach to Him becomes forced and is not
true because he cannot fully believe that God is for him
and has nothing against him. Such fear and doubt undermine
the normal function of intuition, depriving it of the liberty
to fellowship freely with God. The Christian must not have
the slightest accusation in his conscience; he must be assured that his every sin is entirely atoned by the blood of the
Lord and that now there is no charge against Him (Rom.
8.33-34). A single offense on the conscience may suppress
and suspend the normal function of intuition in communing
with God, for as soon as a believer is conscious of sin his
spirit gathers all its powers to eliminate that particular sin
and leaves no more strength to ascend heavenward.

A BELIEVER'S CONSCIENCE

A believer's conscience is quickened when his spirit is regenerated. The precious blood of the Lord Jesus purifies his conscience and accordingly gives it an acute sense that it should obey the will of the Holy Spirit. The sanctifying work of the Holy Spirit in man and the work of conscience in man are intimately related and mutually joined. If a child of God desires to be filled with the Spirit, to be sanctified, and to lead a life wholly after God's will, he must adhere to the voice of conscience. Should he not grant it its rightful place, he shall fall inescapably into walking after the flesh. To be faithful to one's conscience is the first step toward sanctification. Following its voice is a sign of true spirituality. If a Christian fails to let it do its work he is barred from entering the spiritual realm. Even if he regards himself (and is so regarded by others) as spiritual, his "spirituality" nevertheless lacks foundation. If sin and other matters contrary to God's will and unbecoming to saints are not restrained as dictated by its voice, then whatever has been superimposed through spiritual theory shall ultimately collapse because there is no genuine foundation.

Conscience testifies as to whether we are clear towards God and towards men and as to whether our thoughts, words and deeds follow the will of God and are not in any way rebellious to Christ. As Christians advance spiritually the witness of conscience and the witness of the Holy Spirit seem to close ranks. This is because conscience, being fully under the control of the Holy Spirit, daily grows more sensitive until it is attuned perfectly to the voice of the Spirit. The Latter is thereby able to speak to believers through their consciences. The Apostle's word that "my conscience bears me witness in the Holy Spirit" (Rom. 9.1) carries within it this meaning.

If our inward monitor judges us to be wrong we must in fact be wrong. When it condemns, let us repent immediately. We must never attempt to cover our sin or bribe our conscience. "Whenever our hearts condemn us" can we be less condemned by God, since "God is greater than our hearts"

(1 John 3.20)? Whatever conscience condemns *is* condemned by God. Can the holiness of God pursue a lower standard than our conscience? If conscience insists we are wrong, we must be wrong indeed.

What should we do when we are wrong? Cease proceeding to do the incorrect thing if we have not yet done it; repent, confess, and claim the cleansing of the precious blood if we have done it already. It is to be regretted that so many Christians today do not follow these rules. Immediately after the reproof of their inner voice, they lay plans to quench its protest. They usually employ two methods. One is to argue with it, trying to marshal reasons for their action. They suppose that anything reasonable must be God's will and will be condoned by the conscience. What they do not understand is that conscience never argues or reasons. It discerns God's will through intuition and condemns everything which is not according to Him. Conscience speaks for God's will, not for reason. Christians ought not walk by reason but by God's will as disclosed in their intuition. Whenever they disobey any movement there, conscience raises its voice to condemn. Explanation may satisfy the mind but never conscience. As long as the issue condemned is not removed it shall not cease condemning. During the initial stage of a Christian's walk conscience only bears witness to right and wrong; as spiritual life grows, it bears witness as well to what is of God and what is not of God. Although many things appear good to human eyes, they are nonetheless condemned by conscience because they do not originate with God' revelation but are initiated instead by the Christians themselves.

The other method is to ease conscience with many other works. To solve the dilemma of refusing to obey their inner voice of accusation on the one hand but continuing to be afraid of its condemnation on the other, believers resort to many good works. They replace God's will with laudable deeds. They have not obeyed God, yet they insist that what they now do is just as good as what He has revealed—perhaps even better, broader in scope, more profitable, greater in influence. They highly esteem such works; God, however, deems them of no spiritual account whatsoever. He looks neither at the aggregate of fat nor at the number of burnt offerings but solely at the sum of obedience to Him. Nothing, regardless how commendable the intention, can move God's heart if the revelation in the spirit has been neglected. Doubling the consecration will not silence the accusing monitor; its voice must be followed; that and nothing else can ever please God. Conscience simply demands our obedience; it does not require us to serve God in any spectacular way.

Let us therefore not deceive ourselves. In walking according to the spirit we shall hear the directions of conscience. Do not try to escape any inward reproach; rather, be attentive to its voice. By constantly walking in the spirit we are constrained to humble ourselves and to heed the correction of conscience. Children of God should not make a general confession by acknowledging their innumerable sins in a vague manner, because such confession does not provide conscience opportunity to do its perfect work. They ought to allow the Holy Spirit through their conscience to point out their sins one by one. Humbly and quietly and obediently they should permit their conscience to reprove and condemn them of every individual sin. Christians must accept its reproach and be willing, according to the mind of the Spirit, to eliminate everything which is contrary to God. Are you reticent to let conscience probe your life? Dare you let it explore your real condition? Will you allow it to parade before you one after another all the things in your life as they are beheld by God? Will you grant conscience the right to dissect every one of your sins? In case you dare not, in case you are not willing to be so examined, then does not such drawing back prove that there remain many elements in your life which have not been judged and committed to the cross as they ought to have been: that there are still matters in which you have not wholly obeyed God nor fully followed the spirit: that some issues continue to hinder you from having perfect fellowship with God? If so, you cannot contend before God that "there is nothing between You and me."

Only an unconditional and unrestricted acceptance of the reproach of conscience with a corresponding willingness to do what is revealed can show how perfect is our consecration, how truly we hate sin, how sincerely we desire to do God's will. Often we express a wish to please God, to obey the Lord, to follow the Spirit; here is the test as to whether our wish is real or fancied, perfect or incomplete. If we are yet entangled in sin and not completely severed from it, most likely our spirituality is largely a pretense. A believer who is unable to follow his conscience wholly is unqualified to walk after the spirit. Before conscience has its demand realized, what else but an imaginary spirit will lead the person, since the true spirit within him continues to petition him to listen to the monitor within? A believer can make no genuine spiritual progress if he is reluctant to have his evil conscience judged in God's light and clearly dealt with. The truth or falsity of his consecration and service depends on his willing obedience to the Lord—both to His command and to His reproach.

After one has permitted conscience to begin operating, he should allow it to perfect its work. Sins must be treated progressively one by one until all have been eliminated. If a child of God is faithful in his dealing with sin and faithfully follows his conscience, he shall receive light increasingly from heaven and have his unnoticed sins exposed; the Holy Spirit shall enable him to read and to understand more of the law written upon his heart. Thus is he made to know what is holiness, righteousness, purity and honesty, concerning which he had had only vague ideas before. Moreover, his intuition is strengthened greatly in its ability to know the mind of the Holy Spirit. Whenever a believer is therefore reproved by his conscience his immediate response should be: "Lord, I am willing to obey." He should let Christ once again be the Lord of his life; he should be teachable and should be taught by the Holy Spirit. The Spirit shall surely come and help if a person is honestly minding his conscience.

Conscience is like a window to the believer's spirit. Through it the rays of heaven shine into the spirit, flooding the whole being with light. Heavenly light shines in through the conscience to expose fault and to condemn failure whenever we wrongfully think or speak or act in a way not becoming saints. If by submitting to its voice and eliminating the sin it condemns we allow it to do its work, then the light from heaven will shine brighter next time; but should we not confess nor extirpate the sin, our conscience will be corrupted by it (Titus 1.15), because we have not walked according to the teaching of God's light. With sin accumulating, conscience as a window becomes increasingly clouded. Light can barely penetrate the spirit. And there finally comes a day when that believer can sin without compunction and with no grief at all, since the conscience has long been paralyzed and the intuition dulled by sin. The more spiritual a believer is the more keenly alert is his inner monitor. No Christian can be so spiritual as to have no further necessity to confess his sin. He must be fallen spiritually if his conscience is dull and insensitive. Excellent knowledge, hard labor, excited feeling and strong will cannot substitute for a sensitive conscience. He who does not heed it but seeks mental and sensational progress is retrogressing spiritually.

The sensitivity of the conscience can be increased as well as decreased. Should anyone give ground to his conscience to operate, his spirit's window will let in more light next time; but should he disregard it or answer it with reason or works other than what it demands, then his conscience will speak more and more softly each time it is rejected until ultimately it ceases to speak. Every time a believer does not listen to conscience he damages his spiritual walk. If this self-inflicted wounding of his spiritual life continues unabated, he shall sink into the state of being fleshly. He will lose all his former distaste for sin and former admiration of victory. Until we learn to face squarely the reproach which arises from conscience, we do not actually appreciate how meaningful to our walk in the spirit this heeding of the voice of conscience is.

A GOOD CONSCIENCE

"I have lived before God in all good conscience up to this day" (Acts 23.1). This is the secret of Paul's life. The conscience he refers to is not that of an unregenerated person but of a Holy Spirit-filled conscience. Bold in approaching God and perfect in his communion with Him, the Apostle's regenerated conscience gives him no reproach. He does everything according to it. Never does he do anything that his conscience objects to, nor does he ever permit one item to remain in his life which it condemns. He is therefore bold before God and man. We lose our confidence when our conscience is murky. The Apostle "always (took) pains to have a clear conscience toward God and toward men" (Acts 24.16), for "if our hearts do not condemn us, we have confidence before God; and we receive from him whatever we ask, because we keep his commandments and do what pleases him" (1 John 3.21-22).

Believers simply do not realize how very significant their conscience is. Many have the idea that as long as they walk after the spirit all is well. They do not know that an unclear conscience means loss of confidence in approaching God and that this loss in turn means disruption of one's communion with Him. In fact, a muddied conscience can hinder our intuitive communion with God more than anything else. If we fail to keep His commandments and to do what pleases Him our monitor within shall naturally reprove us, rendering us fearful before God and hence keeping us from receiving what we seek. We can serve God only with a clear conscience (2 Tim. 1.3). An opaque one shall surely cause us to shrink back intuitively from God.

"Our boast is this, the testimony of our conscience that we have behaved in the world, and still more toward you, with holiness and godly sincerity, not by earthly wisdom but by the grace of God" (2 Cor. 1.12). This passage speaks of the testimony of conscience. Only a conscience without offense will testify for a believer. It is good to have the testimony of others, but how much better to have the testimony of our own conscience. The Apostle asserts that this is what he is boasting of here. In our walk after the spirit we need to have this testimony continually. What other people say is subject to error because they cannot fully know how God has guided us. Perhaps they may misunderstand and misjudge us just as the Apostles were misunderstood and misjudged by the believers in their day. At times they also may over-praise and over-admire us. Many times men criticize us when we actually are following the Lord; on other occasions they praise us for what they see in us, though it is largely the result of a temporary emotional outburst or a cleverly conceived thought on our part. Hence outside praise or criticism is inconsequential; but the testimony of our quickened conscience is momentous. We should pay extreme attention to how it bears us witness. What is its estimate of us? Does it condemn us as hypocritical? Or does it testify that we have walked among men in holiness and godly sincerity? Does conscience affirm that we already have walked according to all the light we have?

What is the testimony of Paul's conscience? It testifies that he has "behaved in the world . . . not by earthly wisdom but by the grace of God." Conscience in fact can testify to nothing else. What it contends for and insists upon in the believer is solely for that life to be lived by the grace of God and not by earthly wisdom. Earthly wisdom is totally nil in God's will and work. It equally amounts to nothing in a believer's spiritual life. Man's mind is altogether useless in his communion with God; even in his communication with the material world the mind occupies but a subordinate position. A child of God lives on earth exclusively by the grace of God, and grace implies something entirely done by Him, with men having no part in it (Rom. 11.6). Except as one lives exclusively by God—not permitting himself to take any initiative nor allowing his mind to have control over him— can conscience testify that he lives in the world in holiness and godly sincerity. In other words, it operates together with intuition. Conscience bears witness to everything done according to revelation in intuition, but it resists every action which is contrary to intuition, no matter how compatible it is with human wisdom. To sum up, conscience approves only the revelation of intuition. Intuition leads believers, while conscience constrains them to follow their intuition.

A good conscience which attests God's good pleasure in the believer (since there is nothing between him and God) is absolutely essential to a life walked after the spirit. That attestation ought to be the believer's goal: he should be satisfied with nothing less. This indicates what should be a normal Christian's life: as it was the testimony of the Apostle Paul, so must it be with us today. Enoch was a man of good conscience for he knew God was pleased with him. This attestation of God's satisfaction with us helps us to move forward. We must be very careful here, however, lest we exalt our "self" as though we have pleased God. All glory belongs to Him. We should take pains always to have a clear conscience; but should ours in fact be clear, we then must guard against the intrusion of the flesh.

If our conscience consistently attests God's satisfaction with us, we shall have boldness to look to the blood of the Lord Jesus for cleansing each time we unfortunately fail. To have a good conscience we must not depart for a moment from that blood which continually and forever cleanses us. Confessing our sin and trusting in the precious blood are unavoidable. Moreover, because our sinful nature is still within us, we will not be able to recognize many hidden works of the flesh until we have matured spiritually. What we formerly considered harmless may now become sinful to us. Without the cleansing of the precious blood we could never be at peace. But once it is sprinkled on our conscience it shall continue to do its work of cleansing.

The Apostle confides that what he seeks is to have a good conscience towards God and men. These two directions, Godward and manward, are deeply entwined. If we wish to maintain a good conscience towards men, it must first be clear with respect to God. An unclear conscience towards God automatically brings in an unclear one towards men. Consequently all who want to live spiritually must seek to have a clear conscience towards God (1 Peter 3.21). This does not in any way signify that it is unimportant to have a good conscience before men. On the contrary, there are many things which can be done towards God but not towards men. Only a clear conscience towards men effects a good testimony before them. Man's misunderstanding does not affect the testimony: "keep your conscience clear, so that, when you are abused, those who revile your good behavior in Christ may be put to shame" (1 Peter 3.16). Good conduct cannot appease an evil conscience; but neither will much reviling by man cast a shadow over a good conscience.

A good conscience also enables us to receive God's promises. Christians nowadays frequently complain that their little faith is the cause for failure to live a perfect spiritual life. Naturally there are many reasons for not possessing greater faith, but the gravest of these is probably an evil conscience. A good conscience is inseparable from a great faith. The moment it is offended, at that very moment faith is weakened. Let us observe how the Bible joins these two elements: "whereas the aim of our charge is love that issues from a pure heart and a good conscience and sincere faith" (1 Tim. 1.5). Again: "holding faith and a good conscience" (1 Tim. 1.19). Conscience is the organ of our faith. God hates sin intensely, for the apex of God's glory is His infinite holiness. His holiness will not tolerate sin, not even for a moment. If a believer does not purge—according to the dictate of conscience—everything contrary to God's mind, he shall lose his fellowship with God instantaneously. All the promises which God grants us in the Bible may be considered conditional. None are bestowed to gratify one's fleshly lust. No one shall experience the Holy Spirit, communion with God, and answered prayer if he does not deal away with his sin and flesh. How can we claim the promise of God with boldness if our voice within is accusing us? How can anyone, whose conscience does not bear him witness that he has lived on earth in holiness and godly sincerity, be a man of prayer who is able to ask God for unlimited rewards? What is the use of praying if our inward monitor reproves us when we lift up our hands to God? Sin first must be forsaken and cleansed before we can pray with faith.

We need to possess a conscience void of offense, not in the sense that it is better than before or that much evil has been done away but that it is without offense and confident before God. This ought to be the normal condition of our conscience. If we prostrate ourselves before it and allow it to reprove us: if we offer ourselves entirely to the Lord and are willing to perform all His purposes: then our confidence shall increase until it is possible for us to regard our conscience as void of offense. We dare to tell God that now we have nothing left which is concealed from Him. So far as we are concerned we know of nothing between us and Him. In walking by the spirit we should never permit the tiniest offense to stir up our conscience. Whatever it condemns must be confessed immediately, cleansed by the precious blood and forsaken, so that no trace be left behind. Each day we should seek to have a good conscience, because no matter how short a time conscience may be offended it renders great harm to the spirit. The Apostle Paul has set us a good example in always having a good conscience. Therein alone shall we maintain uninterrupted fellowship with God.

CONSCIENCE AND KNOWLEDGE

In abiding by the spirit and listening to the voice of conscience we should remember one thing, and that is, conscience is limited by knowledge. It is the organ for distinguishing good and evil, which means it gives us the knowledge of good and evil. This knowledge varies with different Christians. Some have more while others have less. The degree of knowledge may be determined by individual environment or perhaps by the instruction each has received. Thus we can neither live by the standard of others nor ask other people to live by the light we have. In a Christian's fellowship with God an unknown sin does *not* hinder communion. Whoever observes all the will of God known to him and forsakes everything known to be condemned by God is qualified to enjoy perfect fellowship with Him. A young Christian

frequently concludes that due to his lack of knowledge he
is powerless to please God. *Spiritual* knowledge is indeed
quite important, but we also know that the lack of such
knowledge does not hinder one's fellowship with God. In
the matter of fellowship God looks not at how much we
apprehend of His will but rather at what our *attitude* towards His will is. If we honestly seek and wholeheartedly
obey His desires, our fellowship remains unbroken, even
though there should be many unknown sins in us. Should
fellowship be determined by the holiness of God, who among
all the most holy saints in the past and the present would be
qualified to hold a moment's perfect communion with Him?
Everyone would be banished daily from the Lord's face and
from the glory of His might. That sin which is unknown to
us is under the covering of the precious blood.

On the other hand, were we to permit to remain even
the tiniest little sin which we know our conscience has condemned, we instantly would lose that perfect fellowship with
God. Just as a speck of dust disables us from seeing, so our
known sin, no matter how infinitesimal, hides God's smiling
face from us. The moment the conscience is offended immediately fellowship is affected. A sin unknown to the saint
may persist long in his life without affecting his fellowship
with God; but as soon as light (knowledge) breaks in, he
forfeits a day's fellowship with Him for every day he allows
that sin to remain. God fellowships with us according to the
level of the knowledge of our conscience. We shall be very
foolish if we assume that, since a certain matter has not
hindered our fellowship with God for so many years, it cannot later be of any consequence.

This is because conscience can condemn only to the extent
of its newest light; it cannot judge as sinful that of which it
is not conscious. As the knowledge of a believer grows, his
conscience too increases in its consciousness. The more his
knowledge advances the more his conscience judges. One
need not worry about what he does not know if he but completely follows what he already does know. "If we walk in
the light"—that is, if we are walking in the light which *we*

have already—"as he is in the light, we have fellowship with *one another*, and the blood of Jesus his Son cleanses us from all sin (though many are still unknown to us)" (1 John 1.7). God has unlimited light. Although our light is limited, we shall have fellowship with God and the blood of His Son shall cleanse us if we walk according to the light we have. Perhaps there are still sins today unremoved from our life, but we are not conscious of them; hence we can continue to have fellowship with God today. Let us keep in mind that, important as conscience is, it nevertheless is not our standard of holiness, because it is closely related to knowledge. *Christ Himself* is alone our single standard of holiness. But in the matter of fellowship with God, His one condition is whether or not we have maintained a conscience void of offense. Yet, having fully obeyed the dictates of conscience, we must not visualize ourselves as now "perfect." A good conscience merely assures us that so far as our knowledge goes we are perfect, that is, we have arrived at the *immediate* goal, but not the ultimate one.

Such being the case, our standard of conduct rises higher to the degree our knowledge of the Scriptures and spiritual experience increase. Only when our lives become holier as our light progresses can we preserve a conscience without offense. It shall invariably accuse us if we accompany this year's knowledge and experience with only last year's conduct. God did not cut off His fellowship with us last year because of our sins unknown to us then; but He certainly shall sever it today if we do not forsake the sins unknown last year but now known this year. Conscience is a God-given *current* standard of holiness. Whoever violates that standard is assumed to have committed sin.

The Lord has many words for us, but in view of the immaturity of our spiritual understanding He has to wait. God deals with His children according to their respective conditions. Due to varying degrees of knowledge in the conscience some are not conscious of sins regarded as very great by their fellow-believers. Hence, let us not judge one another. The Father alone knows how to handle His children. He does not expect to find the strength of "young men" in His "little children" nor the experience of "fathers" in the "young men." But He does wait for *each* of his children to *obey* Him according to what he *already knows*. Were we to know for sure (which is not easy) that God has spoken to our brother on a particular matter and that our brother has failed to listen, then we can persuade him to obey. Yet we should never force our brother to follow what our conscience says to us. If the God of perfect holiness does not reject *us* because of our past unknown sins, how can we, on the basis of our current standard, judge our brother who only knows now what we knew last year?

In fact, in helping other people we should not coerce obedience from them in small details but only advise them to follow faithfully the dictate of their own conscience. If their volition yields to God they will obey Him when the Holy Spirit sheds light on the words clearly written in the Bible. As long as his volition is yielded, a believer will follow God's desire the moment his conscience receives light. The same is applicable to ourselves. We should not overextend ourselves to the point of exciting the strength of our soul to understand truths beyond our present capacity. If we are disposed to obey today's voice of God, we are considered acceptable. On the other hand, we should not restrain ourselves from searching any truth which the Holy Spirit may lead us intuitively to search. Such restraint would mean lowering our standard of holiness. In a word, there is no problem for that one who is willing to walk by the spirit.

A WEAK CONSCIENCE

A few moments ago we remarked that the standard of our holy living is Christ, not conscience, though the latter nonetheless is of great significance. It testifies whether or not in our everyday life we have pleased God; it consequently serves as a criterion for the *current* degree of holiness. If we live by what conscience teaches we have arrived at the place we should be for the present moment. It is therefore a prime factor in our daily walk after the spirit. In whatever matter we disobey the dictate of our conscience we shall be reprimanded by it. As a result we shall lose peace and shall be cut off temporarily from having fellowship with God. There is no question that we must follow what conscience demands; but how perfect its demand is remains a question.

As we have seen, conscience is limited by knowledge. It can guide only by the knowledge it possesses. It condemns every disobedience to what it knows, but it cannot condemn what it itself does not know. Hence a vast distance obtains between the measure of conscience and the measure of God's holiness. Just here we find at least two defects. First, a conscience with limited knowledge condemns only what it knows as wrong and leaves untouched in our life numerous matters which are not according to God's will. God and those more matured saints know how imperfect we are, and yet we continue to walk in our old fashion for lack of new light. Is not this an enormous defect? This imperfection is nonetheless bearable because God does not judge what we do not know. Despite this flaw we can fellowship with Him and be accepted if we simply obey whatever our conscience dictates.

But the second defect, unlike the first, *does* interfere with our fellowship with God. Just as a limited knowledge fails to judge what ought to be judged, so it may also judge what should not be judged. Does it mean that conscience is faulty in its guidance? No, the leading of conscience is correct and must be heeded by believers. But there are different degrees of knowledge among the saints. Many things which can be done with knowledge are condemned as sins by the conscience of those who lack knowledge. This manifests the disease of believers' immaturity. The fathers can do many things with perfect liberty for they have advanced knowledge, experience and position, but for the little children to do them would be entirely wrong because they simply do not possess such knowledge, experience and position. This does not imply that there are two different standards for the Christian's conduct. It just shows, however, that the standard of good and evil is bound up with individual position. This law applies to the secular, as well as to the spiritual, realm. Many matters agree perfectly with God's will when done by matured believers, but these very items become sins if copied by immature ones.

The reason for this variance is the different degrees of knowledge in our consciences. When one believer does what his conscience deems good he is obeying the will of God; but the conscience of another person may judge the same thing as evil, and he will be sinning against God if he does it. The absolute will of God is always the same; but He reveals His mind to each person according to the limitation of their spiritual position. Those with knowledge have a stronger conscience and consequently enjoy more liberty; while those without knowledge harbor a weaker conscience and hence experience more bondage.

This is distinctly illustrated in the first letter to the Corinthians. There was much misunderstanding among the Christians at Corinth concerning the eating of food offered to idols. Some of them regarded idols as possessing no real existence since there is no God but One (1 Cor. 8.4). So for them there could be no difference between the food offered to idols and food not so offered: both with propriety could be eaten. But others, having long been accustomed to idols, could not help viewing the food as though it were truly offered to an idol. They felt uneasy when eating it. Because their conscience was weak while eating the food, they were defiled (v.7). The Apostle treated this divergence of view as a matter of knowledge (v.7). The former had light and therefore did not sin when they ate, for their conscience did not bother them; the latter, however, not enjoying such knowledge, felt uneasy while eating and so were guilty. Thus we see the great importance of knowledge. The increase of it sometimes may increase the condemnation of conscience but it may equally decrease its condemnation.

It is advisable for us to beseech the Lord to grant us more knowledge in order that we may not be bound unreasonably, but this knowledge must be kept in humility lest we, like the Corinthians, fall into the flesh. In case our knowledge is inadequate and our conscience continues its censure, we must obey its voice at all cost. We should never philosophize that since this thing is not wrong according to God's highest standard, we can do it in spite of what our conscience says. Let us not forget that conscience is our current standard of God's leading. We need to submit to it, else we sin. God judges whatever conscience judges.

What we have discussed here concerns merely outward items such as food. In those items of a more spiritual character there can be *no* such difference of liberty and bondage, however much our knowledge grows. Only in these external physical matters does God deal with us according to our age. In the young believers He pays much attention to their food, clothing and other external issues, because He desires to put to death the evil deeds of the body. If the young genuinely have a heart to follow the Lord they shall find Him frequently calling them, through their spirit's conscience, to subdue themselves in these matters. But those with deeper experience in the Lord seem to enjoy more liberty in their conscience with respect to these items because they already have learned how to obey Him.

Yet the more advanced ones are confronted by one of the most serious hazards here. Their conscience becomes so strong as to drift into cold numbness. Young Christians who follow the Lord wholeheartedly obey Him at many points, for their conscience is sensitive and easily moved by the Holy Spirit. Old believers, on the other hand, have so much knowledge that they tend to overdevelop their mind so as to numb the sensitivity of the conscience. They are tempted to do things according to the knowledge of their mind and seemingly render themselves immovable by the Holy Spirit. This is a fatal blow to spiritual life. It removes the freshness from a believer's walk and causes it to become old and dull. Regardless how much knowledge we possess, let us be careful not to follow it but the conscience of our spirit. Should we disregard what is condemned intuitively by our conscience and take our knowledge as our standard of conduct, we have already settled into walking after the flesh.

Is it not true that our conscience sometimes can be greatly disturbed when we set out to do what is absolutely legitimate according to the truth we know? That which conscience condemns is reckoned as not in accordance with God's will, even though by the knowledge of our mind it is good. This is because our knowledge is acquired through the searchings of our intellect and not by revelations in our intuition. Hence the leading of conscience and of knowledge can prove to be quite conflicting.

Paul indicates that one's spiritual life shall be impaired enormously if he disregards the reproach of conscience and follows the knowledge of his mind instead. "For if any one sees you, a man of knowledge, at table in an idol's temple, might he not be encouraged, if his conscience is weak, to eat food offered to idols? And so by your knowledge this weak man is destroyed, the brother for whom Christ died" (1 Cor. 8.10-11). Seeing a believer with knowledge eating food offered to idols, the one without knowledge tends to think he too can so eat. But if the latter eats against the voice of his conscience he falls into sin. Let us never for a moment, then, walk by the knowledge we have. However much of it we have accumulated, we ought only to heed the intuition and conscience of the spirit. Perhaps one's knowledge may influence his conscience; even so, what he must follow directly is his conscience. God is looking more for our obedience to His will than for the "correctness" of our conduct. Our listening to the voice of conscience guarantees the genuine character of our consecration and obedience. Through our conscience God examines our motive—whether we desire to obey Him or we seek something else.

Another thing one must guard against is the blocking of his conscience. It often loses its normal operation through a kind of blockage. When we are surrounded by those whose conscience is deadly numb, ours may be numbed also through their argument, conversation, teaching, persuasion or example. Beware of teachers with hardened consciences: beware of man-made consciences: reject all attempts of man to mold yours. Our consciences must be responsible directly to God in all regards. We ourselves must know His will and be responsible for executing it. We will fail if we neglect our conscience to follow that of another.

Let us recapitulate. The conscience of the believer constitutes one of the indispensable faculties of his spirit. We ought to follow its guidance fully. Though it is influenced by knowledge, its voice nonetheless represents God's highest will for His children today. It is well for us to arrive at the highest for today. Other matters we need not worry about. Let us continuously maintain our conscience in a healthy condition. Do not permit any sin to hurt its feeling. If at any time we discover that it has become cold and hard as though nothing can move us, let us recognize by this that we have fallen *deeply* into the flesh. In such a case, all the Bible knowledge we have acquired is but stored in the mind of the flesh and is lacking in living power. We ought to follow the intuition of our spirit unceasingly, being filled with the Holy Spirit, in order that our conscience may increase daily in sensitivity and our repentance may be as instantaneous as our knowledge of anything wrong between us and God. Do not be concerned purely with the mind and neglect the intuitive conscience. The extent of spirituality is measured by the sensitivity to our conscience. Countless are those Christians who have disregarded their conscience in the past and are now unlively, merely holding some dead knowledge in their brain. May we be ever watchful lest we stumble into the same trap. Do not be afraid to be easily moved. Never fear to have the conscience exercised too much; only fear for it not to be moved enough. Conscience serves as a monitor for God. It informs us where something has gone wrong or needs to be repaired. We can avoid much destructive consequences later if we but listen to conscience earlier.

PART SIX

WALKING AFTER THE SPIRIT

1 The Dangers of Spiritual Life
2 The Laws of the Spirit
3 The Principle of Mind Aiding the Spirit
4 The Normalcy of the Spirit

CHAPTER 1

THE DANGERS OF SPIRITUAL LIFE

NOTHING IS MORE VITAL to the Christian life than to walk daily after the spirit. It is this that maintains the Christian in a constant spiritual state, delivers him from the power of the flesh, assists him to obey God's will always, and shields him from the assault of Satan. Now that we understand the operations of our spirit, we must immediately walk by it. This is a moment by moment affair from which there can be no relaxing. In these days we must be keenly alert to the peril of receiving the teaching of the Holy Spirit while subsequently rejecting His leading. On this very point have many saints stumbled and fallen. To acquire teaching alone is not sufficient; we must also accept the leading. We should not be content with just spiritual knowledge but treasure as well the walk after the spirit. Often we hear people drop the words, "the way of the cross"; but what is this way after all? It is in reality nothing else but walking by the spirit, since to walk in that fashion necessitates the committing of our ideas, wishes and thoughts to death. Exclusively following the spirit's intuition and revelation demands our bearing the cross daily.

All spiritual believers know something of the operation of the spirit. Their experience of it, however, is often sporadic because they have not fully understood all the laws which govern its functioning. But with their intuition well-developed they could walk steadily after the spirit without any interference from the outside (note: all that is outside the spirit is considered the outside realm). But not having assimilated the laws of the spirit, they interpret life in the spirit as oscillatory, devoid of rule, and arduous to practice. Many are determined to heed God's will and to follow the leading of the Holy Spirit, but they lack a positive forward-propelling heart because they are not sure if the guidance of their intuition is wholly dependable. They have yet to learn to understand the indication of their intuition as to whether to advance or to stay. They are additionally igorant of what the normal state of the spirit is and are thus incapacitated from being led continually by it. Frequently their inner man loses its power to operate for the simple reason that they do not know how to keep it in a right condition. Though they sometimes do experience revelation in their intuition, they nevertheless wonder why it is, when they are earnestly seeking, that at times their intuition does receive revelation but at other times does not. This of course is due to the fact that on some occasions they unconsciously walk according to the law of the spirit and so obtain revelation whereas at other moments, though asking, they are not asking according to this law and therefore do not secure any revelation. Were they to walk by the law of the spirit continually rather than unconsciously following intermittently, they could always receive the revelation. Unfortunately they are unaware of this possibility. It is nonetheless certain that for us to consistently experience revelation we must know the laws of the spirit and the will of God and must do the things which please Him. Since all movements in the spirit are meaningful, we need to learn their import if we wish to

walk faithfully. Understanding the laws of the spirit is therefore indispensable.

There are countless Christians who consider the occasional
working of the Holy Spirit in their spirit to be the most
sublime of their life experiences. They do not expect to have
such an experience daily because they surmise that such a
special event could happen but a few times in life. Were they
to live by the spirit according to its law, however, they
would discover that these are everyday occurrences. What
they deem extraordinary—something one cannot permanently sustain—is actually the *ordinary* daily experiences of believers. "Extraordinary" indeed if believers should desert this
ordinary life experience and abide in darkness.

Suppose we have received a certain thought. Are we able
to discern whether this comes from our spirit or from our
soul? Some thoughts burn in the spirit while others blaze
in the soul. Believers ought to understand how the various
parts of their being operate or they shall not be able to distinguish the spiritual from the soulical. When thinking, they
should recognize the source of their thought; in feeling,
they should detect the direction from which such feeling
comes; and in working, they should be clear as to what
strength they use. Only thus can they follow the spirit.

We know our soul provides us with self-consciousness.
One aspect of self-consciousness is self-examination. This
is most harmful since it causes us to focus upon ourselves and
thereby enhance the growth of self life. How often self-exaltation and pride are the consequences of such self-examination. But there is a kind of analysis of incalculable help
to the spiritual pilgrimage. Without it we are incompetent to
know who we really are and what we are following. Harmful self-examination revolves around one's own success or
defeat, stimulating attitudes of self-pride or self-pity. Profitable analysis searches only the *source* of one's thought,
feeling or desire. God wishes us to be delivered from self-
consciousness, but at the same time He certainly does not
intend for us to live on earth as people without intelligent
awareness. We must not be overly self-conscious, yet we

must apprehend the true condition of all our inward parts through the knowledge accorded us by the Holy Spirit. It is postively necessary for us to search out our activities with our heart.

Many regenerated believers seem unconscious of possessing a spirit. Though they do have one, they simply are not conscious of it. Perhaps they have spiritual sense but they do not realize such sense arises from the spirit. What every truly born-again person should rely on for living is the life of the spirit. If we are willing to be taught, we shall know what is our spiritual sense. One thing is unmistakable: the soul is affected by outside influences, but not the spirit. For example, when the soul is provided with beautiful scenery, serene nature, inspiring music, or many other phenomena pertaining to the external world, it can be moved instantly and respond strongly. Not so the spirit. If the spirit of believers is flooded with the power of the Holy Spirit, it is independent of the soul. Unlike the latter the spirit does not require outside stimuli by which to be activated but is able to be active on its own initiative. It can move under any circumstances. Hence those who are genuinely spiritual can be active whether or not their soul has feeling or their body has strength. These ones live by the ever-active spirit.

Now as a matter of fact the sense of the soul and the intuition of the spirit are distinctly opposite; nevertheless, occasionally they appear to be quite similar. Their similarity can be so close as to confuse Christians. Should they be hasty to move, they will not easily escape being deceived at these times of similarity. Yet if they would wait patiently and test the source of their feelings again and again, they would be told the real source by the Holy Spirit at the right hour. In walking after the spirit we must avoid all haste.

Soulish Christians generally bend to certain directions. Most of them lean either towards emotion or towards reason. Now when these people become spiritual they tend to fall towards the *opposite* extreme from what they formerly were. Emotional persons will then be tempted to adopt their own cold reason as the leading of the spirit. Because they appreciate how soulish their former passionate life was, they now mistake their own reasoning to be spiritual. Likewise those who were rational believers may subsequently accept their passionate feeling to be the leading of the Holy Spirit. They too are conscious of the soulish cast of their hitherto cold and quiet life; consequently they now interpret their emotion to be of the spirit. These are equally ignorant of the fact that the reversal of position between emotion and reason does not render them a shade less soulish. Let us therefore remember the functions of the spirit. To be led by the spirit is to follow its intuition. All spiritual knowledge, communion and conscience come via the intuition. The Holy Spirit leads the saints by this intuition. They need not themselves figure out what possibly is spiritual; all that is required is to abide by their intuition. In order to listen to the Spirit we must apprehend His mind intuitively.

Some seek the gifts of the Holy Spirit with genuine earnestness. Yet often what they crave is but some joy, for the "I" is hidden behind their quest. They believe if they can feel the Holy Spirit descending upon them or some external force controlling their body or some warm fire burning from head to foot, that then they have been baptized in the Spirit. However true it may be that He does sometimes allow people to so feel Him, it is very damaging for men to seek Him by means of emotion. For this not only can excite their soul life but also may evoke the enemy's counterfeit. What is really valuable before God is not how we emotionally feel the presence of the Lord or how we even feel love towards Him; rather is it how we follow the Holy Spirit and live according to what He has revealed to our spirit. Frequently we meet "Holy Spirit-baptized" people of this kind who continue to live by their natural life and not by their spirit. They lack a sensitive intuition to discern matters in the spiritual world. Not emotion but communion with the Lord in the spirit is what is valuable before God.

Through our lengthy discussion of the functions of the spirit as described in the Bible, we now can realize that the spirit can be as passionate as emotion and as cool as reason.

Only those who are experienced in the Lord can distinguish what is of the spirit and what is of the soul. Those who try to reason out the movement of the Holy Spirit or, as more frequently happens, attempt to feel His movement rather than to seek to truly know God in their intuition and walk accordingly, commit themselves to a life in the flesh. They permit their spiritual life to sink into oblivion.

It may help us to see more clearly the significance of following the spirit's intuition if we examine the life of Paul. God "was pleased to *reveal* his Son *to me*, in order that I might preach him among the Gentiles, (and) I did not confer with *flesh and blood*, nor did I go up to Jerusalem to those who were apostles before me, but I went away into Arabia; and again I returned to Damascus" (Gal. 1.16-17). Revelation, as we have indicated before, is given by God and received in the spirit. When the Apostle John obtained revelation to write, he secured it in the spirit (Rev. 1.10). The Bible consistently testifies that revelation is something which occurs in the believer's spirit. Now the Apostle Paul informs us here that he was walking by the spirit when he received revelation in his spirit to know the Lord Jesus and to be sent to the Gentiles. He did not confer with flesh and blood because he had no need to listen further to man's opinion, thought or argument. He did not go to Jerusalem to see those who were spiritually senior to him so as to obtain their view. He simply followed the leading of his spirit. Since he had received *God's revelation* in his intuition and had known God's will, he no longer sought other evidence. He deemed revelation in his spirit sufficient for guidance. At that time, proclaiming the Lord Jesus to Gentiles was a new departure. Man's soul naturally would suggest amassing more information, especially the opinions of those who had more preaching experience. But Paul followed the spirit alone. He cared not what men, not even the most spiritual apostles, would say.

Thus ought we to follow the direct leading of the Lord in our spirit rather than the words of spiritual people. Does this then imply that the words of the spiritual fathers are use-

less? No, they are most useful. The exhortation and
teaching of the fathers are most helpful, but we nonetheless
ought to "weigh what is said" (1 Cor. 14.29). We must be
instructed by the Lord directly in our spirit. When we are
uncertain whether a movement in the spirit is actually of
God or not, we can be helped greatly by those who have
been taught deeply in the Lord. But if we already *have
known for sure*—as Paul was—that God has so revealed His
mind, then we ought not inquire of men, not even of apostles,
should they still exist today.

From the context of this passage we can see the Apostle
stresses that the gospel he preaches was disclosed to him by
God rather than taught him by other apostles. This is a
point of immense significance. The gospel we preach must
not be just something we hear from men or read from books
or even conceive through our meditation. Unless it is delivered to us by God, it can serve no spiritual utility. Young
Christians today welcome the idea of "instructors" and the
spiritually mature wish to impart an orthodox faith to the
second generation. But who knows what really produces
spiritual value? If what we believe and preach does not originate in revelation it counts for nothing. We can gather from
the mind of others some beautiful thoughts; yet our spirit
remains impoverished and empty. Obviously we are neither
to expect a new gospel nor to demean what the servants of
God teach, for the Bible distinctly instructs us not to despise
prophesying (1 Thess. 5.20). We are simply emphasizing
the utter necessity of revelation.

Without revelation, all that has been written is vain. If we
desire to be spiritually effective in preaching, we initially
must apprehend God's truth in our spirit. Whatever and
however much is acquired wholesale from men counts for
nought spiritually. Revelation in the spirit should occupy a
large place in a Christian servant's life. It is actually the
first qualification for a worker. This alone empowers one to
perform spiritual service and to walk by the spirit. How
multiplied are the workers who trust in their own intellect
and mind for accomplishing spiritual work! Even among the

most evangelical believers it is perhaps chiefly a mental acceptance of the truth and amounts to nothing but death.
Should we not ask ourselves whether what we preach
emerges from God's revelation or comes from men?

THE ATTACKS OF SATAN

In view of the significance of our spirit, which is the site
of communion between the Holy Spirit and the saints, should
we marvel if Satan is most unwilling to let us know the
functions of the spirit for fear we may follow it? The enemy
aims to confine the saint's life within the soul and to quench
his spirit. He will give many strange physical sensations to
believers and fill their mind with various wandering
thoughts. He intends to confuse one's spiritual awareness by
these sensations and thoughts. While confused, God's children are incompetent to distinguish what is of the spirit and
what emanates from the soul. Satan well recognizes that victories of believers rest in their knowing how to "read" their
spiritual sense (alas! how many are ignorant of this principle). He musters his whole force to attack the believer's
spirit.

Let us reiterate that in such spiritual warfare Christians
must never make any move according to their feelings or
sudden thoughts. Never assume that such thoughts cannot
be wrong because we have already prayed. It is a mistake to
consider every notion which comes to us in prayer as being
of God. We seem to innocently think that prayer can right
the wrong and that whatever has been prayed out is bound
to be all right. True, we have sought the will of God, but it
does not mean necessarily that we *have already known* His
will. God makes it known to our spirit, not to our mind.

Satan employs even more drastic measures against believers than that of enticing them into living by the soul instead
of following the spirit. Upon succeeding in luring them—
through their thoughts or feelings—to live by the outward
man, Satan adopts the next step of pretending to be a spirit
in them. He will create many deceptive feelings in the be-

lievers in order to confuse their spiritual senses. If they are ignorant of the wiles of the enemy, they just may allow their spirit to be suppressed until it ceases to function. And then they heed this counterfeit feeling as though they were still following the spirit. Once their spiritual sense grows dull, Satan proceeds further in his deceit. He injects into their minds the thought that now God is leading them by their renewed mind, thus subtly covering up the fault of men in *not using* their spirit as well as covering up the work of the enemy. As soon as man's spirit ceases to operate, the Holy Spirit can no longer find any cooperative element within him; naturally then, all resources from God are cut off. And it is hence impossible for such ones to continue to experience true spiritual life.

Should Christians be insensitive to their condition, Satan assaults them even more mercilessly. He may either mislead them (at a time when they are unconscious of the presence of God) into thinking they are living by faith, or make them suffer without a cause under the delusion that they are suffering with Christ in their spirit. Wherefore Satan by means of a false spirit deceives believers into obeying his will. Such experiences occur to spiritual but undiscerning Christians.

Spiritual ones ought to possess spiritual knowledge so that all their movements can be governed by spiritual reasoning. They should not act impulsively according to fleeting emotion or flashing thought. They should never be in haste. Every action must be scrutinized with spiritual insight in order that only what is approved by the spirit's intuitive knowledge is permitted. Nothing should be done which is propelled by excited feeling or abrupt thought; everything must be carefully and quietly examined before it is executed.

To examine and test our walk is a very important element in following the spirit. Believers should not while away their spiritual life foolishly; they must examine carefully all thoughts, feelings, etc., which come to them in order to discern whether these arise from God or from themselves. The natural inclination is to take life easy, to adapt oneself to whatever happens. If so, one will often welcome what the enemy has arranged. Usually we do not investigate these matters, but Scripture commands us to "test everything" (1 Thess. 5.21). Herein lies both a characteristic and a strength of spiritual believers. They "interpret spiritual truths in spiritual language" (1 Cor. 2.13 RSV marginal). The word "interpret" here means in the original "compare" (RSV marginal), "mixing" or "putting together" (Darby note), or "determined" (Darby note). The Holy Spirit purposely gives spiritual believers such power for them to use to test anything which enters their life; otherwise, under the manifold deceits of the evil spirit, it would be most difficult to live.

THE ACCUSATION OF SATAN

Satan has another way to assault those who set their heart on following the leading of the spirit's intuition. This is by counterfeiting or fasely representing one's conscience with all sorts of accusations. To keep our conscience pure we are willing to accept its reproach and deal with whatever it condemns. The enemy utilizies this desire of keeping the conscience void of offense by accusing us of various things. In mistaking such accusations as being from our own consciences we often lose our peace, tire of trying to keep pace with the false accusations, and thus cease to advance spiritually with confidence.

Those who are spiritual ought to be aware that Satan not only indicts us before God but also to ourselves. He does this to disturb us into thinking we ought to suffer penalty because we have done wrong. He is alert to the fact that the children of God can make no progress spiritually unless they have a heart full of confidence; consequently he falsifies the accusation of conscience in order to make them believe they have sinned. Then their communion with God is broken. The problem with believers is that they do not know how to distinguish between the indictment of the evil spirit and the reproach of conscience. Frequently out of fear of offending God, they mistake the accusation of an evil spirit to be the censure of conscience. This accusation grows stronger and stronger until it becomes uncontrollable if not listened to.

Thus in addition to their willingness to yield to conscience's reproof, spiritual believers should also learn how to discern the accusation of the enemy.

What the enemy charges the saints of may sometimes be real sins, though more often than not they are merely imaginary—that is, the evil spirit makes them *feel* they have sinned. If they actually *have* sinned, they should confess it immediately before God, asking for the cleansing of the precious blood (1 John 1.9). Yet should the accusing voice still continue, it obviously must be from the evil spirit.

Here is a matter of serious consequence. Before one knows how to differentiate between the reproach of conscience and the enemy's accusation, he should ask himself whether or not he *really abhors sin. If* this particular thing is wrong, am I willing to confess my sin and eliminate it? If we truly desire to follow God's will, not having yet heeded the accusing voice, we can be quite confident in our heart for it is not in us to want to rebel against God. Then, having determined to follow God's will, we should examine ourselves as to whether or not we have actually committed that sin. We must know beyond the shadow of doubt whether or not we have done it, because the evil spirit frequently accuses us of many unrelated items. If we have done it, then before we confess to God, we first must find out through the teaching of the Bible and the leading of intuition, whether or not this thing is verily wrong. Otherwise, though we have not sinned, Satan will make us suffer for it just as though we had.

The adversary is skillful in imparting all sorts of feelings to men. He may cause them to feel happy or sad; he may induce in them a feeling of guilt or of none whatsoever. But a child of God should understand that his feeling is not necessarily accurate when he thinks he is not wrong, for often he feels right when actually he *is* wrong. Moreover, he may not be wrong even when so feeling; it may be just his feeling and not be factually grounded at all. Whatever he feels, he must *test it out for sure* so as to know where he really stands. The child of God should adopt a neutral attitude towards every accusation. He should not take any action before he is assured as to the source of it. He must not be hasty; rather, he should wait quietly for assurance as to whether it is indeed the chiding of the Holy Spirit or but the charge of the evil spirit. If it originates with the Holy Spirit, he will then deal with it honestly. The believer's present waiting is due to his uncertainty and not to rebellion. Nevertheless, he absolutely must resist making all confessions to men which are motivated by sheer force from outside, for the enemy often tries to compel him to do this.

Real conviction from the Holy Spirit leads us to holiness while the aim of Satan is solely to accuse. He indicts us to make us indict ourselves. His motive is nothing other than to make Christians suffer. Sometimes after one has accepted the enemy's imputation and confessed accordingly, Satan may next fill him with a false peace. This is no small danger for it deprives the believer of any real contrition over defeat. The reproach of conscience ceases once the sin is confessed and cleansed by the precious blood, but the accusation of the enemy continues even after what is accused has been dealt with. The former leads us to the precious blood; the latter drives us to despair, causing us to reckon ourselves irredeemable. The purpose of Satan is to engineer our fall through accusations: "Since we cannot be perfect," sighs the believer resignedly, "then what is the use?"

At times the accusation of Satan is added to the rebuke of conscience. The sin is real, but when it has been treated according to the mind of the Holy Spirit the accusation continues because the evil spirit has joined his indictment to the reproach of the conscience. It is therefore a matter of utmost concern that we preserve an uncompromising attitude towards sin: not merely yielding no ground to the enemy to indict but also learning how to differentiate between the reprimand of the Holy Spirit and the accusation of the evil spirit and learning how to distinguish what is exclusively the enemy's charge from what is his charge mixed in with the reproach of conscience. We must realize most assuredly that the Holy Spirit never reproves further if the sin is cleansed by the precious blood and forsaken.

ADDITIONAL DANGERS

Other hazards lie in the way of following the spirit besides Satan's counterfeits and his attacks. Often our soul will fabricate or sense something which urges us to take action. Christians must never forget that not all senses emerge from the spirit, for the body, the soul, and the spirit each has its own senses. It is highly important not to interpret soulical or physical senses as the intuition of the spirit. God's children should learn daily in experience what is and what is not genuine intuition. How very easy for us, once perceiving the importance of following the intuition, to overlook the fact that senses exist in other parts of the being besides in the spirit. Actually spiritual life is neither so complicated nor so easy as people usually imagine.

Here then are two causes for alarm: first, the peril of mistaking other senses to be the spirit's intuition; and second, the danger of misunderstanding the meaning of intuition. We meet these two hazards every day. Hence the teaching of the Holy Scriptures is quite essential. To confirm whether or not we are moved by, and walk in, the Holy Spirit, we must see if any given thing harmonizes with the teaching of the Bible. The Holy Spirit never moves the prophets of old to write in one way and then move us today in another way. It is categorically impossible for the Holy Spirit to have instructed people of yesteryear what they ought not to do and yet tell us in our day that we must do these very same things. What we receive in the spirit's intuition needs to be certified by the teaching of God's Word. To follow intuition alone and not in conjunction with the Scriptures will *undeniably* lead us into error. The revelation of the Holy Spirit sensed by our spirit must coincide with the revelation of the Holy Spirit in Scripture.

Since our flesh is continuously active, we must be ever vigilant against its intrusion into our keeping the teaching of the Holy Scriptures. We know the Bible discloses the mind of the Holy Spirit; but were we to observe the Bible perfectly, we still would not necessarily be following the mind of the Holy Spirit. Why? Because often we search the many teaching of the Scriptures with our natural mind and later do them with our strength. Although what is understood and is done agrees perfectly with the Scriptures, it is nevertheless done without dependence upon the Holy Spirit. The whole matter has remained within the realm of the flesh. Wherefore, not only what we know in our spirit concerning the mind of the Holy Spirit needs to be checked by the Scriptures, but also what we know from the Scriptures must be carried out through our spirit. Do we not realize that the flesh craves priority even with respect to keeping the Holy Scriptures? The spirit has intuition; but it also has power. It is consequently null and void if we understand any doctrine in our mind while at the same time it remains unexecuted by the power of the spirit.

One more matter needs to be noticed: a great danger looms before us if we live and walk by the spirit too much. Although the Word does emphasize the believer's personal spirit, the Word also informs us that the significance of one's spirit is due to the indwelling *Holy Spirit*. The reason why we must walk and live in the spirit at all is because our spirit, being the habitation of God's Spirit, is where He expresses His mind. The leading and discipline we receive therein is His leading and discipline. In stressing the significance of the Holy Spirit we are at the same time emphasizing our own spirit since the latter constitutes His base of operation. Our danger, upon apprehending the work and function of man's spirit, is to rely entirely on it, forgetting that it is merely the servant of the Holy Spirit. God's Spirit and not our spirit is the One upon Whom we wait for direct guidance into all truth. If man's spirit is divorced from the divine Spirit it becomes as useless as the other parts of man. We should never reverse the order of man's spirit and the Holy Spirit. It is because many of the Lord's people are ignorant of man's spirit and its operation that we have presented in these pages a detailed account of it. This does not mean, however, that the position of the Holy Spirit in a man is inferior to that of his own spirit. The purpose for understanding this faculty of man is to help us to obey Him more and to exalt Him more.

This should exert great influence on our guidance. The Holy Spirit is given primarily for the benefit of the whole body of Christ. He abides in each individual because He dwells in the whole body of Christ and each is a member of it. The work of the Spirit is corporate in nature (1 Cor. 12. 12-13). He guides individuals because He guides the whole body. He leads each of us for the sake of the body. The movement of one member involves the whole body. The guidance of the Holy Spirit in our individual spirits is related to the other members. Spiritual guidance *is* the guidance of the body. In order that our movements may therefore be related to the body, we need to seek sympathy and agreement from the spirit of "two or three" other members, even after we personally have received guidance in our spirit. This principle must not be neglected in spiritual work. Much of defeat, strife, hatred, division, shame, and pain has been due to the independent moves of those who mean well but who follow merely their own spirit. All who follow the spirit should accordingly test their guidance by its relationship to the spiritual body to determine whether or not it is of the Holy Spirit. In every bit of our work, conduct, faith, and teaching we should be regulated by that relationship of the "members one of another" (Rom. 12.5).

In conclusion, then, along the spiritual pathway lurk many snares. A little carelessness brings in defeat. Yet there is no short cut or bypass we can take. We are not insured because we have learned some knowledge; on the contrary, we ourselves must experience everything. Those who have preceded us can only warn us of the hazards ahead so that we may not fall prey to them. If we intend to bypass part of the pathway, we shall be disappointed, but faithful followers of the Lord can avoid many unnecessary defeats.

CHAPTER 2
THE LAWS OF THE SPIRIT

A CHILD OF GOD must learn to recognize the sense of consciousness of his inner being as the first condition for a life walked after the spirit. If he does not discern what is the sense of the spirit and additionally the sense of the soul, he invariably shall fail to do what the spirit requires of him. For instance, when we feel hungry we know we should eat; when we feel cold we know we should be clothed. Our senses express needs and requirements. We must therefore know what our physical senses mean before we can know how to satisfy them with material supplies. In the spiritual realm, too, one must come to understand the meanings of his spirit's various senses as well as their respective supply. Only after an individual comprehends his spirit with its movements can he walk by the spirit.

There are a few laws of the spirit with which every Christian ought to be acquainted. If he does not understand these laws or fails to see the significance of recognizing the sensations of the spirit, he will miss many of its movements. His failure to discern its senses undermines the proper place of the spirit in his daily walk. Hence once we have known the various functions of the inner man, such as intuition, communion and conscience, we need to identify their movements which can then enable us to walk by the spirit. Being filled with the Holy Spirit, our spirit will be operating actively. But we shall incur loss if we disregard these operations. It is thus imperative that we observe the way the spirit habitually moves. A Christian should know more about the operation of his spirit than about the activity of his mind.

(1) WEIGHTS ON THE SPIRIT

The spirit needs to be kept in a state of perfect freedom. It should always be light, as though floating in the air; only so may life grow and work be done. A Christian ought to realize what the weights laid on his spirit are. Often he feels it is under oppression, as if a thousand pound load were pressing upon his heart. He can unearth no reason for this weight, which usually steals in upon one quite suddenly. It is employed by the enemy to harass the spiritual, to deprive him of joy and lightness, as well as to disable his spirit from working together with the Holy Spirit. If he does not recognize the source of this heaviness and the meaning of the oppression in the spirit, he cannot instantly deal with it and thereby restore his spirit immediately to normalcy.

The believer may be puzzled by such a sensation, interpreting it to be something natural or something occasional. He consequently may disregard it and allow his spirit to come under suppression. How often he continues to work without paying due attention to the weight, and frequently giving the enemy ground to play his trick at will upon him. Many times when this one is supposed to be used by God, he instead is powerless to accomplish God's work because he carries this heavy weight with him. The consciousness of his spirit grows very dull beneath such oppression. That explains why Satan and his evil hosts focus their assault on placing a heavy weight upon the believer's spirit. Alas for the child of God; for he often is unaware that the source of the weight is satanic; and even if he is aware, he may not resist.

With *this* load upon his spirit the Christian is bound to suffer defeat. If he encounters it in the morning and does not deal with it at once, he experiences defeat the whole day long. A free spirit is the basis for victory. In order to fight against the enemy and to live out God's life, we must possess a spirit altogether untrammeled by weight. When it is oppressed the Christian is deprived of his power of discernment and naturally misses God's true guidance. Whenever the spirit suffers oppression the mind cannot function properly. Everything comes to a halt or else everything goes awry.

It is of utmost consequence to deal with the heavy weight or oppression of the spirit *immediately*. Never adopt an attitude of indifference, for if you do you will suffer for it. The weight will grow heavier and heavier. And should it not be dealt away with, it will become a part of your life. Whereupon you will view all spiritual affairs as bitter and acrid, retarding your spiritual advance. In case you do not treat of the weight the first time it will come upon you more easily the next. The way to handle it is to stop the work at hand at once, set your will against this weight, and exercise your spirit to oppose it. Occasionally you may have to utter words audibly against it; at other times with the power of your spirit you should resist in prayer.

It is also indispensible to deal with the cause of such heaviness because the oppressive load shall remain as long as the cause goes unresolved. In addition to resisting the enemy's work there should be the uncovering of the cause behind that work. And if successful, you will thereby regain the place you previously had yielded to the enemy. If you have the power of discernment you will come to see it was because of your failure to cooperate with God at a particular time with regard to a particular matter that the enemy gained ground to crush you with such a heavy weight. The lost ground must be regained. If we resist the enemy by discovering the cause of his working, he shall flee.

(2) BLOCKAGE OF THE SPIRIT

The spirit requires the soul and body as organs for expression. It is like a mistress who must have a steward and a servant working for her to accomplish her wish. It can also be likened to an electric current which requires wire to show forth light. Should the soul and body lose their normality under the attack of the enemy, the spirit shall be shut in and denied any means of outlet. The adversary is familiar with the requirements of the spirit; therefore he frequently acts against the believer's soul and body. When these parts cease to function properly the spirit is stripped of its means of expression and so forfeits its victorious position.

During such a period one's mind may be confused, his emotions disturbed, his will weary and impotent to actively govern the whole being, or his body overly tired and temporarily lazy. He must resist these symptoms at once or else his spirit will be blocked in and he be unfit either to engage the enemy livingly in battle or to retain his ground of victory.

Shortly after his spirit is shut in, the believer loses his "aliveness." He seems to be bashful, seeks to hide himself, and seldom undertakes anything publicly. He likes to withdraw to the back, not wanting to be seen. Perhaps he fancies he has discovered something of himself, not realizing his spirit actually is being blocked. He appears to have no interest in reading the Bible and to have no word in prayer. His past work and experience, whenever recalled, appear to be meaningless, sometimes even laughable, to him. He feels no power in preaching—as though he were merely going through the motions. Should he allow this blockage of the spirit to be prolonged, he shall be attacked even more severely by the enemy. Were not God to intervene, due to his own prayer or that of others, the believer would be suffocated spiritually. For lack of knowledge, his reaction may simply be one of surprise and he may thus assume the all-too-common attitude of giving up. Actually though, because no spiritual experience or sense occurs without a cause, we should search it out carefully and not permit any weight to persist in us.

Satan tries to imprison the spirit in a dark chamber so that the soul is without the guidance of the spirit. As soon as the blockage is lifted, however, the believer once again can breathe easily and be restored to his normal liveliness.

Whenever a child of God is in such a hemmed-in situation, it is vital that he exercise his will towards *audibly uttering* words against the foe, lifting up his voice to proclaim the victory of the cross and the defeat of the enemy. He must wholeheartedly oppose the work of the adversary in both his soul and body. Following such a proclamation he must employ his will actively to resist the blockage. Prayer is one means of opening the spirit. But given the above-described situation, one needs to pray *aloud*. The best thing for the saint to do is to claim the victorious name of the Lord Jesus over every onslaught of the enemy. In addition to prayer he should exercise his spirit to run the blockade so as to reach the outside.

(3) POISONING OF THE SPIRIT

Our spirit can be poisoned by the evil spirit. This poison is the flaming dart of the enemy, aimed directly at our spirit. Into it he shoots sorrow, grief, anguish, woe or heartbreak to cause us to have a "sorrowful spirit" (1 Sam. 1.15 ASV): and a "broken spirit who can bear?" (Prov. 18.14) It is exceedingly hazardous for anyone to accept without objection or question every sorrow which comes upon him and take for granted that these are naturally his own feelings. He has not yet examined the source nor put up any resistance. Let us remember to never accept any thought or feeling lightly. If we wish to walk after the spirit we must be watchful in all points, searching especially the source of every notion and sensation.

Sometimes Satan provokes us to harden our spirit. It can become stiff, unyielding, narrow and selfish. Such a spirit cannot work with God nor can it do His will. And so a believer will abandon his love towards men; he will shed every delicate, sympathetic, tenderhearted feeling towards others. Since he has lost the generosity of the Lord and has drawn a circle around himself, how can the Holy Spirit ever use him mightily?

Frequently the enemy entices Christians to harbor an unforgiving spirit—a very common symptom indeed among God's children. Perhaps the fall of spiritual Christians can be traced chiefly to this very cause. Such bitterness and fault-finding and enmity inflict a severe blow upon spiritual life. If believers fail to see that such an attitude is distinctly from the enemy and *not from themselves,* they shall never be emancipated from the spirit of hatred.

At still other times Satan induces the spirit of God's people to become narrow and confined. He seduces these Christians into separating themselves from others by drawing lines of demarcation. If anyone is blind to the concept of the church as a body he will be devoted to his "small circle," proving that his spirit is already shrunken. The spiritual person, however, does not consider the things of God as his own but loves the whole church in his heart. If one's spirit is open, the river of life overflows; should his spirit shrink, he hinders God's work and lessens his own usefulness. A spirit that is not large enough to embrace all the children of God has been poisoned already.

Often Satan injects pride into the believer's spirit, evoking in him an attitude of self-importance and of self-conceit. He causes him to esteem himself a very outstanding person, one who is indispensable in God's work. Such a spirit constitutes one of the major reasons for the fall of believers: "pride goes before destruction, and a haughty spirit before a fall" (Prov. 16.18).

The evil spirit infects the believer's spirit with these and other venoms. If these poisons are not opposed instantly they soon become "the works of the flesh" (Gal. 5.19). At first these are only poisons from Satan, but they can be transformed into sins of the flesh if the Christian accepts them, even unconsciously, rather than resists them.

If the venom in the spirit is not dealt with it shall immediately become the sin of the spirit, a sin severer than any other. James and John thunderously asked: "Lord, do you want us to bid fire come down from heaven and consume them? . . . And he said, you do not know what manner of spirit you are of" (Luke 9.54,55 marginal). It is most essential that we know of what kind of spirit we are. We often do not perceive that our spirit is prey to the instigation of the enemy. Everything is wrong if it is wrong. From the experience of these two disciples we observe that an erring spirit can manifest itself easily through spoken words. Even so, the words uttered may not reveal nearly as much as the tone assumed. Sometimes the words are correct but the tone is wrong. To assure victory we need to watch even the sound of our speech. Immediately the evil spirit touches our spirit, our voice loses its softness. A harsh, hard, and shrill utterance does not spring from the Holy Spirit; it simply exhibits the fact that the one who speaks has been poisoned already by Satan.

How de we usually speak? Are we able to refer to others without any tinge of condemnation? Our words may in fact be true but lurking behind those words of truth could be the spirit of criticism, condemnation, wrath, or jealousy. Whereas we should speak the truth in love. If our spirit is pure and gentle, then are we able to voice the truth. Now should the spirit of condemning be within us, we most assuredly have sinned. Sin is not only an action; it is also a condition. What is hidden behind things is what matters the most. How many times we sin while doing something for God or men, for darkly hidden away is an unfaithful, unwilling, or grudging spirit.

We must keep our spirit sweet and soft. It must be pure and clean. Do we consider an erring spirit as sin? Do we know when the enemy has attacked our spirit—when our spirit is poisoned? Suppose we do know, are we humble enough to eliminate such sin? The moment we notice our voice has turned harsh, we must stop instantly. With not the slightest hesitation we should turn to ourselves and say, "I am willing to speak with a pure spirit; I am willing to oppose the enemy." If we are reluctant to say to our brethren, "I am wrong," then our spirit remains engulfed in its sin. God's children ought to learn how to guard their spirit from being goaded by the enemy. They should know also how to preserve it in sweetness and tenderness.

In ordinary times the Lord's people should early take the shield of faith which quenches all the flaming darts of the evil one. This implies that we should swiftly exercise living faith to look for God's protection and to withstand the enemy's attack. Faith is our shield, not our extractor: faith is a weapon for quenching the flaming darts, not for pulling them out afterwards. But should anyone be hit by a flaming dart, he at once must eliminate the cause of the dart. He should maintain an attitude of resistance, immediately denying whatever comes from Satan and praying for cleansing.

(4) SINKING OF THE SPIRIT

The spirit sinking or being submerged is largely due to a turning in on oneself. It may be induced by a possessiveness over all the experiences one has had or by an intrusion of the power of darkness or by a self-centeredness in prayer and worship. When anyone's spirit is tilted inward instead of outward the power of God is at once severed and the spirit will soon be surrounded by the soul.

Sometimes this submerging of the spirit in the soul is precipitated by the deceit of the evil foe who supplies the person with physical sensations and various wonderful joyful experiences. He does not perceive that they originate with the evil spirit: he instead construes them to be from God: and thus he unknowingly comes to dwell in a sensuous world where his spirit is drowned in the soul.

Believers may be additionally deceived—and their spirit accordingly descend into the soul—when they do not understand the position of Christ. The Holy Spirit indwells the child of God to manifest the enthroned Christ to him. The books of Acts, Ephesians, and Hebrews speak very plainly on the position of Christ *in the heaven* today. The spirit of the Christian is joined to the heavenly Christ. Because of his ignorance, however, the Christian looks within to find Him. He wishes to be united with the Christ Who is in him. Hence his spirit cannot ascend above the clouds, but rather is oppressed and tumbles into the soulical realm.

All these operations tempt the individual to live in his feelings rather than in his spirit. He needs to know that before he becomes spiritual and actually walks in the spirit the enemy is not compelled at that time to resort to counterfeit; but after the person has experienced the pouring of the Holy Spirit's power into his spirit, he faces a new world never before encountered. And just here is there cause for alarm, for the enemy will work to induce him to cease abiding in the spirit. If he succeeds, the believer will incur great loss. The tactic of the adversary is to deceive him through the feelings of the soul and body into thinking these are spiritual experiences for him to enjoy.

Many who have entered into spiritual living shall meet defeats because of their ignorance of its laws. The enemy foments within them all sorts of physical sensations and supernatural experiences. Should they lean on these super- natural phenomena or on other sensational occurrences which come from the outside, their life in the spirit will be obstructed. They will dwell in their outward soul or body while their innermost spirit is denied the power to cooper- ate with God. Naturally soul and body once again ascend, regain their forfeited authority, and submerge the spirit completely.

While the spirit is submerged its senses are rendered in- operative. When this occurs, many spiritual Christians feel they have lost their spirit. Soul and body occupy such a large place that the entire being can live by their sensa- tions. Man's sensory organs replace the operation of the spirit. The movements of the spirit are buried beneath the powerful sensations of the soul and body. And eventually all spiritual life and work are completely terminated. If such a condition is permitted to last for very long the believer has fallen terribly indeed. He may perhaps be possessed by the evil spirit.

Everything therefore which is capable of impairing spirit- ual consciousness must be denied. We must shun wild laughter, bitter crying, and every other extreme outburst of physical emotion. The body should be kept in perfect calm. We must reject inordinate supernatural or natural sensations, for these propel the mind to follow the body and not the spirit. Never allow anything to hinder us from understanding the small still throb of the spirit.

Because the soul—when the spirit begins to sink—sur- rounds it and reduces it to servitude, the child of God must learn how to keep his spirit continuously outgoing, never permitting it to stagnate. For unless his spirit sallies forth to attack Satan, Satan unquestionably will attack his spirit and cause it to sink. Only as our spirit is flowing out is the Holy Spirit equally able to flow out His life. The moment anyone turns in on himself and sets his spirit to sinking, the torrential flow of the divine Spirit immediately stops. He uses the believer's spirit as His channel for the flowing out of God's life.

A Christian needs to determine what has caused his spirit to slump and then must restore it to its original state. As soon as he discovers a leak in the power of his spirit, he must try to redeem the situation at once.

(5) BURDENS OF THE SPIRIT

The burdens of the spirit differ from the weights on the spirit. The latter proceed from Satan with the intent of crushing the believer and making him suffer, but the former issue from God in His desire to manifest His will to the believer so that he may cooperate with Him. Any weight on the spirit has no other objective than to oppress; it therefore usually serves no purpose and produces no fruit. A burden of the spirit, on the other hand, is given by God to His child for the purpose of calling him to work, to pray, or to preach. It is a burden with purpose, with reason, and for spiritual profit. We must learn how to distinguish the burden of the spirit from the weight on the spirit.

Satan never burdens Christians with anything; he only encircles their spirit and presses in with a heavy weight. Such a load binds one's spirit and throttles his mind from functioning. A person with a burden or concern from God merely carries it; but the one who is oppressed by Satan finds his total being bound. With the arrival of the power of darkness, a believer instantaneously forfeits his freedom. A God-given burden is quite the reverse. However weighty it may be, God's concern is never so heavy as to throttle him from praying. The *freedom* of prayer will never be lost under any burden from God: yet the enemy's weight which forces itself upon one's spirit invariably denies one his freedom to pray. The burden imparted by God is lifted once we have prayed, but the heaviness from the enemy cannot be raised unless we fight and resist in prayer. The weight on the spirit steals in unawares, whereas the concern of the spirit results from God's Spirit working in our spirit. The load upon the spirit is most miserable and oppressive, while the burden of the spirit is very joyous (naturally the flesh does not deem it so), for it summons us to walk together with God (see Matt. 11.30). It turns bitter only when opposed and its demand is not met.

All real works begin with burdens or concerns in the spirit. (Of course, when the spirit lacks any concern we need to exercise our minds.) When God desires us to labor or speak or pray, He first implants a burden in our spirit. Now if we are acquainted with the laws of the spirit we will not continue on carelessly with the work in hand and allow the burden to accrue. Nor will we neglectfully disregard the burden until it is no longer sensed. We should lay everything aside immediately to ferret out *the meaning of this burden.* Once we have discerned its import, we can act accordingly. And when the work called for is done, the burden then leaves us.

In order to receive burdens from God our spirit has to be kept continuously free and untrampled. Only an untrammeled spirit can detect the movement of the Holy Spirit. Any spirit which is already full of concerns has lost the sharpness of its intuitive sense and hence cannot be a good vessel. Due to his failure to act according to the burden which he already has received from God, the believer often finds himself painfully burdened for many days. During this period God is unable to give him any new one. Consequently, it is highly necessary to search out the meaning of a burden through prayer, with the help of the Holy Spirit and the exercise of one's mind.

Frequently the burden or concern in the spirit is for prayer (Col. 4.12). As a matter of fact we are not able to pray beyond our burden. To continue to pray without it can produce no fruit because the prayer must be emanating from our mind. But the *prayer* burden in the spirit can only be lightened *through prayer.* Whenever God concerns us with something, such as prayer, preaching the Word, and so forth, the only way to lessen that concern or burden is to do what it calls for. The prayer burden in the spirit alone enables us to pray in the Holy Spirit with sighs too deep for words. When our spirit is concerned with prayer burdens nothing can discharge that burden except prayer. It is lifted soon after the work is performed.

Because of the large accumulation of prayer burdens we often find it difficult to pray at first, but the longer we pray the more our spirit responds with amens. We should try our best to pour out all the burdens in our spirit by prayer until all of them have left us. The more life is poured out through prayer, the happier we are. A common temptation, however, is to cease praying before the burden is lifted. When we begin to feel buoyant in our spirit we assume our prayer is answered, not realizing we are just beginning to engage in spiritual work. If at that moment we turn away to attend to other matters, then spiritual work will suffer great loss.

A believer should never regard spiritual labor as altogether joyous and jubilant, as though the presence of a burden is going to deprive him of what he considers to be spiritual experience. Quite pitiful is the one who is unaware of what real spiritual exertion in the burden of the spirit is truly like. He who is willing to suffer for God and men does not live for himself; but those who daily seek sensuous pleasures and become apprehensive about bearing burdens for God and the church are living only for themselves. Now in the light of what has just been said, we must not consider ourselves as fallen or as having erred whenever God imparts a burden to us. Satan is extremely pleased if we interpret it as such for he shall thereby escape our attacks. Let us not misunderstand ourselves. And let us not listen to Satan, for if we do we shall be accused and tormented further.

Genuine spiritual work is aggressive towards Satan and travails in birth for believers. These in no wise can be termed joyous undertakings. They require a more thorough death to self. That explains why no soulish Christian is able to engage in true spiritual effort. To enjoy sensuous pleasures daily is no evidence of spirituality. On the contrary, those who go on with God and disregard their own feelings are the truly spiritual ones. When a believer in burden is contending with the enemy he often wishes to be alone, separated from all human intercourse so as to concentrate on spiritual warfare. Before the combat is over he can barely display a smiling face. A spiritual Christian should welcome any burden which the Lord brings his way.

We need to know the laws of the spirit and the way to cooperate with God as well. Otherwise, we may prolong the burden to our disadvantage or else lose the opportunity to labor together with God. Every time we receive a burden in our spirit we should find out immediately through prayer what that burden is. If it is a call to war, to war we go; if a call to preach the gospel, the gospel we preach; and if a call to pray, pray we will. Let us seek how to work together with God. Let the old burden be discharged and the new one come in.

(6) EBBING OF THE SPIRIT

God's life and power in our spirit can recede like a tide. We recognize that anyone soulish usually deems his spiritual life to be at high tide when he *feels* the presence of God; but if he feels low and dry, he is at ebb tide. These are of course but feelings; they do not represent the reality of spiritual life.

Nevertheless, spiritual life does encounter a time of decline, though it is quite unlike any feeling of the soul. After one is filled with the Holy Spirit he can proceed quite well for a period, and then *gradually*, not suddenly, his spiritual life subsides. The difference between a sensuous decline and a spiritual decline lies here: the former is usually abrupt, whereas the latter is gradual. A believer may become conscious that the life and power of God which he once received is gradually ebbing. This may cause him to lose the joy, peace and power which his spirit ought to sustain. Day by day he grows weaker. At this time he seems to lose his taste for communion with God: his Bible reading becomes meaningless: rarely, if at all, is his heart touched by any message or special verse. Moreover, his prayer turns dry and dreary as if there is neither sense nor word; and his witnessing appears to be forced and reluctant, not overflowing as before. In other words, life is no longer as vibrant, strong, buoyant or joyous as before. Everything seems to have receded.

A tide has its ebb and flow. Can God's life and power in our spirit likewise be characterized by such phenomena? By no means! God's life knows no such ebb, because it is forever flowing. It does not rise and fall as the ocean tide, but is like a river ever flowing with living water (John 7.38). God's life in us is not at all like the tide which must ebb at a certain hour, because the source of our inner life is in God with Whom there is "no variation or shadow due to change" (James 1.17). Hence the life in our spirit should flow like a river—incessantly and unto overflowing.

Wherefore if anyone becomes aware that his life is receding, he should understand that life does not subside, it simply ceases to flow. He should know as well that such ebbing is totally unnecessary. Never be so deceived by Satan as to consider it impossible for one who is still in the body to be filled permanently with the life of God. His life in us is like a river of living water. If it is not hindered it shall flow uninterruptedly. A Christian can experience a life forever flowing; an ebb tide is not only unnecessary but abnormal as well.

The question in hand is accordingly not how we may induce spiritual life to rise up after it has fallen; rather, it is how we may get it to flow. The fountain of life remains within the believer, though it is now blocked. Nothing is wrong with the inlet; it is the outlet which is obstructed. The water of life does not spring forth because the flow has no way through. Were the outlet cleared, the water of life would flow unceasingly. What a child of God therefore needs is not more life but more flow of life.

Immediately upon sensing a waning in his spiritual life, a child of God automatically should realize an obstruction must exist somewhere. Satan will accuse you of having retrogressed spiritually; other people will judge you as having lost power; and you yourself will imagine you must have committed some grave sin. These may be true, but they do not form the whole truth. Actually, such a situation is *mostly,* though not entirely, created because of our not knowing how to cooperate with God in fulfilling His conditions for the certainty of a ceaseless flow. Foolishness is a prime factor. Hence a person should immediately pray and meditate over, and test and search out the cause for, such an ebbing. He should wait upon God, asking His Spirit to reveal the reason. In the meantime, he should try to unearth where he has failed to fulfill the condition for the steady flow of life.

Not only should you confess that you have drawn back (such confession is important) but also you should actively ferret out the explanation for the falling back. While the opinions of Satan, others and yourself are undependable, they are still worth considering, since sometimes they *are* real. Upon discovering the cause, you must deal with it without delay. Life will not flow until the cause of obstruction is duly treated.

Consequently, at each ebb tide in spiritual life one must instantly begin to isolate its cause through prayer, meditation and searching. Know the law of the flow of God's life; repulse every attack of the enemy. Then life once again shall flow, stronger than before, breaking through every stronghold of the enemy.

(7) IRRESPONSIBILITY OF THE SPIRIT

Man's spirit can be compared to an electric bulb. When in contact with the Holy Spirit, it shines; but should it be disconnected, it plunges into darkness. "The spirit of man is the lamp of the Lord" (Prov. 20.27). God's aim is to fill the human spirit with light; yet the believer's spirit is sometimes darkened. Why is this? It is because it has lost contact with the Holy Spirit. To perceive whether or not one's spirit is connected with the Holy Spirit, one need only notice if it is shining.

We have said before that God's Spirit dwells in man's and that he cooperates with Him through his own spirit. If the spirit of man has been deprived of its normal condition it will seem to be disconnected from the Holy Spirit, losing all its light. It thus is very necessary for us to maintain our spirit in a healthy quiet state so as to insure its cooperation with the Holy Spirit. If it is disturbed by external forces it automatically is bereft of its power to cooperate with the Holy Spirit and is plunged into darkness.

Now these phenomena cause the spirit to fail in its responsibility of cooperating with the Holy Spirit. As long as it is irresponsible, victory remains impossible. Suppose a person, rising in the morning, feels as though he has lost his spirit. The enemy will perhaps induce him to think it is due to physical weariness lingering from yesterday's overwork. If he takes the enemy's suggestion without question and allows his spirit to become irresponsible, he shall be stripped of all his strength to repel that day's temptations as well as to accomplish that day's work. He should search right away for the real cause, for the spirit ought to be active and powerful enough to regulate the body and not be adversely affected by it. He should acknowledge that his spirit, having been assaulted by the enemy, has become irresponsible. He must seek immediate recovery or else he shall be defeated the moment he meets anyone. Never permit the early irresponsible state of the spirit to continue until midday, for this is a sure way to defeat.

Once realizing his spirit has been irresponsible, a believer should oppose without delay all the works of the enemy as well as the causes for the enemy's work. Should it be purely the attack of the adversary the spirit will regain its freedom after having resisted. But if there is justification for the attack, that is, if the person has given any ground to the enemy, then he must uncover the reason and deal with it. Usually the reason is related to the past history of the individual. He needs to pray over such various matters as his environment, family, relatives, friends, work, and so forth. When his spirit senses a release after a certain matter has been prayed over, then he has isolated the cause for the enemy's assault. Shortly after he has taken care of this matter, the believer's spirit will be freed and restored to its function.

Sometimes, however, the irresponsibility of the spirit is because the Christian has loosened the reins, allowing the spirit to stray off course. But we should note from the Word that "the spirits of prophets are subject to prophets" (1 Cor. 14.32) and "woe to the foolish prophets who follow their own spirit" (Ezek. 13.3). How extremely important for a Christian to control his spirit by exercising his will so that his spirit may not go to extremes but be kept in that state of co-operation with God. Man's spirit can go wild; hence "a haughty spirit" is remarked upon in Proverbs (16.18). The spirit of man can take action independent of God's Spirit if a believer does not exercise mastery over it and make it subject to Him. We accordingly must be watchful lest our spirit veer out of God's orbit, lose its quiet communion with God, and be disabled from laboring with Him.

Occasionally the irresponsibility of the spirit is due to its hardness. God requires a soft and tender spirit to express His mind. Should it grow harsh and unyielding, the operations of His Spirit will be hindered. Only a yielding spirit can fulfill the thought of the divine Spirit: "and every one whom his spirit made willing . . . " (Ex. 35.21 ASV). A Christian ought to be able to yield to Him on the shortest notice. His spirit should be most sensitive so that it can detect the still small voice of God and respond right away. If it is hardened the child of God not only is powerless to follow His will but is also unfit to hear the voice of the Holy Spirit in his spirit. Hence it is necessary to keep one's spirit in a tender and pliable state so as to enable that one always to follow the delicate throbbing therein. This is what the Apostle meant when he wrote: "do not quench the Spirit" (1 Thess. 5.19). A Christian should heed every word, movement, and sense in his inner man carefully. By so doing, his spiritual consciousness will be sharpened and God will be able to make His will known to him.

If a person wishes to walk by his spirit he should recognize when it is irresponsible and unable to cooperate with the Holy Spirit and also determine why. He needs to guard his spirit carefully so as to insure it against all disturbances both from the enemy and from his self life and to assure it a peaceful communion with God.

(8) CONDITIONS OF THE SPIRIT

Let us summarize. A believer should know every law of the spirit if he desires to live by it. If he is not vigilant and loses the cooperation of his spirit with God, then he unquestionably has fallen. To discern the particular condition of his inner man is one of the most central laws pertaining to the spirit. All which we have discussed in the chapter are included in this law.

A child of God ought to know what is and what is not the normal condition for his spirit. Since it should have authority over man's soul and body, occupying the highest position in him and possessing the greatest power, the Christian needs to know if such is the situation in him or not. He should also recognize whether his spirit, if it has lost its normalcy, did so through war or environment. The conditions of the spirit may be classified generally into four types:

(a) The spirit is oppressed and is therefore in decline.
(b) The spirit is under compulsion and so is forced into inordinate activity.
(c) The spirit is defiled (2 Cor. 7.1) since it has yielded ground to sin.
(d) The spirit is quiet and firm because it occupies its rightful position.

A Christian should know at least these four different conditions and also understand how to deal with each one if necessary. Often a person's spirit sinks and is "pushed aside" through his own carelessness as to the enemy's assault. During that time he seems to have forfeited his heavenly position together with its brightness and victory and subsequently feels cold and withered. Due to sadness in his spirit or to any one of a number of other reasons, his inner man is cast down and is denied the joy of floating above. When the spirit is oppressed in this fashion it drops below its normal level.

At other times it may be coerced into running wild. A person can be so stimulated by his soul that his spirit falls under compulsion and is thereby denied its tranquillity. Because of his pursuit of creaturely activities he may develop an "unruly spirit." Too much laughter as well as many other actions may produce an unmanageable spirit. Protracted war with the enemy can provoke the spirit to become overly active. The saint may find his spirit overstretched to the point where it is powerless to stop. Or the enemy may inject strange joy or other feelings into him to entice his inner man to move beyond the acceptable and right counsel of his mind or will. Whenever anyone is incompetent to guard his spirit, then is he open inevitably to defeat.

The spirit on other occasions neither sinks too low nor is elevated too high but is simply defiled. The defilement may be due to its attitude of hardness or unyieldedness; or to sins like pride, jealousy and others; or to the mixing in with the spirit of such soulical functions as natural affection, feeling, thought, and so on. The spirit needs to be purified from its every defilement (2 Cor. 7.1; 1 John 1.9).

If a Christian wishes to walk after the spirit he has to discern exactly what condition his own is in, whether it is quietly occupying its proper place, has fallen too low, is risen too high, or is simply defiled. He must learn, if required, how to uplift his oppressed spirit so that it measures up to the standard of the Holy Spirit, how to exercise his will to prevent his spirit from becoming overly active or to restore it to its normalcy if it is too active, and how to cleanse his defiled spirit that it may work together with God once again.

THE PRINCIPLE OF MIND AIDING THE SPIRIT

IF HE IS TO WALK after the spirit the Christian must understand its every law. Without this fund of knowledge he will not be able to apprehend all the meanings of the different spiritual senses and naturally will be unable to do everything required of him. The demands of the spirit are all expressed through the motions of the spirit. To disregard spiritual movements is to ignore spiritual demands. It is this which establishes the priority of knowing the laws of the spirit in one's spiritual life.

But there is something else of no less importance for anyone wishing to walk after the spirit: the principle of the mind aiding or assisting it. This principle is to be applied constantly. Many defeats in spiritual life can be traced to ignorance of it, even though the laws of the spirit are indeed known. And why? Because these laws can only explain to us the meaning of the spirit's stirring and supply us with ways to satisfy their particular demands. Whenever the spirit senses anything, we are equipped by the knowledge of these laws to fulfill the requirement called for; if the condition is normal, we walk accordingly; and if abnormal, we can correct it. But a problem arises here; which is, that we do not always enjoy such spiritual stirrings. The spirit simply may not speak. Many have experienced an utter silence for quite a few days. It appears as though it is sleeping. Is this to say that during those days when our spirit is inactive we should do nothing? Must we quietly sit for a number of days, neither praying nor reading the Bible nor performing any work? Our spiritual common sense vigorously replies: no; by no means should we waste the time. But if we do anything during that period will it not mean that we labor in the power of the flesh and not according to the spirit?

Now this is just the moment when we should apply the principle of the mind supporting the spirit. But how? When the spirit is sleeping, our mind must come in to do the work of the spirit. And before long we shall see the latter itself joining in the work. The mind and the spirit are closely knit: they are to help each other. Many times the spirit senses something which the mind is made to understand, and then action is taken; while on other occasions the spirit is unmoved and needs to be aroused by the activity of the believer's mind. If the spirit is inactive the mind can induce it to move. And once moved, the believer should follow it. Such inducement of the spirit by the mind is what we here term as the principle or law of the mind aiding the spirit. There is a principle in spiritual life which holds that in the *beginning* we should exercise our spiritual sense to apprehend God-given knowledge, but that afterwards we must keep and use this knowledge by means of the mind. For example, you notice a great need somewhere. According to the knowledge you have received from God, you realize you should pray and petition Him for supply. But at the time you see the need your spirit does not feel at all like praying. What should you do? You should pray with your *mind* instead of waiting for the spirit to move. Every need is a call to prayer. Although at the start you pray despite silence in your spirit, as you pray on you will soon be conscious of something rising within you. It signifies your spirit has joined in at last in this work of prayer.

Occasionally our inner man is so oppressed by Satan or so disturbed by the natural life that we can hardly discern it. It has sunk so low that it seems to have lost its consciousness. We continue to feel the presence of our soul and body, but the spirit appears to be absent. If we should wait for it to stir before we pray, we shall probably never do so, nor shall it regain its freedom. What we must do is pray with what the mind remembers to be the truth we once received and in that prayer resist the power of darkness. If ever we do not sense the spirit we should pray with our mind. Such mental activity eventually will incite our spirit to move.

"Pray(ing) with the mind" (1 Cor. 14.15) can activate the spirit. Although at the outset we may appear to be praying with empty words, divested of any meaning, nevertheless as we pray along with our mind and resist with prayer our spirit soon will ascend. Whereupon the spirit and the mind will work together. And as soon as it comes in, prayer becomes meaningful and quite free. The cooperation between these two elements delineates the normal state of spiritual life.

SPIRITUAL WARFARE

Should a believer in spiritual warfare neglect the law of spirit and mind working together, he will be waiting continually for God's burden instead of warring constantly against the enemy. Because he presently has no sense of war the believer concludes he must delay until he has that sense, and that only then can he begin to pray against the enemy. He does not perceive that if he starts to pray with his mind his spirit shall immediately sense the war. Since we know how wicked the evil spirit is and how he molests the children of the Lord as well as the children of man, and since we should realize also that we must pray against him in order to send him as early as possible to the bottomless pit, how dare we tarry to pray until our spirit acknowledges the urgency? Even though we still lack the consciousness of war, we must pray anyhow. Begin to pray with the mind: curse the evil spirit with the words we have learned already: and our spirit shall soon be activated and shall add its power behind those words of curse. To illustrate. Suppose the Holy Spirit in the early morning anoints you mightily so that you can curse the enemy with your spirit, but at noon you seem to have lost this spirit. What should you do? You should do by your mind now what your spirit had done in the morning. The spiritual principle is that whatever is obtained in the spirit must be preserved and employed by the mind.

RAPTURE

This law of the mind's assistance can be applied as well to

the matter of faith concerning "the rapture." At the beginning you enjoy the "spirit of rapture," but later on you feel as though it is drained of its awareness of the nearness of the Lord's return and the reality of your rapture. In that hour you should recall the law of the mind coming to the aid of the spirit. You ought to pray with the mind even while your spiritual sense is empty. If you merely wait to have your spirit refilled with the sense of rapture, you will never possess it again; but by exercising your mind to think and to pray, you shall shortly be filled with the spiritual awareness you once had.

PREACHING

For the preaching of the truth this principle is vital. Those truths learned in the past are now stored in our brain. Communicating to others what is in our mind simply *by our mind* can produce no spiritual results whatever. No doubt at first we knew those truths in our spirit, but currently the spirit seems to have receded and all which is left are memories. How, then, can our spirit be replenished with these truths so that we may communicate them *by the spirit* to others? By exercising our mind. We should re-meditate on those truths before God and pray over them once again; that is, we should take those truths as centers and pray around them. Shortly thereafter we shall discover our spirit being permeated once more with those truths which had been there before. These initially are possessed in the spirit, later are stored in the believer's mind, and now re-enter his spirit by praying with the mind. Thus are we qualified to preach the truths we once before had known in our spirit.

INTERCESSION

We all appreciate the importance of intercession. Yet often when we have time to spend in intercession our spirit is inactive and fails to supply us with subjects for intercessory prayer. This does not mean we need not pray on that occasion or that we can utilize the time for other matters. On the contrary, it serves as a hint for us to intercede in prayer with the mind and to hope and expect the spirit will be activated into participating. You should accordingly exercise your mind to remember your friends, relatives, and fellow-workers to determine if they are in need. As you remember each one so shall you in turn intercede for them. If in interceding on their behalf your spirit remains cold and dry, then you know you are not to pray for them. But supposing at that same time you recall a special lack in your local church or a number of temptations the church is facing or certain hindrances to the Lord's work in a particular area or some distinctive truths which God's children ought to know today. In that event you should intercede for each of them as they come to your attention. If after praying awhile over these matters your spirit still fails to respond as you are yet praying with your mind, then you realize once again that these are not what the Lord desires you to pray for today. But supposing as you touch upon certain matters in your prayer you feel as though the Holy Spirit is anointing you and your spirit seems to respond: it is at this singular moment that you recognize you are at last interceding for what is on the Lord's heart. Hence the principle calls for the exercise of the mind to help the spirit locate its trend.

Frequently a slight exercise of the mind effects the spirit's response, but on other occasions—due to our narrow-mindedness or our mental dullness—we may be forced to consume considerable time before the spirit cooperates. For example, God would like to enlarge the scope of our prayer to include the nations in order to defeat all the behind-the-scene works of Satan. Or He may want us to intercede for all sinners worldwide or for the entire church. *Your* mind, however, is fixed upon the immediate. It will require some time before our mind is ready to consider these all-embracing issues and begin to pray the prayer of the Holy Spirit. Yet as soon as our spirit joins in, we can and must discharge all the burdens which it has concerning this particular matter. We ought to pray carefully and thoroughly over each and every facet of this matter till our spirit is lightened of its burden. Only thereafter can we turn to intercede for other concerns.

This is indeed an important principle in our spiritual life. Whenever God gives us new prayers they usually are received in our spirit, but afterwards we cannot expect *God* to refill our spirit with those prayers. Instead, *we* should exercise our mind to pray continuously over them until our spirit once more regains its burdens.

KNOWING GOD'S WILL

God's guidance does not always come to us directly; it is sometimes indirect. In direct guidance the Spirit of God moves in our spirit and so enables us to know His will. If our mind is attentive to the movement in the spirit we shall easily understand the will of God. But in the various affairs of life God does not necessarily tell us many things directly. There may be many needs of which we as men are aware. What should we do about these conscious needs? We may be invited to work somewhere or something else may suddenly happen. Such matters as these obviously are not sponsored directly by our spirit, for they come to us from other people. Our mind sees the urgency of solving these problems, yet our spirit is unresponsive. How may we experience the guidance of God in such a situation? Well, when we encounter something of this kind, we must with our mind ask God to lead us in the spirit. By so doing we are experiencing the indirect guidance of God. This is the moment the mind must assist the spirit. When one notices his spirit is inactive he should exercise his mind. It is not necessary for it to assist if the spirit is exuding its thought incessantly: only as the spirit remains silent must the mind fill the gap for it.

In such circumstances the believer should exercise his mind by pondering this unsolved matter before God. Although such prayer and consideration emerge from his mind, before long his spirit will collaborate in the prayer and consideration. His spirit which he did not sense before he now begins to sense, and soon the Holy Spirit will be found leading him in his spirit. We should never sit back because of a lack of early movement therein. Rather should we use the mind to "scoop up" our spirit and activate it to help us know whether or not this matter is of God.

THE PRINCIPLE GOVERNING THE ACTIVITY OF THE SPIRIT

In our spiritual experience the operation of the mind is indispensable. Unlike the ocean tide, the spirit is not filled by spontaneous comings and goings. For it to be filled we must comply with the conditions for its filling. This is where the mind assumes its responsibility: to set in motion what the spirit will soon carry forward by itself. If we endlessly wait for the permeation of the spirit we shall be disappointed. On the other hand we should not too highly esteem the work of the mind. By this time we ought to know that unless our action comes from the spirit it serves no useful purpose. We must not walk after the mind. Why then do we engage the mind? We exercise it not for its sake but for the sake of inducing the *spirit* to work. Hence we continue to esteem the spirit as most important. Now if after our mind has been functioning for some time the spirit still fails to respond, as though there is no anointing, we must cease exercising it. Should we detect in spiritual warfare a prolonged emptiness deep within and our spirit continues to sense nothing, we ought to halt the working of the mind. We should not, however, stop its working because of the unwillingness of the flesh. Occasionally we feel tired and yet we know we must proceed. At other times we know we must cease. There is no fixed law over spiritual matters.

The mind supporting the spirit can be likened to operating a hand water pump. In some pumps it is essential to pour into it a cup of water just to provide suction for the machine while pumping. The relation of our mind to the spirit is similar to that between the cup of water and the water pump. If you do not use this cup of water as a starter you shall be powerless to pump up water from the well. Even so, our spirit will not rise up unless we exercise the mind first. Not to start praying with the mind for the sake of the spirit is like a man who neglects to pour in that cup of water first and concludes after pumping twice that there is not any water in the well.

How varied are the works of the spirit. Oftentimes it is like a lion full of strength; whereas at other times it is like a babe possessing no will of its own. When it is weak and helpless the mind must act as its nurse. The mind is never a subsitute for the spirit; the mind merely helps us to activate it. Should the spirit cease to assert its ruling position, the believed must use the power of his mind in prayer to provoke its reassertion. If the spirit has sunk through oppression he should employ his mind to survey the situation and to pray earnestly until it rises up and regains its freedom. A *spiritual* mind can maintain the spirit in a steady position. It can restrain the spirit from being overly active; it can also uplift the spirit from its fallen state.

Let us elaborate a bit further. As has been said, the spirit can be replenished only with the ministration of the spiritual mind. The principle is that all matters in which the spirit formerly took a hand should now be done by the mind. If the Holy Spirit grants anointing later on, He is attesting to you that you are doing this particular thing in the spirit. In the beginning there was nothing of a spiritual sensing about it but currently the sense in the inner man assures you that this is what it intended in the first place. The spirit was impotent to do it then because it was too weak; now, however, through the help of the mind, it can express what it could not express at the first. We can secure whatever we need in the spirit if we ponder and pray with the mind. This will cause us to be filled again in our spirit.

Another point needs to be observed. In spiritual conflict spirit struggles against spirit. But all the powers of man's entire being should join his spirit in wrestling against the enemy. Of these the mind is the most important. The spirit and the mind join forces in battle. Should the former become oppressed and begin to lose its power to resist, the latter must carry the fight forward on its behalf. As the mind contends and resists in prayer the spirit is thereby replenished and once more rises to the occasion.

THE CONDITION OF THE MIND

Inferior though it be to the spirit, the mind nonetheless can assist it. Besides bolstering a weak spirit, it should be able to read and search out the spirit's thought as well. How necessary, therefore, that the mind be kept in its normal state. Just as the movements of the spirit have their laws, so the activity of the mind is governed by its particular laws. The mind that can work freely is one which is light and lively. If it be expanded too far, like overstretching a bow, it shall sacrifice its effectiveness to work. The enemy well knows how we need our mind to attend the spirit so that we may walk by the spirit. Thus he frequently induces us to overuse it that it may be rendered unfit to function normally and hence be powerless to reinforce the spirit in time of weakness.

Our mind is much more than an organ of assistance to the spirit; it also is the place where we obtain light. The Spirit of God dispenses light to the mind through the spirit. If the mind is overexerted it relinquishes the power of receiving His light. The enemy understands that if our mind is darkened our whole being enters into darkness; he consequently strives with all his effort to provoke us to think so very much that we are unable to work quietly. To walk after the spirit a believer must inhibit his mind from revolving endlessly. If it turns too long around one topic, worries or grieves too much over matters, and ponders too intensively to know God's will, it may become unbearable and hamper its normal operation. The mind needs to be kept in a steady and secure state.

Since the mind occupies such a signal position, the Christian, when working together with others, must be careful not to break into his brother's thought. Such action creates much suffering for that one's mind. When his thoughts are being guided and led on by the Spirit, the believer is terribly apprehensive of interference. Any such act will terminate his thought and set his mind to stretch beyond its proper measure, rendering it unfit to cooperate with the Holy Spirit. Accordingly, not only must we keep our own mind free but we additionally must respect our brother's mind. We first must find out the trend of our brother's thought before we can respond to him; otherwise, we shall cause that brother to suffer unduly.

CHAPTER 4

THE NORMALCY OF THE SPIRIT

AN ERRING SPIRIT is often responsible for much of our incorrect conduct. If anyone desires to walk in a spiritual way he must keep himself continually in a proper state. Just as the mind may become loose and haughty or retreat and grow shy, so may his spirit. Should it not be maintained in the Holy Spirit, then it shall be defeated and his outward conduct shall equally suffer defeat. We ought to understand that numerous outer failures stem from the failure of the inner spirit. Were one's inner man strong and powerful it could control the soul and body and, under any circumstances, inhibit their license; but if it be weak, the soul and body shall oppress the spirit and cause that one to fall.

God is interested in our spirit. It is there that the new life dwells, there that His Spirit works, there that we fellowship with Him, there that we know His will, there that we receive the revelation of the Holy Spirit, there that we are trained, there that we mature, there that we resist the attacks of the enemy, there that we receive authority to overcome the devil and his army, and there that we secure the power for service. It is by the resurrection life in the spirit that our body eventually shall be changed into a resurrection one. As the condition of our spirit is so is the condition of our spiritual life. How essential for us to preserve our spirit in its normal state. What the Lord is especially concerned with in the Christian is not his outer man, the soul, but his inner man, the spirit. No matter how highly developed out outer man may be, if this inner component of ours is abnormal, our whole walk shall go askew.

The Bible is not silent about the normalcy of a believer's spirit. Many matured ones have experienced what the Bible exhorts; they recognize that to retain their triumphant position and to cooperate with God they must preserve their spirit in the proper conditions laid down in the Word. We shall shortly see how it is to be controlled by the renewed will of the believer. This is a principle of great consequence, for by the will one is able to set his spirit in its proper place.

A CONTRITE SPIRIT

"Jehovah is nigh unto them that are of a broken heart,
and saveth such as are of a contrite spirit" (Ps. 34.18 ASV).
"For thus says the high and lofty One who inhabits
eternity, whose name is Holy: I dwell in the high and
holy place, and also with him who is of a contrite and
humble spirit" (Is. 57.15).

God's people often erroneously think that they need a contrite spirit only at the time they repent and believe in the Lord or whenever they subsequently fall into sin. We should know, however, that God wishes us to keep our spirit in a state of contrition at all times. Although we do not daily sin we are nonetheless required by Him to be of humble spirit constantly, because our flesh still exists and may be stirred up at any moment. Such contrition precludes our losing watchfulness. We ought never sin; yet we always should have sorrow for sin. The presence of God is felt in such a spirit.

God takes no pleasure in our repenting over and over again as though this were sufficient; rather does He wish us to live in perpetual contrition. Only a spirit of this kind can equip us to detect and mourn immediately all disharmony with the Holy Spirit present in our conduct and deeds. It also helps us to acknowledge our faults when told of them. This penitent spirit is very necessary, for despite the fact a person has been joined to the Lord to be one spirit, he is not forever afterwards infallible. The spirit can err (Is. 29.24); even if it has not erred, the mind can be so confused as to paralyze it from executing the thought of the spirit. A contrite inner life helps one to confess instantly and to not hide those little points others have noticed in him as being unlike the Lord. God saves those who possess a contrite spirit; others He cannot save for it requires contrition to know His mind. People who cover their faults and excuse themselves do not have a repentant spirit; hence God cannot save them to the uttermost. How we need a spirit susceptible to the correction both of the Holy Spirit and of man, a spirit willing to concede to having lived below par. And then we shall daily experience the salvation of the Lord.

A BROKEN SPIRIT

"The sacrifice acceptable to God is a broken spirit" (Ps. 51.17).

A broken spirit is one which trembles before God. Some Christians do not sense any uneasiness in their inner man after they have sinned. A healthy spirit will be broken before God—as was David's—upon once having sinned. It is not difficult to restore to God those who have a broken spirit.

AN AFFLICTED SPIRIT

"But to this man will I look: to the afflicted and contrite in spirit, and who trembleth at my word" (Is. 66.2 Darby).

The spirit with which God is delighted is an afflicted one because it reverences Him and trembles at His Word. Our spirit must be kept in continual reverential fear of the Lord. All self-reliance and self-conceit must be shattered; the Word of God must be accepted as the sole guide. The believer must possess within him a holy fear: he must have absolutely no confidence in himself: he must be as one whose spirit is so stricken that he dare not raise his head but humbly follows the command of God. A hard and haughty spirit always impedes the way of obedience. But when the cross is working deeply a believer comes to know himself. He realizes how undependable are his ideas, feelings and desires. Hence he dare not trust himself but trembles in all matters, acknowledging that except he be sustained by the power of God he shall unquestionably fail. We must never be independent of God. The moment our spirit ceases to tremble before Him at that precise moment it declares its independence from Him. Except we sense our helplessness we shall never trust in God. A spirit which trembles before Him shields one from defeat and helps him to truly apprehend God.

A LOWLY SPIRIT

"It is better to be of a lowly spirit with the poor than to divide the spoil with the proud" (Prov. 16.19) *"He who is lowly in spirit will obtain honor"* (Prov. 29.23). *"And also with him who is of a contrite and humble spirit, to revive the spirit of the humble"* (Is. 57.15).

Lowliness is not a looking down on one's self; rather is it a not looking at one's self at all. As soon as a believer's spirit becomes haughty he is liable to fall. Humility is not only Godward but is manward as well. A lowly spirit is demonstrated when one associates with the poor. It is this spirit alone which does not despise any who are created by God. God's presence and glory is manifested in the life of the spiritually humble.

A lowly person is a teachable person, easily entreated and open to explanation. Many of our spirits are too arrogant: they can teach others but can never themselves be taught. Many possess a stubborn spirit: they stick to their opinions even if they realize they are wrong. Many are too hard in spirit to listen to an explanation for a misunderstanding. Only the humble have the capacity to bear and forbear. God needs a lowly man to express His virtue. How can a proud man hear the voice of the Holy Spirit and then cooperate with God? No trace of pride should be found in our spirit: tenderness, delicacy, flexibility—these shall be the norm. A tiny bit of harshness in the inner man may hinder fellowship with the Lord, for this certainly is most unlike Him. To walk with the Lord the spirit must be lowly, forever waiting on Him and offering no resistance to Him.

POOR IN SPIRIT

"Blessed are the poor in spirit" (Matt. 5.3).

The poor in spirit views himself as possessing nothing. A believer's peril lies in his having too many things in his spirit. Only the poor in spirit can be humble. How often the experience, growth and progress of a Christian become such precious matters to him that he loses his lowliness. The most treacherous of all dangers for a saint is to meditate on what he appropriates and to pay attention to what he has experienced. Sometimes he engages in this unconsciously. What, then, is the meaning of being poor? Poor bespeaks having nothing. If one endlessly reflects upon the deep experience which he has passed through, it soon shall be debased to a commodity of his spirit and hence become a snare. An emptied spirit enables a person to lose himself in God whereas a wealthy spirit renders him self-centered. Full salvation delivers a believer *out* of himself and into God. Should a Christian retain something for himself his spirit immediately shall turn inward, unable to break out and be merged in God.

A GENTLE SPIRIT

"In a spirit of gentleness" (Gal. 6.1).

Gentleness is a most necessary feature of the inner man. It is the opposite of harshness. God requires us to cultivate a gentle spirit. Amid the most prosperous work anyone with a gentle spirit can instantly stop on short notice from God, just as Philip did when sent from Samaria to the desert. A gentle spirit turns easily in God's hand however He wills. It knows not how to resist God nor how to follow its own will. God needs such a yielding spirit to accomplish His purpose.

A gentle spirit is no less important in human relationships. It is the spirit of a lamb which characterizes the spirit of the cross. "When he was reviled, he did not revile in return;

when he suffered, he did not threaten" (1 Peter 2.23). This is a description of a gentle spirit. Such gentleness is willing to suffer loss; though it has the power of revenge and the protection of the law, it nevertheless has no wish to avenge itself with the arm of flesh. It is a spirit which in suffering harms no one. The one who can boast such a spirit as this lives righteously himself but never demands righteousness from others. He is full of love and mercy; wherefore he can melt the heart of those around him.

A FERVENT SPIRIT

*"In diligence not slothful; fervent in spirit;
serving the Lord"* (Rom. 12.11 ASV).

For a time the flesh may be fervent when it is emotionally excited, but this fervency does not endure. Even when the flesh seems most diligent it actually may be quite lazy, since it is diligent solely in those things with which it agrees; hence the flesh is impelled by emotion. It cannot serve God in matters which do not appeal to it nor when emotion is cold and low. It is impossible for the flesh to labor with the Lord in cloud as well as in sunshine, step by step, slowly but steadily. "Fervent in spirit" is a permanent feature; he therefore who possesses this spirit is qualified to serve the Lord endlessly. We should avoid all fervency of the flesh but allow the Holy Spirit to so fill our inner man that He may keep it perpetually fervent. Then our spirit will not turn cold when our emotion becomes chilled, nor will the work of the Lord collapse into a seemingly immovable state.

What the Apostle stresses here amounts to an order. This order must be taken up by our renewed will. We should exercise it to choose to be fervent. We should say to ourselves, "I want my spirit to be fervent and not to be cold." We should not be overwhelmed by our icy and indifferent feeling; instead we should permit our fervent spirit to control everything, even where our emotion is extremely unconcerned. The sign of a fervent spirit is serving the Lord *always.*

A COOL SPIRIT

"He who has a cool spirit is a man of understanding"
(Prov. 17.27).

Our spirit needs to be fervent yet also to be cool. Fervency is related to "diligence in serving the Lord" whereas coolness is related to knowledge.

If our spirit lacks coolness we often take inordinate action. The enemy purposes to drive us off track in order that our spirit may be deprived of its contact with the Holy Spirit. Frequently we observe saints who, in the hour of a feverish spirit, change their principled life into a sensational one. The spirit is closely knit with the mind. The moment the spirit loses its composure the mind is excited; when the mind becomes heated the conduct of the believer grows abnormal and goes out of control. Consequently it is always profitable to keep the inner man calm and collected. By disregarding the ardor of the emotion, the increase of desire, or the confusion of thought and by measuring every problem with a cool spirit instead, we shall maintain our feet on the pathway of the Lord. Any action taken when our spirit is excited is likely to be against the will of God.

The knowledge of God, self, Satan and all things brings calmness to our spirit; it effects a kind of spirit which soulish believers never experience. The Holy Spirit must fill our inner man while the outer man must be consigned entirely to death; then the spirit will enjoy an unspeakable calm. Neither the soul nor the body nor changing environment takes away that calm. It is like the ocean: although the waves rage on the surface, the bottom of the sea remains composed and undisturbed. Before a Christian experiences the dividing of soul and spirit he will be disturbed and shaken immediately by the slightest perturbation. This is due to lack of spiritual knowledge. Hence to keep the inner and outer man divided is the way to keep the spirit cool. A person with an imperturbable spirit experiences a kind of "untouchableness." However chaotic may be the outside situation he does not lose the calm and peace inside. Though a mountain should fall at his face he remains as composed as ever. Such composure is not achieved through self-improvement but is secured through the revelation of the Spirit Who discloses the reality of all things and through the control the believer exerts over his soul so that it no longer may influence his spirit.

The key, therefore, is the rule of the will. Our spirit must accept this rule. Fervency is what our will desires, but so is coolness. We should never permit our spirit to be in such a condition as to extend beyond the control of the will. We must will both to have a fervent spirit towards the Lord's work and to maintain a cool spirit in executing that work.

A JOYFUL SPIRIT

"My spirit rejoices in God my Savior" (Luke 1.47).

Towards himself a Christian should have a broken spirit (Ps. 51.17), but towards God it should be one of rejoicing always in Him. He rejoices not for its own sake nor because of any joyful experience, work, blessing or circumstance, but exclusively because God is his center. Indeed, no saint can genuinely rejoice out of any cause other than God Himself.

If our spirit is oppressed by worry, weight and sorrow it will commence to be irresponsible, next sink down, then lose its proper place, and finally become powerless to follow the leading of the Holy Spirit. When pressed down by a heavy load the spirit loses its lightness, freedom and brightness. It quickly topples from its ascendant position. And should the time of sorrow be prolonged, damage to spiritual life is incalculable. Nothing can save the situation except to rejoice in the Lord—rejoice in what God is and how He is our Savior. The note of hallelujah must never be in short supply in the spirit of the believer.

A SPIRIT OF POWER

"For God did not give us a spirit of timidity but a spirit of power and love and self-control" (2 Tim. 1.7).

Timidity is not humility. While humility is self-forgetful-
ness completely—a forgetting both its weakness and strength
—timidity recalls all the weakness and hence is self-remem-
bering. God does not delight in our cowardice and withdrawal. He wants us, on the one hand, to tremble before
Him because of our emptiness, yet on the other hand, to
proceed courageously in His might. He requires us to bear
Him witness fearlessly, to suffer pain and shame for Him
valiantly, to accept loss of all things with courage, and to
rely on the Lord's love, wisdom, power and faithfulness with
confidence. Whenever we discover ourselves shrinking from
witnessing for the Lord or withdrawing in other ways where
boldness is demanded, we should realize that our spirit has
abandoned its normal state. We ought to preserve it in a
condition of "dauntlessness."

We need to have a spirit of power, of love, and of self-
control. It should be strong, but not to the point of becoming unloving. It is also mandatory that it be quiet and controlled so that it may not be excited easily. We must have a
spirit of power towards the enemy, a spirit of love towards
men, and a spirit of self-control towards ourselves.

A QUIET SPIRIT

"Let it be the hidden person of the heart with the
imperishable jewel of a gentle and quiet spirit,
which in God's sight is very precious" (1 Peter 3.4).

Granted that this is a word directed towards the sisters,
it nonetheless is spiritually applicable to the brothers as
well.

"To aspire to live quietly" (1 Thess. 4.11). This is the duty
of every Christian. Modern Christians talk far too much.
Sometimes their unuttered words surpass in number those
that are spoken. Confused thought and endless speech set
our spirits to wandering away from the control of our wills.
A "wild spirit" often leads people to walk according to the
flesh. How hard for believers to restrain themselves from
sinning when their spirits become unruly. An errant spirit
invariably ends up with an error in conduct.

Before one can display a quiet mouth he first must possess
a quiet spirit, for out of the abundance of the spirit does the
the mouth speak. We ought to carefully keep our spirit in
stillness; even in time of intense confusion our inner being
should nevertheless be able to sustain an independent quietude. A placid spirit is essential to anyone walking after
the spirit: without it he shall quickly fall into sin. If our
spirit is hushed we can hear the voice of the Holy Spirit
there, obey the will of God, and understand what we cannot understand when confused. Such a quiet inner life constitutes the Christian's adornment which betokens something
manifested outwardly.

A NEWNESS OF SPIRIT

"We should serve in newness of spirit" (Rom. 7.6 Darby).

This too is a serious facet of spiritual life and work. An
old spirit cannot inspire people: the best it can do is pass
on some thought to others: even so, it is weak and therefore powerless to stimulate earnest consideration. An aged
spirit can only produce aged thought. Never can dynamic
life flow out from an old spirit. Whatever issues from a
decrepit spirit (words, teaching, manner, thought, life) are
but old, stale and traditional. Perhaps many doctrines do in
fact reach another believer's mind, but they gain no footing in his spirit; as a consequence, it is impossible to touch
the spirits of others because there is no spirit behind one's
teaching. It is conceivable that the one who harbors an old
spirit has once experienced some of the truths, but they
have now become mere remembrances of the past, purely
pleasant memories. These truths have been transferred
from the spirit to the mind. Or perhaps they have just been
new ideas freshly conceived in his mind, and due to lack
of confirmation in life they simply do not impart the touch
of a fresh spirit to the audience.

Time and again we meet various Christians who habitually
convey something new from the Lord. While we are with
them we feel they have *just* left the Lord's presence, as
though they would bring us right back to the Lord. This is

what newness means; anything else is oldness. Such ones appear to enjoy renewed strength all the time, soaring like eagles and running like youths. Instead of imparting dried, corrupted, and worm-eaten manna of the mind to people, these give fish and bread freshly cooking on the fire of the spirit. Deep and wonderful thoughts never move people as a fresh spirit can.

We must maintain a fresh spirit continually. How can we face people if our inner man does not give the impression of having been newly with the Lord and newly blessed of the Lord? Anything—life, thought, experience—which has reduced itself to a remembrance of the past is old and aged. Moment by moment we must receive everything anew from the Lord. To imitate the experiences of another without ourselves having it in life is forbidden; but to copy from the relics of our own past experience is likewise ineffective. Thus we can grasp the import of what Christ enunciated as recorded in John: "'I live because of the Father" (6.57). Our inner man shall remain unceasingly fresh if we momentarily draw upon the life of the Father to be our life. A stale spirit generates no fruit in work, inspires no walk after the spirit, and achieves no victory in warfare. An old spirit cannot face others because it has not faced God. To enjoy a spirit that is always fresh and new, one's inner being must be in constant touch with God.

A HOLY SPIRIT

"To be holy in body and spirit" (1 Cor. 7.34). *"Let us cleanse ourselves from every defilement of body and spirit"* (2 Cor. 7.1).

For anyone to walk in a spiritual manner it will be necessary for him to keep his spirit holy at all times. An unholy spirit leads people into error. Inordinate thought towards men or things, assessing the evil of others, a lack of love, loquacity, sharp criticism, self-righteousness, refusing entreaty, jealousy, self-pride, and so forth—all these can defile the spirit. An unholy spirit cannot be fresh and new.

In our pursuit of spiritual life we must not overlook any sin, because sin inflicts more harm upon us than does anything else. Even though we already have learned how to be delivered from sin and how to walk by the spirit, we nevertheless must guard against unknowingly returning to the old sinful ways. For such a return renders a walk after the spirit utterly impossible. The child of God therefore needs to maintain an attitude of death towards sin lest it overcome him and poison his spirit. Without holiness no one can see the Lord (Heb. 12.14).

A STRONG SPIRIT

"Become strong in spirit" (Luke 1.80).

Our spirit is capable of growth and should increase gradually in strength. This is indispensable to spiritual life. How often we sense our spirit is not strong enough to control our soul and body, especially the moment the soul is stimulated or the body is weak. Sometimes in helping others we notice how heavily weighed down they are in their spirit, yet ours lacks the power to release them. Or when battling with the enemy we discover our spiritual strength is inadequate to wrestle long enough with the enemy until we win. Numberless are those occasions when we feel the spirit losing its grip; we have to force ourselves to proceed in life and in work. How we long for a more robust inner man!

As the spirit waxes stronger the power of intuition and discernment increases. We are fit to resist everything not of the spirit. Some who wish to walk after the spirit cannot because their inner man lacks the strength to control the soul and the body. We cannot expect the Holy Spirit to do anything for us; our regenerated spirit must instead cooperate with Him. We should learn how to *exercise* our spirit and use it to the limit of our understanding. Through exercise it will become progressively sturdier till it possesses the strength to eliminate all obstructions to the Holy Spirit; such hindrances as a stubborn will, a confused mind, or an undisciplined emotion.

"A man's spirit will endure sickness; but a broken spirit
who can bear?" (Prov. 18.14) Clearly the spirit can be brok-
en or wounded. A wounded spirit must be a very weak one.
Were our spirit sturdy we would be able to endure the stimulation of the soul and *not shake*. Moses' spirit is usually portrayed as being a very strong one; yet because he failed to
keep it continually firm, he found that the Israelites "made
his spirit bitter" (Ps. 106.33) and consequently he sinned. If
our inner being remains vigorous we can triumph in Christ
however much our body may suffer or our soul be afflicted.

The Holy Spirit alone can grant us the strength required
by the inner man. The might of our spirit accordingly derives
from the power of God's Spirit. Ours itself, though, needs
additionally to be trained. After one has learned how to walk
by his spirit, he will then know how to live by its life in place
of soul life, how to use its power instead of his natural power
in performing God's work, and how to apply its strength
rather than his soulical strength in warring against the
enemy. Naturally, such experiences are progressive and must
be entered into progressively. Yet the principle is clear: as
a believer moves according to the spirit he will gain increased power of the Holy Spirit and his inner man will
grow stronger. A Christian ought to maintain his spirit in
strength at all times lest at the critical moment he is powerless to meet the need.

ONE SPIRIT

"Ye stand fast in one spirit" (Phil. 1.27 ASV).

We have observed previously how the life of a spiritual
man flows with that of other Christians. Oneness of the spirit
is a matter of great moment. If by His Spirit God dwells in
the believer's spirit and He fully unites with him, how can
his spirit not be one with other believers? A spiritual man is
not only one with Christ in God but also one with God indwelling each of His children. Should a Christian permit
thought or feeling to control his spirit, it will not be one with
that of other saints. Only when mind and emotion are subject to the spirit's rule can he disregard or restrain differ-

ences in thought and feeling and so be one in the spirit with all children of God. It is necessary for him to guard unceasingly the oneness of spirit with *all* believers. We are not united with a small group—those who share the same interpretation and outlook as we—but with the body of Christ. Our spirit should harbor neither harshness nor bitterness nor bondage but be completely open and entirely free, thus creating no wall in our contact with all other brethren.

A SPIRIT FULL OF GRACE

"The grace of our Lord Jesus Christ be with your spirit" (Gal. 6.18). *"The grace of the Lord Jesus Christ be with your spirit"* (Philemon 25).

The grace of the Lord Jesus Christ is exceedingly precious to our spirit. There we find the Lord's grace to help us in time of need. This is a word of benediction: but this also represents the peak a believer's spirit can ever reach. We should always season our spirit with the grace of our lovely Lord.

A SPIRIT OF RAPTURE

One other facet of the normal spirit needs to be discussed besides those features mentioned already. This one we would term the spirit of rapture. Christians ought to have a spirit which is perpetually in an out-of-this-world and ascending-into-heaven state. Such a spirit as this is deeper than one of ascension, for those who possess the former not only live on earth as though in heaven but also are truly led of the Lord to wait for His return and their own rapture. When a believer's spirit is united to the Lord's and they become one spirit, he commences to live in the world as a sojourner, experiencing the life of a heavenly citizen. Following that, the Holy Spirit will call him to take one further step and will give him the spirit of rapture. Formerly his impetus was "Go forward!"—now it becomes "Ascend up!" Everything about him rises heavenward. The spirit of rapture is that spirit which has tasted the powers of the age to come (Heb. 6.5).

Not all who accept the truth of the Second Coming possess this spirit of rapture. Men may believe in the Lord's return, preach His Second Coming, and pray for His return and yet not have this spirit. Even mature ones do not necessarily possess it. The spirit of rapture is the gift of God. It is sometimes dispensed by God as He pleases and sometimes granted by Him in response to prayers of faith. When possessed of this spirit the believer's inner being seems always to be in a state of rapture. He believes not only in the return of the Lord but also in his being transported. Rapture is more than an article of faith; it is to him a fact. Just as Simeon, through the revelation of the Holy Spirit, trusted that he would not taste death before he had seen the Lord's Christ (Luke 2. 26), so believers should have the assurance in their spirit that they will be transported to the Lord before they die. Such faith is the faith of an Enoch. Now we are not being stubbornly superstitious here; but if we live in the time of rapture, how can we be lacking in such faith? Such belief will help us to understand more of what God is doing in this age as well as obtain heavenly power for our work.

In other words, if the spirit of a Christian is in a state of rapture he will be more heavenly and will not think his way to heaven must necessarily traverse the valley of death.

How frequently God's child, when engaged in spiritual labor, entertains many expectations and plans. He is full of the Holy Spirit, wisdom and power; he believes God will greatly use him; and he looks forward with anticipation that before long his labor shall produce much fruit. However, in the very midst of prosperity the hand of the Lord suddenly sweeps down upon him, suggesting to him that he must conclude all his undertaking and be ready to take another course. This comes as a genuine surprise to man. He naturally asks why it must be so. Is not my power for working? Is not the profound knowledge I have for helping people? Need everything be closed in and cold? Nonetheless, under guidance of this kind the believer learns that the purpose of God for him is an alteration in his course. Previously everything was going forward; henceforth it is to ascend. It does not signify there is no more work; what it does mean is that that work can be concluded at any time.

God continually has employed such circumstances as persecution, opposition, plunder, etc., to cause saints to comprehend that He wishes them to have the spirit of rapture rather than to make progress in the work on earth. The Lord desires to change the course of His children, many of whom do not realize there is this far better spirit of rapture.

This spirit has its definite effect on life. Before one secures it his experience is bound to be changing constantly; after he receives the witness and assurance of rapture in his spirit, however, his life and labor will be sustained on a level worthy of this kind of spirit, thus preparing him for the Lord's return. Such preparation includes more than outward correction: it is making the spirit, the soul, and the body of the believer wholly ready to meet the Lord.

Hence we should pray and petition the Holy Spirit to show us how to obtain this spirit of rapture and how to retain it. We should believe and then be willing to eliminate all obstacles to the realization of such a spirit. And once we have appropriated it we should habitually check our life and work against it. In case we lose this spirit we should determine at once how it was lost and how it can be restored. Such a spirit once obtained can be easily forfeited. This may be due chiefly to our ignorance (at this stage of life) of how to preserve such a heavenly position through special prayer and effort. We must therefore ask the Holy Spirit to teach us the way to retain this spirit. Such prayer usually leads us to seek "the things that are above" (Col. 3.2), and this is one of the requisites for preservation.

Since he now stands at the door of heaven and can be transported at any moment, the Christian should choose to wear the heavenly white garment and perform heavenly work. Such a hope separates him from earthly matters while joining him to the heavenly.

The fact that God wishes a believer to look for rapture does not suggest that he should be concerned only with his rapture and forget the remainder of the work God has appointed him. What God actually designs to convey to him is that he should not permit God-given labor to hinder his rapture. In both his walk and work, heavenly attraction should always be greater than earthly gravitation. The child of God should learn to live for the Lord's service, but even moreso for the Lord's receiving him. May our spirit be uplifted daily, looking for the return of the Lord. May the things of this world so lose their power over us that we do not in the slightest wish to be "worldly"; nay, we even delight in not remaining "in the world." May our spirit daily ascend, asking to be with the Lord earlier. May we so seek the things above that not even the best work on earth can distract our hearts. May we henceforth pray in spirit and with understanding, "Come, Lord Jesus!" (Rev. 22.20)

PART SEVEN

THE ANALYSIS OF THE SOUL—EMOTION

1 The Believer and Emotion

2 Affection

3 Desire

4 A Life of Feeling

5 The Life of Faith

CHAPTER 1

THE BELIEVER AND EMOTION

ALTHOUGH A CHRISTIAN may have experienced deliverance from sin, he shall continue to be soulish—that is, powerless to overcome his natural life—if he fails to experience additionally the deep work of the cross wrought by the Holy Spirit. A limited description of the life and work of soulish Christians has been given earlier. Careful study of the soulish reveals that the conduct and action of such ones stem principally from their emotion. While the soul possesses three primary functions most soulish or carnal Christians belong to the emotional category. Their whole life appears to revolve largely around the impulses of emotion. In human affairs it seems to occupy a greater area than mind and will: it apparently plays a bigger role in daily life than do the other parts of the soul. Hence nearly all the practices of the soulish originate with emotion.

THE FUNCTION OF EMOTION

Our emotion emits joy, happiness, cheerfulness, excitement, elation, stimulation, despondency, sorrow, grief, melancholy, misery, moaning, dejection, confusion, anxiety, zeal, coldness, affection, aspiration, covetousness, compassion, kindness, preference, interest, expectation, pride, fear, remorse, hate, *et al.* The mind is the organ of our thinking and reasoning and the will, of our choices and decisions. Aside from our thought and intent and their related works, all other operations issue from emotion. Our thousand and one diverse feelings manifest its function. Feeling comprises such a vast area of our existence that most carnal Christians belong to the emotional type.

Man's sensational life is most comprehensive, hence highly complicated; to help believers understand it, we can gather all its various expressions into the three groups of (1) affection, (2) desire, and (3) feeling. These groups cover the three aspects of the function of emotion. Should a saint overcome all three, he is well on the way to entering upon a pure spiritual path.

To be sure, man's emotion is nothing but the manifold feelings he naturally has. He may be loving or hateful, joyful or sorrowful, excited or dejected, interested or uninterested, yet all are but the ways he feels. Should we take the trouble to observe ourselves we will easily perceive how changeful are our feelings. Few matters in the world are as changeable as emotion. We can be one way one minute and feel quite opposite the next. Emotion changes as feeling changes, and how rapidly the latter can change. He therefore who lives by emotion lives without principle.

The emotion of man often displays a reactionary motion: a time of activity in one direction will sometimes produce an opposite reaction. For example, unspeakable sorrow usually follows upon hilarious joy, great depression after high excitement, deep withdrawal after burning fervor. Even in the matter of love, it may commence as such but due to some emotional alteration it may end up with a hatred whose intensity far exceeds the earlier love.

A BELIEVER'S EMOTIONAL LIFE

The more one probes the workings of an emotional life the more he will be convinced of its vacillation and undependability. No one should wonder that a child of God who walks by emotion rather than by spirit usually comports himself in a wavelike fashion. He bemoans his existence because it is so unstable. Sometimes he appears to live in the third heaven transcending everything, while at other times he plunges to the low level of an ordinary man. His experience is replete with ups and downs. It does not require an enormous circumstance to change him, for he is unable to withstand even the tiniest mishap.

Such phenomena exist because a person is controlled by feeling and not by spirit. Since the dominant impulse in his walk continues to be emotion, it not having yet been delivered to the cross, his spirit will receive no strengthening of the Holy Spirit. Wherefore this one's spirit is weak, helpless to subdue emotion and through it to govern the whole man. If, however, by the power of the Holy Spirit he has his emotional life crucified and accepts the Holy Spirit as the Lord over all things, he most assuredly can avoid this kind of alternating existence.

Emotion may be denominated the most formidable enemy to the life of a spiritual Christian. We know a child of God ought to walk by the spirit. To walk this way he needs to observe every direction given by his inner man. We know also, however, that these senses of the spirit are delicate as well as keen. Unless the child of God waits quietly and attentively to receive and discern the revelation in his intuition, he never can secure the guidance of his spirit. Consequently, the *total silence* of emotion is an indispensable condition to walking by the spirit. How often its small and delicate motion is disturbed and overpowered by the roaring of one's emotion. On no account can we attribute any fault to the smallness of the spirit's voice, for we have been endowed with the spiritual capacity to be able to hear it. No, it is entirely the mixing in of other voices that causes the

Christian to miss the spirit's voice. But for that person who will maintain his emotion in silence, the voice of intuition can be detected easily.

The upsurge and decline of feeling may not only disqualify a believer from walking in the spirit but may also directly cause him to walk in the flesh. If he cannot follow the spirit he will naturally follow the flesh. Because he is unfit to obtain the guidance of his spirit, he invariably turns to his emotional impulse. Be it therefore recognized that when the spirit ceases to lead, emotion will do so. During such a period the believer will interpret emotional impulses to be motions of inspiration. An emotional Christian can be compared to a pond of sand and mud: as long as no one disturbs the water the pond looks clear and clean; but let it be agitated a moment and its true muddy character appears.

INSPIRATION AND EMOTION

Many saints cannot distinguish inspiration from emotion. Actually these two can be defined readily. Emotion always enters from man's *outside*, whereas inspiration originates with the Holy Spirit in man's spirit. When a believer surveys the beauty of nature, he naturally senses a kind of feeling welling up within him. As he admires the fascinating landscape he is moved with pleasure. This is emotion. Or when he meets his loved one there surges through him an unspeakable feeling as though some sort of power is attracting him. This too is emotion. Both the beautiful scenery and the beloved one are outside the man—hence the stirrings aroused by these external elements belong to emotion. Inspiration, on the other hand, is quite the reverse. It is exclusively effected by the Holy Spirit *within* man. God's Spirit alone inspires; since He dwells in the human spirit, inspiration must come from within. Inspiration may be imparted in the coldest and most tranquil environment; it does not require the encouragement of scenic wonder or of dear ones. Emotion is just the opposite: it withers the instant outside help is removed. And so an emotional person thrives wholly in accordance with the particular environment of the given moment: with stimulation he can press on, without it he folds up. But inspiration needs no such outside aid; on the contrary, it becomes confused should emotion be unduly influenced by external environment.

The Lord's people should be cautious, however, lest they view coldness and absence of constraint to be barometers of spirituality. Such an assumption is far from the truth. Know we not that the mark of emotion is dejection as well as excitation? Know we not that emotion cools as well as stirs? When emotion arouses a man he is elated, but when it mollifies him he feels depressed. Driven by high emotion, the Christian commits many errors. Upon awakening to this fact, however, he tends to suppress his feelings altogether. And so now he conceives himself as spiritual. Yet what he does not realize is that this is but a reactionary impulse of that self-same *emotion* of his which has calmed him down; that following a time of excitement, there is bound to emerge an emotional *re*-action. Such coldness and dullness precipitates the believer to lose interest in God's work: it deprives him as well his brotherly affection towards God's children. Because of the reluctance of the outer man to work, the believer's inner man is imprisoned and the life of the spirit is powerless to flow out. Now during this episode the saint may deem himself to be walking after the spirit, for, he reasons within himself, am I not today an extremely cold person and no longer burning wildly as before? Little does this Christian comprehend that he continues to walk after emotion anyway, only this time after the other extreme of emotion!

Few are the cases, however, of Christians turning cold. Most of them continue to be propelled forward by their high emotion. In the moment of excitement they do many things beyond proper bounds, actions which during subsequent periods of calmness they themselves would deride and consider nonsense. Deeds done under excitement often induce pangs of regret and remorse in retrospect. How distressing that Christians lack the spiritual strength to consign their inordinate feeling to death and to deny its control.

Two reasons can be offered why many walk according to their emotion. First, since they do not understand what walking according to the spirit is nor have ever sought to so walk, they will naturally walk according to the movement of emotion. Because they have never learned how to deny the agitation of their emotion, they are simply swept along by it and do those deeds which they ought not do. Their spiritual sense verily raises its objection, but these individuals so lack spiritual power that they completely disregard its objection and heed their feeling instead. The latter beats stronger and stronger in them until they are completely carried away. They do what they should not; and after having done it they repent for having so done. Second, even those who have experienced the dividing of spirit and soul and who recognize the stirrings of emotion as being soulish and instantly resist can nonetheless walk after emotion. This is due to the success of "spiritual" counterfeit. Before anyone becomes spiritual he is overwhelmed by his powerful emotional feelings; but after he becomes spiritual his emotion often pretends to be his spiritual sense. Outwardly these two are difficult to differentiate, because they appear to be nearly identical. For lack of knowledge, the saints can be deceived. And as a consequence they exhibit many carnal actions.

We should remember that in walking after the spirit all our actions must be governed by *principles*, since the spirit has its own laws and principles. To walk by the spirit is to walk according to its laws. With spiritual principles everything becomes sharply defined. There is a precise standard of right and wrong. If it is "yes" it is "yes" whether the day is clear or cloudy; if it is "no" then it is "no" whether exciting or depressive. The Christian's walk should follow a distinct standard. But if his emotion is not handed over to death, he cannot abide a permanent standard. He will live by the whim of his vacillating feelings and not according to a definite principle. A principled life differs enormously from an emotional life. Anyone who acts from emotion cares neither for principle nor for reason but only for his feeling. Should he be happy or thrilled he may be tempted to undertake what he ordinarily knows is unreasonable. But when he feels cold, melancholy or despondent he will not so much as fulfill his duty, for his feeling fails to go along. If God's children would pay a little attention to their emotion, they would note how changeable it actually can be and how dangerous it therefore is to walk by it. So often their attitude is: if the Word of God (spiritual principle) agrees with their feeling, they observe it; if the Word does not, they simply reject it. What an enemy emotion can be to spiritual life! All who desire to be spiritual must conduct themselves daily according to principle.

One quality which characterizes a spiritual person is the great calm he maintains under every circumstance. Whatever may happen around him or however much he may be provoked, he accepts it all calmly and exhibits an unmovable nature. He is one who is able to regulate his every feeling, because his emotion has been yielded to the cross and his will and spirit are permeated with the power of the Holy Spirit. No extreme provocation has the strength to unsettle him. But if one has not accepted the dealing of the cross upon his emotion, then he will be easily influenced, stimulated, disturbed, and even governed by the external world. He will undergo constant change, for emotion shifts often. The slightest threat from outside or the smallest increase in work shall upset him and render him helpless. Whoever genuinely desires to be perfect must let the cross cut deeper into his emotion.

If the Christian would simply bear in mind that God does not lead anyone who is in turmoil, he might be spared many errors. Never decide on anything or start to do anything while emotion is agitating like a roaring sea; it is in times of great emotional upheaval that mistakes are readily made. Our mind too becomes undependable in such periods because it is easily affected by feeling. And with a powerless mind, how can we ever distinguish right from wrong? Again, during that time even our conscience is rendered unreliable. As emotion pulsates, the mind becomes deceived and conscience is denied its standard of judgment. Whatever is decided and performed in such circumstances is bound to be improper and will be something to be regretted afterwards. A believer should exercise his will to resist and to terminate such fomented feeling; solely when his emotion is no longer boiling but returns to perfect calm can he decide what he should do.

Similarly, one should refrain from doing anything which might stir up his emotion unnecessarily. Sometimes it is peaceful and quiet, but subsequently we do something willfully our own which immediately activates the emotion unduly. Such cases are frequent, with great damage inflicted upon our spiritual life. We must deny all that disturbs the peace of our soul. Not only should we not do anything during emotional crisis; we also should not do anything which tends to induce such a crisis. Does this therefore imply the opposite: that we can do nothing wrong if what we do is decided or performed in a time of emotional quietude? Not necessarily at all, for instead of being led by the spirit we may unfortunately be led by our "cold emotion." If such be the case, the work we do shall soon activate our "warm" emotion. Those who have had experiences along this line may recall how in writing a letter or meeting a person their emotion became greatly agitated, proving that what they were undertaking was out of God's will.

EMOTION AND WORK

Heretofore we have stressed the truth that the spirit alone can do spiritual work, so that any work not achieved by it counts for nothing. This truth is so vital that we feel led to restate it in additional detail.

Today men give much attention to psychology. Even many who serve the Lord feel they *must* diligently study psychology. These believe if only their words, teachings, presentations, manners and interpretations can be made psychologically appealing to people, that many could be won to Christ. Psychology naturally refers in large part to the workings of man's emotion. Occasionally it does seem to be helpful, but a child of God who relies on emotion serves no productive purpose for the Lord.

We recognize already that regeneration of the spirit is the paramount need of man. Any work which cannot quicken man's dead spirit or impart to man God's uncreated life or give him the Holy Spirit to indwell his regenerated spirit proves thoroughly futile. Neither our psychology nor that of the unbelievers can impart life to them. Unless the Holy Spirit Himself performs the work, all is vain.

A Christian should understand that his emotion is wholly natural; it is not the source of God's life. If he in fact acknowledges that no life of God resides in his emotion, he will never attempt to secure the salvation of people by means of his power of emotion through tears, mournful face, cries, or other emotional devices. No efforts of his emotion can affect in the slightest the darkened human spirit. Except the Holy Spirit gives life, man can have no life. If we do not rely on the Spirit and use emotion instead, our work will yield no real fruit.

Those who labor for the Lord need to see distinctly that nothing in man can generate God's life. We may exhaust every psychological method to excite man's emotion, to arouse his interest in religion, to make him feel sorry and shameful for his past history, to create in him a fear of the coming penalty, to foster admiration of Christ, to induce him to seek communication with Christians, or to be merciful to the poor: we may even cause him to feel happy in doing these things: *but* we cannot regenerate him. Since interest, sorrow, shame, fear, admiration, aspiration, pity and joy are merely various impulses of emotion, man can experience all these and his spirit still be dead for he has not yet apprehended God intuitively. From the human viewpoint, might not one be tempted to assert that if a man possesses all these qualities must he not be a first-class Christian? Yet these are but the manifestations of emotion; these do not prove regeneration. The first and foremost sign of new birth in anyone is that he knows God intuitively, for his spirit has been quickened. Let us not be misled or be content in our work if people should change their attitude towards us, become friendly with us, and manifest the above-mentioned expressions. This is *not* regeneration!

If everyone who serves the Lord would take to heart today that our aim is to help people to receive the life of Christ, then none would ever employ an emotional approach to obtain men's approval of the teaching of Christ and their preference for Christianity. Only if we completely acknowledge that what man requires today is God's life—the quickening of the spirit—will we then perceive how vain is any work performed by ourselves. No matter how extensive a man may undergo a change, this alteration effected by emotion occurs exclusively within the pale of his very "self": never does he step outside that boundary and exchange his life for the life of God. May we truly appreciate the reality of the fact that "spiritual aims require spiritual means." Our spiritual aim must be to secure man's regeneration, and to effect that transformation we must use spiritual means. Emotion is altogether useless here.

The Apostle Paul tells us that any woman who prays or prophesies must have her head veiled (see 1 Cor. 11). Many and diverse interpretations surround this matter. We have no intention to join the dispute by deciding on an interpretation. Of one thing we can be sure, however; which is, that the Apostle intends to restrain the operation of emotion. He signifies that everything which can foment emotion must be veiled. It is especially easy for women in preaching to agitate people's emotion. Physically merely the head is covered; but spiritually everything pertaining to feeling must be delivered to death. Although the Bible does not call for the brothers to veil their heads physically, spiritually speaking they should be as veiled as the sisters.

Paul would have no necessity to give such an order of prohibition if emotion were not so greatly being displayed in the Lord's work. Today the power of attraction has developed into nearly the biggest problem in so-called spiritual service. Those who are naturally attractive are more successful; whereas others less attractive experience less success. The Apostle nevertheless insists that everything belonging to the soul, naturally attractive or not, must be covered. Let all the servants of the Lord learn this lesson from the sisters. Our natural appeal does not help us in spiritual work and neither will our lack of natural appeal hinder it. We shall abandon our heart of dependence on the Lord if we stress our power to attract others; likewise, if we pay attention to any lack of power to attract we also shall not walk after the spirit. Far better is it not to think of this matter at all.

What are the servants of the Lord seeking today? Countless ones aspire to spiritual power. But this power is obtained solely by paying a price. Should a Christian die to his emotion he will possess spiritual might. It is because he leans too much on his emotion and is bound too strongly to his desire, affection and feeling that the Christian forfeits real power. Only a deeper operation of the cross can fill us with spiritual dynamite; other than that there is no way to it. When the cross works upon our desire enabling us to live completely for God, spiritual power will naturally be evidenced in us.

A believer's emotion, if not overcome, will additionally hamper him in spiritual work. As long as its influence obtains, his spirit is impotent to control it and consequently unqualified to fulfill the highest will of God. Take physical weariness as an example. We should be able to distinguish (1) the need for rest due to bodily fatigue, (2) the need for rest due to emotional weariness, and (3) the need for rest due to both. God does not intend us to overwork. He wishes us to rest when genuinely tired. Yet we should understand whether we have need to rest due to bodily fatigue or emotional weariness or both. Frequently what we say is rest is merely *laziness*. Our body requires respite and so does our mind and spirit. But a person should never rest because of a laziness which arises from the evil nature in his emotion. How often laziness and emotional distaste for work join to employ physical fatigue as a cover-up. Since man's emotion is highly self-favoring, believers should guard against laziness intruding into what should be exclusively a good and proper kind of rest.

THE PROPER USE OF EMOTION

If God's children permit the cross to operate deeply upon their emotion they shall find afterwards that it no longer obstructs, but rather cooperates with, their spirit. The cross has dealt with the natural life in the emotion, has renewed it, and has made it a channel for the spirit. A spiritual man we have said before is not a spirit, but neither is he a person devoid of emotion; on the contrary, the spiritual man will use his feeling to express the divine life in him. Before it is touched by God emotion follows its own whim. And hence it habitually fails to be an instrument of the spirit. But once it is purified it can serve as the means of the spirit's expression. The inner man needs emotion to express its life: it needs emotion to declare its love and its sympathy towards man's suffering: and it also needs emotion to make man sense the movement of its intuition. Spiritual sensing is usually made known through the feeling of a quiet and pliable emotion. If emotion is pliably subject to the spirit the latter, through the emotion, will love or hate exactly as God wishes.

Some Christians, upon discerning the truth of not living by feeling, mistake spiritual life as one without it. They accordingly try to destroy it and to render themselves as insensate as wood and stone. Because of their ignorance of the meaning of the death of the cross, they do not understand what is meant by handing over one's emotion to death and living by the spirit. We do not say that, in order to be spiritual, a Christian must become exceedingly hard and void of affection like inanimate objects—as though the term spiritual man means for him to be emptied of feeling. Quite the contrary. The most tender, merciful, loving, and sympathetic of persons is a spiritual man. To be entirely spiritual by delivering his emotion to the cross does not denote that henceforth he is stripped of his feeling. We have observed numerous spiritual saints and have noticed that their love is greater than that of others, which demonstrates that a spiritual man is not without emotion and additionally that it differs from that of the ordinary man.

In committing our soul to the cross we must remember that what is lost is the soul *life*, not its *function*. Were its function nailed to the cross we then could no longer think, choose, or feel. We must therefore remember this basic fact: to lose soul life means to doggedly, resolutely, and continuously deny the natural power and to walk exclusively by the power of God; it means to live no longer after self and its desires but to submit unexceptionally to the will of God. Moreover, the cross and resurrection are two inseparable facts: "for if we have become united with him in the likeness of his death, we shall be also in the likeness of his resurrection" (Rom. 6.5 ASV). The death of the cross does not connote annihilation; hence the emotion, mind and will of the soul are not extinguished upon passing through the cross. They only relinquish their natural life in the death of the Lord and are raised again in His resurrection life. Such death and resurrection cause the various operating organs of the soul to lose their life, to be renewed, and to be used by the Lord. Consequently a spiritual man is not emotionally deprived; rather, his emotion is the most perfect and the most noble, as though newly created out of God's hand. In short, if anyone has trouble here, the trouble lies with his theory and not with his experience, for the latter will bear out the truth.

Emotion must go through the cross (Matt. 10.38-39) in order to destroy its fiery nature, with its confusion, and to subject it totally to the spirit. The cross aims to accord the spirit authority to rule over every activity of emotion.

CHAPTER 2
AFFECTION

YIELDING ONE'S AFFECTION TO THE LORD may be viewed by the Christian to be a most difficult task, yet the Lord is concerned with one's affection more than with any other matter. He demands him to present his affection wholly to Him and let Him lord over it. The Lord asks for first place in our affection. We often hear people talk about consecration, but this act is simply the first step in one's spiritual walk. Consecration is not the destination of spirituality, it is but its beginning. It leads a Christian to a sanctified position. In a word, without consecration there can be no spiritual life. Even so, nothing is more paramount in one's consecration than is his affection. Whether or not this has been yielded determines the truth or falsity of consecration. Its acid test is affection. Relatively easy is it for us to hand over our time, money, power, and countless other items; but to offer our affection is exceedingly difficult. This is not to imply we do not love Christ; perhaps we love our Lord very much. Nevertheless, if we grant first place in our affection to another and relegate Christ to second place, or if we love someone else while loving the Lord, or if we ourselves direct our affection, then what we have offered is not considered consecration for we have not yielded our affection. Every spiritual believer appreciates the necessity for affection to be offered first. For without that, nothing really is offered.

God the Father demands absolute love from His children. He is unwilling to share our heart with anyone or anything else: even if He should receive the bigger share, He is still not pleased. God demands all our love. Naturally this strikes a fatal blow to one's soul life. The Lord bids us part with what we ourselves cling to, for it divides our heart. He asks us to love Him totally and to utterly follow Him in love: "You shall love the Lord your God with all your heart, and with all your soul, and with all your mind" (Matt. 22.37). "All" denotes every ounce of it for the Lord. He enjoins us to reserve not one tiny particle of affection which we ourselves can direct. He calls for all. He is a jealous God (Ex. 20.5), therefore He does not allow anybody to steal the love of His children.

Yet how many dearly beloved ones have their claim on the believer's affections besides God! Perhaps an Isaac, a Jonathan, or a Rachel. Wherefore God insists we lay our beloved ones on the altar. He cannot tolerate any competition. Our all must be on the altar. This is the Christian's way to spiritual power. And shortly after the sacrifice is laid on the altar—nay, after the *last* sacrifice is duly placed thereon—fire will come down from heaven. Without the altar, there can be no heavenly fire. How, then, will one ever have the power of the Holy Spirit if he does not take up his cross and offer everyone whom he loves to the Lord? This is not an empty altar, for fire consumes the sacrifice on it. What can the fire consume if there is no sacrifice? Brethren, neither our mental understanding of the cross nor our endless talk about it will give us the power of the Holy Spirit; only our laying everything on the altar will. If we continue to harbor some secret rope uncut, if our heart secretly retains some oxen and sheep and an Agag, we will still not experience the manifestation of the Holy Spirit's power in our lives.

How much the work of God has suffered because of our failure to let the Lord be the Lord of our affections. Many parents cling to their children for themselves and permit the kingdom of God to incur loss. Countless husbands or wives are unwilling to make sacrifice and thus the harvest is left ungathered. Numerous Christians are so attached to their friends that they sit back and let their brethren fight at the front alone. It is deplorable how many think they can love their dear ones and the Lord simultaneously, not comprehending that by loving these, they cannot love the Lord. We persist in living in the soul if we cannot say with Asaph: "Whom have I in heaven but thee? And there is nothing upon earth that I desire besides thee" (Ps. 73.25).

We cannot but stress the significance of our loving the Lord with our whole heart. Nothing satisfies His heart as does our love. The Lord looks not for our laboring for Him but for our loving Him. The church at Ephesus, according to Revelation 2, works and toils for the Lord, yet He is displeased with them because they have abandoned their first love. If our service is rendered for love's sake the Lord will certainly be pleased; but what value is it to Him if we undertake endeavors for Him without truly possessing a heart for Him? We should be aware how possible it is to labor for the Lord and yet not love the Lord. Let us ask God to cast light on the reason for our activity. Is love for the Lord strong within us? What is the use of calling out "Lord, Lord" and working diligently for Him while simultaneously the heart has no love for Him? May we have a perfect heart towards our dearly beloved Lord!

God's children have never fully understood how their loved ones could hinder their spiritual growth. As we begin to have other loves besides a love for God, however, we do discover that He gradually loses significance for us. And even should our loved ones love God, we probably will love Him for the sake of our dear ones rather than because of God Himself. Hence our relationship with God descends from the spiritual to the carnal level. We never ought to love God for the sake of another person or thing; we must love Him for His sake alone. Should a believer love the Lord for his dear one's sake, his devotion towards Him is governed by the one whom he loves. God has thus been done a favor in that the loved one has been responsible for turning the believer's love towards God. And consequently God becomes indebted to that loved one for the devotion He receives from the believer. Today the loved one propels the believer to love God; tomorrow the same one may cause him to abandon his love to God.

Moreover, when we are inclined towards someone we can hardly preserve our heart in quietness; usually we will be stirred by our emotion to seek feverishly to please the other one. Most likely the desire to draw near to God will be less than the desire to draw near to the loved one. In such a case the Christian will doubtlessly exhibit diminished interest in spiritual affairs. Outwardly nothing seems changed: inwardly though his heart is entangled with his dear one. Spiritual interest, if not totally lost, is surely greatly decreased. Furthermore, the Christian's aspiration for the vainglory of this world is excited beyond restraint. In order to obtain the attention of his loved one he will seek to impress that one with the things, fashion, beauty, glory, and other aspects of the world. God and His demands go by the board. Be it therefore known that man can love but one person and serve but one master at a time: if he loves man, he cannot love God. We must sever all secret relationships with man.

Actually, only God can satisfy a Christian's heart; man cannot. The failure of many is to seek from man what can be found only in God. All human affection is empty; the love of God alone is able to fully satisfy one's desire. The moment a Christian seeks a love outside God his spiritual life immediately falls. We can only live by the love of God.

What then? Does this indicate we need not love man? The Bible repeatedly charges us to love the brethren and even to love our enemies. Accordingly we know it is not God's will we should not love man, but He does desire to *manage* our affection towards all men. God does not want us to love others for our sake but to love for His sake and in Him. Our natural likes and dislikes do not have any part here; natural affection must lose its power. God wants us, for love's sake, to accept His control. When He wishes us to love someone, we instantly are able to; should He also desire us to terminate our relationship with someone, we can do that too.

This is the pathway of the cross. Only as we allow it to cut deeply so that we have our soul life delivered to death can we be rid of self in our affections. If we genuinely have undergone death we will not be *attached* to anyone but will be guided solely by the command of God. Our soul life, as it experiences death, loses its power and becomes as much as dead in the matter of affection. God will then direct us how in Him to renew our love for men. God wants us to create in Him a new relationship with those we formerly loved. Every natural relationship has been terminated. New relationships are established through death and resurrection.

How contrary such a course seems to Christians, and yet how blessed it is to those who so experience it! In order to substantiate, for the believer's own profit, his consecration to God, God often "strips" him of that which he holds dear. God endeavors either to secure our love towards Him or to strip us of our love. When He employs the second way He will either cause our loved ones to change their hearts towards us or make it impossible for us to love them by setting up environmental obstacles such as their moving or passing away. If our heart is sincere in consecration, God will deprive us of everything so that He shall be the only One left. To possess spiritual life in reality we must be willing to forsake all we love. Whatever conflicts with our love to God, God demands us to forsake. Spiritual life forbids the dividing of our affection. Any error in our affection—be it an error of intention or purpose or excessiveness—is judged by God to be as wrong as an error in our hatred. Love and hate, when from ourselves, are equally defiled in the sight of God.

Once the believer has passed through a purifying process he will observe how unalloyed his affection towards men *now* is: no longer is self mixed in with his love: all is for God and all is in God. In his former affection he loved others but loved himself more, because he esteemed his own self more important than they. But now he is able to share the sorrow and joy of others, to bear their burdens, and to serve them with affection. No longer does he love what his own self loves, but loves those whom God loves; no more does he count himself above others, but regards them as his own self. He is today in God and loves himself as well as others for God's sake: he can therefore love others as his very self.

Let us understand that the lordship of God over our affection is an indispensable requirement to spiritual growth. How undisciplined and wild is our affection! If it is not subject to God's will it shall endanger our spiritual walk at all times. A mistaken thought may be corrected easily, but an errant affection is nearly unmanageable. We should love the Lord with all our heart, permitting Him to direct our love.

LOVING THE LORD SOULISHLY

Right here we should sound a note of warning. Never think we ourselves can love the Lord. Whatever comes from us is rejected by Him; even loving Him is unacceptable. On the one hand, the believer's lack of deep affection towards the Lord grieves Him greatly; on the other hand, one's loving Him with *soul power* is not welcomed by God either. Our affection, even when used to love the Lord, must be entirely under the spirit's management. Too many love the Lord with a worldly love and too few, with God's pure love.

Nowadays the Lord's people primarily employ their soulical power to absorb the things of God. They speak about their Father God, call the Lord their most beloved Lord, and contemplate His suffering. By so doing their hearts are filled with joy and they feel they are now loving the Lord. They conclude this feeling is from God. Sometimes while meditating on the Lord's cross they cannot withhold their tears because they seem to experience such an unspeakable burning affection for the Lord Jesus. These things nonetheless pass through their lives like ships sailing through the sea: no lasting trace is left behind. Such is the love of countless Christians. But what is this kind of love after all? Such love as this is the sort which only serves to make one's self happy. This is not loving God, it is loving pleasure. The visualization of the Lord's suffering seems to have touched his heart, but its inner truth has not affected his life.

How powerless is the suffering of the Lord in a believer's heart when merely mentally or emotionally conceived! In contemplating His suffering one becomes inflated and proud, viewing himself as loving the Lord far more than do others. He talks as though he is a heavenly man; actually, he has not

moved one breath away from his pitiful self. He gives the
impression of loving the Lord so much, and for this reason
others admire him. Even so, his love is nothing but self-love.
He thinks and talks and desires after the Lord only because
in so doing he can feel happy. His motive is for deriving
pleasure and not for the sake of the Lord. Such meditation
secures to himself a comfortable and pleasant stirring, and
so he continues to meditate. All is soulish and earthly, neither
of God nor of the spirit.

What, therefore, is the distinction between spiritual love
and soulish love towards God? These two are not readily distinguishable outwardly, but inwardly every Christian can
detect the true source of his love. As the soul is our very self
so all which belongs to it cannot draw away from self. A
soulish affection is one in which self is working. To love
God for the sake of personal pleasure is carnal love. If a love
is spiritual it has no self mixed in with loving God. It means
to love God for His Own sake. Any affection which is totally
or partially for one's own pleasure or for reasons other than
for God Himself emanates from the soul.

Another way we can distinguish the source of love is
through its results. If one's love is soulical it does not empower him to be delivered permanently from the world. The
believer must continue to worry and struggle to break away
from the world's attraction. Not so with spiritual love. Here
the things of the world just naturally fade away before it.
The one who participates in that kind of love despises the
world, considering its things abhorrent and abominable.
Henceforth he appears to be unable to see the world because
the glory of God has blinded his physical eyes. Furthermore,
a person who experiences such love as this becomes humble
as though he has dried up before men.

The nature of God's love is unchangeable. Ours alternates
all too readily. If it is our habit to love God with our own
affection we shall turn cold towards Him whenever we are
unhappy. We shall lose our own love should we have to go
through a long period of trial. Our affection towards God will
recede when we cannot obtain the pleasure we expect, because we love Him with our own love and for our own

sake. If it were God's love it would remain in the condition of loving Him through every circumstance. "For love is strong as death, jealousy is cruel as the grave . . . Many waters cannot quench love, neither can floods drown it" (S. of S. 8.6,7). The believer who genuinely loves God will persist in loving Him regardless what he encounters or how he feels. A soulical affection ceases when the movement of emotion ceases; but a spiritual affection is strong, ever unrelenting, for it never relinquishes.

The Lord frequently leads the saint through painful experiences in order that he may not love the Lord for his own sake. When one loves with his own affection and for his own sake he can only love when he senses the affection of the Lord. However, one who loves with God's love and for His sake will be made by God to believe in His love rather than to feel it. At the beginning of a Christian life the Lord uses many ways to attract the believer to, and to assure him of, His love. Later, He desires to guide him further on by withdrawing the feeling of love while leading him on into *believing* His heart of love. Please note that that first step of being attracted by the feeling of the Lord's love is *necessary* for the believer's subsequent deeper walk with the Lord, because unless he has been drawn by the Lord's love he shall be powerless to forsake all and follow Him. During the initial stage on a Christian's spiritual path the feeling of the love of the Lord is vital and helpful, something to be sought diligently. After an appropriate time, though, he ought not *cling* to such feeling, for to do so will bring damage to his spiritual life. Various spiritual experiences are apportioned to different steps in one's spiritual walk. To encounter a certain experience in its corresponding stage of life is both proper and profitable; but to hanker again for those early experiences at a later stage in our walk constitutes retreat or retardation. After the Lord has made a person feel His love, He wishes Him to *believe* in His love. Hence when one has experienced for a time the love of the Lord in his emotion, God will remove that feeling (although not immediately) in order to create in him the essential belief that the love of the Lord never changes. Consequently, let that one not be surprised should he, following a period of feeling the Lord's love, lose that feeling. The time has now arrived for him to believe in the Lord's love.

GUARD AGAINST ONE THING

We have learned that in walking after the spirit we need to keep our emotion calm and quiet; otherwise we cannot hear the voice of intuition. Unless our affection is thoroughly quiet under the will of God our heart will be intermittently disturbed and the guidance of the spirit will hence be interrupted. A believer should always notice in his spirit what person or thing easily activates his affection. Should Satan be impotent to overcome a believer in any other respect, he will tempt him through this particular point involving his affection. Innumerable Christians have failed on just this issue. Great caution must accordingly be exercised.

Nothing activates our affection more than friends, and among friends the opposite sex stirs us the most. Due to differences in natural endowment, the opposite sexes attract each other. Here is not only a physical complement but a psychological one as well. Yet such attraction belongs to the soul: it is natural: it ought to be denied. It is an established fact that the opposite sex can easily stimulate affection. The stimulation by the same sex is much less prevalent than that by the opposite sex. For some psychological reason there is overwhelmingly more attraction to the opposite sex. This is the common and natural tendency. A slight stimulation occasioned by the opposite sex generally stirs up deep affection.

Obviously we are now speaking of the natural tendency of man. For this very reason a Christian who wishes to walk by the spirit must take note of it. In our association with people, especially in the matters of love, if we treat the same sex in one way and the opposite sex in another we know we are already under the operation of the soul. If we treat them differently for no reason other than that one is of the opposite sex, then our affection remains natural. To be sure, such stimulation by the opposite sex can be mixed in with proper motive. A Christian must nonetheless recognize that should

there be such mixed motives in friendship his social intercourse is not purely spiritual.

A worker in his work and while at work needs to watch
lest the thought of the opposite sex makes its intrusion. He
must resist all desire to be glorified among the opposite sex.
All words uttered and mannerisms affected due to the influence of the opposite sex diminish spiritual power. Everything must be done quietly with a pure motive. Remember
that it is not sin alone which defiles; whatever issues from
the soul can defile as well.

Does all this signify, then, that a believer should not have
friends of the opposite sex? The Bible does not so teach. Our
Lord when on earth had friendly fellowship with Martha,
Mary, and other women. So the question fundamentally
must be: is our affection wholly under God's control? Or is
the working of the flesh somehow mixed in with it? It is perfectly proper for brothers and sisters to fellowship; only
there should not be mixed in with it the working of the soul.

To sum up, a Christian's affection must be entirely offered
to God. Whenever we feel it too difficult to hand someone
over to God, we know our soul life has ruled in that area.
Where our affection is unable to yield fully to God's will,
much unspiritual mixture must be there. All soulish affections lead us to sin and draw us to the world. An affection
which is not inspired by the Lord will soon be transformed
into lust. Samson is not alone in the history of man in failing
in this regard. Delilah is still cutting the hair of man today!

We stated earlier that affection is the hardest element
for a believer to offer: *ergo*, its consecration becomes the
sign of true spirituality: *ergo*, this is the greatest test. He
who has not died to worldly affection has not died to anything. Death to natural affection proves one's death to the
world. To covet and to lust after man's affection demonstrates that the Christian has not yet died to self life. His
death to soul life is substantiated by his forsaking every affection other than that for God. How transcendent is a
spiritual man! He walks far above human natural affection.

CHAPTER 3
DESIRE

DESIRE OCCUPIES the largest part of our emotional life: it joins forces with our will to rebel against God's will. Our innumerable desires create such confused feelings in us that we cannot quietly follow the spirit. They arouse our feelings and make for many turbulent experiences. Before one is set free from the power of sin his desire unites with sin in making him love sin and in depriving the new man of his freedom. After he is liberated from sin's outward manifestations the same desire drives him to seek for *himself* many things outside God. And while a person is still in the emotional state he is controlled mainly by his desire. Not until the cross has performed its deeper work and one's desire has been judged in the light of the cross can he wholly live in the spirit and for God.

When a Christian remains carnal he is ruled vigorously by his desire. All natural or soulish desires and ambitions are linked with *self* life. They are for self, by self, or after self. While carnal, one's will is not yielded fully to the Lord, and so he holds many ideas of his own. His desire then works together with his ideas to make him delight in what he wills to have and to expect to have his own ideas realized. All self-delight, self-glory, self-exaltation, self-love, self-pity and self-importance issue from man's desire and render self the center of everything. Can we conjure up anything man himself desires which is not linked to something of self? If we examine ourselves in the light of the Lord we shall see that all our aspirations, no matter how noble, cannot escape the bounds of self. All are for it! If they are not self-pleasing, then they are self-glorifying. How can a Christian live in the spirit if he is engulfed in such a condition?

A BELIEVER'S NATURAL DESIRES

Pride springs from desire. Man aspires to obtain a place for himself that he may feel honored before men. All secret boastings about one's position, family, health, temperament, ability, good looks, and power flow from man's natural desire. To dwell on how differently one lives, dresses and eats and to feel self-content in these differences is also the work of emotion. Even to esteem the gift one receives from God as superior to that of others is inspired by natural desire as well.

How extensively an emotional believer comes to display himself! He loves both to see and to be seen. He cannot abide the restraints of God. He will try every means to push himself to the front. He is unable to be hidden according to the will of God and to deny himself when he is hidden. He wishes others to notice him. When he is not duly respected his desire of self-love suffers a deep wound. But if he is admired by people his heart is overjoyed. He loves to hear praising voices and considers them just and true. He also attempts to elevate himself in his work, whether in preaching or in writing, for his secret self motive goads him on. In a word, this one has not yet died to his desire of vainglory. He is still seeking what *he* desires and what can inflate *him*.

Such natural inclination makes a believer ambitious. Ambition arises through the unleashing of our natural inclination and desire. All ambitions to spread one's fame, become a man above others, and attract the world's admiration proceed from the emotional life. Often in spiritual work the aspirations for success, fruit, power and usefulness are but pretenses for glorifying oneself. The quest for growth, depth, and nobler experience is frequently a search for self-pleasure and the admiration of others. If we trace the course of our life and work back to their source, we may be surprised to discover that our desires are the springs behind many of our undertakings. How we live and work for ourselves!

However good, praiseworthy and effective one's walk and labor may appear to be, if they are motivated by his ambition they are nevertheless judged by God to be wood, hay and stubble. Such conduct and exertion possess no spiritual worth. God deems a believer's craving for spiritual fame just as corrupt as his desiring sin. If one walks according to his natural propensity he will esteem himself well in everything he does; but God is most displeased with this "self."

This natural desire is equally active in other aspects of one's walk. His soulish life hankers after worldly conversation and intercourse. It urges him to see what he should not see and read what he should not read. He may not do these things habitually, yet because of a strong urge within him he sometimes does what he knows he should not. Soulish desire can also be detected in a person's attitude. His soulishness can be spotted even in his mannerism; for instance, in the way he walks. Unquestionably it is discerned most easily in his words and deeds. Now these are admittedly little things, but all who faithfully walk after the spirit realize how impossible it is for them to so walk should they be propelled in these matters by their soulish desire. A Christian needs to remember that in spiritual affairs nothing is too small to hinder his progress.

The more a person is spiritual the more real he becomes, for he has been united with God and is at rest. But when one is goaded by his natural life he becomes very pretentious. He carries a reckless spirit and likes to do daring things in order to satisfy himself and impress others. How he pretends to be mature and wise when actually he is immature in many of his undertakings. He may regret his pretension afterwards but for the moment he feels great. Anyone who pursues such desires cannot avoid going off on a tangent.

Pleasure-loving also is a prominent manifestation of an emotional believer. Our emotion cannot abide living wholly for God; it will most certainly rebel against such a commitment. When a person accepts the demand of the cross in consigning his soulish emotion to death that he may live utterly for the Lord, he will discover experientially how his emotion pleads and maneuvers for a little ground of activity. For this very reason numerous Christians are powerless to walk totally after the Lord. How many Christians, for example, are able to engage in prayer warfare for a *whole day* without reserving some period for recreation, for refreshing their emotion? It is difficult for us to live in the spirit for an entire day. We always set aside for ourselves some time to converse with people in order to relieve our emotion. Only when we are shut in by God—seeing neither man nor sky, living in the spirit and serving Him before the throne—do we begin to appreciate how much emotion demands of us, how imperfectly we have died to it, and how much we yet live by it.

Desire for haste is another symptom of the emotional Christian. One who moves by his natural feeling does not know how to wait on God nor is he acquainted with the leading of the Holy Spirit. Emotion is usually hasty. A Christian emotionally excited acts hastily. It is extremely hard for him to wait on the Lord, to know the will of God, and to walk step by step in that will. Indeed, the Lord's people are incapable of following the spirit unless their emotion is truly yielded to the cross. Let us remember that out of a hundred impulsive actions scarcely one is in the will of God.

Judging by the time we need to pray, to prepare, to wait, and to be filled again with the power of the Holy Spirit, can we really be faultless if we move impulsively? Because He knows the impetuosity of our flesh God frequently uses our fellow-workers, brethren, family, circumstances, and other material factors to wear us out. He wants our hastiness to die so that He can work for us. God never performs anything hurriedly; consequently He will not entrust His power to the impatient. He who wishes to act impulsively must depend upon his own strength. Haste clearly is the work of the flesh. Since God does not desire anyone to walk after the flesh, the Christian must commit his precipitate emotions to death. Each time emotion demands hurry we should tell ourselves: "Emotion is now urging towards hastiness; oh Lord, may Thy cross operate here." He who walks by the spirit must not be hasty.

God takes no pleasure in what we ourselves do, but He is delighted with our waiting on Him, waiting for His orders. Our actions must be ordered by God. Only what is commissioned in the spirit is His undertaking. How impossible this is for the Christian who follows his own inclination. Even when he wants to do God's will he is extremely impatient. He does not comprehend that God has not only a will but also a time. Frequently He reveals His mind but bids us linger for His time to come. The flesh cannot tolerate such waiting. As God's child advances spiritually he shall discover that the Lord's time is as important as the Lord's will. Do not rashly beget an Ishmael lest he become the greatest enemy to Isaac. Those who cannot submit themselves to God's time are unable to obey God's will.

Due to his self-desiring, an emotional believer cannot wait on God. Whatever he undertakes he does in himself, for he cannot trust God nor allow God to work for him. He does not know how to commit a matter completely into God's hand and refrain from employing his own strength. Trust is beyond him because this requires self-denial. Until his desire is restrained, his self will be very active. How he is eager to help God! For God seems to work too slowly, so help Him along he must! Such is the operation of the soul, motivated by natural desire. Often God renders the believer's work ineffectual and thereby seeks to induce him to deny himself.

Self-justification is a common symptom among emotional Christians. The Lord's people often encounter misunderstandings. Sometimes He enjoins them to explain their situations; but unless one is so instructed by the Lord, his explanations are but the agitations of his soul life. More often than not the Lord wishes His people to commit all matters into His hand and not defend themselves. How we like to speak on our own behalf! How awful for us to be misunderstood! It diminishes one's glory and deflates one's self-esteem.

The self in man cannot remain silent when an unjustified fault is leveled at him. He cannot accept what is given him by God nor can he stay for God to justify him. He believes God's justification will come too late; he demands the Lord to justify him at once so that everybody may behold his rightenousness in no uncertain terms. All this is but the ferment of soulish desire. Were the believer willing to humble himself beneath the mighty hand of God at the instance of misunderstanding, he would discover that God wishes to use this occasion to equip him to deny his self more deeply; that is, to deny once again his soulish desire. This constitutes the Christian's practical cross. Each time he accepts a cross he experiences once more its crucifixion. Should he follow his natural concern and rush to defend himself, he shall find the power of self more formidable to subdue on the next occasion.

Before's one natural desire is dealt with he inevitably will pour out his heart to someone in the hour of suffering, discomfort, or despondency. His emotion has been aroused within and he longs to confide his trouble to someone so as to release the miserable pressure upon his breast and thus relieve his burden. Man's soulish inclination is to inform people about his distress as though their very knowledge of it will lessen it. By such action the individual is attempting to derive sympathy and comfort from other people. He yearns intently for this condolence and commiseration for these afford him a certain pleasurable feeling. He does not know how to be satisfied with God knowing his problems: he cannot commit his burdens to the Lord alone, quietly letting Him lead him to deeper death through these circumstances. He seeks man's comfort rather than God Himself. His self life is greedy for what man can give him but despises the ordering of God. Believers should perceive that their soul life will never be lost through *man's sympathy and comfort*— these but nourish that life. The spirit life commences with God and finds in Him its all sufficiency. The power to welcome and endure solitude is the spirit's power. When we locate human ways by which to soften our burdens we are adhering to the soul. God desires us to maintain silence, letting those crosses He has arranged for us work out His purpose. Each time we open not our mouth in suffering, we witness the cross working. To be dumb is the cross! He who loosens not his tongue truly tastes its bitterness! Nevertheless his spiritual life is nourished by the cross!

GOD'S AIM

God aims to have His people dwell exclusively in the spirit, willing to offer their soul life completely to death. To attain this objective He will have to touch severely their natural desire. God wants to destroy their natural inclinations. How often He does not allow His child either to do or to possess things which in themselves are not bad (they may in fact be quite legitimate and good), simply because, as the result of emotional impulses, he wants them for himself. If a Christian walks according to his personal aspirations he cannot avoid being rebellious towards God. Our Lord's aim is to destroy absolutely the believer's craving for anything *besides Himself.* The Lord is not concerned with the nature of a thing; He only asks what directs him to this thing—his own desire or the will of God? The best work or walk, if it arises out of one's desire and not from intuitive revelation, has positively no spiritual value before God. Many works which God had intended to lead His child into He must temporarily suspend because that one is motivated by his own wish. God will begin to lead His child again to these works once he has completely yielded to Him. God longs for His will (made known in our intuition) to be the guiding principle of our life and labor. He does not want us to heed our own propensity even when it seems to agree with His purpose. What we ought to heed is God's will; what we must deny is our own desire. Here is the wisdom of God. Why does He forbid us to follow our inclination even when it coincides with His will? Because it is still *our own desire.* For if we are allowed to obey our good aspirations, does there not remain a place for our "self"?

Despite the fact our desires occasionally agree with His will, God is not delighted with them because they are nonetheless of ourselves. He charges us to break completely with our longings for anything *other than Himself.* This "anything" may include some very excellent desires but He will give no ground to any of them that are independent. We must rely on Him in all matters. What does not emerge from dependence on Him He rejects. Step by step He leads us to deny our soul life.

If anyone wishes to maintain a true spiritual course he must cooperate with God in putting to death his own desire. All interests, inclinations and preferences must be denied. We should gladly accept man's contradicting, despising, discounting, misunderstanding, and harsh criticising and permit these matters which are so antagonistic to natural desire to deal with our soul life. We should learn how to receive suffering, pain, or a lowly place as apportioned us by God. However much our self life feels pained or our natural feeling is hurt, we must bear them patiently. If we bear the cross in practical matters we shall shortly see our self life crucified on the cross we bear. For to carry the cross is to be crucified thereon. Every time we silently accept what goes against our natural disposition we receive another nail which pins our soul life more firmly to the cross. All vainglory has to die. Our longing to be seen, respected, worshiped, exalted and proclaimed needs to be crucified. Any heart for self-display must equally be crucified. Every pretension to spirituality in order to be praised must be cut down; so must all self-importance and self-exaltation. Our desire, whatever its expression, must be denied. Anything which is initiated by ourselves is defiled in the sight of God.

The practical cross which God dispenses runs counter to our desires. The cross aims at crucifying them. Nothing in our total make-up suffers more wounding under the lash of the cross than does our emotion. It cuts deeply into everything pertaining to ourselves. How then can our emotion be happy when our desire is dying? The redemption of God requires a thorough setting aside of the old creation. God's will and our soul's delight are incompatible. For anyone to pursue the Lord he must oppose his own desire.

Since this is God's purpose He therefore arranges to have His children experience many fiery trials so that all these offscourings of desire may be consumed in the fire of suffering. A Christian may aspire to high position, but the Lord brings him low: he may cherish many hopes, yet the Lord allows him no success in anything: he may entertain many delights, but the Lord gradually takes away each of them till none remains: he yearns for glory, yet the Lord inflicts upon him humiliation. Nothing in the ordering of the Lord seems to coincide with the Christian's thought; everything strikes him down as would a beating rod. Though he struggles with all his might he soon deduces that he is heading straight for death. He does not discern at first that it is the Lord Who leads him to this demise. Everything seems to speak of helplessness, seems to remove any hope of life, seems to demand that he should die. During this period when he cannot escape death, he begins to realize he owes this end to God, and so he yields and accepts it with composure. This death, however, bespeaks the cessation of his soul life that he may live utterly in God. To achieve this death in the Christian's life God has worked long and hard. How foolish then for him to resist such an expiration for so long. For is it not true that after he has passed through this death all turns out well and God's aim in him is also fulfilled? Thereafter he can advance rapidly in spiritual growth.

Once he loses his heart for "self" the believer can be wholly God's. He is ready to be molded into any form God wishes. His desire no longer strives against God; nay, he relishes nothing but God. His life has now become quite simple: he has no expectations, no requests, no ambitions other than to be willingly obedient to the Lord's will. A life of obedience to His intent is the simplest kind on earth, because he who so lives seeks nothing but to quietly follow God.

After a person has forsaken his natural longings he obtains a genuinely restful life. Formerly he had many desires.

To satisfy them he planned, plotted and contrived, exhausting every ounce of his wisdom and power. His heart was in constant turmoil. While contriving, he agitated to attain what he desired. When defeated, he agonized because of failure to achieve. How the restful life eludes him! Furthermore, the person who has not yet abandoned what is his and surrendered to what is God's cannot help but be affected by his surroundings. People's capricious attitudes, changing environments, loneliness, and many other elements in the external world work to induce melancholia. This is quite a common trait among emotional saints. But natural desire can also arouse wrath in such a one. When externals go against his wish or do not turn out exactly as he prefers, when matters appear to be unjust and unreasonable to him, he becomes disturbed, anxious, and angry. These different emotional expressions are provoked by external causes. How easily one's emotion can be stirred, perturbed, and wounded. One's natural desire thus seeks out man's love, respect, sympathy and intimacy; but if he fails to realize his desire he murmurs against heaven and cries out against men. Is there anyone exempt from such sorrow and grief? Living in this bitter world as we all do, can anyone realistically expect to have his desire fully realized? If this is impossible, then how can an emotional believer ever secure rest in life? He cannot. But that child of God who purely follows the spirit and seeks not his own pleasure is satisfied with what God gives to him: and his restlessness immediately ceases.

The Lord Jesus speaks to His disciples saying: "Take my yoke upon you, and learn from me; for I am gentle and lowly in heart, and you will find rest for your souls" (Matt. 11.29). The soul here alludes especially to the emotional part of our being. The Lord knows that His Own people must pass through many trials, that the heavenly Father is going to arrange for them to be lonely and misunderstood. As no one understands Him except the Father, so no one will understand His disciples (v.27). Jesus knows that the heavenly Father must permit many unpleasant occurrences to befall the believers in order that they may be weaned from the world. He also appreciates what the feelings in their souls will be like as they are put through the fire. For this reason He tells them in advance to learn from Him so that they may find rest for their emotion. Jesus is gentle: He is able to receive any treatment from men: He joyfully accepts the opposition of sinners. Jesus is likewise lowly: He heartily humbles Himself: He has no ambition of His Own. The ambitious are hurt, angry, and restless when they cannot obtain their wishes. But Christ at all times lives gently and humbly on earth; there is consequently no occasion for His emotion to boil and erupt. He teaches we should learn from Him, that we should be gentle and lowly as He is. He says for us to bear His yoke as a restraint upon ourselves. He bears a yoke too, even the yoke of God. He is satisfied with His Father's will alone; as long as the Father knows and understands Him, why should He be concerned about the opposition of others? He is willing to accept the restrictions given him by God. He explains that we must bear His yoke, accept His restraint, do His will, and seek no freedom for the flesh. If this is done, then nothing can disturb or provoke our emotion. This is the cross. If anyone is willing to receive the cross of Christ and submit completely to the Lord, he shall find rest for his emotion.

This is none other than a *satisfied life*. The Christian cherishes nothing but God; henceforth he is satisfied with His will. God himself has filled his desire. He regards everything God has arranged or given, asked or charged him with, as good. If he can but follow the will of God his heart is satisfied. He seeks his own pleasure no longer, and not because of force but because God's will has satisfied him. Since he is now filled, he has no more requests to make. A life such as this can be summed up in one word: satisfied. The characteristic of spiritual life is satisfaction—not in the sense of self-centeredness, self-sufficiency, or self-filling but in that of the person having found all his needs fully met in God. To him God's will is the very best; he is satisfied. What else need he ask for? Only emotional Christians find fault with God's arrangement and aspire to have more by conceiving numberless expectations in their hearts. But one who has allowed the Holy Spirit to operate deeply in him by the cross no longer yearns for anything according to himself. His desire is fulfilled already in God.

At this point the believer's desire is totally renewed (this does not mean that thereafter there can be no failure); it is united with God's desire. Not only is he, negatively, resisting the Lord no longer; but positively, he is delighting in His delight. He is not suppressing his desires; he is simply delighted with what God requires of him. If *God* desires him to suffer, he asks Him to make him suffer. He finds sweetness in such suffering. If *God* desires him to be afflicted, he willingly seeks such affliction. He loves affliction more than healing. If *God* desires to bring him low, he gladly cooperates with Him in bringing himself down. He delights now only in what God delights in. He covets nothing outside Him. He expects no uplifting if God does not so desire. He does not resist God but rather welcomes whatever He bestows, whether sweet or bitter.

The cross produces fruits. Each crucifixion brings to us the fruit of God's life. All who are willing to accept the practical cross which God gives shall find themselves living a pure spiritual life. Daily there is for us the practical cross God desires us to bear. Every cross has its peculiar mission to accomplish a particular work in our life. May no cross ever be wasted upon us!!

CHAPTER 4

A LIFE OF FEELING

WHEN CHRISTIANS BECOME affectionately attached to the Lord they are usually experiencing a life of feeling. Such an experience for them is most precious. They enter this phase of their Christian walk generally following their emancipation from sin and before their entrance upon a true spiritual life. Because they lack spiritual knowledge, these Christians often assume this kind of emotional experience to be most spiritual and most heavenly since it is encountered primarily after release from sin and affords them great pleasure. The delight it bestows is so satisfactory that they find it difficult to cut loose and forsake it.

During this period the believer senses the nearness of the Lord, so near that the hands can almost touch Him. He is alive to the delicate sweetness of the Lord's love as well as gripped by his own intense love towards the Lord. A fire seems to be burning in his heart; it leave him with an unspeakable joy which makes him feel he is already in heaven. Something is heaving in his bosom, yielding indescribable pleasure, as though he were in possession of a priceless treasure. This sensation continues with him as he walks and works. Whenever the believer passes through this type of experience he wonders where his abode is, for he seems to have shed his earthly tent and now soars away with the angels.

For the moment Bible reading becomes a real delight. The more he reads the more joyous he feels. Prayer is also very easy. How wonderful to pour out his heart to God. The more he communes the brighter the heavenly light shines. He is able to make many decisions before the Lord which indicates how much he loves him. Great is his longing to be quiet and alone with God; if only he could close his door forever and commune with the Lord his joy would be full, for no tongue can speak nor pen can write of the joy that lies therein. Formerly he was gregarious, as though crowds and individuals could satisfy his needs; but today he cherishes solitude because what he could derive from the crowds can never be compared to the joy he now receives when alone with his Lord. He favors seclusion more than companionship for fear that among men he may lose his joy.

Moreover, service assumes considerable spontaneity. Hitherto he appeared to have nothing to say, but now with the fire of love aglow in his heart he experiences multiplied pleasure in telling others of the Lord. The more he speaks the more anxious he is to speak. To suffer for the Lord becomes sweet to him. Since he senses Him so near and dear, he gladly embraces the thought of martyrdom. All burdens turn light and all hardships grow easy.

With such a consciousness of the closeness of the Lord, the Christian's outward conduct also undergoes change. In days gone by he was fond of talking, yet currently he is able to remain silent. In his heart he may even criticize others who talk incessantly. Previously he was rather frivolous, today he is quite serious. Very sensitive is he to any ungodliness appearing in other brethren, for which he judges them sternly. In a word, the Christian at this stage is increasingly careful about his outward deportment as well as possessed with more insight into the shortcomings of others.

Such a person always secretly pities those who are lacking in his experience. He estimates his joy to be most excellent; how pitiable his brethren know nothing of it. While he watches other brothers and sisters serving the Lord coldly and quietly, he considers their lives tasteless. Must not his be the highest life since he is so flushed with the joy of God? It seems to him that he himself is floating on the cloud above the mountains while ordinary saints are plodding along down in the valley.

Does this kind of experience last long however? Can one possess such exultation daily and be happy for life? Most of us cannot maintain such an experience for very long. And so what grieves the believer most is that upon enjoying such an experience—generally speaking, for about a month or two —his most beloved joy suddenly vanishes. He rises as usual in the morning to read his Bible yet where is the former sweetness? He prays as before but finds himself exhausted after a few words. He feels as if he has lost something. Not long ago he was judging others for being far behind him in the spiritual race, but now he considers himself to be one of *them*. His heart has turned cold; the earlier sense of a fire burning within has been smothered. No longer is he conscious of the presence and proximity of the Lord; instead the Lord appears to be quite remote from him. He now begins to wonder where the Lord has gone. To suffer becomes a real suffering now because he cannot sense any more the former joy he had in suffering. Moreover, he has lost interest in preaching: he no longer feels like continuing on after saying but a few words. In sum, during such an episode everything seems to be dark, dry, cold and dead. It appears to the believer as though he has been abandoned by the Lord in a tomb; nothing can comfort his heart. His former expectation of lasting bliss has faded completely away.

At this moment the child of God will naturally surmise that he must have sinned and that the Lord has consequently forsaken him (for if he had not sinned, he reasons, the Lord would not have withdrawn His presence, would He?). Accordingly, he probably sets about scrutinizing his recent conduct, trying to ascertain how he has sinned against the Lord. He hopes that upon confession the Lord will return and replenish him with that previous feeling of intimacy and high spirits. As he examines himself, however, he cannot detect any special sin; he seems to be just the same as before. And so the believer once more resumes his inward inquiry: if today's condition provokes the Lord to depart from me, he asks himself, why did He not forsake me before? And if I have not sinned, then I say again why has the Lord left me? The believer is completely mystified. He can only conclude that he *must* have sinned against the Lord somewhere and hence this forsaken condition. And Satan accuses him too, reinforcing the false notion that he has actually sinned. Wherefore he cries in prayer to the Lord for forgiveness, hoping to regain what he has lost.

The believer's prayer is nonetheless ineffectual. Not only is he unable to have the lost experience instantly restored; he also day by day grows colder and drier in his feelings. He loses interest in everything. Previously he could pray for hours: today even a few minutes becomes forced. He has no inclination to pray at all. The reading of the Bible, which in the past greatly interested him, currently looms before him as a massive rock from which he can derive no nourishment. He experiences no pleasure when fellowshiping with others or undertaking any task; he engages in these affairs merely because a Christian is expected to do them. All is dull and forced.

Confronted by such a sensation some Christians, not all, shrink back. Many matters which they know belong to God's will are left undone because they have fallen into despondency. Many duties go unfulfilled. Their former conduct which they had corrected during the period of ecstasy returns to them. What they pitied others for in earlier days has presently become their own experience. They adopt talkative, frivolous, jesting and fun-loving manners. Although they had undergone a change, that change did not last.

When a child of God is stripped of his joyous feeling, he concludes that all is gone. Since he no longer senses the Lord's presence, surely the Lord cannot possibly be with him. If he does not feel the warm affection of the Lord, he most certainly must have displeased Him. As this experience lengthens, the believer seems to lose even the sense of God. He will therefore seek earnestly to recover what he has lost, so long as he does not faint in his heart. For does he not

love the Lord and has he not longed to be near Him? How
can he abide the absence of the sensing of God's love?

He goes forth to find God. He struggles to free himself
from this desolate state, but without success. Even when he
can force himself into manifesting some good conduct, his
heart secretly condemns him as being hypocritical. It is not
easy for him to succeed in anything for his failures are many.
This naturally intensifies his suffering. If anyone should
praise him at this moment he is keenly embarrassed, because
no one can appreciate how miserable he is inside. On the
other hand if anyone should blame him, he senses the right-
ness of it because he understands his own weakness. He
deeply admires those who are advancing in the Lord and
who are having sweet communion with Him. He looks upon
all others around him as better than he since they each
possess some measure of good while he has not a shred.

Will this barren condition continue forever? Or will he
regain his former experience? What usually happens is as
follows. After awhile, perhaps within a few weeks, the
coveted feeling suddenly returns to him. This may occur at
the hour of listening to a sermon, or following earnest prayer
in his early morning devotion or during his midnight meditation. The time varies but the joy does return. During this
break in the believer's condition, all which had been forfeited is restored. The presence of the Lord is as precious
as before; the glow of love fires up again in his bosom;
prayer and Bible reading become sweet as in days gone by;
and the Lord is so lovely and so approachable that He can
almost be touched. To draw nigh to Him is not a burden but
the pleasure of his heart. Everything is transformed: no more
darkness, suffering and staleness: all is now light, joy and
refreshment. Since he considers his unfaithfulness the reason
for the Lord's departure, he thereafter uses all diligence to
preserve what is regained, lest he be deprived of this life of
feeling all over again. His outward conduct is more careful
than ever; he serves the Lord daily with all his strength,
hoping to sustain his joy and never again fail as before.

Yet strange as it may seem, despite all his faithfulness, the

Lord shortly afterwards leaves the saint once more. His transport of delight has altogether taken flight. He again slumps into anguish, blackness, and barrenness.

If we examine the biography of many Christians we discover that this type of experience is shared by many after they have been delivered from sin and encounter God as a Person. Initially the Lord causes them to sense His love, His presence, His joy. But soon such feeling disappears. It subsequently comes back, rendering them extremely happy; not long afterwards, though, it vanishes a second time. At least several times the Christian undergoes these come and go occurrences. Such phenomena will not happen while he is still fleshly, before he learns to love the Lord; only after he has made some progress spiritually and begun to love the Lord will he meet with this kind of situation.

THE MEANING OF THIS EXPERIENCE

According to the believer's interpretation, he is at his spiritual peak when in possession of the wonderful feeling: he is at his lowest when deprived of it. He often characterizes his walk as full of ups and downs. By this he means that while he is feeling joyful, loving the Lord and sensing His presence he is at his spiritual best; but if his inward sensation is marked by dryness and pain he must be at his spiritual worst. In other words, he is spiritual so long as the warm fire of love is burning in his heart but soulish if his heart turns icy cold. Such is the common notion among Christians. Is it accurate? It is totally inaccurate. Unless we understand how it is wrong we shall suffer defeat to the very end.

A Christian should recognize that "feeling" is exclusively a part of the soul. When he lives by sensation, no matter what the kind, he is being soulish. During the period that he feels joyful, is loving the Lord and senses His presence, he is walking by feeling; likewise, during the period that he feels just the opposite he is *still* walking by feeling. Just as he is soulish whose life and labor are dictated by a refreshing, bright and joyous sensation, so is he equally soulish whose walk and work are determined by a dry, gloomy and painful one. A real spiritual life is never dominated by, nor lived in, feeling. Rather does it regulate feeling. Nowadays Christians mistake a life of feeling for spiritual experience. This is because many have never entered into genuine spirituality and hence interpret happy sensation to be spiritual experience. They do not know that such feeling is still soulical. Only what occurs in the intuition is spiritual experience—the rest is merely soulical activity.

It is here that Christians make one of the grossest mistakes. Under the stimulation of emotion a child of God may feel he has ascended to heaven. And naturally he assumes he has an ascended life. But he does not realize this is solely how he *feels*. He thinks he possesses the Lord whenever he is conscious of His presence, yet he believes he has lost the Lord whenever he cannot sense Him; once more he knows not that this is but the way he feels. He thinks he is truly loving the Lord as he senses a warmth in his heart; but should there be no burning sensation then he concludes that he has veritably lost his love for Him; yet again he is ignorant of the truth that such are only his *feelings*. We know that fact may not agree with feeling for the latter is exceedingly untrustworthy. Indeed, whether one senses much or senses nothing, the fact remains he is *unchanged*. He may feel he is progressing and yet may make no progress at all; he may likewise feel he is regressing and yet may not regress in the slightest. These are simply his feelings. When full of lively stirrings he reckons he is advancing spiritually; this, however, is just a time of emotional excitement which soon will subside to its former state. The working of emotion seems to assist soulical people to advance but the working of the Spirit causes spiritual men to advance. The progress of the former is false; only what is attained in the power of the Holy Spirit is true.

THE AIMS OF GOD

Why then does God impart and later withdraw these feelings? Because He has a number of aims He wishes to fulfill.

First. God grants joy to believers to draw them closer to Him. He uses His gifts to attract men to Himself. He expects His children to believe in His love in every circumstance after He has once shown how gracious and loving He is towards them. Unfortunately Christians love God only when they sense His love and forget Him the moment they do not.

Second. God deals with our lives in this fashion in order to help us understand ourselves. We realize the hardest lesson to learn is that of knowing oneself—to appreciate how corrupt, empty, sinful, and void of good one is. This lesson has to be absorbed *throughout life.* The deeper one learns it the more one perceives the depth of uncleanness of his life and nature in the eyes of the Lord. Yet this is instruction which we do not relish learning nor is our natural life able to learn it. Hence the Lord employs many ways to teach and to lead us into this knowledge of self. Among His numerous ways the most important is this giving of joyous feeling and later taking it away. Through such treatment one begins to comprehend his corruptness. In the state of aridity he may come to see how in the former days of joy he misused God's gift in uplifting himself and despising others, and how he many times acted through the ferment of emotion rather than with the spirit. Such realization evokes humility. Had he understood that this experience is arranged by God to assist him to know himself, he would not have sought blissful sensation so intently as though it were the summit. God desires us to recognize that we may act just as often in dishonoring God's name when in ecstasy as when in anguish. We progress no more during the bright than during the dull period. Our life is equally corrupt in either condition.

Third. God aims to help His children overcome their environment. A Christian should not allow his surroundings to change his life. He whose path is altered by the influence of environment is not deeply experienced in the Lord. We have learned already that what can be affected by environment is emotion. It is when our emotion is influenced by environment that our lives undergo change. How imperative therefore for us to conquer emotion if we wish to overcome environment. To conquer his surroundings the Christian must prevail over all his various sensations. If he cannot surmount his ever vacillating feeling how can he overcome his environment? It is our feeling which is alive to any shift in environment and which varies accordingly. If we do not override our sensation our lives shall oscillate with our changing sensation. Thus do we need to overcome feeling before we can overcome environment.

This explains why the Lord leads one through different feelings in order that he may learn how to quell these feelings and thereby triumph over his surroundings. If he can subdue his strong and contrasting sensations he surely will be able to cope with the changing atmosphere. Thus will he achieve a steadfast and established walk, no longer drifting with the tide. God desires His child to remain the same with or without high feeling. He wants His child to commune with Him and serve Him faithfully whether he is happy or is sad. God's child must not reshape his life according to how he feels. If he is serving the Lord faithfully and making intercession for others, then he should do so in gladness or in sorrow. He should not serve only when he feels refreshed and cease serving when he is parched. If we cannot subdue our many varied sensations then we can in no wise conquer our diverse surroundings. He who fails to surmount his environment is one who has failed to subjugate his feeling.

Fourth. God has another objective in view. He purposes to train our will. A genuine spiritual life is not one of feeling; rather, it is a life of will. The volition of a spiritual man has been renewed already by the Holy Spirit: it now awaits the spirit's revelation before it issues a command to the whole being. Unfortunately the will of quite a few saints is often so weak that either it cannot carry through the commands given it or, under the influence of emotion, it rejects God's will. To train and strengthen the will consequently becomes a very essential step.

A Christian who is excited can easily advance because he has the support of his high emotion. But if he grows despondent he finds the going rough because he then has solely his will on which to rely. God intends to make the volition strong but not to excite the emotion. From time to time He permits His child to experience a kind of weary, barren and insipid feeling so as to compel him to exercise his *will* through the strength of the spirit to do precisely the same thing as he would in a time of emotional stimulation. When stimulated, emotion undertakes the work; but now God aims for the believer's *will* to work in lieu of emotion. The will gradually can be strengthened through exercise only during periods of receiving no aid from feeling. How many mistake sensation for the measure of spiritual life. They erroneously construe the hour of strong feeling to be their spiritual apogee and the hour bereft of such feeling as their spiritual perigee. They are unaware of the fact that one's true life is lived *by his spirit through the will*. The position to which his volition attains in the hour of barren sensation represents the reality of the Christian's attainment. The way he dwells amid drought is his *authentic* life.

Fifth. Via such leading God longs to guide the Christian onto a higher level of existence. If we carefully examine the Chrisitian's walk we shall realize that the Lord at each instance He has desired to lead His own to a higher spiritual plateau first gave that one a taste of such a life in his feeling. We may say that on every occasion that one experiences a life of feeling, he has reached one more station on his spiritual journey. God grants him a foretaste of what He desires him to have: first He arranges for the Christian to sense it and next He withdraws the sensation so that by his spirit through his will he may keep what he has felt. If his spirit can press on with the assistance of his will, the Christian, by disregarding his emotion, can then see that he has made real progress in his walk. This is confirmed by our common experience. While we are pursuing an up-and-down type of existence we usually assume we have not made any advance. We conclude that during these months or years we have simply gone forward and then backward or simply backwards and then forwards. If, however, we were to compare our current spiritual state with that which obtained at the *commencement* of such alternating phenomena, we would discover we have actually *made some progress.* We advance unknowingly.

A great number err because they have not appropriated this teaching. Upon fully consecrating themselves to the Lord for entering upon a new experience such as sanctification or victory over sin, they truly and distinctly step into a new kind of life. They believe they have made progress, for they are brimming with joy, light and lightness. They account themselves already in possession of that perfect course which they admired and sought. But after awhile their new and happy circumstance suddenly evaporates: gone are the joy and thrill. Most of them faint in their hearts. They judge themselves unqualified now for perfect sanctification and unfit to have the more abundant life which others possess. Their judgment is based on the fact that they have lost what they had long admired and had possessed for but a brief moment. What they do not realize is that they have been experiencing one of God's vital spiritual laws, which is: *that what has been possessed in the emotion must be preserved in the will: that only what is retained in the will truly becomes a part of one's life.* God has only withdrawn the feeling; He wants us to exercise our volition to do what we had formerly been stimulated to do by our feeling. And before long we shall discover that what had been forfeited in our feeling has unconsciously become a part of our life. This is a spiritual law. We would do well to remember it so as never to faint.

The whole problem is therefore the will. Is our organ of volition still yielded to the Lord? Is it free to follow the spirit's leading as before? If so, then however much feeling has changed, *it* is of no *concern.* What we must be concerned with always is this: is our will obeying the spirit? Let us not indulge our feelings. Rather let us wisely heed the example of what occurs surrounding the experience of new birth: on that occasion the believer is usually full of joyous sensation; yet soon this sensation disappears; has he consequently perished all over again? Of course not! He has already possessed life in his spirit. How he subsequently feels makes not a particle of difference.

THE DANGER OF THIS LIFE

There is positively no danger if, while having such an experience, we comprehend its meaning and press forward in accordance with God's will. But it can be highly hazardous to spiritual life if we do not apprehend God's will and fail to resist our living by feeling; that is, when we encounter a buoyant feeling we advance unhesitatingly, but in the absence of such sensation we refuse to move at all. Those who make feeling their principle of life expose themselves to many dangers.

Anyone who walks by blissful emotions is usually weak in his will. It is unable to follow the direction of the spirit. The development of spiritual sensing is hampered by substituting his feeling for the spirit's intuition. He walks by his emotion. His intuition on the one side is suppressed by emotion and on the other is left unused; it is barely growing. Now intuition is active solely when emotion is quiet; only then can it communicate its thought to man. It waxes strong if it is often exercised. But the will of that person who leans on feeling is deprived of its sovereign power: his intuition is stifled and cannot transmit a distinct voice. Since the will thereby slips into a withered condition, the believer requires even more *help from feeling* to provoke the will to work. The will turns by feeling. If the latter is high the will is active; but should it be taken away the will suspends action. It is powerless to do anything by itself; it relies on the activation of emotion to propel it. Meanwhile the believer's spiritual life naturally sinks lower and lower until it seems that whenever emotion is absent no spiritual life is indicated at all. The operation of emotion has become an opiate to such ones! How tragic that some remain unconscious of this fact and seek emotion as the zenith of spiritual life.

The cause behind this error lies in the deception which feeling imparts. At the moment of great ecstasy the child of God not only senses love from the Lord but feels an intense love of his own towards the Lord as well. Must we deny our feeling of loving the Lord? Can such a warm sensation of affection towards Him hurt us? This very interrogation discloses the folly of these saints.

Let the question be asked instead: is a person actually loving the Lord when he is full of exultation? Or is it that he loves the *exultant feeling?* Granted, this joy is given us by God; but is it not God Who also takes it away? If we genuinely loved Him we should fervently love Him in whatever circumstances He may put us. If our love is present merely when we feel, then perhaps what we love is not God but our feeling.

Moreover, a person may misinterpret such a feeling to be God Himself, not aware that a vast distinction exists between God and the joy of God. Not until the time of barren feeling shall the Holy Spirit show this one that what he so earnestly sought was not God but His joy. He does not really love God; what he loves is the feeling which makes him joyous. The sensation does in truth give him the sense of God's love and presence, yet he does not love Him for His sake alone but rather does he love because he feels refreshed, bright and buoyant. Thus he craves such feeling again whenever it recedes. What brings him pleasure is the joy of God and not God Himself. Were he actually loving God he would love Him even if he must suffer through "many waters" and "floods" (S. of S. 8.7).

This of course is a most difficult lesson to learn. We must indeed have joy, and the Lord delights to give us that joy. If we enjoy his felicity *according to His will,* such enjoyment is profitable rather than harmful. (This means we do not seek this joy ourselves, though we are thankful should God desire to grant it; yet we are equally thankful if He wishes us to be barren: we shall not try to force the matter). Nonetheless, should we deem it so pleasurable that we afterwards seek it daily, then we already have forsaken God in favor of the joy which He dispenses. The happy feeling God gives can never be separated from God the Giver. Should we try to enjoy the delightful sensation He gives, yet without Him, our spiritual life is in peril. That is to say, we are not able to progress spiritually if we find satisfaction in the joy God gives rather than in God as our joy. How often we love Him not because of Himself but because of ourselves. We love, for in loving God we experience a kind of joy in our hearts. This sharply reveals that we do not actually love Him; what we love is only joy, even if that is the joy of God.

This indicates that we esteem God's *gift* higher than God the *Giver!* It also proves we continue to walk by our soul life and do not appreciate what a true spiritual life is. We deify joyous feeling and incorrectly regard it as pleasurable. To cure His children of this mistake God withdraws the joyous feeling as He wills and topples them into suffering that they may know that pleasure is in Himself, not in His joy. If they verily make *God* their joy they will uplift Him and love Him even in the hour of suffering; if not, they will sink into darkness. God, in so undertaking, aims not to destroy our spiritual life but purposes to destroy all idols we worship other than Himself. He wants to eliminate every obstacle to our spiritual walk. He wants us to live in Him, not in our feelings.

Another danger may arise for those who live by sensation rather than by the spirit through the will: they may be deceived by Satan. This is one matter about which we ought to inform ourselves. Satan is skillful in counterfeiting the feelings which come from God. If with diverse kinds of sensations he attempts to confuse Christians who aspire to walk wholly after the spirit, how much more will he play his tricks on those who desire to follow their feeling. In their pursuit of emotion they fall directly into the hand of Satan, for he delights to supply them with all kinds of feeling which they assume to be from God.

The evil spirit is able to excite or to depress people. Once a person is misled into accepting Satan-dispensed feeling, he has yielded ground to Satan in his soul. He shall continue to be further deceived until Satan has gained control over nearly all his feeling. Sometimes Satan will even induce him to experience supernatural sensations of shaking, electrifying, freezing, overflowing, floating in the air, fire burning from head to foot and consuming all his uncleanness, etc. When anyone has been beguiled to this extent his whole being comes to thrive on feelings, his will is totally paralyzed, and his intuition is entirely surrounded. He exists altogether in the outer man; his inner man is completely bound. At this stage he follows Satan's will in almost everything, for the enemy merely needs to supply him with some particular feeling to goad him to do what he wants him to do. The tragedy is that the believer is not aware he is being tricked by Satan; he instead pictures himself as being more spiritual than others since he enjoys such supernatural experiences.

Supernatural phenomena such as those described damage the spiritual life of many a Christian most severely today. Countless numbers of Gods children have fallen into this pit. They consider these supernatural occurrences—which give them a physical feeling of the power of the spirit and render them happy or sad, hot or cold, laughing or crying and which supply them with visions, dreams, voices, fires and even inexpressible wonderful sensations—as most definitely bestowed by the Holy Spirit, and thus represent the highest attainment of a Christian. They are unable to recognize that these are but the works of the evil spirit. They would never dream that the evil spirit as well as the Holy Spirit could perform such work. Totally ignorant are they of the fact that the Holy Spirit operates in the spirit of men. Whatever induces feeling to the *body* proceeds nine out of ten times from the evil spirit. Why have so many fallen into this snare? Simply because they do not live in the spirit but love to live in their feeling! They accordingly provide the wicked power opportunity to play his tricks. Christians must learn to deny their sensational life or else they shall give ground to the enemy to deceive them.

Let us seriously warn every one of God's children to take note of their *bodily* feeling. We should never allow any spirit to create any feeling in our body against our will. We should resist each of these outward bodily feelings. We should not believe in any of these physical sensations. Rather than follow them we should forbid them, for they constitute the enemy's initial deception. We ought solely to follow intuition in the *depths* of our beings.

A careful observation of a Chritian's life of feeling can uncover an underlying principle in such a life—which is none other than "for the sake of self." Why is joyous sensation so sought after? For the sake of self. Why is barrenness so abhorred? Again for self's sake. Why seek bodily feelings? For self. Why crave supernatural experiences. Also for self. Oh, may the Holy Spirit open our eyes to behold how full of self is a so-called "spiritual" life of feeling! May the Lord show us that when we are filled with joyous emotions our life is still centered on self. It is the love of self-pleasure! The reality or falsity of spiritual life can be gauged by the way we treat self.

CHAPTER 5
THE LIFE OF FAITH

THE BIBLE DISCLOSES for us the normal path of a Christian's walk in such passages as "the righteous shall live by faith"; "the life I now live in the flesh I live by faith in the Son of God"; and "we walk by faith, not by sight" (Rom. 1.17 ASV; Gal. 2.20; 2 Cor. 5.7). By faith are we to live. But while this principle may be quickly grasped in the mind it is not so readily experienced in life.

The life of faith is not only totally different from, but also diametrically opposite to, a life of feeling. He who lives by sensation can follow God's will or seek the things above purely at the time of excitement; should his blissful feeling cease, every activity terminates. Not so with one who walks by faith. Faith is anchored in the One Whom he believes rather than in the one who exercises the believing, that is, himself..Faith looks not at what happens to him but at Him Whom he believes. Though he may completely change, yet the One in Whom he trusts never does—and so he can proceed without letting up. Faith establishes its relationship with God. It regards not its feeling because it is concerned with God. Faith follows the One believed while feeling turns on how one feels. What faith thus beholds is God whereas what feeling beholds is one's self. God does not change: He is the same God in either the cloudy day or the sunny day. Hence he who lives by faith is as unchanging as is God; he expresses the same kind of life through darkness or through light. But one who dwells by feeling must pursue an up-and-down existence because his feeling is ever changing.

What God expects of His children is that they will not make enjoyment the purpose of their lives. God wants them to walk by believing Him. As they run the spiritual race they are to carry on whether they feel comfortable or whether they feel painful. They never alter their attitude towards God according to their sensations. However dry, tasteless or dark it may be, they continue to advance—trusting God and advancing as long as they know this is God's will. Frequently their feeling appears to rebel against this continuation: they grow exceedingly sorrowful, melancholic, despondent, as though their emotions were pleading with them to halt every spiritual activity. They nonetheless go on as usual, entirely ignoring their adverse feeling; for they realize work must be done. This is the pathway of faith, one which pays no heed to one's emotion but exclusively to the purpose of God. If something is believed to be God's mind, then no matter how uninterested one's feeling is he must proceed to execute it. One who walks by sensation undertakes merely what he feels interested in; the one however who walks by faith obeys the complete will of God and cares not at all about his own interest or indifference.

The life of feeling draws people away from abiding in God to finding satisfaction in joy, while the life of faith draws believers into being satisfied with God by faith. They having possessed God, their joyful feelings do not add to their joy nor do their painful sensations render them woeful. A life of emotion induces the saint to exist for himself but a life of faith enables him to exist for God and cedes no ground to his self life. When self is entertained and pleased it is not a life of faith but simply a life of feeling. Exquisite feeling does indeed please the self. If one walks according to sensation it indicates he has not yet committed his natural life to the cross. He still reserves some place for self—wishing to make it happy—while simultaneously continuing to tread the spiritual path.

The Christian experience, from start to finish, is a journey of faith. Through it we come into possession of a new life and through it we walk by this new life. Faith is the life principle of a Christian. This is of course acknowledged by all saints; but strangely enough many seem to overlook this in their experience. They forget that to live and to move by emotion or happy sensations is to do so by sight and not by faith What is the life of faith? It is one lived contrary to a life of feeling because it disregards feeling altogether. If Christians desire to live by this principle they should not alter their demeanor or bitterly cry as though bereft of their spiritual life whenever they feel cold, dry, empty, or pained. We live by faith and not by joy.

THE DEEPER WORK OF THE CROSS

When we forsake physical happiness and mundane pleasures we are apt to conclude that the cross has finished its perfect work in us. We do not perceive that in God's work of annulling the old creation in us there remains a deeper cross awaiting us. God wishes us to die to His joy and live to His will. Even if we feel joyous because of God and His nearness (in contrast to being joyous because of fleshly and earthly things), God's aim nevertheless is not for us to enjoy His joy but to obey His will. The cross must continue to operate till His will *alone* is left. If we rejoice in the bliss God dispenses but renounce the suffering He also dispenses, then we have yet to experience the deeper circumcision by the cross.

Great is the contrast between the will of God and the joy of God. The first is ever present, for we can behold God's mind in His providential arrangement; but the second is *not* always present, since it is experienced only in certain circumstances and at certain times. When a Christian seeks the joy of God he takes simply that part of His purpose which makes him happy; he does not desire the entire will of God. He chooses to obey God's aim when God makes him happy; but if He should cause him to suffer he at once revolts against His will. But the person who receives His will as his life will obey regardless how God makes him feel. He can discern divine arrangement in both joy and suffering.

During the initial stage of a Christian's experience ᴳᵒᵈ allows him to delight in His joy; after he has advanced somewhat in his spiritual walk God withdraws His joy, since this is profitable for the Christian. God appreciates the fact that should the believer seek and enjoy this kind of bliss too long he shall not be able to live by every word which proceeds from His mouth; instead he shall live wholly by that word which makes him glad. Thus he abides in the comfort of God but not in the God Who gives comfort. For this reason God must remove these pleasurable sensations so that His child may live exclusively by Him.

We know that the Lord at the commencement of our spiritual walk normally comforts us during those times we suffer on His behalf. He causes the believer to sense His presence, see His smiling face, feel His love, and experience His care in order to prevent him from fainting. When the believer apprehends the mind of the Lord and follows it He usually gives him great pleasure. Although he has paid some price for following the Lord yet the joy he obtains far surpasses what he has lost and hence he delights to obey His will. But the Lord perceives a danger here: upon having experienced comfort in suffering and happiness in heeding His mind, the child of God naturally looks for such comfort and joy the next time he suffers or obeys the Lord's will or else expects to be helped immediately by His comfort and joy. Hence he suffers or does the Lord's will not purely for His sake but for the sake of being rewarded with consolation and happiness as well. Without these crutches he is powerless to continue. The will of the Lord becomes inferior to the joy which He bestows at the moment of obedience.

God realizes His child is most eager to suffer if he is comforted, and is delighted to follow His will if he is accorded joy. But God now wishes to learn what motivates him: whether he suffers exclusively for the Lord's sake or for the sake of being consoled: whether he heeds God's mind because it should be heeded or because he derives some joy by so heeding. For this reason, after a Christian has made some progress spiritually God commences to withdraw the consolation and delight which He gave him in the hour of suffering and obedience. Now the Christian must suffer without any ministration of comfort from God: he suffers externally while feeling bitter inwardly. He is to do the will of God without the least thing to stimulate his interest; indeed everything is dry and uninteresting. By this process God will learn precisely why the believer suffers on His behalf and obeys His will. God is asking him: are you disposed to endure without being compensated by My comfort? Are you ready to endure just for Me? Are you amenable to perform labor which does not interest you a bit? Can you do it just because it is *My* purpose? Will you be able to undertake for Me when you feel depressed, insipid and parched? Can you do it simply because it is *My* work? Are you able to accept joyfully physical suffering without any compensation of refreshment? Can you accept it because it is given by *Me?*

This is a practical cross by which the Lord reveals to us whether we are living for Him by faith or living for ourselves by feeling. Frequently have we heard people say, "I live for Christ." What does this really convey? Many saints assume that if they labor for the Lord or love the Lord they are living for Christ. This is far from being exactly so. To live for the Lord means to live for His will, for His interest, and for His kingdom. As such, there is nothing for self—not the slightest provision for self-comfort, self-joy, or self-glory. To follow the mind of God because of comfort or joy is strictly forbidden. To recoil from, to cease or delay in, obedience because of feeling depressed, vapid or despondent is positively impermissible. We ought to know that physical suffering alone may not be regarded as enduring for the Lord, for often our bodies will be bearing pain while our hearts are full of joy. If we actually suffer for Him, then not only do our bodies suffer but our hearts feel pained as well. Though there is not the least joyfulness, we yet press on. Let us understand that to live for the Lord is to reserve nothing for self but to deliver it willingly to death. He who is able to accept everything gladly from the Lord—including darkness, dryness, flatness—and completely disregard self is he who lives for Him.

Should we walk by emotion we can perform God's desire only as we have a happy feeling. But should we live by faith we can obey the Lord in all regards. How often we do realize a certain matter is in fact God's will yet we have not the least interest in it. And so we feel parched when we try to perform it. We have no registration that the Lord is pleased nor do we experience His blessing or strengthening. Rather do we feel as if we are passing through the valley of the shadow of death, for the enemy is contesting our way. And alas, without mentioning the innumerable believers who today do not even follow God's will, there are those few following it who more or less only follow that part which interests them. They obey the mind of God solely when it suits their emotion and desire! Unless we advance by faith we shall flee to Tarshish (see Jonah 1.3, 4.2).

We should inquire once again as to what the life of faith is. It is one lived by believing God *under any circumstance*: "If he slay me," says Job, "yet would I trust in Him" (13.15 Darby). That is faith. Because I once believed, loved and trusted God I shall believe, love and trust Him wherever He may put me and however my heart and body may suffer. Nowadays the people of God expect to feel peaceful even in the time of physical pain. Who is there who dares to renounce this consolation of heart for the sake of believing God? Who is there who can accept God's will joyfully and continuously commit himself to Him even though he *feels* that God hates him and desires to slay him? That is the highest life. Of course God would never treat us like that. Nevertheless in the walk of the most advanced Chritians they seem to experience something of this apparent desertion by God. Would we be able to remain unmoved in our faith in God if we felt thus? Observe what John Bunyan, author of *Pilgrim's Progress*, proclaimed when men sought to hang him: "If God does not intervene I shall leap into eternity with blind faith come heaven, come hell!" There was a hero of faith! In the hour of despair can we too say, "O God, though You desert me yet will I believe You"? Emotion begins to doubt when it senses blackness, whereas faith holds on to God even in the face of death.

How few have arrived at such a level! How our flesh resists such a walk with God alone! The natural disinclination for cross-bearing has impeded many in their spiritual progress. They tend to reserve a little pleasure for their own enjoyment. To lose everything in the Lord, even self-pleasure, is too thoroughgoing a death, too heavy a cross! They can be fully consecrated to the Lord, they can be suffering untold pain for Him, they can even pay a price for following the will of God, but they cannot foresake that obviously trifling feeling of self-pleasure. Many cherish this momentary comfort; their spiritual life rests on this tiny twinge of feeling. Were they to exercise the courage to sacrifice themselves to God's fiery furnace, showing no pity or love for self, they would make great strides on their spiritual pathway. But too many of God's people remain subservient to their natural life, trusting what is seen and felt for safety and security: they have neither the courage nor the faith to exploit the unseen, the unfelt, the untrodden. They have already drawn a circle around themselves; their joy or sorrow hinges upon a little gain here or a little loss there; they accept nothing loftier. Thus are they circumscribed by their own petty self.

Were the Christian to recognize that God wishes him to live by faith, he would not murmur against God so frequently nor would he conceive these thoughts of discontent. How swiftly would his natural life be cut away by the cross if he could accept the God-given parched feeling and could esteem everything given him by God as excellent. Were it not for his ignorance or unwillingness, such experiences would deal with his soul life most practically, enabling him to live truly in the spirit. How sad that many succeed at nothing greater in their lives than the pursuit of a little feeling of joy. The faithful, however, are brought by God into genuine spiritual life. How godly is their walk! When they examine retrospectively what they have experienced they readily acknowledge that the ordering of the Lord is perfect: for only because of those experiences did they renounce their soul life. Today's crying need is for believers to hand themselves over completely to God and ignore their feeling.

This should not at all be misconstrued to signify, however, that henceforth we shall become joyless persons. "Joy in the Holy Spirit" is the greatest blessing in the kingdom of God (Rom. 14.17). The fruit of the Holy Spirit, moreover, is joy (Gal. 5.22). If this is so, then how can we reconcile this apparent inconsistency? Simply come to see that though we do lose joy in our feeling, nevertheless the joy we gain issues from a pure faith and cannot be destroyed. Joy of this caliber runs far deeper than emotion. In becoming spiritual we abandon the old desire for self-pleasure and hence additionally the former search for bliss; but the peace and joy of the spirit which arises from faith remains forever.

AFTER THE SPIRIT

To walk after the spirit a Christian must deny every scintilla of his life of feeling. He must move by faith and eliminate the crutches of wonderful sensation to which the flesh naturally clings. When he is following the spirit he neither fears if he receives no help from feeling nor if feeling opposes him. But when his faith is weak and he follows not the spirit, he then will heed the support of the visible, the sensible and the touchable. Emotion replaces intuition in guidance whenever spiritual life grows weak. He who abides in feeling will come to see that, having long sought pleasurable sensations, he shall soon seek as well the help of the world, because feeling rests nowhere save in the world. An emotional Christian often employs his own way and seeks man's help. To follow the leading of the spirit requires faith, for it usually is contrary to feeling. Without faith no one can actually march forward. A soulish person ceases to serve God the moment he becomes depressed; on the other hand one who lives by faith does not delay in serving the Lord until he becomes joyful: he simply goes forward while beseeching God to increase the strength of his spirit that he may overcome any depressed feeling which may descend.

THE LIFE OF THE WILL

The life of faith can be called the life of the will since faith is impervious to how one feels but chooses through volition to obey God's mind. Though the Christian may not *feel* like obeying God, even so he *wills* to obey Him. We find two opposite kinds of Christians: one depends on emotion, the other relies on the *renewed* will. A Christian who trusts in feeling can obey God solely while he is deriving stimulus from his feeling, that is, excitable feeling. The one however who depends on volition determines that he shall serve God amid whatever circumstance or feeling. His will reflects his real opinion whereas his feeling is only activated by outside stimulus. From God's viewpoint not much value accrues in doing His will out of a pleasurable sensation: to do so is merely to be persuaded by the joy of God and not by a wholehearted aspiration to do His will. Except he neither feels a bit of joy nor is stimulated by some wonderful feeling and yet decides to do God's will can the Christian's obedience be counted truly valuable, because it flows from his honest heart and expresses his respect for God and disregard of self. The distinction between the spiritual and the soulish Christian lies precisely there: the soulish primarily considers himself and therefore only obeys God when he feels his desire is satisfied; the spiritual has a will fully cooperating with God and hence accepts His arrangement without wavering even though he has no outside help or stimulus.

Of what have we to boast if we obey God merely while we experience joy in our body? Or how can we brag if we enjoy the cheer of the Lord while suffering? Precious is it in God's sight if we determine to obey His mind and suffer for Him even when the comfort, love, help, presence and joy of the Lord are absent.

A great number of believers are unconscious of the fact that to walk by the spirit is to walk by the will which is joined to God. (A will which is not so joined is untrustworthy and inconsistent; it requires a will that is entirely yielded to God's to always choose what the spirit desires). In the early stage of their Christian experience they heard how other saints enjoyed unutterable bliss during obedience or suffering. They ardently admired such a life, so they too offered themselves exclusively to the Lord with the hope of possessing this "higher" life. In truth, following their consecration they did experience time and again the Lord's intimacy and love, which prompted them to conclude that their hope had been realized. But far too soon did these wonderful experiences become past history.

Because they are unaware that the expression of true spiritual life issues not from feeling but from the will many suffer endless pains, for these believe they have lost their spiritual life when no happy sensation is felt. Such ones, at a time of low feeling, need to ascertain whether their original heart of consecration has been changed or whether they still harbor the desire to do God's will. Are they yet disposed to suffer for Him? Is there any change in their readiness to do anything or go anywhere for God? If these have not been altered, then their spiritual life has not receded. But if these have changed, their life in the spirit has indeed receded.

Just as one's retrogression is not due to any loss of joy but to the weakening of his will in obedience to God, so his progress is not because he possesses many delightful feelings now which he previously did not, but because of a deeper union of his will with God. It is this which renders him more inclined to follow God's will, more amenable to His desires. The touchstone of genuine spiritual life is how much one's volition is united with God's; good or bad sensation, happy or sad feeling does not in the slightest serve as an indicator. If one is willing, however dry he may feel, to be faithful to God even to death, his spiritual course becomes the noblest. Spirituality is measured by our volition because it unfolds our undisguised condition. When our choices and decisions are yielded to God we may safely say we have yielded to God and no longer act as our own sovereign. Self stands in opposition to spiritual life. With self broken down that life grows up: should self remain strong that life will suffer. We accordingly can judge one's spirituality by looking into his will. Feeling, on the contrary, is distinctly different. For even if we possess the most glorious sensations, we are nonetheless full of self, being self-gratified and self-pleased.

Let not those who sincerely strive after spiritual growth be deceived into thinking that feeling is their life principle, because this shall entice them to be mindful always of tingling sensation. Just be certain that the will is utterly offered to God. Joy or no joy is not to be the consideration. God wants us to live by faith. Should He wish us to live by faith and be satisfied solely with His will bereft of consolation or ecstatic delight for long duration, would we be inclined to so live? We should delight in our having obeyed the mind of God, not in being accorded some joy. God's will alone should be sufficient to make us joyful.

THE DUTY OF MAN

While a Christian is governed by feeling he invariably will neglect his duty towards others. This is because he makes himself the center and is consequently unfit to care for the needs of others. For a Christian to fulfill his duty it requires faith and will. Responsibility ignores feeling. Our duty towards men is defined and our responsibility in the mundane affairs of life is certain. These cannot be altered according to one's changing emotion. Duty must be performed according to principle.

During the period that a Christian knows the truth merely in his feeling he certainly cannot fulfill his duty. He is so taken up with the joy from fellowshiping with the Lord that that is all he pursues. His greatest temptation is to want to do nothing but be alone with the Lord and bask in this joy. He does not like the work in which he formerly was engaged because it holds out no other prospect than many trials and troubles. When face to face with the Lord he senses intense holiness and victory, but when he emerges to perform his daily tasks he finds himself as defeated and defiled as before. What he wants is to escape his duties: he hopes that by lingering lengthily before the Lord he can remain holy and victorious the longer. He views these matters of duty as earthy and unworthy of occupying the attention of so pure and triumphant a person as he. Since he cares so much about finding time and place to commune with the Lord and hates so deeply those works which are his duties, he naturally neglects the need and welfare of those around him. Parents and servants who think like this do not, respectively, take good care of their children nor serve their masters faithfully because they judge these duties as worldly, therefore of negligible worth. They believe they must seek something more spiritual. The reason for this unbalanced approach is the believer's failure to walk by faith; he continues to look for self-support. He has not yet been united fully with God. Hence he needs *special* time and *special* place to commune with God. He has not learned to discern the Lord in all matters and to cooperate accordingly with Him. He does not know how to be united with the Lord in the daily details of living. His experience of God is but in his feeling; and so he loves to erect a tent on the mountain and dwell there permanently with the Lord but hates to descend to the plain to cast the demon away.

The loftiest Christian experience is never contradictory to the duties of one's pathway. In reading the letters to the Romans, Colossians and Ephesians we can plainly see how perfectly a Christian must perform his duty as a man. His highest life does not necessitate special hour and situation in order to be manifested; it can be thoroughly expressed at any time or place. To the Lord there is no dichotomy between household work and preaching or praying. The life of Christ can be exhibited through all sorts of activity.

As a consequence to living an emotional life we become dissatisfied with our present position and are loathe to perform the duties connected with that position. We revolt because in those duties we do not find the pleasure we seek. But our life is not for pleasure; why do we therefore look for it again? The path of feeling bids us neglect our duty; the path of faith calls us not to forsake our duty to friends or foes. If we are united with God in every detail of living, we shall know what are our tasks and how we should properly fulfill them.

IN THE WORK OF GOD

To deny the life of emotion and live by faith completely is one of the basic requirements for serving God. An emotional believer is useless in God's hand. He who walks by feeling knows how to enjoy pleasure but not how to work for God. He has not yet attained the status of a worker, since he lives for himself and not for God. Living for the Lord is the prerequisite to working for Him.

A Christian must realize the way of faith before he can be a useful instrument to God and actually perform His work. Otherwise his aim in life is pleasure. He works for the sake of feeling and for that reason he will stop working. His heart is brimming with self-love. If he is placed by the Lord in a field of labor filled with physical and emotional suffering he begins to pity himself and finally gives up. But even as the work of the Lord Jesus was that of the cross, exactly so is the work of a Christian to be. What pleasure is there in such work? Except Christians utterly commit their emotion and their heart of self-love to death, God can hardly find any real workers.

Today the Lord needs men to be His followers who shall trail Him to the end. Too many saints labor for the Lord when the task is prosperous, is suited to their interest, or does not imperil their feeling; but how quickly they retreat should the cross come upon them and require them to die and give them no help except to lay hold of God by faith. We know that if a work is veritably accomplished by God there cannot but be results. Yet supposing one has been commissioned by the Lord and has labored for eight or ten years without achieving any results. Can he continue to labor faithfully simply because God has commanded it? How many saints are there who serve purely because it is God's command? Or how many work just to produce fruits? Since God's work is eternal in nature, He demands men with faith to labor for Him. It is difficult for human beings who live in time to perceive and to understand the work of God, for it is replete with eternal character. How, then, can those who live by feeling ever join in in God's work since nothing in it can please their feeling? Unless the death of the cross cuts penetratingly into the soul of a believer so that he reserves nothing for self, he cannot follow the Lord in work except to a limited extent. Beyond that he is unable to go. God asks for men who are totally broken and who will follow Him even to death to work for Him.

IN BATTLING THE ENEMY

Those who live by feeling are even more worthless in spiritual warfare, because to battle the enemy in prayer is truly a self-denying work. What incalculable suffering is involved! Nothing for satisfying one's self can be found here; it is pouring out one's all for the body of Christ and the kingdom of God. How unbearable must be this resisting and wrestling in the spirit! What pleasure is there for the spirit to be laden with indescribable burden for the sake of God? Is it interesting to attack the evil spirit with every ounce of strength one can summon? This is a prayer warfare. But for whom is the believer praying? Not for himself surely, but for the work of God. Such prayer is for warfare which is thoroughly lacking in interest one usually encounters during ordinary prayer. Is there anything in this that can make him feel comfortable when he must travail in his soul and pray to destroy and to build? No element in spiritual warfare can gladden the flesh—unless of course one is contending merely in his imagination.

An emotional Christian is easily defeated in conflict with Satan. While he is praying to assault the enemy the latter by his evil spirit will attack his emotion. He will set the Christian to feeling that such contesting is painful and such prayer is lifeless. So as he becomes sorrowful, insipid, dark and dry, he immediately stops fighting. An emotional Christian is powerless to war against Satan, for as soon as his feeling comes under attack by Satan he quits the field of battle. If one's emotion has not experienced death, he may provide opportunity to Satan to strike at any hour. Each time he rises to oppose the enemy he is defeated by a satanic touch upon his feeling. Can anyone expect victory over Satan unless he has first overcome his life of sensation?

Spiritual warfare accordingly demands an attitude of total death to feeling and an absolute trust in God. Only a person with this attitude can bear up alone and not seek companions or man's approval in fighting the enemy. Only this caliber of Christian can proceed under all sorts of anguished feelings. He cares not at all for his life nor about death but only cares for the leading of God. He indulges no personal interest, desire or longing. He has offered himself to death already and then lives exclusively for God. He neither blames nor misunderstands Him because he considers all His ways to be loving. This is the class of person who is able to fill the breach. Though he may appear to be deserted by God and forgotten by men, yet he mans his battle station. He is a prayer warrior. He overcomes Satan.

REST

After a believer has thus been dealt with, he can commence the walk of faith which is true spiritual life. And the one who arrives at this position enters upon a life of rest. The fire of the cross has consumed his every greedy pursuit. He at last has learned his lesson: he recognizes that God's will alone is precious. All else, though naturally desirable, is incompatible with the highest life of God. Now he rejoices in relinquishing everything. Whatever the Lord deems necessary to withdraw, he gladly allows His hand to do it. The sighing, mourning and grieving which arose out of his former anticipation, seeking and struggling have today entirely disappeared. He realizes that the loftiest life is one lived for God and one obedient to His will. Though he has lost everything yet is he satisfied with the fulfillment of God's purpose. Though he is left with nothing to enjoy, yet is he humble under the ordering of God. So long as the Lord is pleased he cares not the least what happens to him. He now has perfect rest; nothing external can any longer stimulate him.

Presently the child of God abides by a will which is united with the Lord. His volition, today filled with spiritual strength, is competent to control his emotion. His walk is steady, firm, restful. His former situation of ups and downs has vanished. Even so, we must not now rush to the conclusion that henceforth he shall never again be ruled by emotion, for before we enter heaven itself such sinless perfection is not possible. Nonetheless, in comparing his present state with his former condition, this one can indeed be described as experiencing rest, being established, and continuing firm. He suffers no further from that incessant confusion he encountered heretofore, though occasionally he may still be disturbed by the operation of his emotion. That is why watchful prayer continues to be indispensable. Let us therefore hasten to add: do not misunderstand what has been said to mean that from here on there shall be no possibility of feeling either joy or sorrow. As long as our organ for emotion is not annihilated (it never will be), our feeling shall continue to exist. We still can sense pain, blackness, aridity and sorrow. Yet those sufferings can penetrate our outer man only, leaving our inner man untouched. Due to the clear division between spirit and soul, outwardly our soul may be disturbed and consequently suffer but inwardly our spirit remains calm and composed as though nothing had happened.

Upon arriving at this restful position the believer shall find that all he heretofore had lost for the Lord's sake has today been restored. He has gained God, and therefore everything belonging to God belongs to him as well. What the Lord had withdrawn before he now can properly enjoy in Him. The reason why God at the beginning had led him through many sorrows was because his soul life lay behind everything, seeking and asking too much for *himself*, desiring even things which were outside God's will. Such independent action had to be circumscribed by God. Now that he has lost himself— that is, his natural life—the Christian is in a position to enjoy the bliss of God within its legitimate boundary. Not till today was he qualified to be rightly related to His joy. Hereafter he can thankfully accept whatever is given him, because the eagerness to secure something for self has already been put to nought; he does not petition inordinately for that which was not bestowed upon him.

Such a child of God has advanced onto a pure ground. Where there is mixture there is impurity. The Bible views impurity as something defiled. Before one reaches this ground of no mixture he cannot express a pure walk. He lives for God yet also lives for self: he loves the Lord but loves himself as well: his intention is unto God, yet simultaneously he aims at self-glory, self-pleasure, self-comfort. Such a life is a defiled one. He walks by faith but also walks by feeling, he follows the spirit but also follows the soul. While he does not in fact reserve the larger portion for himself, nonetheless this smaller portion held back is sufficient to render his life impure. Only what is pure is clean; anything mixed with foreign matter becomes defiled.

When a believer has experienced the practical treatment of the cross he finally arrives at a pure life. All is for God and in God, and God is in all as well. Nothing is unto self. Even the tiniest desire for pleasing one's self is crucified. Self-love has been consigned to death. The present aim of existence becomes single: to do the will of God: so long as He is pleased, nothing else really counts: to obey Him becomes the sole objective of life. It does not matter how he feels; what matters is obeying God. This is a pure walk. Although God affords him peace, comfort and bliss, he does not enjoy them for the sake of gratifying his desire. He from now on views everything with God's eye. His soulish life has been terminated and the Lord has granted him a pure, restful, true and believing spiritual life. While it is God Who does destroy him, it equally is God Who builds him up. That which is soulish has been destroyed but that which is spiritual has been established.

THE
SPIRITUAL MAN

Watchman Nee

IN THREE VOLUMES

Christian Fellowship Publishers, Inc.
New York

Available from the Publishers at:
11515 Allecingie Parkway
Richmond, Virginia 23235

THE SPIRITUAL MAN
Volume III

Contents

VOLUME III

EXPLANATORY NOTES   page vi

PART EIGHT: THE ANALYSIS OF THE SOUL —THE MIND

1 The Mind a Battlefield   7
2 The Phenomena of a Passive Mind 30
3 The Way of Deliverance 45
4 The Laws of the Mind 63

PART NINE: THE ANALYSIS OF THE SOUL —THE WILL

1 A Believer's Will   75
2 Passivity and Its Dangers 90
3 The Believer's Mistake 102
4 The Path to Freedom 120

PART TEN: THE BODY

1 The Believer and His Body 139
2 Sickness   158
3 God as the Life of the Body 196
4 Overcoming Death 213

EXPLANATORY NOTES

Volume III of *The Spiritual Man* is a companion book to Volumes I and II of this series of studies. While many other books have been compiled from his spoken messages, this book translated from the Chinese is the only one of any substantial size which brother Watchman Nee himself ever wrote. Perhaps this will account for the difference in style. At the time of writing it he felt this work might be his last contribution to the church, although since then God has graciously overruled. Long after the book's initial publication in Chinese our brother once was heard to express the thought that it should not be reprinted because, it being such a "perfect" treatment of its subject, he was fearful lest the book become to its readers merely a manual of principles and not a guide to experience as well. But in view of the urgent need among the children of God today for help on spiritual life and warfare, and knowing our brother as one who is always open to God's way and most desirous to serve His people with all that God has given him, we conclude that he would doubtless permit it to be circulated in English. Hence this translation.

Translations used. The Revised Standard Version (RSV) of the Bible has been used throughout the text unless otherwise indicated. Additional translations where employed are denoted by the following abbreviations:

Amplified—*Amplified Old Testament*
ASV—American Standard Version (1901)
AV—Authorized Version (King James)
Darby—J. N. Darby, *The Holy Scriptures, a New Translation*
Young's—Young's *Literal Translation*

Soulical and Soulish. The adjectives "soulical" and "soulish" have been used to convey distinctly different meanings. "Soulical" as herein employed pertains to those proper, appropriate, legitimate, or natural qualities, functions, or expressions of man's soul which the Creator intended from the very beginning for the soul uniquely to possess and manifest. "Soulish" appears in these pages to describe that man *in toto* who is so governed by the soulical part of his being that his whole life takes on the character and expression of the soul.

PART EIGHT

THE ANALYSIS OF THE SOUL—THE MIND

1 The Mind a Battlefield
2 The Phenomena of a Passive Mind
3 The Way of Deliverance
4 The Laws of the Mind

CHAPTER 1

THE MIND A BATTLEFIELD

The mind of man is his organ of thought. Through it he is equipped to know, think, imagine, remember, and understand. Man's intellect, reasoning, wisdom and cleverness all pertain to the mind. Broadly speaking the mind is the brain. Mind is a psychological term whereas brain is a physiological term. The mind of psychology is the brain of physiology. Man's mind occupies a large place in his life because his thought easily influences his action.

BEFORE REGENERATION

According to the Bible the mind of man is unusual in that it constitutes a battlefield where Satan and his evil spirits contend against the truth and hence against the believer. We may illustrate as follows. Man's will and spirit are like a citadel which the evil spirits crave to capture. The open field where the battle is waged for the seizure of the citadel is man's mind. Note how Paul the Apostle describes it: "though we live in the world we are not carrying on a worldly war, for the weapons of our warfare are not worldly but have divine power to destroy strongholds. We destroy *arguments* and every proud obstacle to the knowledge of God, and take every *thought* captive to obey Christ" (2 Cor. 10.3-5). He initially tells us of a battle—then where the battle is fought —and finally for what objective. This struggle pertains exclusively to man's mind. The Apostle likens man's arguments or reasonings to an enemy's strongholds. He pictures the mind as held by the enemy; it must therefore be broken into by waging war. He concludes that many rebellious thoughts are housed in these strongholds and need to be taken captive to the obedience of Christ. All this plainly shows us that the mind of man is the scene of battle where the evil spirits clash with God.

Scripture explains that before regeneration "the god of this world (had) blinded the minds of the unbelievers, to keep them from seeing the light of the gospel of the glory of Christ, who is the likeness of God" (2 Cor. 4.4). This verse concurs in what the other verse just quoted said by declaring here that Satan holds on to man's mind by making it blind. Some people perhaps may consider themselves extremely wise in their ability to advance many arguments against the gospel; others may take for granted that unbelief is due to dullness of understanding; but the truth in both cases is that the eyes of man's mind have been covered by Satan. When firmly held by Satan the mind of man becomes "hardened"; man "follows the desires of body and mind (as) children of wrath" and so "is estranged and hostile in mind" because "the mind that is set on the flesh is hostile to God" (2 Cor. 3.14; Eph. 2.3; Col. 1.21; Rom. 8.7).

Upon reading these various passages we can see clearly how the powers of darkness are especially related to man's mind, how it is peculiarly susceptible to Satan's assault. With respect to man's will, emotion and body, the powers of evil are helpless to do anything *directly* unless they first have gained some ground therein. But with man's mind they can work freely without initially persuading man or securing his invitation. The mind appears to be their possession already. The Apostle in comparing men's minds to an enemy's strongholds seems to imply that Satan and his wicked spirits already have established a deep relationship with the minds of men, that somehow they are using them as their bastions in which to imprison their captives. Through man's mind they impose their authority and through the mind of their captives they transmit poisonous thoughts to others so that these too may rise up against God. It is difficult to estimate how much of the world's philosophy, ethics, knowledge, research, and science flow from the powers of darkness. But of one point we are certain: all arguments and proud obstacles against the knowledge of God are the fortresses of the enemy.

Is it strange to behold the mind in such close proximity to the authorities of wickedness? Was not the sin which mankind first committed that of seeking the knowledge of good and evil, and that at the instigation of Satan? Hence man's mind is especially related to Satan. If we were to peruse the Scriptures carefully and to observe the experiences of the saints we would discover that all communications between human and satanic forces occur in the organ of thought. Take, for instance, Satan's temptation. Every temptation with which he entices man is presented to his *mind*. It is true that Satan often uses the flesh to secure the consent of man, yet in each instance of enticement the enemy creates some kind of thought by which to induce the man. We cannot separate temptation and thought. All temptations are offered us in the form of thoughts. Since the latter are so exposed to the power of darkness, we need to learn how to guard them.

Prior to regeneration man's intellect obstructs him from apprehending God. It is necessary for His mighty power to destroy man's arguments. This is a work which must occur at the hour of new birth—and it does happen then in the form of repentance. The original definition of repentance is none else than "a change of mind." Man in his mind is at enmity with God; therefore God must alter man's mind if He would impart life to him. In his unregenerated state man has a darkened mind; at his regeneration it undergoes a drastic change. Because it has been so united with the devil it is vital for man to receive from God a change of mind before he can receive a new heart (Acts 11.18).

AFTER REGENERATION

But even following repentance the believer's mind is not liberated totally from the touch of Satan. As the enemy worked through the mind in former days, so today will he work in the same manner. Paul, in writing to the Corinthian *believers,* confided that he was "afraid that as the serpent deceived Eve by his cunning, your *thoughts* will be led astray from a sincere and pure devotion to Christ" (2 Cor. 11. 3). The Apostle well recognizes that as the god of this world blinds the mind of unbelievers so will he deceive the mind of the believers. Even though they are saved their life of thought is as yet unrenewed; consequently it remains the most strategic battleground. *The mind suffers the onslaughts of the powers of darkness more than any other organ of the whole man.* We should realize that satanic spirits are directing special attention to our minds and are attacking them unrelentingly—"as the serpent deceived Eve by his cunning." Satan did not assail Eve's heart first but rather her head. Similarly today, the evil spirits first attack our head, not our heart, in order to have us corrupted from the simplicity and purity which is towards Christ. They fully understand how it is the *weakest* point in our entire being, for it had served as their fortress before we believed and even now is not yet entirely overthrown. Attacking the mind is the easiest avenue for them to accomplish their purpose. Eve's heart was sinless and yet she received Satan's suggested thoughts. She was thus beguiled through his deception into forfeiting her reasoning and tumbling into the snare of the enemy. Let a believer accordingly be careful in his boast of possessing an honest and sincere heart, for unless he learns how to repulse the evil spirits in his mind he will continue to be tempted and deceived into losing the sovereignty of his will.

Paul continues by telling us from whence this danger comes: "if some one comes and preaches another Jesus than the one we preached, or if you receive a different spirit from the one you received, or if you accept a different gospel from the one you accepted" (v.4). The peril for the Christian is to have false teaching injected into his thought life so as to lead him astray from a sincere and pure devotion to Christ. These are the works the "serpent" is perpetrating today. Satan has disguised himself as an angel of light to lead saints to worship with their intellect a Jesus other than the Lord, to receive a spirit other than the Holy Spirit, and by these to propagate a gospel other than the gospel of the grace of God. Paul pronounces these to be nothing else than the deeds of Satan in the Christian's mind. The adversary translates these "doctrines" into thoughts and then imposes them upon the mind of the Christian. How tragic that few appreciate the reality of these activities! Few, indeed, who would ever think that the devil could give such good thoughts to men!

It is possible for a child of God to have a new life and a new heart but be without a new head. With too many saints, the mind, though their heart is new, is still quite old. Their heart is full of love whereas their head is totally lacking in perception. How often the intents of the heart are utterly pure and yet the thoughts in the head are confused. Having become saturated with a mishmash of everything, the mind lacks the most signal element of all, which is spiritual insight. Countless saints genuinely love all children of God, but unfortunately their brain is stuffed with a hodgepodge of theories, opinions and objectives. Quite a number of God's best and most faithful children are the most narrow-minded and prejudice-filled. Already have they decided what is the truth and what truth they shall accept. They reject every other truth because these do not blend in with their preconceived notions. Their head is not as expansive as their heart. Moreover, there are other children of God whose mind can conceive no thought whatever. No matter how many truths have been heard they can neither remember nor practice nor com-

municate them to others. These have certainly heard a lot,
yet they possess no ability to express any of it. For many
years they have received truths, but not even a little can they
supply for the needs of others. Perhaps they may even brag
how full they are of the Holy Spirit! What creates such symptoms is an unrenewed mind.

Man's head damages people more than man's heart! Were
believers to learn how to distinguish the renewal of heart
from the renewal of head, they would not commit the mistake of believing in man. Christians ought to realize that
even one who maintains a most intimate fellowship with
God may nevertheless unknowingly have accepted Satan's
suggestions in his mind, which consequently precipitate
errors in his conduct, words and viewpoints! Aside from the
plain teaching of the Bible no man's words are entirely trust-
worthy. We must not live by a man's words just because we
admire or respect that man. His utterance and conduct may
be most holy but his thought may not be spiritual. What we
therefore observe is not his speech and behavior but his
mind. Were we to believe, because of one's life conduct, that
what a worker says is God's truth, we would then be making
man's word and demeanor our standard of truth instead
of the Bible. History is strewn with innumerable cases of
sanctified saints who propagated heresies! The simple explanation is that their hearts were renewed but their minds
remained old. We will undeniably acknowledge that life is
more important than knowledge. Indeed, the former is a
thousand times more consequential than the latter. Nonetheless, after some growth in life it is essential to seek the
knowledge which proceeds from a renewed mind. We should
see how urgent it is for both heart and head to be renewed.

If a Christian's mind is not renewed his life is bound to be
lopsided and narrow. Work becomes nigh to impossible for
him. The popular teaching nowadays stresses that there
should be love, patience, humility and so forth in the Christian life. These traits of the heart are highly significant, since
nothing else can replace them. Even so, can we regard these
as meeting *all* our needs? They are important but not inclu-

sive. It is equally vital for a person's mind to be renewed, enlarged and strengthened. Otherwise we shall witness an unbalanced life. Many hold that spiritual Christians should not be common sensical, as though the more foolish they are the better. Now except for the fact that such spiritual believers live a little better than the rest, they have no other usefulness and cannot be entrusted with any work. To be sure, we do not advocate worldly wisdom and knowledge, because God's redemption does not call for employing our former sin-stained mind. But He does desire it to be renewed as is our spirit. God wishes to restore our thought life to the excellent state it had when He created it so that we may not only glorify God in our walk but may glorify Him in our thinking as well. Who can estimate the multipled number of God's children who, due to neglecting their mind, grow narrow, stubborn and obstinate, and even sometimes defiled. They fall short of the glory of God. The Lord's people need to know that if they want to live a full life their mind must be renewed. One of the reasons why the kingdom of God lacks workers today is because too many cannot undertake anything with their head. They neglect to seek its renewal after they are saved and hence permit their work to be obstructed. The Bible declares emphatically that we must "be transformed by the renewal of our mind" (Rom. 12.2).

A MIND UNDER THE ATTACK OF THE EVIL SPIRITS

If we carefully examine the mental experiences of a Christian we shall see that not merely is he narrow-minded but that he contains many other defects too. His head, for instance, may be teeming with all kinds of uncontrollable thoughts, imaginations, impure pictures, wanderings and confused ideas. His memory may suddenly fail; his power of concentration may be weakened; he may be obsessed by prejudices which arise from unknown sources; his thoughts may be retarded as if his mind were being chained; or he may be flushed with wild thoughts which revolve unceasingly in his head. The Christian may find he is powerless to regulate his mental life and make it obey the intent of his

will. He forgets innumerable matters both large and small.
He carries out many improper actions, without knowing why
and without so much as investigating the reason. Physically
he is quite healthy, but mentally he does not comprehend the
explanation for these symptoms. Currently many saints encounter these mental difficulties, but without ever knowing
why.

Should a person discover that he manifests the above-
mentioned signs, he needs to check out a few matters to
determine the origin of those signs. He need only ask himself a few questions: Who controls my mind? Myself? And if
so, why can I not control it now? Is it God who manages my
mind? But according to scriptural principle God never governs the mind for man. (We shall enlarge on this principle
subsequently). If it is neither I nor God who regulates the
mental life, who then is in control? It obviously is the powers
of darkness who foment these mental symptoms. So whenever
a child of God notes that he is no longer able to govern the
mind, he ought to perceive at once that it is the enemy who
is managing it.

One fact which we must always bear in mind is: man possesses free will. God's intention is for man to control himself.
Man has the authority to regulate his every natural endowment; hence his mental processes should be subject to the
power of his will. A Christian ought to inquire of himself:
Are these *my* thoughts? Is it *I* who am thinking? If it is not I
thinking, it must then be the evil spirit who is able to work
in man's mind. Since I will not to think (and my mind
usually follows my will) then the thoughts which presently
arise in my head cannot be mine but rather are those which
emanate from another "person" who uses the ability of my
mind against my own will. The person should know that in
case he has not intended to think and yet there are thoughts
arising in his head, he must conclude that these are not of
him but of the evil spirit.

To determine whether an idea is of himself or of the
wicked spirit, a Christian should observe how it arose. If in
the beginning his mental faculty is peaceful and composed

and is functioning normally and naturally according to the circumstances he is in, but suddenly a thought or a complete idea (having no bearing on his present circumstances or the work in which he is engaged) flashes across his brain, such inordinate and lightning quick thought is most likely the action of evil spirits. They are attempting to inject their thoughts into the believer's head and thus induce him to accept them as his own. It is unmistakable that the notion which the evil spirits introduce into man's mind is a matter he has not thought about at the moment and which does not follow the trend of his thinking. It is entirely "new"—something he never thought of himself. It has arisen abruptly and all by itself. When one gains this kind of thought it is well for him to inquire: Do I really think in *this* manner? Is it really *I* who am thinking? Do I want to think that way? Or is this something which simply becomes activated in my mind all by itself? The child of God should determine whether or not it is he himself who does the thinking. If he has not originated the idea but on the contrary opposses it, and yet it abides in his head, he then can assume that that idea issues from the enemy. Each thought which man chooses not to think and each one which opposes man's will come not from the man but from the outside.

Oftentimes also one's brain is abounding with sundry ideas which he is helpless to stop. His head is like a thought machine, operated by external force; it continues to think but is impotent to desist. The believer may shake his head repeatedly, yet he cannot shake off the thoughts in his mind. They come to him in waves, rolling unceasingly day and night. There is no way to terminate them. He is not aware that this is but the activity of the evil spirit. He ought to understand what a "thought" is. It is something which his *mind grasps at*. But in the case of these unmanageable thoughts it is not that his mind is grasping at something but rather that *something is grasping his mind*. In the natural course of events it is the mind which thinks about matters; now it is these matters which force the mind to think. Frequently a person wishes to set aside a matter but some external power keeps reminding him of it, not permitting him to forget and forcing him to think on further. This is the perpetration of evil spirits.

To summarize, then, we should investigate every *abnormal* sign. Aside from a natural cause such as sickness, all other abnormal indicators have their source with evil spirits. God never interferes with the operation of man's natural ability; He never abruptly mixes in His thought with man's nor does He abruptly restrict or destroy the functioning of man's intellect. The lightning cessation of all thoughts as though the brain has become a vacuum, the flashing interjection of thought at complete variance with the trend then current in the mind, the hasty severance of memory as if a wire had snapped leaving the mind paralyzed: all these are the results of the operation of the enemy. Because the evil spirit has seized hold of the organ of thought, he is able either to force it to cease functioning or by looosening his grip to let it work again. We must recognize that natural causes can produce only natural symptoms. Flash thoughts or loss of memory are entirely beyond the ability or control of our will and are contrary to natural cause and effect: they must therefore be inspired by supernatural evil forces.

In his letter to the Ephesians Paul is found writing about "the spirit that is now at work in the sons of disobedience" (2.2). It is very important to know that the powers of darkness work not only outside but inside the man as well. When men work they can at most do so with their words, gestures or bodily movements; the evil spirits, however, can work with all these but even more. They can act from the outside in the same way as man acts, but they can work additionally from the inside. This means that they can squeeze themselves into man's thought life and work therein. Man is not capable of doing this: he is unable to enter another man's brain, subtly making many suggestions and confusing this matter of the source of the thoughts; but the evil spirits can. They possess an ability in communication which man does not have. They work initially in man's mind and then reach to his emotion, for mind and emotion are closely knit: they operate first in the mind and from there they arrive at man's volition, because mind and will are intimately joined too.

The manner by which these enemy spirits operate is to plant covertly in man's head notions which they enjoy so as to accomplish their aim, or, conversely, they block thoughts which they do not relish so that man cannot think them through. The Bible distinctly indicates that the powers of darkness are able both to impart ideas to man and to steal them from him. "The devil had already *put* it into the heart of Judas Iscariot, Simon's son, to betray him" (John 13.2). This shows that Satan can put his thought into man's mind. "Then the devil comes and takes away the word from their hearts" (Luke 8.12). This attests that Satan removes whatever word man ought to remember and causes him to forget everything. These two verses reveal the two-fold operation of the evil spirits upon the mind of man, either to add something to, or subtract something from, his mind.

THE CAUSES OF THE ATTACK OF THE EVIL SPIRITS

Why is the Christian's mental life so beset by evil spirits? This can be answered in one sentence: believers afford the evil spirits (or the devil) the opportunity to attack. Let everyone clearly understand that it is possible for one's mind to be assaulted by the devil. This is confirmed by the experience of many saints. And the area primarily assailed by him is the thinking faculty, for it has a special affinity towards evil spirits. It either partially or totally has slipped out from under man's sovereignty and has come under their dictate. Accordingly, these powers can switch one's thoughts on or off according to *their* wishes, completely disregarding the victim's ideas. Although the head is still attached to the believer, his sovereignty over it has been supplanted by another. Regardless how extensively he may protest, little can be corrected. Wherever anyone offers opportunity to wicked spirits, he cannot follow his own will any more but must be obedient to another's. When he gives ground to them in his mind he immediately forfeits his sovereignty over it. This also bespeaks the fact that his mental faculty is now being occupied by evil spirits. Had it not been attacked by them his will would continue to control everything: he could think or stop thinking as he willed without difficulty.

Due to this affinity between the mind and evil spirits, the Christian very often gives way to them. The ground gained furnishes these powers with authority to operate unhampered in the believer's head. Let us be aware of this though: that man's mind belongs to *man;* without his permission the enemy would be powerless to use it. Unless man *voluntarily* delivers (knowingly or unknowingly) his mind to the evil spirits they have no right to encroach on man's freedom. This does not imply that these malevolent forces shall never tempt us in our thought (that is unavoidable in this life), but it does signify that upon exercising our will to oppose the tempting thought, it shall be stopped immediately. The defect in many Christians today is that though they often resist with their will, the thought continues. It ought not be this way. It is a sure indication that the evil spirits are at work.

The most crucial factor in relation to their wicked activity is to have *ground* given to them. Without proper footing they cannot operate. The amount of their activity depends on the amount of space yielded to them. It is in the organ of his thought that the Christian supplies territory to evil spirits and hence there that they operate. Generally speaking, the ground in the mind which may be ceded to the enemy is of six kinds. We shall look at each of these now at some length.

(1) An unrenewed mind. The flesh continually furnishes bases for the enemy's operations. If man's mind is not renewed after his spirit is once regenerated, he exposes a great deal of territory to the machinations of the evil spirit. While many saints do have their mentality changed at the time of repentance, nonetheless the eyes of their heart once blinded by Satan have not yet been enlightened entirely and may still be veiled in many areas. These darkened corners are the old operation centers of the evil spirits: though greatly hindered, they have not been eliminated and thus continue to furnish bases for the operations of the unseen hosts of wickedness.

The devil's armies are most careful to cover up their deeds. If a Christian should remain fleshly they will urge upon him notions which seem to agree with his temperament and measure, prompting him to believe these are naturally the result of his thinking. Aware that this unrenewed mind constitutes their best workshop, the enemy forces employ every artifice to keep the believer in ignorance or to thwart him from seeking the renewal of his mind. The yielding of such ground is quite common among Christians. Were this the only type of ground they relinquish they would not suffer too severely in their intellect and memory; but other kinds are involved.

(2) An improper mind. All sins furnish territory to the adversary. If a child of God cherishes sin in his heart he is lending his mind to satanic spirits for their use. Since all sins derive from the dark powers, he is helpless to resist these powers behind whatever sins he allows to persist in his mind. As long as sinful thoughts remain in the heart, precisely that long do the evil spirits work. All unclean, proud, unkind and unrighteous ideas supply bases of activity to these spirits. Once God's child permits such a notion to stay he finds it harder to resist the next time it emerges, because the powers of darkness already have secured an area in his mind.

Besides the sinful ones there are many other improper thoughts which afford the enemy operational bases. Frequently Satan's hosts will introduce an idea into the believer's head. Should he accept it, then this notion will have acquired a footing in his mind. Each unproven theory, vain idea, unknown thought, word casually picked up by ear, or line inadvertently read—all provide ground to the foe as a future site for operations. The adversary may so fill a person with prejudices as to deceive him into opposing God's truth and embracing many heresies.

(3) Misunderstanding God's truth. The Lord's people rarely are aware that every time they accept a lie from the evil spirits they are furnishing fresh ground to the enemy. Should God's followers misconstrue or misinterpret as being natural or caused by their own selves that which the evil spirits have perpetrated upon their bodies, environments or works, they are yielding up precious territory to them for extending their nefarious deeds. A lie embraced forms the

ground for further activity by the satanic elements. In misunderstanding these phenomena to be the results of their own selves, they unconsciously allow these things to remain in their lives. Although this permission is gained through deceit it nevertheless provides sufficient footing for the evil spirits to operate.

On the other hand many Christians misunderstand God's truths. Being ignorant of the true meaning of co-death with Christ, consecration, the movement of the Holy Spirit, and so forth, they conceive in their hearts certain interpretations of these truths and consequently prejudice themselves. Seizing the opportunity, the evil spirits impart to the saints the same thing which they misunderstand and misconstrue of God's truths. They scheme according to the believer's misunderstanding. The latter judges these things to be of God, unaware that they are but a counterfeit from the evil spirits and founded on his misunderstanding.

(4) Accepting suggestions. Multiplied are the suggestions which Satan's hosts plant in the mind of the Christian, especially ideas concerning his circumstances and future. They enjoy prophesying to him, foretelling what will become of him and what will happen to him. Should he be unconscious of the source of such predictions and permit these to dwell in his mind, the evil spirits, at the appropriate time, will work on his environment to precipitate affairs to happen as prophesied. Perhaps the believer may already expect it to be so, not cognizant that everything has been arranged by the enemy powers. The latter merely put their idea into the form of prophecy, then plant it in his head to see if he will accept it or reject it. Should the will of the believer raise no objection, nay, even approve of the prophecy, the spirits of wickedness have obtained a footing for enacting what they have proposed. The fulfillment of the words of fortune tellers is based entirely on this principle.

Occasionally the adversary interjects prophetic utterances concerning the Christian's body, such as foretelling his weakness or sickness. If he absorbs this thought he will be genuinely sick and weak. He thinks he is actually ill. Those with scientific knowledge conclude it to be a psychological illness, but those with spiritual insight know better that it is solely because the person has received the suggestion of the evil spirit and has hence furnished ground for the latter to fabricate the situation. How many of the so-called natural and psychological illnesses are in reality the machinations of the evil spirits. When a Christian does not repel the thoughts which originate with evil spirits he affords them a base for working.

(5) A blank mind. God creates man with a mind to be used—"he who hears the word and understands it" (Matt. 13.23). God desires man to understand His Word with the intellect, from whence the emotion, will and spirit are reached. A lively head is therefore an obstacle to the work of malevolent spirits. One of their greatest aims is to lead a person's mind into a blank state. Blankness means an emptiness inside, the establishment of a true vacuum. The enemy powers employ either deception or force to transform the Christian's mental faculty into a blank entity. They realize that while his head is empty he cannot think. He has been stripped of all reasoning and sense and will accept without question every one of their teachings, regardless of its nature or consequence.

The Christian ought to exercise his mind, for its exercise constitutes such a disadvantage to evil spirits that they are compelled to exert their entire strength to render it blank. Only as his mind is functioning normally is the Christian fit to *discern* senseless supernatural revelations and various implanted suggestions and recognize their alien sources. A vacuous mind provides a foothold for the evil foe. All revelations and notions received by an empty head emanate from enemy sources. If a Christian should at any time not engage his organ of thought, he will discover how eager they are to help him think!

(6) A passive mind. Broadly speaking, an empty mind differs not too much from a passive one. Strictly speaking, the empty head means not using it whereas a passive one means awaiting some external force to activate it. The latter

is a step beyond the former. Passivity is to refrain from moving by oneself and instead to let outside elements move one. A passive brain does not think by itself but allows a foreign power to do the thinking for it. Passivity reduces man to a machine.

A passive state is most advantageous to the evil spirits for it offers them an opportunity to occupy the believer's will and body too. Just as a darkened mind is easily deceived because it knows not what it is doing and where it is going, even so is a passive mind prone to attack since it has no sensitivity whatsoever. Should anyone allow his head to cease thinking, searching, and deciding and to no longer check his experience and action against the Bible, he is practically inviting Satan to invade his mind and deceive him.

In their desire to follow the leading of the Holy Spirit many of the Lord's people feel they do not need to measure, investigate, and judge by the light of the Bible all thoughts which seemingly come from God. They think being led by the Spirit is being dead to themselves and obeying every notion and impulse of their brain. They follow especially those ideas which arise after prayer; hence they arrange for their mind to be passive during and after prayer. They halt their own thoughts and their other mental activities so as to be ready to receive the "thoughts of God." And the result is that they become hard and obstinate, having no reason and carrying out many harsh, pertinacious and irrational things. They do not know: (1) that prayer will not transform our thoughts into godly ones; (2) that to wait for divine thoughts during and after prayer is to invite counterfeits from the evil spirits; and (3) that God's leading is in the intuition of the spirit and not in the mind of the soul. Not a few saints— ignorant of God's will that He does not wish man to be passive but rather to cooperate actively with Him—spend time training themselves to be of a passive mind. They induce themselves to not think in order to possess God's thoughts. How can they not understand that if they themselves are not using their brain neither will God use it nor put His thoughts into it. The principle of God is for men to control the whole

person with their will and to work together with Him. Only
the devil would exploit the opportunity of a passive mind
and seize its control away from men. God has never wanted
men to receive His revelation like a robot; it is the enemy
spirits alone who wish it that way. All passivity profits them,
for they gladly take advantage of the folly and passivity of
God's people to operate in their mind.

PASSIVITY

Any ground ever given to evil spirits invites them to work.
Of these grounds the most serious is passivity. Passivity reflects the attitude of the will which in turn represents the
total being. Passivity provides the liberty for wicked elements to function, though they habitually do so under cover,
trying to deceive the saints. The cause of passivity is the
ignorance of the Christian. He misconceives the role of the
intellect in spiritual life; He thinks too highly of it but at the
same time too lowly of it. Hence he permits his reasoning
powers to settle into inertia and welcomes any thought which
issues from that inert state. How very necessary, therefore,
to clearly apprehend the way God leads.

The passivity of the mind is due to a misconception of the
meaning of consecration and obedience to the Holy Spirit.
Many take for granted that the thoughts in their head hinder
their spiritual walk. They do not perceive that it is a brain
which ceases to function or which functions chaotically that
hinders spiritual life, whereas one which functions properly
is not only profitable but also essential. Such a mind as this
can alone cooperate with God. As has been emphasized previously, the normal path of guidance is in the spirit's intuition and not in the mind. An appreciation of this principle
is exceedingly necessary and should never be forgotten. The
believer must follow the revelation in his intuition, not the
thought in his head. He who heeds the mind is walking after
the flesh and is accordingly led astray. Nevertheless, we have
not said that the mind is utterly useless, that it does not even
exercise a secondary role. True, we make a grave mistake if
we elevate the mind as *the* organ for direct fellowship with

God and for receiving revelation from Him; yet it *does* have
a role assigned to it. That role is to *assist* intuition. Yes, it is
by intuition that we come to know God's will, but we additionally need the mind to inspect our inner sense to determine whether it is from our intuition or is a counterfeit of our
emotions, whether or not it is of God and harmonizes with
the Word. We know by intuition; we prove by the mind.
How easy it is for us to err! Without the assistance of the
mind we shall find it hard to decide what is authentically
of God.

In the normal process of guidance the mind is needed as
well. While the guidance of intuition is frequently quite opposite to reasoning, we still must use the head, though not
to argue with intuition but to examine whether this thing is
really from God. Intuition apprehends the will of God very
quickly; however, we require time for the brain to probe and
prove whether what we apprehend is truly from our intuition
and the Holy Spirit. If it is from God our intuition shall emit
an even more accurate sense while under probing, thus ef-
fecting in us a stronger faith than before that this thing is
in truth from God. The exercise of the intellect in this way—
only in the way of *examinaton*—is both beneficial and proper. But should this sensing be of our fleshly thought and
feeling, then in the process of examination our conscience
will raise its voice of opposition. Consequently, the probing
with our mind to *understand* whether a matter is from God
or not will not interefere but will instead give opportunity
to intuition to prove itself. If it is of intuition what has it to
fear from the probing of the mind? On the other hand, whatever is afraid of being probed is probably out from one's self.
The head should never guide or lead, but it unquestionably
is needed to probe the authenticity of guidance.

Such teaching is in accordance with the Scriptures: "do not
be foolish, but understand what the will of the Lord is" and
"try to learn what is pleasing to the Lord" (Eph. 5.17,10).
The functioning of the mind cannot be set aside unused. God
does not wipe out the various components of man's soul; He
renews them first and then uses them. God wants His child
to know what he is doing when he obeys. He does not desire

a senseless, blind following. It is never His wish that one should follow whatever he hears or feels with a bewildered mind, unaware of what he is about; nor is it ever His way to use any one part of the believer's body without his understanding and consent. God's intention is for the Christian to understand His will and consciously engage the various parts of his body for obedience to God. It is the lazy person who refuses to bear responsibility because he expects to be moved partly or wholly by God only from a passive state. God, however, wants man to examine actively what His will is and next to exercise his own will to obey God. God requires the harmonious working of man's intuition and consciousness.

Even so, a believer, not recognizing this to be God's normal way of guidance, *may* let himself slide into passivity. He may expect God to put His will into his thought; he blindly follows all supernatural leading without employing his intelligence to examine whether it is from God. He even waits for Him to use the parts of his body beyond the sphere of his consciousness; that is to say, he does not engage his mind to understand, or his will to execute in his body, what the will of God is. The consequence of such ignorance is enemy invasion, since passivity is a condition for this phenomenon. (This we shall treat in detail in another place.) If man does not use his intelligence neither will God, because to do so would be contrary to the principle of God's operation. Evil spirits will do so however; they never hesitate to seize the opportunity to use man's mind. It is therefore most foolish for one to allow his mind to sink into a state of passivity because the enemy spirits are on the prowl seeking whomever they may devour.

Let us pursue one step further this matter of passivity as a condition for the operation of evil spirits. We are aware of one class of people who especially relish communicating with these spirits. People usually do not hanker to be demon possessed, but this special class craves to be so possessed. These are the soothsayers, the augurs, the mediums, the necromancers. By accurately observing the cause of their possession we may come to understand the principle of demon possession. These people tell us that in order to be possessed by what they call gods (who actually are demons) their will must present no resistance whatsoever but be favorably disposed to accept whatever comes upon their bodies. To render their will completely passive their mind must first be reduced to blankness. A blank brain produces a passive will. These two elements are the basic requisites for demon possession. Hence a necromancer who is waiting for his "god" to come upon him lets down his hair and shakes his head for a continued period until it is dizzy and his mind completely out of action. As the latter is turning blank his will naturally becomes immobile. At this point his mouth begins to move unconsciously, his body gradually trembles, and before long his "god" descends upon him. This is one way of becoming possessed. Although there may be others, the principle for every spiritist is the same: to achieve passivity of will through a perfectly blank mind; for all spiritists agree that when spirits or demons alight upon them their heads can no longer think and their wills can no longer act. They are unpossessed until this state of an empty mind and an inert will is reached.

Today's so-called scientific hypnotism and religious yogi, which enable people to possess the powers of telepathy, healing, and transforming, are in reality founded upon these two principles. Using the argument that certain methods can be beneficial to mankind, those of this class who perform such techniques as focusing one's attention, sitting silently, contemplating and meditating, are actually employing these devices to reduce their mind to a blank condition and their will to passivity so as to invite supernatural spirits or demons to supply them with many wonderful experiences. Our purpose here is not to inquire whether or not these people realize they are inviting evil spirits to come; we merely wish to observe that they are fulfilling the requirements for demon possession. The consequence is grave; perhaps later they shall awaken to the fact that what they have welcomed are indeed evil spirits.

Our intention here is not a full treatment of this subject. We simply wish to acquaint the Lord's children with the principles behind the practice of the black arts: which are a *blank and passive mind and will*. Evil spirits are overjoyed should these conditions be present, as they can immediately commence to do their dark work.

It is well for every Christian to always bear in mind the one basic and crucially important distinction between the working of evil spirits and that of the Holy Spirit: the Latter works when man fulfills *His* working conditions, while the former work when man fulfills *their* working conditions. If man, even though he may appear to be seeking the Holy Spirit, meets the requirements for evil spirits to operate, God's Spirit will never operate. The wicked spirits wait tirelessly for the opportunity to act. Should anyone be incompetent to distinguish what is truly of God from what is a counterfeit, he need only ask himself one question: what kind of condition was he in when first he experienced such phenomena? If he had fulfilled the prerequisites for the Holy Spirit's activity, it must then have been from God; but had he met the necessary conditions for evil spirits to work, then what he encountered must have been the evil spirit. We do not reject every supernatural phenomenon; what we simply and earnestly desire to do is to separate what is of God from what is of Satan.

The basic distinction between the operating requirements of the Holy Spirit and the wicked spirits can be summarized as follows:

(1) All supernatural revelations, visions or other strange occurrences which require the *total cessation of the function of the mind*, or are obtained only after it has ceased working, are not of God.

(2) All visions which arise from the Holy Spirit are conferred when the believer's mind is fully active. It necessitates the active engagement of the various functions of the mind to apprehend these visions. The endeavors of evil spirits follow exactly the opposite course.

(3) All which flows from God agrees with God's nature and the Bible.

Let us disregard the outward form—it may openly identify itself as devilish or it may disguise itself as divine (such indeed are the terms given)—and simply inquire what the

principle involved is. We need to recognize that every supernatural revelation from the powers of darkness demands the
cessation of the function of the mind; but that whatever
comes from God permits its ability and function to continue
as usual without any interference. Both the vision the Israelites beheld at Mt. Sinai recorded in the Old Testament
and the vision which Peter saw at Joppa mentioned in the
New Testament affirm that these people had complete use
of their heads.

By examining every instance in the New Testament where
God's supernatural revelation is recounted, we find that
everyone there who experiences a revelation does so with his
mind functioning and with the ability *to control himself* and
use any part of his body. But counterfeit supernatural revelations chiefly require the receiver's mind to be totally or partially *passive*, with the receiver no longer able to employ
parts of his body either in part or *in toto*. This constitutes
the fundamental antithesis between what is of God and what
is of the devil. Where the speaking in tongues is related,
for example, the speakers have both control and consciousness of themselves. On the day of Pentecost Peter could *hear*
the mocking of the peoples and *answer* them, proving that
he and his colleagues were not drunk but were filled with
the Holy Spirit (Acts 2). Those who spoke with tongues in
the church at Corinth could count the number of two or
three, could *control* themselves to speak in turn, and if no
interpretation was given could *keep silence* (1 Cor. 14). All
retained their consciousness and could restrain themselves.
This is because "the spirits of prophets are subject to prophets" (1 Cor. 14. 32). But in counterfeit experience the spirits
usually demand the subjection of the prophets to them.
Herein can we see which is of God and which is of the devil.

We have written at length on how to differentiate between
special phenomena given by the Holy Spirit and those given
by evil spirits. We shall conclude by briefly observing how
they differ in *ordinary* occurrences. Let me only illustrate
by using the example of the guidance of God. Now it should
be called to mind that the Holy Spirit wants us to be *en-*

lightened and to *know* (Eph. 1.17-18). God's Spirit never treats men as puppets, summoning them to follow Him without any consciousness. He does not even ask them to do good in that way. He usually expresses His thought in the depth of man, in his spirit. Hence His guidance is never confused, vague, puzzling, or compulsory. But not so with the evil spirits. Simply note how they operate: (1) Their thought always invades from the outside, entering primarily via the mind. It does not come from the innermost being, is not a revelation in the intuition, but is a flashing mental thought. (2) Their thought forces, pushes and coerces man to take action immediately. It never affords man time to think, consider or examine. (3) It confuses and paralyzes man's mind so that it can no longer think.

Consequently, we can see that in all the occurrences of a believer's life, whether special or ordinary, everything which proceeds from evil spirits strips the proper functioning from his mind. The Holy Spirit, however, never does.

CHAPTER 2
THE PHENOMENA OF A PASSIVE MIND

IT IS TO BE SORELY LAMENTED that so many Christians, unaware of the basic difference between the activity of evil spirits and that of the Holy Spirit, have unconsciously permitted the enemy to enter and occupy their minds. Let us touch briefly on the phenomena of a mind under the attack of evil spirits.

FLASHING THOUGHTS

After one's mind has sunk into passivity he will receive many thoughts injected from without, notions which are unclean, blasphemous or confused. These pass through his mind in succession. Although he decides to reject them, he is powerless to stop them or alter the trend of his thinking. His mind is like a perpetual motion machine: once begun, it cannot be halted. Regardless if he opposes with his will, he cannot thrust those thoughts from his head. Notions which are counter to the believer's will are given by evil spirits.

Sometimes these ideas flash into the person's brain like lightning. They enable him to understand or to discover special matters. They may arrive in the form of a suggestion, urging him to do this or that. Often they appear to have arisen from the person himself, but upon close examination he *knows* he has not initiated them; they are but the deeds of evil spirits in a passive mind. The child of God ought to resist flashing thoughts which demand action of him because these do not originate with the Holy Spirit. And should he follow them he will realize how worthless they are.

We know that in these latter times evil spirits especially engage in much teaching (1 Tim. 4.1). The Lord's people should guard against such teachings imparted to passive minds. Not a few think they have obtained new light when they search the Scriptures and that they understand matters which their predecessors did not. These individuals should be very cautious, for it is frequently in the time of meditation that wicked powers flash their ideas into a person or stealthily mix some of *their* thought with his. Not aware of the possibility of accepting the teaching of evil spirits in their minds, Christians assume that anything which has suddenly burst upon them while in meditation is their *own* new discovery of faith. They write and preach these ideas as the fruits of *their* research. Upon hearing or reading these teachings, people marvel at the cleverness of these Christians. But do they perceive that many of these doctrines in reality emanate from the bottomless pit? Diverse heresies, numerous so-called "spiritual teachings," sundry interpretations of the Word which tear the church of Christ into pieces originate with these lightning thoughts during Scripture study. We should not be impressed with how excellent such sudden enlightenment may be; rather should we ask *whence* this light came. Was it revealed by the Holy Spirit in our intuition? Did it arise out of our own thinking? Or were these ideas fomented by evil spirits?

Should one's mind be passive, it will be easy for the enemy to inject nonsensical notions into him, for instance telling him: "You are God's special vessel" or "Your work will shake the whole world" or "You are much more spiritual than the rest" or "You should take another course" or "God will soon open a wide door for your preaching" or "You should step out to live by faith" or "Your spiritual usefulness is unlimited." Heady thoughts like these disarm all the vigilance of the saint. He thrives day and night on these ideas—dreaming how great and marvelous he is. Not employing the rationalism of his mind, he fails to realize how harmful and how laughable these notions can be in his spiritual walk. He indulges in them by continuously imagining how glorious his future is going to be.

Some who deliver messages for the Lord are often governed by these bursting thoughts. They preach what has been revealed to them suddenly. They construe their sudden thoughts to be from God and so accept them passively. They do not understand that God neither gives sudden revelation nor imparts it to the mind. Despite the fact such words are sometimes seemingly full of meaning, they nevertheless come from the powers of darkness. Furthermore, occasionally as a believer is preaching, many Scripture verses abruptly swarm into his brain and his thinking; the audience appears to be touched; yet following the meeting no practical help in life is experienced by those who have heard. It is like a dream. This too can be the action of the powers of darkness.

Having yielded territory in his mind to evil spirits, the child of God will realize that they are able to provoke any thought in him. Among fellow-workers, evil spirits often sow a groundless doubt or divisive thought in the mind of one worker so as to separate him from the others. Upon their wicked instigation the worker concludes without foundation that so-and-so thinks such-and-such of him, and so comes the separation. Actually there is no basis for such a thought. If the child of God only knew how to examine the source of such imaginings and how to resist them, there would be no separation. How sad that he regards it as his own thought, not recognizing that the evil spirits have planted it in him.

PICTURES

The adversary also can project pictures onto the screen of a believer's mind. Some are clear and good and are welcomed by him; others are impure and sinful, much detested by his conscience. Whether good or bad, liked or disliked, the sad fact is that he has no strength to prohibit these pictures from entering his head. Against the opposition of his will, there lingers before his eyes past experiences, predictions of future events, and many other matters. This is because his power of imagination has slumped into passivity. He cannot control his imaginative powers but has allowed the evil spirits to manipulate them. The child of God should be aware that whatever does not emerge from his *own* mind proceeds from supernatural enemy forces.

DREAMS

Dreams can be natural or supernatural. Some are inspired by God while others are generated by the devil. Beyond those which are produced by man's physiological and psychological conditions, the rest are supernatural in origin. If one's mind has been open to evil spirits his night dreams become for the most part just another form of the "pictures" he encounters during the day. The wicked unseen powers create pictures in the day and dreams in the night. To determine whether or not his dreams derive from the devil the believer simply should inquire of himself: is my mind *usually* passive? If so, these dreams are untrustworthy. Moreover, dreams and visions which God inspires enable man to be normal, peaceful, steady, full of reasoning and consciousness; but what the evil spirits precipitate are bizarre, rash, fantastic, foolish, and render a person arrogant, dazed, confused, and irrational.

The reason why satanic powers can impart innumerable strange dreams to the Christian is because his mental life is passive. To that one whose mental faculty is already passive none of his dreams proceed from God or from natural causes but are from wicked spirits. At nighttime the brain is not as active as in the day, hence more passive and more liable to being manipulated by the devil. Such night dreams cause him to wake up the next morning with a heavy head and a despondent spirit. His sleep does not replenish his strength because through his passive mind the evil spirits have affected adversely the well-being of the whole man. Anyone who suffers from such night dreams is subject to the nefarious activity of the evil spirits in his mind. If he resists their deeds day and night he shall regain his freedom.

INSOMNIA

Insomnia is one of the common ills of the saints; it is likewise a particularly distinctive work of the enemy in the mind of man. Many find that as they lie in their beds endless thoughts pour into their head. They continue to think about their day's work or to recall past experiences or just to fill their minds with a hodgepodge of unrelated matters. They appear to be considering a thousand different ideas such as what they should do, how they should do it, and what should be the best plan. They think ahead to the affairs on the morrow: how to plan, what might happen, or how to handle a variety of situations. Considerations like these inundate them in waves. Though these people know that bed is the place for sleep and not one for thinking as is a desk, nonetheless their brain revolves incessantly. They appreciate the importance of sleep for the next day's task; they really want to sleep and not think; and yet, due to cause unknown, they cannot. Their mind works relentlessly on and sleep escapes them. Some saints may have suffered the anguish of countless nights of insomnia: as usual when night has fallen they have laid down all concerns and have prepared to rest their minds; nonetheless, no matter how weary they may have been their mind has not been able to rest. For like a machine which cannot be turned off, it continues to operate. Their will has no control over their brain. They are helpless to stop their thinking and can only wait till somehow their mind ceases to work so that they can secure some sleep. In the natural course of events sleep revives one's spirit; but when one has experienced untold nights of insomnia such a believer will come to dread sleep, bed and the night. He has to rest, yet each morning he feels as though he is emerging from a terrible world: his head is heavy, his will is numbed, and he seems to have no energy.

In a situation like this, the child of God is inclined to believe it is due to his physical condition or to the stimulation or overexertion of his nerves. Frequently these reasons are merely suppositional. If they were real, then following rest or some other natural remedy he would experience restoration. But he does not because the evil spirits employ those natural reasons to obscure their unseen activities. Thus when a believer senses thoughts galloping through his head during the night, let him inquire of himself on this wise: where do these thoughts originate? Are they mine or are they foreign? Am I thinking? Do *I* think this way? Could it be from myself when I do not even want to think? Who gives me such multiplied, confused, unclean, oppressive thoughts? Who, indeed, except evil spirits!

FORGETFULNESS

Due to the devil's attack quite a few saints are deprived of their power of memory and suffer from forgetfulness. They forget even what they have just said or done. They cannot locate the article they have just put aside that same day. They forget the promises made not so long ago. They behave as though they are without brain, for nothing seems to remain in their mind. These saints may conclude that their memory is worse than anybody else's, without realizing that their mind is actually under the disturbance of evil spirits. Consequently they must rely on notes. They become slaves to notebooks and memoranda as a means of reminder. Now we are not suggesting that a person should be able to remember everything. We grant that matters can be forgotten after many years or forgotten immediately when they leave no deep impression. Even so, many events which have happened not too long ago and which have arrested one's attention *ought* to be recalled within a certain time limit and under certain appropriate circumstances. Why are they forgotten, lost without leaving any shadow, and beyond recall? The explanation cannot be natural; it must be due to the invasion of malevolent forces. Some matters are quite naturally forgotten, others do not so naturally vanish. All unnatural loss of memory suggests the subtle attack of Satan's hosts. Many Christians undergo this kind of assault. How many endeavors are destroyed by this. And how many jokes are inspired by this forgetfulness. Confidence and usefulness are damaged.

Another phenomenon can be noticed: a believer usually may possess a fine memory, but at various critical moments it unexpectedly fails. His mind seems to have faltered abruptly and he cannot remember anything, plunging him into great difficulties. Such sudden cessation of this function of the mind may appear to be mystifying to him but he may interpret it to be the result of a temporary deficiency in physical strength, something which can happen once in a while. What he does not comprehend is that this is a symptom of his mind undergoing an attack of evil spirits.

LACK OF CONCENTRATION

Satan's minions often interfere with the Christian's power of mental concentration. We acknowledge that different individuals possess varying degrees of this power. Yet from our observations of the experiences of Christians we note that this power in most of them has suffered a greater or lesser degree of loss through the dissipating work of evil spirits. Some appear to be totally powerless to concentrate when trying to think; others are better but their thoughts take flight everywhere after but a few moments of concentration on a particular matter. Especially during times of prayer, Bible reading, or listening to messages do Christians discover their thoughts wandering. Although they will to concentrate, they fail to do so. They may succeed for a short while in arresting their galloping thoughts by their will, but such an effect does not last long. Sometimes they lose all control. It is obviously the enemy who is at work. The reason for the devil's exertions lies in the fact that the believer has made provision in his mind for the evil spirits. What a pity to see a person wasting the power of his mind, accomplishing nothing from dawn to dusk. As the wasting of physical strength is harmful, so the wasting of mental power is damaging too. Today a large number of Christians expend a great deal of time without producing much result. Their minds are assailed by evil spirits and so they cannot concentrate.

Because of the onslaught of these dark forces God's people experience a peculiar kind of inattentiveness. The mind should be focusing on a particular matter, yet abruptly it turns blank and subsequently drifts elsewhere. They are unconscious of what they are doing or what they are reading. They may hold to the opinion that they must have been thinking about other affairs, but can such thoughts be originated by their *own* will? The Christians who all of a sudden cannot hear anything during meetings are numberless. Enemy spirits try to prevent them from hearing what would be profitable, yet not by stopping the operation of their minds but by forcing them to think of other things.

Once the mind has been attacked by the devil believers find it troublesome to listen to others. Oftentimes they miss several sentences or words. To listen attentively they must wrinkle their foreheads, trying to understand what others mean. They frequently fail to comprehend the simplest words; they often misapprehend the teachings given them. All this is due to the disturbances in their minds. With many prejudices have they been stuffed already by evil spirits, and everything has been interpreted already to them. For this reason many a Christian is averse to hearing what others have to say. Before people can finish he is interrupting impatiently, for the evil spirits already have inspired him with countless thoughts and desire him to listen to theirs and then spread them around to others. Such individuals actually are listening both within and without: listening within to the suggestions of the enemy and listening without to people speaking with them. The voice within their minds speaks louder than the one in their ears so that they can barely hear the outside voice. Such symptoms as inattentiveness or heedlessness signify in reality that their hearts are occupied by satanic elements. Believers occasionally experience a sudden state of heedlessness; the fact is, their hearts have been snatched away by the wicked ones. Until they are liberated from the activity of evil spirits they will be powerless to concentrate.

Because of these disturbances in their minds Christians often will shake their heads, trying to rid themselves of these unsettling thoughts. They have to speak aloud to themselves in order to leave an impression on their mind. They must likewise think aloud, else their darkened mind will not understand. They additionally need to read aloud to acquaint themselves with what they have read. All these are consequences of the lack of concentration.

INACTIVITY

Upon being fiercely attacked, the mind of the believer loses its ability to think. It falls almost entirely into the hands of evil spirits so that he himself can no longer use it. He cannot think even should he want to, for he is incapable of initiating any thought of his own. Actually myriads of thoughts over which he has no control pass through his mind; he has no power to halt these and initiate his own. The foreign ideas are too overpowering for him to entertain his own. Occasionally he may locate an opening in his mind through which to insert his thought, but he discovers it is very toilsome to continue thinking. So many voices and so many subjects are there already that these simply squeeze his out. If any person desires to think, he must possess memory, imagination and reasoning power; but the Christian has presently lost these powers, hence is unable to think. He cannot create, deduce or recollect, nor can he compare, judge and apprehend. Therefore he cannot think. And should he attempt to do so he experiences a kind of dazed sensation which stifles any productive thought.

Since his mental process is now under bondage, the believer naturally will develop an inordinately off-balanced viewpoint. A mound looms up before him as a mountain. Everything appears to be as arduous as ascending a stairway to heaven. He is especially fearful of anything which requires thought. He does not like to converse with people because this is too demanding of him. To proceed steadily and diligently at his daily job seems to require his life. He is gripped by an intangible chain which others fail to recognize. He feels as uncomfortable as a slave who wants to revolt but never succeeds.

Thus the Christian lives as in a dream. His time is dissipated, spent without thought, imagination, reasoning, or consciousness. As the mind is assailed the will becomes affected automatically, for the former is the light of the latter. He passively allows himself to be tossed to and fro by his environment and makes no choice for himself. When he is filled with unsettling notions and has no peace, he cannot break through his bondage to emancipation. He seems to be restrained by an unseen impediment. Numerous things he wants to do; yet in the midst of trying to do them he is overwhelmed by an impulsive feeling to stop because all tasks have become impossible in his eyes: to him his life has become nothing but a succession of insurmountable obstacles. How can he ever be satisfied?

Inactivity like this is sharply at variance with the ordinary type. Should one's mind be quiescent he can activate it whenever he wants. But should the inactivity of the brain be due to the oppression of evil spirits, then no matter how much he desires to be active he cannot stir it one iota. He simply cannot think! His head seems to be loaded down by some heavy weight. Such is the phenomenon of a mentality deeply affected by evil spirits.

Many a saint who is continuously worrying contracts this illness of mental inactivity. Yet were we to delve into his environment and position we would inescapably conclude that here is one who certainly ought to be satisfied and happy; but the fact is that he is full of worries and unhappy thoughts. Ask him to give the reason for this and to him nothing whatever can be a sufficient one. Suggest to him to get rid of such thoughts and he finds himself utterly unable. He himself does not understand his plight. He appears to have sunk into a quagmire from which he cannot extricate himself. Hs is so used to worrying that he has no strength to rise above it. This of course is the heavy hand of the enemy. If it were a matter of natural worry there would have to be a *cause of sufficient reason*. All worries without natural cause or sufficient justification are precipitated by evil spirits. The believer has slumped so low because at the beginning he accepted the notions of the wicked ones and now is powerless to free himself. His mind has settled thoroughly into passivity so that it can no longer be active. Such a person is aware of this bondage because he is loaded with burdens. He cannot glimpse the blue sky nor can he comprehend the true picture of anything. He cannot exercise his reasoning power. He is as a prisoner cast into the dungeon, eking out his days in darkness. Evil spirits enjoy seeing men suffer. Everyone who falls into their hands will be so treated by them.

VACILLATION

While the mind of a believer is dominated by enemy powers his thoughts are totally unreliable, since most of them come from the wicked spirits. Few of them are his own. These spirits may generate in him one kind of thought but very shortly afterwards beget an opposite kind. In following such shifting notions the Christian naturally turns into a vacillating person. Those who are with him or work with him consider him unstable in character because he is everlastingly changing positions. Fundamentally though, it is the wicked spirits who change his thoughts and alter his opinions. How frequently we find Christians who say at one moment "I can" but at the next "I can't." They declare in the morning "I want" and shift in the afternoon to "I don't want." The reason is that at first the evil spirits plant in the mind the thought of "I can" and induce him to believe he genuinely can; nonetheless, they next inject into him another and contrary thought of "I can't" and cause him to think he really is unable. So it is not he himself who has altered what he initially declared.

In these numerous shifting attitudes we can detect the adversary at work in the mind of man. Saints may abhor living such a vacillating life, but they have no way to stabilize themselves because they are not their own. If they refuse to follow the alien suggestions the wicked powers shall falsify the voice of conscience and accuse them of not following God. Now to avoid being accused, these saints have no choice but to shift their positions before men. These alternating and unsteady traits all proceed from the same source. In listening in their heads to the suggestions of the evil spirits Christians commence abruptly to undertake many tasks, but as the enemy powers change their proposals the Christians correspondingly shift their labor.

Beyond these occurrences, evil spirits additionally often provoke people to think at inappropriate occasions. They will awaken them at midnight, for example, instructing them to perform such-and-such a matter. If one refuses to obey they will begin to accuse him. Or else in the deep of night they may suggest to him a shift in course, so that an exceedingly important decision is made during a time when the mind is most susceptible to confusion. By tracing the origin of many of these sudden turns of events we will discover evil spirits at work in the mind of men.

TALKATIVENESS

Those of God's people whose minds are assaulted by Satan frequently shy away from conversing with people because they have not the strength to *listen;* for while they are trying to listen to others, thoughts over which they have no control drift through their brains like wind-blown clouds. They are usually most talkative, however. Since their heads are bursting with thoughts, how can their mouths not be abounding with words too? A mind which cannot listen to others but demands that others listen to it is a sick mind. While it is true that some Christians are talkative by nature, nevertheless, unknowingly they may in fact be instruments in the hands of evil spirits. Many Christians are like talking machines which are run by outside powers.

How many there are who cannot restrain their tongues from gossiping, jesting and backbiting. Their heart is clear but they are unable to end or restrict these unprofitable words. It seems that as soon as ideas have moved into their mind and before there has been any opportunity to think them through, they have already become words. Thoughts rush in in waves, compelling the person to speak. The tongue is out of control of the mind and the will. A torrent of words is uttered without *thinking* or choosing. Sometimes they are spoken against the intent and will of the speakers. Later reminded by others, they wonder why they thus spoke. These are all due to the passivity of the mind. Satanic elements can engage man's tongue through man's immobilized mind. They begin by mixing their thoughts with man's thought, and then they proceed to mix their words with man's words.

The Christian must unmistakably understand that all his utterances have to be the result of his own thinking. Any word which bypasses the process of thinking is formulated by the wicked spirits.

OBSTINACY

After a person's mental faculty has declined into passivity and is occupied by the powers of darkness, he categorically refuses to listen to any reason or evidence once he has made a decision. He views any attempt by anyone to make him understand better as an encroachment on his liberty. He deems them most foolish, for they can never know what *he* knows! His concepts may be totally wrong, yet he thinks he has *inexplicable* reasons. Since his mind is entirely immobile, he knows not how to examine, distinguish and judge with reason. He uncritically swallows anything which the evil spirits propagate in his mind, esteeming it to be most excellent. When such an individual hears a supernatural voice he automatically accepts it as God's will; to him the voice already has become his law; it therefore transcends the investigation of reason. Whatever be the thought or voice or teaching he deems it infallible and positively safe. He refuses to test, examine, or consider; he tenaciously holds on to it and is unwilling to heed anything else. No amount of reasoning and conscience of his own or the explanation and evidence of others can move him one bit. Once he believes it to be God's leading, his mind is sealed against any change. And since he does not employ his reasoning power he can be deceived readily by evil spirits. Those who have a little understanding see the danger but he devours it all as candy. To restore such a person as this is certainly not easy.

THE SYMPTOM OF THE EYES

A mind which is passive and assailed by evil spirits can be identified readily through the eyes. Man's eyes reveal his mind more than any other part of his body. If the mind is passive a person reading may look at a book and yet no idea will enter his brain nor make any impression in his memory, While he converses with people his eyes tend to wander around, up and down, flitting in all directions. It is surely a most impolite manner, but he cannot look straight into another's face. On another occasion he may act in the opposite extreme by gazing at another's face without so much as blinking, as though transfixed by some unknown power.

Such gazing can be most serious because the devil uses this means to induct the believer into the attitude of a necromancer. Frequently, upon gazing long at the speaker's countenance the believer begins to listen no longer to what he is saying but is instead intent upon listening to the many thoughts which the malevolent powers at that moment are begetting in him.

We need to observe whether the movement of our eyes follows the consciousness of our minds or acts independently of the intent of our heart. When a mind is passive the person's eyes become dazed. He is apt to behold many unsought and peculiar sights while unable to concentrate on seeing what he wishes to see.

FINALLY

To recapitulate. The phenomena of a Christian's mind under the attack of evil spirits are manifold and various. One principle, however, underlies them all: the person has lost his control. According to the ordering of God, each of man's natural abilities (among which is the thought process of the mind) should be subject completely to man's own rule. But should a Christian unknowingly give ground to evil spirits they may occupy his mental life and take direct action therein, unhampered by the victim's will. Consequently, if ever the Chrisitian discovers any independent action in his mind he should realize he is under the assault of the powers of darkness.

Inactivity in place of activity, disquietude instead of calm, restlessness due to overflowing thoughts, inability to concentrate or distinguish or remember, confusion beyond control, labors without fruit, worklessness during the day and dreams and visions in the night, insomnia, doubts, unwatchfulness, fear without reason, disturbance to the point of agony—one and all are nefariously inspired by the evil spirits.

CHAPTER 3

THE WAY OF DELIVERANCE

WHEN ONE'S MIND HAS fallen victim to the phenomena discussed in the previous chapter, he should seek the way of deliverance. What was described in that chapter were but general symptoms of a passive mind. We cannot set forth everyone's condition in detail because there are variations in the degree of passivity, the extent of the evil spirit's attack, and hence the measure of damage to the mind. Nevertheless it should be stated that as soon as one realizes he has encountered any of the aforementioned phenomena, he must exercise extreme caution because he may have given ground to evil spirits and so is being assaulted. He should look for deliverance.

Few are the believers who are not surprised at their ignorance of the damage done to their mind. It is on the contrary a matter of great surprise to them that they have been unconscious of the fallen condition of their organ of thought. They seem to understand a lot about many matters, but as regards their own mind they know next to nothing. They do not even realize how serious has been the damage inflicted until someone else has pointed it out to them. Why have these not discerned it before? Is it not that this very lack tells us that our mind and the evil spirits possess some special relationship which consequentially weakens our knowledge concerning our mind? Let any who have suffered such damage answer this question.

THE WILES OF THE EVIL SPIRITS

If his eyes have been opened to see his condition, the believer will naturally search for deliverance. Realize, though, that the evil spirits are not going to let their captives go free without a fight. They will apply every ounce of strength upon the person to prevent him from securing deliverance. The evil spirits will suggest many lies to serve as excuses:

> Those sudden beautiful thoughts of yours are from God.
> Those flashing revelations are the fruits of spirituality.
> That bad memory is due to your ill-health.
> It is natural for you to become abruptly forgetful.
> Your over-sensitiveness is because of your temperament.
> Your weak memory is inherited.
> Insomnia is an outgrowth of sickness.
> You are simply tired.
> You cannot think because you have worked too hard.
> That incessant contemplation at night stems from your mind's overexhaustion in the daytime.
> Impure thoughts arise from your sins.
> You already have fallen.
> You cannot listen to others because of your particular environment and because of their faults.

The evil spirits can manufacture sundry other excuses. Unless God's children realize they are *really being attacked* and have actually fallen from the normal state, the enemy will engage these and other excuses like them to cover up the ground they have gained. But the true reason lies in the fact that the mind is passive and vacuous, and thus occupied by these satanic spirits. Every one of these phenomena is the effect of their pernicious working. We grant the possibility of natural causes being mixed in with these excuses, but the experience of so many saints confirms that the powers of darkness are extremely subtle in operating alongside natural causes so as to deceive the saints into accepting these natural causes—such as temperament, physical condition and environment—as the only explanation, forgetting altogether the subtle mixing in by the evil spirits. The latter are very delighted in hiding their works behind some little natural cause. There is one test which can be brought to bear here, however; and that is, that if the cause is natural the man's condition will be restored to normal once the natural factor is eliminated: but were there something supernatural added to the natural, then the man will not recover even though the natural element is removed. If you have insomnia, for example, the enemy will suggest it is due to your overwork and your mind's overexhaustion. You listen to this and cease working and rest for a period without exercising your mind at all. Nonetheless thousands of thoughts continue to crowd your mind and pass to and fro through your brain during sleep. This demonstrates that your illness is not entirely due to natural cause: a supernatural one is mingled in with it somewhere. If you do not take the time to deal with the supernatural aspect, your removal of the natural element will serve no purpose.

It is of paramount importance that brethren today *examine* the source of these excuses. The wicked powers are highly skilled in misleading people into explaining their evil devices in terms of natural phenomena. They goad them into imagining they themselves are wrong. These individuals thus unconsciously cover up the perpetrations of the evil spirits. Consequently whatever excuse comes into his head the Christian must examine it carefully. Every reason must be scrutinized and every symptom of the mind must be traced. Otherwise, in his mistaking supernatural work to be natural he will cede increased ground to the enemy. Every opinion he entertains about himself needs to be proven, lest he yield new territory to the evil spirits even before the old is recovered.

Because of his long capitulation a person may easily commit the fatal error of defending the malevolent operations of the evil spirits. This must be guarded against, for in so doing he assists them in veiling the true cause of their attack. Although he is in distress, nevertheless he is siding with the evil spirits in preserving their ground.

The devil's hosts at this juncture are inciting the believer's flesh to cooperate with them. Actually the flesh always works together with the devil. For the sake of saving face or for some other reason, the Christian refuses to believe his mind could possibly be occupied by the devil and objects to hearing anything about him or his works. Such distaste of examination for fear that he may lose his "spiritual experience" is a great hindrance to deliverance. He may retort in any one of a number of ways: "I don't *need* deliverance, why should I *want* to be delivered?" or "I have overcome through Christ; He has overcome Satan already, so now I need pay no attention to him but just leave him to God. I focus my attention on Christ." or "I know nothing about satanic matters." or "I concentrate on preaching the gospel, why should I notice Satan?" With these or many other responses the believer dismisses the actions of the evil spirits in him. And to those who try to help him he may even say: "All right, you resist for me and pray for me." He is not speaking with sincerity; he merely desires to live in ease and let others sweat out deliverance for him.

Yet in all this, it should be asked why anyone should object to hearing about Satan and his works? Can it be that his mind has in fact been worked on by Satan and hence is apprehensive about facing the situation once it might be exposed? The truth is that he is familiar with too many things already concerning the devil and does not care to know any thing more. Yet the gospel of Jesus Christ saves people not only from sin but from the devil as well. Why then be afraid if the devil be mentioned when the gospel is preached? Is it not similar to the person who has committed a certain crime and is afraid to have anyone mention that particular crime? Due to his preoccupation with the devil the believer resents people mentioning him. Deep down in his heart he harbors a fear lest his true condition should be revealed. Supposing I am indeed invaded by evil spirits, he gravely muses, then what in the world can I possibly do about it now? Thus he speaks to others as we have indicated above both to cover up and to comfort himself.

But should a believer receive and accept the light and begin to look for freedom, the evil spirits will commence to pour into his mind loads of accusations which charge him with all sorts of errors and which condemn and reprimand him in such a fury that he is left with no energy to recover his lost ground. They know he has obtained light and that they can no longer *deceive* him. They therefore change their tactics to a ceaseless chain of accusations: "You are wrong, you are wrong." During this time the believer, because there is no help in view, feels like sinking into a pit of sin. But if he could recognize this as simply Satan's lie he would rise up and resist. He shall overcome.

Experience teaches us that directly after one apprehends the truth of his having lost the sovereignty over his mind and accordingly begins to seek to regain it, he shall suffer many times over that of previous days. The evil spirits will attempt one final struggle for him. They will employ their customary lying tactic by hinting to him that he cannot possibly regain his freedom since he has sunk too deeply into passivity or that God is not disposed to grant him grace again or that he will fare better if he does not resist or that in any case he can never see the day of deliverance so why bother to strive and suffer anyway. Every child of God ought to know, however, that he should not live by satanic grace. He mūst have liberty even should he die retrieving it. No one can have fallen into passivity to such an extent that he is beyond deliverance. God is for him and he shall be set free.

Once knowing the truth and acknowledging that his mind has never been released or only partially released from the power of darkness, the child of God naturally will rise up to do battle against the evil spirits in order that their stronghold in him may be overthrown. Then and there he learns that the weapons of war must be spiritual, for fleshly ones avail him nothing. He cannot free himself by making resolutions or by adopting measures to improve his memory or thinking. His mind is captive to supernatural powers that cannot be cast out or destroyed by carnal devices. The believer never dreams that the powers of darkness could have so profoundly usurped his head until he learns the truth for himself and prepares to retrieve the lost territory which these wicked powers will accordingly be stirred to defend. The child of God thus comes to see how dark, dull, passive, and out of control his head truly is. The devil will use every means to torture his mind, threatening him not to take any action to recover the lost territory. This convinces the believer more than ever that his mental life is definitely a stronghold of the enemy and that he has not had complete control over it. He perceives how the enemy attempts to prevent it from understanding truths he desires to learn, for he is able to remember non-essential matters but is totally powerless to comprehend or recall the vital ones. He senses that there is an opposing force in his head which is against the truth to which he already has given consent.

Now begins the war for liberation of the mind. Is the Christian content to remain the stronghold of the evil spirits? If not, then who must solve the problem? God? No, it is man himself. He must choose whether to offer himself wholly to God or allow his thinking apparatus to remain a concession of Satan's. Will the powers of darkness be permitted to utilize his mind? Are they going to be permitted to pour forth their perverted thoughts through the mind of the saved? Will they be allowed to fill his head with the fire from hell? Can they propagate at will their teachings through his mind? Is it henceforth going to be possible for them to resist God's truth by manipulating him in his intellect? Can they harm and torment him via the mind? The Christian himself must decide the issue. Is he willing to be a permanent puppet of the evil spirits? *He* must make the choice, else there can be no possibility of deliverance. To be sure, any decision for God does not then signify he has already overcome. It only indicates whether he is really opposing the attack of the enemy.

THE LOST GROUND TO BE RECOVERED

We will recall that because the believer has given ground to the evil spirits, they have been able to operate on his mind. Earlier we had grouped this lost ground under six headings; now we shall reduce them to three main types:

(1) an unrenewed mind, (2) acceptance of the evil spirits'
lies, and (3) passivity. The believer should examine himself
carefully to find out which of the three grounds he has furnished to the evil spirits. Is it the unrenewed mind? or the
passive mind? or the acceptance of the lie of the evil spirits?
Or has he yielded on all three counts? Judging by the experience of Christians, a large number have supplied all
three to the devil and his minions. Upon isolating the point
or points by which he has ceded territory to the evil spirits,
he must set out immediately to recover all the ground he
has lost. This is his only salvation. Since he has degenerated
into his present state through surrendering this or that foothold to the evil spirits, he will be free solely when these footholds are all regained. The unrenewed mind must be renewed; the lie accepted must be spotted and denied; and
passivity must be turned into free action. We shall discuss
them one by one.

THE MIND RENEWED

God desires not only a change in the mind of His children
at the time of conversion; He desires also a mind that is
totally renewed, which is transparent as crystal. We find this
commanded in the Word of God. The reason Satan can work
is that the Christian has not been liberated entirely from a
carnal mind. He may start out with a narrow mentality
which cannot tolerate others or a darkened mentality that
cannot comprehend deeper truth or a foolish mentality
which cannot bear any important responsibility; and afterwards he slips into deeper sins. This is because "the mind
that is set on the flesh is hostile to God" (Rom. 8.7). Once
knowing the teaching of Romans 6 many Christians see
themselves as having already been freed from their carnal
mind. What they do not appreciate is that the cross must
operate minutely in every area of the man. "Consider yourselves dead to sin" must be followed by "let not sin therefore
reign in your mortal bodies" (Rom. 6.11-12). Following the
change of mentality there must be the bringing of "*every
thought captive to obey Christ*" (2 Cor. 10.5). The mind

must be renewed completely, since any residue of its carnality is hostile to God.

For us to have our intellects renewed we must draw near to the cross. This is plainly called for in Ephesians 4. The Apostle Paul describes the darkness of man's carnal mentality in verses 17 and 18; but in verses 22 and 23 he informs us how the mind can be renewed: "Put off your old nature which belongs to your former manner of life and is corrupt through deceitful lusts, and be renewed in the spirit of your mind." We know our old man has been crucified with the Lord already (Rom. 6.6). Here we are exhorted to "put off" so that our mind might be renewed. This brings the cross into view as the instrument for its renewal. A believer should understand that his old brain too is part of that old man which God wants us to put off entirely. The salvation which God imparts through the cross includes not only a new life but the renewal of every *function* of our soul as well. The salvation which is rooted deeply in our being must gradually be "worked out." A serious lack among Christians today is in not perceiving the need for their minds to be saved (Eph. 6.17); they conceive salvation in general and somewhat vague terms. They fail to recognize that God desires to save them to the uttermost in that all their abilities are to be renewed and fit for His use. The mind is one of man's natural endowments. God calls His own to believe that their old man was crucified on the cross; thereafter they need to accept single-mindedly God's judgment towards the old man and exercise their will to resist or to put off its deeds including their old thoughts. They must come to the foot of the cross, willing to forsake their traditional mentalities and trusting God to give them a new mind. Brethren, the old one needs to be thoroughly put off. Yes, its renewal is God's work, but the putting off—the denial, the forsaking—of your old organ of thought is what you must do. If you perform your part, God will fulfill His. And once you put off specifically, you should just as thoroughly believe that God will renew your mind, despite the fact you know not how.

How many of God's children, although hitherto saved and possessed of a new life, still carry about them an old head.

Nothing of their former theories, thought processes, or prejudices has been altered: only a Christian casing has been added. They use their old brain to search, to accept and to propagate spiritual truth. Is it any wonder they fall into countless errors and precipitate endless conflicts in the church? Just as God is displeased with the wicked man who uses his own strength to do the Lord's work, so He is displeased with the wicked man who uses his own mind to apprehend God's truth. An unrenewed mentality is spiritually dead; hence everything which proceeds from it is likewise none other than dead. Many may boast in the depth of their Bible knowledge and in the excellency of their theological tenets, but those with spiritual discernment are aware that it is dead.

Upon recognizing the staleness of his mind and being willing to put it off by the cross, the Christian now should practice denying all carnal thoughts daily. The renewal will otherwise be impossible. For how can God ever succeed in His responsibility of renewing the believer's mind if the latter still thinks according to the flesh?

Patiently and decisively must the Christian examine every one of his thoughts—but in the light of *God*. Whatever is not of Him or is contrary to His truth must be "squeezed" or "pressed" out of his head. Mere mental understanding of truth similarly must be rejected. Paul has mentioned how our unrenewed mind is filled with arguments and proud imaginations (2 Cor. 10.5). These prevent men from arriving at true knowledge of God. Christians must bring all these thoughts captive to obey Christ. The Apostle says "every thought"; consequently one must not allow so much as a single thought to escape such treatment. He should not rest until every idea is brought into subjection to Christ. The examination of his thought should determine whether (1) it comes from his old mind or (2) it emanates from the ground given away, and whether (3) it will yield new ground to the evil spirits or whether (4) it issues from a normal or renewed mind. He should inquire why his thinking is confused, prejudiced, rebellious, or infuriated—why he opposes certain truth before he even examines it—why he is against some Christians whom he has merely heard about (does he have sufficient warrant for so withstanding or does he detest them purely out of a natural mind?). During such a period of investigation every idea and imagination needs to be scrutinized so that those which arise from the old creation may be detected and discarded. To those who live out their days foolishly such a regimen no doubt appears to be unbearable. Being managed by the powers of darkness, their mind is loose and wild. But we must face the fact that a war is on. And unless we fight, how can we retake the fortresses of the enemy which are in the mind? The enemy is very real; how then can we be less vigilant?

LIES DENIED

As the saved one places himself beneath God's light he will discover that often in the past he has accepted lies from the evil spirits which triggered his falling into that condition in which he now finds himself. Sometimes he adopted a wrong *attitude* or *action* due to misunderstanding God's truth by believing in the enemy's lie. For instance, by misunderstanding the relationship between God and man he inadvertently may believe that God dispenses His thought directly to him. So he passively waits and tarries and then accepts those registrations he assumes are from God. The evil spirits are thereby successful in their counterfeit and are able to supply him frequently with innumerable identical thoughts. Or, on another occasion, by appropriating what the enemy has suggested concerning his health or other matters directly involving him, he finds the conditions of his body and related affairs turn out to be exactly as he was told. The evil spirits, for example, may hint to the person's mind that certain things will happen to him. If he does not resist or if he unquestioningly receives the suggestion, he will find before long that whatever the evil spirits have appointed invariably does come to him.

By exercising himself the child of God will uncover many vexations, weaknesses, sicknesses, and other similar phenomena in his life today to be due to his directly or indirectly having accepted lies planted in him in the past by evil spirits. They either are caused directly by believing in these lies or are induced indirectly after believing in them. To secure one's freedom the Christian must experience God's light which is God's truth. Since he formerly lost ground by believing lies, he now must recover this ground by denying all lies. As light dispels darkness, so truth destroys lies. The saint must therefore seek to apprehend every truth concerning himself, God, and the evil spirits. He should pay a price to possess these truths. He should pray singleheartedly for light that he may behold his precise condition (the truth) and thereby know where he has been deceived and has accordingly suffered. He next should scrutinize all his physical and environmental sufferings. Whence does each stem? What has provoked these troubles; was it through believing Satan's lie or by adopting a wrong action through acceptance of any lie? He should trace the source and then *quietly* and *prayerfully* wait to be illuminated by God's light.

The devil abhors light and truth because these remove the ground of his working. Each word of truth has to be fought for in the believer's mind. The evil spirits try to keep from him the truth about their operations. They moreover attempt to disown the *particular* phenomenon which results from accepting a *particular* lie. Their operating principle is ever and anon "to keep them from seeing the light" (2 Cor. 4.4). A Christian must be very thorough in spotting the truth concerning all matters. Truth means at the very least the *true condition*. Even should he be helpless to drive away the enemy, his siding with the truth causes the latter to forfeit his ground. The believer at minimum can declare by his will that he *wants* the truth, that he wants to know and obey the truth. By prayer and by choice of will he ought to resist every satanic lie, whatever form it may take— a thought, an imagination or an argument. In so doing the Holy Spirit is afforded opportunity to lead his darkened mind into the light of God's truth. In practical experience the believer sometimes may spend months before discerning *one* satanic lie. He first must resist in his will every ground of the evil spirits and afterwards overthrow one by one the lies which he *formerly believed but now disbelieves*. In this way he gradually will recover all the surrendered territory. He will not believe, not even in the slightest degree, what the evil spirits say. So shall they lose their power.

NORMALCY RECOGNIZED

If one has plunged into all sorts of vexations due to passivity or believing the lie of the evil spirits, he urgently needs to determine what is normal for him. Except for the unrenewed mind, both passivity and assent to lies furnish such footholds to evil spirits that the Christian's mental state will deteriorate steadily in every direction. His powers of thinking, of recall, of physical endurance, and so forth will all continually fail. If he realizes his danger he ought to rise up and seek liberation. But what should he regard as "liberation"? It is this: he needs to be restored to his *original* state. Hence it is essential for anyone who seeks restoration to determine what his original state was. Each person has his normal condition, that state he had before he fell through the deceit of the enemy. He must be made reaware of his normal state. Upon discovering he is not as he was before, he should ask himself such questions as: What was my former condition? How far am I today from it? How can I be restored to it?

Your former state is your normal state. The condition from which you fell is your measuring rod. Should you be ignorant of what is normal for you, you need to inquire of yourself on this wise: Was my mind born so confused or was there a time when I was not confused? Was my memory habitually so poor or was there a period when I could remember well? Was I usually so sleepless or did I once sleep well? Did I always have so many pictures passing before my eyes like movies on a screen or were there some clear moments? Have I always been weak or was there a time when I was stronger? Is it true I could never control myself or could I once manage myself much better? By answering these questions the person ought to be able to perceive whether he lacks his normal state, is under attack, or has grown passive. He in addition will be helped in delineating what his normal state is.

To define what his original condition was, a person must acknowledge and believe initially that he *does have* a normal state. Though he has fallen today, he nonetheless once experienced a better life. Precisely that is his normal state towards which he should aspire to be restored. Normalcy means nothing but one's normal state. If he finds it difficult to decide what his normalcy is, then let him recall the best experience of his life when his spirit was strong, memory and thought clear, and body most healthy. Let him adopt that as his normalcy. It can afford him a minimum measure to which he ought to attain. He should not be content with any measurement less than that condition. And there is no reason why he should not be able to arrive at that state since he once was there. Yet even that is still not his highest possibility. Consequently he must at least regain his normalcy and refuse to ever again descend from it.

By comparing his present situation to that of his former days the Christian can determine how far he is now from what he once was. He whose mind is being assaulted can now see how weak his memory and thinking have become. And he whose body is being attacked can well appreciate how low his strength today is in comparison with his former strength. Upon realizing he has fallen from his normalcy he immediately should exercise his will to resist the present abnormal condition and strive to be restored to his normal state. Usually the evil spirits will withstand such attempted overthrowing of their strongholds. They will begin to suggest to the believer: You are now old, naturally you cannot expect to have as strong a mind as a youth; man's ability deteriorates according to years. Or, if you are young, they will intimate: Due to an inborn deficiency you of course cannot, like the others, enjoy the blessing of an active mind for long. Or, they will hint to you that you sank into this condition because you worked too hard. They may even grow so bold as to tell you your present state is what you really are, that you are inferior to others because you received a lesser gift. The aim of the evil spirits is to mislead the child of God into believing the explanation for his weaknesses is *natural, necessary* and unsurprising. If God's child neither is deceived nor is passive but is absolutely free, those words perhaps might be worthy of investigation; but should he be deceived and passive, those excuses are utterly unbelievable. He who has been redeemed to enjoy a better life than this poor condition should not allow the powers of darkness to hold him down in a lower state. He decisively should reject their lies.

One point should be noticed: a mind which is weakened through sickness is altogether different from one which is undermined by ceding ground to evil spirits. In the first case, man's nervous system is damaged; in the second, the work of the enemy does not upset the constitution of the nerves but merely inhibits their proper functioning. If a man's mind is not organically damaged but is only temporarily out of normal operation, he can be restored to his former state once the evil spirits are cast out. Many insane people have had their nervous system damaged through natural illness first before they are disturbed by the evil spirits; hence it is more difficult for them to be restored.

PASSIVITY OVERTURNED

After determining what one's normalcy is, the Christian's next important step is to battle for recovery. We should not forget, however, that the adversary will try his best to retain the ground he has won exactly as earthly rulers jealously guard their territories. We cannot expect the powers of darkness to surrender their citadels without a struggle. Quite the reverse, they will fight to the very end. Let us realize that, while it is most easy to cede any ground, it requires an enormous effort to recover it. Yet we should pay particular attention to this observation: that just as each nation has laws and their legal judgments must be absolutely obeyed, so in God's universe there are spiritual laws whose legal judgments are so authoritative that even the devils cannot disobey. If we learn these spiritual laws and act on them the evil spirits will be forced to return what they have taken.

The most basic and consequential law of the spirit realm is that nothing pertaining to man can be accomplished without the consent of his will. It is through ignorance that a child of God accepted the deceit of the evil spirits and permitted them to work in his life. Now he must recover the relinquished territory; and to do so he must exercise his will to overturn his earlier consent by insisting that he is his own master and will not tolerate the enemy manipulating any segment of his being. In such a warfare as this the evil spirits cannot violate spiritual law; and hence they must retreat. At the beginning the believer's mind was usurped by the wicked powers through its passivity; this in turn ushered in the passivity of the will. Now the believer should declare by God's law that his mind belongs to him, that he is going to use it and will not permit any outside force to instigate, employ or control his mind. If he relentlessly retreats from passivity and exercises his mind, the latter gradually shall be liberated till it attains to its original state. (Later we shall have more to say on recovering the ground and its battle.)

In this conflict the child of God must exercise his mind. He must take the initiative in each action and not depend on anyone else. If possible he must make his own decision, not waiting passively for other people or for more conducive environment. He must not glance back at the past nor worry concerning the future but learn to live just for this moment. Prayerfully and watchfully must he proceed step by step. He must exercise his mind and *think*: think what he should do, speak, or become. He must throw away every crutch, not allowing any worldly element or means to be substituted for the ability of the mind. He must use it to think, reason, remember and comprehend.

Because the individual's mental life has been protractedly passive, the battle for freedom likewise requires a protracted period. Let him understand that before he regains his liberty many of his thoughts will not be conceived by him but rather will be inspired by evil spirits who usurp his mind. For this reason he must scrutinize every notion lest he unconsciously furnish new ground to the evil spirits before the old is wholly recovered. During this period, therefore, accusations which arise may not necessarily be due to his faults nor praises be due to his merits. He should not abandon hope if his head is full of despondent thoughts; neither should he be elated if it is filled with exalted ideas.

The believer in addition should assail the lies of the evil spirits. Every suggestion from the enemy must be met resolutely with the truth of the Bible. Answer doubts with the texts of faith; respond to despair with words of hope; reply to fear with words of peace. If he does not know the appropriate verse, let him pray for direction; if he recognizes that something is from his foes then he can say to them, "This is your lie, I will not accept it." Victory is obtained by wielding the Sword of the Spirit.

During the struggle he must never forget the position of the cross. He must stand on Romans 6.11, reckoning himself dead to sin but alive to God in Christ Jesus. He already has died and has therefore been delivered from the old creation. The evil spirits cannot now do anything in his life, for what ground of operation they had has hitherto been taken away on the cross. Each time the Christian exercises his mind and resists the devil he is depending completely on what the cross has accomplished. He perceives that his death with the Lord is a fact; hence he strongly maintains that position before the enemy. He has died; the evil spirits have no authority over a dead person. Pharaoh could not hurt the children of Israel who were on the other side of the Red Sea. Resting on the Lord's death gives the Christian an immense advantage.

FREEDOM AND RENEWAL

As the believer retrieves the ground inch by inch, the effect gradually will be manifested. Although at the beginning situations may appear to turn worse as he attempts to recover, nonetheless if he persists he shall witness the adversary steadily losing his power. Various symptoms will decrease as the territory is increasingly regained. He will detect his mind, with its memory, imagination and reasoning powers, gradually becoming free so that he can use it again. But let him beware of one hazard at this point: he could become self-content and cease to fight to the end, to that point where all lost ground is recovered. And thus he would leave the evil spirits with a foothold for perpetrating some new future action. The believer must continue to restore his sovereignty until he is utterly emancipated. Should he stand on the foundation of the cross and exercise his mind to resist the enemy's usurpation, he shall soon be delivered completely. He shall become master of his own mental life.

Let us briefly recapitulate the process from passivity to freedom:

(1) The Christian's mind was originally normal.

(2) He sank into passivity because he wanted God to use his mind.

(3) He was deceived into thinking he now possesses a new mind.

(4) In point of fact he had fallen below normalcy through the assaults of the evil spirits.

(5) His mind grew weak and powerless.

(6) He battles to regain the lost ground.

(7) His mind seems to become more corrupt and confused than ever.

(8) Actually he is gradually regaining freedom.

(9) He insists on his sovereignty and determines to recover from his passivity.

(10) Passivity is overturned; he is recovered.

(11) By maintaining his will, he has not only succeeded in thereafter retaining his normalcy, but also

(12) His mind is so recovered that he can do what he could not do before.

Let us see that a renewed mind is something deeper than simply a freed one. To regain the strongholds forfeited through passivity and believing the enemy's lie means merely to restore what has been lost; but to be renewed includes not only restoration of what was relinquished but also a coming into possession of something higher than he originally had. To have a mind renewed is to arrive at the highest possibility which God has ordained for his mind. God wants the Christian's mind not just to be unshackled from the power of darkness by becoming wholly self-controlled, but in addition to be *renewed* so that it can cooperate completely with the Holy Spirit. God desires the mind to be full of light, wisdom and understanding, with all its imaginations and reasonings purified and brought to perfect obedience to God's will (Col. 1.9). Let us therefore not be content with but a little gain.

CHAPTER 4

THE LAWS OF THE MIND

WITH HIS MIND RENEWED, the child of God may marvel at its power. He is emancipated from sluggish and non-essential activities. His ability to concentrate becomes much sharper, his understanding more perceptive, his memory more alert, his reasoning more explicit, and his outlook less confined. He works more effectively, thinks more comprehensively, and grasps the thought of others more easily. In addition, he receives spiritual knowledge with an open mind because he is now free from the language of his own petty experience and released into the boundless world of spiritual knowledge. Every prejudice and preconceived notion towards God's work are removed, enabling his mind to undertake the work which before was impossible and to bear responsibility two or three times that which he formerly could bear.

The reason the Christian's mind is ineffective today is because it has not yet been renewed. Yet even once renewed, there is no guarantee that it may not again be harassed by the old mentality. If the Christian does not relentlessly oppose his traditional way of thinking he shall unconsciously turn back to it. As he needs to deny the work of the flesh and daily follow the spirit, so he must resist the old mental way and daily think according to the renewed mind. Such vigilance is absolutely essential; otherwise he will return to his old state. Retrogression is all too possible in spiritual life. Unless a child of God is watchful following his mental renewal, he can still believe in the enemy's lie and once again through passivity give him ground. In order that he may maintain his mind continually in the renewed state, it being renewed day by day, he needs to appropriate its laws. As the spirit has its laws, so the mind has too. We shall mention a few of these, the practice of which will assure victory to the believer.

THE MIND WORKING WITH THE SPIRIT

In analyzing the discerning-understanding-performing process of a *spiritual* Christian, we can identify these steps: (1) the Holy Spirit reveals God's will in one's spirit that he may know what it is; (2) through his mind he comprehends the meaning of this revelation; and (3) with his volition he engages his spiritual strength to activate the body that it may execute God's will. Nothing in a person's life is closer to the spirit than his mind. We know it is the mechanism for learning matters in the intellectual and material realms while the spirit is the component for perceiving realities in the spiritual realm. A Christian knows all things about himself through the intellect whereas he knows the things of God through the spirit. Both are organs of knowledge, hence their relationship is manifestly closer than are others. In walking after the spirit we shall find the mind to be the best helper to the spirit. It is therefore necessary to understand how these two work together.

The Bible speaks most distinctly about the coordination of the spirit and the mind: "that the God of our Lord Jesus Christ, the Father of glory, may give you a spirit of wisdom and of revelation in the *knowledge* of him, having the eyes of your hearts enlightened, that you may *know* . . . " (Eph. 1.17-18). We have explained the meaning of "a spirit of wisdom and of revelation" before; it means that God makes Himself and His will known to us by giving revelation in our spirit. But now we wish to note how the revelation obtained intuitively in our spirit works together with our mind.

"The eyes of your heart" points figuratively to the organ of our reasoning and understanding, that is, our mind. In this passage the word "know" or "knowledge"—used twice—

serves to convey two distinctive notions: the first one is a knowing intuitively, the second is a knowing or understanding mentally. This spirit of revelation is located in the depth of our being. God reveals Himself to our spirit that we may truly apprehend Him by our intuition. Thus far, however, this is but intuitive knowledge; that is to say, the inner man knows while the outer man remains ignorant. The communication to the outward man of what has been known by the inward man is an indispensable step, the lack of which prevents united action by the inner and outer man together. How then can there be this communication? The Scripture informs us that our spirit will enlighten our mental faculty to make it understand the meaning of the revelation in the intuition. Since our outward man depends on the mind in order to comprehend things, the spirit must convey what it knows intuitively to the mind so that the latter can deliver the message to the entire being and enable the child of God to walk according to the spirit.

We first come to know the will of God in our intuition and then our intellect interprets that will to us. The Holy Spirit moves in our spirit, producing in us a spiritual sense; afterwards we exercise our brain to study and to understand the meaning of this sense. It requires the cooperation of both spirit and mind to comprehend fully the will of God. The spirit enables our inner man to know, while the mind causes our outer man to understand. Such cooperation occurs in a second, although it takes longer to describe with pen and ink. They operate like two hands: and in the twinkling of an eye the spirit already has made known to the mind what it has seen. All revelations come from the Holy Spirit and are received not by the mind but by man's spirit, so that man may know by intuition; they are then studied and understood by his mental powers.

We consistently ought to refuse to allow the mind to serve as the prime element for receiving God's will, yet we must not inhibit it from serving as the secondary apparatus for understanding that will. A carnal Christian mistakes the thought of the head to be the criterion for his conduct because he has not yet learned how to walk after the spirit. A spiritual Christian follows the spirit, but he also permits his mind to comprehend what the spirit means. In true guidance these two elements are one. Ordinarily the leading in the spirit opposes what men call reasoning; however, to the person whose rational power has been renewed such reasoning works together with his spirit, thus his guidance seems perfectly logical to *his* reasoning. But the rationality of the person whose inner man has not yet attained this lofty position frequently will withstand the leading of the spirit.

We have observed in Ephesians 1 how the spirit aids the mind. Upon receiving revelation from God the believer's spirit enlightens the intellect. The mind of a spiritual man does not rely upon natural life; it depends instead on the enlightening of the spirit's light. It lapses into darkness otherwise. A renewed mentality needs to be directed by the light of the spirit. This explains why a person may find his thoughts confused and his whole being dissipated if his inner man is blocked by evil spirits. The brain of a spiritual man is sustained by the spirit. Should the latter fall under a seige, its power cannot reach directly to the brain and so the mind immediately loses some control. The preservation of these two elements in their proper relationship requires an alertness lest our spirit be beseiged by the evil spirits and cause our mind to relinquish its normal functioning.

A believer's mind is the outlet of the Holy Spirit. How does He Who dwells in man's spirit express Himself? He is not satisfied with man only believing that He is present in the human spirit. His aim is to manifest Himself through man that others too may possess Him. There are a thousand and one things for which the Holy Spirit requires the co-operation of *man*. It is not enough for Him to *dwell* in man's spirit, He desires additionally to *express* Himself through it. What expresses man's spirit is the mind. Should it be obstructed, the spirit shall be deprived of its means of expression, and then God's Spirit cannot flow from man's inner being to other people. We need the mind, moreover, to read the meaning of our intuitive knowledge, thus opening the way for God to communicate His thought through us. If our mentality is narrow and foolish the Holy Spirit finds Himself unable to fellowship with us in the way He desires.

MIND, THE SPIRIT, AND A SPIRITUAL MIND

The more spiritual a child of God becomes the more he is conscious of the significance of walking according to the spirit and the dangers of walking according to the flesh. But how is he actually to walk by the spirit? The answer given in Romans 8 is to mind the spirit and to possess a spiritual mind: "they that are after the flesh mind the things of the flesh; but they that are after the Spirit the things of the Spirit. For the mind of the flesh is death; but the mind of the Spirit is life and peace" (vv. 5-6 ASV). To walk after the spirit means to have the mind set on the things of the spirit; it also means to have the spirit rule the mind. Those who act according to the spirit are none other than those who are occupied with the things of the inner man and whose mind is therefore spiritual. Walking by the spirit simply denotes that a mind under the control of the spirit sets itself on the things of the spirit. This implies that our mentality has been renewed and has become spirit-controlled and thus qualified to detect every movement and silence of the spirit.

Here we see once more the relationship between these two component parts—"they that are after the flesh mind the things of the flesh; but they that are after the spirit the things of the spirit." Man's head is able to mind the flesh as well as the spirit. Our mental faculty (soul) stands between the spirit and the flesh (specifically here, the body). Whatever the mind sets itself on is what the man walks after. If it occupies itself with the flesh, we walk after that; conversely, if it sets itself upon the spirit, we follow after it. It is therefore unnecessary to ask whether or not we are walking after the spirit. We need only inquire if we are minding the spirit, that is, noticing the movement or silence therein. Never can it be that we set ourselves on the things

of the flesh and yet walk after the spirit. On whatever the
mind sets itself, that do we follow. This is an unchangeable
law. What does our mind think and notice in our daily experience? What do we obey? Are we heeding the inner man
or do we obey the flesh? Being occupied with the affairs of
the spirit will make us spiritual men, whereas occupying
ourselves with the affairs of the flesh will turn us into fleshly
people. If our mind is not governed by the spirit, it must
be governed by the flesh; if not guided by heaven, it must
be guided by earth; if not regulated from above, it must
be regulated from beneath. Following the spirit produces
life and peace, while following the flesh results in death.
From God's point of view, nothing arising from the flesh contains any spiritual value. A believer is capable of living in
"death" though he still possesses life.

Why is *minding* the realities of the spirit so important to a
life which walks after the spirit? Because that is the most
conspicuous condition for securing guidance in the spirit.
How many of God's children wait for Him to arrange their
circumstances while concomitantly overlooking the need to
heed the spirit; that is, they pay no heed to the prompting of
their inner depths. Often God Who indwells us already has
led us within our spirit, yet because of the dullness of our
mental faculty we just do not appreciate it. He has truly
given revelation to our intuition, but our intellect is dwelling
on a thousand and one matters other than on the movement
in the spirit. We are neglecting our spiritual sense. Sometimes our spirit is normal but our mind errs, so we are incapacitated from following the spirit. Whatever is expressed
by its intuition is delicate, quiet and gentle; unless we habitually mind its realities, how can we ever know the thought
of the spirit and accordingly walk? Our mind ought to be
alert like a watchman, always on the lookout for the movement in the inner man so that our outer man may be yielded
wholly.

All the leadings of God are transmitted via small delicate
sensations in the spirit. God never employs anything like a
compulsory, overwhelming feeling to try to force man into

obedience. He invariably affords us an opportunity to make our choice. Anything which is forced upon us comes not from God but is a work of the evil spirits. Until we fulfill the essentials for the working of the Holy Spirit, He will not work. Hence it necessitates more than merely waiting for His guidance. Our spirit and mind must function actively together with the Holy Spirit if we expect Him to lead us. We will walk after the spirit if we exercise our inner man to cooperate with the Holy Spirit and use as well our outer man to follow the movement or silence in our spirit.

AN OPEN MIND

Besides experiencing God's direct revelation, we also frequently receive truth through the preaching of the Word by other children of God. Such truth is first received in the intellect before it reaches the spirit. Since we make contact with the utterances or writings of others with the mind, there is hardly any possibility of this kind of truth reaching our life except through the channel of the mind. An open mind is consequently of paramount importance to spiritual life. If our brain is full of prejudice towards the truth or towards the preacher, truth will not enter it nor will it extend to our life. No wonder some believers derive no help—already have they decided what they would like to read or hear.

If a Christian is familiar with the process whereby truth is translated into life he will perceive the significance of a mind being unimpeded. Truth is understood initially by the mind; next it enters and stirs the spirit; and lastly, it is manifested in practical living. A closed mind prevents truth from entering the spirit. A closed mentality is a prejudiced one; it opposes and criticizes any item differing from its idea; its notion becomes the standard of truth; anything contrary cannot be truth. Such a mentality deprives the opportunity for many of God's truths to penetrate into the man; consequently it damages the believer's spiritual life. Many experienced saints can testify to the necessity for an unprejudiced mind in regard to revelation of truth. Oftentimes enough truth has been communicated to us, but we simply have not comprehended it because of the lack of an open mind. How many are the years that God must expend in removing all obstacles before we can accept truth. An unobstructed mentality in conjunction with a free spirit aids us the most in knowing the truth.

If the mind is open the individual will soon perceive the preciousness of a truth which initially appeared rather dull to him but now is illumined by the spirit's light. This is the way a child of God often receives truth: at the beginning it seems quite meaningless; after a while, though, the light of the spirit shines upon his mind and equips him to comprehend the depth of that truth. Although he may not have at his command the proper words to explain it, yet inwardly he has understood perfectly. An open mind lets in the truth, but the illumination of the spirit's light renders the truth profitable.

A CONTROLLED MIND

Every part of the Christian's life needs to be under reins; that includes the mind even following its renewal. We ought not toss the reins to it lest the evil spirits take advantage. Let us remember that *thought is the seed of action.* Carelessness here invariably leads to sin there. An idea sown will eventually grow, however prolonged such growth may require. We can trace all our presumptuous and unconscious sins to those seed thoughts we allowed to be planted before. If a sinful notion is allowed to stay in the head, then after a time, perhaps a few years, it will result in a sinful act. Suppose, for example, we conceive an evil thought against a certain brother. If it is not eradicated and cleansed immediately, it ultimately will produce its unsavory fruit. The Christian must exert his utmost strength to deal with his thoughts. Should his mental life be left uncontrolled, he cannot possibly control anything. Hence Peter exhorts us to "gird up (our) minds" (1 Peter 1.13), by which he means to say that we must regulate all our thoughts and never let them run wild.

God's objective is to "take *every* thought captive to obey Christ." Hence we ought to scrutinize every one of our thoughts in the light of God, not allowing one to escape our observation or judgment. Whatever the notion may be, it must be examined and controlled.

In gaining dominion over his mental life the Christian should not allow any improper thought to remain in him. Every inappropriate item must be driven out. Further, he must not permit his mind to lie idle. Every matter should be weighed carefully so that he may be both a sensible and a spiritual person. He should not allow his mind to drift off at random lest he provide opportunity for the evil spirits to work. It must not be lazy, doing nothing; rather should it always be functioning actively. Even after the Christian has received revelation in the spirit, he still needs to exercise his intellect to examine, to test, and to ascertain whether this is of God or of himself. He also needs to discover whether, by taking any action, he would be following the spirit entirely and according to God's timing, or whether there would be any element of his own mixed in with it. Such mental activity helps the spirit to clarify the revelation received in its intuition as well as to uncover any discrepancy. Any thought which centers on self hinders us from knowing God's will; only whatever disallows self is effective. God never wants us to follow blindly; He insists upon our lucidly apprehending His mind. Anything lacking clarity is unreliable.

When the mind is functioning, beware lest it do so alone, that is, beware lest it operate independently of the spirit's rule. A selfless mind aids the Christian in understanding God's will, but an independent one merely exhibits the corruption of the flesh. For instance, many search the Scriptures with their brain, depending upon their own intellectual ability. Yet the truth they claim to know is but there in their heads. Such independent mental action is quite dangerous, for it accomplishes nothing in the Christian's life other than to furnish some additional information for his thoughts and some additional ground for his boasting. We should sincerely reject all truths which are solely mental, for such knowledge provides Satan with an opportunity to work. We must restrain any desire which seeks mere intellectual knowledge.

The brain ought to function, but it likewise needs to rest. If a believer were to allow it to work incessantly without any occasion for rest, it eventually would become sick just as the body does. He must regulate its activity, forbidding it to grow overactive and go out of control. The defeat Elijah encountered under a broom tree was due to the excessive working of his mind (1 Kings 19).

A Christian should keep his mind in the peace of God at all times. "Thou dost keep him in perfect peace," noted Isaiah, "whose mind is stayed on thee, because he trusts in thee" (26.3). A restless brain is a disturbed brain that is harmful both to spiritual life and to spiritual service. It has led many into numerous errors. An unpeaceful mind cannot operate normally. Hence the Apostle teaches us to "have no anxiety about anything" (Phil. 4.6). Deliever all anxious thoughts to God as soon as they arise. Let the peace of God maintain your heart and mind (v.7). But Paul also exhorts us to put our heads to work and not just let them lie fallow: "brethren, whatever is true, whatever is honorable, whatever is just, whatever is pure, whatever is lovely, whatever is gracious, if there is any excellence, if there is anything worthy of praise, think about these things" (v.8).

The mind is not to be ruled by the emotions. It should rest calmly in God and work by faith. This is the meaning of "a sound mind" which Paul entreats us to cultivate (2 Tim. 1.7 AV). A believer should follow the intuition of the spirit. He must let God's rule of right and wrong judge in all cases.

The head needs to be kept in a humble state. A proud thought easily leads one astray. Any self-righteous, self-important or self-sufficient notion can bring in error. Some have a background of extensive knowledge and yet they fall into self-deceit because they think too much and too highly of themselves. Any who genuinely desire to serve the Lord must do so "with all lowliness of mind" (Acts 20.19 ASV).

He must cast off every self-deceptive consideration and ascertain his place in the body of Christ as appointed by God.

A MIND FULL OF GOD'S WORD

"I will put my laws into their minds," declares God (Heb. 8.10). We should read and memorize more of the Word of God, lest we be unable to find it at the moment of urgent need. If we diligently read the Bible God will fill every thought of ours with His laws. We shall recall instantly what the Bible says when we are in need of light for our way. Many are unwilling to exercise their minds in reading the Word. They like to open the Bible at random following prayer and take whatever is before them as being from God. This is extremely untrustworthy. But if our mind is abounding in His Word, the Holy Spirit is able through our spirit's intuition to enlighten our mind at once by bringing to our remembrance some appropriate verse. We do not require anyone to tell us we should not steal, for we know the Word of God has said so. Such a word is already in our mind. This is true in other matters as well; so if we are united with the Bible in this way, we shall be able to apprehend the mind of God in all regards.

A CRY FOR A CLEANSED MIND

The Christian continually ought to ask God to purify his mental life and keep it fresh. He should request God to root out every evil thought towards Him and all excessive notions as well so that what he believes is completely of God. Pray that you may not only think of Him but in addition think rightly. Pray that no thought will issue forth from your evil nature, but that if it does it will be exposed and disposed of by God's light immediately. Ask God to keep you away from your old pattern of thinking in order that the church of God may not be divided by special doctrines. Ask Him too to check you from accepting any special teaching with your mind which would separate you from His other children. Entreat Him to make you of one mind with the others; and if in any matter this one mind is lacking, then wait earnestly and patiently for it. Beseech Him not to permit you to hold any erroneous idea or teaching in your new life. Implore Him to render you dead not only to this evil nature of yours but also to your evil mentality. Plead with Him that your thought may not in any way be the cause of division in the body of Christ. Beg Him not to allow you to be deceived again. Supplicate on behalf of other children of God that they too may live by Him, no further provoking and no further scattering each other, that all may truly enjoy one life and one mind.

PART NINE

THE ANALYSIS OF
THE SOUL—THE WILL

1 A Believer's Will
2 Passivity and Its Dangers
3 The Believer's Mistake
4 The Path to Freedom

CHAPTER 1

A BELIEVER'S WILL

A MAN'S WILL IS his organ for decision-making. To want or not to want, to choose or not to choose are the typical operations of the will. It is his "helm" by which he sails upon the sea of life.

The will of a man can be taken as his real self, for it truthfully represents him. Its action is the action of the man. When we declare "*I* will," it is actually our volition which wills. When we say "*I* want, *I* decide," again it is our volition which wants and decides. Our volition acts for the entire man. Our emotion merely expresses how we feel; our mind simply tells us what we think; but our will communicates what we *want*. Hence, it is the most influential component of our entire person. It is deeper than emotion and mind. So in seeking spiritual growth the believer must not neglect the volitional element in him.

Many commit the error of treating "religion" as a matter of emotion; they believe that it merely soothes and gladdens men's emotions. Others insist that "religion" ought to be compatible with reason and not overly emotional; only a kind of rational religion is acceptable to these. What both these groups do not know is that true religion *per se* does not aim at emotion or reason but aims to impart life to man's spirit and to lead his will to be completely yielded to God's will. Unless our "religious" experience produces in us a *willing* acceptance of the whole counsel of God, it is very superficial. What can it profit a man if along his spiritual pathway the will exhibits no proper sign of grace? Or if the will is not touched?

True and perfect salvation saves man's will. Whatever is not sufficiently thorough to embrace the salvation of man's volition is but vanity. All pleasant feelings and all lucid thoughts belong exclusively to the external realm. Man may experience joy, comfort and peace in believing God, he may understand His majesty and amass much wonderful knowledge; but does he possess any genuine union with Him if his will is not united with God's? The joining of wills forms the only true union. Consequently, upon receiving life the believer should be attentive not only to his intuition but likewise to his volition.

A FREE WILL

In discussing man and his will we particularly should bear in mind that he exercises a free will. This means that man is sovereign, that he has a sovereign will. What he disapproves of should not be forced on him, what he opposes should not be coerced. Free will signifies that man can choose what he wants. He is not a mechanical toy to be run by others. He is responsible for all his actions; the will within controls all matters both inside and outside him. He is not governed automatically by an external force; rather, he houses a principle within him which determines his acts.

This was the state of man when created by God. The man the Creator fashioned was not something mechanical; for it will be recalled that God said to him: "You may *freely* eat of every tree of the garden; but of the tree of the knowledge of good and evil you shall not eat, for in the day that you eat of it you shall die" (Gen. 2.16-17). How did God command him? God persuaded, prohibited, yet never coerced. If Adam were disposed to listen and not eat the forbidden fruit, it would be *Adam* who so willed. But if he would not listen and would eat, even God would not restrain him. That is free will. God put this responsibility of eating or not eating upon man for him to choose according to his untrammeled will. God did not create an Adam who was incapable of sinning, rebelling or stealing, since to have done so would have been to make man into a piece of machinery. God could advise, prohibit and command; however, the responsibility of hearing or not lay with man. Out of love, God gave the command beforehand; out of righteousness, he would not force man to do what the latter did not wish to do. For man to obey God, it requires a willingness on his part, because God never compels him. He could verily employ sundry means to make man willing; nevertheless, until he gives his consent God will not make His way into the man.

This is an exceedingly vital principle. We shall see later how the Creator never works against this principle, whereas the evil spirits consistently do. By this can we distinguish what is of God and what is not.

THE FALL AND SALVATION

Unfortunately, mankind has fallen. By this plunge man's unfettered volition suffered prodigious damage. We may say that there are two massive contradictory wills throughout the universe. On the one side stands the holy and perfect will of God; on the other is arrayed the defiled, defiling and opposing will of Satan. In between subsists the sovereign, independent, free will of man. When man listens to the devil and rebels against God he seems to render an eternal "no" to God's will and an abiding "yes" to Satan's. Since man employs his volition to choose the will of the devil, his volition falls captive to the devil. Therefore all his acts are governed by Satan's will. Until he overturns his early subjection, man's will remains unquestionably oppressed by the enemy power.

In this fallen position and condition man is fleshly. This flesh—by which his will, together with his other organs, is ruled—is thoroughly corrupted. How can anything pleasing to God ever result from such a darkened will? Even his questing after God springs from the realm of the flesh and therefore lacks any spiritual value. He may invent many ways of worshiping God at this time, yet all are his own ideas, all are "will-worship" (Col. 2.23 ASV), totally unacceptable to Him.

Let us realize, then, that except a man receive God's new life and serve Him therein, every bit of service for God is but the work of the flesh. His intention to serve and even to suffer for Him is vain. Before he is regenerated, his will, even though it may be inclined towards good and God, is futile. For it is not what fallen man intends to do for God but how He Himself wishes man to do for Him that really counts in God's eyes. Man may devise and initiate countless notable works for God; nonetheless, if they do not originate with God they are nothing more than will-worship.

This is true with respect to salvation. When man lives carnally even his desire to be saved is not acceptable to God. We read in the Gospel of John that "to all who received him, who believed in his name, he gave power to become children of God; who were born, not of blood nor of the will of the flesh nor of the *will of man*, but of God" (1.12-13). Man is not regenerated because he wills it so. He must be born of God. Nowadays Christians entertain the incorrect concept that if anyone wishes to be saved and seeks the way of life he undoubtedly will be a good disciple of Christ, for nothing can be better than this desire. God nonetheless affirms that in this matter of regeneration as well as in all other matters related to Him, the will of man is totally nonefficacious.

Many children of God cannot understand why John 1 asserts the will of man to be noneffective whereas Revelation concludes by saying, "Let him who *desires* take the water of life without price" (22.17), as though man himself is entirely responsible for his salvation. And does not the Lord Jesus

Himself give as explanation for the Jews not being saved the following declaration: "You *refuse* to come to me that you may have life" (John 5.40)? Here again, the responsibility for perdition apparently rests on man's will. Can the Bible be contradicting itself? Is there any special meaning behind these apparent inconsistencies? A comprehension of this matter will help us to appreciate what God requires of us in our Christian life.

We will recall that God wishes no one to "perish but that all should reach repentance" because He "desires all men to be saved and to come to the knowledge of the truth" (2 Peter 3.9; 1 Tim. 2.4). No problem arises concerning whom God wants to save or whom He will let perish. The problem before us is, rather, what is the sinner's attitude towards God's will? If he decides to be a Christian because he is naturally inclined towards "religion," naturally contemptuous of the world or naturally influenced by his heredity, environment or family, he is as far from God and His life as are other sinners. If the sinner chooses to be a Christian at the moment of excitement or enthusiasm, he may not fare better than the rest. It all reduces itself to this: what is his attitude towards *God's* will? God loves him, but will he accept this love? Christ calls him, but will he come? The Holy Spirit wants to give him life, but is he willing to be born? His will is useful only in choosing God's will. The question now is, and solely is, how does his volition react towards God's will?

Have we noticed the difference here? If man himself commences the search for salvation, he is yet perishing. Various founders of religions belong to this category. But if man, upon hearing the gospel, is *willing* to accept what God *offers* to him, he shall be saved. In the one case, man originates; in the other, he receives. The one does the willing himself while the other accepts God's will. John 1 speaks of man himself willing, whereas John 5 and Revelation 22 refer to man's *accepting* God's will. Hence no contradiction exists between these two; rather is there a very crucial lesson for us to learn.

God is instructing us that in such a paramount and excellent matter as salvation anything which proceeds from self cannot be accepted but is rejected by Him. Indeed, if we

wish to advance in our spiritual development we must understand and bear in mind every vital principle God used
in dealing with us at the time of regeneration. These initial
principles betoken how we ought to continue in our spiritual
life. What we have just now discussed constitutes one of the
greatest of these principles. Anything which issues from us,
that is from our flesh, is utterly unacceptable to God. Even
should we seek such an indispensable and sublime a matter
as salvation, our pursuit is nonetheless rejected. What we
need unceasingly to remember is that God looks not at the
appearance of a thing—whether good or bad, big or small—
but looks instead to see whence it originates, from Him or
not. In salvation, we are saved not because we want to be
saved but because God wants to save us; and so is it to be
throughout our lives. We need to see that aside from what
God does through us, all other activities, however commendable they may be, are utterly nonefficacious. If we fail to
learn this life principle at the initial stage of salvation, we
shall encounter endless defeats thereafter.

Moreover, according to the actual condition of man, while
he is a sinner his will is rebellious against God. Therefore
God must bring men to Himself as well as grant him new
life. Now just as the will of man represents the man—for it
is the essence of his being, so the divine will personifies God
—it being His very life. To say that God will bring man to
Himself is to say that He will bring man to His will. No
doubt this takes a lifetime to fulfill, but even at the outset
of salvation God commences working towards that end.
Hence when the Holy Spirit convicts a man of sin, that conviction is such that the man would not have a word to say
even should God condemn him to hell. Then when that man
is shown by God His definite plan in the cross of Christ he
will gladly accept it and express his readiness to receive the
salvation of God. Thus do we observe that the first stage of
salvation is essentially a salvation of the will. A sinner's faith
and acceptance is but his *desire* to take the water of life and
be saved. Similarly his opposition and resistance are his *unwillingness* to come to the Lord for life, and accordingly he

perishes. The battle whether to be saved or to perish is fought out in the will of man. Man's original fall was due to the rebellion of his will against God's; and so his present salvation is effected by having his volition brought into obedience to God.

Although at the moment of new birth man's will is not yet fully united with God, his fallen will nonetheless is uplifted through his acceptance of the Lord Jesus and his denial of Satan, self, and the world. By believing God's Word and receiving His Spirit, his will is also renewed. After a man is born anew he obtains a new spirit, a new heart, and a new life; his will receives a new master and is henceforth under new management. If his will is obedient it becomes a part of the new life; if it resists, it turns out to be a formidable enemy to the new life.

This renewed will is much more vital than the other parts of the soul. A mind may be misled and emotion can be inordinate, but the will can ill-afford to be wrong. For it to be wrong brings in serious consequences, since it is man's very self and controls all other organs of man. If it is wrong, God's will cannot be realized.

A SUBMISSIVE WILL

What is salvation? It is none other than God saving man out of himself into Himself. Salvation has two facets: a cutting off and a uniting with. What is cut off is self; the uniting is with God. Whatever does not aim at deliverance from self and union with Him is not genuine salvation. Anything which cannot save man from self and join him to God is vanity. A true spiritual beginning involves release from animal life and entry into divine life. Everything belonging to the created one must be relinquished so that the created one will enjoy all things solely in the Creator. The created one must vanish in order that true salvation may be manifested. Real greatness rests not on how much we have but on how much we have lost. Authentic life can be seen only in the abandonment of self. If the nature, life and activities of the created one are not denied, the life of God has no way to express itself. Our "self" is often the enemy of God's life. Our spiritual growth shall be stunted severely if we have no intention nor experience of losing ourselves.

What is self? That is extremely difficult to answer, nor can our answer be fully correct. But were we to say "self" is "self-will," we would not be too far from the mark. Man's essence is in his volition because it expresses what man fundamentally is, desires, and is willing for. Before God's grace has done its work in man all which a man has, whether he be sinner or saint, is generally contrary to God. It is because man belongs to the natural, which is exceedingly antithetical to God's life.

Salvation, then, is to deliver man from his created, natural, animal, fleshly, and self-emanating will. Let us make a special note of this: that aside from God giving us a new life, the turning of our will to Him is the greatest work in salvation. We may even say that God imparts new life in order for us to abandon our will to Him. The gospel is to facilitate the union of our will with God. Anything short of this is failure of the mission. God aims his arrow of salvation not so much at our emotion or our mind but at our will, for once the latter is saved, the rest are included. Man may be united with God in mind to a certain degree; he may agree with Him in his feeling towards numerous things; but the most consequential and most perfect union is that of his will with the divine will. This accord embraces all other unions between God and man. Anything short of the union of wills is inadequate. Since our total being moves according to our will, it is obvious that it constitutes the most influential part of man. Even so noble an organ as the spirit must yield to the rule of the will. (We shall enlarge on this subsequently). The spirit does not symbolize the whole man, for it is but his organ for communication with God. The body cannot stand for man either, because it is only his apparatus by which to communicate with the world. But the will embodies man's authentic attitude, intention and condition. It is the mechanism in him that most nearly corresponds to the man himself. Now unless this will is united with God, all other unions are shallow and empty. Once this ruling will of man is joined completely to God, the man is spontaneously and fully submissive to Him.

Our union with the Lord has two steps: the union of life and the union of will. We are united with Him in life at the time we are regenerated and receive His life. As He lives by His Spirit so shall we thereafter live by the Holy Spirit. This is the bond of life. It indicates we share one life with God. This uniting is an internal one. But what *expresses* that life is the will; consequently there needs to be an external union, one of the will. To be joined with the Lord in will simply denotes that we have one will with Him. These two unions are related, neither is independent of the other. The one of new life is spontaneous, for this new life is the life of God; but the one of will is neither so simple nor spontaneous because our will is clearly our self.

As we have remarked before, God intends to destroy the life of the soul but not its function; so upon being joined with the Lord in life, He launches forth to renew our soul with its various parts in order that our soul may be one with our new life and consequently one with His will. Our will being what it is, God of course daily seeks its union with His will. Salvation cannot be complete until man's will is united entirely with God's. Without that perfect bond *man's self* is yet at odds with Him. He wants us to have His life, but He also wants us to be united with Him. Since our will most closely represents us, our union with Got cannot be complete without the joining of our will to Him.

A careful reading of the Scriptures will yield the fact that a common denominator underlies all our sins: the principle of disobedience. Through Adam's disobedience we perish; through the obedience of Christ we are saved. Formerly we were sons of disobedience; today God wants us to be sons of obedience. Disobedience means to follow one's own will; obedience means to follow God's will. The purpose of divine salvation is to encourage us to deny our will and be united with Him. Right there lies a big mistake among modern Christians. They envisage spirituality to be joyous feeling or profound knowledge. They spend time craving various sensations or questing after mental knowledge of the Bible, for they regard these as highly superior. Meanwhile, acting upon their feelings and thoughts, they go about performing many good, grand and notable tasks which they believe must be quite pleasing to God. They do not comprehend, however, that He asks not how they feel or reason; He only seeks the union of their wills with His. His delight is in having His people desire what He desires and do what He says. Except for a believer's unconditional surrender to God with the believer disposed to accept His will entirely, all else which is labeled spirituality—such as holy and happy feelings or prize-winning thoughts—is but an outward show. Even visions, dreams, voices, sighings, zeal, work, activity, and toil are external. Unless the believer is determined in his volition to finish the course God has set before him, nothing is of any worth.

If we are really united with God in will, we shall cease at once every activity which emerges from ourselves. Hereafter there can be no independent action. We are dead to self but alive to God. No longer do we act for Him under our impulse and according to our way. We act solely after we are moved by God. We are set free from every motion of self. Such union, in other words, is a change of center, a new beginning. In the past all activities focused on self and began with it; today everything is of God. He does not ask the nature of whatever we start; He simply inquires who started it. God discounts every element not yet freed from self, no matter how good it may appear to be.

THE HAND OF GOD

Because many believers are saved but not absolutely yielded to God's will, He uses many ways to effect obedience. He moves His own by His Spirit and touches them with His love that they may obey Him alone, desiring nothing outside His will. But often these do not produce the desired attitude in His children. God consequently must use His hand to lead them to where He desires them to be. His hand is seen primarily in environment. God lays His hand heavily on His people to crush, to break, or to bind—that their wills may be hardened no more against Him.

The Lord is not satisfied until we are thoroughly united with Him in will. To achieve that end He permits many disagreeable things to come to us. He lets us grieve, groan, and suffer. He arranges for many practical crosses to traverse our path that through them we may bow our heads and capitulate. Our volition is naturally exceedingly stubborn; it refuses to obey God until it is heavily disciplined. By submitting ourselves under His mighty hand, willingly accepting His discipline, our will experiences one more cut and is once again delivered to death. And if we continue to resist Him, greater affliction awaits us to bring us into subjection.

God purposes to strip all that is ours away. All believers, after they are truly regenerated, conceive the notion of observing the will of God. Some openly promise such; others secretly entertain this idea. To prove and see whether this promise or thought is real or not, God puts His children through various unpleasant strippings. He causes them to lose material things: health, fame, position, usefulness. What is more, He even causes them to be deprived of joyous feeling, burning desire, the presence and comfort of God. He must show them that everything except His will must be denied. If it is God's will, they should be willing to accept pain and suffering upon their physical bodies. They must be ready to embrace dryness, darkness, and coldness if He seems pleased to so treat them. Even if He should strip them of everything, of even so-called spiritual effectiveness, they must accept it. He wishes His own to know that He saves them not for *their enjoyment* but for His Own will. In gain or loss, joy or sorrow, consciousness of His presence or that of His rejection, Christians must contemplate God's will alone. Suppose it were His will to reject us (which it never is), could we gladly accept rejection? When a sinner first trusts in the Lord his objective is heaven. This is permissible during *that* particular period for him. After he has been taught in God, however, he knows that he has come to be-

lieve in Him solely for the sake of His will. Even if, by believing, he were to end up in hell, he would still believe in
God. He is no longer mindful of his own gain or loss. If his
going to hell would glorify God, he is ready for that. Obviously this is but a hypothetical case. Yet Christians must
understand that they live on earth not for themselves but
for His will. Their greatest blessing, highest privilege and
supreme glory lies in rejecting their corrupt volition of flesh
and blood in order that they may be united with God's volition for the accomplishment of His heart's desire. The gain
or loss, glory or shame, joy or pain of the created one is nothing to be concerned about. If only the Highest can be satisfied, it matters not to what degree the humble be brought
down. This is the only way for believers to lose themselves
in God!

TWO MEASURES

Two measures are necessary in being joined to God in will.
The first is for God to subdue the activities of our will; the
second is to conquer the life of our will. Quite often our volition is subservient to the Lord only in a number of particular matters, which nonetheless prompts us to think that we
are fully obedient to Him. Down within us, however, hides
a secret tendency which shall rise to the surface when the
opportunity is provided. God's intent is not merely to curtail
the movement of our will but also to smash its inner tendency so that its very quality seems to be transformed. Strictly speaking, an obedient will and a harmonious one are very
different: obedience is related to activity whereas harmony
is related to life, nature and tendency. The obedient will of a
servant is seen in his executing every order of his master,
but the son who knows the father's heart and whose will is
one with the father's not only fulfills his duty but fulfills it
with delight as well. An obedient will puts a stop to one's own
activity, yes, but a harmonious will is in addition one heart
with God. Only those who are in harmony with Him can actually appreciate his heart. If a person has not arrived at
this perfect harmony between his own and God's will, he

has yet to experience the summit of spiritual life. To be obedient to the Lord is indeed good, but when grace completely conquers the natural life the Christian will be fully attuned to Him. As a matter of fact, the union of wills is the zenith of anyone's spiritual walk.

Numerous saints conclude they already have lost their wills entirely. Nothing could be farther from reality. When the moment of temptation and trial comes they will discover that an obedient will is not the same as a harmonious one, that nonresistance does not necessarily mean no will of their own self. Who is there who does not care for a little gain, who does not withhold a little something for himself? Who really desires no gold or silver, honor, freedom, joy, advantage, position or whatever? One may think he cares nothing for these items; while he has them he may not be conscious of their hold upon him; but let him be on the verge of losing them, and he shall soon discover how tenaciously he wants to hold on to them. An obedient will may agree with God's will on many occasions, but at some time or other there is bound to be a mighty struggle between the life of the believer's will and the will of God. Unless His grace realizes its fullest work, the saint can hardly overcome.

Obviously from this an obedient will cannot be viewed as perfection. The volition, though broken and deprived of the strength to resist God, has yet to achieve concord with Him. We of course acknowledge that to arrive at the point of being powerless to resist God is itself the fruit of His great grace. And ordinarily we say that an obedient will is already dead in itself. Yet strictly speaking it still possesses a thread of life which is unbroken. There continues to be a hidden tendency, a secret admiring of the former way of life. That is why on certain occasions it finds itself less joyful, less ardent and less diligent in obeying the Lord than at other times. While the will of God is in fact obeyed, there nevertheless remains a difference in personal like and dislike. Had the life of self genuinely and completely been consigned to death, the attitude of the believer towards every part of the will of God would be *exactly the same*. Any disparity in speed, feeling and effort shows a lack of concord in one's will towards God's will.

We may illustrate these two conditions of the will by citing Lot's wife, the Israelites, and the prophet Balaam. The departure from Sodom of the wife of Lot, the exodus of the Israelites from Egypt, and the blessing of Israel by Balaam can all be regarded as obeying the will of God. All these were men and women subdued by the Lord, not following their own opinions; even so, their inward tendencies were not harmonious with Him; hence every one of them ended in failure. How frequently the direction of our footsteps is correct but our secret heart differs with God. And so we ultimately fall.

THE WAY TO SURMOUNT

God never obeys us. He is pleased with nothing but with our obeying Him, that is, obeying his will. However noble, grand and indispensable a thing may be, it cannot be substituted for His will. What He desires us to do is His will. He does it Himself and requires us to do the same. From His view He sees nothing except corruption wherever man's self is present. If acts are performed under the guidance of the Holy Spirit they are good and profitable; but if the same acts are performed by man alone their value is greatly diminished. Consequently the cardinal point is not man's intention nor the nature of the thing, but purely the will of God. This is the first point to keep in mind.

Let us next inquire how man's will can be attuned to God's. How can man effect the transfer from having self-will as his center to having the will of God as his center? It all hinges on the natural life. The measure of our being unshackled from the control of the soul life determines the measure of our union with God, for nothing hinders that union more than the energy of the soul. The more the soul's vitality is crushed the more our will centers on God. The new life in us inclines towards Him, but it is suppressed by

the old life of the soul. Committing the soul life to death
is therefore the way to mount the peak of spirituality.

The man outside God is lost and the thing outside God is
vain. Whatever is outside God comes from the flesh. Any
strength or thought other than His is accursed. The believer
must deny his own strength as well as his own pleasure. He
should disregard himself completely in every respect. Let him
do nothing for himself but trust God in all matters. Let him
proceed step by step according to His way, waiting for His
time, and fulfilling His conditions. Let him receive willingly
from God his strength, wisdom, righteousness, and work.
Let him acknowledge God as the source of all things. Thus
shall harmony be attained.

How this indeed is the "narrow gate" and the hard way!
It is narrow and hard because God's will must be the standard for each footstep. It has but one rule: make no provision
for self. The least deviation from this rule shall take man out
of the way. Nevertheless it is not impossible, for as the soul
life is lost by its habits, tastes, desires and longings being
gradually broken, there shall remain no more resistance to the
Lord. How lamentable that so many Christians have never
passed through this gate and walked along this path; while
others may have entered, yet do not patiently walk thereafter. Regardless how long or how short that difficult period
may be, this alone is the way of life. This is God's gate and
God's way. It is true and secure. Anyone who esteems the
abundant life must become its pedestrian.

CHAPTER 2

PASSIVITY AND ITS DANGERS

"MY PEOPLE ARE DESTROYED FOR lack of knowledge" (Hos. 4.6) is certainly applicable to our day. Christians nowadays generally are lacking in two kinds of knowledge: (1) a knowledge of the conditions by which evil spirits work; and (2) a knowledge of the principle of spiritual life. Ignorance here is furnishing Satan and his evil spirits an incredible advantage and is inflicting enormous harm on the church of God. What grieves our hearts is that, even as folly is prevailing, Christians continue to boast of their familiarity with the Bible and of the abundance of their experience. They do not realize that their much so-called knowledge is mere human reasoning, quite devoid of usefulness. Humility before the Lord and eagerness in seeking the revelation of God's truths are almost unknown. While boasting in the richness of their knowledge, they themselves sink into the very quicksand from which they can neither extricate themselves nor rescue others. It is indeed a most dreadful scene.

THE LAW OF CAUSE AND EFFECT

For each and every thing God has created there is a law. All actions are governed by laws. Hence evil spirits also operate according to definite laws, one of which is that certain causes will produce certain effects. Now should anyone fulfill the conditions for the working of evil spirits (whether he fulfills them willingly, such as the witch, the medium, or the sorcerer—or unwittingly, such as the Christian), then he has definitely given ground to them to work on him. Notice that the law of cause and effect is involved here. Fire scorches, water drowns: these are laws: none escapes scorching if he falls into fire, nor can any escape drowning if he jumps into water. Likewise everyone who meets the requirements for the operation of evil spirits will be harmed by them. Hence the same law of cause and effect is operative here. It pays no heed to whether one is a Christian or not; once the conditions are met, the evil spirits do not fail to act. Just as a Christian cannot avoid being scorched or drowned if he falls into fire or water, so he cannot escape the danger of being hurt if he ignorantly supplies the prerequisities for the working of evil spirits. The fire scorches everything put into it; the water drowns all who are immersed in it; and evil spirits attack all who give them ground. One will not escape simply because he is a child of God. If he provides the enemy the opportunity, he will not hesitate to assault him. What, then, are the conditions for the working of the enemy? What facilitates this malevolent working? This is the crucial question. The Bible characterizes such conditions as "place" (Eph. 4.27 ASV) or "opportunity" (RSV). It can additionally be denoted as "ground." It means any portion of *empty* space marked off in man for the evil spirits. This place or ground constitutes their foothold. The degree of invasion is determined by the degree of the foothold. The evil spirits will commence to penetrate into any man, be he "heathen" or Christian as soon as he has obtained a footing in him. Whatever affords the evil spirits an opportunity or a foothold by which to attack or invade may be termed as "ground." If ground is given, invasion is unavoidable. The particular cause brings in the particular effect. A Christian who yields ground to evil spirits and yet envisages himself to be beyond attack has been gravely deceived already by the enemy.

Now to put it simply, the ground or territory which the believer furnishes to the evil spirits is sin. Sin includes all the possible grounds. In retaining sin he retains as well the evil spirits that hide behind it. All sin yields territory to them. But there are two kinds of sin, one is positive and the other negative. Positive sins are those which a person commits: his hands perform bad acts, his eyes see evil scenes, his ears hear wicked voices, and his mouth speaks unclean words. These render opportunity to evil spirits in varying degree to take hold of the hands, eyes, ears and mouth of the saint. Whichever part of him sins, that is what invites the enemy to come and occupy it. If occupation stems from *sinning,* the child of God needs to forsake unrelentingly so as to recover the lost territory. Else the evil spirits will increase their hold gradually until the entire person is occupied. *One reason why some who hitherto have accepted the fact of the co-death of the cross find it difficult to lay aside the sin which clings so closely is because aside from the problem of the "flesh" they also have the problem of having been assaulted by supernatural evil powers.*

This kind of positive sin which presents a working opportunity to the evil spirits is by and large understood by most Christians and consequently we shall not enlarge upon it. Let our attention now be focused on the second type, on negative sin. This is largely *mis*understood. Since it is within the scope of the will, we shall discuss it in detail.

The popular notion is that only the positive kind are sins; negative ones are not counted as such. The Bible nonetheless holds that not only all manner of unrighteousness which a man actively *commits* is sin but that "whoever knows what is right to do and fails to do it, for him it is sin" as well (James 4.17). The Word of God treats what man *commits* and what man *omits* both equally as sin. Sin gives footing or ground to the work of evil spirits. And besides the positive sin, the negative kind—that of omission—likewise provides ground for their work.

The particular sin of omission which gives ground to the evil spirits is the believer's passivity. Disuse as well as misuse of any part of one's being is a sin in the sight of God. The Lord endows us with all sorts of abilities none of which are to be misused or go unused. For a person to cease engaging any part of his talent but to allow it to sink into inertia is to provide occasion for the devil and his army to exercise it for him. This is the ground for their sinister operations.

All Christians are aware of sin as a condition for the enemy's assault, but an innumerable number of them are unaware that passivity is also a sin and a condition for his assault. Once place is given, penetration becomes inevitable and sufferings naturally follow.

PASSIVITY

What primarily precipitates the enemy's invasion among the "heathen" and among carnal Christians is willful sin; but "the primary cause of deception . . . in surrendered believers may be condensed into one word, passivity; that is, *a cessation of the active exercise of the will in control over spirit, soul and body, or either, as may be the case.*" The organ of volition ceases to choose and decide matters referred to it. "The word passivity simply describes the opposite condition to activity; and in the experience of the believer it means, briefly, (1) loss of self-control—in the sense of the person himself controlling each, or all, of the departments of his personal being; and (2) loss of free-will—in the sense of the person himself exercising his will as the guiding principle of personal control, in harmony with the will of God."* The passivity of a saint arises out of the non-use of his various talents. He has a mouth but refuses to talk because he hopes the Holy Spirit will speak through it. He has hands but will not engage them since he expects God to do it. He does not exercise any part of his person but waits for God to move him. He considers himself fully surrendered to God; so he no longer will *use* any element of his being. Thus he falls into an inertia which opens the way for deception and invasion.

Upon accepting the teaching of their union with God's will, Christians often develop a wrong concept of what this union signifies. They misconstrue it to mean to obey God passively. They think their will must be cancelled out and that they must become puppets. They maintain that they must not employ their own volition any more nor that their

---

*(Mrs.) Jessie Penn-Lewis in collaboration with Evan Roberts, *War on the Saints*, 7th ed. (Bournemouth, England: "Overcomer" Book Room, n.d.), 69, 70. (Hereinafter cited as Penn-Lewis, WOTS)

will should exercise control over any other segment of their body. They no longer choose, decide, or activate with their will. At first it appears to be a great victory, for amazingly "the 'strong-willed' person suddenly becomes passively yielding." (Penn-Lewis, WOTS, 73) He is as weak as water. He holds no opinion on any affair but obeys orders absolutely. He exercises neither mind, nor will, nor even conscience to distinguish between good and evil, for he is a person of perfect obedience. Only when he is moved does he move; a perfect condition (and an invitation too) for the enemy to come in.

By falling into this state of inaction the Christian now ceases from every activity. Indeed, he waits quietly all the time for some external force to activate him. And unless this force compels him to move he shall remain decidedly inert. If such a situation is permitted to continue this one will discover that sometimes when he knows he should act he cannot because the external force has not come upon him. Moreover, even when he wants to act he finds he is unable to do so. Without that outside power he cannot move a step. His will is suppressed and he is bound; he can move only after that alien force has come to move him.

THE BELIEVER'S FOLLY

The evil spirits take advantage of one's inactive state to accomplish their wiles, while he himself persists in esteeming such inertia as real obedience to God and perfect union with His will. He does not realize that God never demands passivity; it is the powers of darkness which have propelled him into this state. Furthermore, God wants His own to exercise their wills actively to cooperate with Him. This is what is implied in such Scriptures verses as: "if any man's *will* is to do his will, he shall know . . ." (John 7.17) and "ask whatever you *will*, and it shall be done for you" (John 15.7). God never disregards our volition.

We human beings enjoy a free will. God never encroaches on that will. While He does expect us to obey Him, He nevertheless respects our personality (note: the word "personality" as employed in this book has always had in view the person of man, not his character). He wishes us to desire what He desires. He will not usurp our desiring and reduce our volition to deathly inactivity. He needs our most positive cooperation. His pleasure is in the created one reaching his summit, that is, perfect freedom of will. In creation God ordains man to an unfettered will; in redemption He recovers that will. Since He did not *create* man to obey mechanically, how could He expect *redeemed* man to be a robot acting under His remote control direction? The greatness of God is certainly manifested in His not requiring us to turn into wood and stone that we might be obedient. His way is to make us obey Him willingly through the working of His Spirit in our spirit. He refuses to will in place of us.

In a word, the *law* that governs the working of God and the working of Satan in man is exactly the same. God delights in seeing man have free will, so He creates him with such a capacity. It means that humanity has the power to choose and decide all matters concerned. Though God is the Lord of the entire universe, yet is He willing to be restricted by a non-encroachment on man's free will. He never forces man to be loyal to Him. And Satan likewise is unable to usurp any part of man without the latter's *consent* granted either knowingly or unknowingly. Both God and the devil require man to be persuaded before operating in him. When man "desires" good, God will accomplish it; but when he "desires" evil, the wicked spirit will fulfill it. This is what we see in the Garden of Eden.

Before regeneration man's volition was enslaved to Satan and therefore not free. But in a regenerated and overcoming Christian the volition is free and therefore able to choose what is of God. Naturally Satan will not let go, so he devises sundry ways to recapture him. He is fully cognizant that he shall never secure permission openly; hence he uses wiles to obtain the necessary consent. Now mark this well: Satan must gain the believer's permission but the latter will never yield it to Satan; the devil is therefore compelled to resort to deception in order to extract this consent from him.

The evil spirits cannot enter without the acquiescence of man's will and they can penetrate only as far as his will approves.

If the believer knows the principle of spiritual life as well as the conditions for the working of evil spirits he will not fall into such danger. It is because he is unconscious both of the advantage the adversary secures through inertia and of the necessity (in spiritual life) of an active will cooperating with God that he allows his volition to be passive. What we must remember always is that God never substitutes His will for man's. Man himself must be responsible for what he does. God does not decide for him.

If the evil spirits do not operate in some passive persons, then most likely the passivity of these individuals in fact amounts to nothing more than laziness or inactivity. Usually those who are inactive in this way (that is, without the working of the evil spirit) *can* become active at any time. However, if they plunge into such a passivity as to be occupied, then they will be unable to be active even if their will *should* desire it.

Here then is the antithesis between the working of God and the working of Satan. Though God wants man to be yielded completely to Him, He also wants him to use every talent he possesses in cooperation with the Holy Spirit. Satan, on the other hand, demands total cessation of man's will and actions that his evil spirits may operate in his stead. The contrast is truly sobering: God calls man to choose actively, consciously and willingly to do His will so that his spirit, soul, and body may be free; Satan coerces him to be his passive slave and captive: God appoints man to be autonomous, free to be his own master; Satan forces man to be his puppet, a marionette altogether manipulated by him: God never requires man to cease his activities before He can work; Satan bids man to be utterly passive and inactive: God asks man to work together with Him consciously; Satan charges man to obey him passively. It is true that God does require man to cease from his every sinful activity without which he cannot cooperate with the Holy Spirit; but

Satan compels him to cease *all* his activities, including the functioning of his soul, so that his minions can act in place of man. Man is thus reduced to a mere piece of machinery without any conscious responsibility.

It is a terrible circumstance that Christians do not know the fact of God's living in them and the principle of His working in them. They think He wants them to be like pawns on a chessboard that He may maneuver them around as He pleases. They feel they must be absolutely passive, possessing no power to choose or decide, but just to be managed insensibly by God. They forget that when God first created man He made him with a free will. God obviously is not pleased if man wills things other than Himself, but neither is He pleased if man were to obey Him mechanically and unconsciously. He is satisfied when a person wills what He wills, and never wants him to become a will-less person. Many matters must be executed by believers *themselves;* God will not do these for them. It is taught that we must hand everything over to God and let Him do it instead of us—that we must not lift our hands nor move our feet—that we must be so surrendered to the indwelling Holy Spirit that He can arrange everything in lieu of ourselves—that we must let God move us. We grant there is some truth in such teaching but the error therein mixed is perhaps more potent than is the truth. (We shall speak more on this point in the next chapter.)

THE DANGERS

A Christian in his ignorance may be deceived by the powers of darkness, may unwittingly tumble into the trap of Satan, and fulfill the conditions for his working. Let us observe the order of this process, for it is highly important: (1) ignorance, (2) deception, (3) passivity, and (4) entrenchment. Ignorance is the primary cause of this process. Satan can deceive because the saint is unfamiliar both with the demand of the Holy Spirit and the principle of satanic working. Were Christians to apprise themselves of how to cooperate with God and what His procedure of working is, they would never accept Satan's deception. But once deceived, they surmise that for God to live and work through them means for them to remain passive; and so they accept as being from God many supernatural manifestations from evil spirits. The deception grows deeper, finally resulting in an entrenchment of alarming proportions.

It is a vicious cycle: each time ground is given, the evil spirits are encouraged to come in; upon entering, they manifest themselves through sundry activities; and if the believer misinterprets these activities, not knowing that they originate with the devil, he will cede even more place to the evil spirits since he has believed already in their lies. This cycle goes round and round, daily augmenting the degree of penetration. Once he descends into passivity by furnishing a foothold to evil spirits, the dangers can easily multiply.

After one has slipped into inertia and ceases to choose for himself, he will passively succumb to whatever circumstance comes to him. He assumes that it is God Who now is deciding everything for him; all that is therefore required of him is but to passively submit. Whatever happens to him is given and arranged by God; it is His will, hence he must silently accept all things. Shortly afterwards the believer loses all power of choice in his daily life; he can neither decide nor initiate anything which falls within his duty. In addition, he is afraid to express his opinions and is even more unwilling to divulge his preference. And so others must choose and determine for him. Such a victim of the enemy is like seaweed adrift in the ocean waves. He very much hopes that others will decide for him or that his environment will be such that only one alternative is open for him to follow, thus relieving him from the responsibility of having to make a decision. He seems to be happy when forced to do anything, for this keeps him from anxiety which would arise from indecision. He would rather be driven by circumstance than be free to choose his circumstance since making a choice is so trying for him.

In such a condition of inertia, to decide a small matter becomes a tremendous chore! The victim looks for help everywhere. He feels quite embarrassed because he does not know how to cope with his daily affairs. He seems hardly to understand what people say to him. Painful is it for him to recall anything; agonizing is it to make a decision; terrifying, to consider any task. His inert will is impotent to bear such a heavy responsibility. Because of its gross weakness he is compelled to wait for assistance through environment or through men. If he is helped by any particular person he rejoices in receiving such help, yet resents beholding the capture of his will. Who can tally up the hours consumed in waiting for outside aid? Are we suggesting that such a passive believer does not like to work? Not at all; for when compelled by an external force he is able to work; but just have the compulsion terminate and he will halt right in the middle of his labor, feeling himself insufficient in strength to carry on. Innumerable unfinished jobs form the sad testimonials of a passive will.

How inconvenient must this state of inaction be! A believer has to rely on multiplied notes to help him remember; he has to talk aloud to concentrate; he has to devise hundreds of "crutches" to assist him along in life. His senses gradually grow dull until finally he unconsciously develops many idiosyncrasies and queer habits such as not looking straight while talking, bending while walking, exercising little or no mind in any undertaking, either attending too much to physical needs or excessively suppressing bodily requirements, and so forth.

In his foolishness the Christian does not perceive that all these symptoms flow from passivity and invasion but instead believes that they are merely his natural weaknesses. He comforts himself with the thought that these are not too surprising since he is not as gifted or well-endowed as others. He fails to discern the lies of the evil spirits and allows himself to be further deceived. He dare not undertake any task nor do any work because he is so afraid, so nervous, so inarticulate, so dull in mind, or so weak in body. He has never examined why other believers fare so differently. People less talented than he can do far more. And even he himself was much better before. How then can he attribute these symptoms to heredity, natural temperament, and so forth? Know that these are caused by the evil spirits whether one perceives it or not.

Being well acquainted with the believer's current condition, the powers of darkness will foment many troubles in his environment to disturb him. Because his will is passive already and powerless to work, the evil spirits usually will maneuver him into a situation where the exercise of volition is necessary so as to embarrass him and subject him to derision. During such a time, the victim is being harassed by the evil spirits as they please, just like a caged bird that is teased at will by naughty boys. They instigate many difficulties that these may wear out the saint. How distressing that he has not the strength to protest and resist. His circumstances wax worse. He has the authority to deal with the evil spirits, yet he cannot utter a word. The powers of darkness have gained the upper hand, all because their victim has fallen from ignorance to deception, from deception to passivity, and from passivity to the sufferings of deep entrenchment. Nevertheless, he has not yet discerned that such a situation has not been given by God; and so he continues on in his passive acceptance.

When the Christian has sunk into such a state he unconsciously *may even rely upon the help of the evil spirits.* He cannot will anything by himself, hence looks for outside forces to help him. He is troubled often by the evil spirits, yet he innocently expects these same spirits to come to his aid. This is the reason why they desire to make him passive. Holding in their hands the various talents that a believer possesses, they are able to express themselves whenever these talents are exercised. They like to do the willing in place of the person. And the evil spirits certainly are not going to hesitate to exert themselves wherever they are so welcomed. They delight in enticing a person to follow outside revelation blindly without using either thought or will; they therefore often impart a host of strange and supernatural phenomena to men.

The Christian, unaware of the principle of God's working, assumes he is being obedient to *God* when actually he is a prey to deception. Let us be advised of this verse in Romans 6: "Do you not know that if you yield yourselves to anyone as obedient slaves, you are slaves of the one whom you obey . . .?" (v.16) If we offer ourselves in name to God but in actual practice are yielding to the evil spirits we cannot escape being the latter's slave. True, we are deceived; even so, we have yielded openly to the false one and are consequently responsible. The Christian should realize that if he does not commune with God in accordance with the proper conditions for divine fellowship but instead fulfills the requirements for the working of the evil spirits, he will then be enslaved by them.

We ought to review one final time this process culminating in entrenchment. As a person is coveting the physical sensations of God's presence and other similar experiences (as earlier described in Parts Three and Seven) he may be deceived by evil spirits and accorded many counterfeit workings. He naïvely accepts these as from God and accordingly gets himself into a state of passivity. He concludes that he must not make any move, for is it not God Who will move him? He terminates all actions, believing God will act in place of him. But God never does so because He wants man to cooperate actively with Him. However, the believer unwittingly has fulfilled the conditions for the operations of the evil spirits and they do not hesitate to step in and act. Man himself does not act, neither does God act, so the evil spirits act for him. Let the Christian mark this well that once he has perceived the will of God in his spirit's intuition his whole being needs to be employed actively in executing God's will. He should not be passive.

CHAPTER 3

THE BELIEVER'S MISTAKE

We must not fall under the misapprehension that those believers who are deceived by evil spirits must be the most defiled, degenerate, and sinful. They are on the contrary oftentimes fully surrendered Christians spiritually more advanced than ordinary believers. They strive to obey God and are willing to pay any cost. Unwittingly do they stumble into passivity because of the fact that although they are wholly consecrated they know not how to cooperate with God. Those who are less serious about spiritual matters do not face the danger of passivity, for how could anyone sink into inactivity and eventually into the grip of the enemy when, though professing to be utterly consecrated, he persists in living according to his own ideas? He might give ground to evil spirits in other respects but certainly not in the matter of yielding to God's will by delivering a passive ground to the enemy. Only those committed ones who disregard their own interests are open to passivity. Their will can easily slip into this state since they are most eager to obey all orders.

Many will wonder why God does not protect them. Is not their motive pure? How can God permit such faithful seekers of His to be deceived by evil spirits? Many people will contend that He ought to safeguard His Own children under any circumstance; they do not realize that to enjoy God's protection one must fulfill His conditions for protection. Should a person fulfill the conditions for the working of the evil spirits God cannot forbid the latter to work, for He is a law-abiding One. Because the Christian intentionally or unintentionally has surrendered himself to the evil spirits God will not hinder them from the right to control that one. How many hold to the idea that a pure motive safeguards them from deception! Little do they realize that the people most deceived in the world are those with good intentions. Honesty is no condition for not being deceived; but *knowledge* is. Should the believer neglect the teaching of the Bible, failing to watch and pray even though trusting his pure motive to keep him from deception, he shall be deceived. How can he expect God to protect him when he is providing the prerequisites for the working of evil spirits?

Countless saints consider themselves beyond deception because they have had frequent spiritual experiences. This very element of self-confidence betrays the deception they are in already. Unless they are humble enough to acknowledge the possibility of being deceived, they shall be deceived perpetually. Deception is neither a matter of life nor of intention but one of knowledge. It is difficult for the Holy Spirit to point out the truth to that person who has absorbed too many idealistic teachings in the early stages of his Christian experience. Equally hard is it for others to supply him with necessary light if he already has developed a prejudiced interpretation of the Scriptures. The danger of such false security is to give opportunity for the evil spirits to work or to continue to work.

We saw earlier how ignorance is the cause of passivity and passivity, the cause of entrenchment. The latter condition would never occur if a Christian had the right knowledge. Actually passivity is a *mistaken* obedience or consecration. It may additionally be said to be an *excessive* obedience or consecration. Had he recognized how the evil spirits require man's inertia for their working he would not have allowed himself to descend into passivity. Had he realized that God does not reduce man to a marionette in order to work, then he would not wait passively to be moved. Ignorance accounts for today's tragic plight among the saints.

A Christian requires knowledge in order to distinguish God's working from that of Satan's. He should know the principle of divine operation as well as the condition for satanic operation. He who possesses such knowledge guards himself from the powers of darkness. Since Satan assails the believer with lies, he must be met with the truth. Because he intends to keep the believer in darkness, he must be countered with light. Let us learn by heart that the principle governing the working of the Holy Spirit and that of the evil spirit are diametrically opposite. Let us also remember that each operates *according to his respective principle.* Although the evil spirits are skillful in a variety of camouflages, their working principle remains the same. By examining the inward principles we are able to differentiate what is of the Holy Spirit from what is of the evil spirit, for each invariably acts in accordance with his particular principle.

Let us now consider in some detail a number of erroneous conceptions which Christians more than not commonly hold.

A MISTAKEN NOTION CONCERNING CO-DEATH WITH CHRIST

The conditions for passivity in a believer may come about through a wrong interpretation concerning the truth of "death with Christ." Paul says that "I have been crucified with Christ; it is no longer I who live, but Christ who lives in me; and the life I now live in the flesh I live by faith in the Son of God, who loved me and gave himself for me" (Gal. 2.20). Some misconstrue this to connote self-effacement. What they deem to be the summit of spiritual life is "a loss of personality, an absence of volition and self control, and the passive letting-go of the 'I myself' into a condition of machine-like, mechanical, automatic 'obedience'." (Penn-Lewis, WOTS, 86)* They thereafter must harbor no feelings; they should instead renounce all consciousness of personal wishes, interests and tastes. They must aim at self-annihilation, reducing themselves to corpses. Their personality must be totally eclipsed. They misapprehend the command of God to mean a demand for their self-effacement, self-renunciation and self-annihilation so they may no longer

---

*See previous Chapter for full bibliographical citation.

be aware of themselves or their needs but may be conscious only of the movement and operation of God in them. Their misconception about being "dead to self" means for them the absence of self-consciousness. So they endlessly deliver their self-consciousness to nought till they sense nothing but the presence of God. Under this mistaken notion they assume they must practice death; on each occasion therefore when they become aware of "self" or are conscious of personal wants, lacks, needs, interests or preferences they consistently consign these to death.

Since "I have been crucified with Christ," they argue, then *I* no longer exist. And since it is "Christ who lives in me," then *I* no longer live. *I* having died, I must practice death—that is, I must not harbor any thought or feeling. Because Christ is alive within me, He will think or feel in my place. My personality is annihilated, therefore I will obey Him passively, permitting Him to think or feel for me. Unfortunately these people overlook what Paul further said about "the life I now live in the flesh." Paul died, and yet he has not died! This "I" has been crucified, nevertheless "I" still lives in the flesh. Paul, upon having passed through the cross, still declares of himself that "I now live"!

This confirms that the cross does not annihilate our "I"; it exists forever. It is "I" who will one day go to heaven. How can salvation ever benefit *me* if somebody else goes instead of me? The true purport of our accepting co-death with Christ is that we are dead to sin and that we deliver our soul life to death; even the most excellent, most righteous and most virtuous soul life we deliver to death. God beckons us to deny the desire to live by our natural power and to live instead by Him, leaning upon His vitality moment by moment for the supply of every need. This does not in anyway imply that we are to destroy our various functions and settle into passivity. Quite the reverse is true: such a walk with God requires us to exercise our will daily in an active, consistent and believing manner for the denial of our own natural energy and the appropriation of divine energy. Just as neither the death of today's physical body means annihilation nor the death of the lake of fire suggests extermination, so co-death with Christ in the spirit cannot denote effacement. Man as a person must exist; his will must continue: only his natural life must die. This is the teaching of the Holy Scriptures.

The consequences of a misconception of the truth such as this are (1) the believer himself ceases to be active; (2) God cannot use him because he has violated His operating principle; therefore (3) the evil spirits seize the opportunity to invade him since he unwittingly has fulfilled the prerequisites for their working. Due to his misinterpretation of the truth, and his practicing of death, he becomes a tool of the enemy who has disguised himself as God. Alas and alack, this misapprehension of the teaching connected with Galatians 2 has come to be in many cases the prelude to deception.

After such a "death" as this the individual is deprived of any feeling. He cannot feel for himself, nor can he feel for others. He gives those around him the impression of being like iron and stone, utterly devoid of feeling. He does not sense the suffering in others nor is he sensitive to how much pain he has given people himself. He has no ability to sense, to distinguish or to discern things within or without. This person is totally unaware of his own manner, attitude, and action. He speaks and acts without exercising his will and knows not from whence his words, thoughts and feelings originate. Without having made any decision through his own volition these words and feelings nonetheless flow like a river. All his actions are mechanical; no knowledge has he of their sources; he is only spurred on by an alien power. Strange to say, however, unconscious of self as he is, yet is he most sensitive to the treatment accorded him by others. He tends to misunderstand and hence to suffer. In any case, this "unconsciousness" forms both the condition and the consequence of the enemy's penetration. By it the evil spirits are enabled to work, to attack, to suggest, to think, to press or to suppress without the slightest resistance from the believer who is completely unaware of anything.

Let us consequently keep in mind that what people commonly term "death to self" in essence signifies death to the life, power, exercise and activity of self; in no way does it refer to the death of one's personality. We must not efface ourselves and render our personalities non-existent. This is a distinction we must comprehend. When we say without self, we mean without any self-activity, not without self-existence! If a Christian accepts the interpretation which envisages a loss of personality and refuses to think, feel or move, he shall live as one in a dream. Though he conceives himself to be truly dead, entirely selfless, and intensely spiritual, his consecration is not towards God but is as to the evil spirits.

GOD'S WORKING

Another text easily mishandled is Philippians 2.13: "it is God who worketh in you both to will and to work, for his good pleasure" (ASV). To some this passage seems to teach that God performs both the willing and the working; that is, that He puts into His child what He has willed and worked. Since God wills and works instead of him, he himself need not do so. The believer has become a kind of superior creature having no need to will and to do work now that God has done so for him. He is like a mechanical toy which exercises no responsibility of its own to will and do. These saints do not see that the correct substance of this verse is that God works in us up to the point of our readiness to will and to work. He undertakes only to that point and no farther. He never wills or acts in place of man. He merely endeavors to bring man to the position of being disposed to will and to do His excellent will.

Man himself must perform the willing and the working. The Apostle carefully states, "*you* both to will and to work" —not God wills and works, but *you;* your personality continues to exist and hence you yourself must will and act because the responsibility is yours. God is indeed at work, but never does He substitute Himself for us. To choose and to do belong to the man. God wants to move us, melt us and encourage us, so that our hearts may bend towards His will, yet he does not will instead of us to do His will. He turns us towards His desire, then leaves us to make up our will. What the Word teaches here is that one's volition requires the support of God's power. How ineffectual and fruitless are deeds done according to one's own volition apart from Him. God does not will in man's stead, but neither does He desire man to will independently. He calls him to will in His power, which is to say, to will according to His working in man.

Not comprehending the correct meaning of this passage the believer surmises that he need not will. He thus allows another volition to control his being. He dare not decide any issue, choose any action, or even resist any power, but passively waits for the will of God to come to him. When an external volition decides for him he passively accepts it. He quenches whatever proceeds from his own volition. And the result: neither he himself uses his volition nor God uses it to choose and decide for him, since He requires active co-operation. But the evil spirits seize his passive will and act instead of him.

We need to see the difference between God willing for us and our volition cooperating with God. If He were to choose and decide *in lieu* of us we would have no real connection with the act or deed done because our hearts would not have been exercised towards it. And when we come to ourselves afterwards we would know that it was not done by *us*. But if we exercise our volition and actively cooperate with God, *we* undertake to do the thing ourselves though in the divine power. A person under deception may consider himself the doer, speaker and thinker, but when enlightened by God he realizes he does not really want to so do, speak and think. He knows he has no connection with these acts because they were performed by the enemy.

It is not God's purpose to annihilate our volition. If we say we henceforth shall have no volition of our own but shall let His will be manifested in our body we have not offered ourselves to God; instead, we have covenanted with the evil spirit since God never substitutes His will for ours. The right attitude is this: that I have my own will, yet I will the will of God. We should put our volition on His side—and even this is to be done not by our own strength but by the life of God. The truth of the whole matter is that the life which formerly energized our volition has now been committed to death so that now we engage our volition in the energizing life of God. We do not eliminate our will; it is still there; only the life has changed. What has died is our own life; the function of the will continues although renewed by God. Hereafter the volition is energized by the new life.

THE WORK OF THE HOLY SPIRIT

Those believers are numberless who have plunged into passivity and enslavement because of not understanding the work of the Holy Spirit. What follows are some of the most common misunderstandings.

1. *Obey the Holy Spirit.* Believers think Acts 5.32 suggests that they must obey the Holy Spirit—"the Holy Spirit whom God has given to those who obey him." But they fail, according to the command given in the Bible, to test all the spirits to see if they are of truth or of error (1 John 4.1,6). They instead accept as being the Holy Spirit every spirit which comes to them. They think this obedience must be highly pleasing to God. What they do not know is that the Scripture here does not teach us to obey the Holy Spirit but to obey God the Father through the Spirit. In verse 29 of Acts 5 the Apostles when under questioning by the council replied that they "must obey *God.*" Should anyone make God the Spirit his object of obedience and forget God the Father he tends to obey the spirit in him or around him instead of obeying through the Holy Spirit the Father Who is in heaven. This will set him on the road to passivity and in addition provide the evil spirits the chance for counterfeit. Overstepping the bounds of the Word of God ushers in countless perils!

2. *The Rule of the Holy Spirit.* We will recall from our past discussion how God rules our spirit through the Holy

Spirit and how our spirit rules our body or the entire person through the soul (or will). This may sound simple, yet the spiritual implication is enormous. The Holy Spirit influences our intuition alone to make His will known. Only our spirit does he fill and nowhere else. *Never does He control or fill our soul or body directly.* This point should be carefully underscored. We should *not* therefore expect God's Spirit to think through our mind, feel through our emotion, or decide through our volition. He makes His will known to our spirit's intuition in order that we ourselves may think and feel and act according to His will. It is a grave blunder to think we must offer our mind to the Holy Spirit to let Him think through it. The truth is He never uses man's mind directly instead of man. He never asks him to offer himself passively to Him. What God wishes is cooperation with him. He does not work for man, because even His movement in working for him could be quenched by the believer. He never forces anyone to do anything.

The divine Spirit does not directly control man's body either. If man desires to speak he has to engage his *own* mouth—to walk, his *own* feet—to work, his *own* hands. The Spirit of God never interferes with man's freedom of will. Aside from working in man's spirit (which is God's new creation), He does not use any part of man's body apart from the consent of the latter's own volition; nay, even if man is willing, He does not exercise any of his bodily parts for him. Man should be his own master. He must exercise his own body. This is God's law which He will not violate.

We often say that "the Holy Spirit rules over man." By this we mean He works in us to make us obedient to God. But if we should mean that He directly controls our total being we are in complete error. We can distinguish right here between the work of the Holy Spirit and that of evil spirits. The Holy Spirit indwells us to witness that *we belong to God* whereas evil spirits manipulate people to reduce them to robots. God's Spirit asks for our cooperation; evil spirits seek direct control. Hence it is plain that our union with God is in the spirit and not in the body or soul. Should we misunderstand the truth and expect God to move our mind, emotion, volition, and body directly, we open wide the door to the counterfeit of evil spirits. While a Christian should not follow his own thought, feeling or preference, nevertheless after he has received revelation in his spirit he ought to *execute* with his mind, emotion and will this charge which has come to his spirit.

SPIRITUAL LIFE

Among the various misconceptions relating to spiritual life can be found the following.

1. *Speaking*. The text used is Matthew 10.20: "it is not you who speak, but the Spirit of your Father speaking through you." Christians often assume that God will speak for them. Some imagine that while delivering a message in a meeting they must not employ their mind and will but simply offer their mouths passively to God, letting Him speak through them. Needless to say, however, the words of Jesus recorded in this particular passage are to be applied only to the time of persecution and trial. It does not suggest that the Holy Spirit will speak instead of the believer. The experience of the Apostles Peter and John in the council fulfills this prediction.

2. *Guidance*. Text: "And your ears shall hear a word behind you, saying, 'This is the way, walk in it'" (Is. 30.21). Saints do not perceive that this verse refers specifically to the experience of God's earthly people, the Jews, during the millennial kingdom when there shall be no satanic counterfeit. Unaware of this fact they view supernatural guidance in a voice to be the highest form of guidance. They esteem themselves more spiritual than the rest and hence receive supernatural guidance of this type. They neither listen to their conscience nor follow their intuition; they merely wait in a passive manner for the supernatural voice. These believers hold that they do not need to think, ponder, choose or decide. They simply need to obey. They permit the voice to be substituted for their intuition and conscience. And the consequence is that "(a) he does not use his conscience; (b)

God does not speak to him for automatic obedience; (c) evil spirits take the opportunity and supernatural voices are substituted for the action of the conscience." (Penn-Lewis, WOTS, 121) The outcome is that the enemy gains more ground in the believer. And "from this time (forward) the man is not influenced by what he feels or sees, or by what others say, and he closes himself to all questions, and will not reason. This substitution of supernatural guidance for the action of the conscience explains the deterioration of the moral standard in persons with supernatural experiences, because they have really substituted the direction of evil spirits for their conscience. They are quite unconscious that their moral standard is lowered, but their conscience has become seared by deliberately ceasing to heed its voice; and by listening to the voices of the teaching spirits, in matters which should be decided by the conscience in respect to their being right or wrong, good or evil." (Penn-Lewis, WOTS, 121-22)

3. *Memory.* Text: "But the Counselor, the Holy Spirit, whom the Father will send in my name, he will teach you all things, and bring to your remembrance all that I have said to you" (John 14.26). Christians do not grasp that this verse means the Counselor will enlighten their mind so that *they* may remember what the Lord has spoken. They instead think it instructs them not to engage their memory because God shall bring all things to their minds. They accordingly allow their memory to degenerate into passivity; they do not exercise their wills to remember. And what is the outcome?— "(a) the man himself does not use his memory; and (b) God does not use it, because He will not do so apart from the believer's co-action; (c) evil spirits use it, and substitute their workings in the place of the believer's volitional use of his memory." (Penn-Lewis, WOTS, 121)

4. *Love.* Text: "God's love has been poured into our hearts through the Holy Spirit which has been given to us" (Rom. 5.5). Believers misconstrue this to signify that they are not themselves to love but to let the Holy Spirit dispense God's love to them. They petition God to love through them

that His love may be supplied abundantly so as to fill them with divine love. They no longer will love for hereafter it is God Who must make them love. They cease to exercise their faculty of affection, permitting its function to sink into total paralysis. With the result that (a) the believer himself does not love; (b) God will not bestow supernatural love upon him in disregard of the man or the operation of his natural affection; and so (c) evil spirits substitute themselves for the man and express their love or hate through him. And once he has abandoned the use of his will to control his affection the evil spirits put their counterfeit love in him. Thereafter he behaves like wood and stone, cold and dead to all affections. This explains why many saints, though holy, are scarcely approachable.

"You shall love the Lord your God with all your heart, and with all your soul, and with all your mind, and with all your strength," says the Lord Jesus (Mark 12.30). Now *whose* love is this? Exactly whose heart, soul, mind and strength is brought into view here? It is of course ours. Our natural life needs to die, but these natural endowments and their functions remain.

5. *Humility*. Text: "Not that we venture to class or compare ourselves with some of those who commend themselves" (2 Cor. 10.12 ff.). Believers misjudge this long passage from verse 12 to 18 as signifying a call to hide themselves to the extent that they are left without a proper self-regard, one which God unquestionably permits us to have. Not a few instances of self-abasement are essentially a disguise for passivity. Consequently: (a) the believer effaces himself; (b) God does not fill him; and (c) evil spirits exploit his passivity to render him useless.

When the Christian is self-abased under the enemy's penetration his surroundings appear entirely dark, hopeless and desolate to him. He gives the impression of being deadly cold and dishearteningly melancholic to all who are in contact with him. He himself easily faints and is discouraged. At critical moments he deserts the fight and withdraws, thus embarrassing others. God's work is not too important to him.

In speech and work he tries hard to hide himself, but this only manifests his self the more—to the great sorrow of the truly spiritual. Due to his excessive disregard for himself he stands by watching when there is such great need in the kingdom of God. He exhibits perpetual inability, hopelessness, and wounded feelings. While he may envisage this to be humility he does not realize it is but the work of the evil spirits. True humility is able to look at God and proceed on.

GOD'S ORDERING

We know that besides man's will there are two other totally antagonistic wills in the world. God calls us to obey Him and to resist Satan. Twice in the Bible do we find these two sides mentioned together: (1) "submit yourselves therefore to God," exhorts James, and then he follows immediately with "resist the devil" (4.7); (2) "humble yourselves therefore under the mighty hand of God," enjoins Peter, and continues by charging his readers to "resist (the devil), firm in your faith" (1 Peter 5.6,9). This is the balance of truth. A believer certainly must learn to submit himself to God in all matters, acknowledging that what He orders for him is the best. Though he suffers, yet he heartily submits to the will of God. This, however, is just *half* the truth. The Apostles understood the danger of being lopsided; hence we find them right away warning the Christian to resist the devil once he submits to God. This is because there is another will besides His, that of Satan's. Frequently the devil counterfeits the will of God, especially in the things which happen to us. If we are unaware of the presence of a will other than God's, we can easily mistake Satan's to be God's and so fall into the devil's trap. For this reason God wants us to resist the devil when we submit to Him. Resistance is done by the *will*. Resistance means our volition opposes, disapproves, and withstands. God wishes us to exercise our volition, therefore He exhorts us to "resist the devil." He will not resist for us; we ourselves must do so. We have a will; we should use it to take heed to God's Word. So teaches the Bible. Thinking that God's will is revealed in His orderings, the Christian may accept anything which comes to him as His will. In that event he naturally will not employ his volition to choose, decide or resist. He just quietly accepts everything. This sounds good and appears right, but it contains a serious fallacy.

Now we do acknowledge the hand of God behind everything, and we do confess we must submit fully under His hand. But the point at issue here is more one of attitude than of conduct. If what happens to us is the direct will of God, would we object to it? This is a matter of our heart intention. But after we are assured of our obedience to God we should inquire further: does this emanate from the evil spirit or is it but God's permissive will? If it is His commanded will, we have no objection; if otherwise, we will resist it together with God. Hence this never implies that we should submit to our environment without daily examination and testing. Our *attitude* remains the same at all times, but our *practice* comes only after we are sure of God's will, for how could we submit to Satan's will?

A Christian ought not act as one who is without a brain, passively driven by his environment. He actively and consciously should examine the source of every item, test its nature, understand its meaning, and decide the course to take. It is important to obey God, but not blindly. Such active investigation is not a sign of rebellion against God's ordering, because our heart's intent continues to be one of submission towards God. We only wish to be sure that in our submission we are verily obeying *God*. A definite lack in an obedient attitude exists among believers today. Though they perceive God's will, they nevertheless fail to yield. Contrariwise, those who have been broken by God run to the other extreme by unquestioningly accepting whatever occurs to them. The truth lies in the center; *obey* in heart and *accept* after being assured of the source.

How sad, though, that many fully consecrated believers do not discern this difference. Such a Christian therefore passively submits to his environment, surmising that *everything* happens to him by the order of God. He gives ground to the evil spirits to torment and hurt him. These spirits provide environment (their snares) by which to trap the saint into performing their will or raise up circumstances to trouble him. Believers may misunderstand this to be what Matthew 5.39 enjoins when it says "do not resist one who is evil," not recalling that God summons them to struggle against sin (Heb. 12.4). By overcoming environment they are ovecoming the spirit of this world.

The factors in such a misapprehension of God's ordering are that (a) believers do not use their will to choose and decide; (b) God certainly does not oppress them with environment; and (c) the evil spirits utilize the environmental circumstances as a substitute for their passive will. Rather than obeying God these believers actually are obeying the evil spirits.

SUFFERINGS AND WEAKNESSES

Having fully surrendered to God the Christian naturally concedes that he should walk in the way of the cross and suffer for Christ's sake. He additionally acknowledges the futility of his natural life and is willing to be weak in order that he may be strengthened by the power of God. These two attitudes are commendable but they can be utilized by the enemy if they are not rightly understood.

Having recognized that there is something of great profit in suffering, the Christian following consecration may submit passively to whatever comes to him without question. He simply believes he is suffering for the Lord and that therefore it is both profitable and rewarding. Little does he understand that, unless he intentionally exercises his will both to accept what God allots and to resist what the enemy dispenses, his passive acceptance of *all* suffering will surely afford an excellent opportunity to the evil spirit to torment him. Suffering at the hand of the evil spirit while believing the satanic lie that his suffering emanates from God merely gives the enemy the right to prolong the assault. The person is unaware that his suffering does not arise from God but arises out of his fulfilling the conditions for the working of evil spirits. He still pictures himself as suffering for the church that he may complete what is lacking in Christ's afflictions for the sake of His body. He conceives himself a martyr whereas in fact he is a victim. He glories in these sufferings, yet they constitute but symptoms of the adversary's entrenchment.

We should notice that all these afflictions which flow from the work of the evil spirits are meaningless—positively fruitless and purposeless. Apart from the fact that one is suffering, there is no sense to it. The Holy Spirit does not bear witness in our intuition that this proceeds from God.

Should the believer investigate a little he may discover that he did not encounter such experiences before he offered himself to the Lord and *chose to suffer.* Having made the choice, he automatically accepted all sufferings as from God, although most are triggered by the power of darkness. He has surrendered ground to the evil spirits; he has believed their lies; and his life is consequently marked by unreasonable and ineffectual sufferings. Knowing the truth concerning the deep workings of the evil spirit helps the individual not only to overcome sins but to eliminate unnecessary afflictions as well.

The child of God may hold this same erroneous concept concerning weakness. He thinks he should maintain a condition of weakness if he is ever to possess God's strength. For has not the Apostle Paul asserted that "when I am weak, then I am strong" (2 Cor. 12.10)? He accordingly *wills* to be weak that he too may be strong. He does not observe that the Apostle has not *willed* to be weak but that he is merely relating to us his experience of how the grace of God strengthens him in his frailty for the accomplishment of God's purpose. Paul has not desired this infirmity; yet he is strengthened by God in that infirmity. Paul is not to be found persuading a strong believer to *purposely choose* weakness in order that God may strengthen him afterwards. He simply is showing the *weak* believer the way to strength!

Choosing weakness and choosing suffering both fulfill the requirements for the operation of evil spirits since by so doing man's will is placed on the enemy's side. This explains why countless children of God who enjoyed good health in the beginning find themselves weakened daily after they have chosen to be weak. The strength they expect does not emerge: they soon become a burden to others: they are useless in God's work. Such a choice does not draw down God's power; rather does it furnish the evil spirits ground for attack. Unless these saints persistently resist this debility they shall encounter prolonged weakness.

THE VITAL POINT

What we have described may be applied primarily to serious cases; many other people have not gone to such an extreme. The principle involved is nonetheless the same for all. The devil does not fail to act whenever there is *passivity of will* or a *fulfillment of his working conditions*. Although some Christians may not specifically choose suffering or weakness, they nevertheless *unwittingly* allow themselves to sink into passivity, thus ceding place to the enemy and falling into a perilous situation. Let anyone who has the above experience ask himself whether he has fulfilled the operating requirements of the evil spirits. This will save him from many counterfeit occurrences and unnecessary sufferings.

We know the enemy makes use of the truth, yet he overextends it beyond its bounds. Which of the following is not of truth: self-denial, submission, waiting for God's ordering, suffering, and so forth? Even so, evil spirits exploit the believer's ignorance of the principle of spiritual life to divert him into fulfilling their operating requirements. If we fail to judge the underlying principle of any teaching, as to whether it meets the conditions of the Holy Spirit or that of evil spirits, we shall be deceived. Any overextension of the truth is most precarious. Let us be very cautious in this regard.

By now we should be acquainted fully with the basic distinction between the working of God and that of Satan: (a) *God wants the believer to cooperate with Him by exercising his will and using all his abilities in order that he may be filled with the Holy Spirit;* but that (b) *to facilitate his work the evil spirit demands the believer to be passive in his will and to deny the use of either part or all of his abilities.* In the first case, God's Spirit fills the spirit of man and imparts life, power, release, enlargement, renewal, and strength to the man that he may be free and unshackled. In the second case, Satan occupies man's passive organs and, if undetected, proceeds to destroy his personality and will by reducing him to a puppet, subduing his soul and body, and leaving him bound, oppressed, ravaged and imprisoned. The Holy Spirit enables the believer to know the will of God in his intuition so that he may understand it afterwards with his mind and carry it out later by freely exercising his will. The satanic spirit, however, so puts the person under the oppression of an external power that it appears to him to represent God's will and compels him to act like a machine devoid of thought or decision.

Today many of God's children have fallen unknowingly into passivity: their will and mind cease to function; hence they experience untold sufferings. All simply happens according to law. Just as there is a law to everything in the natural realm, so is there also a law to everything in the spiritual realm: certain actions produce certain results. God Who establishes these laws is Himself law-abiding. Whoever violates one of these laws, willfully or unintentionally, must reap the corresponding consequence. But if man exercises his will, mind and strength to cooperate with God, His Spirit will then work, for this too is a law.

CHAPTER 4
THE PATH TO FREEDOM

IT IS POSSIBLE FOR a consecrated Christian to be deceived into passivity for some years without ever awakening to his dangerous plight. The degree of inactivity will increase in scope until he suffers unspeakable pain in mind, emotion, body and environment. To present the true meaning of consecration to these ones thus becomes vitally important. The knowledge of truth is absolutely necessary for deliverance from passivity, without which freedom is *impossible*. We know that a believer falls into passivity through deception but this latter in turn is caused by a lack of knowledge.

THE KNOWLEDGE OF TRUTH

The very first step to freedom is to know the truth of all things: truth concerning cooperation with God, the operation of evil spirits, consecration, and supernatural manifestations. The child of God must know the truth as to the source and nature of the experiences he may have been having if he expects to be delivered. Since his descent was (1) deception, (2) passivity, (3) entrenchment, and (4) further deception and passivity, then the way to release will be initially the uncovering of deception. Once the early deceit is dissolved, passivity, entrenchment and further deceit will disintegrate. Deception unlatches the gate for the evil spirits to rush in; passivity provides a place for them to stay; and the result of these two is entrenchment. To dispossess them requires an ending of passivity which in turn needs the exposure of deception, and this is brought about by nothing else save the knowledge of truth. Knowledge of truth is therefore the first stage towards freedom. Only the truth can set people free.

We have cautioned our readers repeatedly about the danger of supernatural experience. We are not suggesting that every such manifestation must be categorically resisted, forsaken and opposed: this would be at variance with Biblical teaching since the Scriptures record numerous supernatural acts of God. Our purpose simply has been to remind Christians that there can be more than one source behind supernatural phenomena; God can perform wonders, but so can evil spirits imitate! How crucial for us to distinguish what is of God from what is not of God. If one has not died to his emotional life but earnestly seeks sensational events, he will be easily duped. We do not urge people to resist all supernatural manifestations, but we do exhort them to resist every supernatural occurrence which derives from Satan. So what we have tried to point out throughout this Part of the book has been the basic differences between the operation of the Holy Spirit and that of the evil spirit so as to help God's children discern which is which.

It can be stated that present day Christians are particularly susceptible to trickery in supernatural matters. Our earnest hope is that in their contact with supernatural phenomena they shall first undertake the task of discriminating lest they be beguiled. They must not overlook the fact that when the supernatural experience is authored by the Holy Spirit they are still able to engage their own mind; it is not required that they be totally or partially passive before they obtain such an experience. And afterwards too they are still able to exercise their conscience freely to distinguish good and evil without the least inhibition. But should the experience be authored by the evil spirit, then the victims must settle into passivity, their mind be blank, and their every action be performed under outside compulsion. Such is the essential difference. The Apostle Paul mentions in 1 Corinthians 14 various spiritual gifts among which are revelation, prophecy, tongues and other supernatural manifestations. He ac-

knowleges these gifts as flowing from the Holy Spirit, yet he
defines the nature of these God-given gifts in these words:
"the spirits of prophets are subject to prophets" (v.32). If
what the prophets (believers) receive is from the Holy Spirit,
then the spirits they receive will be subject to them. This
means that the Holy Spirit Who bestows diverse supernatural
experiences upon men will not infringe on their rights by
manipulating any part of their bodies against their wills.
They continue to retain the power of *self-control*. Only that
spirit which is subject to the prophet or believer is from
God; any spirit which demands the prophet to be subject
to it is not from God. Although we should not oppose all
supernatural elements, we nonetheless should judge whether
these supernatural spirits require a man's passive subjection or not. The workings of the Holy Spirit and those of
the evil spirit are fundamentally opposite: the Former
wishes men to be sovereignly free; the latter requires him
to be altogether passive. The believer should judge his experience by this criterion. Learning whether he has been
passive or not can be the solution to all his problems.

Should the child of God desire freedom his folly must be
removed. In other words, he must know the truth. He needs
to appreciate the real nature of affairs. Satanic lies bind, but
God's truth unshackles. Naturally the knowledge of truth is
going to be costly, for it will shatter the vainglory one has
assumed due to his past experiences. He looks upon himself
as far more advanced than others, as being spiritual and
infallible. How hard hit he will be if he confesses the possibility of his being invaded or if he is shown to have been so
invaded! Unless God's child sincerely adheres to all the truth
of God, it becomes very rough for him to accept this kind
of painful and humiliating truth. One encounters no difficulty in accepting that truth which is agreeable; but it is not
easy at all to take in a truth which blasts one's ego. To acknowledge himself as liable to deception is relatively easy;
whereas to confess that he is entrenched by the enemy already is most difficult. May God be gracious, for even after
a person has known the truth he may yet resist it. The ac-

ceptance of truth is thus the first step to salvation. The child
of God must be willing to know all the truth concerning
himself. This requires humility and sincerity. Therefore let
him who vehemently opposes such truth beware lest unknowingly he actually be enslaved.

The roads to truth are many and various. Some are awakened to their true state upon discovering that they have lost
their liberty in all respects through their protracted and
serious satanic bondage; others whose experiences may be
ninety per cent of God and only ten per cent impurity come
to know the truth when they begin to doubt their experience;
still others are brought to a knowledge of their condition
through the truth given them by other believers. In any
event, the Christian should not refuse the first ray of light
which shines upon him.

Doubting is the prelude to truth. By this is not meant
to doubt the Holy Spirit or God or His Word but to doubt
one's own past experience. Such doubt is both necessary and
scriptural because God commands us to "test the spirits" (1
John 4.1). Believers often embrace a wrong idea: they are
afraid to examine the spirits lest they sin against the Holy
Spirit. But it is He Himself Who desires us to make the test.
Now if it turns out to be the Holy Spirit He can stand the
test; if however it is the evil spirit its true nature will accordingly be exposed. Is it God Who has in fact caused you
to fall into today's position? Does the Holy Spirit ever work
contrary to His law? Are you really infallible in all matters?

Having received some light as to the truth, the believer
next can readily admit that he is susceptible to deception.
And this affords the truth a working opportunity. The worst
fallacy one can ever commit is to reckon oneself infallible.
To maintain that others may be wrong but never he is to be
duped to the very end. Only after he is self-abased will he
be able to see that he is genuinely deceived. By comparing
the principle of divine working against the conditions of satanic working, he concludes that his past experiences were
obtained through passivity. He had fulfilled the requirements
for the working of the evil spirits, hence was given those many

strange manifestations which made him happy initially but which pained him ultimately. He had not cooperated actively with God but had instead passively followed that will which he had taken for granted must be God's. Both his happy and painful experiences must have originated with evil spirits. He consequently now admits how deceived he has been. The child of God not only must accept the truth but in addition must admit his condition in the light of that truth. In this way the lie of the enemy shall be annulled. Thus one's experience here is to (a) acknowledge that a *believer* is open to deception; (b) admit that *he* too is subject to duplicity; (c) confess that *he* is deceived; and next (d) further inquire as to why he was beguiled.

THE DISCOVERY OF GROUND

We may now infer that ground must have been furnished the evil spirit. But what is the ground which a believer supplies? Before he considers what ground he has given, let him first review exactly what ground is.

The believer ought to realize that besides sin there are other elements which can afford ground to evil spirits: the acceptance of a counterfeit, passivity of will, and assent to the enemy's flashing thought. For the present we focus our attention on passivity, that is, on allowing our mind or body to sink into a coma-like state, ceasing to exercise conscious control over the mind, and inactivating the proper functions of the will, conscience and memory. Passivity, though there are various gradations of it, forms the principal ground. The scope of the enemy's penetration is determined by the degree of passivity. As soon as the person becomes aware of an inert condition—whatever its degree—he must recover that ground at once. Firmly, intently and persistently he should oppose the enemy's attempt to maintain any footing in him, especially in the areas where he has been deceived. It is indispensable that he know the ground and recover it.

Upon realizing he has been deceived, the believer should next seek light concerning the ground he has lost and try to recover it. Since evil spirits maintain their position on the territory surrendered to them, they shall leave once that area is cleared away.

Because the Christian has fallen into passivity and deception by not using his will in self-control, he now must exercise his will actively to resist through the power of God the powers of darkness in every temptation and suffering and to cancel his earlier promises to them. Since passivity came in gradually, it will be eliminated gradually. The measure of one's detection of his inertia is the measure of that one's emancipation. If the duration of his inactivity has been long, the longer will it take to be delivered. To descend a mountain is always easier than to ascend it; in like manner, to become passive is easy but to regain freedom is painstaking. It requires the cooperation of the total man to retake all forfeited ground.

The child of God definitely should ask God to show him where he has been deceived. He must sincerely desire to have *all* the truth about himself revealed. Generally speaking, whatever the believer fears to hear will probably pertain to the ground given the enemy. What he is afraid to deal with is the very item he should dispense with, for nine out of ten times the enemy has established his footing right there. How necessary that the Christian beseech God to shed light on his symptoms and their causes so that he may recapture the lost territory. Enlightenment is a "must"; without it the believer tends to interpret the supernatural as being something natural, the spiritual (of the evil spirits) as being something physical. And so he provides ground for the enemy.

THE RECOVERY OF GROUND

One common principle underlies the way all ground is relinquished to evil spirits: it is through passivity, the inactivity of the will. If lost ground is ever to be recovered it is mandatory that the volition be reactivated. The Christian henceforth must learn (a) to obey God's will, (b) to resist the devil's will, and (c) to exercise his own will in collaboration with the will of the other saints. Responsibility for recovering ceded territory rests chiefly on the will, It is the volition which became passive, hence it must be the volition which dispels passivity.

The first measure the will undertakes is to *resolve*, that is, to set itself towards a definite direction. Having suffered much at the hands of evil spirits but now enlightened by the truth and encouraged by the Holy Spirit, the child of God is led naturally to a new position of abhorring those wicked spirits. He accordingly resolves against all their works. He is determined to regain his freedom, be his own master, and drive off his enemy. The Spirit of God so works in him that his fury against the evil spirits gathers momentum. The more he suffers the more he hates; the more he ponders his plight the more furious he becomes. He resolves to experience a complete emancipation from the powers of darkness. Such a resolve is the first step towards the recovery of lost ground. If this resolution is real he will press on towards the goal no matter how fierce a fight the enemy may put up. The entire man supports his resolve to henceforth oppose the adversary.

The Christian also should engage his will to choose, that is to decide the future he desires. In days of spiritual battle this choice can be very effective. He should ever and anon declare: I choose freedom; I want liberty; I refuse to be passive; I will use my own talents; I insist on knowing the wiles of the evil spirits; I wish for their defeat; I will sever every relationship with the powers of darkness; I oppose all their lies and excuses. Such a declaration of the will is highly beneficial in warfare. It expresses his *choice*, not simply his resolve, on these particular matters. The powers of darkness pay no attention to one's resolve, but should he choose with his will to oppose them through the power of God then they most certainly shall flee. All this is related to the principle of the freedom of man's will. Just as in the beginning the believer permitted the evil spirits to enter, so now he chooses the very opposite, the undercutting of any footing of the enemy.

During this period of conflict the Christian's will must be engaged actively in various operations. Beyond resolving and choosing, he also ought to *resist*. That is to say, his will must exert its force to contend with the evil spirits. He moreover should *refuse*—shut the door against—the entry of the enemy. By resisting he prohibits the evil spirits from further working; by refusing he cancels the former permission he had granted them. Refusal in addition to resistance practically immobilizes all the perpetrations of the enemy. Resisting is our attitude regarding what lies ahead of us; refusing is our position regarding what lies behind. For instance: by proclaiming that "I will to have my freedom" we are refusing the evil spirits; yet we need as well to resist, that is, to exert strength in combating the enemy so that we may keep the freedom we have just obtained through refusal. Both refusal and resistance must be continued until complete emancipation is won.

To resist is truly a battle. It requires all the strength of the spirit, soul and body. Nevertheless, the main force is the will. To resolve, choose and refuse are primarily questions of attitude; but to resist is a matter of overt practice. It is a conduct expressive of an attitude. It is wrestling in the spirit, which is to say, that the will through the strength of the spirit *pushes* the evil spirits off the ground they presently occupy. It is an assault against the enemy line. In resisting, one employs one's will power to drive, push and chase off. The enemy spirits, even should they perceive the believer's hostile attitude against them, will not budge an inch from the ground they occupy. They must be driven out with real force. The child of God must mobilize spiritual power to immobilize and remove the enemy. He must *exercise* his will to chase them away. A mere declaration of intention is insufficient. It needs to be coupled with practical measures. Resistance without refusal is similarly ineffective, because the ground originally promised to the enemy must be recovered.

In retaking surrendered territory the believer must use his will on the one side to resolve, choose and refuse and on the other to resist. He should resolve to fight, choose freedom, refuse ground, and resist the enemy. He must contend for his sovereignty. This element of free will should never be lost sight of. God has granted us an unhampered volition that we may be our own masters, but today the evil spirits have usurped our members and talents. They have become man's master; he has lost his sovereign rights. To oppose this the believer enters the fray. He continually declares: I am not willing to let the evil spirits encroach on my sovereign rights; I will not allow them to invade my personality; I will not permit them to possess me; I will not follow them blindly; I will not consent to their manipulating me; I will not, I verily am unwilling; I intend to be my own master; I know what I do; I resolve to control myself; I prefer to have my entire being subject to myself; I resist all the works of the wicked ones as well as their right to work on me. In resolving, choosing and refusing with our will we arrest any further working of the enemy. Thereafter we must resist with our will.

The believer commences his life anew following the recovery of his ground. The past is over, and now marks a new beginning. What was offered to the evil spirits has all been reclaimed. The spirit, soul and body of the whole person are retrieved from the enemy's hand and are rededicated to God. Every inch of the territory surrendered through ignorance has today, one upon another, been recovered. The sovereign power of man is once again returned to him. And how is this done? By rejecting what once was accepted; disbelieving what once was believed; withdrawing from what once he drew nigh to before; destroying what once was erected; canceling what once was covenanted; retrieving what once was promised; dissolving what once was joined; resisting what once was obeyed; uttering what once went unspoken; opposing what once was cooperated with; and denying what once was given. Every past consideration, counsel, and permission must be overthrown; even past prayers and answers must be denied.

Without a doubt every one of these dealings runs directly against the evil spirits. Formerly an intimate association had been formed with these spirits through mistaking them for the Holy Spirit; presently, with the newly added knowledge, all which was yielded to them in ignorance must be retrieved. Just as each ground *one after another* was ceded, so now all must be reclaimed *specifically*. The greatest hindrance to complete liberty is the believer's unwillingness to recover all territory carefully: point by point, one after another. He tends to exercise his will in a general, vague and inclusive way to retake all ground. Such general opposition merely indicates the correctness of the believer's attitude. To be set free he must restore everything specifically. This may seem laborious but if he genuinely wills to be released and prays for God's light, the Holy Spirit gradually shall reveal the past to him. By resisting them one by one, all eventually shall be dissolved. By patiently pressing forward he shall experience deliverance in one area after another. He is on his way to freedom. To resist in a general way shows we do really oppose the evil spirits; but only resisting in specific fashion can force them to desert the ground they occupy.

Step by step the will of the Christian had descended downhill till it became totally passive. Now he must reverse the process and step by step ascend to freedom. He must retrace all the stages by which he descended, only this time his direction will be upward. Previously he was deceived into passivity by degrees; he now needs to reactivate his will in the same manner. All his earlier passivity must be restored one by one. Each movement upward bespeaks some regaining of ground. Whatever was most recently lost to the evil spirits is usually the first ground to be recovered, just as in climbing stairs we ascend the last step of our descent first.

The child of God must reclaim all footholds until he arrives at the freedom he first enjoyed. He should know *from where* he has fallen since it is to that place that he must be restored. He ought to understand what was hitherto normal for him—how active his will and how clear his mind were in the beginning—as well as what his current condition is. By comparing these two states he will be able to ascertain how far he has descended into passivity. Whatever his normal state was, that must he now set before himself as the minimum standard or goal of his ascent. He should not be satisfied until his will is restored to its original state, that is, until it actively controls every part of his being. He should never deem himself free before his normalcy has once more been regained.

Hence the child of God needs to recover completely every function of his being which has toppled from normalcy into passivity—whether that function be to think, to recall, to imagine, to discern right from wrong, to resolve, to choose, to refuse, to resist, to love, or whatever. Everything over which he has relinquished control must be restored to his personal sovereignty. He should exercise his volition to oppose inertia as well as to make use of all these functions of man. When he tumbled into passivity the evil spirits seized upon his passive organs and used them instead of him. The attempt to reclaim lost areas and regain personal use of his organs may be exceedingly difficult for the believer. This is due to the facts that (a) his own will is necessarily weak yet and hence powerless to direct every portion of his being; and (b) the evil spirits contend against him with their full strength. If for example he has been passive in the matter of decision he will now cancel the ground given and forbid the evil spirits to work any more. He is determined to decide for himself without any of their interference. But he finds (a) that he cannot decide and (b) that the evil spirits do not let him decide and act. When the believer refuses them permission to control him, they will not allow their captive to act without their permission.

Right here must the believer choose: is he going to be forever passive, is he going to let the evil spirits act forever for him? He of course will not permit them to manipulate him any longer. Though temporarily he is unable to decide anything, he nonetheless will *not allow* the evil spirits to control his power of decision. The battle for freedom has now been joined. This is a contest of the *will*, for it is through its passivity that all the parts of the man have fallen into the hands of the evil spirits. Hereafter the will must rise up to (a) oppose the rule of the evil spirits, (b) recover all lost ground, and (c) work actively with God for the use of every part of his person. Everything hinges on the volition. The evil spirits will withdraw if the believer's volition withstands them and forbids them to occupy his organs any further.

Every foot of surrendered territory must be recaptured; each bit of deception must be uncovered. The child of God needs to contend patiently with the enemy over each and every matter. He must "fight through." All ground is not necessarily removed at the moment of refusal. The evil spirits will yet mount their last struggle; the children of God must be strengthened through many battles. "The refusing must therefore be reasserted, and the believer refuse persistently, until each point of ground is detected and refused, and the faculties are gradually released to act freely under the will of the man. The faculties let go into passivity should regain their normal working condition, such as the operation of the mind kept to true and pure thinking so that any subject being dealt with is mastered, and does not dominate beyond control. So with the memory, the will, the imagination, and the actions of the body, such as singing, praying, speaking, reading, etc." (Penn-Lewis, WOTS, 193)° The will must be engaged as the master of the entire man. All talents must be able to function properly according to one's normal condition.

In addition to refusing any ground to the powers of darkness, the child of God will have to refuse all their operations. If by his volition he maintains this antagonistic attitude the endeavors of the enemy will be spoiled. He should ask God for light on the enemy's exertions so as to resist them one by one. Since the operation of the evil spirits in the child of God is (a) to act in place of him and (b) to influence him to act according to their will, he must (a) refuse to let them act for him and (b) resist their influence on him. He needs to re-

---

°See Part Nine, Chapter 2 for full bibliographical citation.

fuse to let in the enemy spirits as well as refuse any ground that will maintain them in him. As he resists, the foe shall contend in every way. He must therefore battle with *all his strength* until he is restored to his normalcy and freedom. When he first begins to fight he may find himself temporarily incapacitated; but if he struggles on with all his might, his volition will turn from passivity to activity and control his whole being. Thus shall passivity and the enemy's entrenchment be destroyed in battle.

"The 'fighting through' period is a very painful time. There are bad moments of acute suffering, and intense struggle, arising out of the consciousness of the resistance of the powers of darkness in their contest for what the believer endeavors to reclaim." (Penn-Lewis, WOTS, 194) In exercising his volition to (a) resist the rule of the evil spirits and (b) reinstate his own office, the Christian shall meet stiff opposition from his enemy. Initially he may not be aware of the depth to which he has fallen; but once he commences, point by point, to fight his way back to a normal state, then does he discover how far he has plunged. Because of the resistance of the enemy he may find at the initial stage of combat that his symptoms grow *worse* than before, as though the more he fights the less strength his will has and the more confused becomes the particular area over which the engagement is being fought. Such a phenomenon is nonetheless the sign of *victory!* Though the believer does feel worse, in reality he is better. *For it demonstrates that the resistance has had its effect: the enemy has felt the pressure and is consequently making his last stand. If one continues to exert the pressure the evil spirits will depart.*

During the battle it is positively essential that the believer stand on Romans 6.11, acknowledging himself as *one* with the Lord: the Lord's death is his death. Such faith releases him from the authority of the evil spirits since they can have no power over the dead. This position must be firmly taken. In conjunction with such a stand as this there must be the use of God's Word against all the lies of the enemy, because at this juncture the adversary will lie to the saint by suggesting that he has fallen beyond any hope of restoration. If he listens to this guile he will surely tumble into the greatest peril of all. He should remind himself that Calvary has destroyed Satan and his evil hosts already (Heb. 2.14; Col. 2.14-15). The work of salvation is finished that all may experience deliverance out of the powers of darkness into the kingdom of the Son of God's love (Col. 1.13). Suffering for the sake of recovering ground assures a person of that which the enemy is afraid of, and how urgent that the ground be recovered. Consequently, whenever the wicked powers inflict new and greater afflictions upon the believer, let him perceive that these are from the enemy and then let him refuse and disregard them, neither worrying nor talking about them.

If the Christian patiently endures temporary discomforts and courageously exercises his volition to recapture surrendered territory, he shall find himself progressively being freed. Little by little as the ground is refused to the enemy and restored to the believer the degree of penetration will correspondingly decrease. If he does not cede any *new* ground to the enemy the latter's power to harass him shall diminish as the ground dwindles. While it may require some time before he is set free completely, even so he is now on the road to liberation. He begins to be conscious of himself, his need for food, his appearance, and other such elements of awareness which were relinquished through the enemy's attack. But he must not misconstrue these to be a retrogression in his spiritual life. On the contrary, the restoration of consciousness is evidence that the former invader has departed from his senses. Thus at this stage he should proceed faithfully until full freedom has been restored. He should be wary of contentment with a little gain; he should not stop until his normalcy is recovered entirely.

TRUE GUIDANCE

We need to comprehend the true way by which God leads man, and the relationship between man's will and the will of God.

The obedience of the Christian to God ought to be unconditional. When his spiritual life reaches the summit his
will shall be perfectly one with God's. This does not imply,
however, that he has no more volition of his own. It is still
there; only the fleshly control of it is gone. God always requires man's volition to cooperate with Him in fulfilling His
will. By beholding the example of our Lord Jesus we can
be assured that the volition of anyone fully united with God
is still very much with him. "I seek not my *own* will but the
will of him who sent me"; "not to do my *own* will but the
will of him who sent me"; "nevertheless not *my* will, but
thine, be done" (John 5.30, 6.38; Luke 22.42). Here do we
see the Lord Jesus Who, though one with the Father, yet
possesses His *Own personal* will apart from that of the
Father. He has His Own will but neither seeks nor does
that will. The implication is obvious that all who truly are
united with God should place their will alongside His. They
should not annihilate their organ of volition.

In true guidance the Christian is not obligated to obey
God mechanically; instead he must execute God's will
actively. God takes no pleasure in demanding His own to
follow blindly; He wants them to do His will in full and
conscious exercise of their total beings. A lazy person would
like God to act for him so that he can simply follow passively. But God does not desire His child to be lazy. He
wishes him to prepare his members actively and obey actively after he has spent time in examining the will of God.
Wherefore in the practice of obedience the believer goes
through the following steps: (a) *willingness* to do God's will
(John 7.17); (b) *revelation* of that will to his intuition by
the Holy Spirit (Eph. 5.17); (c) strengthening by God to
will His will (Phil. 2.13); and (d) strengthening by God to
do His will (Phil. 2.13). God never substitutes Himself for
the believer in carrying out His will; consequently, upon
knowing the will of God he must will to do it and then
draw upon the power of the Holy Spirit to work it out.

Why must the Christian draw on the power of the Holy
Spirit? Because standing alone his will is very weak. How

true are those words of Paul: "I can will what is right, but I cannot do it" (Rom. 7.18). One must be strengthened by the Holy Spirit in the inner man before he can practically obey God. Hence *God* first works in us to will and then works in us to work for His good pleasure (Phil. 2.13).

God reveals His will in our spirit's intuition and there supplies strength to us both to will and to work out His will when our volition is united to Him. He demands that we be one with Him, but He never uses our will for us. The purpose of God's creation and redemption is to give man a perfectly free volition. Through the salvation accomplished by the Lord Jesus on the cross we Christians now can choose freely to do the will of God. All the charges in the New Testament concerning life and godliness are to be either chosen or rejected as we so wish and will. Such charges would mean nothing if God were to annihilate the operation of our volition.

A spiritual Christian is one who has full authority to exercise his own volition. He always should choose God's will and reject Satan's. While at times he is uncertain whether something is from God or from the devil, yet he is able to choose or reject. He can declare: Even though I know not if this is of God or of Satan, yet I choose what is God's and reject what is Satan's. He may continue to be uninformed but he can continue to maintain the attitude of wanting what is God's and rejecting what is the devil's. A child of God ought to exercise this right of choosing or rejecting in all respects. It does not matter too much if he is unaware, as long as he decides to choose the will of God. He may say: whenever I know what God's mind is, I shall do it; I always choose God's will and reject Satan's. This attitude affords the Spirit of God opportunity to work in him until his will against the devil daily grows stronger and Satan daily loses his influence in him. In this way God secures another faithful servant in the midst of a rebellious world. By persistently maintaining the *attitude* of rejecting the enemy's will and continually beseeching God to prove what is of Him, the be-

liever begins before long to appreciate the great effectiveness
of such an attitude of will in spiritual life.

SELF CONTROL

The summit of a Christian's spiritual walk is self-control.
What commonly is spoken of as the Holy Spirit ruling in us
does not mean that He directly controls any part of man.
Any misunderstanding of this can result in either deception
or despair. If we know that the aim of the Holy Spirit is to
lead man to the place of self-control, we shall not fall into
passivity but shall make good progress in spiritual life.

"The fruit of the Spirit is . . . self-control" (Gal. 5.22-23).
The work of the Holy Spirit is to bring the believer's outward
man into perfect obedience to his self-control. The Holy
Spirit rules the believer through his renewed will. When a
child of God walks after the flesh his outward man is
rebellious to the spirit and so he becomes a disintegrated
person. But when he walks in the spirit and produces spiritual fruit he manifests the power of self-control as well as
love, joy, kindness and so forth in his soul. The outward
man, once dissipated and confused, is now thoroughly subdued and perfectly submissive to the man's self-control
according to the mind of the Holy Spirit. What the Christian
must therefore control by his will are:

(a) his own spirit, maintaining it in its proper state of
being neither too hot nor too cold. The spirit needs the control of the will just as do the other parts of man. Only when
one's volition is renewed and is filled with the Holy Spirit is
he able to direct his own spirit and keep it in its proper
position. All who are experienced agree that they must engage their will to restrain the spirit when it becomes too
wild or to uplift it when it sinks too low. Only so can the
believer walk daily in his spirit. This is not contradictory to
what we mentioned before about man's spirit ruling over the
whole person. For when we say the spirit rules the total man
we mean that the spirit, by knowing the mind of God intuitively, *governs* the whole being (including the volition)
according to God's will. Whereas in stating that the will con-

trols the man we mean the will *directly controls* the entire
man (including the spirit) according to the will of God. In
experience these two perfectly agree. "A man without self-
control is like a city broken into and left without walls"
(Prov. 25.28).

(b) his own mind and all the rest of his soul's abilities.
All thoughts need to be subjected fully to the control of the
will; wandering thoughts must be checked one by one—
"take every thought captive to obey Christ" (2 Cor. 10.5).
And "set your minds on things that are above" (Col. 3.2).

(c) his own body. It ought to be an instrument to man,
not his master by virtue of unrestrained habits and lusts.
The Christian should exercise his volition to control, discipline and subdue his body in order that it may be entirely
submissive, ready to do God's will and hindering not. "I
pommel my body and subdue it" (1 Cor. 9.27). Once the believer's volition has achieved a state of perfect self-control
he will not be hindered by any part of his being, because
the moment he senses God's will he immediately performs
it. Both the Holy Spirit and man's spirit need a will under
self-control by which to execute God's revelation. Hence on
the one hand we must be united with God and on the other
hand subdue our whole being so as to render it obedient to
us. This is imperative to spiritual life.

PART TEN

THE BODY

1 The Believer and His Body
2 Sickness
3 God as the Life of the Body
4 Overcoming Death

CHAPTER 1

THE BELIEVER AND HIS BODY

We should know what place our physical body occupies in the purpose and plan of God. Can anyone deny the relationship between the body and spirituality? In addition to a spirit and a soul we also have a body. However healthy may be the intuition, communion and conscience of our spirit and however renewed the emotion, mind and will of our soul, we can never develop into spiritual men and women—never be perfected but continually lacking in some way—if our body is not as sound and restored as are our spirit and soul. We should not neglect our outer shell while attending to our inner components. Our life shall suffer if we commit this blunder.

The body is necessary and important; otherwise God would not have created man with one. By accurately searching the Scriptures we can discover how much attention God pays to man's body, for the Bible has a lot to say about it.

Most singular and awesome of all is the fact that the Word became flesh: the Son of God took upon Himself a body of flesh and blood: and though He died He wears this garb forever.

THE HOLY SPIRIT AND THE BODY

Romans 8.10-13 unfolds to us the condition of our body, how the Holy Spirit helps it, and what ought to be our right attitude towards it. If we appropriate these verses we will not misunderstand the place of a believer's body in God's plan of redemption.

"If Christ is in you, although your bodies are dead because of sin, your spirits are alive because of righteousness" (v.10). Initially both our body and spirit were dead; but after we believed in the Lord Jesus we received Him into us to be our life. The fact that Christ by the Holy Spirit lives in the believer forms one of the essential tenets of the gospel. Every child of God, however weak, has Christ dwelling in him. This Christ is our life. And when He enters to make His abode in us, our spirit is made alive. Formerly both the spirit and the body were dead; now the spirit is quickened, leaving only the body dead. The estate common to *every believer* is that his body is dead but his spirit is alive.

This experience produces a wide disparity between the Christian's inward and outward state. Our inner being is flowing with life while the outer man is still full of death. Being full of the Spirit of life we are very much alive, yet we exist in a shell of death; in other words, the life of our spirit and the life of our body are radically unalike. The former is life indeed, but the latter is verily death. This is because our physical frame is still the "body of sin": no matter how advanced a Christian's spiritual walk is, his flesh is nonetheless the "body of sin." We have yet to possess a resurrected, glorious, spiritual frame; "the redemption of our bodies" (Rom. 8.23) awaits us in the future. Today's body is just an "earthen vessel," an "earthly tent," a "lowly body" (2 Cor. 4.7, 5.1; Phil. 3.21). Sin has been driven out of the spirit and the will but it has not been expunged from the body. Because sin remains there, it is therefore dead. This is the purport of "your bodies are dead because of sin." Simultaneously, however, our spirit is alive. Or to phrase it more correctly, our spirit receives life because of the righteousness which is in Christ. When we trust in Him we receive Him as our righteousness and we also are justified by God. The former is Christ imparting to us His very Self (a substantive transaction); the latter is God justifying us for Christ's sake (a legal transaction). Without the impartation there can be no justification. The moment we receive Christ we obtain the legal position of being justified before God and additionally the practical experience of having Christ imparted to us. Christ comes into us as life so that our dead spirit may be made alive. This is the import of "your spirits are alive because of righteousness."

"If the Spirit of him who raised Jesus from the dead dwells in you, he who raised Christ Jesus from the dead will give life to your mortal bodies also through his Spirit which dwells in you" (v.11). Verse 10 explains how God quickens our spirit; this verse tells us how God gives life to our body. The tenth verse speaks of the spirit being made alive, with the body still dead; the eleventh verse goes further by saying that after the spirit is made alive the body too may live. The first part announces that the spirit lives because of Christ dwelling in us; this part declares that the body will live because of the Holy Spirit abiding in us. The Holy Spirit will give life to our bodies.

The body is dead not in the sense that this outer shell is, but in the sense that it is traveling towards the grave; spiritually speaking it is counted as dead. According to man's thought the body possesses life; yet according to God even that life is death because it is abounding with sins—"your bodies are dead because of sin." On the one hand, although there is strength in the body we must not permit it to be manifested. It should not have any activity, for the activation of its life is but death. Sin is its life, and sin is spiritual death. The body lives by spiritual death. On the other hand, we know we should witness, serve and labor for God. These require bodily strength. Now inasmuch as the body is spiritually dead and its life is nothing but death, how then can we ever engage it to respond to the demands of spiritual life without concomitantly drawing upon its death-life? It is obvious that our body cannot and will not do the will of the Spirit of life within but will oppose and fight against Him. How can the Holy Spirit therefore induce our body to answer His call? He must Himself give life to our bodies of death.

The One "who raised Christ Jesus from the dead" is God. Why is He not directly named? It is to emphasize the *work* which God did in raising the Lord Jesus from the dead. It aims at calling the attention of believers to the feasibility of God raising their *mortal* bodies since God hitherto has raised the *dead* body of Jesus. The Apostle indirectly says this Spirit of God is the Holy Spirit, Who also is the Spirit of resurrection. He again employs the word "if"—"if the Spirit of Him . . . dwells in you he . . . will give life to your mortal bodies." He is not doubting that the Holy Spirit is in the believer, for he mentions in verse 9 that anyone belonging to Christ has the Spirit of Christ. What he means is: you have the Holy Spirit indwelling you; therefore your mortal bodies should experience His life. This is the privilege shared by all who possess the indwelling Spirit. He does not wish any saint to miss this blessing through ignorance.

This verse in reality teaches that if the Spirit of God abides in us, then through this indwelling Power God also gives life to our mortal bodies. It is not speaking of a future resurrection because that is not the subject here. It simply compares the resurrection of the Lord Jesus with our receiving life today in our body. If the verse were touching upon resurrection it would use the term "the body of death"; but only the mortal body is in view here, one which is subject to death *though not yet died*. The believer's body is spiritually dead, for it marches towards the grave and must die. This is quite distinct from one already deceased in the literal sense. Just as the Holy Spirit indwelling us is an ever current affair, so the Holy Spirit giving life to our mortal bodies must be a current experience too. We should realize further that it is not speaking of our regeneration here either, for the Holy Spirit is not imparting life to our spirit but is instead giving life to our bodies.

By this verse God informs His children of their bodily privilege, which is life to their mortal frames through His Spirit Who indwells them. It does not assert that the "body of sin" has become a holy body or that our "lowly body" has been transformed into a glorious one or that this mortal body has put on immortality. These cannot be realized in this life. The redemption of our earthen vessels must wait till the Lord comes and receives us to Himself. To change the nature of our body in this age is impossible. Therefore the real meaning of the Holy Spirit giving life to our bodies is that: (1) He will restore us when we are sick and (2) He will preserve us if we are not sick. In a word, the Holy Spirit will strengthen our earthly tents so that we can meet the requirements of God's work and walk in order that neither our life nor the kingdom of God will suffer through the weakness of the body.

This is what God has provided for all His children. Yet how many Christians day by day genuinely experience this life given by His Spirit to their mortal bodies? Are there not many whose spiritual life is endangered by their physical condition—many who fall because of their physical weakness —many who cannot work actively for God because of the bondage of illness? The experience of Christians today does not correspond to God's provision. Various reasons of course account for this discrepancy: some refuse to accept God's provision for they maintan it has nothing to do with them; while others know and believe and desire this provision but have not presented their bodies a living sacrifice. These hold instead that God has furnished them strength to live through themselves. But those who truly wish to live for God and claim this promise and provision by faith shall experience the reality of the fullness of life in the body as given by the Holy Spirit.

"So then, brethren, we are debtors, not to the flesh, to live according to the flesh" (v.12). This verse fully describes the proper relation between the believer and his body. Countless brethren are slaves to their fleshly frames. The spiritual life of many is totally imprisoned in their bodies! They exist as two different persons: when they withdraw to the inner man they have a feeling of being spiritual, nigh to God and abounding in life; but when they live in the outer flesh they feel fallen, carnal and alienated from God because they are obeying their bodies. Their body becomes a heavy burden to them. A little physical discomfort can alter their life. A slight illness or pain will perturb them and flood their hearts with self-love and self-pity. Under these circumstances it is impossible to follow a spiritual course.

The Apostle in using the words "so then" is merely continuing beyond what he has enunciated before. We believe this verse directly follows upon verses 10 and 11. The tenth declares the body is dead; the eleventh states the Holy Spirit gives life to the body. On the basis of these two bodily conditions, the Apostle can consequently conclude by saying: "so then, brethren, we are debtors, not to the flesh, to live according to the flesh." First, since the body is dead because of sin, we *cannot* live by following the body. To do so would be to commit sin. Second, because the Holy Spirit has given life to our mortal frames we *need not* live according to the flesh, since it has no authority any longer to bind our spiritual life. By this provision of God's Spirit our inner life is competent to directly command the outer frame without interference. Previously we seemed to be debtors to the flesh—incapable of restricting its demands, desires and lusts—and lived according to the flesh by committing many sins. But now we have the provision of the Holy Spirit. Not only the lusts of the flesh have no control over us, even its weakness, illness and suffering have lost their grip.

Many argue that we should fulfill the legitimate desires and demands of the flesh, but the Apostle contends we owe nothing to it. Beyond preserving our earthly tents in a proper condition as God's vessels, we owe the flesh nothing. Naturally the Bible never prohibits us from taking care of the body, else we would have to allot even more time and attention to it because of unnecessary sickness. Clothing, food and lodging are requisites; rest is also necessary. Nonetheless, what we stress is that our life should not be occupied solely by these concerns. True, we should eat when hungry, drink when thirsty, rest when weary, clothe ourselves when cold. Yet we must not permit these affairs to penetrate so deeply into our hearts that we make them partial or total objectives in our life. We must not love these necessaries. They should come and go according to *need*: they should not stay in us and become desires within. Sometimes for the sake of God's work or some other overriding need, we must pommel our body and subdue it despite its own requirement. The Disciples' love of sleep in the Garden of Gethsemane and the Lord's endurance of hunger by the well of Sychar present a contrasting picture of defeat and victory over the legitimate requirement of the body. Because we are debtors to the flesh no longer, we ought not sin according to its lusts nor slacken in spiritual work due to physical weakness.

"For if you live according to the flesh you will die, but if by the Spirit you put to death the deeds of the body you will live" (v.13). Should Christians reject God's provision and live by the flesh instead, they certainly will be punished.

"If you live according to the flesh you will die." This word "die" and the word "live" in the next clause have several meanings. We will mention only one, which is the death of the body. According to sin our body is "dead"; according to consequence it is a "body of death"—that is, it is doomed to death; if we live by the flesh this body of death shall become a dying body. In following the flesh we on the one side are unfit to receive the life given to the body by the Holy Spirit, while on the other we shorten the days of our life on earth because all sins are harmful to the body. All sins manifest their effectiveness in the flesh, and that effect is death. Through the life given to our body by the Holy Spirit we should resist the death which is in it; if not, death will quickly complete its work there.

"But if by the Spirit you put to death the deeds of the body you will live." We should receive the Holy Spirit not only as the Giver of life to our earthen vessel but also as the Executor of its deeds. How can we expect to have Him give life to our fleshly frame if we neglect the work of putting to death its deeds? For only by putting to death its deeds through the Holy Spirit can we *live*. For the body to live its doing must first be put to nought, or else death shall be the immediate result. Herein do we discover the mistake of many. Christians assume they can live for themselves—using their fleshly frames for the things they wish to do—but at the same time expect the Holy Spirit to give life to their frames so that they can be healthy and without infirmity. Would He give life and strength to men to empower them to live for themselves? How utterly ridiculous! The life God gives to our body is for the purpose that we may thereafter live for Him. If the Holy Spirit were to grant health and strength to us who have not offered ourselves wholeheartedly to God, would that not bolster us to live more energetically for ourselves? Innumerable Christians seeking the Holy Spirit as life for their mortal frames should now see that they do not have this experience because they have neglected this essential point.

We cannot ourselves control our body, but through the Holy Spirit we can. He will empower us to put to death its many deeds. Believers have all experienced their lack of strength to deal with the fleshly lusts which provoke the members of the body to perform deeds gratifying to the flesh. But by the Holy Spirit they are fit to cope with the situation. This is very important to know. It is useless to try to crucify one's self. Today many grasp the truth of being crucified with the Lord on the cross, yet few exhibit its reality. The truth of co-crucifixion is but a teaching to many saints. This is essentially due to a lack of clear understanding concerning the place of the Holy Spirit in the scheme of salvation. They do not apprehend how the Spirit moves together with the cross. We must realize that the cross without God's Spirit is absolutely ineffective. *Only the Holy Spirit can take what the cross has accomplished and make believers experience it. If we hear the truth of the cross but do*

*not allow Him to work this truth into our lives, then we know
nothing but a theory and an ideal.*

A recognition "that our old self was crucified with him so
that the sinful body might be annulled" (Rom. 6.6 Darby)
is indeed good; but we remain shackled by fleshly deeds if
"by the Spirit" we have not "put to death the deeds of the
body." We have seen too many saints who understand most
lucidly the truth of the cross and have accepted it yet in
whom it is not one whit effective. They begin to wonder
whether the reality of the *practical* salvation of the cross can
ever be experienced in their lives. But they should not be
surprised at all since they have forgotten that only the Holy
Spirit can translate the cross into experience. He alone can
substantiate salvation, nonetheless they forget Him. Unless
believers abandon themselves and trust completely in the
power of the Spirit to lay to rest the deeds of the body, the
truth they profess to know will persist as mere theory. Only
a putting to death by the power of the Holy Spirit will give
life today to our mortal frame.

GLORIFY GOD

The passage in 1 Corinthians 6.12-20 sheds additional
light on this matter of the believer's body. Let us consider
this passage verse by verse.

"All things are lawful for me, but not all things are helpful. All things are lawful for me, but I will not be enslaved
by anything" (v.12). As substantiated by the verses following, the Apostle Paul is here writing about the body. He
judges all things to be lawful because according to nature
every demand of the body—such as eating, drinking or sex—
is natural, reasonable and lawful (v.13). Yet he further
judges that not every one of them is necessarily helpful nor
should any enslave man. In other words, according to man's
natural existence the Christian may be permitted to do many
things with his body, but as one who belongs to God he is
additionally able *not* to do these things for the glory of God.

"Food is meant for the stomach and the stomach for food
—and God will destroy both one and the other. The body is

not meant for immorality, but for the Lord, and the Lord for the body" (v.13). The first half of this verse corresponds to the first half of the preceding verse. Food is lawful, but since food and stomach will eventually be destroyed, none is eternally useful. The latter half of the verse corresponds to that half of the preceding verse too. The Christian is capable of rising completely above the urge of sex and yielding his body wholly to the Lord (1 Cor. 7.34).

"The body is for the Lord." This is a word having enormous import. Paul is speaking to us firstly about the issue of food. In the matter of eating and drinking the Christian is afforded a chance to prove in practice that "the body is for the Lord." Man originally fell on this very point of food; the Lord Jesus was tempted in the wilderness on this same issue as well. Numerous Christians do not know how to glorify God in their eating and drinking. They do not eat and drink simply to keep their body fit for the Lord's use but indulge to satisfy their personal desires. We should understand that the body is for the Lord and not for ourselves; hence we should refrain from using it for our pleasure. Food ought not hinder our fellowship with God since it is to be taken purely to preserve the body in health.

The Apostle mentions the subject of immorality too. This is a sin which defiles the body: it directly contravenes the principle that "the body is for the Lord." Immorality here includes not just looseness outside the marriage relationship but overindulgence within marriage as well. The body is for the Lord, wholly for the Lord, not for oneself. Thus license even in legitimate sexual intercourse is prohibited also.

The Apostle Paul's intent in this passage is to show us that any excess of the flesh must be thoroughly resisted. The body is for the Lord; the Lord alone can use it. The indulgence of any part solely for personal gratification is not pleasing to Him. Other than as an instrument of righteousness, the body is not to be used in any other way. It, like our entire being, cannot serve two masters. Even in such natural affairs as food and sex the body should be engaged exclusively to fill *needs*. While needs do require satisfaction, the body is nonetheless for the Lord and not for food and sex. Nowadays many Christians aspire to sancification of their spirit and soul, not fully appreciating how greatly sanctification in these realms depends on sanctification of the body. They forget that unless all nerve responses, sensations, actions, conduct, works, food and speech which belong to the body are utterly for the Lord, they can never arrive at perfection.

"The body is for the Lord." This signifies that though the outer flesh belongs to the Lord it is entrusted to man for him to maintain for Him. How few are those who know and practice this truth! Many saints today are stricken with sickness, weakness and suffering; God is chastening them that they may present their bodies to Him a living sacrifice. They would be healed if they yielded them completely to God. God wants them to know that the body is for the Lord, not for themselves. If they continue to live according to their wishes they shall see the scourge of God remain upon them. All who are sick should take these words seriously to heart.

"And the Lord for the body." This is an incredibly wonderful statement! We usually think of the Lord as saving only our spirit and our soul, but here it is said that "the Lord (is) for the *body*." Christians look upon the Lord Jesus as having come to save their spirit and soul alone, that the body is useless, having no value in spiritual life and not graciously provided for in God's redemptive scheme. But it is plainly enunciated here that "the Lord is *for* the body." The Lord, affirms God, is equally for the earthen vessel which man lightly esteems.

Why do believers overlook their fleshly frames? It is because they erroneously look upon the Lord Jesus as saving them merely from their sins and not also from the sickness of their body. Hence they can only resort to human methods for the cure of their physical weakness and illness. When they look into the four Gospels they find that the Lord Jesus healed more bodies than He saved souls; yet they spiritualize the affair entirely by interpreting these infirmities as being spiritual sicknesses. They may concede that the Lord Jesus did heal physical sicknesses while on earth, but they believe too that He heals only spiritual diseases today. They are willing to hand their spiritual ills over to the Lord for healing but take it for granted that they must go elsewhere for their physical ills, concluding that the Lord will have nothing to do with those. They forget that "Jesus Christ is the same yesterday and today and forever" (Heb. 13.8).

It is quite customary among today's saints to assume the attitude that God apparently has made no provision for the body. They limit the redemption of Christ to the spirit and the soul and cross out the body completely. They disregard the facts that the Lord Jesus healed physical ills in His day and that the Apostles continued to experience this power of healing in their day. No other explanation for their attitude can be put forward than that of unbelief. The Word of God, however, declares the Lord is also for the body.

This is related to what was said just before. Our body is for the Lord and simultaneously the Lord is for our body too. We see in this the joint relationship of God and man. God gives His Own Self totally to us that we may offer ourselves completely to Him. Upon offering ourselves to Him He will again give Himself to us according to our measure of committal. The Lord wishes us to know that He has given His body for us; He also wants us to know that if our body is genuinely for Him we will experience Him for it. The meaning of the body for the Lord is that we present ours wholly to Him to live for Him; while the Lord for the body implies that, having accepted our consecration, He will grant His life and power to our bodily frames. He will care for, preserve and nourish this physical frame of ours.

Aware of its weakness, uncleanness, sinfulness and deadness, it seems scarcely conceivable that the Lord is also for the body. This we shall nonetheless understand if we contemplate God's way of salvation. When the Lord Jesus was born the Word became flesh. He possessed a body. While on the cross, "he himself bore our sins in his *body* on the tree" (1 Peter 2.24). United to Him by faith, our bodies were crucified with Him as well; and thus has He released them from the power of sin. In Christ this fleshly tent of ours has been resurrected and ascended to heaven. The Holy Spirit is presently dwelling in us. Therefore may we say that the Lord is for our body—not just for our spirit and soul but for our body too.

The Lord for the body embraces several meanings: (1) It conveys the idea that the Lord will deliver the body from sin. Nearly every sin is related somewhat to it. Quite a few sins arise from special physiological causes. Feasting for example is an indulgence of one's physical taste and drinking is a catering to one's bodily lust. Many moments of anger are triggered by physical discomforts. Oversensitive nerves may cause people to be brittle and harsh. Peculiar personalities often result from a peculiar physiological make-up. Many notorious sinners physically are constructed differently from normal persons. Even so, with all these manifestations, the Lord is still for the body. If we offer ours to Him, acknowledging Him as Lord of everything and claiming His promise by faith, we shall see how the Lord can deliver us from ourselves. Irrespective of how we physiologically are made, even possessing special weaknesses, we can overcome our sins through the Lord.

(2) The Lord is additionally for our physical ills. As he destroys sin so will He heal diseases. He is for every matter related to our body; He is consequently for our sicknesses also. Diseases are but the manifestation of the power of sin in our bodies. The Lord Jesus is able to deliver us from sicknesses as well as from sins.

(3) The Lord is also for our living in the body. He will be its strength and life so that it may live by Him. He desires us to experience in our daily walk the power of His resurrection in order that our body too may live by Him.

(4) The Lord is equally for the glorification of the body. This pertains to the future. Today we attain great heights if we walk by Him, yet that does not change the nature of our body. But the day shall come when the Lord shall redeem it and transform this lowly frame into a likeness of His glorious body.

We must underscore the significance of the body being for the Lord. If we yearn to experience the Lord for the body we first must practice the body for the Lord. It is impossible to experience the Lord for the body if we use our bodies according to our wants and for our pleasure instead of presenting them for living entirely unto the Lord. Yet were we to hand ourselves over completely to God, yielding our members as instruments of righteousness and conducting ourselves in all matters according to God's order, He most surely would accord us His life and power.

"And God raised the Lord and will also raise us up by his power" (v.14). This is to explain the last clause of the preceding verse which is "the Lord for the body." The resurrection of the Lord is a *bodily* one: our future resurrection will therefore be *bodily* too. As God has already raised the body of the Lord Jesus so will He also raise ours from the dead. These two facts are equally certain. Hence this is how the Lord is for our body: He will raise us up by His power. It is yet future, nevertheless today we may foretaste the power of His resurrection.

"Do you not know that your bodies are members of Christ? Shall I therefore take the members of Christ and make them members of a prostitute? Never!" (v.15). The first question is noticeably unusually phrased. In other places, such as 1 Corinthians 12.27, it merely states "*you* are the body of Christ and individually members of it"; but only in this passage does it say "your *bodies* are members of Christ." Our whole being is indeed a member of Christ; why, then, is the body specified here? We naturally assume that our spiritual life is a member of Christ for is it not spiritual? But how can this corporeal frame be considered a member of Christ? We are verily witnessing an exceedingly wonderful truth.

We must understand our union with Christ. God does not look at believers individually; He includes them together within His view of Christ. No Christian can exist outside of Christ, because his daily strength to live is supplied by Him. To God, the union of believers with Christ is an altogether definite reality. The "body of Christ" is not just a spiritual term, it is truly a fact. Just as a physical body is joined to a head, so believers are joined to Christ. In God's eye, our union with Christ is perfect, unlimited and absolute. To word it another way, our spirits unite with the spirit of Christ (most important of all), our souls unite with the soul of Christ (the union of wills, the union of affections, and the union of minds), and our bodies unite with the body of Christ. If our union with Christ is *complete* how can the corporeal part of our being be excluded? If we are the members of Christ our bodies too are the members of Christ.

Unquestionably perfect union will not be achieved until the time of future resurrection. Even so, our union with Christ is already a present verity. This teaching is vital, for what comfort we have when we know that *the body of Christ is for our bodies*. All truths may be experienced. Do we have any physiological defect, sickness, suffering or weakness? Remember, Christ's body is for our bodies. Ours are united to His; accordingly we may draw life and strength from His body for the supply of our physical needs. Everyone who has bodily defects should stand on this union with Christ by faith and draw from His resources for their fleshly needs.

The Apostle marvels that the Corinthian believers could be ignorant of such a clear truth. Had they truly apprehended this teaching they would have encountered many spiritual experiences as well as dealt responsibly with various practical warnings; such as, if these bodies are members of Christ could we have dared make them members of a prostitute? For the Apostle right away inquires: "Do you not know that He who joins himself to a prostitute becomes one body with her? For as it is written, 'The two shall become one'" (v.16). Paul develops this doctrine of union most effectively. "He who joins himself to a prostitute becomes one body with her," that is, he becomes a member of the prostitute. A believer has been united with Christ, hence he is a member of Christ. Where will this leave Christ if this member of His becomes a member of a prostitute? The Apostle forbids such a thing.

"But he who is united to the Lord becomes one spirit with him" (v.17). In verses 15-17 we can behold the mystery of

our body's union with Christ. The thought of this seven-
teenth verse is that if man in joining his body to that of a
prostitute becomes one *flesh* and also a member of her, how
could our bodies not become the members of Christ if we are
united to the Lord and become one spirit with Him? To join
the body to a prostitute will effect the union of the two bodies: how much more must the two bodies become one if our
whole being is joined to Christ!

Paul views the first step in uniting with the Lord as becoming "one spirit with Him." This is a union in the spirit.
But he does not regard the believer's body as something unrelated. He concedes that the primary union is in the spirit,
yet this fusion of the spirit will consequentially cause the believer's body to be a member of Christ. This ultimately
proves that the body is for the Lord and the Lord is also for
the body.

The issue before us is union. The children of God ought
to perceive clearly their position in Christ, how there is not
the slightest gap in their union with Him. Their bodies
are members of Christ through which His life may be exhibited. They could not expect much if the Lord were weak
and sick; but since the opposite is true, they undeniably can
obtain health, power and life from him.

We need to call to mind one point, however. We should
at no time harbor the thought that because the *body* is the
member of Christ we must therefore physically feel every
spiritual fellowship and affair there as though we must have
evidence in the body. If we must feel the presence of God
in our fleshly frame—if He must take direct control of it and
shake it—if the Holy Spirit must fill our frame and make
His will known through it—or if the Holy Spirit must assume
management of the tongue of the body and speak—then
our body has supplanted our spirit in the latter's works. And
the result will be that our spirit loses its operation as its
work is taken over by the body. But our earthen vessel is
not capable of enduring such strenuous labor, hence it often
becomes weakened. Furthermore, the evil powers as disembodied spirits crave human bodies. Their chief aim is to
possess man's physical frame. A Christian who has his body

extended beyond its normal capacity gives opportunity to the evil spirits to work. This is in accordance with the law of the spiritual realm. Assuming that God and His Spirit will commune with him in the *body*, the Christian naturally anticipates experiencing such fellowship there. But God and His Spirit never communicate directly with one's body; God communicates through His Spirit in the believer's spirit. If a child of God persists in seeking to experience God in his body, the evil spirits shall seize the opportunity to come in and shall accord him what he naïvely seeks. The consequences can be none other than occupation by evil spirits. But as to the union of the believer's body with Christ, this fact explains how it is able to receive God's life and be strengthened. Owing to the spirit's noble position, one must be doubly cautious lest he allow his body to usurp its work!

"Shun immorality. Every other sin which a man commits is outside the body; but the immoral man sins against his own body" (v.18). The Bible considers immorality or fornication as more serious than other sins because it has a special relationship to our bodies which are the members of Christ. Need we wonder why the Apostle emphatically and persistently persuades Christians to avoid fornication? We look at it in terms of a moral uncleanness, but the Apostle stresses a far different aspect of it. No sin other than fornication can occasion our body to be united with another; wherefore this is a sin against the body. This implies that no sin but fornication can render a member of Christ a member of a prostitute. Fornication is sinning against the members of Christ. Since Christians are united with Christ, fornication becomes doubly abominable. Or to view it from another perspective: by seeing the abomination of fornication we can appreciate how very real is our body's union with Christ.

"Do you not know that your body is a temple of the Holy Spirit within you, which you have from God?" (v.19) This is the second instance the Apostle Paul asks "Do you not know?" The first occurred in verse 15 which spoke of "the body for the Lord." In this second instance he is referring to "the Lord for the body." Earlier Paul had expressed it in a general way as "*you* are God's temple" (3.16); now he says specifically that "*your body* is a temple of the Holy Spirit." It indicates that the habitation of the Holy Spirit is extended beyond the spirit to the body. We commit a signal error if we consider the body His primary dwelling place, for He dwells initially in our spirit where He holds fellowship with us. However, this does not preclude His life flowing from the spirit to make our body alive. We are deceived if we expect the Holy Spirit to descend primarily on our bodies; but we shall suffer loss, too, if we limit His dwelling place to our spirits.

We should recognize the place of the body in God's design of redemption. Christ sets apart our fleshly frames that we may be filled with the Holy Spirit and become His instruments. Because He has died, been resurrected and been glorified, He is now qualified to give His Holy Spirit to our body. As in the past our soul life permeated our body, so now His Spirit shall permeate it. His life will flow into every member, and He will give us life and power far abundantly beyond what we can think.

That our body constitutes a temple of the Holy Spirit is a sure fact; and it can be livingly experienced as well. Yet many are like the Corinthian believers who forgot this glorious possibility. Though God's Spirit does dwell in them, He seems non-existent to them. We need to exercise faith to believe, to acknowledge and to accept this fact of God. If we *draw* on this fact by faith we shall discover that the Spirit will bring not only the holiness, joy, righteousness and love of Christ to our souls, but also life, power, health and strength to our weak, weary and sick bodies. He will give to our earthen vessels the life of Christ together with the vital elements of His glorious body. When our body has truly died with Christ, that is, when it is subject completely to Him, all self-will and independent action denied and nothing sought but to be a temple of the Lord, then the Holy Spirit shall assuredly manifest the life of the risen Christ in our mortal

frame. How good it is for us to genuinely experience the
Lord in healing and in strengthening, in His being our
health and life! If we see our tent as a temple of the Holy
Spirit we shall follow Him in wonderment and in love!

"You are not your own; you were bought with a price. So
glorify God in your body" (vv.19-20). You are members of
Christ, you are a temple of the Holy Spirit, you are not your
own. You were purchased by God with a price. Everything
of yours belongs to Him, especially your body. The union of
Christ with you and the seal of the Holy Spirit within you
proves that your body particularly is God's. "So glorify God
in your *body*." Brethren, God wishes us to honor Him there.
He wants us to glorify Him both through the consecration of
this "body for the Lord" of ours and also through the grace
exhibited by the "Lord for the body" of His. Let us be sober
and watchful lest we use our bodies for ourselves or permit
them to fall into a condition as though the Lord were not for
the body. Thus we shall glorify God and allow Him to demonstrate His power freely in delivering us from weakness,
sickness and suffering as well as from self-interest, self-love
and sin.

CHAPTER 2
SICKNESS

SICKNESS IS A COMMON occurrence in life. For us to know how to keep our body in a condition which glorifies God, we first must know what attitude to take towards sickness, how to make use of it, and also how to be healed. Because sickness is so prevalent we cannot avoid having a serious lack in our life if we do not know how to deal with it.

SICKNESS AND SIN

The Bible discloses a close relationship between sickness and sin. The ultimate consequence of sin is death. Sickness lies between sin and death. It is the sequel to sin and the prologue to death. If there were no sin in the world, there would be neither sickness nor death. Had not Adam sinned, sickness would not have come upon the earth: of this we can be most certain. Hence as with every other woe, sickness was ushered in by sin.

Human beings are made up of two natures: the non-corporeal and the corporeal. Both suffered from man's fall. The spirit and soul were damaged by sin and the body was invaded by sickness. The sin of the spirit and soul together with the sickness of the body attest that man must die.

When the Lord Jesus came to save, He not only forgave man's sin but also healed man's body. He saved bodies as well as souls. From the outset of His ministry He healed man's sickness; at the conclusion of His labor He became a propitiation on the cross for man's sins. Behold how many sick people were healed by Him during His earthly days! His hands were ever ready to touch the sick and raise them up.

Judging both by what He Himself did and by the command
He gave His disciples, we cannot help but see that the salvation He provides includes the healing of sickness. His
is the gospel of forgiveness *and* healing. These two go together. The Lord Jesus saves people from sins and sicknesses
that they may know the love of the Father. In reading the
Gospels, the Acts, the Epistles or the Old Testament, we
continually witness how healing and forgiveness run parallel
to each other.

We all know Isaiah 53 forms the clearest chapter in the Old
Testament on the gospel. Various places in the New Testament make reference to this particular chapter when the
fulfillment of its prophecies concerning the redemptive work
of the Lord Jesus is in view. "The chastisement of our peace
was upon him; and with his stripes we are healed" (v.5
ASV). It tells us in unmistakable terms that both the healing
of the body and the peace of the soul are accorded us. This
is made even plainer when we consider the two different
uses of the verb "bear": "he bore the sin of many" (v.12)
and "he has borne our griefs (Hebrew: sicknesses)" (v.4).
The Lord Jesus bears our sins; He also bears our sicknesses.
Because He has borne our sins, we need not bear them again;
in like manner, since He has borne our sicknesses, we need
no longer bear them either.° Sin has done damage to our soul
and body, so the Lord Jesus saves both. He saves us from
sicknesses as well as from sins. Believers today can offer
praise with David: "Bless the Lord, O my soul; and all that is
within me, bless his holy name! . . . Who forgives all your
iniquity, who heals all your diseases" (Ps. 103.1,3). What a
shame that so many Christians can utter but half a praise for
they know but half a salvation. It is a loss to both God and
man.

Let us note that God's salvation would not be complete if
the Lord Jesus simply forgave our sins but did not heal our
sicknesses too. How could He save our souls and yet leave

°Now of course there is a difference in scope between the Lord's bearing
sins and His bearing sicknesses. This is enlarged upon in the author's message on sickness and healing which has been included as an addendum to
Chapter 2 of this Part.—Translator.

our bodies to be tormented by infirmities? Did He not stress both while He was on earth? Sometimes He forgave first and then healed; at other times, just the reverse. He does according to what man is able to take in. In perusing the Gospels we find that the Lord Jesus performed more healing than any other works, because the Jews at that time seemed less able to believe in the Lord's forgiving them than in the Lord's healing (Matt. 9.5). Christians today, however, are precisely the opposite. In those days men believed that the Lord had power to heal sickness but they doubted His grace of forgiveness. Today's saints believe His forgiving power and doubt His healing grace. They confess that the Lord Jesus came to save people from sin, yet ignore the fact that He is equally the Savior Who heals. Man's unbelief divides the perfect Savior into two, though the truth remains that Christ is forever the Savior of man's body and soul, competent to heal as well as to forgive.

In our Lord's thought, it is not enough that a man be forgiven and not healed too. Hence, we find Him commanding, "Rise, take up your bed and go home" after His declaration to the paralytic, "Man, your sins are forgiven you" (Luke 5. 24,20). But as to ourselves, although we are people plagued by both sins and sicknesses, we count forgiveness from the Lord sufficient, leaving illness to be borne by ourselves and to be healed by other means. The Lord Jesus, however, did not want people to have to take the paralytic home still confined to a bed after his sins had been forgiven.

The Lord conceives a contrary view from us with respect to the relationship between sin and sickness. Our thought is that sin belongs to the spiritual realm, something disliked and condemned by God, whereas sickness is merely a mundane phenomenon having nothing to do with Him. On the other hand, the Lord Jesus considers both the sins of the soul and the infirmities of the body to be the works of Satan. He came "to destroy the works of the devil" (1 John 3.8), therefore He casts out demons and heals sicknesses. When Peter under revelation speaks of the Lord's *healing ministry*, he declares that He "went about doing good and healing all that were oppressed by the devil" (Acts 10.38). Sin and sickness are as intimately associated as are our soul and body. Forgiveness and healing complement each other.

THE CHASTISEMENT OF GOD

Having seen something of the Lord's thought regarding sickness, we now turn our attention to the causes of the sickness of *believers*.

"That is why many of you are weak and ill, and some have died. But if we judged ourselves truly, we should not be judged. But when we are judged by the Lord, we are chastened so that we may not be condemned along with the world" (1 Cor. 11.30-32). Paul explains here that sickness is one type of the Lord's chastening. Owing to their having erred before the Lord, believers are chastened with illness to prompt them to judge themselves and eliminate their mistakes. In chastening His children God deals graciously towards them that they may not be condemned with the world. If Christians repent of their faults God will no longer chasten them. Can we not then avoid sickness through self-judgment?

We often conclude sickness to be merely a physical problem and to have no relation to God's righteousness, holiness and judgment. But the Apostle tells us quite plainly in this passage that sickness is an effect of sin and a chastisement of God. Christians like to cite the story of the blind man in John 9 to support the contention that their sickness is not God's chastisement due to sin. Yet the Lord Jesus has not said there that sin and sickness are unrelated; He simply is warning His disciples not to condemn each and every sick person. If Adam had not sinned, that man in John 9 would never have been blind. Moreover, that particular man was *born* blind, so the *nature* of his illness is quite unlike that of a believer's sickness. The infirmities of those who are born infirm are perhaps not due to their own sins; but according to the Scriptures sickness after we have believed in the Lord is usually related to sin. "Therefore confess your sins to one another, and pray for one another, that you may be healed" (James 5.16). Sins must first be confessed and then there will be healing. Sin is the root of sickness.

Illness is frequently the chastisement of God employed to draw our attention to some sin which we have overlooked so that we may forsake it. God *permits* these sicknesses to fall upon us that He may discipline us and purge us from our faults. God's hand bears down on us to direct our eyes to some unrighteousness or some debt, some pride or love of this world, some self-reliance or greediness in work, or some disobedience to God. Sickness is consequently God's open judgment of sin. Yet we are not to infer from this that the one who is ill is necessarily more sinful than others (cf. Luke 13.2); quite the opposite, they who are chastened by the Lord are usually the holiest. Job is a prime example.

Each time a believer is chastened by God and becomes sick he is open to great blessing, for the Father of spirits "disciplines us for our good, that we may share his holiness" (Heb. 12.10). Sickness prompts us to recollect and examine the past as to whether there be any hidden sin, obstinacy or self-will. Then and there we can detect if any barrier exists between us and God. As we search the depths of our heart we come to realize how full of self and unlike the holiness of God has been our past life. These exercises enable us to advance in spiritual development and to obtain God's healing.

Hence the first action one should take when ill is not to scurry around in search of healing and the means of healing. He should neither be anxious nor afraid. What he should do is place himself completely in God's light for examination, having an honest desire to learn if he is being chastened because of some lack. He should judge himself. Thus the Holy Spirit shall point out to him where he has failed. And whatever he is shown, it must be immediately confessed and forsaken. If that sin *has done harm to others* then he must *do his best* to make it up, meanwhile believing that God has accepted him. He should offer himself afresh to God and be disposed to obey His will fully.

God "does not willingly afflict or grieve the sons of men" (Lam. 3.33). He will cease chastening when He realizes the objective of self-judgment is attained. God is most happy to withdraw His chastisement when no longer needed. The Bible assures us that if we judge ourselves we will not be judged. God desires us to be freed from sin and self; once that end has been reached the sickness will disappear because it has accomplished its mission. What the Christian needs to understand today is that God chastens him for a specific purpose. Accordingly, always allow the Holy Spirit to uncover what the sin is so that the aim of God may be achieved and the chastisement may no longer be necessary. Then will God heal.

Once the saint has confessed and forsaken his sin and in addition believed for forgiveness, he can trust God's promise and know without fear that He will make him well. With a conscience void of accusation he has the boldness to approach God for grace. It is when we are far away from Him that we find it hard to believe or that we dare not believe; but after sin is forsaken and forgiven through the enlightening of, and obedience to, the Holy Spirit, we have free access to God. Since the cause of the sickness has been removed, the sickness itself shall be removed. Now the sick believer has no difficulty in believing that "the chastisement of our peace was upon (Christ); and with his stripes we are healed." At that moment the presence of the Lord will be manifested abundantly and the life of the Lord will enter his body to make it alive.

Are we really aware that the heavenly Father is not pleased with us in many areas? He uses sickness to help us perceive our shortcomings. If we do not suppress the voice of conscience the Holy Spirit shall most certainly show us the reason for the chastisement. God delights to forgive our sins and heal our ills. The great redemptive work of the Lord Jesus includes both forgiveness and healing. He will permit nothing between us and Him; He wants us to live by Him as never before. Now is the time to trust and obey Him totally. The Heavenly Father does not wish to chastise. How willing He is to heal us that through seeing His love and power we may hold closer communion with Him.

SICKNESS AND SELF

All evil and adverse environment has the effect of exposing our true condition. These do not add any particular sin to us; they only reveal what is in us. Sickness is one of these environments through which we can read our true condition.

We never realize how much we are living for God and how much for self until we are sick, especially if that sickness is a protracted one. During our ordinary days we may declare with great conviction in our hearts that we will obey God with our whole heart and will be satisfied with whatever treatment we receive from Him; only at the time of sickness, though, do we discover how much of that declaration is genuine. What God wishes to accomplish in His children is that they be satisfied with His will and way. He does not want His children to murmur against His will and way because of their *own* immature feelings. For this reason God permits sickness to descend upon His dearest children time and again in order to make manifest their attitude towards His specially arranged will.

How pitiful is the Christian who for the sake of his own desire murmurs against God when under trial. He does not accept what God gives as the best for him; instead his heart is flooded with the desire for early healing. (What we mean by sickness given by God is in reality sickness permitted by God, for the one who directly gives sickness is Satan. But whatever illness befalls a Christian comes through God's permission and comes with a purpose. The experience of Job is a perfect example.) Because of this, God must prolong the sickness. He will not withdraw His instrument before He has achieved His purpose. The end in all communications between God and the believer is to bring the latter to an unconditional submission to Him, gladly welcoming any treatment from Him. God is not pleased with that person who praises Him in prosperity but complains against Him in adversity. God does not want His own to doubt His love or misunderstand His acts so easily: He wants them to obey Him even to death.

God intends His children to recognize that everything which comes upon them is given by Him. However dangerous is the physical or environmental circumstance, it is measured by His hand. Even the falling of a hair is within His will. Should a person resist what comes upon him he cannot but be resisting as well the God Who permits these occurrences. And should he develop a heart of hatred following a painful period of sickness, he cannot but be hating the God Who allowed it to happen to him. The question under discussion is not whether a believer ought to be sick but whether he is opposing God. God wants His own to forget their sickness when ill. Yes, forget their sickness and look away steadfastly at God. Suppose His will is for me to be sick and to continue to be so; am I ready to accept it? Can I humble myself beneath the mighty hand of God and resist not? Or do I covet in suffering a health which is outside God's present purpose? Can I wait until His end is fulfilled before asking in His will for healing? Or will I seek other means of healing while He is chastening me? Am I, in the time of deep suffering, striving for what He presently will not grant? These questions should pierce deeply into the heart of every sick believer.

God takes no pleasure in His children's sickness. Rather does His love make Him desire smooth peaceful days for them. But He knows the danger: in time of ease our love towards Him, our words of praise and our service for Him, are conditioned by peaceful living. He knows how easily our hearts can turn from Him and His will to His gifts. He consequently permits sickness and similar phenomena to come upon us that we may see whether we want Him or purely His gifts. If in days of adversity we seek nothing else, then it indicates we genuinely want God. Sickness readily discloses whether one seeks his own desire or the arrangement of God.

We still harbor our personal desires. Such aspirations prove how flushed with our own thoughts our daily life is. Both

in the work of God and in our dealings with people, we hold
tenaciously to many thoughts and opinions. God is compelled to bring us near the door of death in order to teach
us the folly of resisting Him. He lets us pass through deep
waters that we may be broken and may forsake our self-
will—that behavior of ours which displeases Him immensely.
How numerous are the Christians who ordinarily seem to
follow nothing of what the Lord has said but become
obedient only after their bodies are afflicted. The way of
the Lord must therefore be this: He chastises after love's
persuasion has lost its effectiveness. The purpose of His
chastisement is to break down self-will. Every sick Christian should judge himself seriously in this respect.

Besides self-desire and self-will, what God additionally
hates is a heart of *self-love*. Self-love endangers the spiritual
life and destroys spiritual works. Except God expunge this
element from us, we cannot run our spiritual race swiftly.
Self-love has a special relationship to our body. To say we
love ourselves means we cherish our bodies and our life.
Hence to destroy this odious trait God often permits sickness to come upon us. Because of our love of self we are
fearful lest our body be weakened; yet God weakens it; He
allows us to experience pain. And when we expect to get well
our sickness becomes the more serious. We wish to keep
on living, but that hope appears to fade. God of course deals
differently with different people—some drastically, some
relatively lightly; nonetheless, the purpose of God in removing the heart of self-love remains the same. How many *strong*
ones must be brought near the gates of death before their
love of self dissolves: what else is left to be loved now that
his body is ruined, his life is endangered, sickness has progressively devoured his health, and pain has swallowed up
his power? By this time the person is actually willing to die;
he is hopeless but also self-loveless. It would be the height
of tragedy were he at this moment not to return and claim
God's promise of healing.

The heart of a believer is far from God's. God permits him
to be ill that he may forget himself; but the more ill he

grows the more self-loving he becomes; he endlessly dwells
on his symptoms in his anxiety to find a cure. Almost all
thoughts revolve about himself! How attentive he now is to
his food, what he should or should not eat! How worried he
is when anything goes awry! He takes great care for his comforts and rest. He agonizes if he feels a bit hot or cold or
has suffered a bad night, as though these were fatal to his
life. How sensitive he is to the way people treat him: do they
think enough of him, do they take good care of him, do they
visit him as often as they should? Countless hours are exhausted in just this way of thinking about his body; and so
he has no time to meditate on the Lord or on what the Lord
may be wanting to accomplish in his life. Indeed, many are
simply "bewitched" by their sickness! We never truly know
how excessively much we love ourselves until we become
sick!

God is not delighted with our self-love. He desires us to
comprehend the far-reaching damage it inflicts upon us. He
wishes us to learn in the hour of sickness how to be en-
grossed not in our symptoms but exclusively in Him. It is
His desire that we commit our body entirely to Him and
allow Him to care for it. Every discovery of an adverse
symptom should warn us not to be occupied with our body
but to mind the Lord.

Due to love of self the believer seeks healing as soon as
he is sick. He does not perceive that he ought to rid his
heart of wicked deeds before beseeching God to heal. His
eyes are fixed upon healing. He does not bother to inquire
why God has permitted this sickness, what he should repent
of, or how he should let God's work be perfected in him. All
he can contemplate is his own weakness. He longs to be
strong again, so he searches everywhere for the means of
healing. That he may be cured speedily, he entreats God and
inquires of man. With the sick believer in such a state as
this, it is impossible for God to accomplish His purpose in
him. That is why some are made well only temporarily;
after a while their old infirmity returns. How can there be
lasting healing if the root of sickness is not removed?

Sickness is one of the methods by which God chooses to speak to us. He does not want us to grow anxious and seek immediately for cure; instead He asks us to pray obediently. What a pity it is for that person who eagerly expects to be healed while simultaneously is unable to say to the Lord, "Speak, Lord, for Your servant hears." Our sole aim is merely to be delivered from pain and weakness. We rush to find the best remedy. Sickness prompts us to invent many cures. Each symptom frightens us and sets our brain to work. God appears to be far from us. We neglect our spiritual welfare. All thoughts center upon our sufferings and the means of cure. Should the medicine work, then we praise the grace of God. But should the cure be delayed we lapse into misunderstanding our Father's love. Yet let us ask ourselves: if all we desire is to be delivered from pain, are we being led by the Holy Spirit? Do we think we can glorify God with the power of the flesh?

MEDICINE

Self-love naturally produces self-means. Instead of solving the root of the sickness in God, Christians covet cure through man's drugs. We do not intend to waste a lot of time here in arguing whether or not a believer can use medicine. Yet we do want to say that since the Lord Jesus has provided for the healing of our body in His salvation, it seems to be ignorance, if not unbelief, if we turn to the aid of man's invention.

Many debate whether or not the saints should take medicine. They seem to imply that if this question is resolved all questions are solved. But are they aware that the principle of spiritual living is not in "can or can't" but in whether or not God has so led? Our question, therefore, is: when a believer, because of self-love, depends on medicine and eagerly seeks healing, is he being guided by the Holy Spirit or is it exclusively his own activity? According to human nature, until one has experienced many adverse circumstances he is reluctant to be saved by faith; he usually strives to be saved by his works. Is it not equally true with the healing of one's body? Perhaps the struggle over divine healing is even more intense than that over forgiveness of sin. Believers will acknowledge that unless they trust the Lord Jesus for salvation they cannot gain entrance to heaven; but why, such ones will ask, must they depend on the salvation of the Lord for healing when they can employ many other medical means? So our attention is not focused upon whether medicine can be used but upon whether in using it through one's own activity he has demeaned God's salvation. Has not the world spun out sundry theories for saving man from sin? Does not the world supply many schools of philosophy, psychology, ethics and education as well as countless rituals, rules and practices to assist people to be good? Can we as believers accept these means as perfect and workable? Are we for the finished work of the Lord Jesus on the cross or for these ingenious human devices? In such a similar manner has the world invented multiplied kinds of drugs to relieve people from ailments; yet the Lord has equally accomplished on the cross that work of salvation pertaining to the body. Shall we therefore seek cure according to human methods or shall we rely on the Lord Jesus for healing?

We do acknowledge that occasionally God utilizes intermediaries to manifest His power and glory. Judging from the teaching of Scripture and the experience of Christians, however, we are forced to confess that after the fall of man our feelings seem to control our lives, which prompts us naturally to incline towards the intermediaries than towards God Himself. Hence we observe that during the period of illness Christians direct more attention to medicine than to the power of God. Although their lips may proclaim a trust in God's power, their hearts are almost totally wrapped up in medicine—as though without its help God's power cannot be released. No wonder they exhibit signs of unrest, anxiety and fear, hotly pursuing the best means of cure everywhere. These ones lack the peace which springs from trusting in God. With their hearts thus absorbed in the use and application of medicine, they turn to the world and sacrifice the presence of God. God has purposed through sickness to bring people *nearer to Him*, yet precisely the *opposite* seems to be the effect. Perhaps some indeed are able to use medicine without damaging their spiritual life, but such ones are few. Most of God's people tend to rely on intermediaries more than on Him and consequently their spiritual life is harmed through the use of drugs.

There is a vast distinction between cure through medicine and healing by God. The power of the first is natural while that of the second is supernatural. The way of obtaining the cure is likewise distinguishable: in using medicine the trust rests in human cleverness; in depending on God the confidence is in the work and life of the Lord Jesus. Even should the physician be a believer who entreats God for wisdom and for blessing in the drug used, he is nonetheless powerless to impart spiritual blessing to the one healed, for unconsciously the latter already has pinned his hope of cure on medicine rather than on the power of the Lord. Though he be healed physically, his spiritual life shall suffer loss. If the person verily trusts in God he will commit himself to His love and power. He will inquire and investigate the cause of his sickness—wherein has he displeased the Lord. So that when he is healed he shall be blessed spiritually as well as bodily.

Many argue that since medicine is given by God they certainly can use it. But this is what we want to emphasize: does God lead us to use medicine? We do not wish to debate whether or not medicine comes from God; we instead wished to inquire whether or not the Lord Jesus is given by God to His children as the Savior of their physical ills: should we seek a cure through the natural power of drugs as unbelievers or weak Christians do, or should we accept the Lord Jesus Whom God has prepared for us and trust in His name?

Trusting medicine and accepting the life of the Lord Jesus are absolutely diametrical. We grant the effectiveness of medicine and other medical inventions, but these cures are natural, short of the best God has provided for His own. Believers may ask God to bless the drugs and be cured; they may also thank God after being cured by these, regarding themselves as having been healed by God Himself; yet such healing is not the same as accepting the life of the Lord Jesus. For by so doing they are taking the easy way out, quitting the battlefield of faith. If, in our conflict with Satan, healing were the only objective to attain in sickness then we could employ any available means of cure. But should there be more important purposes than mere healing to be realized, then must we not be quiet before God and await His way and time?

We do not want to state dogmatically that God never blesses medicine. We know God has blessed many times, for He is so kind and generous. Christians who trust in medicine are nevertheless not standing on the ground of redemption. They are assuming the same position as do worldly people. They cannot testify for God in this particular matter. Swallowing pills, applying ointments, and taking injections will not afford us the life of the Lord Jesus. In trusting God we are elevated to a place higher than that of the natural. Cure by medicine is often slow and painful; the healing of God is quick and blessed.

One observation is certainly beyond dispute, which is: that were we to be healed by dependence on God, we would derive such spiritual profit from it as a cure by medicine could never accord us. When sick in bed how deeply people repent of their past lives; but once they are healed through use of medicine they drift further away from God. Yet they would not fall into such an after-effect were they to be healed like others by waiting and trusting in God. These latter ones confess their sins, deny themselves, trust in God's love, and depend on His power; they accept the life and holiness of God; and they establish a new indivisible relationship with Him.

The object lesson God purposes us to learn in sickness is to cease from all our own activity and trust Him thoroughly. How often in anxiously seeking cure we are driven on by a heart of self-love. We forget God and the lesson He wishes to teach us. For if God's children were void of self-love, would

they so eagerly strive after healing?—if they have truly
ceased from their activities, would they turn to the assistance
of human medicine? Not at all. They would examine themselves quietly before God, seeking to understand first the
meaning of their sickness, and afterwards asking *Him* for
healing on the basis of the Father's love. The contrast between leaning on medical help and leaning on God's power
is that in the former case the person anxiously seeks for a
cure while in the latter case he calmly aspires to ascertain
God's will. It is because believers are full of self-love, im-
petuous desire and their own strength that they so seek for
a cure when sick. They would react differently were they
to learn to depend on God's power. To trust in God for
healing, believers must honestly confess and forsake their
sins and be willing to offer themselves utterly to Him.

Many today are sick. In each of these sicknesses the Lord
has a special purpose. Whenever "self" relinquishes its
power, the Lord will heal. If Christians refuse to bow, if
they refuse to gladly receive the sickness as the best from
God, and if they search for means other than God, they will
be filled with sickness again even after being cured. If they
cling to self-love and are mindful of themselves all the time,
God will give them increased cause to pity themselves. He
will show them that earthly medicine cannot permanently
heal. God intends His children to know that *a strong and
healthy body is neither for the sake of pleasing one's self
nor to be used in accordance with one's desires but is wholly
for God.* The spirit of healing is a spirit of holiness. What we
lack is not healing but holiness. What we need to be delivered from initially is not sickness but self.

When a child of God has denied the use of human means
and medicine and has trusted in the Father with singleness
of heart, he notices his faith waxing stronger than usual. He
has launched upon a new relationship with God; he begins
to live by that life he formerly did not trust. He commits
his body as well as his spirit and soul to his heavenly Father.
He discovers that the will of God is to manifest the power
of the Lord Jesus and the love of the Father. He is led to

exercise faith unto proving that the Lord redeems the body as well as the spirit and soul.

"Therefore I tell you, do not be anxious about your life" (Matt. 6.25). The Lord will care for whatever we commit to Him. If we secure instant healing, let us praise God. Should our symptoms grow more severe, let us not doubt but let us look away instead to God's promise and furnish no occasion for self-love to be revived. God may be using this very situation to extinguish the last drops of our love for self. Were we to regard our body we would commence to doubt; but if we behold God's promise we will draw nearer to Him, our faith will be increased, and healing eventually will come to us.

We must nevertheless be careful lest we fall into extremes. Though God aims for us to rely exclusively upon Him, yet once we have definitely denied our own activities and trusted Him in perfect faith, He may delight in our using some natural means to render help to our body. We mean such articles as "a little wine" prescribed for Timothy. Timothy possessed a weak stomach and was afflicted frequently with ailments. Instead of scolding him for lack of faith and failure to be cured directly from God, Paul persuaded Timothy to use a little wine for it would be beneficial to him. What the Apostle here enjoins us to use is some such element as wine, something neutral in its innate character.

From this case we may learn a lesson. We must, it is very true, believe and depend on God (even as Timothy must have done); even so, we at the same time should not go to extremes. If our body is weak we should learn to be led by the Lord to eat some singularly nourishing food. By using a little of such nourishments according to the leading of the Lord, our body shall be strengthened. Before our body is fully redeemed we continue naturally to be human beings who yet possess a physical body. We should therefore be attentive to its natural needs.

Such use of nutrients is not contradictory to faith. Only, believers need to be cautious lest they know merely these nutrients and do not trust in God.

BETTER TO BE HEALED

Some of God's saints have run to extremes. They were naturally hard and obstinate but were broken by God through sickness sent them. By submitting themselves to the purpose of God's chastisement they became most gentle, kind, soft and holy. However, since sickness has been so effective in transforming their lives, they begin to relish sickness more than health. They view sickness to be an enzyme to spiritual growth. They aspire no more to be healed but accept unnaturally instead the sickness which comes to them. They now contend that were they meant to be whole, God would step in Himself and heal them. According to their reckoning, it is less troublesome to be godly in sickness than in health, one is nearer to God in inactivity and suffering than in activity, and it is more excellent to lie in bed than to run to and fro. Consequently, they have no desire to seek divine healing. How can we help them to know that health is *more profitable* than weakness? We acknowledge that many believers do forsake their wickedness and enter upon a deeper experience during sickness; we admit that a number of invalids and infirm persons possess unusual godliness and spiritual experiences; but we must additionally confess that many Christians are rather unclear on several points.

The sick may be holy, but such holiness is a little unnatural. Who knows but what, once he was recuperated and again had the freedom of choice, he would return to the world and to himself? In sickness he is holy; in health he becomes worldly. The Lord has to keep him in prolonged illness in order to keep him holy. His holiness hinges on his sickness! Let us understand, however, that life with the Lord need not at all be restricted to illness. Never, never entertain the thought that unless one is under the yoke of sickness he has no strength to glorify God in his daily duties. On the contrary, he should be able to manifest the life of God in an ordinary daily walk. To be able to endure suffering is good, but is it not even better if one can obey God when he is full of strength?

SICKNESS **175**

We should recognize that healing—divine healing—is
something which belongs to God. In striving to be cured
by human medicine we naturally are separated from Him;
but in aspiring to be cured by God we will be drawn closer
to Him. He who is healed by *God* glorifies Him more than
he who is always sick. Sickness can glorify God, for it
presents Him with an opportunity to manifest His healing
power (John 9.3); yet how can He be glorified if one remains protractedly ill? When we are healed by God we
witness His power as well as His glory.

The Lord Jesus never portrayed sickness as a blessing
which His followers ought to endure to their death. Hs never
suggested it was an expression of the Father's love. He calls
His disciples to take up the cross, but He does not allow
the sick to remain ill for long. He tells them how they should
suffer for Him but never says they should be sick for Him.
The Lord foretells we shall have tribulation in the world,
yet He does not view illness as tribulation. How truly He
suffered while on earth, yet never was He sick. Moreover,
on every occasion when He met a sick person He healed him.
He avows that sickness comes from sin and the devil.

We must differentiate suffering from sickness. "Many are
the afflictions of the righteous," notes the psalmist, "but the
Lord delivers him out of them all. He keeps all his bones;
not one of them is broken" (Ps. 34.19-20). "Is anyone among
you suffering?" asks James. Then "let him pray" that he may
obtain grace and strength; but, the Apostle continues, "is
any among you sick? Let him call for the elders of the
church" that he may be healed (5.13-14).

1 Corinthians 11.30-32 deals with the relationship of believers to sickness most comprehensively. Sickness is the
chastening of God. If a Christian is willing to judge himself, God shall withdraw the illness. God never desires His
own to persist long in it. No chastisement is permanent
Once the cause of it is removed, the chastisement itself will
follow suit. "For the moment all discipline seems painful
rather than pleasant; *later* . . . "—believers tend to forget
God's "later"—"it yields the peaceful fruit of righteousness

to those who have been trained by it" (Heb. 12.11). Thus we find chastisement is only momentary; afterwards it will produce the most excellent fruit of righteousness. Do not let us misconstrue the discipline of God as being punishment. Strictly speaking, believers are no longer judged. The passage of 1 Corinthians 11.31 supports this statement. The concept of *law* should no longer be with us as though sin must always be answered with a corresponding degree of punishment. What we have here is not a judicial, but a family, problem.

Let us return to the positive teaching of the Bible concerning our body. One verse in Scripture which can completely overthrow the idea some have is 3 John 2: "Beloved, I pray that all may go well with you and that you may be in health; I know that it is well with your soul." This is a prayer of the Apostle John as revealed to him by the Holy Spirit, so it expresses the eternal thought of God in regard to the body of the believer. God has no intention for His children to be sick throughout their lives, unable to serve Him actively. He wishes them to be in bodily health even as their souls are well. Accordingly, we can conclude beyond doubt that prolonged illness is not God's will. He may chasten us temporarily with sickness, but He has no pleasure in protracted sickness.

Paul's word in 1 Thessalonians 5.23 additionally confirms that inordinately long illness is not God's will. As the spirit and soul are, so should be the body. God is not satisfied to have our spirit and soul sound and blameless while our body remains weak, sick and racked with pain. His purpose is to save the whole man, not just a part of him.

The work of the Lord Jesus also reveals the will of God concerning sickness, because He did nothing but the will of God. In the healing of the leper He especially unveils to us the heart of the heavenly Father towards the sick. The leper pleaded, "Lord, if you *will*, you can make me clean." Here we see a man knocking at the gate of heaven inquiring if it is God's will to heal. The Lord stretched out His hand, touched him, and said, "I will; be clean" (Matt. 8.2-3).

Healing often represents God's mind. He who thinks God is reluctant to heal does not know His will. The earthly ministry of the Lord Jesus included "healing *all* who were sick" (v.16). How can we arbitrarily claim that He now has changed His attitude?

The aim of God for today is for His "will (to) be done on earth as it is in heaven" (Matt. 6.10). God's will is carried out in heaven: is there sickness there? No! God's will is altogether incompatible with sickness. What a serious fault it is for Christians, upon having asked healing of God and having given up hope, then to utter the words, "May the Lord's will be done" as if the will of the Lord were synonymous with sickness and death. God does not will for His children to be ill. Though He sometimes permits them to be sick for their profit, His determinate counsel forever is health for His people. The fact that there is no sickness in heaven fully proves what the will of God is.

Were we to trace the source of sickness we would be doubly persuaded to seek for healing. All who were sick "were oppressed by the devil" (Acts. 10.38). The Lord Jesus described the woman who was bent over and could not fully straighten herself as one "whom Satan bound" (Luke 13.16). When He healed Peter's mother-in-law He "rebuked the fever" (Luke 4.39) in the same manner as He rebuked the demons (cf. vv. 31-41). In reading the book of Job we learn that it is the devil who caused Job's sickness (Ch. 1 & 2); but it is God Who healed him (Ch. 42). The thorn that harassed and weakened Paul was "a messenger of Satan" (2 Cor. 12.7); the One Who made him strong is God. He who has the power of death is the devil (Heb. 2.14). We know illness ripens into death, for it is one of the facets of death. As Satan has the power of death, he has the power of sickness too, for death is but the ultimate step beyond sickness.

We cannot avoid concluding from these passages that sickness originates with the devil. God *permits* Satan to attack His children because they contain some defects in their lives. If they refuse to forsake what God has demanded and

thus allow illness to continue in their lives, it is as if they
have forsaken what God has ordered and have welcomed
sickness instead. In so doing they voluntarily place themselves under the oppression of Satan. Who is so illogical as
to return to bondage after he has obeyed the revealed will
of God? Realizing that sickness proceeds from the devil, we
ought to resist it. We should be clear that it belongs to our
enemy and hence is not to be welcomed by us. The Son of
God comes to set us free, not to have us bound.

Why does God not remove our infirmity when it is no further needed? This is a question posed by many saints. Let
us give heed to the principle of God's dealing with us which
is always that of "be it done for you as you have believed"
(Matt. 8.13). Often God wishes to make His children well,
but He has to let sickness remain with them because of their
unbelief and lack of prayer. If God's saints accede to sickness
—nay, even welcome it—as though it would deliver them
from the world and make them holier, then the Lord can do
nothing except grant them what they ask. God frequently
deals with His own according to what they are able to
receive. God may be most delighted to cure them; yet for
the lack of believing prayer this precious gift is not the
portion of all.

Are we wiser than God? Should we exceed what the
Bible reveals? While the sick room may at times be like a
sanctuary where the inner man is deeply moved, illness
nonetheless is not God's ordained will nor is it His best.
Should we follow our emotional whim and disregard the
revealed will of God, He can only let us have what we
desire. How many of the Lord's people piously say: I leave
myself in God's hand for healing or for sickness; I allow God
to do what He wills. But these are generally people who
use medicine. Is this committing everything to God? How
contradictory is such a life! Their submission is but a sign of
spiritual lethargy. In their hearts they long for health, but
mere desire will not prompt God to work. They have accepted sickness passively for so long that they simply succumb to it, forfeiting all courage to seek freedom. The best

for them would be for other people to believe on their behalf or for God to confer upon them the faith to believe. However, faith given by God shall not come unless their will becomes active in resisting the devil and in holding on to the Lord Jesus. Many are infirm not out of necessity but for lack of strength to lay hold on God's promise.

Be it therefore apprehended that the spiritual blessing we receive in sickness is far inferior to what we receive in restoration. If we rest on God for healing, then naturally after being cured we will continue to walk in holiness so as to preserve our health. By making us well the Lord possesses our body. Unspeakable is the joy found in a new relationship and a new experience with Him, not because of sickness cured but because of a new touch with life. In such a time believers glorify the Lord far more than in the time of ill-health.

God's children should accordingly rise up and strive after healing. First hear what God has to say through our sickness, then do as has been revealed with singleness of heart. Moreover, commit your body afresh to the Lord. If there are near you elders of the church who can anoint you with oil (James 5.14-15), then call them and follow the *injunction* of the Holy Scriptures. Or else quietly exercise faith to lay hold of the promise of God (Ex. 15.26). God will heal us.

[*Translator's note*: It was thought profitable for the reader that the following message on sickness and healing, spoken by Mr. Nee in 1948, should be included at this point as an addendum to what has just been set forth in this section on the subject by the author. Although some duplication does appear, it was felt best to include the message in its entirety.]

There are a few matters concerning sickness we would like to consider together before God:

1. The Relation between Sickness and Sin

Before the fall of mankind no infirmity of any kind existed; sickness arose only after man had sinned. One can say generally that both sickness and death resulted from

sin; for by one man's tresspass sin and death came into the
world (Rom. 5.12). Sickness spread to all men just as did
death. Though not all sin in the same way as Adam did,
yet because of his transgression, all die. Where there is sin
there is also death. In between these two is that which we
usually call sickness. This, then, is the factor common to
all disease. However, there is actually more than one cause
to account for sickness coming upon people. Some sicknesses
spring from sin, while others do not. So far as *mankind* is
concerned, sickness does come from sin; but in relation to
the *individual* it may or may not be the case. We need to
distinguish between these two applications of sickness. Now
it is entirely true that were there no sin there could neither
be death *nor* sickness; for if there were no death in the world,
how could there ever be sickness? Death arises through sin,
and sickness through the inception of death. Even so, this
cannot be specifically and indiscriminately applied to every
individual, because while many do fall ill through sin there
are others who become ill for reasons other than sin. In this
matter of the relationship of sin to sickness we must therefore make a careful distinction between the application of
this relationship to mankind as a whole and its application
to individual men.

We will recall in such Old Testament books as Leviticus
and Numbers that God's promise was, that if the people of
Israel obeyed Him, walked in His way, rebelled not against
His laws and did not sin against Him, then He would keep
them from many diseases. These words plainly teach that
many maladies derive from sin or rebellion against God. Yet
in the New Testament we discover that some sicknesses are
not caused by the person having committed any transgression at all.

Paul once wrote that he would deliver to Satan for the
destruction of his flesh that man who had sinned by living
with his father's wife (1 Cor 5.4-5). This definitely indicates that some sickness proceeds from sin. The consequence of sin is either sickness if the sin is light or death
if it is serious. Judging from the words of 2 Corinthians 7

this man was not sick to the point of death because, out of godly grief, he produced a repentance which led to salvation and brought no regret (vv.9-10). Paul charged the church at Corinth to forgive such a man (2 Cor. 2.6-7). In 1 Corinthians 5 mention is made of delivering this man's flesh (not his life) to Satan; he was to be sick but was not to die.

Paul further wrote that those in the church at Corinth who ate and drank of the bread and the cup of the Lord without discerning the Lord's body had become weak and ill and some even had died (1 Cor. 11.29-30). This reveals that disobedience to the Lord was the provocation for their sickness.

The Scriptures have served sufficient notice that many (but not all) are ill because of sin. Hence the first action we must take when sick is to examine ourselves to determine whether or not we have sinned against God. By searching, many find that their illness is in fact due to sin: on a particular occasion they had rebelled against God or had disobeyed His Word. They had gone astray. Just as soon as that particular sin is found out and confessed, however, the sickness will be over. Countless brothers and sisters in the Lord have encountered such experiences. Shortly after the cause is discovered before God the illness is gone. This is a phenomenon beyond the explanation of medical science.

Sickness does not necessarily issue from sin, yet much of it actually does. We acknowledge that many diseases have their natural causes, but we equally maintain that we cannot attribute all sickness to natural reasons.

I am reminded of one brother, a professor in a medical school, who once lectured his students as follows. We have isolated many natural explanations for illnesses. For instance, a certain type of coccus causes a particular kind of disease. As medical doctors, he continued, we can determine which type of organism produces what kind of disease, but we have no way to explain why among certain equally exposed people some are infected while others remain immune. Suppose, for example, ten persons enter the same room simultaneously and are exposed to the same type of coccus. We would expect the physically weak to be infected; yet the fact may be that the weak are spared and the strong are the ones stricken. We have to acknowledge, he concluded, that aside from natural causes there is additionally the control of Providence. Personally I think well of what this brother has said. How often people grow sick in spite of every preventive measure.

I also recall what one of my schoolmates related to me about his experience at Peking Medical College. There was a certain professor in the college who was profound ir learning yet short on patience. Hence he usually posed very simple questions in examinations. Once he asked why people contracted tuberculosis. This was a simple enough question; yet many failed to supply the proper answer. Most replied by writing that certain people had tubercle bacillus. All of *these* answers were marked incorrect. The professor explained that the earth was full of tubercle bacilli but that not everybody was felled by tuberculosis. It is only under certain favorable conditions, he reminded them, that these bacilli cause the disease called tuberculosis. The bacillus alone cannot cause the disease. Most students forgot the importance of these favorable conditions. Let us be aware, therefore, that despite the presence of many natural factors Christians become sick only by God's permission given under appropriate conditions.

We unreservedly believe that there are natural explanations for sickness; this has been proven scientifically. We confess nonetheless that many illnesses among God's children are the consequences of sinning against God such as in the case cited in 1 Corinthians 11. It is consequently essential to ask for forgiveness first, then for healing afterwards. We frequently can detect, soon after we have been struck down with sickness, where we have transgressed against the Lord or how we have been disobedient to His Word. When the sin is confessed and the problem resolved, the sickness fades away. This is truly a most marvelous event. Thus the initial point we need to know is the relation between sin and sickness. Generally sickness results from sin; and individually, too, it may result from sin.

2. The Lord's Work and Sickness

"Surely he has borne our griefs and carried our sorrows; yet we esteemed him stricken, smitten by God, and afflicted. But he was wounded for our transgressions, he was bruised for our iniquities" (Is. 53.4-5). Of all the Old Testament writings this 53rd chapter of Isaiah is quoted most often in the New Testament. It alludes to the Lord Jesus Christ, especially to Him as our Savior. Verse 4 affirms that "he has borne our griefs and carried our sorrows" whereas Matthew 8.17 declares that "this was to fulfil what was spoken by the prophet Isaiah, 'He took our infirmities and bore our diseases'." The Holy Spirit indicates here that the Lord Jesus came to the world to take our infirmities and bear our diseases. Prior to His crucifixion He had already taken our infirmities and borne our diseases; which is to say that during His earthly ministry the Lord Jesus made healing His burden and task. He not only preached, He also healed. He preached the glad tidings on the one hand, but on the other hand strengthened the weak, restored the withered hand, cleansed the leper and raised the palsied. While on earth the Lord Jesus devoted Himself to the performance of miracles as well as to the ministry of the Word. He went about doing good, He healed the sick, and cast out demons. The purpose of His work was to overthrow sickness, the result of sin. He came to deal with death and sickness as well as with sin.

Psalm 103 is familiar to many of God's children; I myself love to read it. David proclaims, "Bless the Lord, O my soul; and all that is within me, bless his holy name!" Why bless the Lord? "Bless the Lord, O my soul, and forget not all his benefits." What are His benefits? "Who forgives all your iniquity, who heals all your diseases." (vv.1-3) I wish brothers and sisters to see that sickness is coupled with two elements: death on the one side, sin on the other. We have mentioned earlier how death is the result of sin, with sickness included therein. Both sickness and death flow from sin. Here in Psalm 103 we find that sickness is coupled with sin. Because of sin in the soul there is disease in the body. Along with the forgiveness of our iniquity comes the healing of our disease. The trouble in the body is sin within and disease without. But the Lord takes both away.

There is a basic dissimiliarity, however, between God's treatment of our iniquity and His treatment of our disease. Why this difference? Our Lord Jesus bore our sins in His body on the cross. Does any sin remain unforgiven? Absolutely none, for the work of God is so complete that sin is entirely destroyed. But in taking our infirmities and bearing our diseases while He lived on earth, the Lord Jesus did not eradicate all diseases and all infirmities. For note that Paul never says "when I sin, then am I sanctified," but he does declare that "when I am weak, then I am strong" (2 Cor. 12.10). Hense sin is thoroughly and unlimitedly dealt with whereas sickness is only limitedly treated.

In God's redemption the handling of sickness is unlike that of sin. With the latter, its destruction is totally uncircumscribed; with the former, this is just not so. Timothy, for instance, continued to have a weak stomach. The Lord permitted this weakness to remain with His servant. So in God's salvation sickness has not been eradicated as totally as has sin. Some maintain that the Lord Jesus deals solely with sin and not with illness too: others conceive the scope of His treatment of disease to be as broad and inclusive as His treatment of sin. Yet the Scriptures manifestly indicate to us that the Lord Jesus deals with both sin and sickness; only His dealing with sin is limitless while that with sickness is limited. We must behold the Lamb of God taking away *all* the sin of the world—He has borne the sin of each and every person. Sin's problem is therefore already solved. But meanwhile sickness still pervades God's children.

Nonetheless, we contend that since the Lord Jesus has actually borne our diseases there should not be so much sickness as there is among the children of God. While Jesus was on earth he unmistakably devoted Himself to the healing of the sick. He included healing in His work. Isaiah 53.4 is fulfilled in Matthew 8, not in Matthew 27. It is realized *before* Calvary. Had it been realized on the cross, healing would be unbounded. But no, the Lord Jesus bore our diseases prior to crucifixion, with the result that this aspect of His work is not as unlimited as was His bearing of our sins.

Even so, numberless saints remain ill because they have missed the opportunity of being healed; they do not see that the Lord has borne our diseases. Let me add a few more words on this point. Unless we have the assurance as did Paul upon praying thrice that his weakness would stay on because it was profitable to him, we should ask for healing. Paul accepted his weakness only after he had prayed the third time and had been shown distinctly by the Lord that His grace was sufficient for him and that His strength would be made perfect in his weakness. Until we are sure that God wants us to bear our weakness, we should boldly ask the Lord Himself to bear it and take away our disease. The children of God live on earth not to be sick but to glorify God. If to be sick will bring God glory, well and good; but many diseases do not necessarily glorify Him. Consequently, we must learn to trust the Lord while sick and must realize that He bears our sickness too. He healed a great number while He was on earth. And He is the same yesterday, today and forever. Let us commit our infirmity to Him and ask for His healing.

3. *The Believer's Attitude towards Sickness*

Every time the believer falls ill the first thing he should do is to inquire after its cause before the Lord. He should not be overanxious in seeking healing. Paul sets a good example in showing us how he was most clear about his weakness. We must examine whether we have disobeyed the Lord, have sinned anywhere, owe anybody a debt, have violated some natural law, or have neglected some special duty. We ought to know that frequently our violation of natural law can constitute a sin against God, for God sets up these natural laws by which to govern the universe. Many are afraid to die; upon becoming sick they hurriedly seek out physicians, for they are anxious to be cured. Such ought not to be the Christian's attitude. He should first attempt to isolate the cause for his malady. Alas, how many brothers and sisters do not possess any patience. The moment they fall sick they search for a remedy. Are you so afraid to lose your precious life that through prayer you lay hold of God for healing yet simultaneously lay hold of a physician for drugs and an injection? This reveals how full of self you are. But then how could you be less full of self in sickness if you are filled with self during ordinary days? Those who are ordinarily full of self will be those who anxiously seek for healing just as soon as they get sick.

May I tell you that anxiety avails nothing. Since you belong to God, your healing is not so simple. Even if you are cured this time, you will be ailing again. One must solve his problem before God first; and then can be solved the problem in his body.

Learn to accept whatever lesson sickness may bring to you. For if you have dealings with God many of your problems will be resolved quickly. You will find out that often your illness is due to some sin or fault of yours. Upon confessing your sin and asking for forgiveness, you may expect healing from God. Or, should you have walked further with the Lord, you may discern that involved in this is the enemy's attack. Or the matter of God's discipline may be associated with your unhealthy state. God chastises with sickness so as to render you holier, softer or more yielding. As you deal with these problems before God you will be enabled to see the exact reason for your infirmity. Sometimes God may allow you to receive a little natural or medical help, but sometimes He may heal you instantaneously without such assistance.

We should see that healing is in God's hand. Learn to trust Him Who heals. In the Old Testament God has a special name which is, "I am the Lord, your healer" (Ex. 15.26). Look to Him and He will be gracious to His own ir this particular regard.

The initial step which the believer should therefore take when sick is to ferret out the cause; afterwards he may resort to several different ways for healing, one of which is to call the elders of the church to pray and anoint him with oil. This is the only command in the Bible concerning sickness.

Is any among you sick? Let him call for the elders of the church, and let them pray over him, anointing him with oil in the name of the Lord; and the prayer of faith will save the sick man, and the Lord will raise him up; and if he has committed sins, he will be forgiven. (James 5.14-15)

Make no haste in seeking a cure, but rather have dealings with God at the outset. One of the things to be done is to call for the elders of the church to anoint you with oil. This speaks of the flowing of the oil from the Head to you as one of the members of the body. The oil which the Head receives runs down upon the whole body. As a member of the body of Christ, one can expect the oil on the Head to flow to him. Where life flows, sickness is swept away. The purpose of anointing is hence to bring down oil from the Head. Through disobedience, sin or perhaps some other reason the believer has gotten himself out of the body circulation and has departed from the body protection. Accordingly, he needs to call the elders of the church to reinstate him into the circulation and life flow of the body of Christ. This is just as in the physical body; for when any of its members is out of joint the life of the body cannot flow freely into it. Thus the anointing is to restore such a flow. The elders represent the local church; they anoint the believer on behalf of the body of Christ so that the oil of the Head may flow to him once again. Let the oil on the Head come upon that member through which life has been obstructed! Our experience tells us that such anointing may raise the seriously sick up instantly.

At times one identifies the explanation for his illness to be his individualism. This may well be the chief cause for illness. Some Christians are highly individualistic. They do everything according to their own will. They do it all by themselves. If the hand of God comes upon them they grow sick, for the supply of the body does not reach such members. I dare not over-simplify these matters. The reasons for sickness can be many and varied. One sickness may be due to disobeying the Lord's command, refusing to carry out His will; another may be caused by committing some particular sin; but still another may be the consequence of individualism. Now in the case of certain individualists God overlooks and does not discipline; but especially in the case of those who know the church, He chastens them with illness if they commence to act independently. The Lord will not let these go without some discipline.

It is also possible that infirmity is the consequence of a defiled body. Should anyone defile his body, God will destroy that temple. Many are infirm because they have corrupted their bodies.

By way of summing up, then, no sickness occurs without a cause. If the Christian contracts an illness he should try to locate its cause or causes. After he has confessed them one by one before God he should summon the elders of the church so that they may confess to one another and pray for one another. The elders will anoint the sick one with oil that the life of the body of Christ may be restored to him. The influx of life will swallow up the disease. We believe in natural causes, but we additionally must affirm that spiritual causes have priority over the natural. If the spiritual are taken care of, the sickness shall be healed completely.

4. God's Chastening and Sickness

An amazing fact is found in the Bible: that it is relatively easy for a "heathen" to be healed, but healing for a Christian is not so easy. The New Testament overwhelmingly shows us that whenever an unbeliever seeks the Lord he is cured immediately. Now the gift of healing is for the brethren as well as for the unbelievers. Yet the Bible tells of some believers who are not healed; among them are Trophimus, Timothy and Paul. And these are the best of the

brethren. Paul left Trophimus ill at Miletus (2 Tim. 4.20).
He exhorted Timothy to use a little wine for the sake of his
stomach and his frequent ailments (1 Tim. 5.23). Paul himself experienced a thorn in his flesh from which he suffered
much and was reduced to great weakness (2 Cor. 12.7).
Whatever the nature of that thorn, be it eye trouble or some
other disease, it pricked his flesh. One feels great discomfort should a little finger be pricked by a thorn. Paul's, however, was a big thorn, not a tiny one. It gave him such
discomfort that he could only describe his physical condition
as weakness. These three are brethren par excellence, yet
none was healed. They had to endure sickness.

It is quite evident that sickness is different from sin in its
outworking. Sin does not produce any fruit of holiness, but
sickness does. The more a person sins the more corrupt he
becomes; sickness, though, bears the fruit of holiness because
the chastening hand of God is upon the sick. Under such circumstances it behooves a child of God to learn how to submit himself under the mighty hand of God.

If one is ill he ought to deal with every cause of his illness
before the Lord. If, after all has been dealt with, the hand of
God still remains upon him, then he should understand that
this illness is for the purpose of restraining him from being
proud or loose or for some other purpose. He should accept
it and learn its lesson. To be sick is valueless if the lesson is
not learned. Sickness itself does not make a man holy, but its
lesson if accepted produces holiness. Some grow worse spiritually during illness; they become more self-centered. That
is why one must discover the lesson in such a period. What
profit or fruit can be derived from it? Is the hand of God
upon me to keep me humble as He did with Paul, "to keep
me from being too elated by the abundance of revelations"
(2 Cor. 12.7)? Or is it because God desires to weaken my
stubborn individuality? What is the use of sickness if it does
not provoke me to learn the lesson of weakness? Many are
sick in vain because they never accept the Lord's dealing
with their particular problems.

Do not look upon sickness as something terrible. In whose
hand is this knife? Remember that it is in God's hand. Why
should we be anxious over our infirmity as though it were
the hand of the enemy? Know that God has measured out all
our sickness. To be sure, Satan is the originator of them; it
is he who makes people ill. Yet all who have read the Book
of Job realize that this is only through God's permission and
is completely under the restriction of God. Without God's
permission Satan cannot make anyone sick. God permitted
Job to be attacked with ill-health, but note that He did not
allow the enemy to touch his life. Why then are we so agitated, so full of despair, so anxious to be cured, so afraid we
will die when we are struck down with ill-health?

It is always well for us to bear in mind that all sickness is
in God's hand. It has been both measured and circumscribed
by Him. After Job had fulfilled the course of his trial his
sickness was over, for it had accomplished its purpose in
him—"Ye have heard of the patience of Job, and have seen
the end (purpose) of the Lord, how that the Lord is full of
pity, and merciful" (James 5.11 ASV). What a shame that
so many are ill without realizing its purpose or learning its
lesson. All infirmities are in the Lord's hand and are measured out to us that we may learn our lessons. The sooner we
learn them the quicker these infirmities pass away.

May I put it bluntly: many are sick simply because they
love themselves too much. Unless the Lord removes this self-
love from their hearts He cannot use them. Therefore we
must learn to be those who do not love ourselves. Some people can think of nothing but themselves. The whole universe
seems to revolve around them. They are the center of the
earth as well as the hub of the universe. Day and night are
they occupied with their own selves. Every creature exists
for them, everything circles around them. Even God in
heaven is for them, Christ is for them, and the church is for
them. How can God destroy this self-centeredness? Why is it
that some maladies are hard to be cured? How intently they
solicit men's sympathy! If they should spurn human sympathy their ailments would soon be healed.

A startling fact is that many are ill because they like to be ill. In sickness they receive the attention and love which they do not usually enjoy in health. They frequently become ill that they may habitually be loved. Such people need to be severely reprimanded; and should they be willing to receive God's dealing in this particular matter they shall soon be well.

I know a brother who always expected love and kindness from others. Whenever people inquired after his well-being, he habitually responded with complaints about his physical weakness. He would give a detailed report of how many minutes he suffered from fever, how long it was he had a headache, how many times per minute he breathed, and how irregular was his heartbeat. He was continually in discomfort. He loved to tell people of his distress so that they might sympathize with him. He had nothing to relate except his tale of endless sickness. And at times he wondered why he was never healed.

Now it is difficult to speak the truth. And sometimes it can be costly. One day I was inwardly strengthened to tell him candidly that his long illness was due to his love for sickness. He of course denied it. Nevertheless I proceeded to point out to him: You are afraid that your sickness might leave you. You crave sympathy, love and care. Since you cannot secure these in any other way, you obtain them by being sick. You must rid yourself of this selfish desire before God will ever heal you. When people ask how you are, you must learn to answer that "all is well." Would this be telling a lie if the night before had been ill-spent? Recall the story of the woman in Shunem. She laid her dead child on the bed of the man of God and went to see Elisha. When she was asked, "Is it well with you? Is it well with your husband? Is it well with the child?", she replied, "It is well." (See 2 Kings 4.26) How could she say that, knowing the child had died already and was laid on Elisha's bed? Because she had faith. She believed that God would raise up her child. So today you too must believe.

Whatever may be the cause, be it intrinsic or extrinsic, the sickness will be over once God has obtained His end. People like Paul, Timothy and Trophimus are exceptions. Although their sicknesses were long-sustaining, they acknowledged that this was profitable to their work. They learned how to take care of themselves for the glory of God. Paul persuaded Timothy to drink a little wine, to be careful in eating and drinking. In spite of their frailties the work of God was not neglected. The Lord gave them sufficient grace to overcome their disabilities. Paul labored in weakness. By reading his writings we can conclude easily that he accomplished as much as ten persons could have. God used this weak man to exceed ten strong persons. Though his body was frail, God nevertheless gave him strength and life. These though are the exceptions in the Bible. Some of God's special vessels may receive the same treatment. But the rank and file, especially beginners, should examine whether they have sinned; and upon confessing their sins they shall see their sickness readily healed.

Lastly, I wish you to see before the Lord that sometimes Satan may launch a sudden attack or sometimes you unwittingly may violate some natural law. Even so, you still can bring it to the Lord. If it is the enemy's assault, rebuke it in the name of the Lord. Once a sister had a protracted fever. After discovering that it was a satanic attack, she rebuked it in the Lord's name and the fever left her. If you violate a natural law by putting your hand in the fire, you surely shall be burnt. Take good care of yourself. Do not wait until you are sick before you confess your negligence. It is important to take care of your body during the ordinary days.

5. The Way to Seek Healing

How should men seek healing before God? Three sentences in the Gospel of Mark are worth learning. I find them especially helpful, at least they are very effective for me. The first touches upon the power of the Lord; the second, the will of the Lord; and the third, the act of the Lord.

a) The Power of the Lord: "God can." "And Jesus asked

his father, 'How long has he had this?' And he said, 'From childhood. And it has often cast him into the fire and into the water, to destroy him; but *if you can* do anything, have pity on us and help us.' And Jesus said to him, '*If you can!* All things are possible to him who believes'" (9. 21-23). The Lord Jesus merely repeated the three words which the child's father had uttered. The father cried, "If you can, help us." The Lord responded, "If you can! Why, all things are possible to him who believes." The problem here is not "if you can" but rather "if you believe."

Is it not true that the first problem which arises with sickness is a doubt about God's power? Under a microscope the power of bacteria seems to be greater than the power of God. Very rarely does the Lord cut off others in the middle of their speaking, but here he appears as though He were angry. (May the Lord forgive me for phrasing it this way!) When He heard the child's father say "If you can, have pity on us and help us," He sharply reacted with "Why say if you can? All things are possible to him who believes. In sickness, the question is not whether I can or cannot but whether *you believe* or not."

The initial step for a child of God to take in sickness therefore is to raise up his head and say "Lord, you can!" You remember, do you not, the first instance of the Lord's healing of a paralytic? He asked the Pharisees, "Which is easier, to say to the paralytic, 'Your sins are forgiven,' or to say, 'Rise, take up your pallet and walk'?" (Mark 2.9) The Pharisees naturally thought it easier to say your sins are forgiven, for who could actually prove it is or is not so? But the Lord's words and their results showed them that He could heal sickness as well as forgive sins. He did not ask which was more difficult, but which was easier. For Him, both were equally easy. It was as easy for the Lord to bid the paralytic rise and walk as to forgive the latter's sins. For the Pharisees, both were as difficult.

b) The Will of the Lord: "God will." Yes, He indeed can, but how do I know if He wills? I do not know His will; perhaps He does not want to heal me. This is another story in

Mark again. "And a leper came to him beseeching him, and kneeling said to to him, 'If you will, you can make me clean.' Moved with pity, he stretched out his hand and touched him, and said to him, 'I will; be clean' " (1.40-41).

However great the power of God is, if He has no wish to heal, His power shall not help me. The problem to be solved at the outset is: Can God?; the second is: Will God? There is no sickness as unclean as leprosy. It is so unclean that according to law whoever touches a leper becomes himself unclean. Yet the Lord Jesus touched the leper and said to him, "I will." If He would heal the leper, how much more wills He to cure *our* diseases. We can proclaim boldly, "God can" and "God will."

c) The Act of the Lord: "God has." One more thing must God do. "Verily I say unto you, Whosoever shall say unto this mountain, Be thou taken up and cast into the sea; and shall not doubt in his heart, but shall believe that what he saith cometh to pass; he shall have it. Therefore I say unto you, all things whatsoever ye pray and ask for, believe that ye receive (Gr. *received*) them, and ye shall have them" (11. 23-24 ASV). What is faith? Faith believes God can, God will, and God has done it. If you believe you have received it, you shall have it. Should God give you His word, you can thank Him by saying, "God has healed me; He has already done it!" Many believers merely *expect* to be healed. Expectation regards things in the future, but faith deals with the past. If we really believe, we shall not wait for twenty or a hundred years, but shall rise up immediately and say, "Thank God, He has healed me. Thank God, I have received it. Thank God, I am clean! Thank God, I am well." A perfect faith can therefore proclaim God can, God will and God has done it.

Faith works with "is" and not "wish." Allow me to use a simple illustration. Suppose you preach the gospel and one professes that he has believed. Ask him whether he is saved, and should his answer be, I wish to be saved, then you know this reply is inadequate. Should he say, I will be saved, the answer is still incorrect. Even if he responds with, I think I shall definitely be saved, something is yet missing. But when he answers, I am saved, you know the flavor is right. If one believes, then he is saved. All faith deals with the past. To say I believe I shall be healed is not true faith. If he believes, he will thank God and say, I have received healing.

Lay hold of these three steps: God can, God will, God has. When man's faith touches the third stage, the sickness is over.

CHAPTER 3
GOD AS THE LIFE OF THE BODY

We noted earlier how our body is the temple of the Holy Spirit. What arrests our attention is the special emphasis the Apostle Paul gives to the body. The common concept is that the life of Christ is for our spirit, not for our body. Few realize that the salvation of God reaches to the second after He gives life to the first. Had God desired that His Spirit live solely in our spirit so that only it might be benefited, the Apostle would simply need to have said that "your spirit is the temple of God" and not mention the body at all. By now, however, we should understand that the meaning of our body as the temple of the Holy Spirit is more than its being the recipient of a special privilege. It likewise means being a channel for effective power. The indwelling of the Holy Spirit strengthens our inner man, enlightens the eyes of our heart and, makes our body healthy.

We have also noted how the Holy Spirit makes alive this mortal frame of ours. To wait until we die before He raises us up is not necessary, for even now He gives life to our mortal body. In the future He will raise from the dead this *corruptible* body, but today He quickens the *mortal* body. The power of His life permeates every cell of our being so that we may experience His power and life in the body.

No more need we look upon our outer shell as a miserable prison, for we can see in it the life of God being expressed. We now can experience in a deeper way that word which declares that "it is no longer I who live but Christ who lives in me." Christ has presently become the source of life to us.

He lives in us today as He once lived in the flesh. We can thus apprehend more fully the implication of His pronouncement: "I came that they may have life, and have it abundantly" (John 10.10). This more abundant life suffices additionally for every requirement of our body. Paul exhorts Timothy to "take hold of the eternal life" (1 Tim. 6. 12); surely Timothy is not here in need of eternal life that he may be saved. Is not this life that which Paul subsequently describes in the same chapter as "the life which is life indeed" (v.19)? Is he not urging Timothy to experience eternal life today in overcoming every phenomenon of death?

We would hasten to inform our readers that we have not lost sight of the fact that our body is indeed a mortal one; even so, we who are the Lord's can verily possess the power of that life which swallows up death. In our body are two forces in action: death and life: on the one side is consumption which brings us nigh to death; on the other side is replenishment through food and rest and these support life. Now extravagant consumption weakens the body because the force of death is too powerful; but by the same token excessive supply reveals signs of congestion because the force of life is too strong. The best policy is to maintain these two forces of life and death in balance. Beyond this, we should understand that the weariness which believers often experience in their body is in many respects distinct from that of ordinary people. Their consumption is more than physical. Because they walk with the Lord, bear the burdens of others, sympathize with the brethren, work for God, intercede before Him, battle the powers of darkness, and pommel their body to subdue it, food and rest alone are insufficient to replenish the loss of strength in their physical frame. This explains in a measure why many believers, who before the call to service were healthy, find themselves physically feeble not long afterwards. Our bodily strength cannot cope with the demands of spiritual life, work, and war. Combat with sin, sinners, and the evil spirits saps our vitality. Solely natural resources are inadequate to supply our bodily needs. We must depend on the life of Christ, for this alone can sustain us. Should we rely on material food and nourishment and drugs we will be committing a serious blunder. Only the life of the Lord Jesus more than sufficiently meets all the physical requirements for our spiritual life, work, and war. He alone furnishes us the necessary vitality to grapple with sin and Satan. Once the believer has truly appreciated what spiritual warfare is and how to wrestle in the spirit with the enemy, he will begin to realize the preciousness of the Lord Jesus as life to his body.

Every Christian ought to see the reality of his union with the Lord. He is the vine and we the branches. As branches are united with the trunk, so are we united with the Lord. Through union with the trunk the branches receive the flow of life. Does not our union with the Lord produce the same results? If we restrict this union to the spirit, faith will rise up to protest. Since the Lord calls us to demonstrate the reality of our union with Him, He wishes us to believe and to receive the flow of His life to our spirit, soul, and body. Should our fellowship be cut off, the spirit most assuredly will lose its peace, but so will the body be denied its health. Constant abiding signifies that His life continually is filling our spirit and flowing to our body. Apart from a participation in the life of the Lord Jesus there can be neither healing nor health. The call of God today is for His children to experience a deeper union with the Lord Jesus.

Let us therefore recognize that, though phenomena do occur to us in the *body*, they are in truth spiritual matters. To receive divine healing and to have our strength increased are spiritual and not purely physical experiences, although they do take place in the body. Such experiences are nothing less than the life of the Lord Jesus being manifested in our mortal frame. As in the past the life of the Lord caused this dead spirit of ours to be resurrected, so now it makes alive this mortal body. God wants us to learn how to let the resurrected, glorious and all-victorious life of Christ be expressed in every portion of our being. He calls us to renew our vigor daily and hourly by Him. This is precisely our true life. Even though our body is still animated by our natural soul life, we no longer live by it because we have trusted in the life of the Son of God Who infuses energy into our members far more abundantly than all which the soul life could impart. We lay great stress on this "life." In all our spiritual experiences this mysterious yet wonderful "life" enters into us abundantly. God desires to leads us into possessing that life of Christ as our strength.

The Word of God is the life of our body: "Man shall not live by bread alone, but by every word that proceeds from the mouth of God" (Matt. 4.4). This substantiates the thought that God's Word is able to support our body. Naturally speaking man must live by bread, but when the Word of God emits its power man can live by it too. Herein do we behold both the natural and the supernatural way of living. God does not say that henceforth we need not eat; He simply informs us that His Word can supply us with life which food cannot. When food fails to produce or to sustain the desirable effect in our body, His Word can give us what we need. Some live by bread alone, some by it *and* the Word of God. Bread sometimes fails, but God's Word never changes.

God hides His life in His Word. Inasmuch as He is life, so also is His Word. Should we view God's Word as a teaching, creed or moral standard, it shall not prove very effective in us. No, God's Word must be digested and united with us in the same manner as is food. Hungry believers take it it as their food. If they receive it with faith the Word becomes their life. God claims His Word is able to sustain our life. When natural nourishment fails we can believe God according to His Word. Then shall we perceive Him not only as life to our spirit but as life to our body as well. Christians nowadays experience great loss in not noticing how bountifully God has provided for our earthly tent. We confine God's promises to the inner spirit and overlook their application to the outer flesh. But do we realize our physical requirement is no less needful than that of the spiritual?

THE EXPERIENCES OF THE SAINTS OF OLD

God never wants His children to be weak; His ordained will is for them to be robust and healthy. His Word affirms that "as your days, so shall your strength be" (Deut. 33.25). This naturally points to the body. As long as we live on earth the Lord promises to give us strength for it. God never presumes to grant us an extra day of life without in addition providing extra stamina for that day. Because of the failure of His children to claim this precious promise by faith, they find their vitality unequal to their days on earth. In order to provide as much energy for His children as the days He gives require, God promises to make Himself their strength. As God lives and as we live, so shall be our strength. Believing God's promise, we can say each morning upon arising and seeing the dawn that as God lives so shall we have enablement for the day, enablement physical as well as spiritual.

It was a common occurrence for the saints of old to know God as the strength of their body or to experience God's life permeating their body. We can observe this first in Abraham: "He did not weaken in faith when he considered his own body, which was as good as dead because he was about a hundred years old, or when he considered the barrenness of Sarah's womb" (Rom. 4.19). By faith he begot Isaac. The power of God was displayed in a body as good as dead. The crux of the matter here is not so much the condition of our body as the power of God in that body.

The Scriptures describe the life of Moses by saying that he "was a hundred and twenty years old when he died; his eye was not dim, nor his natural force abated" (Deut. 34.7). This is speaking beyond question about the power of God's life in Moses' body.

The Bible also mentions the physical condition of Caleb. After the Israelites had entered Canaan Caleb testified:

> Moses swore on that day, saying, 'Surely the land on which your foot has trodden shall be an inheritance for you and your children for ever, because you have wholly followed the Lord my God.' And now, behold, the Lord has kept me alive, as he said, these forty-five years since the time that the Lord spoke this word to Moses, while Israel walked in the wilderness; and now, lo, I am this day eight-five years old. I am still as strong to this day as I

was in the day that Moses sent me; my strength now is as my
strength was then, for war, and for going and coming. (Josh. 14.
9-11)

To this one who followed the Lord wholeheartedly God became his strength as He had promised, so that even after
forty-five years he did not diminish in vigor.

In reading the book of Judges we learn about the physical
prowess of Samson. Though Samson performed many immoral acts and though the Holy Spirit may not impart such
towering strength to every believer, yet one point is sure:
if we depend on the Holy Spirit we shall find His power
supplying all our daily needs.

From what David sang as recorded in his psalms, we can
ascertain that the power of God was in David's body. Note
the following passages:

"I love thee, O Lord, my strength. . . . the God who girded me
with strength and made my way safe. He made my feet like
hinds' feet, and set me secure on the heights. He trains my
hands for war, so that my arms can bend a bow of bronze"
(18.1,32-34)
"Jehovah is the strength of my life; of whom shall I be afraid?"
(27.1 ASV)
"May the Lord give strength to his people!" (29.11)
"Summon thy might, O God; show thy strength, O God, thou who
hast wrought for us. . . . the God of Israel, he gives power and
strength to his people" (68.28,35)
"Who satisfies you with good as long as you live so that your
youth is renewed like the eagle's" (103.5)

Other psalms record also how God became strength to His
Own people, for example: "My flesh and my heart may fail,
but God is the strength of my heart and my portion for ever";
"Blessed are the men whose strength is in thee"; and "With
long life I will satisfy him, and show him my salvation" (73.
26, 84.5, 91.16).

Elihu related to Job the chastening of God and its after
effects.

Man is also chastened with pain upon his bed, and with continual strife in his bones; so that his life loathes bread, and his

appetite dainty food. His flesh is so wasted away that it cannot be seen; and his bones which were not seen stick out. His soul draws near the Pit, and his life to those who bring death. If there be for him an angel, a mediator, one of the thousand, to declare to man what is right for him; and he is gracious to him, and says, 'Deliver him from going down into the Pit, I have found a ransom; let his flesh become fresh with youth; let him return to the days of his youthful vigor.' (Job 33.19-25)

This signifies how the life of God can be manifest in one who is near the gate of death.

The prophet Isaiah too bears testimony concerning this matter:

Behold, God is my salvation; I will trust, and will not be afraid; for the Lord God is my strength and my song, and he has become my salvation. (12.2) He gives power to the faint, and to him who has no might he increases strength. Even youths shall faint and be weary, and young men shall fall exhausted; but they who wait for the Lord shall renew their strength, they shall mount up with wings like eagles, they shall run and not be weary, they shall walk and not faint. (40.29-31)

All this stamina is shown in the body, for the power of God is generated in those who wait on Him.

When Daniel beheld the vision of God he whispered: "No strength was left in me; my radiant appearance was fearfully changed, and I retained no strength" (10.8). But God sent His angel to increase Daniel's strength. So in recording this incident Daniel explained how "again one having the appearance of a man touched me and strengthened me. And he said, 'O man, greatly beloved, fear not, peace be with you; be strong and of good courage.' And when he spoke to me, I was strengthened and said, 'Let my lord speak, for you have strengthened me' " (10.18-19). Once more we see how God supplies power to man's body.

The Lord's children today ought to know that He does care for their body. God is not only strength to our spirit, He is equally so to our body. Even in the Old Testament time when grace was not manifested as much as it is today, the saints experienced God as strength to their outer flesh.

Can today's blessing be less than theirs? We should experience at least the same divine invigorating power as they did. If we are uninformed as to the riches of God, we perhaps may restrict them to what concerns our spirit. But those who have faith will not limit His life and power to the spirit by neglecting their application to the body.

We wish to underscore the fact that God's life is adequate not only to heal sickness but also to preserve us strong and healthy. God as our might enables us to overcome both illness and weakness. He does not heal so that we may live afterwards by our natural energy; *He* is to be energy to our body that we may live by Him and find power for all His service. When the Israelites left Egypt God promised them by saying, "If you will diligently hearken to the voice of the Lord your God, and do that which is right in his eyes, and give heed to his commandments and keep all his statutes, I will put none of the diseases upon you which I put upon the Egyptians; for I am the Lord, your healer" (Ex. 15.26). Later we find this promise wholly fulfilled as noted in Psalm 105: "there was not one feeble person among his tribes" (v.37 ASV). Let us hence understand that divine healing includes both God's curing our sicknesses and His withholding diseases from us that we may remain hardy. If we are totally yielded to God, resisting His will in nothing but believingly receiving His life as strength to our body, we shall yet prove the fact that Jehovah heals.

THE EXPERIENCE OF PAUL

If we accept the Biblical teaching that our bodies are the members of Christ, we cannot but also acknowledge the teaching that the life of Christ flows through them. The life of Christ flows from the Head to the body, supplying energy and vitality to it. Since *our* bodies are members of *that* body, life naturally flows to them. This however needs to be appropriated by faith. The measure of faith by which we receive this life will determine the measure in which we actually experience it. From the Scriptures we have learned that the life of the Lord Jesus can be appropriated for the believer's body, but this requires faith. Doubtless Christians, when first exposed to such teachings, are struck with surprise. Yet we cannot dilute what the Word distinctly teaches. An examination of Paul's experience can assure us of the preciousness and reality of the teaching.

Paul, in referring to his physical condition, remarked about a thorn in his flesh. Three times he entreated the Lord concerning this, that it should be removed. But the Lord answered him, "My grace is sufficient for you, for my power is made perfect in weakness." And in response the Apostle said, "I will all the more gladly boast of my weaknesses, that the power of Christ may rest upon me . . . for when I am weak, then I am strong" (2 Cor. 12.9-10). We need not inquire what that thorn was because the Bible does not divulge it. One point however is certain: the consequence of this thorn on the Apostle was that it weakened his body. The "weakness" here referred to is physical in nature. The same word is used in Matthew 8.17. The Corinthians were well acquainted with Paul's bodily frailty (2 Cor. 10.10). Paul himself acknowledged that when he was with them the first time he was physically weak (1 Cor. 2.3). His debility cannot be due to any lack of spiritual power, for both Corinthian letters reveal a powerful spiritual vigor in the Apostle.

From just these few passages we can gain insight into Paul's physical condition. He was very weak in body, but did he remain long therein? No, for he informs us that the power of Christ rested upon him and made him strong. We notice a "law of contrast" here. Neither the thorn nor the weakness which came from the thorn had left Paul; yet the power of Christ inundated his frail body and gave him strength to meet every need. The power of Christ was in contrast to the weakness of Paul. This power did not waft the thorn away nor did it eliminate weakness, but it abided in Paul to handle whatever situation with which his weakened frame could not cope. It may be likened to a wick which though kindled with fire is not consumed because it is saturated with oil. The wick is as flimsy as ever, but the oil supplies everything the fire requires of it.

Thus do we apprehend the principle that God's life is to be our bodily enablement. His life does not transform the nature of our weak and mortal body: it merely fills it with all its necessary supplies. As to his natural condition, Paul was unquestionably the weakest physically; as to the power of Christ which he possessed, he was the strongest of all. We know how he labored day and night, pouring out his life and energy, performing work which several strong-bodied men could not stand. How, then, could a weak man like Paul undertake such work unless it were that his mortal frame was made alive by the Holy Spirit? It is an established fact that God imparted strength to Paul's body.

How did God do it? Paul was speaking about his body when he related in 2 Corinthians 4 how he and those with him were "always bearing about in the body the dying of Jesus, that the life also of Jesus may be manifested in our body. For we who live are always delivered unto death for Jesus' sake, that the life also of Jesus may be manifested in our mortal flesh" (v.10-11 ASV). What particularly arrests our interest is that verse 11 in relation to verse 10, though seemingly redundant, is not repetitious. Verse 10 is concerned with the life of Jesus being manifested in our bodies whereas verse 11 is concerned with the life of Jesus being exhibited in our *mortal flesh*. Many are able to express the life of Christ in their bodies but fail to advance further to do so in their mortal flesh. The distinction is far-reaching. When Christians fall ill many are truly obedient and patient and voice no complaint or anxiety. They sense the presence of the Lord and exhibit His virtues in their countenance, speech, and act. Through the Holy Spirit they genuinely manifest the life of Christ in their bodies. Nevertheless, they do not appreciate the healing power of the Lord Jesus nor have they heard that His life is also for their lowly bodies. They fail to exercise faith for the healing of their bodies as they previously did for the cleansing of their sins and the quickening of their dead spirits. They are therefore powerless to manifest the life of Jesus in their *mortal* flesh. They receive grace to endure pain but do not receive healing. Verse 10 they have experienced, yet verse 11 goes untried.

How does God heal us and strengthen us? By the life of Jesus. This is most significant. When our mortal flesh is revitalized the nature of our body is not changed to immortality—it remains the same. The life which supplies the vitality to this body, however, is changed. Whereas in days past we lived by the power of our natural life, now we live by the energy of that supernatural life of Christ. Because His resurrection power is sustaining our body, we are empowered to perform our appointed tasks.

The Apostle did not suggest that once having lived by the Lord he would never again be weak. Not at all, for whenever the power of Christ did not cure him he would be as weak as ever. We can forfeit the manifestation of the life of the Lord Jesus in our bodies through neglect, independence, or sin. Sometimes we may be weakened through the attack of the powers of darkness against whom we have boldly advanced. Or we may suffer affliction for the sake of Christ's body if we are deeply involved with it. But only in the life of deeply spiritual persons do both of these occur. In any case, we are certain that, weak though we may yet be, God's will is never for us to be invalids unable to work for Him. The Apostle Paul was often weak, but never did God's work suffer because of his weakness. We acknowledge the absolute sovereignty of God, but Christians cannot use that as their excuse.

"Always bearing about in the body the dying of Jesus" is the basis for "the life of Jesus (to) be manifested in our body." In other words, our own life must be denied totally before that of the Lord Jesus will be manifested in our bodies. This unfolds to us the intricate relationship between a spiritual selfless walk and a sound healthy body. The power of God is used exclusively for Him. When God exhibits His life in our bodies He does so for the sake of His Own work. He never dispenses to us His life and strength that we may consume it selfishly. He does not give His energy to our bodies that we may waste it; nor does He do so to accomplish our purpose. How then will He ever bestow this power upon us if we do not live entirely for Him? Right there do we locate the reason for many unanswered prayers. Believers too often covet health and vitality solely in order to enjoy themselves. They seek God's strength for their bodies that they may dwell more comfortably, joyfully, conveniently. They want to be able to move freely without any impediment. That is why up to this very moment they are still weak. God will not furnish us His life for us to wield independently. For would we not live even more for ourselves, and would not the will of God incur even greater loss? God is waiting today for His children to come to *their* end that He may grant them what they are seeking.

What is meant by "the dying of Jesus"? It is that life of the Lord which always delivers its self up to death. The entire walk of our Lord was characterized by self-denial. Right through to His death the Lord Jesus never did anything by Himself but always executed His Father's work. Now the Apostle informs us that by his letting the dying of Jesus so work in his body the life of Jesus was manifested also in his mortal flesh. Can we receive this teaching? Presently God is waiting for those who are willing to accept the dying of Jesus so that He may live in their bodies. Who is inclined to follow God's will perfectly? Who will not initiate anything by himself? Who dares to attack the powers of darkness incessantly for God? Who refuses to use his body for his own success? The life of the Lord Jesus shall be manifested in the bodies of such believers as these. If we take care of the death side God will look after the life side: we offer our weakness to Him and He gives His strength to us.

NATURAL POWER AND THE POWER OF JESUS

If we have presented ourselves utterly to God we can believe that He has prepared a body for us. We often imagine how nice it would be had we had control over how we were made. What we most want is that our bodies shall not contain many inherent defects but possess a greater resistance instead in order that we may live long without pain or illness. But God has not consulted us. He knows best what we should have. We should not judge our ancestors for their faults and sins. Neither should we doubt God's love and wisdom. Everything which concerns us is ordained before the foundation of the world. God fulfills His excellent will even in this body of pain and death. His purpose is not for us to desert this body as though it were a burdensome weight. Rather, He urges us to lay hold of a *new* body through the Holy Spirit Who indwells us. In preparing whatever body He gives us God is fully aware of its limitations and dangers; nonetheless He wants us through painful experiences to desire a new body so that we may no longer live by our *naturally possessed* power but by the power of God. Thus we shall exchange our weakness for His strength. Even though this body of ours has not been transformed, the life by which it lives is already a new one.

The Lord delights in flooding every nerve, capillary, and cell of our body with His might. He does not transform our enfeebled nature into a vigorous one, nor does he dispense a great deal of strength to be stored in us. He wants to be the life to our mortal flesh so that we may live *momentarily* by Him. Perhaps some may think that to have the Lord Jesus as life to our body means God miraculously grants us a large measure of bodily power that we may never again suffer or be sick. But this was evidently not the experience of the Apostle, for does he not definitely declare that "we who live are always delivered unto death for Jesus' sake, that the life also of Jesus may be manifested in our mortal flesh"? Paul's flesh was frequently weakened, but the strength of the Lord Jesus continuously flowed into him. He lived momentarily by the life of the Lord. To accept Him as life for our body requires *constant trust*. In ourselves we cannot meet any situation at any time; but by trusting continually in the Lord we receive moment by moment all the necessary strength.

This is what is meant by the words spoken by God through Jeremiah: "I will give you your life as a prize of war in all places to which you may go" (45.5). We are not to deem ourselves safe and secure because of our own inherent

strength; we must instead commit ourselves to the life of the
Lord for every breath. In this alone is safety, for He alone
ever lives. We do not possess any *reserve* power which enables us to move as we wish; each time we need strength we
must draw from the Lord. A moment's drawing is good for
that moment's living; there is no possibility of holding a little
in reserve. This is a life completely united with, and exclusively dependent upon, the Lord. "I live because of the
Father, so he who eats me will live because of me" (John 6.
57). Precisely there is the secret of this life. Were we able to
live independently of the life-giving Lord, we would renounce this heart of utter reliance and live according to our
own will! And would we not then be like those of the world,
wasting our strength? God wants us to have a constant trust
as well as a constant need. Just as the manna long ago had to
be gathered daily, so our bodies must momentarily live by
God.

By walking in this fashion we will not limit our work by any
inherent power nor will we always be anxious because of the
body. If it is God's will, we must dare to walk this way, however much man's wisdom may consider it risky. For God is
our strength; and we are but waiting to be sent. In ourselves
we have no power to undertake any task, yet our eyes are
upon the Lord. We are absolutely helpless, nonetheless
through Him we shall go forth and conquer. Alas, how many
of us are too powerful in ourselves! We know not how to distrust our strength that we thereby may know how to trust in
Him. His strength is made perfect in our weakness. The more
helpless we are (this pertains to attitude), the better is His
power demonstrated. Our strength can never cooperate with
the Lord. If we try to reinforce His strength with ours we
shall reap nothing but defeat and shame.

Since the Lord demands such a trust in Him, this practice should not be limited to the naturally weak situation in
us but should include the naturally strong in us too. Perhaps some Christians who currently can boast robust and
healthy bodies assume they need not seek this experience
until they become weak. This is a misjudgment, for both the

naturally weak and the naturally strong require the life of God. Nothing we receive in the old creation is satisfactory to Him. Were believers deeply taught by the Lord they would lay down their own power to accept God's, even should their bodies be strong and seemingly have no need for His life. This is not a *choosing* of weakness with their will but is rather a *disbelieving* in their own strength just as they distrust their own talents. Such consecration will preserve them from self-exaltation founded on natural energy— a common ill among many servants of the Lord. They will not dare move beyond what He orders. They will act as the naturally weak do; without the strengthening of the Lord they dare not move one step. They will refrain from overworking and avoid careless living, just as though they were weak naturally.

In such a way of life it is imperative that "self" be imprisoned by the Holy Spirit; otherwise we certainly shall be defeated. Some genuinely admire the self-denying life but are unable to cease completely from their own energies. Hence they disregard God's purpose and move along according to their desire. They may reap the temporary admiration of men but their bodies shall finally collapse. God's life refuses to be enslaved to man's will. That work which He has not ordered He shall never give His strength to supply. If we should become active outside the realm of God's will we shall discover the life of God is apparently leaking away and that our fragile body must undertake the task In order to live by Him we must not be presumptuous; we should begin to move only upon being assured that it is truly God's will. Solely through obedience will we experience the reality of His life for us. Else would He ever give us His strength to rebel against Him?

THE BLESSING OF THIS LIFE

Were we to receive the life of the Lord Jesus to be the life of our body, we would today experience our bodies being strengthened by the Lord as well as our spirits being prospered by Him.

As far as our knowledge is concerned we already realize that our body is for the Lord; yet because of our self-will He is unable to fill us completely. But now we commit our all to Him that He may deal with us in whatever way He wishes. We present our bodies a living sacrifice; therefore we control neither our life nor our future. Now we truly understand what is meant by the body for the Lord. What worried us before cannot now shake us. The enemy may tempt us by reminding us that this way is too risky or that we are being too unmindful of ourselves; even so, we are not frightened as we used to be. One thing do we know: we belong to the Lord absolutely: nothing can therefore befall us without His knowledge and permission. Whatever attack may come is but an indication of His special purpose and His unfailing protection. Our bodies are no longer ours. Every nerve, cell, and organ has been handed over to Him. No more are we our own masters, hence we no longer are responsible. If the weather abruptly changes, this is His business. A sleepless night does not make us anxious. No matter in what unexpected way Satan assaults, we remember the battle is the Lord's and not ours. Then and there the life of God flows out through our bodies. At such an hour others might lose peace, grow despondent, become worried, and desperately seek some remedial measure; but we quietly exercise faith and live by God, for we know we henceforth live not by eating, drinking, sleeping, and so forth, but by the life of God. These things cannot hurt us.

Understanding now that the Lord is for his body, the Christian is able to appropriate all the riches of God for his needs. For every urgent requirement there is always His supply; his heart is accordingly at rest. He does not request more than what God has supplied, but neither is he satisfied with anything less than what He has promised. He refuses to use his own strength in any matter to help God ahead of His time. While worldly people are anxiously running for help because of the suffering and pain of the flesh, he can wait calmly for God's time and God's riches due to his union with

Him. He holds not his life in his own hand but looks for the Father's care. What peace this is!

During this period the believer glorifies God in every respect. He takes whatever may happen as an opportunity to manifest His glory. He does not use his own ways and thus interfere with the glory which is due God. But when the Lord stretches out His arm to deliver, then is he ready to praise.

The aim of the child is no longer the blessing from the Father. God Himself is far more precious than all His gifts. If healing would not express God then he does not want to be healed. Should we merely covet the Father's protection and supply, should we cry out only for deliverance from temptation, we already have fallen. God as our life is not a business proposition. Those who genuinely know Him do not beg for healing but always seek the Father. If health might lead him astray and take away from God's glory, he would rather not be healed. Believers continually should remember that whenever our motive is to covet God's gifts rather than God Himself, we already are beginning to falter. Should a Christian live perfectly for the Lord he will not be anxious to seek help, blessing, or supply. He will instead commit himself unconditionally to God.

CHAPTER 4

OVERCOMING DEATH

The experience of overcoming death is not unusual among saints. By the blood of the lamb the Israelites were protected from the hand of the death angel who slew the first-born of Egypt. In the name of the Lord David was saved from the paws of the lion and the bear and also from the hand of Goliath. By casting some meal into the pot Elisha drove death out of it (2 Kings 4.38-41). Shadrach, Meshech and Abednego suffered no harm in the fiery furnace (Dan. 3.16-27). Daniel witnessed God shutting the mouths of the lions when he was thrown into their den. Paul shook off a deadly viper into the fire and experienced no harm (Acts 28.3-5). Enoch and Elijah both were raptured to heaven without tasting death—perfect examples of death being overcome.

It is God's aim to bring His children through the experience of overcoming death now. To triumph over sin, self, the world, and Satan is necessary; but victory is not complete without a corresponding triumph over death. If we wish to enjoy a complete victory we must destroy this *last* enemy (1 Cor. 15.26). We will leave one foe unconquered if we fail to experience the triumph over death.

There is death in nature, death in us, and death from Satan. The earth lies under a curse; it is therefore ruled by that curse. If we desire to live victoriously on this earth, we will have to ovecome the death which is in the world. Death is in our body. On the day we are born it begins to work in us; for which of us from that day onward does not commence traveling towards the tomb? Do not view death merely as a "crisis"; it is pre-eminently a progressive matter. It is already in us and is gradually and relentlessly devouring us. Our release from this earthly tent is but the crisic consummation of the protracted working of death. It can strike at our spirit, depriving it of life and power; it can strike at our soul, crippling its feeling, thought and will; or it can strike at our body, rendering it weak and sick.

In reading Romans 5 we find that "death reigned" (v.17). Death not only exists, it also reigns. It reigns in the spirit, in the soul, in the body. Although our body is still alive, death already is reigning in it. Its influence has not yet reached its zenith, but it is reigning nonetheless and pushing its frontiers so as to engulf the whole body. Various symptoms which we discover in our body demonstrate how much its power is upon us. And these lead people to that ultimate demise—physical death.

While there is the reign of death, there is also the reign of life (Rom. 5.17). The Apostle Paul assures us that all who receive the abundance of grace and the free gift of righteousness "reign in life," a force which far exceeds the operative power of death. But Christians today have been so occupied with the problem of sin that the problem of death has virtually been forgotten. Important as the overcoming of sin is, the overcoming of death—a related problem—should not be neglected. We know Romans Chapters 5 to 8 deal very distinctly with the matter of overcoming sin, but it gives equal attention to the question of death: "the wages of sin is death" (6.23). Paul deals with the consequence of sin as well as with sin itself. He not only contrasts righteousness and trespasses but also compares life and death. Many Christians stress overcoming the various manifestations of sin in their character and daily life, yet they fail to emphasize how to overcome the result of sin, namely, death. The Apostle, however, is used by God in these few chapters to discuss not so much sin's manifestations in daily life as sin's consequence which is death.

We must see clearly the relationship between these two elements. Christ died to save us not only from our sins but

from death as well. God is now calling us to subdue both
these phenomena. As sinners we were dead in sins, for sin and
death reigned over us; but the Lord Jesus in His death for
us has swallowed up our sin and death. Death at first reigned
in our body, but being identified with His death we have
died to sin and been made alive to God (6.11). Because of
our union with Christ "death no longer has dominion over
him (us)" nor can it bind us anymore (6.9,11). The salvation of Christ replaces sin with righteousness and death with
life. Since the main objective of the Apostle in this portion
of Scripture is to deal with sin and death, our acceptance
cannot be complete if we absorb only half the theme. Paul
describes the full salvation of the Lord Jesus in these terms:
"the law of the Spirit of life in Christ Jesus has set me free
from the law of sin and death" (8.2). Granted we have a
great amount of experience in overcoming sin, yet how much
have we experienced the overcoming of death?

Having received the uncreated life of God in our spirit,
we who have believed in the Lord and are regenerated undeniably have as a result some experience in triumphing
over death, but must our experience be limited to just this
little measure? How much can life overcome death? Unequivocally most of the Lord's saints have not enjoyed the
full extent of this particular experience which God has provided for them. Must we not confess that death works more
potently in our body than does life? We ought to be as attentive to sin and death as is God. We must overcome death
as well as sin.

Since Christ has conquered death, believers *need not* die
though they *may* yet die. It is the same as the fact that
Christ condemned sin in the flesh so that believers *need not*
sin any more even though they *may* yet sin. If a Christian's
goal is not to sin then not to die should likewise be his goal.
As his relationship with sin is regulated by the death and
resurrection of Christ, so must his connection with death
be regulated by them. In Christ the Christian has conquered
completely both sin and death. Hence God now calls him to
triumph over these two experientially. We usually assume

that since Christ has conquered death for us we need not pay any further attention to it. How can we then exhibit the victory of the Lord experimentally? To be sure, there is no basis for our victory apart from that of Calvary; yet to not claim what Calvary has accomplished for us is certainly not the way to victory. We do not conquer sin by being passive, neither can we conquer death by disregarding it. God desires us to be serious about overcoming death; that is, through the death of Christ we actually must overcome the power of death in our body. We heretofore have subdued many temptations and also the flesh, the world, and Satan; now we must rise up to defeat the power of the last enemy.

If we determine to resist death in the same way we have resisted sin, our attitude towards the former will be changed completely. Mankind is marching towards the tomb, and because death is the common lot of the entire fallen race, we naturally tend to adopt a submissive attitude. We have not learned to rise against it. Despite our knowledge of the soon return of our Lord and the hope of not passing through the grave but being raptured to heaven, most of us still prepare to wait out death. When the righteousness of God works in us we abhor sin; but we have not allowed God's life to so work in us that we equally begin to hate death.

To overcome death believers must alter their attitude from one of submission to one of resistance towards it. Unless we cast off our *passive* approach we will not be able to overthrow death but will be mocked by it instead and finally come to an untimely end. Numerous saints today misapprehend passivity for faith. They reason that they have committed everything to God. If they ought not to die, He verily shall save them from it: if they ought to die, then He doubtless shall allow them to die: let the will of God be done. Such a saying *sounds* right, but is this faith? Not at all. It is simply a lazy passivity. When we *do not know* God's will, it is fitting for us to pray: "not my will, but thine, be done" (Luke 22.42). This does not mean we need not pray *specifically*, letting our requests be made known to God. We should not submit passively to death, for God instructs us to work together actively with His will. Except we *definitely know* God wants us to die, we must not passively permit death to oppress us. Rather, we must actively cooperate with God's will to resist it.

Why should we adopt such an attitude as this? The Bible treats death as our enemy (1 Cor. 15.26). Consequently, we must resolve to oppose it and subdue it. Since the Lord Jesus has faced and overcome death on earth for us, He wants us personally to conquer it in this life. We should not petition God to grant us strength to put up with the power of death; we should petition instead for might to overthrow its power.

As death has come from sin, so our victory over death has come from the work of the Lord Jesus Who died for us and saved us from sin. His redemptive work is closely related to death—"Since therefore the children share in flesh and blood, he himself likewise partook of the same nature, that through death he might destroy him who has the power of death, that is, the devil, and deliver all those who through fear of death were subject to lifelong bondage" (Heb. 2.14-15). The cross is the basis for victory over its power.

Satan has this power, which power he derives from sin: "as sin came into the world through one man and death *through sin,* and so death spread to all men because all men sinned" (Rom. 5.12). But the Lord Jesus invaded the domain of death and through His redemptive act removed its sting which is sin, thus disarming Satan of his power. By Christ's death, sin lost its potency, and so death was deprived of its power too. Through the crucifixion of Christ we henceforth shall overthrow the power of death and lift its siege around us by claiming the victory of Calvary.

Three different ways are open for Christians to overcome death: (1) by trusting we will not die until our work is finished; (2) by having no fear of death even should it come because we know its sting has been removed; and (3) by believing we will be delivered completely from death since we shall be raptured at the Lord's return. Let us ponder these one by one.

DEATH AFTER OUR WORK IS FINISHED

Unless a Christian plainly knows his work is finished and he no longer is required by the Lord to remain, he should by all means resist death. If the symptoms of death have been seen already in his body before his work is done, he positively should resist it and its symptoms. He should believe that the Lord will undertake in what he has resisted, for He has work for him yet to do. Hence before our appointed task is discharged we can trust in the Lord restfully even in the face of dangerous physical signs. In cooperating with the Lord and resisting death we will soon see Him work towards the swallowing up of it by His life.

Notice how the Lord Jesus resisted the jaws of death. When people tried to push Him down a cliff He passed through the midst of them and went His way (Luke 4.29-30). On one occasion "Jesus went about in Galilee; (but) he would not go about in Judea, because the Jews sought to kill him" (John 7.1). On another occasion the Jews "took up stones to throw at him; but Jesus hid himself, and went out of the temple" (John 8.59). Why did He thrice resist mortality? Because His time had not yet come. He knew there was an appointed hour for the Messiah to be cut off; He could not die in advance of God's appointed moment nor could He die at any other place than at Golgotha. We too must not die before our time.

·The Apostle Paul likewise had the experience of resisting death. The powers of darkness pressed for his premature departure; yet he overcame them in each instance. Once when he was imprisoned with death as the possible outcome, he confessed as follows:

> If it is to be life in the flesh, that means fruitful labor for me. Yet which I shall choose I cannot tell. I am hard pressed between the two. My desire is to depart and be with Christ, for that is far better. But to remain in the flesh is more necessary on your account. Convinced of this, I know that I shall remain and continue with you all, for your progress and joy in the faith. (Phil. 1.22-25)

Paul was not afraid to die, nevertheless before the work was done he knew by faith in God he would not die. This was his victory over death. And towards the end, when he said "I have fought the good fight, I have finished the race, I have kept the faith," he also knew that "the time of (his) departure (had) come" (2 Tim. 4.7,6). Before our race is fully run we must not die.

Peter knew the time of his departure too: "I know that the putting off of my body will be soon, as our Lord Jesus Christ showed me" (2 Peter 1.14). To concede—by a sizing up of our environment, physical condition, and feeling—that our time has come is an error on our part; we instead need to possess definite indications from the Lord. As we live for Him, so must we die for Him. Any call for departure which does not come from the Lord ought to be opposed.

In reading the Old Testament we find that all the patriarchs died "full of years." What is meant by this phrase? It means they totally lived out the days appointed them by God. God has apportioned each of us a particular age (John 21). If we do not live to that age we have not conquered death. How are we to know the span appointed us? The Bible offers a general yardstick—"the years of our life are threescore and ten, or even by reason of strength fourscore (Ps. 90.10). Now we are not suggesting that everybody must live to be at least seventy, for we cannot encroach on God's sovereignty like that; but in case we receive no registration of a shorter period, let us accept this number as standard and repulse any earlier departure. By standing on the Word of God we will see victory.

NO FEAR IN DEATH

In speaking of overcoming death we do not mean to imply that our body shall never die. Though we believe "we shall not all sleep" (1 Cor. 15.51), yet to say that *we* will not die is superstitious. Since the Bible suggests the common span of life as seventy years of age, we can expect to live that long if we have faith. But we cannot hope to live forever because the Lord Jesus is our life. We know God frequently has His exceptions. Some die before the age of seventy. Our faith can only ask God that we do not leave before our task is finished. Whether our life be long or short, we cannot perish like sinners before half our appointed days are over. Our years should be sufficient enough to accomplish our life work. Then when the end does come we can depart peacefully with the grace of God upon us, as naturally as the falling of a fully ripened melon. The book of Job describes such a departure in this manner: "You shall come to your grave in ripe old age, as a shock of grain comes up to the threshing floor in its season" (5.26).

Overcoming death does not necessarily mean no grave, for God may wish some to overcome it through resurrection just as our Lord Jesus did. In passing through death believers, like their Lord, need have *no fear of it*. If we seek to overcome the jaws of death because we are afraid or unwilling to die, we already are defeated. It may be that the Lord will save us from death altogether by rapturing us alive to heaven; we nonetheless should not ask for His speedy return out of a fear of mortality. Such apprehensiveness shows we are defeated already by death. Let us come to see that even should we go to the grave we are merely walking from one room to another room. There is no justification for unbearable inward pain, fear and trembling.

We originally were "those who through fear of death were subject to lifelong bondage" (Heb. 2.15). The Lord Jesus, however, has set us free and therefore we fear it no more. Its pain, darkness and loneliness cannot frighten us. An Apostle who had experienced victory over death testified that "to die is gain. . . . My desire is to depart and be with Christ, for that is *far better*" (Phil. 1.21,23). Not a wrinkle of fear could be detected there. The victory over death was actual and complete.

RAPTURED ALIVE

We know that at the return of the Lord Jesus many will be raptured alive. This is the last way of overcoming death. Both 1 Corinthians 15.51-52 and 1 Thessalonians 4.14-17 discuss this way. We realize there is no set date for the

Lord's coming. He could have come at any time during the past twenty centuries. Hence believers always could cherish the hope of being raptured without passing through the grave. Since the coming of the Lord Jesus is currently much nearer than before, our hope of being raptured alive is greater than that of our predecessors. We do not wish to say too much, but these few words we can safely affirm; namely, *should* the Lord Jesus come in our time, would we not want to be living so as to be raptured alive? If so, then we must overcome death, not letting ourselves die before our appointed hour so that we may be raptured alive. According to the prophecy of Scripture, some believers shall be raptured without going through death. To be thus raptured constitutes one more kind of victory over death. As long as we remain alive on earth we cannot deny we may be the ones to be so raptured. Should we not therefore be prepared to overcome death completely?

Perhaps we *will* die; nonetheless, we are not necessarily under any obligation so to do. The words the Lord Jesus variously proclaimed make this teaching crystal clear. On the one hand our Lord asserted: "he who eats my flesh and drinks my blood has eternal life, and I will *raise* him up at the last day" (John 6.54). On the other hand, yet on the same occasion, Jesus also affirmed this: "This is the bread which came down from heaven, not such as the fathers ate and died; he who eats this bread will *live for ever*" (v.58). What the Lord is saying is that among those who believe in Him, some will die and be raised up while others will not pass through death at all.

The Lord Jesus expressed this view at the death of Lazarus: "I am the resurrection and the life; he who believes in me, though he die, yet shall he live, and whoever lives and believes in me shall never die" (John 11.25-26). Here the Lord is not only the resurrection but also the life. However, most of us believe Him as the resurrection, yet forget that He also is the life. We readily admit He will raise us up after we die, but do we equally acknowledge that He, because He is our life, is able to keep us alive? The Lord Jesus explains to us His two kinds of work, yet we only believe in one. Believers throughout these twenty centuries shall have experienced the Lord's word that "he who believes in me, though he die, yet shall he live"; certain others shall enjoy in the future His other word that "whoever lives and believes in me shall never die." Thousands and thousands of believers already have departed in faith; but God says some shall never die—not some shall never be raised again, but, some shall *never die*. Consequently we have no reason to insist that we first must die and subsequently be resurrected. Since the coming of the Lord Jesus is nigh, why should we die beforehand and wait for resurrection? Why not expect the Lord to come and rapture us that we may be delivered totally from the power of death?

The Lord indicates He will be resurrection to many but also life to some. Marvelous though it is to be raised from the dead, as was the experience of Lazarus, this by no means exhausts the way of victory over death. The Lord has another method: "never die." We are appointed to walk through the valley of the shadow of death; on the other hand God has erected a floating bridge for us that we might go directly to heaven. This floating bridge is rapture.

The time of rapture is drawing near. If anyone desires to be raptured alive he here and now must learn how to overcome death. Before rapture, the last enemy must be overcome. On the cross the Lord Jesus entirely overcame that enemy; today God wants His church to experience this victory of Christ. We all sense we are living in the end time. The Holy Spirit is presently leading us to wage the last battle with death before the rapture comes.

Realizing his days are numbered Satan exerts his utmost strength to block Christians from being raptured. This explains in part why God's children are being assaulted so fiercely in their bodies today. Due to the severity of these physical attacks, they seem to breathe into themselves the air of death, thereby relinquishing any hope of being raptured alive. They do not perceive this is but the challenge of the enemy, aimed at hindering their ascension. However, should they receive the call of rapture, they naturally soon come to possess a combative spirit against death. For they sense in their spirit that death is an obstacle to rapture which must be overcome.

The devil is a murderer (John 8.44). The purpose of Satan's work against the saints is to kill them. He has a special tactic for the last days: to "wear out the saints" (Dan. 7.25). If he can add just a little anxiety to the believer's spirit, increase just a trifle the restlessness in his mind, cause the saint to lose sleep one night, eat less the next time and overwork still another time, then he has made inroads with his power of death. Although a single drop of water is powerless, continuous dripping can indisputably wear a hole in a rock. Being well acquainted with this truth, Satan incites a little worry here, a little anxiety there, or a little neglect elsewhere to literally wear out the saints.

Sometimes the devil directly attacks believers and causes them to die. Many deaths are assaults such as these, though few recognize them for what they are. Perhaps it is merely a cold, sunstroke, insomnia, exhaustion or loss of appetite. Perhaps it is uncleanness, wrath, jealousy or licentiousness. Failing to perceive that the power of death is behind these phenomena, the full victory for Christians is jeopardized. Were they to recognize them as the assaults of death and resist aright, they would triumph. How often saints attribute these to their age or to some other factor and miss the real import of it all.

The Lord Jesus is returning soon. We must therefore wage a total war with death. Even as we fight against sin, the world and Satan, so must we fight against death. We should not only ask for victory; we should also lay hold of it. We should claim the triumph of Christ over death in all its fullness. Were we to review our past experience beneath the light of God we would discover how many times we have been assailed by death without our knowledge. We endlessly attributed happenings to other causes and thereby lost the power to resist. If we had recognized certain events to have been the assaults of death, we would have been strengthened by God to have experientially overcome death. In that case our experience would have been like passing over broken bridges and torn-up roads: for in that experience all our surroundings appear to demand our death—yet we *cannot die*: time and again we despair of life, still *we cannot die*: we ask ourselves why we *now* must die, for though the battle fiercely escalates, we do not feel like dying: we seem instead to cry out—I do not *want* to die! What is the implication of this kind of experience? Simply that God is leading us to fight our last battle with death before we are raptured. These assaults are designed for no other purpose than to frustrate our being raptured alive.

We should clamp shut the wide-open gates of hades with the victory of Christ. We should stand against death, forbidding it to make any inroad in our bodies. Resist everything possessing the disposition of death. View sickness, weakness and suffering with this attitude. Sometimes the body may not be conscious of anything, yet death is at work already. Anxiety in the spirit or sorrow in the soul may produce death as well. God is now calling us to the rapture; accordingly, we must subdue whatever might hinder that event.

God places His children in various circumstances which impel them hopelessly and helplessly to commit their lives by a thread of faith into the hand of the Lord. For his hand is their only hope. And during such a period it is as though they were crying out, "Lord, let me live!" Today's battle is a battle for life.

Murderous evil spirits are working everywhere. Unless the saints resists and pray they shall be defeated. They shall die inescapably if they continue to remain passive. Should you pray "Lord, let me conquer death," He will respond with "If you resist death, I will let you conquer it." Prayer alone is futile if the will is passive. What you should say is: "Lord, because of your conquest over death, I now resist all its onslaughts. I am determined to conquer death immediately. Lord, make me victorious."

The Lord will enable you to overcome death. So lay hold of the promises God has given you, ask for life, and trust that nothing can harm you. Do not concede to the power of death, or else it will touch you. For instance, you may be staying in a disease-infected area; yet you can withstand all diseases and not permit anything to come upon you. Do not allow death to attack you through sickness.

No longer can we wait passively for the Lord's return, comforting ourselves with the thought that we will be raptured anyway. We must be prepared. As in every other matter, rapture requires the cooperation of the church with God. Faith never lets affairs follow the line of least resistance. Death must be singularly resisted and rapture must be claimed wholeheartedly. Faith is necessary, but that does not mean passively deserting responsibility. If we only believe mentally that we can escape death yet passively continue to submit ourselves to its power, how are we benefited?

MORTAL SIN

The Bible mentions a kind of mortal sin or "sin unto death" which believers may commit (1 John 5.16). The death here does not point to spiritual death, for the eternal life of God can never be extinguished; nor can it be an allusion to "the second death" since the Lord's sheep cannot perish. It necessarily signifies the death of the body.

Now let us especially notice what the essence of mortal sin is. To do so will enable us to know how to keep ourselves away from it so that (1) our flesh may not be corrupted, (2) we may not forfeit the blessing of being raptured before death, or (3) we may still finish the Lord's appointed work before our days are fulfilled and we die, if He should tarry and we must pass through the grave. May we say that because of their negligence in this matter quite a few of God's children have had their years shortened and their crowns lost. Many of God's workers, had they given attention to this, might yet be serving the Lord.

The Word has not spelled out concretely what this sin is. It only assures us that such a sin is possible. From the Scripture records we understand that this sin varies according to people. A particular sin for some is mortal, yet to another person it may not be a sin unto death, and vice versa This is because of differences in grace received, light accepted, and position attained among different believers.

While the Bible never identifies this sin, we can nevertheless observe that any sin which results in death constitutes a mortal one. The people of Israel committed such a sin at Kadesh (Num. 13.25-14.12). Although they had tempted the Lord many times before (14.22), He always simply forgave them. But this time, though He still forgave them after they refused to enter Canaan, He additional caused their *bodies* to fall in death in the wilderness (14.32).

At the waters of Meribah Moses was provoked to speak "words that were rash" (Ps. 106.33): this was his "mortal sin": he died outside Canaan. Aaron committed the same offense as Moses and he likewise was forbidden to enter the holy land (Num. 20.24). The man of God who journeyed from Judah to Bethel disobeyed the commandment of the Lord with regard to eating and drinking; in so doing he committed his mortal sin (1 Kings 13.21-22). In the New Testament we learn how Ananias and Sapphira were punished with death because they committed what for them was their mortal sin, because they attempted to lie to the Holy Spirit by keeping back part of the proceeds from their land (Acts 5). The man in Corinth who lived with his father's wife was guilty too of this kind of sin, forcing the Apostle Paul to pronounce judgment by telling those at Corinth "to deliver this man to Satan for the destruction of the flesh" (1 Cor. 5.5). Not a few of the brethren in Corinth died because they were guilty of profaning the body and blood of the Lord (1 Cor. 11.27,30). They had committed the sin unto death.

To overcome mortality we must persistently overcome sin, for the former results from the latter. If we wish to live till our days are accomplished or till the Lord returns, we should be careful not to sin. Negligence in this has driven many to the grave prematurely. The mortal sin is not any particular terrifying transgression, because it is nowhere fixed or specified. Such a sin as fornication, of which the Corinthians were guilty, may be counted as mortal; but so too may rash words such as Moses uttered become a sin unto death (for note how the Scriptures characterized Moses: "now the man Moses was very meek, more than all men that were on the face of the earth" Num. 12.3; therefore no sin could be overlooked in this man's life).

Now is the day of grace. God is full of grace. So let our hearts be comforted. Do not allow Satan to accuse you, hinting that you have committed the mortal sin and hence must die. Although the Bible does not encourage us to pray for others who have sinned this mortal sin, God will forgive us if we judge ourselves and genuinely repent. The man in 2 Corinthians 2.6-7 is believed by many to be that very one who had lived with his father's wife. In 1 Corinthians 11.30-32 we also are reminded that even though we may have committed the sin unto death, we can nevertheless escape death if we judge ourselves truly. Therefore never permit any sin to reign in your body lest it become your mortal sin. Our flesh can be weakened, yet we must never lose the heart of self-judgment. We must judge our sin without mercy. It is true that we can never attain to sinless perfection in this life, but frequent confession and trust in God's grace are indispensable. God will yet forgive us. Those who seek victory over death need to remember this.

> Then he declares to them their work and their trangressions, that they are behaving arrogantly. He opens their ears to instruction, and commands that they return from iniquity. If they hearken and serve him, they complete their days in prosperity, and their years in pleasantness. But if they do not hearken, they perish by the sword, and die without knowledge. The godless in heart cherish anger; they do not cry for help when he binds them. They die in youth, and their life ends in shame. (Job 36.9-14)

THE TEACHING OF PROVERBS

The Proverbs is a book about the believer's practical daily walk. It teaches much on the ways of keeping one's life. We shall center our attention around its instruction concerning the way to overcome death.

"My son, do not forget my teaching, but let your heart keep my commandments; for length of days and years of life and abundant welfare will they give you" (3.1-2)

"It will be healing to your flesh and refreshment to your bones" (3.8)

"Let your heart hold fast my words; keep my commandments, and live" (4.4)

"Hear, my son, and accept my words, that the years of your life may be many" (4.10)

"Keep hold of instruction, do not let go; guard her, for she is your life" (4.13)

"For (my words) are life to him who finds them, and healing to all his flesh" (4.22)

"Keep your heart with all vigilance; for from it flow the springs of life" (4.23)

"He who commits adultery has no sense; he who does it destroys himself" (6.32)

"He who finds (wisdom) finds life and obtains favor from the Lord" (8.35)

"By (wisdom) your days will be multiplied, and years will be added to your life" (9.11)

"Righteousness delivers from death" (10.2)

"The fear of the Lord prolongs life, but the years of the wicked will be short" (10.27)

"In the path of righteousness is life, but the way of error leads to death" (12.28)

"The fear of the Lord is a fountain of life, that one may avoid the snares of death" (14.27)

"A tranquil mind gives life to the flesh, but passion makes the bones rot" (14.30)

"The wise man's path leads upward to life, that he may avoid Sheol beneath" (15.24)

"He who ignores instruction despises himself" (15.32)

"In the light of a king's face there is life" (16.15)

"He who guards his way preserves his life" (16.17)

"He who keeps the commandment keeps his life; he who despises the word will die" (19.16)

"The fear of the Lord leads to life" (19.23)

"The getting of treasures by a lying tongue is a fleeting vapor and a snare of death" (21.6)

"A man who wanders from the way of understanding will rest in the assembly of the dead" (21.16)

"He who pursues righteousness and kindness will find life and honor" (21.21)

As the Spirit of God leads us to overcome death we discover new meanings to these verses. We are accustomed to viewing "life" as a kind of terminology. But when we have been enlightened we begin to realize our physical life shall be extended if we fulfill God's conditions. And contrariwise, should we disobey these commandments our life shall gradually fade away. For instance, God exhorts you to "honor your father and mother that it may be well with you and that you may live long on the earth" (Eph. 6.2-3). Now if we disobey, our years on earth shall be cut short by sin. God wishes us to hearken to His words, to possess wisdom, to seek righteousness and to keep our hearts, that we lose not our life. If we would have life we must learn to obey.

THE POWERS OF THE AGE TO COME

We are told that in the future kingdom the Lord Jesus is to be the sun of righteousness with healing in its wings (Mal. 4.2). And "no inhabitant will say, 'I am sick'" (Is. 33.24). At that time we *believers* will enjoy what the Scriptures foretell: "the perishable puts on the imperishable, and the mortal puts on immortality, (and) then shall come to pass the saying that is written, 'Death is swallowed up in victory'" (1 Cor. 15.54). To Christians, the characteristic of the kingdom age is that there is no more weakness, sickness or death, because our bodies will have been redeemed and Satan trodden under foot.

We are equally instructed by the Scriptures that we may foretaste the powers of the age to come now (Heb. 6.5). Though our bodies yet wait to be redeemed, we today through faith can taste in advance the powers of the coming age in having no weakness, no sickness, and no death. This is a very deep experience, but if the Christian meets God's requirements and fully trusts in His Word, he is able to enjoy such an experience. Faith is timeless: not only can it draw upon what God has done for us in the past, it can claim as well what God will do for us in the future.

Paul the Apostle describes the change in our bodies in this manner: "while we are still in this tent, we sigh with anxiety; not that we would be unclothed, but that we would be further clothed, so that what is mortal may be swallowed up by life. He who has prepared us for this very thing is God, who has given us the Spirit as a guarantee" (2 Cor. 5.4-5). The word "guarantee" here connotes the idea of "down payment"—a payment to guarantee future payment in full. The Holy Spirit in us is God's guarantee that "what is mortal is swallowed up by life." Though we have not experienced this victory fully today, we nonetheless do experience it partially for we possess the Holy Spirit as the down payment. The giving of the Spirit is that we may foretaste the future triumph of life.

"Now (God) has manifested (himself) through the appearing of our Savior Christ Jesus, who abolished death and brought life and immortality to light through the gospel" (2 Tim. 1.10). Life and immortality, declares the Apostle, are the common portion of all who receive the gospel. Wherefore the question arises, how far is the Holy Spirit able to lead a believer into possessing his portion? Death has been abolished; consequently, believers ought to experience something of this. Now this age is soon to be over; with the rapture in view the Holy Spirit intends to bring believers to experience more of possessing this possession.

Let us believe it is possible to foretaste the powers of the age to come. When Paul exclaims, "Thanks be to God, who gives us the victory through our Lord Jesus Christ" (1 Cor. 15.57), he is pointing to the *present* and he is concerned with the problem of *death*. Although he is referring to future total victory over death, even so he is not content to leave such an experience entirely to the future. He claims we may overcome through the Lord Jesus now!

God has among His principles this one—that what He intends to do in a certain age He first exhibits in a few. What all will experience in the millennium, the members of Christ should currently be experiencing. Even in past dispensations there were people who experienced in advance the powers of the coming age. How much more must the church today have the experience of Christ's victory over death. God desires us to thrust through the boundaries of hades now. The Lord calls us to overcome death for His body's sake. Unless we conquer the last enemy our battle is not concluded.

Let each of us therefore seek the Lord's mind concerning our future. We entertain no superstitious concept that we will not die. But if now is the end time and the coming of Christ will tarry no more but will be consummated in our lifetime, then we should exercise faith to lay hold of God's Word and trust that we shall not die but shall see the Lord's face alive. And let us who thus hope in Him purify ourselves as He is pure. Moment by moment let us live for Him and draw upon His resurrection life for the needs of our spirit, soul and body.

"By faith Enoch was taken up so that he should not see death" (Heb. 11.5). Let us likewise believe. Believe that death is not necessary, that rapture is certain, that the time will not be long. "Now before (Enoch) was taken he was attested as having pleased God" (Heb. 11.5). How about us?

Oh how excellent is the future glory! How perfect is the salvation which God has prepared for us! Let us arise and go up. May "heaven" so fill us that the flesh finds no ground nor the world holds any attraction! May the love of the Father so be in us that we hold no more communication with His enemy! May the Lord Jesus so satisfy our hearts that we desire none else! And may the Holy Spirit create in each believer the prayer, "Come, Lord Jesus!"